Sixty-One
in '61

Sixty-One in '61

*Roger Maris Home Runs
Game by Game*

Robert M. Gorman

McFarland & Company, Inc., Publishers
Jefferson, North Carolina

ALSO OF INTEREST
BY ROBERT M. GORMAN AND DAVID WEEKS

*Death at the Ballpark:
More Than 2,000 Game-Related Fatalities
of Players, Other Personnel and Spectators
in Amateur and Professional Baseball,
1862–2014*, 2d ed. (McFarland, 2015)

All photographs are from the National Baseball Hall of Fame, Cooperstown, New York, unless otherwise mentioned.

LIBRARY OF CONGRESS CATALOGUING-IN-PUBLICATION DATA

Names: Gorman, Robert M., author. | McFarland & Company.
Title: Sixty-one in '61 : Roger Maris home runs game by game / Robert M. Gorman.
Other titles: Sixty-one in 1961
Description: Jefferson, North Carolina : McFarland & Company, Inc., Publishers, 2019. | Includes bibliographical references and index.
Identifiers: LCCN 2019041366 | ISBN 9781476672625 (Paperback) ∞
ISBN 9781476638270 (eBook)
Subjects: LCSH: Maris, Roger, 1934–1985. | Baseball players—United States—Statistics. | Pitchers (Baseball)—Biography. | American League of Professional Baseball Clubs—History. | Major League Baseball (Organization)—History. | Baseball—United States—History.
Classification: LCC GV865.M34 G67 2019 | DDC 796.357092 [B]—dc23
LC record available at https://lccn.loc.gov/2019041366

BRITISH LIBRARY CATALOGUING DATA ARE AVAILABLE

ISBN (print) 978-1-4766-7262-5
ISBN (ebook) 978-1-4766-3827-0

© 2019 Robert M. Gorman. All rights reserved

No part of this book may be reproduced or transmitted in any form or by any means, electronic or mechanical, including photocopying or recording, or by any information storage and retrieval system, without permission in writing from the publisher.

Front cover: Roger Maris hitting his 61st home run in the last game of the season at Yankee Stadium on October 1, 1961 (National Baseball Hall of Fame, Cooperstown, New York)

Printed in the United States of America

*McFarland & Company, Inc., Publishers
Box 611, Jefferson, North Carolina 28640
www.mcfarlandpub.com*

To my beautiful wife Jane—
your unwavering love and support sustained me
as I fulfilled my childhood dream

Acknowledgments

This book was three years in the making, and it would not have been possible at all without the help and support of many others. First, I would like to thank all those librarians out there who supplied me with the books, journals, and newspapers that were essential to the completion of my research. Special thanks to Philip Hays, who oversees interlibrary loan operations at Dacus Library, Winthrop University. He spent untold hours cajoling, begging, and beseeching libraries around the country into lending the documents I so sorely needed.

I would also like to express my deep appreciation to pitchers Terry Fox, Johnny James, Dick Stigman, and Jerry Walker and to catcher John Romano who so willingly shared memories of their careers in general and the 1961 season in particular. You all actually lived the dream; I thank you for making me a part of it. This book is a whole lot richer because of you.

I am again indebted to my great friend Dr. Jason Silverman, renowned historian, Lincoln scholar, and baseball enthusiast, who proofread the entire volume, not only catching errors and typos, but also making many excellent suggestions for improvement. You're the best.

And a special thanks to Sandy and John Britt for proofing the final document. Your tireless efforts to improve this text are much appreciated.

Of course, nothing would have been possible without my wonderful wife, Jane, who tolerated my obsession with Roger Maris as I spent hours at a time squirreled away while researching and writing on my boyhood hero. She patiently read through what I wrote and was there with her advice when I was uncertain how to proceed. You are the love of my life.

Table of Contents

Acknowledgments vi

Preface 1

Introduction 3

1. Overcoming Obstacles 5
2. Roger Maris Before 1961 41
3. April–May 58
4. June 92
5. July 134
6. August 187
7. September 228
8. October 280

Aftermath 295

Appendix: Roger Maris by the Numbers 301

Chapter Notes 303

Bibliography 327

Index 333

Preface

Much has been written about Roger Maris over the years. The first work appeared before the 1961 season was even complete. Several other I-was-there accounts were published the following spring, most important of which was his story, *Roger Maris at Bat*. Although not a literary masterpiece, it did allow the much-maligned player an opportunity to respond to his detractors in the press and the public. It was much like the man himself—straightforward, honest to a fault, blunt, uncompromising. A slew of other works appeared after his untimely death in late 1985, including reflections by his Yankee teammates and some of the journalists who covered him at the time. Even more popped up after the release of the Billy Crystal film, *61**, in 2001. Most recently, Tom Clavin and Danny Peary wrote the definitive biography of him, *Roger Maris: Baseball's Reluctant Hero*.

So why write another book on this often misunderstood player? I have read dozens of monographs (including works of fiction) and hundreds of articles about him, beginning with Leonard Shecter's *Roger Maris: Home Run Hero*, which I purchased from my neighborhood drugstore when it first appeared in the fall of 1961 (and which I still have). All of them cover that season broadly with occasional descriptions of some of his milestone home runs, but none have gone into much detail about each of the homers and the 48 pitchers who surrendered them.

One of the great debates that year concerned the quality of American League pitching. Many argued that the noticeable increase in home run production in the junior circuit was the result of diluted pitching because of the addition of two new teams. "Expansion from eight to 10 teams has unquestionably weakened the American League," contended Walter Bingham in *Sports Illustrated*. "There are 25 percent more pitchers in the league than last year, minor league pitchers by the old standard, and they are a big help to good hitters." But was that really the case? Did Roger Maris feast off a bunch of has-beens and never-weres while Babe Ruth faced nothing but the *crème de la crème* of the American League? Exactly who were these starters and relievers and how good were they?

The book begins with a discussion of the various obstacles and problems he had to confront to achieve what many thought an impossible task. Issues such as his personality, a new style of sports journalism which was much more invasive and demanding than in the past, the Ford Frick directive, the ghost of Babe Ruth, the relationship between Maris and Mickey Mantle, the overall quality of the pitching he faced, the debate about juiced balls and lively bats, the nature of the stadiums in which he played, and the playing conditions under which he labored are all explored to provide some context for his amazing feat.

The bulk of the work looks at each of the home runs, including the one that did not count and the game-winning World Series dinger. Brief biographies of each pitcher cover his pitching style and his career both before and after 1961 and the circumstances under which the games were played. It is my hope that the reader will come to appreciate, as I have, that Roger Maris faced some really fine pitching that season in spite of what was asserted then (and even now). Yes, there were marginal hurlers in the group, but Babe Ruth, as one sportswriter admitted, "clobbered his share of umbays [bums]" as well.

I used a variety of resources in writing this book—primary first-person accounts, major secondary sources, magazine, newspaper, and journal articles, and player interviews when possible. I have tried to keep statistics to a minimum, but no good baseball book is complete without a few basic ones. I used Baseball-Reference.com as my main source for these stats, but any mistakes are, of course, mine alone. The *SABR Baseball Biography Project* (sabr.org/bioproject) website was useful as a starting point for my research on the 48 pitchers Maris homered off of that summer. All the biographies in this volume are uniquely mine, however, and have a different focus entirely from the ones appearing on the website. And there are several I wrote that are not presently included in the project at all. Some of the SABR biographies provide information drawn from player interviews; cited in the notes and in the bibliography are those nine from which I used comments made by the players themselves.

The Sporting News is a basic resource for any baseball-related research, but I also drew from daily newspapers around the country, especially those published in the 10 American League locations (Baltimore, Boston, Chicago, Cleveland, Detroit, Kansas City, Los Angeles, Minnesota, New York, and Washington, D.C.).

Player interviews are essential as well. Sadly, more than half of the 48 pitchers are deceased and many others suffer from debilitating illnesses that prevent them from being interviewed. I did have the opportunity to speak with pitchers Terry Fox, Johnny James, and Dick Stigman and with catcher John Romano, who willingly shared their memories with me. Roger Maris passed away in 1985, but he did leave his account of that season, *Roger Maris at Bat*, and a slew of interviews from which I drew comments made by him. I also used first-person accounts published by teammates Tony Kubek, Mickey Mantle, Bobby Richardson, and Ralph Terry and by manager Ralph Houk. Pitchers Russ Kemmerer and Milt Pappas, both deceased, wrote books that included valuable information about the 1961 campaign.

Introduction

It was early June 1998 and my wife, Jane, and I were on the last leg of a month-long road trip out West that started from our home in Charlotte, North Carolina, and wandered through Oklahoma, Texas, New Mexico, Arizona, Utah, Wyoming, and Montana before reaching North Dakota. We were in Fargo, standing before the grave of Roger Eugene Maris, my childhood hero. A gentle breeze blew through Holy Cross Cemetery as I gazed upon his beautiful headstone in the shape of a baseball diamond, lost in that magical summer of 1961 when I was 12 and baseball was the world to me. Carved in the middle was his last name; below that was a silhouette of that picture-perfect left-handed swing of his with "61" engraved above the barrel of the bat and "61" below it. Inscribed on the base was the phrase that captured the true essence of that historic season—"Against All Odds."

America in 1961 was a fascinating time. We had a young president, the Cold War was in full bloom, the Civil Rights movement was entering a new phase, American astronauts rocketed into outer space for the first time, and two baseball players entranced a nation as they pursued another who was viewed as a god by many fans of the game. Arguably no other sporting event in the nation's history was more widely covered, discussed, and hotly debated as the home-run battle between Roger Maris and Mickey Mantle as they pursued Babe Ruth's single-season record.

My love of the Yankees began the year before. I grew up in the Miami area, and there was no local major league team to which I could pledge my allegiance. But the Saturday afternoon "Game of the Week" almost always was New York versus some other lesser club. I loved Yogi Berra and Mickey Mantle, but it was Roger Maris who captured my imagination. There was just something about him—the way he stood at the plate, his gorgeous swing, how he ran the bases, head down and all business—that appealed to me. I thrilled with other Yankee fans as they poured it on to capture the flag late in the 1960 season and died along with them when, in Game 7 of the World Series, light-hitting Bill Mazeroski smacked a walk-off home run over the left-field wall to end it all. To add insult to injury, I had bet my father, a Pirates fan, a dollar that the Yankees would prevail; it was a hard pill to swallow when I handed over what was two weeks' allowance. (A number of years ago I meet Yankee catcher John Blanchard at a card show and told him how I cried like a baby when Maz hit that improbable dinger. He looked up at me and responded, "So did I.")

The 1961 season was a time of redemption for the Yankees in general and Roger Maris in particular. He blossomed in 1960, hitting 39 round-trippers (second most in the American League behind Mickey Mantle's 40) before a late season injury to his ribcage knocked him off his stride. Most saw him as the missing ingredient that took the Yankees from third place in 1959 to the World Series in 1960. He won his first American League Most Valuable Player Award as a result, defeating teammate Mantle by three votes. Still, some doubted he had any real staying power.

The 1961 campaign did not start off well for the second-year Yankee. He did not hit his first home run until his eleventh game and managed only three in total through the first 28. It was beginning to look like 1960 was a fluke and that he would be lucky to hit even a dozen homers that year. Then he suddenly caught fire and the pursuit of Babe Ruth was on. While most of the country pulled for Mickey Mantle, I remained a Maris loyalist. I did not realize at the time how unusual it was to root for Maris over Mantle, nor how much guff Maris had to put up with for simply doing his job.

He never wanted the fame forced upon him. He hated being in the spotlight. He was a private man who wanted to be left alone and was totally unprepared for the intense scrutiny he was placed under that season. To make matters even worse, so many seemed to be against him, either because he, a sub-.300 batter, had the audacity to challenge the immortal Babe or because he was not Mickey Mantle, whom most saw as the "true" Yankee. The scorn, the constant denigration of his abilities, the outright nastiness heaped upon him was unlike anything any other baseball player before him had ever experienced. Yes, the way he handled the attention and relentless questioning added to his problems, but he did not deserve the outrageous sniping he received during and after the season. No one does. It soured the whole experience for him to the point that, even though he was proud of breaking the record, he never ever wanted to go through that again.

"Roger Maris never pretended to be anything other than what he was—a man who wanted nothing more than to excel at his chosen profession," baseball historian Maury Allen wrote after the passing of the Yankee slugger at the age of 51. "He never asked to be famous. He only wanted to be appreciated." And he never once compared himself to Babe Ruth (or to Mantle, for that matter). "I have never imagined myself as a Babe Ruth, nor have I ever claimed that I am a Babe Ruth. I'm just Roger Maris, a guy trying to do the best he can," he said time and again. But for five years he was one of the preeminent players in the game, and for that one glorious summer surpassed the best of them, against all odds.

1

Overcoming Obstacles

To fully appreciate the struggles and ultimate triumph of Roger Maris in 1961, one must first understand the context and conditions under which he achieved what many thought was an impossible task: surpassing the single-season home run record of the iconic and beloved Babe Ruth. Who was Roger Maris and what were the obstacles he faced as he pursued the immortal Bambino? How different from Ruth were the fan and press responses to Maris' assault on the record and what role did both play? What impact did baseball commissioner Ford Frick's ruling on the number of games allowed to officially break Babe Ruth's record have on Maris? In what ways was the 1961 game different from the one played in 1927? Because 1961 was an expansion year for the American League—two new teams were added—many postulated that the pitching was watered-down and thus the hurlers Maris faced were decidedly inferior to the ones Ruth confronted. But was that really the case? Some argued that Maris and other sluggers hit so many home runs in 1961 because the ball was juiced, or the bat was livelier, or the stadiums were smaller than in 1927. How accurate were these suppositions? And was he a one-dimensional flash-in-the-pan player that some then—and now—thought him to be? How Roger Maris was able to confront and overcome these and other obstacles while fully cognizant that many in the press and among the fans belittled him and did not want him to succeed is the true miracle of that summer.

Personality

In many ways Roger Maris was an unlikely hero, a man ill-equipped for the task ahead of him. Whereas Ruth was outgoing and gregarious, Maris was reserved and somewhat introverted. He abhorred being in the limelight. He preferred playing in relative anonymity in Kansas City rather than being the center of attention, as was his lot in New York. In his first-person account of the 1961 season, *Roger Maris at Bat*, he talked about how he felt like "a freak in a sideshow":

> Everywhere I went I knew eyes were on me. When I went out to eat, when I walked into the hotel lobby, as soon as I appeared on the field there were always eyes, eyes, eyes.... It made me very uncomfortable. When you know every eye is on you, it is impossible to feel natural or comfortable.
>
> It had now reached the point where the only time I relaxed was during a ball game. It was a pleasure when the games started. There was no one around, no questions. Even standing alone in the outfield was a relief ... it was like an oasis. I was able to stand there alone and sort of collect my thoughts, get ready for the next question spree. There was no one out there except a few loud-

mouthed fans, but they couldn't bother me now. I had so much on my mind that I didn't hear them most of the time.[1]

Roger Maris was at heart a family man, someone who disliked being away from his wife and children for long periods of time. One of the reasons he was unhappy being traded to New York at the end of the 1959 season was that it meant even longer separations from his loved ones. When word reached him of the trade, he told one reporter, "Kansas City is my home now. I've got nothing against the Yankees, but I'm sorry to leave here. And I'll expect more money."[2]

Maris simply hated being on the road far away from the comfort and security of his family. "It really doesn't take much to get me thinking about what's going on at home; what I would be doing if I were there; what the kids are doing." He admitted that there were many times during his professional career when he seriously thought about "packing up and going home" because "I just don't like being away from home. I would love to be able to come home every night and be with my family. Yet, most of the time I am buried away in a strange town and in a lonely hotel room."[3]

Maris liked playing baseball, but not all the hoopla surrounding it. More than anything he saw it as a means of financial protection for his loved ones. "I don't think that I am money-hungry," he asserted, "except as it can help me reach the financial security which I hope to attain for my family. To me it seems quite natural that a man will always set himself a financial goal that would prove good for his family. That has always been my goal in baseball—to set up a good life for my wife and children."[4]

When he was just 14 years old, Maris and his older brother began working summers as a laborers on the railroad where his father was employed. This experience was central to the development of his work ethic. "It proved very valuable to me," he stated years later. "[I]n fact, it had a great deal to do with the way I think and the way I act":

> It was during that period that I learned the hard way the value of a dollar. I learned to appreciate the value of money and what it can do for you. That is why I am so anxious to reach a point where I feel I have financial security. I don't mind working for it, but it has become one of my goals in life.
>
> I also learned at that early age how to take orders from a boss and that when you have a job to do you must do it to the best of your ability. Although I was merely a laborer on the railroad, I was able to get satisfaction from doing my job well and from being able to follow instructions.
>
> Another valuable lesson I learned was that there are times when you must take things, but that there is also a point where you don't have to take any more. I believe it was here that I began to develop into a man, a man who would fight for whatever he thinks is right.[5]

These attitudes were reflected in his approach to the game itself. Maris loved to "joke and kid around with the boys" in the clubhouse, but once he put on the uniform and walked onto the field, "my mood changes":

> Baseball is my business, and I take it seriously. When I put that uniform on my mind is completely centered on the game just ahead of me. I know that I have to go out on the field and do my job. Not just do a job, but do it as well as I can possibly do it. I don't have any time to do any goofing around.
>
> Perhaps I take it more seriously than I should, perhaps more seriously than anyone should take it. I can't help it, that's the way I feel. When anything or anyone distracts me from the job at hand then, certainly, my temper can flare up. I'm in no mood for clowning around at this time.[6]

Unlike the image of him as an angry man, one promoted primarily by the press, Maris was open and fun to be around. He maintained that he was totally different away from the ballpark. "I like people and like to be around them." For those who knew him intimately—his teammates, childhood friends, and others he met over the years—that was indeed the case. His wife, Pat, was particularly confused by this caricature of him. "[O]ne thing I can never understand is the stories of him being red-necked or the Last Angry Man. He is nothing like that when he is around home." He was very reserved when first meeting someone, which may have been off-putting to some. If he got to know you and liked you, however, you were a friend for life. "Usually when I meet someone for the first time," he confessed, "I'll stay in the back seat on the outside until I make up my mind about him." According to him, "There is no halfway with me. When I take a liking to someone, then I really like him and stick by him unless one day he proves I was wrong in the first place." Whitey Herzog, a teammate from Maris' years with the Athletics, confirmed this aspect of his personality to be the case. "He didn't make friends easy. He was always afraid of being taken advantage of. But if he liked you, if you didn't cross him … brother, you had a friend."[7]

Maris had a quiet generosity about him that he tried to keep private from the press. Julie "Big Julie" Isaacson, a New York labor leader and celebrity-fixer who became good friends with Maris, told a story of how the right fielder helped him come up with a bar mitzvah gift for the son of a friend. "Give him me," the Yankee slugger suggested. After the game that day, Maris appeared at the hotel where the initiation ceremony was held. Approaching the youngster, he asked, "Are you the Yankees fan who became a man today?" Maris, who was Catholic, even participated in the singing of "Hava Nagila" ("Let Us Rejoice"), a traditional Jewish folk song frequently sung at celebratory events. "I couldn't even sing the words myself," Big Julie recalled. "Roger just worked hard to show his friends he cared." Maris had a special affection for children, regularly taking time to visit them in the hospital or respond to their fan letters. In one instance, the parents of a wayward boy wrote, asking him if he would correspond with their son in the hopes that his advice might help the boy change his ways. With four children of his own at that time, he knew the predicament the parents were in and gladly did so. They responded later, expressing their "deep gratitude" for this gesture, remarking, "A boy's hero has become a very real person in our household."[8]

There is no question that Maris could be irritable and defensive at times. When it came to dealing with the press and responding to criticism, he was frequently his own worst enemy. The story is told about teammate Whitey Ford, joking around in the clubhouse one day, proclaiming that if he were president, he would appoint Maris his "Secretary of Grievances." Baseball historian Robert Creamer noted that "Maris tended to alienate people. He was too sensitive to criticism to attract affection and admiration, and his personality would not reshape itself to meet the demands of people he came into contact with. He never forgot grudges." Maris took particular offense at those fans and members of the press who criticized him for not having a better batting average, arguing that a .270 hitter was not supposed to hit so many home runs:

> I was getting sick and tired of reading how odd it was for someone unable to come close to .300 as a hitter, but still hitting homers at a record pace; I was fed up with letters from crackpots telling me that I was a lousy hitter who had no business hitting home runs.
>
> Having people say the things they did hurt my pride as a ballplayer. I definitely didn't like to have the things said. I would never go around knocking anyone just because he might be fortunate enough to be going good.
>
> It wasn't only my pride that was hurt, but also my feelings as a professional. I have never knocked another player in my life. I never knock anyone unless he proves to me that he is no good. If anyone is doing a good job at his profession, then I don't see where anyone gets the right to say: "You're a lousy hitter, or you're a lousy dentist, or doctor or lawyer."[9]

But Maris was hypercritical of himself, which is why he so often appeared to be angry. He had an especially difficult time maintaining his equilibrium and emotions when he was in a slump or had a bad day and was much more sensitive to criticism, deserved or not, during periods when things were not going as well as he expected. In an article published in the *New York Times* the day after he hit his sixty-first home run, Maris was referred to as the "Angry King of Swat" and "the Mad Bomber." He admitted that "even the Yankee clubhouse attendants think I'm tough to live with. I guess they're right. I'm miffed most of the time regardless of how I'm doing." "Maybe I'm a lot of things people say I am," he mused. "I just don't like to lose. When I think I'm not doing the best I can, I get steamed."[10]

True to his Midwestern upbringing, Maris was forthright, blunt, and honest, almost to a fault. Jimmy Cannon, renowned sports commentator for the *New York Journal-American*, described Maris as "a candid man who holds onto the truth as he sees it. There is no deceit in Maris and he doesn't duck into the sanctuary of evasion when you ask him a difficult question. I don't know a more honest man in sports." Part of the problem in his dealings with the press during his career, especially during the Yankees years, was that he spoke his mind, oftentimes before he had thought things through. "Sometimes when I get wound up on a subject I am liable to say too much. I always believe that an honest question deserves an honest answer, but sometimes you can get into trouble by saying the wrong thing ... even if you are being completely honest."[11]

Frankness was another feature of the Maris personality. He felt staying true to one's self was essential, no matter the cost:

> I don't care for a phony person myself and can't be that way. I am always frank, unless it might hurt someone and then I'll just clam up and say nothing. It doesn't always work out for the best, however, for sometimes I have been ripped up pretty good just because I was frank ... although I was telling the truth. Some people don't like to hear the truth.
>
> Sometimes it is said that people think I'm tough to get along with just because I say what I think and don't follow the crowd. That's all right with me. If people are going to like me they are going to have to take me as I am. If they don't like me, then there is no way I can change them. In fact, I wouldn't even make an attempt. My friends know me and understand me. The others don't count anyway.[12]

"If there is any failure Maris has in his public relations," sportswriter Tom Meany concluded after interviewing him in 1960, "it is bluntness. He hasn't been around long enough to be diplomatic. While he can fend off leading questions, he is apt to be frank when he is asked for his opinion on a certain subject or, more dangerous still, a certain individual." But while Meany found Maris to be outspoken, it was not "in a noisy sense, as a Leo Durocher or Jimmy Piersall might be, but outspoken in delivering his opinions. He doesn't play games with interviewers." Echoing those same sentiments, Robert Creamer observed that Maris "had almost no sense of public relations. He could not give easy, glib answers to anything. While this didn't bother Maris's teammates, who both liked and admired him, it disturbed many reporters and broadcasters. Maris spoke the literal truth, and that jarred and upset people expecting ritual responses to their questions." Bob Cerv, who played with Maris in Kansas City and roomed with him and Mickey Mantle during the 1961 season, agreed that Maris was too direct for his own good. While expressing his amazement at how patient his friend was in his dealings with the press, Cerv observed that Maris was "frank, very frank. Too much, at times. If only he'd think a little more about some of the things he says. But no, he punches it right out, whatever they ask him."[13]

Maris was a fighter, someone who did not back down if he thought he was in the right:

> When I think I am right, there is no man who is going to tell me that I am wrong unless he can PROVE IT [emphasis Maris] to me. As long as I know I am right I'm going to put up an argument regardless of the consequences. I don't care how big the person is I am arguing with or how much power he has. If I believe I'm right, then he's going to get a battle. It has already happened many times during my baseball career.

As Maris well knew, this combative attitude was present throughout his career and led to some thinking he was a malcontent or, in sports parlance, a "red-ass" or "redneck." He claimed that if people had that impression of him, it "doesn't bother me ... not even a little bit." In the eyes of some managers and front office personnel, Maris was not deferential enough. It was primarily for this reason that he was sometimes labeled a troublemaker and a complainer, not because he could not get along with his teammates. He had the audacity to stand up for himself, to fight for a better salary, to assert himself when he felt he was not being managed or treated properly. He played during a time before free agency when players had little say over what they were paid, for whom they played, or to which team they were traded. Contracts were signed yearly; one could either choose to play under the contract offered or leave organized ball entirely. Even the superstars had limited influence over their baseball destinies. But from the very beginning of his career, Maris was not intimidated by the powers-that-be. If he believed he was being benched too often, he told his manager or the team owner to "play me or trade me." If he did not like the salary he was offered, he threatened to walk. And he meant it. In his first year of professional ball, in fact, he demanded he be assigned to play his inaugural season in Fargo or he would leave. Indians management was shocked by this ultimatum, but knew he was serious and accommodated the youngster as a result. While this behavior was tolerated because of his talent, it did not endear him to those in charge.[14]

Maris did not like being told what to do. There is a revealing, and oft told, story about the newest Yankee's arrival in New York. He was met at the airport by Julie Isaacson, who Maris did not know at the time. According to Isaacson, Maris was dressed like a country bumpkin, including wearing what he termed "Pat Boone white bucks." Big Julie was aghast and informed Maris that Yankees did not dress that way. "If they don't like the way I dress," Maris purportedly stated, "they can send me back to Kansas City." Isaacson insisted that at the very least Maris should buy new shoes. The following day when Isaacson picked him up, Maris asked to be taken to a shoe store. Thinking that he had at least won the shoe argument, Big Julie was taken aback when Maris emerged with not one, but two, new pairs of the same style shoe he had been wearing the day before. According to Isaacson, that was Roger Maris in a nutshell.[15]

Jimmy Cannon, who savaged Maris in his column the following spring for what he perceived to be a snub, in late 1961 wrote with admiration of how Maris had remained true to himself during that long and trying season. "But you have held on to the truth of your character. Your attitude was shaped in outraged obscurity. You're brusque and candid and often belligerent with those who you think are trespassers on your dignity. You didn't change your character, as if it were a uniform, when you were traded [to the Yankees]." Maris "has fought to keep his personality and has retained his character," the writer noted on another occasion. "In some ways this is as great a feat as hitting 60 home runs."[16]

Historian David Halberstam described Maris as "a small-town boy" who "remained a small-town boy the rest of his life. He did not lightly accommodate to anything that was different, nor was he ever anxious to change his ways. The more he was pressured to change, the more he resented that very pressure, and the less flexible he became. Confronted with any kind of resistance, he tended to bristle and pull in." Or, as one teammate observed, Maris was someone "who never heard the cheers but always remembered the boos."[17]

The Press

These personality traits and attitudes were not ones likely to make for smooth relations between Roger Maris and the press. He was not Babe Ruth and he was not Mickey Mantle, which damned him in the eyes of many sports journalists.

Ruth reveled in publicity and recognized that the press was essential in building and promoting his image as a superhero. And sports writers loved him. He was open, colorful, and eminently quotable. They mostly avoided writing about his personal life—his excesses, transgressions, and misbehavior—instead choosing to focus on, and exaggerate, his exploits on the field. Some of them, including future baseball commissioner Ford Frick, were fawning sycophants who saw the Babe as a deity. Unquestionably he was one of the greatest ballplayers of all time, so it was easy to become blinded by his accomplishments. And they showered him with glowing nicknames—The Sultan of Swat, The Great Bambino, and other such sobriquets—as a sign of their adoration. Maris was afforded no such laudatory labels from the reporters who covered him.

When Ruth passed away in 1948, the press acted as if a god had met his demise. "No death since Franklin Roosevelt's had moved the people—and the press—to such maudlin excess," wrote *Time* magazine. "Between the pumped-up sentimentality of the public mind and the morticianly manners of the public prints, it was impossible to decide which influenced the other more. The genuine tributes to flamboyant George Herman Ruth were drowned in a messy fog of tear-jerking pictures and prose." And *Time* was as guilty of these excesses as the rest of the press. Accompanying this critical commentary was a reprinted Rube Goldberg illustration of three young boys with slumped shoulders bowing their heads in tribute as a ghostly Babe Ruth, bat slung aside after hitting one of his patented home runs, streaks through the heavens shouting, "So long, kids."[18]

Ruth clearly benefited from this style of sports journalism. Noted author Paul Gallico, who early in his career wrote for the New York *Daily News*, described it this way: "We sing of their muscles, their courage, their gameness and skill because it seems to amuse readers and sells papers, but we rarely consider them as people and strictly speaking, leave their characters alone because that is dangerous ground." Stanley Walker, one-time editor of the *New York Tribune*, labeled it "Gee Whiz" reporting wherein athletes were bigger-than-life and could do no wrong. While there was a more critical attitude toward ballplayers at the time—what Walker termed the "Aw Nuts" approach—it was not nearly as popular with the reading public as its competitor. And since newspapers were the primary source of information during that era, the public readily bought into the mythical Babe Ruth persona created by the "Gee Whiz" press.[19]

A whole generation of baseball fans, many of them still alive when Maris played, embraced this image of the herculean and god-like Babe Ruth, which predisposed them to take a disliking to anyone who challenged their hero. And Roger Maris, with his aversion to being the center of attention, his sometimes curt response to questions, his distrustful attitude toward the press, and his colorless personality, as some unfairly described him, paled in comparison to the mighty Babe in the opinion of many reporters and fans, dooming him from the get-go. As Jimmy Cannon so aptly stated it, "You're Roger Maris, not Babe Ruth, and that disturbs a lot of people."[20]

Sports journalism changed dramatically over the intervening years between Ruth and Maris. Whereas coverage of baseball players in the earlier era was deferential and rarely concerned with players' personal lives, it had become much more invasive by the time Maris hit his stride. Television, too, was now on the scene, allowing more fans to actually see the game as it was played on the field. As a consequence, print media moved more toward analysis and behind-the-scenes reporting. New York, in particular, with its plethora of newspapers competing for paid circulation, was the center of this new style of journalism. The older generation of reporters—their eyes filled with the wonders of Ruth, Gehrig, Cobb and Foxx—were still around, while a new type of expose-anxious journalists, more concerned with the story behind the game, were just coming into their own. Derogatorily labeled "chipmunks" by veteran reporter Jimmy Cannon, these younger scribes, anxious to make a name for themselves, scurried around poking their noses into the players' private lives. Maris "was caught in the middle of a clash between two schools of sportswriting thought: younger writers, hungry for every angle, who were unwilling to canonize him ... and older writers who resented Maris' temerity for chasing the mighty Babe," maintains Pulitzer Prize–nominated journalist Alan Schwarz. For someone like Maris who hated publicity and resented personal questions, this more aggressive form of journalism was a living hell.[21]

Some reporters were looking for the sensational, and in doing so frequently crossed the line with Maris. The slugger bristled at such audacity, which made him even more distrustful of the press. These "weird questions," as he described them, were sometimes salacious in their intent. Late in the season, Maris was being interviewed for a magazine article when the reporter suddenly asked, "When you are on the road, do you like to play around?" Aghast, Maris, who was a devoted husband and dedicated family man, responded, "I'm married." Refusing to drop this line of inquiry, the reporter admitted, "So am I, but I still like to play around when I'm traveling." All the furious Maris could reply was "I don't," as he abruptly ended the interview by turning and walking away. He explained to Jimmy Cannon after the incident, "Anyone fools with my family had better watch out. If anyone writes lies about me where my family is concerned, I'll deck him."[22]

Maris did not stack up well against his teammate Mickey Mantle in the eyes of many of their contemporaries in the press. While Mantle could be churlish and mercurial with reporters at times, he could also be quite approachable and friendly. One correspondent proclaimed Maris as "a real sobersides" compared to Mantle, who he described as "something of a comedian when not playing ball." It was not that Mantle did not receive vicious press criticism. Throughout his career, reporters often referred to him in disparaging terms, calling him a loafer, a quitter, even a draft dodger because he was classified as 4-F due to osteomyelitis from a childhood injury. But in 1961, everything changed. Suddenly Mantle was the media's darling. In the eyes of many journalists and fans, if anyone were to beat Ruth's record, it should be Mantle, the "true" Yankee, not that interloper Maris. "Mantle is the symbol of a Yankee," acknowledged one New York reporter. "If Maris hits 61 homers, he'll smash the image of Mantle and Babe Ruth in the same season. That's too much for New Yorkers to take ... so they're rooting against Maris." Baseball historian

Robert Creamer concurred with that observation. Even though Maris was the reigning American League MVP and was matching Mantle homer-for-homer, "he was clearly the villain in the Chasing Babe Ruth drama. Mantle got the early season publicity … and even after Maris caught up and passed him, Mantle seemed the obvious choice to eventually finish on top. But Maris did, and the fans and the press resented it."[23]

Both Mantle and Maris were quite aware that most Yankee fans and members of the press preferred the Mick over the man from Fargo. "I became an American hero in 1961 because he [Maris] beat me," Mantle opined to biographer Jane Leavy. "He was an ass, and I was a nice guy. He beat Babe Ruth and he beat me, so they hated him. Everywhere we'd go, I got a standing ovation. All I had to do was walk out of the dugout." As Mantle himself once noted, it took Roger Maris to make him beloved in the eyes of the public.[24]

Maris' rocky relationship with the press grew even more problematic the latter part of the season as it became apparent that he was posing a serious challenge to Babe Ruth's home run record. Reporters swarmed around him at his locker after the game, even when he had not hit a home run or had not contributed to a Yankee win. He hated being bombarded with questions and often told those assembled to talk with a teammate who had had a much better day. "He was hounded by the media in ways no player ever had been before, pinned to his locker like a caged animal," asserts Alan Schwarz.[25]

Maris frequently lashed out at the press and fans in these situations. In early September after the Yankees had swept the Detroit Tigers in a crucial three-game series in New York, the Bombers took on the hapless Washington Senators in a Labor Day doubleheader at the stadium. Maris went hitless in both games and was in a sour mood when he entered the locker room. He was angry at himself for not performing to his own high expectations and irritated at some fans who had been heckling him during the game. It was an explosive situation as the press began firing questions at him:

> They had me surrounded in the clubhouse. I had done nothing. There were plenty of guys for them to talk to, but they were on me. Some of them started to get a little raw in their questions, and I got hot under the collar. For some reason I started to put the rap on the fans.
>
> That was just what the writers were waiting for … me to pop off. I guess I said too much. In fact, I know that I said too much. I said things I had no business saying because there are many more good fans than bad ones. I was a bit surprised to read what I had said in the papers.

Surprised he may have been, but he did not deny what he was quoted as saying. He referred to Yankees enthusiasts as "a lousy bunch of front runners" who cheered when he homered but booed when he played poorly. "Give me the fans in Kansas City any time. There's no place where the fans can compare to the people out there," he complained. When he was reminded that spectators paid to get in, he fired back, "I didn't ask them to come. If they keep giving me a hard time, I'll do my job on the field and give them what they pay to see. But they better not come around after the game bothering me for autographs. I can walk through fifteen million of them and never look at one of them."[26]

This was Roger Maris at his most combative. While he later apologized for what he had said and tried to clarify by claiming he was not referring to all fans, but just the "few fans that are really bad," the damage had been done. Sadly, while this type of impulsive response to the pressures of the season may have been especially harsh and imprudent, it was not untypical of how he responded when feeling cornered. The press loved these unguarded moments and delighted in reporting them to the public. It, of course, had the desired effect of painting Maris as a whiner who did not deserve the season he was having.[27]

Part of the problem was that Maris was convinced that reporters were deliberately "trying to create excitement and juggle words to make a better story." He complained, "Many times I would be answering a question, but another writer would come in about halfway through the answer. He'll only hear part of it, yet he'll base his story on that.... Many times, however, a word or two gets twisted and then it comes out bad. That's what I don't like." A couple of years after he retired from baseball, Maris expressed regret that he did not handle these group press interviews differently. "If I had that to do over again, I wouldn't say a word until all the writers were there. Then I'd talk for 15 minutes and quit."[28]

For whatever reason, Maris read these articles about himself, although he claimed that he did not go out of his way to "see what they said about Roger Maris." Mantle, on the other hand, apparently read only the headlines and looked at the game results and standings on the sports pages, ignoring the contents of the articles. Undoubtedly it would have been much better for Maris' peace of mind had he followed Mantle's example.[29]

The conflict between Maris and the press grew worse as he closed in on Ruth's hallowed record in September. As author Jack Orr described it, these critical stories by reporters and columnists had a snowballing negative impact on the public's perception of Maris. "The stories made the fans react against Maris," Orr explained, "and he was less than a popular hero. He snapped back at fans and reporters and that led to further taunts and an even rougher press, which led to Maris snapping more sharply."[30]

There were times, though, when Maris and members of the press corps got along quite well. He was most comfortable around those he knew and who covered him regularly, like the *New York Post*'s Leonard Shecter. Maris "enjoys exchanging banter with reporters," the columnist noted, finding the Yankee outfielder "charming" in those moments. One day late in the season a reporter was talking to Maris about his lack of home runs in Los Angeles. The unidentified journalist told Maris about how the Dodgers' Wally Moon hit all his "Moon shots" at the Los Angeles Memorial Coliseum by swinging at the bottom half of the ball. "Maris found this hilarious," Shecter observed. "He kidded the reporter about it for days. 'Know what I swing at?' he said. 'The C in Cronin's name on the ball.' He laughed uproariously." Sid Gray, another of New York's many sportswriters, found Maris to be "cooperative, talkative, literate and affected with a wholesomeness that comes from being truthful and sincere."[31]

While those reporters who understood Maris and recognized the pressure he was under treated him fairly, numerous others disliked him and looked for any statement or behavior they felt reflected badly on him. A prime example was George Frazier at the *Boston Herald*. In late September as the stress on Maris was at its peak, the slugger, in an unguarded moment, acknowledged to the press that he was exhausted both mentally and physically. It was an honest statement of how he felt, but Frazier and others saw it as a sign of weakness and went for the jugular.

In his column entitled "Maris Talented with Bat but a Champion? Nay!" Frazier prayed that his sons "never be like Roger Maris. Anything, please, God but that—not even if he were to hit a 100 home runs!" Calling Maris a "whiner" and claiming he lacked "grace under pressure," Frazier compared him unfavorably to teammate Mickey Mantle, "who had been out there day after day through the long season with never a whimper, with only the knifing of the pain inside his body, with only his immense skills and his consummated grace under pressure." Implying that Maris was a baby, Frazier nastily concluded his rant against him by calling on fans to "observe a moment of silence while we burp Roger Maris, home run hitter and endorser of many emoluments, none of them, ironically, a diaper service. Now then, if you will please pass the pablum."[32]

Jim Ogle, who covered Maris throughout the 1961 season, later confirmed that these types of nasty, personal attacks on the Yankee slugger were all too common among some in the media. "Never did so many who knew so little do so much to destroy a man's image to the public than some sports writers did to Maris," he wrote in 1967. "Maris was ripped time after time by writers who not only didn't know him, but had never spoken to him."[33]

Many of these confrontations could have been prevented, or at least defused, if the Yankee front office had provided their star with guidance and shelter from the onslaught of a demanding press. But they did not. They left Maris to fend for himself, which he often did badly. "The Yankees, completely unprepared for the media circus, gave him no help, offered him no protection, and set no guidelines," wrote David Halberstam. "They let him, stubborn, suspicious and without guile, hang out there alone, utterly ill prepared for this ordeal." In fact, it was not until late in the season that Yankee manager Ralph Houk began controlling press access to the clubhouse. By then it was too little, too late. The image of Maris as a bitter, angry, ungrateful man was firmly implanted in the public mind.[34]

Ford Frick

One of the biggest obstacles Roger Maris faced in his pursuit of Babe Ruth was the commissioner of baseball, Ford Frick. When it became apparent in mid-summer that both Maris and Mickey Mantle were making a serious run at Ruth's single-season record, Frick made his infamous 154-game ruling on July 17: "Any player who may hit more than sixty home runs during his club's first 154 games would be recognized as having established a new record. However, if the player does not hit more than sixty until after his club has played 154 games, there would have to be some distinctive mark in the record books to show that Babe Ruth's record was set under a 154-game schedule and the total of more than sixty was compiled while a 162-game schedule was in effect." Contrary to myth, Frick was not the one to suggest an asterisk as the distinctive mark. That dubious honor belonged to Dick Young, columnist for the New York *Daily News*. "Maybe you should use an asterisk on the new record," Young purportedly remarked when Frick made his announcement to the assembled reporters. "Everybody does that when there's a difference of opinion."[35]

In early August, Frick had to amend his earlier dictate because the question of tied games came up. The Yankees played 155 games in 1927 and 163 in 1961 because there was a tie game in both seasons: ten innings on April 14, 1927, seven innings on April 22, 1961. Had Ruth, Maris, or Mantle hit a home run in their respective tied games, it would have counted toward their season totals. While none of them did, Maris and Mantle each lost a home run in the second game of a doubleheader in Baltimore on July 17 when it was rained out before the regulation five innings were completed. There is no indication that Ruth lost a home run in 1927 due to a called game.[36]

Frick decided that it made "no difference how many tie games are played. When the Yankees or any other club has a total of 154 games won or lost, then they will have finished a 154-game schedule as far as the records go. The ties are just rub of the green, a break in favor of the men who get an extra chance." Thus, Maris and Mantle had until game

155 to "officially" break or tie Ruth's record since the Yankees played the same number of games in 1927. Yet this so-called clarification failed to account for any other seasons in which more than 154 games were played to completion. In 1951, the New York Giants and the Brooklyn Dodgers played 157 games, which included the three playoff games against each other at the end of the established 154-game season. Bobby Thomson hit two home runs in those three games and both counted toward his regular-season totals. As Leonard Koppett stated in the *New York Post*, "how totally useless baseball statistics would become if Frick's quaint idea that a 154-game portion of a 10-team 162-game schedule can somehow be related to an eight-team 154-game schedule."[37]

One reason the 162-game schedule was so controversial was that the 154-game schedule had been around for over 50 years and was considered by many to be sacrosanct. The fact that the National League did not adopt the new schedule until the following season when it, too, expanded to ten teams also made the 1961 American League schedule seem aberrant in the minds of some. In addition, there were some who believed that this longer season would not last and that both leagues would eventually revert to playing 154 games. Dick Young postulated that baseball was going through a "transitory stage" and "that eventually, perhaps in five more years, further expansion will produce 24 teams and a return to the 154-game sked. Therefore, all records should be preserved on the 154-game basis—with a special section for these interim years of 162."[38]

In the fall of 1960 before the implementation of this new schedule in the American League, Frick was much more sanguine about the prospects of records being broken because of the longer season. "But the longer I thought about it the more convinced I became that our fears are groundless. Certain records are bound to be affected but I doubt that the great marks we treasure will even be approached, despite the eight extra games." As for the single-season home run record, "I don't think the Babe's record is vulnerable. I'll grant you that Hank Greenberg and Jimmie Foxx came reasonably close with fifty-eight each. Could they have gone the rest of the way if each had eight more games? I'm not too sure." But he did temper his "conviction" by indicating he would "ask the rules committee to study this problem and try to soften the impact wherever necessary. My own idea is that some records might deserve to be listed in two categories." He also recognized that "comparisons today aren't always valid because of changes in playing fields, the bringing in of outfield fences, the raising or lowering of screens. We've survived all that—and so have most of the records." His 1960 sentiments were perfectly in line with the existing practice of listing new records without regard for length of the season. When Babe Ruth, for example, set a new major league record in 1919 by belting 29 home runs in 136 games during a postwar-shortened 140-game schedule, no one then noted that he surpassed the previous record of 27 homers set in 1884 when the season was only 112 games long.[39]

Clearly he had a change of heart midway through the 1961 season. His decision, done without consulting the records committee, was a calculated ruling designed to protect Babe Ruth, as evidenced by the fact that he had no apparent concerns with other records that might be broken in 1961. For example, when in game 151 Sandy Koufax surpassed Christy Mathewson's single-season strikeout record which was set in 1903 during a 140-game season, Frick did not make a pronouncement that Koufax's achievement would carry a distinctive mark. Jim Gentile hit his fifth grand slam in the Baltimore Orioles' game 155, the same number as Ernie Banks hit in the shorter 1955 season. While Frick was forced to announce that it would not be recognized as a tie, no such notation was ever made in any record books.

By way of illustration, the *Baseball Guide and Record Book* published by the Sporting News in 1962 states without qualification that "Gentile socked five of the bases-loaded four-baggers, matching the Big Time mark set by Ernie Banks of the Chicago Cubs in 1955." When it came to Maris' achievement, the *Guide* declared, "Ruth's 60 Homers Still Tops: Maris Set 162-Game Season High with 61." As Shirley Povich of the *Washington Post* noted, "Because of the longer season, the records for assists and putouts, team and individual, are in danger as well. Lacking a directive of Frick, it appears they are not worth his concern." Frick never commented on these other records. And, to be fair to the commissioner, no one in the press or among the fans seemed to be much concerned about any other records either. A sports columnist might raise the question on occasion, but all anyone really cared about was the single-season home run record.[40]

On the day Frick announced his decision, Maris had 35 home runs and Mantle 33. Both were well ahead of Ruth's 1927 pace and the commissioner was terrified that one or both of them would out-homer the Babe. Frick, writes baseball historian Maury Allen, "had been close to Babe Ruth in the 1920s and 1930s, ghosted articles and books about him, dined with him often, told endless stories about him and enjoyed being in the glow of the light the great baseball eminence radiated in his lifetime and beyond. He could hardly be described as an impartial man when it came to protecting the glory of the Babe." Frick made much of the fact that he was at Ruth's bedside the day before he died of cancer, claiming that the Bambino had asked to see him specifically. Allen poses the crucial question: "Could that possibly be a man who could fairly rule on the significance of what Roger and Mickey Mantle were doing in the summer of 1961?"[41]

The impact of this ruling was two-fold. First, by imposing an arbitrary time limit on the accomplishment, it significantly increased the pressure on Maris as the days wound down. "[I]n Roger's case," commented sportswriter Milton Gross, "Frick's ukase works a concentrated injustice because that much more pressure has been thrust upon him willy-nilly. It would seem there is pressure enough upon him riding the wheel of history without having to gear himself for 162 games, but try only for 154."[42]

Gross' observation was on the money. The specter of the 154-game limit haunted the right fielder as he approached it in mid-September. He was constantly badgered by reporters who asked him repeatedly if he could do it in 154 games. While claiming the ruling did not bother him, he did acknowledge that it "made everyone more conscious of the record, especially the pitchers. It put the spotlight on the record and, therefore, started more talk about it, more questions. I didn't like that..." Clearly, though, Frick's decision did affect Maris in ways both physical and mental. By early September he admitted that he was weary and feeling "blah." "I'm not feeling too good," he told reporters after hitting his fifty-fifth home run on September 7. It was around this time that he noticed his hair was falling out in patches and decided to see a doctor about it. Maris was informed that his hair loss was "because of nervous tension, strain, and being upset. It was then I first discovered what the home-run chase had really been doing to me."[43]

The ruling had the added effect of delegitimizing the accomplishment should Maris tie or exceed Ruth's record after game 155. And this was exactly what it did in the eyes of many in the press and among some fans, especially Ruth loyalists. Article after article congratulated Maris after he hit home runs 60 and 61, but nearly all of them noted that he had done it in games 159 and 163 respectively as if somehow he was a failure for not doing it in 154 games. In actuality, Maris hit 60 home runs in fewer plate-appearances (684) than did Ruth (687). That fact was rarely mentioned in press accounts of his feat.

The Sporting News, baseball's "bible," took particular delight in declaring "Maris Finishes Second to Babe's No. 1" in an editorial published on September 27. "Babe Ruth still is the king," the editorialist smugly proclaimed. "In 154 games, he still has hit more home runs than any other man in the game. In happier times, with a more settled league, where every player would be an established major leaguer, a man tying or beating his record would be better accepted." While agreeing, somewhat condescendingly, that Maris was "a tremendous competitor," the editorial concluded with a reiteration of Maris' "failure": "As it stands now, Ruth still is Number One. But Roger Maris is Number Two, only one away from the mighty Babe. It is an equitable finish, one that should be satisfying to almost everyone who followed Maris' valiant effort." Joe Trimble of the New York *Daily News* hit the nail on the head when he wrote, "Frick, by opening his mouth and putting his foot in it, has put unnecessary pressure on Maris—who certainly has about all that one man can stand at this point," adding that that Frick's "dictum" had "stigmatized" any home run record that might occur after 154 games.[44]

Initially, even Maris himself bought into this notion that he had fallen short. "I had given it my best shot," he wrote in his account of the season. "I had tried and I failed." Nearly 20 years later, Maris still harbored resentment over how he was treated for breaking Ruth's record. "They acted as though I was doing something wrong, poisoning the record books or something," he stated in 1980. It cast a cloud over what Maris had accomplished, one that was not entirely eliminated until 1991 when commissioner Fay Vincent and a panel on statistical accuracy overturned Frick's pronouncement. "This change allows Roger Maris to receive the recognition he deserves," Vincent stated when he announced their decision nearly six years after Maris' death from cancer.[45]

Frick's proclamation was controversial and drew a battle-line between those who revered the Babe and those who felt that no distinction should be made. Maris, of course, was well aware of the brouhaha surrounding Frick's decision and clearly understood that many fans and sports writers agreed with the commissioner. A poll conducted by *The Sporting News* among members of the Baseball Writers' Association found that 37 respondents supported Frick, 18 did not.

"The slugger who equaled or surpassed Ruth's record with the help of a 162-game schedule should not be allowed to inherit Ruth's crown," opined Shirley Povich of the *Washington Post*. "At best it would be artificial or synthetic." Bob Broeg of the *St. Louis Post-Dispatch* used the questionable analogy of foot races in supporting the commissioner: "You can't compare times for a 100-yard dash or a 100-meter dash because of different distances, either." Many who agreed with Frick felt that *all* records prior to the longer 1961 season, not just the season home run record, should be put in a different category. Hy Hurwitz of the *Boston Globe* concurred, adding that the ruling should have been made prior to the season, not in mid–July when Ruth's record appeared to be in jeopardy. Even many in the New York press, such as Dan Parker of the *New York Mirror*, Dick Young of the *Daily News*, Jack Butler of the *Brooklyn Tablet*, Joe King of the *New York World-Telegram*, and Max Kase of the *New York Journal-American*, stated their agreement with the commissioner to one extent or another.[46]

But others in the press expressed outright and vociferous opposition to Frick's ruling. Jimmy Powers of the New York *Daily News* called the decision "ridiculous." "There have been so many changes through the years, playing habits, the physical layout of the parks, encroachments on space in so many ways that the record book would be full of asterisks if we tried to reduce everything to a certain era or 'freeze' it," he argued. The *Washington*

Star's Francis Stann acknowledged that "Commissioner Frick is a nice man but he is going to make blithering idiots of us all if records are going to be departmented [*sic*]. I don't feel a 154-game restriction should be placed to protect any record." Bob Stevens of the *San Francisco Chronicle* stated simply, "records are made to be broken, conditions to the contrary notwithstanding." He also asserted that "99 per cent of them [records] are overrated anyway." Eugene Fitzgerald, sports columnist for the *Fargo Forum and Moorhead News*, Maris' hometown newspaper, questioned Frick's assumption that a longer season gave Maris the edge. "Frick can never prove that there is an advantage in playing a 162-game schedule, involving long air jumps, numerous night games, twi-night doubleheaders and pack eight additional games into the same number of days as in 1927 when Babe Ruth hit his 60 in a schedule which included all day games, played at a more leisurely pace."[47]

And Walter Bingham in *Sports Illustrated* labeled Frick's ruling "a foolish, pathetic little statement, foolish because it makes so little sense, pathetic because it will be ignored." Bingham also envisioned a bizarre scenario that was raised by others as well: if one of the M and M Boys were to hit 61 homers by game 154 and the other did not, that individual would be considered the new single-season home run king under Frick's imposed limit. But what if the one who came in second under Frick's dictate were then to pass the official champion in the last eight games? Who would be the undisputed record holder, the one who hit 61 within the limit or the one who hit the most home runs that season?[48]

Surprisingly, many players at the season's second All-Star game in Boston voiced support for the commissioner. The 12 expressing agreement included Maris teammates Whitey Ford, Stan Musial, Dick Donovan, John Roseboro, Norm Cash, Jim Gentile, and Warren Spahn and Eddie Matthews of the Milwaukee Braves. Of course, since none of them were in danger of being impacted by Frick's decision, they had nothing to lose in backing him. Curiously, even Mickey Mantle agreed with the ruling, stating, "I think it's right. Ruth set it in 154 games and you should beat it in the same number of games. If I should break it in the one hundred and fifty-fifth game, I wouldn't want it." Years later, Mantle retracted this earlier statement when he wrote, "I thought it was a ridiculous ruling. It made no sense at all."[49]

Five others, such as Roy Sievers, Ernie Banks, and Al Kaline, voiced their opposition. Roger Maris was more cautious in his response, as was typical of him when it came to this topic. "I think Mick has a good chance to break it," he stated. "I think the commissioner shouldn't have made any 154-game ruling when he did. But if Mick breaks it, I hope he does it in 154. The same goes for me." As for Yankee manager Ralph Houk, he fully supported his two sluggers, terming Frick's pronouncement "a joke." Contending, as did many others, that "a season's a season," the Yankee skipper declared that "if the commissioner's going to make special rulings for this record, then they'd better throw out the whole record book and make special rulings for every other record in it."[50]

One of Ford Frick's most vocal critics was Joe Cronin, President of the American League. "I respect the commissioner's feelings on the matter," Cronin announced, "but as far as I'm concerned, it will be a record if either or both do it in 162 games." Cronin noted that when baseball expanded to 154 games, no one challenged existing records from earlier seasons when far fewer games were played. He gave the example of Hugh Duffy, who in 1894 set a National League record when he batted .440 in 125 games. "[T]here was no talk of not recognizing a new mark should someone better Duffy's figure in more games than he played." And when Maris hit his sixtieth home run, Cronin made no bones about the fact that he considered Maris as having legitimately tied Babe Ruth. "Marvelous, just marvelous," Cronin declared about the achievement. Even Happy Chandler, Frick's immediate predecessor as baseball commissioner, was critical of his dictum. "Mantle? Maris? They ought to break Babe's record," he told Bob Considine of the *Washington Post*. "Why should anybody object? It would be a pretty sad circumstance in this country if we didn't root for new young fellows coming along to do things better than the men of the past." He called Frick's decision "nonsense," proclaiming, as many others did, "A season's a season, and now the season's 162."[51]

Naturally the fans were drawn into the controversy as well. In late September the *New York Times* did an informal man-in-the-street poll of 25 New Yorkers as to how each felt about Frick's declaration. Fifteen came out strongly in favor of making a distinction, nine strongly disagreed, and one said he did not care one way or the other. Those voicing agreement made statements like "Maybe Ruth would of hit seventy in 162 games" and "They've been doctoring the ball and moving the fences. What the Babe wouldn't [sic] have done today!" Opponents argued, "He gets the record if he does it this season. Do the Yanks have to win the pennant in 154 games? No" and "If Maris breaks the record in 162 games, the people will accept it." Even fans as far away as Cuba and Japan chipped in their two cents' worth.[52]

Some criticized Frick for arbitrarily making such a consequential decision without consulting, let alone deferring to, the seven-member Records Committee of the Baseball Writers' Association like former commissioner Warren Giles had done several years earlier when it came to Stan Musial setting a new National League record for consecutive games played. As baseball historian Allen Barra pointed out, at that time major league baseball did not maintain an "official" record book and Frick had zero authority to dictate to private publishers like the Elias Sports Bureau, *The Sporting News* and others how they must list baseball records. He was basically using his "bully pulpit" as commissioner to convince them to do as he wanted.[53]

Dan Daniel, one of the committee members and a Frick supporter, stated then that "the Records Committee should be reorganized and that it should determine if it wanted to pass on the matter [of the single-season home run record] or refer it to the BBWAA as a whole." Members Joe Reichler of the Associated Press and John Drebinger of the *New York Times*, both of whom opposed Frick's ruling, threatened to resign if the matter were not referred to the committee for consideration. When asked if he would accept the decision of the Records Committee if such a vote were held, Frick responded adamantly, "No, I don't recognize it." Even though the writers association did authorize the committee to confer with Frick at baseball's winter meeting in December, the rebellion fizzled when Frick defiantly stated before his appointment with committee members Dan Daniel and Joe Reichler, "They're mistaken if they think they're going to win in the Maris matter." Consequently, Frick's directive stood until it was overturned 30 years later.[54]

In his autobiography, Frick had little to say about his controversial decision. He claimed that he only made a ruling because newspaper reporters kept pressing him to do so. He also confirmed that it was Dick Young of the New York *Daily News* who first raised the question of an asterisk. As for the ruling itself, he proclaimed, "No apologies! Just two official records of two great baseball accomplishments that fans will never forget. I still think it was the right decision."[55]

The Babe Ruth Factor

> "I have never imagined myself as a Babe Ruth, nor have I ever claimed that I am a Babe Ruth. I'm just Roger Maris, a guy trying to do the best he can. I know better than anyone that I'm no Babe Ruth and I'd certainly have a lot of nerve if I ever tried to claim that I was."—Roger Maris, *Roger Maris at Bat*

While it is impossible to measure with any exactitude the psychological impact the Ruth legend had on those who pursued him, it was there nevertheless. As two-time Pulitzer Prize–winning journalist James Reston so aptly expressed it,

> Frick, the high commissioner, merely thought about the mathematics and not the philosophy of the Maris Case, and he did nothing about the psychology of it at all. The essential difference between Ruth and Maris is ... that Maris had to worry about Ruth and Ruth didn't have to worry about Maris. The Babe swung with a free mind, as I remember it, often with an empty mind. The difference wasn't that Maris had a livelier bat or ball than Ruth, but that he had a livelier imagination—and that is no advantage to a ball player under savage pressure in a howling stadium.[56]

When Ruth hit 60 homers in 1927, the only record he was breaking was his own. He did not experience any of the type of mental and emotional stress his challengers did, nor was there all the press and fan brouhaha surrounding his feat as there was in 1961.

Babe Ruth, ca. 1920. Says Roger Maris: "I have never imagined myself as a Babe Ruth, nor have I ever claimed that I am a Babe Ruth. I'm just Roger Maris, a guy trying to do the best he can"—*Roger Maris at Bat* (author's collection).

Even commissioner Ford Frick, self-appointed protector of the Babe, admitted that the response in 1927 was more low-keyed. "It was just another home run for the Babe," Frick stated, "and I don't remember that there was any great excitement, either from the fans or from the sports writers." Many out-of-town papers covered the record-breaking homer only in passing while even New York tabloids were somewhat subdued in their coverage. The headline on the sports page of the *New York Times*, for example, read, "Home Run Record Falls as Ruth Hits 60th; Pirates Lose; Giants Out of Race," covering the event in just one column that did not even include a statement from the Babe.[57]

Most took it in stride because they expected Ruth to hit even more the following season. Long-time Yankee equipment manager Pete Sheehy, who was there the day Ruth broke his own record, told Bob Considine that "60 didn't seem something very special, for Babe. We figured he'd hit 65–70 the next year." The slugger himself saw his accomplishment as routine. "Relax kid," Frick remembered Ruth telling him after hitting number 60, "I'll get a couple more tomorrow." And when Ruth was reminded by a reporter that he was "the new champion," he responded, "There's no new champion, just the old champion."[58]

Jimmy Cannon recognized the tremendous challenge confronting Maris or any player who dared assail the Great Bambino:

> The immortals make death seem like a brief nap lying on a couch in the middle of an endless day. There is no night for them. The grave is not the final abode. Part of them endure. In his own way, Maris understands the frustration of poets and playwrights who challenge Shakespeare with the same 26 letters of the alphabet.... Now he suffers from the purposeless spite of men who regard Ruth as others in a nobler profession honor Einstein. Where the undisputed great all come alone and unwanted to the incandescent place where the undisputed great dwell everlastingly. He trudges the lonliest [sic] road man takes.[59]

Without question Ruth was one of the greatest players in the history of the game. He seemed to be able to do it all—hit for average, hit for power, even pitch. Few in his generation or succeeding ones came up to the standards set by the Sultan of Swat. Roger Maris was not the first to labor under the unremitting burden of being compared to Ruth. Hack Wilson, Jimmie Foxx, and Hank Greenberg all came close, but in the end fell short, in part because they, too, had the specter of Babe Ruth hovering over them. The "august image of the Babe," wrote Joe King in *The Sporting News*, is "the most formidable barrier of all." One advantage these previous contenders had was that Ruth was still alive and his persona not yet at the mythical proportions it reached after his demise. As Arthur Daley reminded his readers in 1961, "the ghost of Babe Ruth keeps growing ever stronger, mocking those who would challenge him."[60]

Some in the press were unrelenting in comparing Maris to Ruth, reminding him over and over again about his "lowly" batting average, that his homers were not as prodigious as those blasted by Ruth, that he lacked Ruth's gregarious and bigger-than-life personality, that he was not even a "real" Yankee. *New York Journal-American* columnist Frank Graham scolded Maris, telling him to "stop being annoyed by those who insist upon holding the image of Babe Ruth before you. You can't really beat him, ever, no matter how many home runs you hit." Dan Parker, sports editor for the *New York Mirror*, was adamant that Maris and Mantle could not hold a candle to the mighty Babe:

> The strongest feeling I have on the subject, and I give voice to it without meaning to disparage, is that if you added Mantle and Maris and multiplied by 10, you might have a two-ply entity that would equal Babe for color, personality and all the other intangibles which separate an athlete of heroic mold from the rest of the pack.... Neither of them has Babe's down to earth appeal, utterly uninhibited nature, immunity against pressure and natural aptitude for getting along with people.... Anyway, neither the Mick nor the Rajah was cast in Babe's heroic mold. Of the Babe it has often been said: "There'll never be another like him." So far there hasn't been.[61]

As would be expected, most of the players from the Ruth era were quite protective of their contemporary. Many considered Maris a second-rate player, someone they thought unworthy in his assault on the Ruth record. Maris was well aware of their opinions and it irritated him. "It gets me sore," he confessed to journalist Roger Kahn. "[T]hey keep comparing me to Ruth, running me down, and I'm not trying to be Ruth. It gets me damn sore."[62]

Hall-of-Famer Rogers Hornsby in particular took umbrage with Maris, declaring that "it would be a shame if Ruth's record got broken by a .270 hitter." Implying that it was easy to get Maris out, Hornsby advised pitchers to "[t]hrow the first two inside and make him foul them, then come outside so he can't pull." He also said "that there was only one thing Maris could do better than the Babe—that was, run." Maris, in keeping with his nature, responded angrily to these comments, cursing Hornsby before reminding him that "they been trying that on me all year and you see how well it works." The ill-will between the two festered during the off-season, finally erupting into a nasty confrontation during spring training the next year when Maris refused to have his picture taken with Hornsby, who had become a coach with the New York Mets. This refusal infuriated Hornsby, who commented that he had "posed with some real major leaguers, not some bush leaguer like he is." Maris, he continued, "couldn't carry my bat," adding that he was a "little punk player" and a "swelled up guy."[63]

Those thinking Maris undeserving because of his batting average ignored, or were not aware of, the fact that as the consummate team-player, his batting average soared when hitting with runners on base. With bases empty, he batted .241 in 316 at-bats; with runners on, it was .303 in 274 at-bats; with runners in scoring position in 128 at-bats he maintained a .328 batting average; and with runners on and two outs, he hit .333 in 87 at-bats. Not too shabby for someone widely criticized for being a mediocre .270 batter.[64]

Maris did have his supporters among players of the earlier generation. Hank Greenberg was especially vocal in expressing his respect for what Maris was doing. "I have a proprietary feeling toward Roger—a pride of authorship, you may call it—because I was the one who brought him into baseball." He particularly resented the "great inclination on the part of many to deprecate the feat even before it is accomplished. They speak of the lively ball, expansion, dilution of pitching strength, smaller ball parks and all that nonsense." He firmly believed that Ruth "was not subjected to the strains of night-and-day baseball, the constant travel and the frantic publicity commotion that has to be unsettling to the two young men [Maris and Mantle]. I'm convinced that the accomplishment of breaking the record is greater now than it ever was." As the most recent player to have come close to toppling the Babe, Greenberg knew firsthand the pressures of which he spoke, including, in his case, suffering a torrent of anti–Semitic epithets hurled at him by spectators.[65]

Several years after the 1961 season, Jimmy Cannon perhaps best described the psychological pressure Maris faced pursuing an icon like Babe Ruth:

> You're Roger Maris who isn't Babe Ruth.... People expected you to be like Ruth when you hit the 61 home runs in 1961. He was regarded as a national resource. He was flattered by crowds and responded to adulation. You shrank from all that. It was as if you didn't believe it. Yet you turned in one of the great achievements in baseball.... Sometimes it seemed you were being attacked by a man already in the grave. Old-timers rapped you because a .269 batter had hit one more home run than Ruth. You didn't break Ruth's record because you had your cuts across a schedule of 162 games. He struck 60 in a tournament of 154 games. The pitcher threw the ball, and you hit it. It was what Ruth did. But they wanted you to have more style. Fame became drudgery for you. It all went sour.... It was you up against Mickey Mantle. But your real opponent was Ruth.[66]

Mickey and Roger

Throughout most of that summer, Mickey Mantle and Roger Maris ran neck-and-neck in the home run race. Mantle began the season blistering hot while Maris started ice cold. By late May, though, Maris found his groove and the two great competitors changed the lead back and forth with each successive home run. It was not until mid-September when Mantle began to fade and then ground to a halt completely because of leg injuries and a bleeding abscess on his thigh that Maris became the sole pretender to the Ruth crown. That was when the long season and the glare of publicity focused on him alone really came down hard on the Yankee right fielder.

Much was written that summer about the supposed ill-will between the two Yankee powerhouses. It was pure invention by some of the reporters who were trying to generate controversy. Since it was rumored that Babe Ruth and Lou Gehrig did not get along in 1927, then that must be the case with Mantle and Maris they reasoned. Nothing could have been further from the truth. Yankee pitcher Ralph Terry, who had been a teammate of Maris during his tenure with the Athletics, summed up these press stories of strife between Maris and Mantle in one simple, straightforward phrase, "That's all bullshit."[67]

While some in the press described the Mantle-Maris relationship as, at best, "a peaceful coexistence," others thought it was much more than that. Bob Considine insisted, "There is no tension between the two, as has been written. They live together when their families are away, ride to work together, operate side-by-side in the outfield of the team they are hammering toward the World Series." Whether or not they were close personal friends only they knew for sure, but as David Halberstam stated it, "there was no animosity, though, and no hard words."[68]

Mantle and Maris got along quite well in fact. For most of the summer, they shared an apartment together along with Bob Cerv, a move that was initiated by Maris with the help of his friend, Big Julie Isaacson. The union leader was convinced that "Roger actually saved Mickey" by allowing Mantle to live with him and Cerv. According to Big Julie, Mantle spent his spare time bar-hopping. One day Isaacson got a call from a friend who owned the bar at the St. Moritz Hotel telling him that Mantle was dead drunk and to come and get him. Maris and Isaacson went to work on Mantle until they convinced him that he needed to change to a more stable living environment. All three players drove to the stadium in Mantle's car. Both sluggers saw the apartment as "a haven in the wilderness," as Maris described it. "Here we could come back after a ball game and be alone. We listened to music, especially Mickey's hillbilly stuff, watched television and talked." Mantle saw their rooming together in the same way. "No matter where I go they ask me if Rog and me are bad friends," the Mick told Jimmy Cannon. "We're roomies. We live together with Bob Cerv. The last day off we were together every minute. I can't cook and neither can Rog. Bob got to make ham and eggs."[69]

Mantle also said that they rarely talked about the home run race, but when they did, it was done in a joking manner. "I hope Maris hits 80," he told one reporter, "and I hit 81." On another occasion he described the friendly banter between the two of them: "I told him if he comes up to try for 60, I'm going to ask the umpire to look at his bat and tell him to throw it out of the game. You know what Rog says? He says if he's on base and I hit 60, he's going to turn around and run past me the wrong way on the bases, so I'll be automatically out. But nobody wants to believe we're real good friends. Do you think I'd live with someone I didn't like?"[70] These are hardly the words of two men who disliked each other.

More than anything, the two were congenial co-conspirators in their pursuit of the Babe, two highly trained professionals who supported each other in word and deed and who pushed each other to do their best. As shortstop Tony Kubek described it, "Roger and Mickey were fighting for the home run record, but it was the healthiest form of competition because they drove each other to excellence." Both players acknowledged that the competition between them helped them hit all the home runs they did. In early

September, Mantle spoke to the fact that it was a rivalry, but "a friendly one. Anything you do you want to do better than someone else." When asked if he thought he would have hit as many homers as he had to that point if Maris were not in the lineup, he admitted he did not think so. "I doubt if I'd played as many games as I had," he told the interviewer. As for Maris, he expressed on more than one occasion his admiration for Mantle and his belief that the long-time Yankee stalwart was the one most likely to catch Ruth. "If anybody breaks it, it will be number 7," he told Bob Considine in mid–August. Maris also contended that both were "enjoying the dingdong chase after the home-run lead."[71]

The 1961 Yankees were a cohesive team with players who liked each other and got along well together. On some other teams, there might have been some bitterness over two teammates getting such a massive amount of publicity as was heaped on the M and M Boys, but nothing like that was present in the Yankee clubhouse. Jimmy Cannon, who covered the team extensively that season, swore that there was no conflict with the other players. "It is a tribute to their [Mantle and Maris] decency that they are not resented by the other[s].... I've sat around with a lot of them and they are grateful to Mantle and Maris for the runs their homers have created during the tournament for the pennant. I haven't heard one complaint about them being selfish or egotistical."[72]

Understandably, though, most of the Yankee players were pulling for Mickey Mantle to break Ruth's record. "We weren't anti–Roger at all," explained second baseman Bobby Richardson. "It's just that we had known Mickey longer.... When Mickey eventually fell out of the home run race, all of us—including Mickey—threw our full support behind Roger." Tony Kubek concurred, noting that because Maris had not come up through the Yankee system, "it was almost like he was an outsider." However, that did not mean that he and the other Yankees were not supportive of the man from Fargo. "But once Mickey got hurt, we rallied around Roger, and I think Roger felt better about going for the record. And even before that, we were behind Roger because of the pressure he endured." Maris himself was aware of the preference for Mantle, but that did not bother him in the least. "All my teammates were pulling for me, and they helped a lot when the pressure became almost unbearable," Maris affirmed.[73]

Many believe Maris may not have hit as many home runs had he not been hitting in front of Mantle most of the 1961 season. Intentional walks have often been held up as proof of the advantage Maris derived by batting third in the order. And indeed, Maris was never intentionally passed even once in the regular season because to do so would generally mean facing the switch-hitting Mantle next. Mantle, on the other hand, received nine free passes that year. Mantle supporters felt this batting order was unfair to their hero. Manager Ralph Houk received multiple letters from Yankee fans demanding he bat Mantle in front of Maris. Houk, of course, was not about to change so successful a lineup. "I want Mickey in between Rog and Yogi [who were both left-handed hitters]," he quite reasonably explained.[74]

Clearly, Maris benefited from batting in front of Mantle. Analysts with the Elias Sports Bureau found that in 475 at-bats in which Mantle was batting behind him, Maris batted .293 with 54 home runs. Games in which Maris did not bat in front of Mantle (115 at-bats), he hit just seven homers with a .174 batting average. But, as they pointed out, this lower production was in part because early in the season he often batted seventh against left-handed pitching due to his greater difficulty with southpaws. It was also during a time when he was swinging a cold bat against right-handed pitching as well. After he found his stroke, he had better success against lefties. Nevertheless, the Elias researchers did conclude that "it's doubtful Maris could have achieved such season-long success" had Mantle not been behind him. Their response: "So what?" Babe Ruth had Lou Gehrig batting behind him, they noted. "Great hitters bat in the middle of the order, surrounded by the best of their teammates. Only Maris hit 61 home runs."[75]

Finally, it should be noted that the previous season Mantle batted in front of Maris more often (52 games) than Maris batted in front of Mantle (36 games) and both seemed to thrive under that arrangement. In fact, Mantle finished first (40 home runs) and Maris second (39 home runs) in the American League in 1960. That season, Mantle was intentionally walked six times, Maris four. Only once was Mantle given a free pass in order to pitch to Maris. "I'm glad to have him in the same batting order as me," Mantle informed Tom Meany. "If I hit ahead of him, they can't walk me with Roger coming up next, and if I bat behind him, I've got a chance to raise my own RBIs. They've got to pitch to one of us or the other. They can't walk both of us. That helps the club." As for the total number of homers that year, Maris could conceivably have hit even more had it not been for a ribcage injury that knocked him out of the lineup for nine games in mid–August. At that point he was batting .295 with 35 home runs while Mantle had a .273 batting average with 27 four-baggers. When Maris returned nearly two weeks later, he never really got back on track, hitting just four more homers and batting .239 for the remainder of the season. While it was only conjecture, Leonard Koppett calculated that had Maris hit at the same rate he was before he incurred the injury, his home run total would have been 55.[76]

The Pitchers

The one-two punch used by those in the press and among the fans then—and even now—in questioning the legitimacy of Maris' accomplishment is the length of the season and the quality of the pitching. It was very common for those who were critical of Maris to assert that the pitching of the American League in 1961 was watered down because of expansion. "Expansion from eight to 10 teams has unquestionably weakened the American League," argued Walter Bingham in *Sports Illustrated*. "There are 25 percent more pitchers in the league than last year, minor league pitchers by the old standard, and they are a big help to good hitters." Bingham's assertion became gospel among those who wanted to deny Maris his due for bettering Ruth. Interestingly, none addressed the issue of how many "minor league" batters there were in the American League that year because of expansion. How accurate was their contention and how did 1961 pitching measure up to that in 1927? Did Maris face weaker pitching than Ruth?[77]

Looking at American League pitching from 1959 to 1962, when both leagues had expanded to ten teams, one can see only a slight rise in the average ERA in 1961. In 1959 it was 3.86, in 1960 it was 3.87, in 1961 it was 4.02, and in 1962 it was 3.97. American League batting averages barely changed at all with expansion. In 1959 it was .253, in 1960 it was .255, in 1961 it was .256, and in 1962 it was .255.

If diluted pitching were a significant factor in batter success during the years of expansion, would not one expect to see an increase in ERAs and batting averages in the National League in 1962 as well? Francis Stann at the Washington *Evening Star* certainly thought so, predicting, quite wrongly as it turned out, that in 1962 the senior circuit would see "the most prolific home run year in history" because of all the "fugitives from the bushes," his term for the pitchers he thought National League batters were likely to face. He even prophesized that someone would join Maris as "a wrecker of Ruth's record." In 1962, however, the National League's average ERA actually declined, from 4.03 in 1961 to 3.94 in 1962. Batting averages declined as well, from .262 in 1961 to .261 in 1962. And while National League home run totals in 1962 did exceed 1961 totals by some 253 dingers, the leader in home runs that season was Willie Mays with 49.[78]

Maris hit his 61 regular-season home runs off of 46 pitchers whose average ERA was 4.30, somewhat above the league average for all pitchers that season. He hit 26 homers off of pitchers who had ERAs below the league average and 35 off of pitchers who had ERAs above the league average. These pitchers had 396 wins and 425 losses for a combined .482 winning percentage. As to winning records, 28 were hit off of pitchers with records of .500 or above, 33 off of pitchers with losing records. Five of the pitchers were rookies, one was pitching in his final season, and two were rookies who were also pitching in their only seasons. Maris loved facing the White Sox, hitting 13 homers off of Chicago pitching. Next came the Washington Senators with nine home runs, followed closely by Cleveland and Detroit with eight apiece. Red Sox pitchers surrendered seven homers, followed by the Athletics with five, the Angels and the Twins with four apiece, and ending with the Orioles with three.[79]

The researchers at Elias looked at how well the pitchers Maris homered off of in 1961 had pitched in 1960 (before expansion). Their reasoning was that pitchers not doing well the season before might have continued to pitch in 1961 because their careers were extended due to expansion. What they found was truly fascinating: in 1961 against pitchers who had 25 starts or were credited with 10 saves in 1960, Maris batted .343 and hit 23 home runs in 166 at-bats (one home run for every 7.2 at-bats); against those who had not performed as well in 1960, he batted a significantly lower .241 and hit 38 home runs in 424 at-bats (one home run in every 11.2 at-bats). They also found that "[a]gainst pitchers who worked fewer than 75 innings—the group that most closely approximates those who wouldn't have pitched in the majors in an eight-team league—Maris hit slightly worse than he did against others." In fact, if Maris had hit as well against these weaker pitchers as he did the better ones, he would have hit a mind-boggling 82 home runs. The numbers "indicate overwhelmingly that Maris did not exploit lesser pitchers" and that "nothing in Maris's record indicates that he would have hit fewer than 61 home runs against a more experienced or more talented set of pitchers," the Elias Sports Bureau researchers concluded.[80]

In terms of quality, the pitchers that Babe Ruth homered off of were not dissimilar to the ones Maris faced. Ruth hit 60 home runs off of 33 pitchers whose average ERA was 4.24, somewhat above the league's average ERA of 4.14. He hit 28 homers off of pitchers who had ERAs below the league average and 32 off of pitchers who had ERAs above the league average. These pitchers had 346 wins and 370 losses for a combined .483 winning percentage. As to winning records, 26 were hit off pitchers with records of .500 or above, 34 off pitchers with losing records. It should be noted that the league's average ERA in 1927 (4.14) was higher than that in the expansion year of 1961 (4.02). Also, the league's batting average in 1927 was .286, considerably higher than that in 1961 (.256). Ruth victimized the same pitchers far more frequently than did Maris: two pitchers gave up four home runs each, seven gave up three home runs each, and seven gave up two home runs each. Maris, on the other hand, hit three homers each off of three pitchers and two homers each off of nine pitchers. Maris hit solo shots off of 34 pitchers, Ruth off of 17 pitchers. As Jerry Nason wrote in the *Boston Globe*, "You cannot with clear conscience put the rap on the pitching the Yankees' present M squad faces without knocking the pitching Ruth faced."[81]

One factor that is rarely raised in judging the quality of pitching Maris faced in 1961 versus that which Ruth confronted in 1927 was baseball's color barrier. Ruth played in the days of segregated baseball, never having to tackle the great African American and black Latino pitchers of his era except in the occasional exhibition game. How many home runs would Ruth have hit if he were confronting the likes of Satchel Paige, Smokey Joe Williams, Bill Foster, or Bullet Rogan instead of inferior white pitchers like Ernie Wingard (2–13, 6.56 ERA, one home run), Slim Harriss (14–21, 4.18 ERA, three home runs), Milt Gaston (13–17, 5.00 ERA, four home runs), or Tom Zachary (8–13, 4.13 ERA, three home runs, including number 60)? Would these pitchers have even been in the big leagues if black pitchers were allowed to play? While organized ball in 1961 was still struggling with full integration, Maris did face a number of excellent black hurlers including Mudcat Grant (15–9, 3.86 ERA, one home run), Bennie Daniels (12–11, 3.44 ERA, one home run), and Juan Pizarro (14–7, 3.05 ERA, one home run). The question posed by Emory University law professor Anita Bernstein strikes at the heart of the matter: "How about an asterisk for ... the Bambino himself, for excelling against competitors who would have played in the minor leagues where they belonged but for the boost of racism?"[82]

Balls and Bats

Early Wynn, who surrendered one of Roger Maris' 61 homers, was convinced the ball that year was juiced. "[J]ust cut it open and you'll find a carburetor," he complained. "[T]his home run craze is going to end when a pitcher is killed or crippled by one of those baseballs they're hitting," warned the future Hall-of-Famer. Dizzy Dean concurred. "Oh, no, it ain't lively. Then how come I hear its heartbeat?" he quipped. While Joe DiMaggio did not think the ball was livelier, he did believe that the way it was constructed favored the hitters. "I compared the 1948 ball with one for 1961" and "[t]here were fewer and bigger, broader stitches on the older ball. These give the pitchers better control," he claimed.[83]

Sports columnist Murray Robinson disagreed, noting that the "rabbit ball," as he called it, was introduced in the Ruth era and thus "any number of batters of that time thereupon became mighty home-run sluggers overnight." "The M Boys' detractors," he asserted, believed that "the rabbit ball was concocted by schemers just in time for the 1961 season in a plot to dethrone the Babe." To him, the only real question was whether or not the 1961 ball was "rabbitier" than the 1927 version. "I don't think it is," he concluded. Edwin Parker, president of A. G. Spalding and Brothers, the company that manufactured the baseballs used by both the American and National Leagues, insisted that the ball they produced was "unchanged. The specifications are exactly the same as in 1926."[84]

So, was the 1961 ball livelier or not? That question was so pervasive in the late summer of 1961 that the *New York Times* hired Foster D. Snell, Inc., an engineering firm, to test seven balls, including one from 1927, which was a ball that was hit for a home run by Babe Ruth that season, one from 1936, one from 1960, and one "from the current batch being launched at Yankee Stadium." The other three were official American League baseballs purchased in a local sporting goods store. According to A. G. Spalding and Brothers, the American and National League balls were exactly the same, the only difference being the labeling stamped on the balls—"Reach" on the American League balls, "Spalding" on the National League balls. The balls sold in sporting goods stores were the same as those used in the major leagues.

All seven were subjected to a battering ram test before two of these balls were dissected. "The 1961 ball is slightly larger, slightly lighter and slightly livelier than one 1927 ball," the engineers concluded. But, they cautioned, these results "might be due more to age deterioration than to differences in manufacture." In spite of the wear on the Ruth ball, however, they did find that it and the 1961 ball "appeared amazingly similar." The fact that the researchers were given only a small sample of balls and that they were not permitted to cut open the Babe Ruth ball added to this tentative conclusion. They did note that the 1961 ball was slightly lighter than the 1927 and 1936 balls, but again they qualified their findings by suggesting that the weight differences might be due to the older balls absorbing more moisture over the years. "A complete storage history would be required, of course, to certify the point."

What they did discover was that a "baseball hit on the seams will travel further" than one struck on the ball's smooth surface. "[I]t is possible that, as far as the baseball is a factor, more balls are now being seam-struck than in previous years," the engineers speculated. "The only valid conclusion which can be drawn from the data herein is that there are differences in construction between 1927 and 1961 baseballs. The effect of these differences cannot be estimated in the absence of a sufficient quantity of test samples." The bottom line on whether or not the 1961 ball was livelier, as the *New York Times* pointed out, was "maybe it is, and maybe it isn't."[85]

Sports Illustrated hired a different firm to study the 1961 balls and came to a more definitive conclusion. Joseph S. Ward and Associates compared balls from 1952 and 1953 with those used in 1961. In 1953 Ward tested six unused balls from 1952 and six new balls from 1953 at the request of Max Kase, then sports editor for the *New York Journal-American*. In this earlier investigation, Ward found that the 1952 ball "averaged an 8-foot rebound and the 1953 ball 8 feet 7½ inches. Thus the 1953 ball had 8 percent more resiliency than the 1952 ball." His "tentative engineering conclusion" at the time was that the 1953 ball was a "jack rabbit" compared to the ball used in 1952.

Using this earlier examination as a base—with the 1961 examination taking place in a different facility and with newly-constructed equipment that "would allow him [Ward] to duplicate the exact conditions of the previous tests" conducted in 1953—the firm then acquired twelve 1961 baseballs in a sealed box delivered directly from Spalding for testing. They found the average rebound of the 1961 ball to be 8 feet, 9½ inches, making the rebound average 2 percent greater than the 1953 ball and 10 percent greater than the 1952 ball. To put it another way, "a 300-foot drive in 1952, under the same impact force, would result in a distance of 324 feet in 1953 and 330 feet in 1961." Based on these results, the biggest change in the ball occurred between the 1952 and 1953 seasons, not between the 1953 and 1961 seasons.

Unlike the Snell study, Ward researchers did not test any balls from the 1960 season when the average number of home runs per game was less. That would seem to be a more significant comparison if one is arguing that an even livelier ball was first introduced in the 1961 season. In fact, the Snell researchers tested one ball from 1960 and four from 1961 finding only a slight difference between the rebound inches of the 1960 ball (31.4

inches) and the average for the four 1961 balls (32.18 inches). Ward and Associates also found that the weight of the 1961 balls was heavier (5.29 ounces) than the maximum allowed under the official baseball rules (5.25 ounces). They thought this weight discrepancy when compared to the 1952 and 1953 balls was the "most significant thing," concluding that "[t]he difference in weight must mean there is a difference in some part of the composition of the [1961] ball. This was reflected in the performance tests showing a livelier ball."[86]

Leonard Koppett, for one, was disparaging of this second study. He was especially outraged that the sampling size was so small and that all the 1961 balls came from the same box. The *Sports Illustrated* "story states with either shock or glee, but certainly pride, these six balls were taken from a single sealed box provided by the manufacturer— and that each was a fraction of an ounce heavier than the maximum allowed by baseball rules. Now you and I, not being engineers, might wonder at that point whether or not we had a box of typical or defective baseballs on our hands and might try to find out by comparing them with some other boxes," which the researchers did not do. "But then, suppose these overweight balls did turn out to be typical (which would be a better story, if proved). What sort of sampling procedure is it to test six baseballs when the two major leagues use up 160,000 or so every season?" Although Koppett was confusing Ward's earlier study—when six balls from each of the two seasons were compared—with his firm's more recent study—when a dozen 1961 balls were analyzed—his concern about the number of balls compared is spot on. Indeed, sampling size was the underlying problem with all these investigations.[87]

A third study was conducted by *Popular Mechanics* in conjunction with the Armour Research Foundation; the results were reported in the December 1961 issue of the magazine. Twelve "verified game balls from 1909 to 1937" were compared to 12 balls taken from a lot of new balls owned by the Chicago White Sox. Both groups were subjected to chemical and mechanical tests to determine if there were significant changes over the years that would account for the increase in home runs. First, the researchers found that "there have been changes in yarns, rubber and cork core materials, and manufacturing processes" between the two groups of balls as well as "inconsistencies" within each group. "While the effect of these irregularities on 'liveliness' is hard to predict, it's almost certain that they would not have performed identically," they concluded. Impact tests were used to test the "liveliness" of each ball, that is, "their ability to rebound from a blow." To their surprise, they found that even though the 12 newer balls were from the same carton, "their coefficients of restitution [liveliness] varied from .50 to .68; enough variation to account for a 12 percent difference in distance when hit by a bat at the same speed." In other words, even within the same group of 1961 balls, some were "livelier" than others. They also determined that there was less such variation within the older-ball group.[88]

In addition, their measurements revealed that the older balls "had a much different seam structure than the 1961 sample balls. The older seams were narrower, tighter, seemed to be sewn with lighter thread, and were much flatter than the 1961 seams. As a result, the contour of the older balls was smoother." Using wind-tunnel tests, they determined there was less "drag" on the newer balls. In fact, the older balls "showed 10 to 15 percent *more drag* [their emphasis] than the 1961 balls.... That's enough to boost a 350-foot fly ball to a 385-foot home run."[89]

Perhaps the most astounding finding was that the older balls "showed almost exactly the same coefficient of restitution as the new balls *at high bat speeds* [emphasis added].

But at lower [their emphasis] *bat speeds, the 1961 balls were much 'bouncier' than the older samples, and the slower the bat speed, the greater the difference. So the light hitter, not the home run king* [emphasis added], *is the one who should really be profiting from a livelier ball."* Thus, according to their findings, "the ball *isn't* [their emphasis] much livelier for the 'home run king' types like Ruth and Mantle and Maris. But it responds better to the lesser efforts of lighter, less powerful players. Coupled with the other factors that affect home run hitting, this low-speed liveliness could explain the increase in overall home run hitting while, at the same time, individual performance has not improved."[90]

So there you have it. Three different tests, three different results, all conducted using a small sample size. While none of them definitively answered the question about whether or not the ball used in 1961 was any different from those used in the decade prior to that, it appears that if there was a difference, it was so slight as to be insignificant.

There is one final point concerning whether or not the ball was juiced. Both the American League and the National League used the same Spalding baseballs. Why, then, did not the senior circuit experience a significant increase in home runs over previous seasons? In the National League in 1959, there were 1,159 home runs, in 1960 there were 1,042, and in 1961 there were 1,196, indicating a slight, but statistically insignificant, increase in this offensive category. League batting averages over the same period were .260 in 1959, .255 in 1960, and .262 in 1961. Again, there was a minor fluctuation upwards, but not so much so that 1961 stood out as an anomalous season offensively. In fact, if one excludes Maris and Mantle, the number of home runs produced by the top ten home-run hitters in 1961 was not that much different from previous seasons. The most homers hit by a National League player in 1961 were 46 by Orlando Cepeda, which tied him for third place overall with Jim Gentile and Harmon Killebrew from the American League.

Others argued that it was not the ball that gave Maris and Mantle an advantage over the Babe, it was the type of bat used by players in 1961. Was the 1961 bat "livelier" than the ones swung by Ruth and his contemporaries? That was certainly what Joseph Sheehan at the *New York Times* believed. "A second go-round on a pioneer research tour several years ago has strengthened the conviction that the current rash of homer hitting is attributable to revised qualities of the bat, rather than the ball," adding that the increase in home runs in both leagues was "because today's players are taking heavier swings with lighter bats at more or less the same old ball."[91]

These lighter bats were not unique to the 1961 season, however. In fact they had been in vogue for at least a decade. And while the average number of home runs per game showed a significant increase over the Ruth era, it varied from season to season. In 1950, for example, the average in the American League was 0.78 per game. The following season it had dropped to 0.68. It remained roughly in that range until 1955 when it again reached the height of the 1950 season, 0.78. The next year it increased significantly to 0.87, fluctuating slightly above or below that average through the 1960 season (0.88). The average jumped to 0.95 in 1961 and 0.96 in 1962, again averaging in that range until it began to decline again during the 1965 season (0.85). Interestingly, the home run average per game in the National League was often higher during that same period. In 1950 it was 0.89, declining somewhat until the 1953 season when it increased to 0.96. In 1955 it skyrocketed to 1.03, varying from 0.98 to 0.93 until the 1960 season (0.84). In 1961, the average was actually higher (0.97) than the expansion-year American League (0.95). Curiously, in 1962 when the senior circuit added two teams, the average dropped to 0.89 and, with the exception of the 1987 season (0.94), remained below that average until 1994.[92]

Clearly, the lighter bats used since the late 1940s to early 1950s were, in part, responsible for the jump in home runs over the Ruth era. With the exception of 1929 (0.61) and 1930 (0.72), yearly averages ranged from a low of 0.19 (1919) to a high of 0.56 (1940) until a significant increase began in the immediate post–World War II years. It was during the Ruth period that the heavy bat was the typical weapon used by the home-run hitter. According to records maintained by the Hillerich and Bradsby Company (manufacturers of the Louisville Slugger), Ruth "favored a forty-two-ounce bat in his prime and never used one that weighed less than thirty-eight ounces." In comparison, Maris used a slightly thick-handled 33-ounce bat while Mantle preferred a thinner-handled bat of the same weight.[93]

Ruth initiated the home-run era, but it took a while for baseball to completely evolve from the small-ball approach to the game. Once he demonstrated that "home run hitters drive Cadillacs," other players began to follow suit and to look for ways to improve home run output. Sluggers at that time believed that the heavier the bat, the greater the distance the ball was driven. Some players even hammered nails and needles into the barrel of the bat to increase the bat's weight. And, indeed, bats of greater mass do tend to drive the ball farther.

But recent studies have shown that while a heavier bat can result in increased distance, bat speed is actually more important in enhancing batted-ball speed (BBS) than the weight of the bat. "Boosting two factors—the mass of the bat and the speed of the swing—can raise batted ball speed (BBS), which adds distance to a hit. But swing speed can affect BBS more dramatically." Therefore, "[i]n terms of turning a hit into a homer: Against a 94-mph fastball, every 1-mph increase in swing speed extends distance about 8 ft." The ideal would be for the player to swing a heavy bat at great speed, but that is not realistic because "it takes more effort to swing a heavy bat with the same speed as it does a lighter bat, and most players cannot swing a heavy bat as quickly as they can a bat which is half the weight." A lighter bat also results in greater bat control and allows the batter to wait just a little longer before initiating his swing.[94]

Interestingly, in 1962 Roger Maris participated in a "faintly scientific experiment" on bat weight and ball distance that was later reported in the *American Journal of Physics*. During this test conducted in Fort Lauderdale during spring training, Maris used five different bats ranging in weight from 47 ounces to 33 ounces. Each of the bats were replicas of the models used by players from different eras: a 46-ounce, 37-inch, untapered model bat used by Pete Browning (1882–1894); a 47-ounce, 34-inch, untapered model bat used by Frank "Home Run" Baker (1908–1922); a 42-ounce, 34½-inch model bat used by Ty Cobb (1905–1928); a 44-ounce, 35½-inch model bat used by Babe Ruth (1914–1935); and Maris' own 33-ounce, 35-inch, comparatively thin-handled, tapered model bat.

Maris then hit five balls with each of the bats and the distances of those that were fly balls hit to the outfield were then measured and correlated to the weight of the bat. Maris regularly hit the ball farther with the heavier bats than he did with the model bat he used in 1961. Of the five longest hits, first (405 feet) and third places were with the Ty Cobb model bat, second place (365 feet) was with the Babe Ruth model bat, fourth place was with the Pete Browning model bat, and fifth place (357 feet) was with the Maris model bat. Ranked according to total distances for all flies was the Ty Cobb bat (1,621 feet), the Home Run Baker bat (1,549 feet), the Pete Browning bat (1,541 feet), the Babe Ruth bat (1,524 feet), and the Maris bat (1,523 feet). The sample is small and perhaps Maris' bat speed decreased as his arms tired from more swings with the heavier bats, thus reducing distance, but nonetheless it demonstrated that a lighter bat alone is not a sufficient explanation for his outstanding season. As he once said, "The weight of the bat isn't the most important thing. What counts more is how you swing it." There are just too many other variables involved in hitting—including the type, speed, and location of the pitch; launch angle; batter stance; reaction time; visual acuity, eye-hand coordination, wrist snap, and so forth—to attribute any batter's home run success to just one thing.[95]

The Stadiums

There was quite a debate at the time about whether or not Maris and the other sluggers in 1961 had an edge because, it was argued, they were playing in stadiums with shorter fences than in 1927. Many saw Yankee Stadium as custom-designed for a dead-pull hitter like Maris, believing that to be the reason for his home-run-hitting prowess. But Maris actually hit more of his regular-season home runs on the road (31) than he did at "The House That Ruth Built." The same was true for Ruth in 1927 when he smashed 32 of his 60 homers away from home. Interestingly, during his Yankee career Maris hit 94 home runs at home, 109 on the road. Even the Babe as a Yankee hit only four more home runs (259) at the stadium than he did at other parks (255). So it appears that neither of them took special advantage of the relatively short right-field porch—some 296 feet down the line to the foul pole—at Yankee Stadium.[96]

So what about the other ballparks? Did Maris play in bandboxes while Ruth had to deal with mammoth coliseums? The short answer is "No." According to the researchers at Elias, the two best "home-run producers" in 1961 were Metropolitan Stadium, home of the Minnesota Twins, and Wrigley Field in Los Angeles, home of the Angels. Wrigley in particular was home-run-friendly with its 345-foot power alleys which were only a few feet longer than down the lines—338 feet to the right field foul pole, 340 to the left field pole. There were 248 home runs launched at the Los Angeles stadium that summer, a new major league record that stood until 1996. Playing half their games at this former minor league park was one of the reasons the Angels were second only to the Yankees in homers that year with 189. Elias calculated that Wrigley, which served as the Angels' home field just for the 1961 season, "doubled the home-run potential of the typical major-league player." Did Maris use Wrigley as his personal launching pad? The answer again is "No." He hit only two home runs there all season. The same held true for Minnesota's stadium; Maris hit just one dinger in Bloomington.

"Had Maris hit eight or 10 home runs at Wrigley Field, and another four or five at Metropolitan Stadium, the objection that he played in small ballparks might have had some merit," argued the Elias Sports Bureau. Clearly that was not the case. Maris hit five home runs each at Cleveland Stadium, Comiskey Park, and Tiger Stadium; four each at Fenway Park, Griffith Stadium, and Municipal Stadium; two at Wrigley Field (Los Angeles); and one each at Metropolitan Stadium and Memorial Stadium. Maris himself was puzzled by the fact that he did not hit as well as expected at either Los Angeles or Minnesota. "I can't understand it. They look like good ballparks. The fences aren't that far. The ball seems to sail nicely enough. Everybody else hits homers there. I don't."[97]

Ruth had more than his share of batter-friendly stadiums as well. As *Sports Illustrated* writer Walter Bingham noted in 1961, the Babe's "cozy parks" included League Park in Cleveland with its right field barrier just 290 feet distant—240 feet when roped off to accommodate fans at sold-out games—and its right field power alley a minuscule 319 feet. Ruth hit four of his homers there, including his tenth which was one that barely left the field. About that particular four-bagger, James Harrison of the *New York Times* quipped, "On a field less tiny than the Cleveland enclosure the right fielder would have camped under this blow and had plenty of time for a ham sandwich and a bottle of pop." In Harrison's estimation the ball traveled 600 hundred feet, "300 up and 300 down," clearing "the high [45 foot] right field screen with almost six inches to spare. George actually blushed as he loped around the bases." In comparison, Cleveland Stadium where Maris competed was 320 feet down the lines and 389 feet in the power alleys.[98]

Ruth also had the advantage of playing in Sportsman's Park in St. Louis when facing the Browns, the site of another four of his homers. It was 310 feet to right field and 354 to right center. The distance to the 11½-foot high right field fence was so short, in fact, that in mid-summer 1929, two years after Ruth's historic season, the Browns added a 25-foot screen atop the existing structure to reduce the number of cheap home runs. That change was made on July 5 shortly after the visiting Detroit Tigers had bashed eight homers in a four-game series. When the Browns moved to Baltimore to become the Orioles, the team played in Memorial Stadium, a much more spacious facility. There the foul poles were just 309 feet away (with a 14-foot high wall), but the power alleys were some 380 feet distant.[99]

Then there was Shibe Park in Philadelphia where Ruth launched five dingers. It was 307 feet to the right field foul pole and 354 to right center. When the Athletics relocated to Kansas City, they played at Municipal Stadium. Right field at Maris' former home park measured out at 353 feet, including 338 down the right field line and 387 to right center. Maris himself observed, "How can you compare different eras? Everything is different now. It is the same as trying to compare Jack Dempsey with Joe Louis. There just is no way to do it."[100]

Playing Conditions

Many of the old-timers complained that they had to deal with rougher playing conditions than did players in 1961. Just like the assertions that Maris faced weak pitching while using a lively bat to hit a rabbit-ball, this was another of the claims made that, intentional or not, tended to minimize his phenomenal season. Johnny Mize was one who firmly believed the modern big leaguer was pampered, especially when compared to the ballplayers of his and Ruth's eras. Dismissing night baseball as being any sort of a problem, Mize maintained that he "played often with the temperature 100 and it used to get that high and stay there for 10 days at a stretch in St. Louis.... Back in the days when the players had few of the comforts they have now, I remember well how many times we'd play a double-header in St. Louis and then have to leave on a road trip. And we would have to walk the mile or so to the station." Former Cardinals pitcher Ted Wilks agreed: "And then get on a railroad car that had been standing in the sun all day and was about 50 degrees hotter than an oven." Mize asserted that when traveling by train, one had "the choice of sitting there with the windows closed and suffocating or opening the windows and inhaling soot and smoke; when you did that you arrived the next morning with your face as black as night and you'd blow coal dust out of your nose for a day."[101]

Even the sleeping accommodations on road trips were a hardship according to Mize.

The hotel rooms would be so hot, "you couldn't go to bed earlier than 1 or 2 o'clock in the morning." Players had to take cold showers to cool off before going to bed. "Usually, that didn't work so you'd throw some cold water on the bed and jump on that. And maybe around 2 or 4 o'clock you'd go to sleep. And you'd have to be up at 8 o'clock and ready to get out to the ball park not too long after breakfast." He thought the modern player had it much easier. "Nope, don't tell me about how much better the old-timers had because they played in the daytime," observing that they had "no air conditioning, no planes." And to him, night baseball was no big deal. "They [the lights] don't affect many hitters, it's cooler at night. You go back to the hotel and your room is air-conditioned. You get on a train and the cars are air-conditioned or you fly."[102]

While night games may not have been particularly onerous for some ballplayers, as Johnny Mize contended, that was not the case with Roger Maris. In 81 day contests, he batted .288 with 35 homers in 299 at-bats; in 80 night games his average dropped to .251 with 26 dingers in 291 at-bats. Projecting from these figures how well he might have done had all his games been in the daylight, he would have hit nearly 70 home runs that season. Why did Maris hit considerably better in the day than at night? It could be that he saw the ball better in natural sunlight than in artificial light or it could have been that his reduced production at night was because he was one of those individuals commonly known as a "morning person."

All of us have internal biological clocks known as circadian rhythms. Some of us prefer daytime hours, others function better at night. According to neurologist Jeffrey Ellenbogen, "Circadian timing influences every aspect of our physiology, including our behavior and physical performance. And just as genetics governs different hair color for different people ... our genes partly determine our individual differences in peak performance at certain times of day." A recent study of 16 major league players from seven teams demonstrated that players who preferred daylight hours performed better in games that began before 2:00 p.m. (.267 batting average) than the "evening-type" player (.259 batting average). During mid-day games (2:00 p.m. to 7:59 p.m.) the evening types surpassed the morning types (a .261 batting average versus a .252 batting average) in offensive production. And for games starting after 8:00 p.m.—usually as a result of rain delays—the batting average for those preferring evening hours jumped to .306 while the morning types remained at .252. While the researchers acknowledged that their data was "not statistically significant due to low subject numbers," they did feel that their preliminary results showed "a trend toward morning-type batters hitting progressively worse as the day becomes later, and the evening-types showing the opposite trend."[103]

In addition, the combination of alternating day games with night ones can be wearying and could impact performance. Yankee manager Ralph Houk observed "that the sudden shifts in time are disrupting. Between that and night games followed by an afternoon game the next day, it is impossible for a player to live a fairly regular life." This was not a problem that Ruth, Mize and others of their generation had to confront. Shift work, especially rotating frequently from day to night and back again, often leads to what is known as shift work sleep disorder (SWSD). According to the Cleveland Clinic, SWSD "commonly affects those who work non-traditional hours, outside the typical 9 a.m. to 5 p.m. work day." One of the underlying factors impacting our circadian rhythms is light, which serves as "a time cue." Once it becomes dark, the body begins to wind down, to move toward a state of rest.[104]

Disrupting this natural cycle can lead to negative side effects, including sleepiness, reduced energy levels, difficulty concentrating, and mood swings. Those who change work schedules often frequently experience the most difficulty. A study of air traffic controllers who rotated between night and day workhours during the week, for example, found that over half of those examined "reported periods of severe fatigue or exhaustion and symptoms of gastrointestinal disturbance typically found among shift workers." With the coming of lights to ballparks and the scheduling of night games mixed with day games, for all intents and purposes ballplayers became rotating shift workers.[105]

What follows was a typical schedule of play experienced by Roger Maris in late May and early June, a period when he had found his swing and was beginning to display his home-run hitting abilities. He played in 17 games in a two-week period that included three doubleheaders—two of the "twi-night" variety (night/night games) and one traditional day/day twin bill—all with no days off:

Monday, May 29, in Boston—9:20 p.m. start time (rain-delayed) and lasted two hours, nine minutes. Maris was zero for four.

Tuesday, May 30, in Boston—a day game lasting two hours, 56 minutes. Maris was three for five with two home runs.

Wednesday, May 31, in Boston—a night game lasting two hours, 52 minutes. Maris was one for four with one home run.

Thursday, June 1, in Boston—a day game lasting three hours, eight minutes. Maris was zero for four.

Friday, June 2, in Chicago—a night game lasting two hours, six minutes. Maris was one for four with one home run.

Saturday, June 3, in Chicago—a 13-inning day game lasting three hours, 26 minutes. Maris one for five with one home run.

Sunday, June 4, in Chicago—a day game lasting two hours, 38 minutes. Maris was two for four with one home run.

Monday, June 5, in New York—twi-night doubleheader. Game One started at 6:04 p.m. and lasted two hours, 28 minutes. Maris was zero for three. Game Two started at 9:06 p.m. and lasted two hours, 31 minutes. Maris was zero for two.

Tuesday, June 6, in New York—8:03 p.m. start time and lasted two hours, 44 minutes. Maris was one for four with one home run.

Wednesday, June 7, in New York—2:03 p.m. start time and lasted two hours, 14 minutes. Maris was one for four with one home run.

Thursday, June 8, in New York—twi-night doubleheader. Game One started at 6:02 p.m. and lasted two hours, 12 minutes. Maris was zero for three. Game Two started at 8:45 p.m. and lasted two hours, 32 minutes. Maris was zero for five.

Friday, June 9, in New York—8:13 p.m. start time and lasted two hours, 34 minutes. Maris was two for four with one home run.

Saturday, June 10, in New York—2:04 p.m. start time and lasted two hours, 12 minutes. Maris was zero for four.

Sunday, June 11, in New York—day doubleheader. Game One started at 2:03 p.m. and lasted two hours, 19 minutes. Maris was one for four. Game Two started at 4:56 p.m. and lasted two hours, 21 minutes. Maris was two for four with two home runs.

In seven away games, Maris went eight for 30 in 33 plate appearances with six home runs and 13 RBIs for a .267 batting average. In 10 home games, Maris went seven for 37 in 42 plate appearances with five home runs and 11 RBIs for a .189 batting average. In the 17 total games, the Yankees won 13 and lost four. And while Maris hit 11 homers, his combined batting average was .224, considerably below his season average of .269. One can easily surmise from this that he felt the wear-and-tear of the day/night game schedule variation and the three doubleheaders as is reflected in his failure to hit in six of the 17 games, including all four games of the two twi-night doubleheaders in New York.

Maris played in 23 doubleheaders, Ruth in 18. The reason there were more doubleheaders in 1961 was because of the eight extra games being played in the same number of calendar days (April 11–October 1) as in 1927 (April 12–October 1). In 1927, doubleheaders were often scheduled on consecutive days to reduce the amount of travel time. Of Ruth's 18 twin bills, 10 were played back-to-back: May 27–28 in New York, May 30–31 in Philadelphia, June 21–22 in Boston, July 8–9 in Detroit, and September 5–6 in Boston. Maris had only one instance when he played doubleheaders on consecutive days: September 14 in Chicago followed by a twi-night stand in Detroit on September 15. The September 14 contest with the White Sox had not been scheduled in advance; it was the result of a rain-out on September 13. The first game was during the day, the make-up game at night. All of Ruth's twin contests were played during the day. Maris, on the other hand, had six twi-night competitions and seven more in which the first game was in the day, the second at night.

Doubleheaders were a distinct disadvantage for Maris, especially ones involving night games. He hated twin bills and typically performed poorly in those situations, with the exception of the two July 25 games, which will be discussed later. He failed to hit in five of them, and had only one safety in each of six others. Although he did hit 13 home runs in those 46 games, the Yankee right fielder batted just .229, 40 points below his season average. Maris did much better when both games were in the day (.292 batting average with eight home runs) than when the first game was in the day and the second at night (.212 batting average with one home run) or in twi-night affairs (.152 batting average with four home runs). In fact, his performance when both games were at night would have been much worse had it not been for the uncharacteristic July 25 battle against the White Sox in New York in which he had five hits, four of them home runs. Ruth, on the other hand, seemed to thrive when playing two games on the same day. He batted .391 with 17 homers in those 36 consecutively-played matchups. These figures underscore the fact that Maris would have hit much better if all his doubleheaders were in the daylight like they were for Ruth.[106]

Jet lag was another of the difficulties to which Ruth and the other old-timers did not have to adjust. Train travel may have been somewhat uncomfortable in Ruthian days, but at least he and the others did not have to travel back and forth across multiple time zones to play distant teams. The most they had to deal with was crossing over one time zone, not three like those playing on the east and west coasts in 1961 had to do. "When we rode trains," Ralph Houk noted, "the change in time wasn't so noticeable. But it's pretty hard to tell a ballplayer he ought to be in bed because it's midnight when his watch still says it's only 9 or 10."[107]

Anyone who has traveled from coast-to-coast or internationally can relate to what Houk was saying. But does jet lag impact performance? According to researchers Alex Song, Thomas Severini, and Ravi Allada, it does. They analyzed 20 years of data from Major League Baseball involving over 46,000 games. According to their findings, jet lag—which they defined as crossing two or more time zones—had a definite negative impact on both offensive and defensive performance in very specific areas. "Surprisingly, we found that jet lag impaired major parameters of home-team offensive performance, for example, slugging percentage, but did not similarly affect away-team offensive performance," which was most "evident after eastward travel with very limited effects after westward travel."

In other words, eastern-based teams like the New York Yankees would experience the biggest negative impact after returning home from playing the Los Angeles Angels, while the Angels traveling to New York would experience much less of a fall-off in offensive production. According to one of the researchers, "One of the more surprising things we found was that in some cases we would see effects on home teams and not away teams. We don't typically think of home teams as suffering jet lag, but that's what we observed." These findings confirmed what earlier studies found; that is, "misalignment is especially strong when a person's day is shorter than it should be—which happens whenever people travel east." Conversely, "when you travel west you adjust by waking up later and going to bed earlier in relation to your home city time and your internal biological clock."[108]

Early in the 1961 season, John Drebinger of the *New York Times* wrote about the difficulties teams faced in traveling to away games. It was not a bed of roses as Johnny Mize implied. "[T]here is another side to the life of a modern ballplayer that one may just as well know about before he gets the notion it's all luxurious hotels and flitting through the blue from town to town. This can become, instead, a nightmarish jumble of chasing trains, planes and buses." He gave as an example the Yankees' away trip that began with a doubleheader in Washington on April 30 and ended with a night game against the Athletics on May 10 before returning to New York for a home-stand against the Tigers on May 12.

On April 30, the Yankees were in Washington where they split a daytime doubleheader against the Senators, the Bombers winning the first game, the Senators the second. Because the afternoon game scheduled for May 1 was a rainout, the Yankees went to the airport early hoping to catch their charter flight to Minnesota. Unfortunately, there was no flight crew available, so the team had to wait until later that night, arriving in Minneapolis at 1:00 a.m. on May 2. Later that afternoon, they beat the Twins, 6–4, in a 10-inning contest that lasted three hours. On May 3 they played another day game, this time beating Minnesota, 7–3. After again conquering the home team in an early afternoon game, the squad was delivered by bus to the airport in Minneapolis, planning to get a jump on the flight to Los Angeles for a contest scheduled for the following night. Once again misfortune reared its head: the charter plane had engine trouble, causing a delay of two and a half hours.

Arriving in L.A. at 2:00 a.m. on May 5—5:00 a.m. New York time—the team had little time to rest before a night game against the Angels. They won that battle, 5–4, but lost the following night, 5–3. They were defeated by the same score the following afternoon, May 7, before returning to their hotel. Since they had to be at the Los Angeles airport at 7:30 a.m. on May 8 for a flight to Kansas City, their sleep-time was shortened due to an early wakeup call. Fortunately, because their first game against the Athletics was not scheduled until the night of May 9, the weary travelers did get the day of their arrival to catch up on some much-needed sleep. They lost the May 9 game, 5–4, but did manage to defeat Kansas City the next evening by a score of 9–4. After staying over in Kansas City, the Yankees arrived back in New York on May 11, giving them the remainder of that day—shortened by one hour due to a change in time zones—to recuperate before they had to confront the league-leading Tigers at the Stadium the next night. As pitching coach Johnny Sain quipped afterwards, "Who was it once said, 'You can't beat the hours'?"[109]

While one can debate whether or not it was more exhausting to travel by train in the earlier period as Johnny Mize described it, no one can deny that this type of hectic pace involving crossing up to three time zones during a 162-game season could wear down any player. All of them felt it, but Roger Maris' big mistake was to verbalize it to the press. "I'm tired, plain old fashioned tired," the Yankee slugger announced in late August. The main reason for his exhaustion, he said, was "the heavier schedule. They added games but compressed it into the same period of time as before." Admitting that he "need[s] lots of rest," he considered asking for some days off, "but how could I do that now. The Tigers are right on our tail, only two games away, and all of us have to play every minute we can." As a result of statements like these, some reporters were quick to jump all over him, calling him a whiner and implying he was a baby, which was what George Frazier of the *Boston Herald* labeled him.[110]

Exhaustion at the end of a long season is a very real condition most players experience. Dr. Scott Kutscher from the Vanderbilt University Medical Center led a study of how fatigue impacts performance as the season unfolds. What he found was that "strike-zone judgment" for most batters was noticeably worse in September than in April. "Plate discipline—as measured by a hitter's tendency to swing at pitches outside of the strike zone—got progressively worse over the course of a Major League Baseball season, and this decline followed a linear pattern that could be predicted by data from the six previous seasons." He and the other researchers "theorize that this decline is tied to fatigue that develops over the course of the season due to a combination of frequency of travel and paucity of days off."[111]

Such was the case with Roger Maris who fit this pattern exactly, hitting 15 home runs in June, 13 in July, 11 in August, and 10 in September/October. Clearly, Babe Ruth, with his 17 home runs in September/October after hitting only nine in each of the previous three months, was the rare exception to this rule. Maris' problems at the plate were exacerbated after the Yankees clinched the American League pennant on September 20. After that was accomplished, his main objective was to surpass Babe Ruth's single-season home run record. By this stage of the season, though, Maris was physically and emotionally drained. He started pressing, swinging at pitches outside the strike zone. "I wasn't swinging normally," he wrote. "I knew that the chase after the home-run record had fouled up my swing." As a result, he "had been swinging at bad pitches. I was doing what the pitchers hoped I would do. I felt that if I hit another home run this season it would be only if the pitchers made a mistake." In spite of the many obstacles facing him, though, Maris was able to accomplish what Hack Wilson, Jimmie Foxx, and Hank Greenberg before him failed to do, conquer the Babe.[112]

Was Roger Maris a One-Season Wonder?

Robert Creamer asserted that Maris "was probably the most misunderstood and least appreciated of American sports heroes." Part of the reason so many in the press and among the fans objected to him was that they saw him as a flash-in-the-pan, a player who came out of nowhere and was having a freak season. He was just a redneck country boy from nowheresville, some contended. He doesn't hold a candle to the immortal Babe.

He isn't even a true Yankee like his teammate Mickey Mantle. He's not that good of a fielder either. Yeah, he can hit a homer on occasion, but he has a lousy batting average. And so the argument went.

Oliver Kuechle, sports editor for the *Milwaukee Journal*, verbalized this dismissive attitude after Maris was unsuccessful in hitting home run number 60 during the 154-game-limit dictated by Ford Frick. His failure to do so "evokes no great regrets here." If Ruth's record were to be broken, "it should be by somebody of greater baseball stature and of greater color and public appeal." Maris, Kuechle asserted, "is not more than a good big league ball player. He is colorless. He has never hit .300 in the majors. He has little of the imposing physique at the plate commonly associated with the true slugger. He has been only average in the field. He is often surly.... There just isn't anything deeply heroic about the man."[113]

The contention that Roger Maris was a one-dimensional player who was just lucky enough to be playing in a year with juiced balls and mediocre pitching—which some believe to this day—is not only unfair, it is totally inaccurate. Roger Maris had long been scouted by the Yankee brass. It was an open secret that when he was traded by Cleveland to Kansas City, it would not be long before he was wearing the Yankee pinstripes. His career was often plagued by injuries, which disguised his true abilities from undiscerning eyes. In his first game with the Bombers, he hit two home runs. He was batting near .300 that 1960 season until suffering a debilitating injury late in the year. He was leading Mickey Mantle in both home runs and batting average at the time and quite conceivably could have hit even more homers had he remained injury-free. In spite of the fact his offensive production declined noticeably after mid–August as a result, he still managed to hit 39 home runs, just one behind Mantle, good enough for second-place in the American League. In addition, he led the league in slugging percentage (.581), at-bats per home run (12.8), extra-base hits (64), and runs-batted-in (112), all while missing 26 games.

Many thought his acquisition by the Yankees was the main reason they went from third place in 1959 to the World Series in 1960. He won his first MVP award at the end of the season. And while his offensive production in 1962 declined from 1961, he was still in the top 10 in the American League in slugging percentage (ninth), total bases (seventh), home runs (tied for fifth), runs-batted-in (eighth) and extra-base hits (tied for third). Baseball historian Allen Barra maintained that Maris in 1962 "was pretty good, too, hitting 33 home runs, driving in 100 runs and generally supplying much [of] the glue the team needed with Mantle out for much of the season. So his value was probably much greater that year than the simple statistics indicate." From 1959 to 1962, Maris was an All-Star and a two-time MVP winner, averaging 37 home runs and 106 RBIs per season during that period.[114]

As Leonard Koppett pointed out, Maris' 100 home runs over two consecutive summers was more than any other earlier slugger hit in back-to-back seasons with the exceptions of Babe Ruth, who "was in a class by himself," Jimmie Foxx (106 in 1932/1933), and Ralph Kiner (101 in 1949/1950). "If it's so easy, and the ball is so lively ... how come all those other fellows playing every day haven't done it, too?" Koppett wanted to know. Nobody then or now had a definitive answer to that trenchant question. One can only conclude that while 1961 was clearly a career-year never to be repeated, Maris definitely was not a flash-in-the-pan.[115]

As for his defensive work, many consider him one of the best right fielders in Yankee history and rate the strength and accuracy of his arm second only to Al Kaline among his American League contemporaries. Those of us of a certain age well remember the fielding play he made in Game 7 of the 1962 World Series in San Francisco. With the Yankees clinging to a 1–0 lead going into the bottom of the ninth, Matty Alou led off with a bunt single. Two outs later, Willie Mays hit a double into the right-field corner. Normally the fleet-footed Alou would have scored from first, but Maris quickly retrieved the ball and fired a bullet to cutoff man Bobby Richardson who pegged it home to hold Alou at third. Willie McCovey then hit a liner to Richardson at second, thus securing another Yankee World Series win.

Or look at his base-running smarts in Game 3 of that same series. It was the bottom of the seventh, no score, with Mantle on second, Tom Tresh on third. Maris singled to right to drive in two runs, advancing to second on a Willie McCovey error. When Elston Howard flied out to Willie Mays in center, Maris tagged and beat the throw to third. He then raced home on a Clete Boyer groundout to short. The Yankees won, 3–2. As *New York Times* sports columnist George Vecsey later wrote, "Maris's feet and Maris's glove and Maris's arm had saved two of the victories, and nobody put an asterisk on that."[116]

Many were the times that Maris, who played all-out, all the time, crashed into a fence or fell into the seats in pursuit of a fly ball or slid hard into second to break up a double play. "There are a number of other myths about Roger Maris that need to be done away with," Allen Barra argued, "such as the notion that his only contribution to his team was the ability to hit home runs. Maris was regarded as a fine outfielder with an excellent arm…. He was considered an excellent baserunner, too." From 1960 to 1962, "Roger Maris was a terrific ballplayer," Barra concluded, "and for several others he was very good to good."[117]

2

ROGER MARIS BEFORE 1961

Roger Eugene Maris (originally Maras) was born in Hibbing, Minnesota, on September 10, 1934. His father, Rudy, who worked for the Great Northern Railway, moved the family to Grand Forks, North Dakota, then to Fargo, while Roger was still a youngster. It was there that the future "Sultan of Swat" developed his athletic prowess. He and Rudy Jr., his older brother by a year, played multiple sports together. As a sophomore at Fargo Central High School, the elder brother was a standout halfback and linebacker on the school's football team. The following year Roger hoped to play on the same team as his brother, but that was not to be. When the football coach benched Rudy and consigned Roger to the B team, both brothers transferred to Bishop Shanley, Fargo's Catholic high school. The move split the community, with many supporters of Fargo Central resenting the brothers for what they did. This joint action by the siblings was in keeping with a core aspect of Roger Maris' personality: he fought when he thought he was being wronged, no matter the cost. As he stated years later, "I have never been the type of person to let anyone give me the business. I felt that Bud [Rudy's nickname] and I were getting the short end of the stick and decided to do something about it."[1]

As much as Roger excelled at football—in one game, he scored five touchdowns: two on kickoff returns, one on a punt return, a fourth on a 32 yard run from the line of scrimmage, and the fifth on an interception—he also was a fine baseball player. The brothers played American Legion ball during the summers, where both were outfielders. One season Roger batted .367 as he helped lead Fargo to the North Dakota state championship.[2]

Upon graduation, Maris was courted by both the University of Oklahoma to play football and by the Cleveland Indians. The young athlete initially decided to take the full scholarship offered by the Sooners, but after a few days at the university he concluded that college life was not for him. "As soon as I got to Oklahoma and got into the exams," Maris explained, "I lost my patience. I said the hell with it." Upon returning home, Maris contacted Hank Greenberg, Indians general manager, and the future home run king signed for $5,000.[3]

Roger's rise through the Indians farm system was not without its conflicts. Beginning with his first spring training in 1953, Maris set a pattern in which he "argued and demanded his own way with managers and general managers at every stage of his career." While such obstinate behavior was typically career-ending, that was not the case with Roger Maris. Toward the end of camp in Daytona Beach, Florida, in 1953, for example, Maris made it known that he wanted to play his inaugural season at home with the Class C Fargo-Moorhead Twins. Mike McNally, the Cleveland farm director, had other plans for the 18-year-old. He felt that beginning a career playing in front of family and friends would put undue pressure on the rookie and insisted that Maris stay in Daytona Beach to play for the Indians' Class D franchise there. Displaying the stubbornness that was so much a part of his personality, Maris stated that he would leave if he did not get his way on the matter. "It kind of surprised me," McNally said later. "You're used to having your own way with the youngsters." Management eventually caved, but at a cost to Maris. It was this incident, he concluded years later, that established his reputation as stiff-necked and unyielding, an image that was not entirely undeserved.[4]

If there was any pressure from playing in front of the home crowd, it certainly did not show in his performance. Maris had an outstanding season with Fargo, batting .325 with nine home runs, 13 triples, 80 RBIs, and 14 stolen bases. He was one of the reasons that the Twins won the Northern League championship that year. At the end of the season he was voted the league's Rookie of the Year. Only Hank Aaron the year before received more total votes than did Maris. A beaning incident earlier that season had implications for his later batting style. Maris was out for a week after sustaining a blow to the head by a ball thrown by southpaw Burt Ostby during a game against the Grand Forks Chiefs on August 4. He was taken to the hospital as a precaution, but suffered no lasting physical damage from the beaning. While the incident did not result in him becoming intimidated by pitches inside—which sometimes happens when a batter suffers such a severe injury— he did begin standing further from the plate. That proved not to be a problem, though, because he had the ability to pull an outside pitch without having to crowd the plate.[5]

The following season, Indians management wanted him to remain at Fargo for further development, but Maris balked, insisting that he be promoted or he would walk. Once again, management backed down and the 19-year-old slugger was assigned to the Class B Keokuk (Iowa) Kernels. It was a fortunate move for all concerned for it was there that the youngster came under the influence of Kernels manager Jo-Jo White. The Indians intended for Maris to change his batting style, to learn to pull the ball for power instead of remaining the spray hitter that he was and that was exactly what White set out to do. "I liked him right away," White said in 1961. "He was a real tough monkey. And he had what it takes to be a ballplayer—great desire. It stuck out all over him."[6]

Maris responded positively to White's guidance, later crediting him for his success as a home-run hitter. "If he hadn't turned me to pulling, then certainly I wouldn't be hitting so many homers," Maris ruminated in 1962. "I almost felt like going up to Jo Jo and thanking him for what he had done for me. Who knows? If it hadn't been for him, perhaps no one would have ever heard of me. Certainly I wouldn't be with the Yankees." White asserted that he "knew damn well he [Maris] could be a big leaguer." The former Kernels manager considered Maris to be a multi-tool player. "He had everything. Some guys can hit but they can't run. Some can't throw. Some can do all those things but they can't think too well. Roger could do everything—hit, run, throw, think. When those guys make it, they become great."[7]

It was in Iowa that Maris began developing what became that beautiful left-handed swing of his. An article in the *Athletic Journal* described Maris as "a picture of explosive power and strength." Maris, standing back from the plate, knees slightly bent with the bat positioned behind his head, "holds [the bat] high, with his hands at the end. Striding 3 to 5 inches, Maris' body bends into the swing, bringing his hip and shoulders around together. The ball is being met out in front by a level bat. Roger's cocked wrists roll over at contact with the ball. The weight which is transferred from his left foot to his right

Roger Maris launches number 61. "He's got a swing that is grooved for any right field stands or fence in baseball. He has learned how to pull almost any pitch in the strike zone ... and that's practically an impossible job"—Bob Scheffing, manager of the Detroit Tigers.

foot gives him the follow-through necessary to send the ball sailing over the fences." Getting out in front of the ball, of course, was critical. Doing so "gives the swing maximum power and enables the eyes to judge the ball better. The front hip must be open and turned quickly to enable the hitter to get around."[8]

In a detailed photo essay of his swing, *Look* magazine concluded that "Maris's muscularity, balanced and elastic, is superior" to that of Mickey Mantle. "But his power traces mainly to the exceptional co-ordination and timing of his swing, with its accentuated wrist and forearm snap. Much of this snap flows from the unusual way in which Roger cocks his left wrist. In the grip most batters use, the front knuckles of the top hand are in direct line with the back knuckles of the lower hand." Maris, however, turned his left hand slightly so that the knuckles were not in perfect alignment.[9]

Detroit Tigers manager Bob Scheffing said of Maris, "He's got a swing that is grooved for any right field stands or fence in baseball. He has learned how to pull almost any pitch in the strike zone ... and that's practically an impossible job." Maris rarely hit the ball to left field. In fact, only one of his homers in 1961 cleared the left field fence. "He pivots in such a style that many times his arms actually seem to be locked," remarked one observer. "That's because he pivots his entire body toward right field with his arms merely leading the way on the outer end of his sweeping motion. When he is in this groove, his follow-through is the envy of any golf professional." This follow-through was essential for his success as a hitter; failure to do so usually ended with an out. As one example, there was a game against the Tigers in late September 1961 in which he did not complete "his swing, or his pivot. As a result, the ball was popped to short center or short left."[10]

The Yankee right fielder was prone to extended slumps, often exacerbated by him obsessing about it when his hitting went south. "Maris' only drawback is that he lingers too long in a batting slump," commented Jo-Jo White. "He'll have to conquer that problem." Leonard Shecter asserted that when Maris was not hitting well, it "makes him unhappy which in turn makes the slump even worse." Consequently, when a manager removed him from the lineup, his "face would grow stormy, his swing, even during batting practice, would become more vicious and as a result his slump would become deeper and deeper." Maris, though, denied that was ever the case. "I don't brood just because I hit a bad streak," he claimed. "I just become more determined to get straightened out. Why brood? It doesn't help."[11]

Often times he went into prolonged dry spells after suffering a debilitating injury. Maris noted that "any slump is a matter of timing. That's why it's so hard for a player to maintain the rhythmic swing you've got to have for good hitting if he isn't in the line-up every day. Any time I've been out, I've found it takes quite awhile to adjust my timing after I get back." Maris was what he referred to as a "groove" hitter. "I just swing in a groove. When I'm going good I hit anything—any kind of pitch, lefty or righty pitcher. When I'm going bad I can't hit anything at all." Maris claimed he never tampered with his batting stance or swing when in a slump, nor did he attempt to predict the pitch. "I'm no guesser up there. I don't try to outsmart the pitcher." Oftentimes, these frustrating slumps were followed by incredible hitting streaks. He had no explanation for why this was so. "As far as I'm concerned I'm doing the same thing I always did."[12]

Jo-Jo White was uncomfortable with the notion that he made Maris the hitter he later became. "I only made a suggestion, that's all," he told one reporter. Clearly his influence was much more than that because Maris thrived under the manager's tutelage. By mid–July he was second in the Three-I League in batting average (.351) and led the league in home runs (19, including three grand slams), total bases (180), hits (98), and RBIs (69). Whereas in the previous season the young slugger had hit just nine home runs, by the end of 1954 he had blasted 32 (second in the league), all the while maintaining a .315 batting average. He also plated 111 runs (third in the league) and stole 25 bases, five more than his league competitor, the speedy Luis Aparicio.[13]

In 1955 Maris was promoted to the Class AA Tulsa Oilers where he again came into conflict with authority, this time with team manager Dutch Meyer. Maris maintained that Meyer "kept trying to change everything I did. According to him I couldn't do anything right. I was really getting fouled up." This conflict negatively impacted the 20-year-old's performance in the field as well as at the plate. In the 25 games he played for the Oilers, he batted a miserable .233 with just one home run. Things came to a head when, the day after Maris cost his team the game by overthrowing third base, the manager forced the outfielder to field and throw ball after ball to the bag while his teammates were warming up. Maris made nearly two dozen of these plays before deciding he had had enough. Turning his back on the manager, he started walking off the field. An incensed Meyer raced toward his player shouting, "Where the hell do you think you're going?" Maris, equally furious, informed his manager, "Off the field. You're not ruining my arm for me." He then proceeded to the owner's office where he demanded that he be sent elsewhere.[14]

Once more, the front office obliged by reassigning him to the Class A Reading Indians where he was reunited with Jo-Jo White. For his part, Meyer was fired as team manager a short time later. Even during the height of this 1961 home run chase Maris vividly recalled the incident. "I threw about 15 times and told him to go jump in the lake. If that arm pops, your career is over.... You never know when you're going to hurt it. Even now I never throw in practice. If I'm going to throw it out, I'll do it in a game, when it means something."[15]

While the move to Reading was a demotion, it proved to be the correct decision. As was the case in Keokuk, Maris flourished under White's leadership. In 113 games, the future Yankee batted .289 with 19 home runs, 78 RBIs, and 24 stolen bases. In recognition of his performance, the regional baseball writers' association elected him to the Eastern League All-Star team. The Indians ended up winning the league pennant, but lost in the first round of the playoffs. Most importantly, the Reading period restored Maris' self-confidence and helped prepare him for the jump to Triple-A the following spring. And it brought him to the attention of the Yankee brass for the first time. Yankees general manager George Weiss wanted a left-handed pull-hitter and Maris fit the bill in his eyes. "He had all the potential of what we wanted," Weiss stated. "We began following him. Watched him the next year in Indianapolis."[16]

As with previous promotions, Maris' tenure with the Indianapolis Indians had a rocky start. In Maris' eyes, he felt he was being benched too often and thus informed manager Kerby Farrell to either play him or send him elsewhere. Apparently Farrell kept his cool for he agreed that he would allow Maris to play for 10 days straight, promising him that "no matter how you do, you're in the lineup." Maris delivered and, except for a foot injury that sidelined him for six games in early August, never rode the pine the rest of that season. In 131 games, he batted .293 with 17 home runs, 75 RBIs, and seven stolen bases and successfully drag bunted 17 times out of 18 attempts.[17]

Maris' advancement to the big club was pretty much assured by his performance during the regular season as well as his crucial role in the Indians' four-game sweep of the Rochester Red Wings for the Junior World Series title. In the first game of that contest he threw out the potential tying run at the plate in the bottom of the ninth to help secure a 3–2 victory and in the second game drove in seven of the 12 Indianapolis runs on a single and two homers. Indians General Manager Hank Greenberg said of Maris that his slugger was "one with a chance to be not merely a good major league outfielder, but an outstanding one.... He's strong, fast, and hard-nosed," while Farrell, who managed Maris in Cleveland the following season, described him as having "the raw potential of a Mickey Mantle."[18]

Maris' reputation for being demanding and stubborn preceded him when he reported to the Indians 1957 spring training camp in Tucson, Arizona. There was little question he had what it took to be an outstanding big leaguer, but there was concern on the part of a few that he might be too difficult to handle. "A young man described by some as a spoiled brat and by others as a reformed mamma's boy will be the most closely inspected young Indian in Tucson starting Monday," wrote Hal Lebovitz in the *Cleveland News*, who based his reporting partly on hearsay. Former Indians skipper Al Lopez, for one, was not impressed by Maris' personality or performance. Calling him a "spoiled kid" (not the loaded word "brat" as Lebovitz reported) who "appeared to sulk," Lopez claimed Maris "came to camp with the reputation of being a power hitter and a speed boy, [but] did little except run fast." Since there was conflict between Lopez and Maris during the previous year's spring training camp, it may have colored the ex-manager's opinion of Maris to some extent.[19]

When Lebovitz saw Maris in action, however, he formed an entirely different opinion about the outfielder. Apparently the reporter was called on to substitute for an ailing umpire during one late–February intrasquad spring training game while in Tucson, which afforded him the opportunity to observe Maris up-close. He was especially impressed by Maris' aggressive play even though he had been ill the two previous days. "This is a kid who had just come out of a sick bed, who had wobbly knees, had been prematurely branded a jaker [loafer]," Lebovitz remarked. "I'll take him. He showed me plenty yesterday."[20]

Others among the Cleveland press and within the Indians' organization viewed Maris in an entirely different light. Hank Greenberg was a strong supporter of the youngster as was Kerby Farrell, the incoming Indians manager. Acknowledging that Maris struggled early in Indianapolis, Farrell stated that "once he started he was my boy. The greatest two-out hitter I ever saw." He added that Maris "was the hottest thing in the minor leagues" and that once he made the big club "the Cleveland fans will really see something." Jimmy Doyle, the *Cleveland Plain Dealer*'s doggerel-writing sports columnist, had nothing but praise for the young prospect: "A Redskin rook of promise rare is/The swift and stalwart Roger Maris/Good wood man and good glove man, too/As Kerby Farrell says, he'll do." And, contrary to what critics like Al Lopez thought, the *Plain Dealer*'s Harry Jones found Maris "to be solid in the sense that he maintained proper balance. He didn't press, or swing wildly, or brood." For Maris to be effective, Jones argued, he "must play every day." The journalist was convinced Maris was "the one player who can make the greatest difference in the ball club. If he is given full opportunity and succeeds, this young man can add speed to the club and punch to the attack."[21]

The 22-year-old rookie outfielder made his first major league appearance with Cleveland on April 16, 1957, playing left field. He was impressive in this inaugural game, going three for five and scoring one of the Indians two runs in a 10-inning, 3–2 loss to the White Sox. All three hits were against southpaw Billy Pierce, including two with two strikes against him. His performance in his next outing was even more notable. With the game in Detroit knotted at three going into the eleventh inning, Maris, who had struck out in three previous at-bats, launched his first major league grand slam into the right-field bleachers to give the Indians an 8–3 victory.

The event garnered front-page headlines in the *Cleveland Plain Dealer* and caused would-be poet Doyle to wax lyrically: "The kid shook off a fanning bee/(Three times he'd been struck out)/And slammed one that was grand to see/A four-mast, four-run clout." Even the irrepressible Bill Veeck got into the act, claiming that "the minute Maris hit his grand slam homer in Detroit, the sun came out in Cleveland." Hal Lebovitz, who earlier had expressed some concerns about the outfielder's personality, was now solidly in the Maris camp. He "displayed so much promise during spring training and the first week of the season, that this writer, for one, considers him the hottest candidate in the American League for Rookie of the Year honors." The columnist went on to add that he found "no trace of moodiness or surliness in Maris this spring…. In truth we have come to know him as a friendly young man who tells only what is in his heart."[22]

This was pretty heady stuff for a youngster who had appeared in only two games. Manager Farrell, recognizing that such effusive praise could result in overconfidence, cautioned the press to keep things in perspective. "But it's still early. For his sake, let's not make a Mickey Mantle out of him yet." Maris, though, seemed to handle the sudden attention well. While admitting he "felt awful good," he added that he could not "help remembering how foolish I looked striking out three times. And missing by a couple feet, too."[23]

The slugger continued this torrid pace through early May, maintaining a .315 batting average to go along with his five home runs. Then adversity struck, as it would so often over the years. Maris was one of those players who seemed to be stalked by physical misfortune. Things would be going well then something would happen—appendicitis, ribcage damage, a fractured hand—that caused everything to come to a screeching halt.

He suffered so many debilitating injuries that analysts with the Elias Sports Bureau postulated these were what prevented him from generating the career statistics necessary for election to the Baseball Hall of Fame. While they admitted their statistical projections as to what his performance numbers could have been had he remained injury-free were "still somewhat short of certain Hall of Fame status," they contended these numbers "combined with the single-event value of hitting 61 home runs ... would have been plenty." While their assertion is certainly open to debate, clearly one of the reasons Maris was so successful in 1961 was that he suffered no long-term physical ailments that season.[24]

The main reason Maris suffered so many injuries was his style of play. He often referred to his baseball career as a job, one he engaged in primarily as a means of securing a sound financial future for his wife and children. But he also loved playing the game, if not all the hoopla surrounding it. His work ethic dictated that when he played, he played to win, which meant he was aggressive on the base paths and daring when pursuing fly balls. In addition, his experience playing football conditioned him to literally put his entire body into whatever he did, consequences be damned. There were many occasions during his years as a professional ballplayer when he would collide into a second baseman or short stop to break up a double play or crash into a wall or flip over a fence to pull in a potential home run. Jo-Jo White was particularly impressed with his physicality. "I liked his nerve, the way he'd run into fences for you, the way he slid. Oh God, he'd rip that bag and the man right along with it." But White also expressed concern about the long-term consequences of this type of play. "I told him that running into fences wasn't going to do him any good," White explained. "I told him, 'You got to protect yourself.'" His response was classic Maris: "I'd just as soon stay away from them [fences and walls]. All you can do is get hurt. But if a ball is there you have to try."[25]

So during a game on May 10, 1957, Maris was just being Maris when he slid hard into Milt Graff, Kansas City's second baseman, as teammate Rocky Colavito raced toward first on a grounder to third. Graff, upended by the collision while trying to catch a wild throw from the third baseman, came down hard on Maris, his elbow cracking two of Maris' ribs. And that was the pivotal event in his first season of major league ball. Maris, who had hit a go-ahead two-run homer the inning before, was now out for two weeks. When he returned, he was not nearly as productive as he was prior to the accident. In the Indians' final 134 games, which included another two-week stint on the disabled list after he injured his right foot in late June, he hit just nine more home runs and his batting average plummeted to a miserable .235.

As Maris later acknowledged, "When I came back [from the ribcage injury], I couldn't do a thing. My timing was way off and my average melted. [M]ost of the time I was helpless at the plate." Of course, any dreams of being Rookie of the Year evaporated along with this subpar performance. And it was all for naught. While he was successful in taking out the second baseman, Indians shortstop Chico Carrasquel, following Colavito in the batting order, brought the inning to a halt when he grounded into a 3–6–1 double play.[26]

Before the end of the season, Kerby Farrell received his walking papers. He was replaced by the "brash" Bobby Bragan, who himself had been terminated as manager of the seventh-place Pittsburgh Pirates earlier that year. Two weeks later, Hank Greenberg was out as general manager of the Indians, only to be replaced by the controversial Frank "Trader" Lane, seen by many as "the most volatile personality in the executive branch of baseball today." Neither move boded well for Roger Maris' continued association with Cleveland. Lane, whose sobriquet indicated his willingness to trade any player at any time, began his tenure as Indians general manager by announcing the only two players he would not consider dealing were Herb Score and Roger Maris. If that was his true position, it did not last long into the 1958 season.[27]

Lane and Maris quickly came into conflict over two issues. First, the new general manager wanted his outfielder to play center field. To that end, he expected Maris to learn the position during winter ball in the Dominican Republic. Maris, who had a miserable time playing in the DR the year before, had no desire to leave his family to repeat that experience. He refused to go despite Lane's financial enticements. "He kept bugging me to play winter ball in the Dominican Republic," Maris recalled a few years later. "I didn't want to. He insisted. That made no difference to me. It was my privilege to refuse and I did." It may have been his right to refuse, but Maris realized that by doing so, it would cost him. "I knew I had two strikes against me when I came to spring training in Tucson."[28]

Second, Maris, along with several other players, decided to haggle with Lane over his 1958 salary, something that did not sit well with "Frantic Frank." In addition, Maris and Bobby Bragan never hit it off. The new manager, who thought his outfielder "surly" and a loafer, was unimpressed with either Maris' fielding—he was convinced Maris was "wall-shy"—or batting. As a result, Bragan admitted he "didn't find much playing time for him once the season started." For his part, Maris resented the manager's criticisms and thought Bragan was doing Lane's bidding, an opinion which undoubtedly was reinforced by the general manager's habit of sitting next to Bragan in the dugout. But Bragan had been hired by Greenberg, not Lane, and never was Lane's man. Bragan and the players found the general manager to be both hypercritical and a shameless self-promoter. "He didn't offer advice, or even constructive criticism," Bragan declared. "All Lane wanted to do was blow his own horn and denigrate everything and everybody else."[29]

Things only grew worse as the season progressed. Bragan began platooning Maris more often, frequently using him as a pinch-hitter and a late-inning replacement, which only served to increase the tension between the two men. By the middle of June Maris' batting average had plummeted to .225. The fact that Maris pulled a muscle in his lower back in late April and was out of the lineup for over a week likely contributed to this offensive decline. By then the die was cast; on June 15 Maris was traded to the Kansas City Athletics. As for Bobby Bragan, Lane fired him as manager less than two weeks later, replacing him with Joe Gordon.

Maris found new life in Kansas City. He loved the city and the city loved him. He felt comfortable in Cowtown, a Midwestern city more like his North Dakota home than Cleveland or New York ever were. He immediately bought a house in suburban Raytown, fully expecting to stay with the team the rest of his career. It was the ideal place for someone like Maris who hated being in the spotlight.

Ernest Mehl, sports editor for the *Kansas City Star*, seemed pleased with the trade that brought Maris to the Athletics. Stating he preferred Maris over teammate Rocky Colavito, he asserted "it is quite obvious the A's now will be more dangerous at bat.... Maris is fleet, has power and can throw." His only concern was how "adept" the newest Athletic would be covering center field. That fear, though, proved to be for naught as Maris played almost exclusively in right.[30]

Maris started off slowly with his new team. He did not hit his first home run in an A's uniform until June 22, but as the summer progressed, he heated up as well. From mid–July through mid–August he batted over .300 with 10 home runs. Being the streaky hitter he was, though, he cooled off again. By the end of September he had slugged 19 four-baggers and driven in 53 runs for the A's, ending the 1958 season with a total of 28 homers and 80 RBIs between the two teams. His overall batting average remained low (.240), but he did raise it from .225 with the Indians to .247 with the Athletics.

Maris felt that overall he had a good year. "The only thing is the average," he proclaimed, "and they can take that and shove it. A lot of guys would have liked to have my year. The average is just for show." The Yankees certainly were not put off by Maris' performance that season. They had tried to acquire him from Cleveland earlier that year, but they could not pull off a deal with Frank Lane. By season's end the American League powerhouse was again making noises about securing the youngster, and that, too, failed to materialize. But as even the fans knew all too well, it was just a matter of time before Maris was patrolling right field for the Bombers.[31]

The following season Maris began to come into his own. Until the end of July he destroyed American League pitching, sporting a league-best .344 batting average to go along with his 14 homers. And he did all of this in spite of missing a month from late May to late June due to an emergency appendectomy. Suddenly, though, things began to unravel for the first-time All-Star. From late July through the end of the season, he batted a hideous .167 while hitting just two more home runs. He ended his season on September 27 with a .273 batting average and 16 homers. What happened? Maris was always a streak hitter prone to extended slumps and that undoubtedly was at play. And he may have been dealing with health issues, perhaps as a consequence of this earlier attack of appendicitis.

Certainly Maris was aware that his late-season nosedives often followed an injury or illness, stating, "I was never able to get back into stride" in those situations. He felt his surgery may have been at least a part of the reason for the falloff. "I had that operation," he told reporter Leonard Shecter a couple of years later. "I just ran out of gas." Conceivably the pressure and exposure from being an offensive league-leader was a factor as well. Many thought he made matters worse by overcompensating, which took him out of his natural rhythm. He came to understand this later. "I was pressing in the last part of 1959," he explained to writer Tom Meany. "Everybody was telling me I was, but I couldn't see it then. I realize it now." Interestingly, the Kansas City fans remained supportive in spite of his difficulties at the plate, which Maris deeply appreciated; that was not the case in New York. Ultimately, though, Maris himself was uncertain as to why he experienced so precipitous a decline. When *New York Times* columnist Arthur Daley asked the future

Yankee what caused this end-of-the-season crash, Maris responded, "I still don't know what happened."[32]

One thing the disastrous end of his 1959 season did not do was make him any less attractive to the New York Yankees. In fact, it may have encouraged Kansas City management to make a trade, fearing that if he had another season like that again, he would no longer be desirable to other clubs. It was an open secret at the time that when the Yankees wanted a player on the Athletics roster, they got him. Over a five-year period there were 15 trades between the two franchises that involved nearly 60 players. Later, it was disclosed that there was an "arrangement"—what Bill Veeck so aptly termed "an unholy alliance"—between Arnold Johnson, owner of the A's, and Yankees owners Del Webb and Dan Topping, all three of whom were business partners in the Automatic Canteen Company of America.

Until Johnson's untimely death in early 1960, the Athletics often acted as a feeder team to the powerful New York club. So when Roger Maris was traded to Kansas City in the middle of the 1958 season, it was clear to everyone in the know that he would soon end up in New York. In fact, some of the more conspiracy-minded believed the Yankees were behind the trade that brought Maris to the Athletics in the first place. Frank Lane on at least one occasion speculated that may have been the case. The Yankees "had their eyes on him for years," he contended. "I'm not at all certain they didn't tell [Arnold] Johnson to get Maris from me." In keeping with Lane's erratic and self-serving behavior, however, that accusation conflicted with his later claim that he was the one who talked Johnson into taking Maris over Rocky Colavito, asking only of the Athletics owner that he "promise me he wouldn't pass Maris right on to New York that year, although I knew he'd wind up with the Yankees in any event." Yankees general manager George Weiss, though, seemed to confirm Lane's earlier suspicions when he admitted he once told Arnold Johnson "if he ever landed Maris, I'd make him a real deal to bring Roger to the Yanks."[33]

Of course, the Kansas City brass denied that there was ever such an understanding between the two clubs. Parke Carroll, the Athletics general manager, was infuriated by such talk. "We deal with the Yankees because we feel we can help our club," he asserted. "Or you can put it this way. We deal with the Yankees because they deal with us. That's more than you can say about other clubs, including those in the National League." Carroll claimed his team had arranged to send Maris to the Pittsburgh Pirates for Dick Groat, but the Pirates backed out at the last minute. "So the Yankees came into the picture. They wanted Maris. We wanted ball players. I don't care what they say. I think we made a good deal."[34]

The 1959 season for the Bronx Bombers was a miserable one. Sporting a 79–75 record, the team finished third behind the Chicago White Sox and the Cleveland Indians, 15 games out of first place. Fresh blood was needed and with a short right-field porch in Yankee Stadium (296 feet), Roger Maris, a dead-pull hitter, seemed the perfect fit. Whatever the truth of the matter concerning the Athletics-Yankees relationship may have been, on December 11, 1959, the two teams completed a multi-player trade that proved to be decidedly in the Yankees' favor. Kansas City received Don Larsen, Marv Throneberry, Norm Siebern, and an aging Hank Bauer for Roger Maris, Kent Hadley, and Joe DeMaestri.

Maris, who apparently heard about the trade second-hand, initially was not happy about becoming a Yankee. By some accounts, he was greeting customers in a Kansas City grocery store as part of an off-season job when either the store manager or a customer informed him of the transaction. He was the quintessential family man and did not relish being away from his wife and children for extended periods of time. He also was intensely private and preferred the modest attention he experienced in Kansas City to the high level of exposure he received playing in New York

Always blunt and to-the-point, he told one reporter, "I've got nothing against the Yankees, but I'm sorry to leave here. And I'll expect more money." He also expressed concerns about how he would fit in with his new club and the Yankee way of doing things. "I don't believe I'd be happy playing there," he said when rumors about a prospective trade first reached his ears. "They get on their ballplayers a lot and try to make them do things the way they want. When someone gets all over me I just get mad."[35]

His sentiments, of course, did nothing to endear him to the New York press or Yankees fans. If indeed he heard about the move from a third party and not directly from the Yankee front office, one can hardly blame him for being angry over such an affront. Oddly, New York sportswriter Tom Meany thought comments of this nature were made by Maris "in jest" and "facetiously," which seems highly unlikely. He made too many similar responses that winter for them not to be accurate expressions of his true feelings at that point in time.[36]

In spite of any reservations he may have had, Maris did report to the Yankee spring training camp ready to play. As expected, he held out signing his contract until the salary issue was resolved. In this instance, both sides could claim victory: Maris did receive a raise, but at a slightly lesser amount than he had wanted. Being the professional that he was, Maris had mellowed about the swap that brought him to the Bronx. "Looking at the good side of it, I think it's a break getting a shot to play with a better ball club. I think you do better yourself and then there's a chance to pick up extra money [by playing in the World Series]," the ever-practical player noted. He did admit to feeling somewhat ill-at-ease being the new kid on the block. "One thing I hate about going to the Yankees is leaving the friends I made on this club [the Athletics] here. You may not realize it but it takes a long time for a player to be accepted after he goes to a new team." But he knew he would eventually be embraced by his new teammates. "It was the same when I came over here [Kansas City] and it will be the same with the Yankees."[37]

In addition to adjusting to unfamiliar surroundings, Maris also had a new manager he had to please. Highly successful, but oft times outrageous and inscrutable, Casey Stengel expected a lot out of the newest Yankee. The longtime Yankee skipper was pleased with the acquisition of Maris, but stated he "is going to have to carry a big load. In the first place, there will be the big publicity. Then, there will be the necessity of hitting and fielding in the style we expected of him when we made the trade." "The Old Perfessor" planned to convert Maris into a left fielder, which made the slugger uneasy to say the least. He was comfortable playing right field, which he considered his natural position.[38]

But Maris was first and foremost a team player, and he never balked or made any protests beyond expressing his understandable concerns. "If Stengel feels that the welfare of the club demands my shifting to left, well, left it will be," he announced. "I know that this field is especially tough in the Stadium. But others have overcome the problem. So will I." The only thing he asked was to play consistently there for every inning of every spring training game and not be moved around in the outfield. That wish was granted and by the end of camp Maris had developed into a fine left fielder. For reasons known only to Stengel, though, when the regular season began Maris was moved back to right field, remaining there from then on except when he patrolled center on those occasions when Mantle was out of the lineup.[39]

In spite of his preferences and concerns, the slugger had an outstanding spring, batting over .300, which carried over into opening day. In his inaugural game as a Yankee, he went four for five with two home runs and four RBIs in an 8 to 4 Yankee win in Boston. By mid–June he was batting a robust .354 and led the American League with 47 RBIs and both leagues with 18 home runs.

It was around that time reporters began to ask the inevitable question that haunted him throughout the 1961 season: "Are you going to break Babe Ruth's single-season home run record?" His response was one he used consistently the following season. Claiming he was not thinking about the Ruth record, he insisted he was "only interested in having a good year for [himself] and seeing the Yankees win the pennant." And as a variation on this theme, he told another interviewer, "I don't care about Babe Ruth's record. I don't give a damn if he hit 900 home runs. It doesn't help me or the team any." Maris hated being the center of attention, so these comments, while sincere, were also attempts to deflect the spotlight away from himself as he went about his business.[40]

Not only was Maris having a brilliant season at the plate, he was also demonstrating to all doubters that he was one of the best right fielders in the game. Indeed, many thought his glove and arm were as much a factor in the Yankees' success that season as was his bat. There was a game in mid-summer that is often cited as an example of how this was true. In early July the Yankees, who had been in first place, went into a significant slump. On July 5, they were holding on to a slim one-game lead over the Indians when things started to go south. They lost a three-game series to Boston, then three out of four to the Tigers. On July 22, they were to play a four-game set against the White Sox who now held first by a few percentage points. Chicago took the first two games as well as the first game of a July 24 doubleheader, leaving the Yanks in second place, two games out. The evening match-up thus became a do-or-die contest. If New York won, they would be just one game behind; if they lost, it would mean a three-game separation.

The Yankee rotation, which had not been performing well, was depleted as Casey Stengel used four pitchers in the earlier game. The manager thus had no choice but to go with Eli Grba, a young relief pitcher burdened with a 5.11 ERA who was making just his second start of the season. With one in, one on, and one out at the top of the second inning, Gene Freese unloaded on the pitcher, sending a long fly ball to the deep right center field gap between Mickey Mantle and Maris. In all likelihood it would have gone for extra bases had Maris not come streaking over to snag the ball at the last moment.

It was an important play. Had it landed safely, not only would it have meant another run, but Stengel might have lost confidence in his pitcher, resulting in a call to an exhausted bullpen. But as it was, Grba induced a comebacker to the mound for the third out, thus limiting the damage to only one run. He settled down after that, pitching a complete-game Yankee victory. It set in motion a streak in which New York won 10 of their next 14 games, moving them back into first place during that two-week stretch. Later, Yankee ace Whitey Ford was to point to this game as the possible turning point in the team's 1960 season. "It may seem silly to say this but there is always a game you can look back on, maybe even one play, and say to yourself, 'This is the one.' We could have been, and I'm certainly not saying we would have been, but we could have been out of it if Roger hadn't caught the ball Freese hit."[41]

The right fielder went into one of his periodic slumps after the All-Star break. From mid–July through mid–August, he batted just .234, but he did manage to hit seven homers and drive in 24 runs during that period. In fact, all the Yankee batters seemed to be a bit off-stride. Over those same four weeks, Mantle's batting average was higher (.271), but he hit fewer home runs (six) and produced fewer RBIs (16) than did Maris.

In spite of this bump-in-the-road offensively, by the middle of August Maris was hitting a very respectable .295 with 35 homers and 95 RBIs while more often than not batting fourth behind Mantle. Then on August 14, he was injured sliding into second base during the second game of a doubleheader. Suffering from bruised ribs after a collision while attempting to break up a double play, Maris was out of the lineup for over a week. He never quite got back to form, belting only four more home runs to end the season with 39, just one less than Mantle who led the American League with 40. In spite of missing 19 games, he still plated a league-best 112 runs on a .283 batting average while winning the Gold Glove Award for his defensive skills in right field. Most importantly, he helped lead the Bombers to the 1960 American League pennant, quite a turn-around from the year before when they placed third.

Many believed his presence in the lineup was the key ingredient to the Yankees again becoming a championship club. Dan Daniel of the *New York World-Telegram* stated simply, "Without Maris the Bombers would not have won this pennant." And Paul Richards, who was voted the American League Manager of the Year for piloting the Baltimore Orioles to a surprising second-place finish that season, was even more adamant in his assessment of Maris' contribution to the Yankees. "Without Maris the Yankees would be just where they were last year," he declared. At the end of the season the slugger was voted the American League's Most Valuable Player, the first of two MVP awards he would receive in his major league career.[42]

Finally, the arrival of Roger Maris had a profound and positive impact on Mickey Mantle. The 1959 season had been a miserable one for the Yankees and many laid the blame squarely on Mantle for the team's third-place finish. He definitely had a subpar season by his standards, producing the lowest batting average (.285) and lowest RBI total (75) since his rookie season. To top that all off, he hit just 31 home runs, the fewest since 1954, and he lead both leagues in strikeouts (126). Even he admitted he had "a lousy season." His frustration over this lack of production often was reflected in his behavior. It was not uncommon for him to throw his bat or kick the water cooler when he failed to perform to his own expectations, which only served to make matters worse. For whatever reason, Maris seemed to change much of that. Perhaps it was because his offensive production took some of the pressure off of Mantle. There was someone else to share the limelight, someone else who would feel the heat if the Yankees were not playing well.[43]

As Mantle was to acknowledge many times, it took Roger Maris to make him popular with Yankee fans. From the very beginning, the two got along well. Naturally, they were competitive, but it was of a healthy sort, one which encouraged the best from each other. "They sit around the locker together exchanging little scraps of information," observed Yankee infielder Gil McDougald. "It's as though Mickey's trying to tell Maris how glad he is. Kind of welcome to the club." There was an observable change for the better in Mantle's demeanor and attitude as the season progressed. "Maris being around and playing the way he has made Mickey a better ballplayer," McDougald added. "You see it in so many little different ways. He's not getting down on himself so easily. When he strikes out he doesn't throw things around so much. He doesn't walk out to his position. He runs out. I think the best thing that's happened for Mickey is having Maris around." Mantle's improvement in this regard was of immense benefit to the entire team. As everyone knew, how Mantle went, so went the Yankees. There is little doubt that the Maris/Mantle relationship was crucial to both their and the Yankees' success in 1961.[44]

New York ended the 1960 regular season in typical Yankee fashion. After changing the league lead back and forth through most of the summer, in mid-September New York found itself tied with the upstart Orioles for first place; the White Sox were third, just two games behind them both. Postseason was certainly not guaranteed. But then the Bombers caught fire, winning all of their last 15 games to close out the season eight games ahead of second place Baltimore. The Bombers ended up losing to the Pittsburgh Pirates in what proved to be one of the strangest and, for the Yanks, must frustrating World Series ever. New York outscored Pittsburgh 55 to 27, winning their three games by the scores of 16–3, 10–0, and 12–0, before losing Game 7 by a score of 10–9 on a walk-off homer in the bottom of the ninth inning by the light-hitting Bill Mazeroski.

After returning home to Raytown, Missouri, Roger Maris was surprised to learn he had won the American League's Most Valuable Player Award, surpassing teammate Mickey Mantle by a razor-thin vote of 225 points to 222. When contacted by telephone about winning the award, Maris responded, "I thought it was possible, but I wasn't expecting to win it. This is a happy feeling. Every player in the American League likes to win this at least once before he retires." But as with so many events in Maris' life, his triumph was not without controversy. Three of the 24 voters did not include Mantle on their secret ballots at all (Maris was omitted from one ballot), leaving many in the press to feel the Mick was somehow cheated out of an award he deserved more.

Jack Lang of the *Long Island Press* said as much, claiming the vote was "the latest 'jobbing'—this time of Mickey Mantle." He was convinced that the three voters who omitted Mantle's name were doing so because they favored what he considered to be a lesser candidate. He speculated that it was a trio of scribes from Baltimore who, as supporters of Brooks Robinson, "ganged up on the Yankee center fielder. But whatever Mickey's detractors had in mind, it didn't work. Mantle didn't win but Maris did and Robinson finished far up the track."[45]

Arthur Daley, sports columnist for the *New York Times*, was even more adamant that Mantle merited the award more than Maris. "Maris was a tremendous ball player for the first half of the season, but as soon as he passed the midway point he went strictly downhill, finishing with an average of .283 and a home run total of 39." He contrasted Maris' offensive production before and after the All-Star break, concluding that "his decline is readily discernable." Not only was "Master Mickey ... much more consistent," he argued, he was proficient even when the going got tough. "When the Yankees needed productive hitting most, Mantle delivered. He continually came through with key homers that won ball games, directly or indirectly. He delivered the big hits that kept rallies going. And he was to contribute the same ferocious brand of batting in the World Series, even though Series play has no bearing on the balloting." By contrast, one must infer from his arguments on behalf of Mantle that Maris was more or less a dud the second half of the season. It was Mantle's performance that delivered the pennant. But how accurate was his contention?[46]

From July 15 to September 14, the day before the Yankees caught fire, there was no question that Maris cooled off. During these two months, which saw him play in just 49 games because of the injury he suffered in mid-August, Maris batted a lowly .221. Mantle, on the other hand, batted .286 while playing in 64 games. However, if one looks at other offensive categories, Mantle was only slightly more productive than Maris in spite of appearing in over a dozen more games. From mid–July through mid–September, Mantle belted 14 home runs and drove in 39 while Maris had 11 homers and 33 RBIs.

Certainly Maris was experiencing one of his periodic batting slumps, undoubtedly exacerbated by the ribcage injury. Prior to the All-Star break, he batted .320 with 27 homers and 69 runs driven-in. Afterwards he dropped to .240 with 12 home runs and 43 RBIs. Mantle, on the other hand, remained remarkably consistent throughout the season. He batted .274 with 20 home runs and 45 RBIs in the first half of the season, then .277 with 20 home runs and 49 RBIs in the second half.

During the last two weeks of the regular season when the Yankees won 15 straight games to take the pennant, Maris showed signs of breaking out of the doldrums. While he hit only one home run during that period, perhaps because of his sore ribs, he did hit a double and two triples while driving in 10 on a .293 batting average. Mantle's average dropped noticeably during that same time frame. He batted .234, but did hit six homers. His RBI production, however, was exactly the same as Maris' (10) and he had no extra-base hits other than the dingers.

Both Mantle and Maris were deserving of the award. The Yankees would not have reached postseason had either of them not performed as well as they did that season. But there are two intangible factors that should be considered in deciding who was the most worthy of the two. First, Mantle had an outstanding World Series. Although the Yankees ended up losing, it was not because of him. He batted .400 with three home runs and 11 RBIs. While Maris had a decent enough Series, batting .267 with two solo homers for two RBIs, Mantle was by far the better and more consequential of the two. But as Arthur Daley pointed out, what a player did in the World Series should not be a factor in voting for the season's Most Valuable Player. Without a doubt Mantle's play in the Series added luster to his overall record that year. How much influence that had on the voted can never be determined, but it was possible his Series performance increased his standing with some voters.

Second, most Yankee players and the journalists who covered them recognized that Maris had a positive impact on Mantle's improvement that season. Even Mantle partisan Arthur Daley admitted as much. "If Maris had not performed so proficiently in the beginning, though, it's conceivable that Mantle might not have had the inspirational lift to carry on. Mickey hustled harder, fielded better and was a finer all-around ball player this year," he admitted. "Perhaps Roger deserves extra credits for stirring the Mick to a high degree of productiveness." A number of Yankee teammates thought that way. "I believe Maris actually carried the club the first half of the season. Maybe if it wasn't for him Mantle wouldn't have had the incentive in the second half," one player said. Another noted, "Maris was a tremendous help to us. Even when he wasn't hitting he was fielding great. Some guys fall off at the plate, they slump in the field too. Another thing was that Maris played when he was hurting. You have to admire him for that." Whether Maris should have won over Mantle is a matter of opinion, but no one can argue with any authority that he was undeserving of the award.[47]

At the end of November, Maris added to his accomplishments by winning *The Sporting News*' Gold Glove Award for his outstanding play in right field. Being selected by his fellow players from the other American League teams added to the significance of the honor. "The Yankee winner combines speed, good judgment on fly balls and a strong arm," wrote *The Sporting News*. "Throwing ability in right field is especially important in preventing first-to-third advances from singles hit in that direction. The threat of Maris' arm is enough to keep most runners from moving up the extra base." Then in January 1961, he was named the "Sultan of Swat" by the Maryland Professional Baseball Players Association. The award, created in honor of Babe Ruth, included a $2,000 (the equivalent of nearly $17,000 in 2018 dollars) "diamond studded crown." As part of this acknowledgment, Maris attended the awards banquet where he endured the ribbing of the sportswriters. In a skit entitled "Sign on the Dotted Line" sung to the tune of "I Love Paris," reporters poked fun at Maris' desire for a significant salary increase: "I love money in the springtime/I love money in the fall/ They love Maris in the summer, when they play me/But in the winter I must fight for what they pay me/I want 50 thousand this year/'Cause I didn't get it last." Roger Maris had truly arrived.[48]

1961 Spring Training

Maris was not the only player seeking a significant raise. Because the expansion Washington Senators and Los Angeles Angels had to pay $75,000 apiece for each of the 56 players they selected from the existing American League clubs, there was every expectation that the salaries of those players remaining on the other teams would go up as well. "The magnates believe that salaries reached their peak in 1960," wrote Dan Daniel in *The Sporting News*. "They are off, way off. Player salaries are going much higher."[49]

Bill Skowron, the Yankees' first baseman, was the first to publicly state the view of the majority of players on this issue. "Far be it from me to cast any aspersions on the 56 players who were drafted. But it seems to me that the situation calls for a decent salary increase for me. I have not received a raise in three years. If I told you what I got last season [$21,500, which was the equivalent of $180,000 in 2018 dollars], you wouldn't believe me." After batting .309 with 26 home runs and 91 RBIs in 1960, the Moose was adamant that he expected much more. "I am not going to take a contract for $30,000. The time has come for me to get paid what I am worth. It looks as if I will have to turn holdout."[50]

Maris got nowhere near the $50,000 that the sportswriters were kidding him about at the awards banquet in January. When he signed his contract a few weeks later, the speculation was that he received $32,000 ($268,000 in 2018 dollars), up from the $18,000 he was paid the year before. Mantle's 1961 salary, on the other hand, was $70,000 ($587,000 in 2018 dollars), which was $10,000 more than in 1960 and the same as it was in 1959. Maris may have wanted more, but he seemed to accept the 1961 figure without complaint because, as he acknowledged, he went "sour" in the last half of the 1960 season. As for Moose Skowron, he was able to secure a $35,000 contract from the Yankees, $3,000 more than Maris, the 1960 MVP.[51]

Maris' 1961 campaign began in ominous fashion. Hoping to enjoy a few days of family vacation in St. Petersburg, Florida, before reporting to the Yankees' spring training camp, he bundled his wife, Pat, and their three young children into the family car and started the long drive from Missouri. Along the way the car broke down in rural Georgia and was towed 25 miles to the nearest garage. Traveling over country roads, the front of the car kept banging into the back of the tow truck, jostling the entire Maris family who were sitting in the broken down vehicle. Pat Maris, who was two-months pregnant, was adversely affected by the constant swaying and bumping.

Fearing that she might lose the baby (they had experienced a miscarriage earlier in their marriage), Mrs. Maris was hospitalized as soon as the family reached their destination. Although she was released several days later, the possibly that she still might miscarry remained. She was ordered to rest and not to engage in any taxing activities for at least three weeks as a precaution. In the meantime, Maris' mother arrived from Fargo to take over supervision of the three children so that he could report to camp. So it was with serious concern for the health of his wife and unborn child that Maris entered the Yankee clubhouse in early March. "I went to the ball park and went through the drills every day," he recalled, "but I'm quite sure that I wasn't concentrating on the business at hand. My mind was often back at the house. How I was wishing we would soon learn something definite about my wife's condition; whether or not the baby was safe."[52]

This near-tragic event could not help but prey on the slugger's mind as he went through the pre-season ritual of getting into shape. His batting suffered as a result. "You can't hit if your mind isn't concentrating on the pitchers ... and my mind wasn't doing that too often," he admitted. Over the next several weeks he batted barely above the Mendoza Line, not even hitting his first—and only—spring training home run until late March. The Yankees as a team performed poorly and Roger Maris was not the only player having trouble at the plate. Just Mickey Mantle, Moose Skowron, and Hector Lopez were doing well offensively.[53]

But Maris did show signs of heating up toward the end of camp. In addition to his homer against the Pirates' Bob Friend on March 28, he hit a game-winning walk-off single in the bottom of the eleventh inning to defeat the St. Louis Cardinals, 5–4, during the Yankees' final exhibition game in St. Petersburg. Manager Ralph Houk did not seem too perturbed about the performance of either Maris or the team as a whole that spring. "I know our won-loss record [9–19] has been anything but spectacular," he acknowledged. "But I've never been concerned about that. Our primary purpose this spring was to get in shape for the pennant race. With this in mind, I'm completely prepared to go with what we have." He made a special point of expressing confidence in his right fielder. "He's hitting the ball hard and with Mickey Mantle, Bill Skowron, Yogi Berra and others also meeting the ball, we're going to score some runs."[54]

3

April–May

In spite of Houk's conviction, though, Maris' batting woes carried over into the first six weeks of the regular season, beginning with the home opener against the Minnesota Twins on April 11. A minuscule crowd of 14,607 braved 50-degree temperatures to see the Yankee sophomore receive his 1960 MVP Award before the game. After that, it all went downhill for both the player and his team. Whitey Ford, who had won five straight opening-day starts, lost to the Cuban-born Pedro Ramos, 6–0, giving the newly-relocated franchise a first-season victory. The Yankee hurler even suffered the embarrassment of surrendering a two-run single to his mound counterpart before being lifted with one out in the top of the seventh. Maris, who batted fifth, failed to get a hit in three plate-appearances, although he did reach base in the second on an error. It was not an auspicious beginning for New York or its right fielder.[1]

For the first ten games of the new season, Maris continued to labor at the plate, batting an atrocious .161 with five singles and just one RBI on a sacrifice fly. With the exception of Mickey Mantle, the rest of the lineup was cold as well. By April 25 New York was a mediocre 5–4, relegated to fourth place, three games out of first. The matchups the Yankees were able to win were due mainly to Mantle, the team captain.

It was as if Mantle and Maris had decided to switch roles from the previous season. In 1960 Maris carried the team during the first half while Mantle struggled. Now it was the Mick who was belting home runs literally left and right while Maris was in the doldrums. During the first ten games the Yankee stalwart batted .344 with five home runs and 11 RBIs. Mantle was so hot, in fact, a comparison to Babe Ruth's single-season home run record appeared in the press for the first time. While noting that on April 21 Mantle was 18 games ahead of the Bambino's 1927 pace, the *New York Times* suggested that although "it might be a trifle early to start making predictions … in the Yankee camp there is a pronounced feeling that this could be Mantle's greatest season." As accurate as that prognostication turned out to be, no one then had the slightest inkling that Roger Maris would be experiencing the season of his life as well.[2]

Manager Ralph Houk blamed much of the team's poor start on the frigid, wet weather, which caused postponements of a number of games. After the opener on April 11, for example, New York did not play again until April 15. Not only did it disrupt the pitching rotation but, as Houk explained, "you can't expect a fellow to play one day and be off two and still keep his timing. I'm sure that when the weather gets better and we start playing every day, you'll see these fellows hit the way they should."[3]

Home Run # 1—Game 11—April 26—Day Game

After a 4–1 loss to the Baltimore Orioles on April 23, the Yankees caught a chartered flight immediately after the game to open a three-game series against the league-leading Detroit Tigers. The following afternoon they faced their long-time nemesis, Frank Lary. Although the Tiger ace gave up two runs in the top of the first inning, the Bengels tied it up on the bottom of that same inning. Lary settled down after that, pitching a complete game 4–3 win for the Tigers eighth straight victory. "His fast ball blazed, his sinker dipped, his curve clipped, his slider slid," said Ralph Houk about the right-hander's performance. In other words, it was a typical outing by a pitcher who consistently dominated the Yankees. That win gave him a lifetime 24–8 record over the Bombers, thus confirming the accuracy of his sobriquet "The Yankee Killer." Maris, who usually hit Lary well—in 1960 he batted .412 with two home runs against the Tiger ace—had only one hit in four at-bats, although he scored one of the Yankee runs. With drizzle and 40 degree temperatures the following day, the scheduled game had to be postponed, the fifth such rainout for the Yankees since opening day two weeks earlier.[4]

It was another cold, wet day when the Yankee bus pulled into Tiger Stadium for an afternoon contest on April 26. With temperatures in the low 40s, fewer than 5,000 Detroit fans bothered to show up to see if their beloved Bengels could run their winning streak to nine games. What they witnessed instead was a wild affair where the lead see-sawed back and forth for over three hours before the hometown team finally succumbed to Mickey Mantle's mighty bat in the tenth inning. Roger Maris lent his two cents' worth as well.

Dom Mossi was the starter for Detroit, but gave up five runs in the first, in large part due to two errors on the part of Chico Fernandez, the shortstop. In the bottom of the second, the Tigers staged a comeback, scoring four that included a throwing error by Whitey Ford. Mossi was lifted after four innings with the Yankees up, 7–5.

Paul Foytack, who was in his eighth season with Detroit, was called in to stop the Yankee onslaught. The 30-year-old Scranton, Pennsylvania, native spent most of his early career in the Tiger bullpen. Part of his problem was that he was inconsistent, pitching a great game one outing, then a disaster the next. In 1955, for example, he was relegated to the role of spot-reliever because manager Bucky Harris did not think much of his young pitcher. "He hasn't shown me enough to be a starter. And he doesn't have the control a relief pitcher requires," Harris explained. He appeared in only 22 games that season, almost always in relief. And the one start Harris did allow him to make, he lasted just four innings after having surrendered four earned runs. He ended that year with a thoroughly unimpressive 5.26 ERA that included 36 walks to go along with 38 strikeouts. But that frustrating season was not the end of the road of the troubled hurler.[5]

The right-hander had the good fortune to come under the tutelage of Detroit coach Jack Tighe, who worked assiduously with the youngster on improving his control. Foytack already had an outstanding fastball—what he referred to as his "bread-and-butter pitch"—but lacked mastery over his other pitches. "Jack tried to impress on me that I have a good fastball and a curve and that I could throw a palm ball as my 'off' pitch. So he ordered me to lay off the slider. There's no question it has improved my control," Foytack declared.

All his hard work paid off. In 1956 Foytack became the Tiger's fourth starter, making the most of his opportunity to pitch on a regular basis. He went 15–13 in 43 games, ending the season with a very respectable 3.56 ERA. He was fourth in the American League in innings pitched (256) and third in strikeouts, but still had a tendency to walk too many batters and give up too many long balls (24, fifth in the league). "Up-and-Down Foytack," as one sportswriter called him, had at last come into his own.[6]

Over the next three seasons, he became a workhorse, pitching 682 innings in 116 games, mostly as a starter. He fashioned a 43–38 record with a 3.77 ERA over that time period. But he continued to allow a disproportionate number of free passes and four-baggers, placing in the top ten in those two categories from 1957 through 1959. He seemed, however, to have settled in as a reliable hurler with the Detroit staff. Then it all collapsed in 1960. At the end of the 1959 season he experienced shoulder problems which reappeared the following spring. He ended up pitching just a little over 92 innings in 28 games, splitting time between starting and relieving. He ended the season with an atrocious 2–11 won-loss record on a bloated 6.14 ERA. And home runs remained a problem: on his final start on September 10, he gave up three bombs, including a monster shot by Mickey Mantle that landed in a lumber yard outside the stadium. By some estimates it traveled an incredible 643 feet. Amazingly, though, 1960 did not spell the end of his career.[7]

He worked hard over that winter to strengthen his arm. While eventually he would get back to his earlier form, at the start of the year he was still struggling. Because there was still some concern about the state of his arm, he did not make his first appearance of the season until that April 26 game. He was idle so long that he quipped, "Twenty more minutes of pitching in batting practice and I'll earn my letter." So he was rusty when he took the mound at the top of the fifth to face the bottom of the Yankee order.[8]

He got Elston Howard to ground to short, but then Maris, hitting in the seventh slot, stepped into the box with his less-than-imposing sub–Mendoza average. Maris was familiar with Foytack, having faced him on several occasions in the past. In 1958 he had one homer off him, but went just three for 18 overall that season. The following year Maris did somewhat better, hammering two homers and going four for 18. In 1960, though, the Yankee slugger failed to get a single hit in eight plate appearances, although he was walked four times.

The right fielder singled in the first inning, so he was showing some signs of life when he strode to the plate, a slumping slugger confronting a struggling pitcher. Maris came out the victor in that early encounter, parking the ball in the right-field seats for his first homer of the season. Although it added a run to the Yankee lead, it was only temporary as the Tigers came roaring back in the bottom of the seventh to go ahead, 11–8. Once again it was Mickey Mantle's bat that secured an important win for the Bombers. Batting left-handed in the eighth inning with New York down, 11–9, he hit a two-run homer to tie it up. Then batting right-handed in the tenth, he again hit a two-run blast to give his team the lead for good. He now had seven round-trippers to Maris' one.[9]

That was the only run Foytack gave up over the two innings he pitched. It was a good enough outing to earn him his first starting assignment on April 30. Unfortunately, that did not turn out well as he allowed four earned runs with three long balls over seven innings to take a loss. It was a rough outing, but eventually he crafted a decent season, ending with an 11–10 record on a 3.93 ERA. But home runs remained a problem. He allowed 27 in just 170 innings pitched, making him eighth in the American League that year. He played another two and a half years with Detroit before being traded to the Los Angeles Angels in the middle of the 1963 season. His final outing as a major leaguer was on May 7, 1964, a disastrous affair in which he allowed three earned runs on two home runs in two innings of relief. Over 11 seasons in the majors, mostly with second division teams, he compiled a record of 86 wins and 87 losses with a cumulative 4.14 ERA. As for Roger Maris, he never hit another home run off of him although he faced him 14 more times after that April 26 contest.

Maris experienced a modicum of relief after getting his first home run of the season. It was a drop in the bucket, but at least it was a beginning. The slump that started in the second half of the 1960 season continued to haunt him for the next several weeks. Sportswriters began asking, "What's wrong with Maris?" Other than confirming he was pressing too hard and trying to pull the ball too much, especially at Yankee Stadium, he had no real explanation for what was happening. He tried to remain positive, however. "It's easy to be out front when you're going good," he said after hitting that first homer. "It's hard to be a gay blade when you're going bad but we gotta do it."[10]

Unlike Mantle, he never threw helmets or bats or had tantrums during the down times. He just kept plugging along. "I know I can hit. It's just a question of going out and doing it. You can't go bad forever. It might take a week, a day, a month or all year. But it'll come back as long as you can keep it out of your mind." No matter how poorly he was doing offensively, he never let his plate troubles affect his performance in the field. "He is the same spectacular man on defense he was when he was slugging the ball last year," observed Dan Daniel in *The Sporting News*. "Not all players react that way. But he is fortunate in having the unyielding temperament."[11]

Everyone had a theory as to why he was struggling. Dan Daniel observed that "his timing is way off. Then there is the arrogance which the pitchers of the opposition adopt toward a slumping hitter with a reputation. They are getting away with pitches they wouldn't dare throw to Maris if he were right." Manager Ralph Houk continued to express confidence in his right fielder, but he could not help but be a little concerned. He knew that the success of the Yankees depended in large part on a productive Maris. He was aware that Maris was a streak hitter, as he believed all sluggers to be. "They swing hard, and it's like flipping a penny. If they miss the ball by a quarter inch, it's the difference between a long-distance clout and a pop-up." He truly believed, though, that Maris would eventually rediscover his swing.[12]

Home Run # 2—Game 17—May 3—Day Game

Before he got back on track, however, Maris still had some less-than-productive games ahead of him. It was nearly a week before he hit another homer. In that time, though, the Yankees went on a mini winning streak, taking four of their next five games. Maris crossed the Mendoza Line for the first time that season, raising his batting average to a less-than-inspiring .212. Although he had only four hits in 17 at-bats, two of those were for doubles. He scored two and plated two others to help the Yanks win some closely-fought battles.

Mantle continued to sparkle both in the field and at bat. In addition to clouting another home run, giving him a seven-run lead over his partner, he drove in seven and saved the April 27 game against the Indians with his speed and glove. After driving in what proved to be the winning run with a triple in the bottom of the seventh, he was patrolling his position in center when, with one on and one out in the top of the ninth, Cleveland third baseman Bubba Phillips smashed an Art Ditmar pitch into deep right-center. It appeared to be a game-tying extra-base hit, "but at the last split second, the galloping Mantle lunged, slipped and skidded after the ball and made a gloved-hand catch" to seal a Yankee victory. For the first time, Mantle began hearing far more cheers than boos. Most importantly, the four victories moved New York into second place, just one game behind league-leading Detroit. Things were beginning to look up.[13]

On May 2, Maris had a decent outing against the Twins in Minnesota. In addition to hitting a double in three at-bats, he was walked twice and scored two runs to help the Yanks to a 6–4, 10-inning victory. His second run occurred in the top of the tenth on a Mickey Mantle grand slam. In the second game of the series, the Yankees faced veteran right-hander Pedro Ramos.

Known as "The Cuban Cowboy" for his wild antics and fondness for Western movies and cowboy hats, the right-handed side-arming Ramos produced a 15-year career in spite of having winning records in just two of those seasons. His performance as a major league pitcher

Pedro Ramos, "The Cuban Cowboy," was noted for his wild antics and fondness for Western movies and cowboy hats. The right-handed starter for the Minnesota Twins gave up two homers to Maris in 1961, numbers 2 and 17. He also led the league in losses (20), hits (265), and home runs (39) that season.

was erratic, to say the least. He led the American League in losses from 1958 to 1961, while also having the most game starts in two of those years. Relying on a fastball and his patented "Cuban palm ball" (a type of spitball), Ramos was particularly fond of serving up home runs in bunches. In fact, he led the league in long-balls allowed in 1957 (43), 1958 (38), and 1961 (39).

Ramos claimed that while he was "a sneaky pitcher" at times, the reason he allowed so many round-trippers was because ultimately he was "too honest and just threw a fastball down the middle when I had two strikes." He was convinced he had a cannon for an arm. "Early in my career, I thought I could get everyone out with my fastball. If I'd been smarter, I would have monkeyed around instead of always challenging batters when I got ahead." Eventually he did smarten up. Because he believed his curveball, which he frequently threw side-arm, "wasn't that effective," he developed his special palm ball when he "needed another pitch to help me get by in tough situations when I didn't want to use my heater. I needed a ball that would sink so I could get double-play grounders instead of 2-run homers."

His most famous dinger was the one Mantle came a foot from hitting out of Yankee Stadium on May 30, 1956. Naturally, it came on a two-strike, two-ball pitch. One can only surmise that he decided to be "too honest" with the Mick that day. The comical Cuban said of that shot, "I thought the ball was going to New Jersey." The 1958 season was of particular note; not only did he surpass all American League pitchers in losses, hits, earned runs, and home runs (38), but he was first in game starts and batters-faced.

From 1964 until his final major league season in 1969, he pitched mainly in relief for a number of teams, including spending a little over two seasons with the Yankees. His lifetime record was 117 wins against 160 losses with a 4.08 ERA and 316 homers surrendered. Regardless of the situation, stadium, outcome, or how well he did, Ramos loved pitching. "When I was on the mound, I didn't even know how many people were in the stands.... I didn't care if the mound was high or low.... I went hitter by hitter, inning by inning.... I pitched quickly. I didn't give the batter too much time to think. I knew what I was going to throw. My best pitch every time." Sadly, he led a less-than-enjoyable post-baseball life. He experienced a series of arrests for drug trafficking and possession, carrying concealed weapons, drunk driving, and parole violations; these numerous misdemeanors and felonies resulted in a three-year sentence to a Florida federal penitentiary in the early 1980s.[14]

Maris batted well against Ramos over the seven seasons they faced each other, hitting a cumulative .288 with seven long balls. In his first year as a Yankee, he batted an impressive .389 against the righty, including two dingers, a triple, a double, and five RBIs. While his average dropped to .200 in 1961, that would not be the case with his run production. In their first confrontation on opening day, however, Ramos dominated Maris just as he did the other Yankee batters. The right fielder failed to get a hit, only reaching base on a fielding error. Their second meeting of the season was a different matter altogether.

Ramos came into the game sporting a 2–0 record with a 3.12 ERA over his previous four appearances, but he had yielded five homers in those four games. He was about to add to that total. The afternoon contest started in fine fashion for the Cuban hurler. The Twins plated a run in the first while Ramos held the Yanks in-check over the first three innings, giving up just three meaningless singles. The righty's cause was helped when Maris grounded into an inning-ending double play in his first plate appearance. Then in the fourth two errors and a couple of timely hits put the Yankees up, 3–1.

Ramos corralled the Bombers after that until the seventh inning, which proved his undoing. It began with a Bobby Richardson single followed by a Harmon Killebrew error on what should have been a sacrifice by pitcher Bob Turley. A sac-bunt by Tony Kubek, again fielded by Killebrew, ended with a force at first and runners on second and third. After a single by Lopez produced a run, Maris walked to the plate for his fourth appearance of the day, this time with runners on the corners and determination in his eyes.

"He [Ramos] had gotten me out three times, but this time I got him out," Maris recalled later. The right fielder hammered a line shot deep into the right-field seats for three runs and his second homer of the 1961 campaign. "Maybe it was a lot of pent-up frustration that I put behind that swing. Whatever it was, the ball went out of the park.... It really felt great." His three RBIs proved to be the nail in the Twins' coffin. Ramos was replaced by Ted Sadowski who managed to close out the inning with no more Yankee runs, but it was too little, too late. Minnesota attempted a comeback in the bottom of the inning, scoring two runs, but the Yankee lead was just too much to overcome. The Bombers won, 7–3, with four of the Yankee runs unearned. The win moved New York into a tie for first place with Detroit. For Maris, it was his first home run at Metropolitan Stadium, a venue that proved to be unfriendly to him. It was the only four-bagger he would hit there that season.[15]

Home Run # 3—Game 20—May 6—Night Game

The following day, the Yankees faced the Twins for the third and final time. Having yet to find the batting order he felt worked best, manager Ralph Houk moved players around depending on who was pitching against them any particular day. He usually placed Maris in the seventh slot whenever a lefty took the mound, which was the case on May 4 when Jim Kaat started the game for the home team. It was a practice that stopped once Maris found his stroke two weeks later. After that Maris batted third in front of Mantle except for those games when Mantle was out of the lineup. On that day, though, Houk's decision was right on target as Maris went hitless against the young left-handed pitcher.

Fortunately for the Bombers, Mickey Mantle was still on a tear, driving in two runs, one of which was his ninth homer of the year off of reliever Ted Sadowski in the sixth inning. The Mick's performance insured a sweep of Minnesota. Afterwards, the team jetted to the West Coast for the first time that season to face the newly-minted Los Angeles Angels in a nighttime affair. While Maris did slightly better than the day before by walking three times and scoring twice, the hero that game was the light-hitting third baseman Clete Boyer, whose two-run blast with Maris aboard in the top of the ninth resulted in a one-run Yankee victory. Mantle, unfortunately, went hitless, thus ending his 16-game hitting streak. The following evening saw the Yankees' consecutive wins end at four as the Angels defeated them, 5–3. Although the loss once again moved New York to second place behind Detroit, for Maris it proved to be another sign that he was moving out of his three-week-old slump.[16]

The Angels starting hurler the night of May 6 was righty Eli Grba, who had the distinction of being the first player selected in the expansion draft held at the end of 1960. He pitched parts of his first two major league seasons with the Yankees where he was used as a spot starter and a reliever. In 1960, his second year with New York, he compiled a winning record in 24 game appearances, going 6–4 with a 3.68 ERA after he was called up from Richmond in mid–June. Known in the minor leagues as "Let 'em Fly, Eli" because of his fastball, he had a good curve, slider, and changeup as his secondary pitches. His biggest problem was control, generally issuing more walks than strikeouts. He was no automatic out at bat either. He hit .234 with two homers, three doubles, and 11 RBIs in 80 plate appearances in his first season with the Angels.

On April 11, 1961, he toed the rubber in the first game in Angels history, beating the Orioles in Baltimore, 7–2, in nine complete innings. Considering that he labored for a second division club, Grba had a decent season in 1961, winning 11 and losing 13 with an ERA of 4.25. He did allow 26 home runs that year, tying him for ninth place in the American League in that category, in large part because of where he played his home games. Los Angeles' Wrigley Field was a notorious home-run-friendly park with its 345-foot power alleys which were only a few feet longer than down the lines (338 feet to the right field foul pole, 340 to the left field pole).

In 21 games at home, Grba gave up 19 four-baggers while in 19 road contests only seven. In fact, all batters took advantage of the friendly confines of the Angels' home field, clouting a total of 248 homers there that summer, a major league record that stood until 1996. Playing half their games at Wrigley was the main reason the Angels were second only to the powerful Yankees in total team home runs. Oddly, though, Maris hit only two round-trippers in what should have been his personal launching pad, which greatly puzzled the slugger. "I can't understand it.... The fences aren't that far. The ball seems to sail nicely enough. Everybody else hits homers there. I don't."[17]

The bespectacled right-hander showed a lot of potential, but, sadly, he had a serious drinking problem. "I was drinking heavy and I didn't care about anything," he explained to an interviewer. "My priorities were all gone." (He stopped drinking in 1981, remaining sober from then on.) He lasted two more seasons with Los Angeles, ending his major league career in 1963 with a cumulative record of 28 wins and 33 losses on a 4.48 ERA. As for Maris, Grba generally handled him well. In 23 plate appearances over three seasons, Maris batted .250, hitting two home runs, both of which came in his historic 1961 season. The first of those occurred on the night of May 6.[18]

The first time Grba faced his old team was on April 20 in New York. That outing did not go as well as his opening day assignment. He served up two monster home runs to Mickey Mantle for five RBIs before he was lifted after six innings of work. The Yankees defeated the Angels, 7–5, with Grba taking the loss. He was hoping to exact a measure of revenge on this next confrontation with the Bombers.

He stumbled a bit in the first, giving up a run on a Maris single, but in the bottom of the inning the Angels took a 2–1 lead on a Leon Wagner triple followed by a run-scoring groundout by first baseman Ted Kluszewski. The Yanks tied it at two in the third inning on a Moose Skowron single to right that plated Maris from second after he was walked to start the inning. The Angels came roaring back with two solo home runs in the bottom of that inning to make it 4–2. Then Maris came to the plate with one out and none on in the top of the fifth.[19]

Grba delivered a high outside fastball that Maris hammered over the wall just to the left of the 412-foot marker in center field. "It was one of the few times I didn't try to pull that type of pitch," Maris later said. "I went with it and hit it over the left-center-field fence. It was a real thrill to see that one go out." He was particularly pleased that for once he did not try to pull an outside pitch. "My power is any place I can get a ball to pull, but this was away from me. It convinced me that I had the power to hit the ball out in any direction, not just right field, if I would just go with the pitch." As true as that statement was, it would be the only home run he would hit in that direction all season. "Pulling the ball, however, is actually a force of habit. Regardless of where the ball is pitched, usually I'm pulling. Many times I get way out front and the ball just twists off the bat and goes foul."[20]

That home run was particularly important for another reason—it was the 100 of his career. Noting that it was "an added thrill" as a result, it was the first ball he ever wanted to have back as a memento. "There was no chance, however, for it went over the fence, bounced into the street, and was gone forever," he remembered with some regret.[21]

That was the last run the Yankees scored that night. Angels left fielder Leon Wagner hit his second home run of the game in the bottom of the sixth making the final score, 5–3, in favor of Los Angeles. In spite of the loss, Maris "was feeling pretty good that night. After hitting only one home run in fifteen games, now I had hit two in four days. Perhaps I had reached the turning point. I was even in a mood to kid with the writers about the whole thing. I had told them that I was having an early slump just to foul them up." Maris now stood at three home runs to Mantle's nine.[22]

Maris may have thought he had "reached a turning point" after that May 6 contest, but he played eight more games before that hope became a reality. From May 7 through May 16, he batted a pathetic .188, getting only six hits in 36 plate appearances while driving in just two runs. As a sign that he was truly pressing during that period, he struck out (six times) twice as much as he walked (three times), which was unusual for him. As he well knew, his timing was off and he was swinging at bad pitches. The Yankees as a team slumped during that period as well, winning just three of the eight games, leaving them four games out and just one ahead of Minnesota. Even Mickey Mantle had cooled; in 10 games from May 5 through May 16, he hit .226 and, while he did hit another homer to give him 10, he had only two RBIs.

Ralph Houk claimed not to be overly worried. "I was neither up nor down," in part because he was certain Maris was at last starting to come around. "Like a long-dormant volcano he was beginning to rumble" was how baseball historian Robert Creamer described it. In the meantime, Houk continued to shuffle the lineup in the hopes of coming up with the perfect combination.[23]

Maris was desperate to figure out why he had not completely broken out of his slump. He was grateful that Houk was being patient with him, but he was worried that he might be benched or worse, traded, as he was in the past when he was not producing as expected. "As this horrible start extended so long, I began to wonder if I did have any security. I knew there were now ten teams in the league and began to wonder if I would eventually be on all ten of them. I wondered if the Yankees were disappointed in me, perhaps already looking around for a trade. The Yankees don't hang on to outfielders hitting .200." He felt added pressure because of his performance the season before. "Not only was I with the Yankees, but I was no longer just one of the mob. I had won the Most Valuable Player award and had been the RBI champion last season. Now when I was slumping it created attention and debate." And Maris hated being the center of attention. But just as he thought his plate troubles might last all season, two things happened which had a profoundly positive effect.[24]

Houk believed Maris was burdened by his concern over his wife's health, that it was weighing on him, impacting his performance. Maris always had the safety and security of his family foremost in his mind, so he could not help but be troubled by the lingering threat to his wife's pregnancy. It was around this time that he learned his wife and unborn child were out of danger, which greatly relieved the worried outfielder. "Now I was able to put my mind on baseball," he stated.[25]

Then a summons from the front office in mid–May put Maris further at ease. He was already beginning to get his act together when he was notified that Yankee co-owner Dan Topping and general manager Roy Hamey wanted to talk with him. "You can imagine my thoughts about that," he said later. "I thought perhaps I was to be traded. I figured that I was going to at least be called on the carpet for something." He went to lunch with the two, fully expecting them to "lower the boom" on him. Instead, they wanted to assure him that his job was secure, but to forget about his batting average "and to go out and swing for home runs. We would rather see you hit a lot of homers and drive in runs than hit .300." Verbalizing their expectations took a lot of the pressure off of Maris. "I guess that was the turning point," he said later. "I quit pressing and homers started to come." Unfortunately, they also "suggested" he have his eyes examined just in case there was a problem with his vision, never bothering to inform Ralph Houk about it. That directive created tension between him and the rookie manager.[26]

The Yankees suffered their second loss in three games against the Angels the following afternoon by the same score as the evening before. Home runs were again their undoing as Yankee starter Art Ditmar gave up two and the usually-reliable Luis Arroyo one. With May 8 an off-day, the team flew to Kansas City for a short two-game series against the sixth-place Athletics.

Just before game time, New York pulled off a trade with Los Angeles that brought them reserve outfielder Bob Cerv and reliever Tex Clevenger for pitchers Ryne Duren and Johnny James, along with rookie outfielder Lee Thomas. The Cerv acquisition was of particular import to Maris. The two were teammates and friends while playing for the Athletics and became roommates once Cerv moved to New York. They and Mickey Mantle soon ended up sharing an apartment in Queens, which seemed to have a positive calming effect on both the Yankee sluggers. There they could have some semblance of normalcy in their private lives hidden away from demanding fans and the hounding press.[27]

The trade, however, was of no immediate help. The Yankees lost that night by a lone run after starter Whitey Ford was charged with three earned runs and reliever Arroyo with another, all in the bottom of the eighth, for a third straight New York loss. Even Cerv failed to deliver when he led off the ninth with a groundout in his first pinch-hitting assignment as a Yankee. Mantle went hitless for the fourth consecutive game, dropping his batting average to .284. Maris was 0-for-4 as well, but did remain above the Medoza Line with a .225 average. Concern was growing in the Yankee clubhouse.[28]

Thanks to timely one-hit relief by newly-acquired Tex Clevenger, the Yankees were able to end their three-game losing streak by turning the tables on the Athletics, scoring five runs in the top of the eighth. In that fateful inning, Mantle broke out of his hitless-slump with a single and a run-scored while Maris, batting seventh again, came through with a run-scoring single of his own off lefty Jim Archer. New York had an off-day on May 11 before flying home to play the league-leading Tigers in a crucial four-game series at the Stadium.[29]

The Bombers first had to figure out Frank Lary if they hoped to catch Detroit. His May 12 performance was not a pretty one, but once again "The Yankee Killer" prevailed. He surrendered 11 hits, issued seven walks, hit one batter, threw two wild pitches, and offered up a two-run homer to Hector Lopez over the nine innings, but was able to strand 14 Yankee baserunners. Adding insult to injury, he hit a ninth inning solo shot over the left-field wall that turned out to be the winning run in a 4–3 victory.

The following afternoon saw another Yankee defeat, this time thanks mainly to Rocky Colavito's two dingers and four RBIs. "The Rock" generated even more excitement when he was evicted from the game in the eighth after he rushed into the stands to protect his father, who was being assaulted by a drunken fan. "What would you do if you saw someone belting your 60-year-old father? My dad is here today, and if the same thing happened again I would act the same way," he said afterwards.[30]

Fortunately, the Yankees were able to secure a split with the Tigers when they took both ends of the May 14 doubleheader, winning by scores of 5–4 and 8–6. Neither Maris nor Mantle contributed much in that series, driving in just one run apiece, although Mantle was 5-for-10 in those four games. Clearly his batting slump was in the past. Maris had to wait one more game.

Home Run # 4—Game 29—May 17—Day Game

On May 16 and 17, the Yankees played host to the new version of the Washington Senators for two games. Expecting a sweep of the seventh-place club, they were the victims instead. In the first game, starter Bill Stafford gave up three runs in the third inning, which was all Washington needed to defeat the Yankees, 3–2. The only bright spot was Mantle's tenth home run of the season, a solo shot in the sixth. A sense of doom descended upon players and management alike when New York dropped an 8–7 decision the following day.

When pressed by reporters after that second defeat, Ralph Houk responded in frustration. "What would you have me do in my spot?" he asked them. "Name me one change you would make. I mean it. Tell me one thing I could do to stop all this." Part of the problem was that the Yankees were not hitting well with runners on base. The Bombers left 37 stranded in the four-game homestand against the Tigers and another 20 in the two games with the Senators. "Our defense is good and our pitching for the most part hasn't been bad," Houk argued. "But crimineys, how can we go along without getting that one hit when we need it?"[31]

"The Yankee players seem to be losing patience, too—with themselves," noted one sportswriter. What no one realized at the time, however, was that Roger Maris' bat was about to catch fire. It was as if someone had lit a fuse and both Maris and the Yankees exploded. Over the next six weeks, beginning with that May 17 loss until the end of June, he slammed 24 home runs and drove in 54, raising his batting average from .208 to .260 in those 45 games. New York ignited as well, going 29–16 during that month and a half. They would be just two games out of first when the dust settled.[32]

The Senators' starting pitcher that May 17 game was left-hander Pete Burnside. Because he would be facing a southpaw, Maris was again relegated to the seventh position in the lineup. It was the tenth, and final, time that season. From then on, he typically batted third except for those games when Mantle was out of the lineup.

The southpaw came up through the New York Giants farm system. A Dartmouth graduate, he made his first major league appearance as a starter on September 20, 1955. He lasted only 3⅔ innings, giving up seven runs, but only two of them were earned. He made one more appearance five days later, pitching a complete game for his first major league win. The following season was spent in the minors before returning to the big club at the start of the 1957

Left-hander Pete Burnside of the Washington Senators was one of Maris' favorite pitchers that summer. The slugger's three dingers (numbers 4, 29, and 42) accounted for over a fourth of the total home runs (11) Burnside surrendered in 1961.

season. After a masterful complete-game shutout in his first start that year, things turned sour and he was consigned back to the minors for further work. After a brief, and unsuccessful, start with the Giants in 1958 season, he was again sent down. By the end of the year he was wearing a different uniform.

Burnside was what some might refer to as a "four-A" player. He pitched extremely well in the minors and in winter ball, but was never quite able to put it all together for a successful major league career. He had good stuff, so that was not the issue. His blazing fastball was his dominant pitch. "There are those graybeards who even suggest his fast ball is more 'live' than were those of Walter Johnson and Bob Feller," observed one sportswriter. And the great Carl Hubbell ranked him "as the most promising pitcher in the chain of the New York Giants."

Playing for the Dallas Eagles in the Double-A Texas League during the 1955 season, he compiled an 18–11 record that included 235 strikeouts in 255 innings pitched. In addition, he had a good curve to go along with the hard one. His main problem seemed to be one of control, especially with the hook. Bucky Walters, pitching coach for the Giants in 1957, noted exactly that: "Now, if he can hold the plate with that jug [curveball] of his, he may do." Like any pitcher, Burnside needed to be in the rotation on a set and consistent basis to maintain his sharpness. As he well knew, "getting a chance to pitch regularly ... makes a lot of difference." Unfortunately for him, he rarely had that opportunity. One outing he would start, the next relieve, a pattern which could not help but be disruptive. It was no coincidence that his best ERA (3.77) in the majors was in 1959 when he was used only in relief, never as a starter. Being shifted back and forth between the majors and minors, as he was in his early career, was hardly conducive to effective pitching either.

In addition, he was plagued by a series of injuries over the years which occurred at crucial points in his development. Hall-of-Famer Hubbell, however, believed the underlying issue was one of him trying too hard. "He puts everything he's got on every pitch up there [in the majors]. He does better down with the Millers because he relaxes more." Burnside admitted as much when he said, "I probably wanted to make the grade so much I over-extended myself."[33]

In 1959 he was traded to the Detroit Tigers where he went 1–3 with a 3.77 ERA in 30 games, all out of the bullpen. The following season was the only time in his major league career he did not end up with a losing record, going 7–7 in 31 games, nearly half of them as a starter. Left unprotected by Detroit, he was selected by the new Washington Senators in the expansion draft at the end of 1960, their eighth selection overall. Although he had a disappointing year in which he was 4–9 with a 4.53 ERA in 33 games, the Senators still saw him as vital to their success in 1962. He had a great end to the season, going 3–3 with a minuscule 1.80 in his final six decisions, which was why the club was not interested in trading him. "Primary among [the reasons] are Burnside's brilliant finish last season, when he won four [sic] of his six starts, and was more effective than any lefty in the league except Whitey Ford during that period," sportswriter Shirley Povich reported.[34]

Washington did not feel that same way about their 31-year-old left-hander at the end of the 1962 campaign. After a discouraging season in which he won just five while losing 11 in 40 game appearances, Burnside's contract was not renewed. He ended his major league career the following year, appearing in six games for the Baltimore Orioles before being signed as a free agent by the Senators after he was released by the Birds. He toed the rubber in 38 games for the Nats, all but one in relief, ending up with an 0–1 record to go along with a huge 6.15 ERA. Over parts of eight major league seasons, he compiled a disappointing record of 19 wins, 36 losses and a less-than-impressive 4.81 ERA.

Burnside was one of Roger Maris' favorite victims in 1961. Prior to that season, Maris failed to park one off of the lefty in 16 plate appearances, but in 1960 he did bat .417 with five singles in 12 at-bats. In their first confrontation on April 30, Burnside induced a Maris groundout in the bottom of the ninth inning to secure a 2–1 Senators win. Their next battle occurred on May 17 when Burnside started the game for Washington. For the first seven innings, the lefty appeared untouchable. He held the Yankees to just one run while his teammates added eight of their own to give him a very comfortable seven run cushion. All Maris managed to do against him offensively was a fielder's-choice grounder in the second, a lineout to right in the fourth, and a bunt single in the sixth. "The first two times up I had done nothing," commented Maris. "Perhaps I was getting a little panicky. Whatever it was, I had suddenly decided that I'd try bunting when I batted in the sixth. At least I could still bunt." While this successful at-bat came to nothing score-wise, it may just have been the very thing he needed to restore a little self-confidence.[35]

With the Senators seven runs ahead going into the bottom of the eighth, the roof suddenly caved in on the hard-luck pitcher. After allowing a lead-off single to Mickey Mantle, Burnside struck out Moose Skowron. A wild pitch moved Mantle to second, followed by an Elston Howard single that scored the center fielder. With one on and one out, Maris took his fourth turn at the plate.

"Then I came up hoping I could keep the rally going," Maris recalled. "Should I bunt again? That wouldn't help now, so I went for broke. Burnside came in with a nice fat fast ball. I timed it perfectly, swung, and almost jumped as I saw it heading for the seats." The ball landed deep into the right-field bleachers for two runs. "It was only my fourth home run, but I felt like a million. It was a great feeling of relief. It had come off a left-handed pitcher and was my first of the year at the Stadium."[36]

Burnside was lifted after delivering two more singles, replaced by Marty Kutyna who allowed two more to score before stopping the damage at five Yankee runs. New York added another run in the ninth, ending with a 8–7 loss and a win for Burnside. While the defeat left the Yankees five games behind the Tigers, Houk was not displeased because his Bombers had suddenly started living up to their reputation. "That was a real pleasure to see," the manager said afterwards. "Our pitching wasn't up to par today, but in the past our hitters hurt us the most."[37]

To top it off, Maris made a sparkling fielding play to go along with his success at the plate that day. Washington third baseman Billy Klaus, who homered off of Art Ditmar to open the first inning, came within an eyelash of doing so again in the fifth, this time with a runner on. He hit a long fly ball that Maris, with one foot on the ground and his back bent awkwardly over the short right field wall, snagged at the last moment. All in all, it was not a bad day for either the slugger or the Yankees.

Home Run # 5—Game 30—May 19—Night Game

Ralph Houk was quite prophetic when he spoke to the press before heading to Cleveland the next day for a two-game series. "All we need is for two or three of our big men to get hot at the same time," he contended. "Of course, Mickey Mantle has been hitting well all year, but we need a couple of more fellows to get hot with men on base and drive in the big runs for us. I can't help but think it's bound to happen, and I've got a feeling it's going to happen soon." If by "soon" he meant after two more losses, then he was right on target.[38]

The May 19 game in Cleveland was started by another of Maris' favorite pitchers, Jim Perry, older brother of Hall-of-Fame pitcher Gaylord Perry. The hard-throwing right-hander had a distinguished, if somewhat erratic, 17-year career in the majors that saw him pitch for Cleveland, Minnesota, Detroit, and, at the end, Oakland. In his 1959 rookie season he posted a 12–10 record with an outstanding 2.65 ERA while alternating between starting and relieving. He came in second in the Rookie of the Year voting.

He had a breakout year with Cleveland in his sophomore season. Winning 18 against 10 losses with a decent 3.62 ERA, he was first among all American League pitchers in wins, games started, and shutouts, while placing in the top 10 in innings pitched, complete games, and winning percentage. He was named "Sophomore of the Year" and "Man of the Year" by the Cleveland branch of the Baseball Writers' Association of America for his efforts that season.[39]

Cleveland Indians right-hander Jim Perry, brother of Gaylord Perry, had a distinguished 17-season major league career in which he recorded 215 wins against 174 losses. He was another of Maris' favorites, surrendering three round-trippers to the Yankee right fielder (numbers 5, 21, and 49).

He had one major flaw, though, that would haunt him throughout his career—he allowed too many home runs. He led the American League twice in that category with 35 in 1960 and 39 in 1971 and placed sixth in 1961 with 28, three of those belonging to Roger Maris. The Yankees as a team regularly feasted off of Perry in that department. In 1960 they clobbered him with 15 long balls, establishing a new major league record for the most homers allowed by a single pitcher to one team in a season. Four of those dingers occurred in just one game at Yankee Stadium.

Commented Cleveland sportswriter Hal Lebovitz, "He threw so many home-run pitches [in 1960] there was a fear he might become punchy from the bombardment. But Jim, fortunately, has the proper temperament. He's a fighter, a confident one. If a hitter beats him once, Jim seems eager for a return bout." Perry tried to keep a positive attitude about his penchant for offering up gopher balls. Referring to his off-season job of selling bomb shelters around his hometown of Williamston, North Carolina, Perry wisecracked to one reporter, "The way I was bombed last summer [1961], I ought to get one for myself."[40]

His 1961 season with the Indians was one of his off-years. He won just 10 games while losing 17, third most in the league, and led all American League pitchers in earned runs. His home-runs-allowed total that season was the third most of his career. He surrendered 308 round-trippers over 17 years, placing him in the top 50 (fiftieth) among all pitchers in both leagues in that category. In early May 1963 he was traded to the Minnesota Twins, which turned out to be the beginning of the most productive period of his career.

Over the next ten seasons he compiled an excellent 128–90 record with an earned-run average just over 3.00. His superb 1969 season (20–6, 2.82 ERA) was exceeded only by the 1970 campaign. That year the 34-year-old right-hander received the Cy Young Award and placed ninth in MVP voting after winning 24 while losing only 12 out of the 40 games he started. In 1974, the next to last season of his career, he was traded back to Cleveland after spending the previous summer with the Detroit Tigers. It was an especially exciting year for him: he was teamed up with his younger brother, Gaylord, for the first, and only, time. Together they won 38 out of the Indians 77 victories, Jim going 17–12 and Gaylord 21–13. The right-hander ended his career after playing for both Cleveland and the Oakland A's in 1975. During those 17 summers, he compiled a very respectable record of 215 wins against 174 losses with a cumulative 3.45 ERA in 630 games, pitching a little over 3,285 innings in those outings.[41]

According to John Romano, Perry's frequent battery-mate in Cleveland, his dominant pitches were his fastball and his slider. When facing a batter for the first time, Perry relied on his slider as his go-to pitch. "When in doubt you come in with your best pitch. I figure mine is the slider." His curveball early in his career was far less imposing than his other two pitches. It was not until he came under the tutelage of Twins pitching coach Johnny Sain that he developed a sharper-breaking curve and a fastball that "sailed inside to righthanded batters."[42]

His delivery style was described by some as "herky-jerky" and by others as "flapping wings." "His arms flop around, hiding the ball. Suddenly it's coming at you," explained Charlie Maxwell, longtime Tiger outfielder and first baseman. "He fools you," expounded Red Wilson, another of Perry's Cleveland catchers. "From the dugout he doesn't look overpowering. And the ball doesn't blaze into the catcher's mitt. But he throws a surprisingly large number of pitches past the hitters. The ball is on top of them before they know it." As with most pitchers, good control was basic to his success. "He throws for spots and his control is excellent," Wilson noted. "And he knows how to mix up his speeds. The batter never knows what to expect."[43]

Perry was blessed with a self-confidence not usually found in young players. During spring training in 1959 when he was there just to pitch batting practice, he was overheard to say, "They won't send me back. I'm going to make the club." And during that same spring when Cleveland farm director Hoot Evans tried to talk to him about the salaries he might expect to receive as he moved up the ladder in the minor leagues, he responded, "Oh, it doesn't matter. I'll make the big club, so I'll get a new contract anyway." "Perhaps Perry was just as frightened as any other rookie who tried out with a big league club," suggested one sportswriter, "but he gave the appearance of complete self-assurance, almost to the point of cockiness." Perry was convinced poise and believing in one's self were just as important as pitching ability. "You need confidence to be a winning pitcher. Everything else is secondary. You can have all the stuff in the world, but you won't win a game without confidence in your ability."[44]

Many believed the right-hander's tendency to over-analyze the game was the root cause of his periodic episodes of ineffectiveness on the mound. Jimmy Dykes, his manager through most of the 1961 season, firmly believed that was the case. "I keep telling Jim to rear back and fire and the heck with the cute stuff. Be he won't do it. He's thinking too much and that's his trouble."

Sportswriter Hal Lebovitz was one who agreed with that assessment. "Generally Jim has good control. But when he tries to get too fine, he is inclined to become less effective." Echoing those same sentiments, one mound opponent insisted Perry would be better off if "he just reared back and fired." "But he just isn't made that way," concluded Lebovitz.[45]

Roger Maris had great success against Perry over the seven seasons the two faced each other. In the 1960 campaign when the Yankees hit those 15 round-trippers off of him, Maris contributed three of them. In 1961 he did even better against the righty, batting a cool .417 while adding another three homers to his career total of nine. So it was to no one's surprise, least of all Perry's, when the Yankee slugger took him deep in the night of May 19.

Although the Indians came into the contest with a winning record that placed them just one game behind the powerful New York club, no one expected much out of the hometown favorites that night. Cleveland, as their fans knew all too well, held the dubious honor of having lost 11 straight decisions to the Yankees, including their first two games earlier in the season. Conquering them in this twelfth matchup seemed a near-impossible task. And so it appeared that was indeed the case by the time the Yankees completed their at-bats in the top of the first inning. It began in fine fashion when Perry induced leadoff batter Tony Kubek to hit into a first baseman-pitcher groundout to open the frame. But then shortstop Woodie Held bobbled a ground ball off the bat of Hector Lopez to put a runner on first, setting the stage for Maris' heroics.

When the two met for the first time that season, Maris drove in two runs on a sacrifice fly and a single to help New York win, 4–2. He was about to add two more. "Suddenly all my worries and cares began to disappear," he reminisced about the game, "and, against my old team, I found my long-lost timing. I got into the groove." Maris' blast landed deep into the right-field seats, giving the Yankees a temporary 2–0 lead. Perry settled down after that, limiting New York to just those two runs, one of which was unearned. After responding with two runs on a Vic Power single and a bases-loaded walk to Woodie Held in the bottom of that inning, the score remained knotted at two until the sixth when Maris led off the top of that inning with a single. Mickey Mantle then walked, followed by a Yogi Berra homer that put the Yanks ahead, 5–2. Perry got the next three batters, but that ended his outing.[46]

Cleveland, however, kept the game interesting by coming back with two runs of their own in the bottom of the sixth, one of those off of reliever Luis Arroyo, to cut the visitor's margin to one run. Lopez then hit a solo shot in the top of the seventh to give New York a two-run lead, followed by a Moose Skowron single in the eighth, scoring Mantle to provide the Bombers with what appeared to be an insurmountable 7–4 lead. But fate was smiling on the hard-pressed Indians that day. In the bottom of the eighth, the usually untouchable Arroyo surrendered his second run of the game, while relievers Tex Clevenger and Jim Coates combined to allow four more runners to cross home plate, the last two on a two-out, bases-loaded hit batsman and a heads-up Vic Power steal of home. When reliever Bob Allen induced Maris to fly to right for the third out of the ninth inning, Cleveland had an improbable 9–7 victory that put an end to the embarrassing Yankee winning streak against them.[47]

Home Run # 6—Game 31—May 20—Day Game

The Yankees faced Cleveland again the following afternoon before returning to New York to take on the Baltimore Orioles in a May 21 doubleheader. The Indians starter in the midday affair was 24-year-old right-hander Gary Bell who, like Maris, was a product of the Cleveland farm system. Bell and his minor league teammate, Jim "Mudcat" Grant, were among the crop of young hurlers Cleveland hoped would prove to be successful replacements for the club's aging pitching staff of Bob Feller, Bob Lemon, Early Wynn, and Mike Garcia. That was the main reason Bell signed with the Indians in spite of offers from other teams. "I figured that would be a good place to go, because by the time I was ready they would be on the way out," he told one interviewer.[48]

In 1956, just his second year of professional baseball, Bell went 13–8 with a 2.84 ERA and set a new Eastern League record with 192 strikeouts. The following year he was promoted to the Mobile Bears in the Double-A Southern Association, then to the San Diego Padres in the Pacific Coast League. Bell continued to blossom while with the Bears. On July 14 he pitched a nine-inning no-hitter against the Little Rock Travelers and, at the time of his trade to the Padres, was fast approaching the Southern League record for strikeouts of 237 with his 178 Ks. While he struggled a bit pitching at the Triple-A level, he managed to compile a season-long record of 11 wins, 12 losses with a 3.73 ERA and 232 strikeouts between the two teams.[49]

After opening the 1958 campaign with San Diego where he went 6–2 on a minuscule 1.80 ERA, Bell was called up to the big club, making his major league debut on June 1 against the Kansas City Athletics. By season's end, the right-hander won 12 and lost 10 while maintaining an earned-run average of 3.21 with 110 strikeouts over 182 innings pitched. He was a front-runner for the American League Rookie-of-the-Year Award, ultimately finishing third in the balloting.

His success that first year was due in large part to Joe Gordon, who became manager after Bobby Bragan was fired about a third of the way through the season. Bragan had the habit of alternating the young pitcher between relieving and starting and of taking him out of a game when the going got tough, which undermined his self-confidence. Gordon changed all of that. While Bell still relieved at times, his manager allowed him to pitch through the rough spots. In a July 6 contest in Cleveland against the Athletics, for example, Bell suddenly ran into trouble. The righty was cruising along with the Indians up eight to nothing when, in the top of the sixth, he surrendered a three-run homer. Under Bragan he would have been lifted, but Gordon walked out to the mound and told Bell, "I'm not taking you out of the game. You are going to stay in and finish even if you get killed." Bell did not allow another run after that, pitching all nine for the first complete game of his major league career. He went on to pitch nine more complete games, ending his rookie season with ten in all. "That game meant a lot to me," he said afterwards. "I didn't expect to pitch because I lost my last two starts, so I felt pretty good when Joe started me and I won."[50]

The following season Bell again had a winning record (16–11), but his ERA jumped to 4.04, in large part because home runs became a problem. He was fourth in the league with 28 dingers allowed. He and Indians catcher Russ Nixon thought they knew what the problem was that season—control. Bell had a devastating slider, his best pitch, according to Nixon, but "he just couldn't get it over the plate." Ill-tempered Early Wynn thought that Bell's underlying problem was that he was too nice a guy. "Gary Bell could be a great pitcher if he'd only learn to be mean," contended the future Hall-of-Famer. What Wynn meant was that Bell had to start throwing at batters if he wanted to win consistently. But that went against the right-hander's innate personality. "I've brushed hitters back a few times, but I really don't enjoy doing it."[51]

The 1960 season began well. He was a member of the All-Star team for the first time and had a winning recorded (7–6) and a decent ERA (3.24) by mid-year, but then he developed shoulder inflammation that ended his season in late August. He finished with nine wins and 10 losses and an ERA of 4.13. Oddly enough, he pitched great when facing the Yankees, winning three out of four appearances after going 0–5 the previous two years against the mighty Bombers. That was not the case in 1961.[52]

Indians catcher John Romano thought Bell's best pitch was his fastball. One sportswriter said that when Bell "lets the ball fly, it goes f-a-z-o-o-m past the hitter. The fact that he throws effortlessly adds to his deceptiveness." Padres manager George Metkovich thought his right-hander had "one of the greatest arms I ever saw." Bell praised Cleveland's pitching coach, Mel Harder, for helping him adjust his delivery to make his heater more effective. "He changed my motion so I get more hip action." Bell also had a first-rate slider. Battery-mate Russ Nixon claimed it was his best pitch after his fastball. When in control of it, his slider "broke with the speed and deception of a rattlesnake." According to Nixon, "If he gets his slider over this year [1960] to go along with his good fast ball, that big dipsy-doodle curve and the change-up curve, he'll win 22 games." Using this repertoire of pitches, Bell had a good, if not spectacular, major league career. He appeared in 519 games as a starter or reliever, winning 121 and losing 117 while maintaining a 3.68 ERA over 12 seasons, most of them in an Indians uniform.[53]

Roger Maris did quite well over the previous three summers Bell and he had faced each other. In 47 plate appearances against Bell from 1958 through 1960, Maris batted a cumulative .312 with a homer in each of those years. The May 20 game was the first time in 1961 the two confronted one another. Bell had not been pitching well when he took the mound that day. He lost his first four starts before winning his first game of the season on May 10, an 11-inning, complete-game affair against the White Sox. Part of Bell's problem was that he was still tentative about airing out his fastball because he was still concerned about the shoulder problems he encountered at the end of the 1960 campaign. On top of that, he lacked his usual control, thus making some of his pitches "too fat." The advantage, therefore, was definitely in Maris' favor that game. In his first plate appearance of the afternoon, Maris was hit by an errant pitch after Bell struck out the first two batters of the inning. The slugger took his second at-bat in the top of the third, again with two away. This time, though, he took revenge for the earlier plunking by getting every bit of the ball. "Maris lofted his sixth homer of the year … over the right-field fences," reported the *New York Times*.[54]

With New York up by one, starter Ralph Terry suddenly imploded in the bottom of the fourth, allowing three Cleveland runners to score, one of whom crossed home on a Mantle fielding error. The score remained 3–1 in favor of the Tribe until Bell hit a wall in the top of the eighth. After singles by Tony Kubek and pinch-hitter Jesse Gonder, Maris lifted a long sacrifice fly to right which allowed Kubek to score from third. Bell then walked Mantle, followed by a Berra single to fill the bases with New Yorkers.

At that point, rookie reliever Frank Funk took the mound and, after a groundout scored Gonder to tie the game, he retired Bob Cerv on a foul out to the third baseman to end the Yankee uprising. The Indians, though, reclaimed the lead in the bottom of that inning when catcher John Romano hit a run-scoring double off of Bill Stafford, who replaced Terry an inning earlier. That was all Cleveland needed. With two gone in the top of the ninth, Kubek tripled, but was stranded at third when Funk induced Hector Lopez to fly out to right field. While Bell did not get the win, he was effective enough to allow Cleveland to claim its sixth victory in its last seven games. The loss dropped the Yankees into fourth place while propelling the Indians into a tie for second.

Home Run # 7—Game 32—May 21—Day Game/ Doubleheader

The Yankees returned home in a funk, having lost four straight games to second-division teams. Though the season was barely a quarter over, there was a growing concern that the pennant was beginning to slip away from them. For one thing, Mantle, who carried the club in the early goings, appeared to be in a mini-slump of his own. In the 14 games stretching from May 4 through the team's second loss to the Indians, he batted a lowly (for him) .267 with just two home runs and four runs batted in. Maris was showing signs of heating up, belting four round-trippers and knocking in 10 runs during those two weeks, but he still had a ways to go before he was firing on all cylinders.

On top of that, erratic pitching and a number of blown opportunities resulted in the loss of nine of those 14 games. Starting pitching was a particular problem. "Bullet" Bob Turley, winner of the 1958 Cy Young Award, was experiencing arm trouble and never would regain use of the incredible fastball that made him so unhittable. By the end of May his ERA had exploded to an uncharacteristic 5.15. By August he was on the disabled list for the remainder of the season. And the usually dependable Art Ditmar, who had won 15 games for the Yanks the year before, was struggling as well.

The Yankees were still above .500, but just barely. As Ralph Houk said, "Pennants aren't won by playing .560 ball." (In actuality, the Yankees' winning percentage was even worse than that. It was .533 after the second defeat in Cleveland.) Fortunately, though, New York was at a major turning point in its frustrating season. Houk took a chance and replaced Turley and Ditmar with rookie Rollie Sheldon and untested Bill Stafford, a relief pitcher in just his second season who Houk converted into a starter. It was a risky move that paid off; together they won 25 games. With the starting rotation steadied and Maris and Mantle beginning to hit again, the Bombers were about to live up to their name.[55]

On May 21, New York played host to the Baltimore Orioles in a daylight doubleheader. The Birds were in fifth place, just a half a game behind the Yankees. The Orioles starting pitcher in the first game was Chuck Estrada, a member of Baltimore's youthful pitching staff affectionately referred to as the "Kiddie Korps." In 1960 this talented group of young hurlers (Estrada, Steve Barber, Milt Pappas, Jerry Walker, and Jack Fisher), all under the age of 23, propelled the Orioles into a surprising second-place finish, winning Paul Richards the American League Manager of the Year Award as a result.[56]

Estrada tore through the minor leagues. In 1957, his first year in pro ball, he went 17–11 for the Class C Salinas Packers. In 1958, he was 15–11 for the class A Knoxville Smokies. And in 1959 he won 14 while losing only six for the Triple-A Vancouver Mounties even though he suffered from a reoccurring blister on a pitching-hand finger throughout that season. The National Association of Baseball Writers voted him the "outstanding right-hander" at the Triple-A level for his accomplishments that year.[57]

It was no surprise to anyone when the 22-year-old right-hander made the jump to the major leagues in 1960. Starting out in the bullpen, by May he was used mainly as a starter, a role that he relished. On May 1 he pitched his first complete game, a 9–5 win over the Yankees. In his 25 starts that season, nearly half (12) were complete games, which tied him for fifth most in the American League. He was also fifth in strikeouts, third in strikeouts per nine innings pitched, ninth in innings pitched, ninth in batters faced, and first in fewest hits per nine innings pitched. His 18 wins tied him with Jim Perry for most victories in the American League, a significant accomplishment for a rookie. If he had a down side, it was control and wildness. He was third in walks and second behind Detroit's Frank Lary in hit batsmen.

Estrada lived and died off his high fastball. Many thought he was the hardest thrower on the Orioles pitching staff during that time. Indeed, Orioles pitching coach Harry Brecheen was convinced the right-hander was the hardest thrower in the league. "Very definitely there is no one in the league any quicker than he is," claimed Brecheen. He "has a smooth, easy motion which makes his speed more deceptive. Other fast-ballers, like Ryne Duren, muscle up when they throw and a batter is braced for it. Estrada's fast ball is by 'em before they know it." Teammate Brooks Robinson believed Estrada to be "the hardest worker of the pitchers" in the years they played together.[58]

In 1961 Estrada had another good season. He went 15–9, a better winning percentage than the year before, but he led the league in walks with 132 in 212 innings pitched. At the root of his control problems was a sore elbow that flared up during spring training. Out of fear that it would be a permanent condition and that he might be labeled a whiner, he told no one about his pain. He aggravated his elbow by throwing too hard in the early part of training camp. "I rushed it. One day I threw batting practice and I just couldn't throw," he recalled. "I used to go to bed and my elbow woke me up. It felt like somebody was stabbing me with a toothpick. I was really worried. I didn't know what to think."[59]

He was the starter on opening day, but could not even complete the inning. He gave up five earned runs on three walks and a home run. In his next start he did better, pitching a little over six innings while allowing only one earned run on a homer to Mickey Mantle. His outings were up and down through the early part of the summer, until he decided not to favor his elbow anymore. In a June 6 game in Baltimore against the Angels, "I just let go and finally the soreness came out."[60]

That event was the turning point in his season. He went from a dismal record of 2–4 with a 6.07 ERA to a winning season with a respectable 3.69 ERA. Little did he realize at the time that it was just a brief respite from his struggles. He labored through the 1962 season, pitching some 223 innings in 33 game starts, but posted a losing record of 9–17. He was tied for first in the American League in the games-lost category. The following season was even worse. In early June, his pain was so bad he was shut down for the remainder of the year. In September he underwent elbow surgery to remove a bone spur, but his arm was never the same after that. He fought to make it back, but his major league career came to a sad end in mid–June 1967 as a reliever for the New York Mets. In spite of his elbow problems, Estrada did post a respectable career record of 50 wins against 44 losses with a 4.07 ERA.

Estrada owned Roger Maris during the 1960 season. The Yankee slugger managed only one hit in 14 plate appearances against the Oriole hurler. The following season, though, Maris turned the tables on the righty, hitting an outrageous .571 that included one home run, the only one he hit off of Estrada over the four seasons they confronted each other. Maris had only seven plate appearances against Estrada as the two matched up in just two games that year. In the April 23 contest, the right fielder had one hit (a meaningless single) off the starter in his six innings of work. Baltimore beat New York, 4–1, that day, giving Estrada his first victory of the season. The second time they met, Estrada was not so fortunate.

The May 21 game started in fine fashion for Maris. With two gone and the bases empty in the bottom of the first inning, he smacked the ball into the right-field seats near the 340 marker, giving him four homers in four days and his seventh of the season. The ball traveled some 350 feet, flying over the short outfield wall just out of the reach of a leaping Earl Robinson, who ended up falling into the stands in a vain attempt to catch it. But Maris was not done yet. In his next at-bat, he hit an infield single to first base after Hector Lopez put the Yankees up, 2–1, with a single of his own that scored Tony Kubek from third. Pitcher Whitey Ford added another run with a single in the bottom of the fourth to make the score 3–1 in the Yankees' favor. After flying out to open the bottom of the fifth inning, Maris plated a second run off of Estrada in the bottom of the seventh, punching a single to right that scored Kubek from second base, giving New York a 4–1 advantage. The Orioles added a run of their own on a Dick Williams solo shot off of Ford in the top of the eighth, but that was all she wrote for the Birds. The cunning lefty stopped Baltimore from scoring again for his fifth win against just one loss. It was the first complete game of season for a Yankee starter.[61]

While the Bombers lost the second half of the twin bill, they did move into a tie for third place. Maris did not get a hit, but did drive in a run on a sacrifice fly. The split did not help them gain ground against Detroit, however. New York remained five and a half games back after the Tigers beat the Athletics, 5–3. But things were definitely looking up. Maris, for one, seemed to have found his stroke at last. He now had 20 RBIs against Mantle's 26 and had raised his batting average to .248. In the five games since hitting the first of his four home runs, he batted .471 with 9 RBIs. "For the first time all spring, I was feeling good," he stated. "I felt as if I were finally on the beam. Forgetting all the early troubles, I began to feel that perhaps now I was possibly straightened out and off and running for a good year after all." With Mickey Mantle holding at 10 homers, Maris was just three behind his partner in crime.[62]

A week before the sudden home run splurge, Maris had his lunch meeting with Roy Hamey and Dan Topping in which they directed him to have his eyes examined. The visit was set for the afternoon of May 22, just hours before an evening battle against the Orioles. Maris felt obligated to keep the appointment even though his recent performance made it clear that nothing was wrong with his eyes. When the bosses tell you to do something, however, you do it, most especially if you are feeling appreciative for their patience during the weeks you struggled at the plate. As it turned out, not only was the eye exam totally unnecessary, it caused a slight rift between manager and player when Maris had to be taken out of that night's game because of a reaction to the prescribed eye drops.

The ophthalmologist at Lenox Hill Hospital found nothing wrong with Maris' eyesight. According to Maris, the examining physician told him his vision was so good, "I could be flying jets." There was some eye strain, so Maris was given drops to use every few hours. "Just before taking the field, I dropped some of the solution into my eyes. Then I went into right field." Within a matter of minutes his vision was so blurred he could not even see Art Ditmar on the mound. Calling time, the right fielder ran to the dugout to inform Houk of his difficulties seeing.[63]

That was when the manager first learned of Maris' visit to the ophthalmologist earlier that day. Unaware that he had gone to the doctor at the behest of the Yankee front office, Houk directed his anger at Maris. "I have a player hitting the best he has all year and he picks that time to go to the eye doctor," he grumbled afterwards. The game was delayed for several minutes while Maris had his eyes irrigated, but he still had difficulty seeing. Hoping that his vision would clear quickly, Houk sent the slugger back to his position in right with instructions "to tell Mantle that if he saw a ball hit toward right field to get over there and fast." Fortunately, that did not become necessary. Houk decided to bench Maris before his first at-bat, but he was not happy about doing so. "[H]e shows up here blind, for baseball purposes, and I have to sit him down," he complained. "I was a little scared," Maris admitted later. "I knew Ralph was angry at me, but I was just following orders." The fact that the Yankees won that evening helped diminish the manager's irritation. And once Houk became aware that it was not Maris' decision about whether or when to have his eyes examined, he calmed down completely. Maris' vision cleared later that night, so there was no lasting damage done and he was able to play against Boston after a day off for New York.[64]

Home Run # 8—Game 35—May 24—Day Game

With the eye drop incident behind him, Maris resumed his torrid home-run hitting pace. On May 24 New York played an afternoon game at home against their archrivals, the Boston Red Sox. It was the first time that season the two teams had faced each other. While Boston was relegated to the second division with a 15–18 record, the games between the two teams were always fiercely fought. The Boston starter that day was 6-foot-8 Gene Conley, the tallest man in the major leagues. He held another distinction in addition to his intimidating size: he was a power forward in the National Basketball Association for six seasons, four of which were with the Boston Celtics led by the legendry Red Auerbach. At the time he played for both the Red Sox and the Celtics, he became the first man to play two major sports in the same city.

The king-sized right-hander had a meteoric rise through the

At 6-foot-8, Boston Red Sox starter Gene Conley was the tallest player in the major leagues at the time. He also played for the Boston Celtics in the winter. That high leg kick and gigantic stride toward home plate bothered a lot of players, but not Maris who blasted two off the intimidating pitcher (numbers 8 and 10).

Braves farm system. Beginning his professional baseball career at the age of 20, he went 20–9 on a 2.16 ERA with the Hartford Chiefs in the Single-A Eastern League in 1951. The Braves foolishly rushed him to the majors the following spring, but after a three-loss start with a horrendous 7.82 ERA, he was sent down to the Triple-A Milwaukee Brewers where he posted a respectable 11–4 record. At season's end Conley made his NBA debut, appearing in 39 games as a reserve player for the Boston Celtics that winter. The following spring, the Braves decided to keep him at the Triple-A level for further development when their minor league franchise relocated to Toledo. There he posted an outstanding record of 23 wins against only nine losses with an impressive 2.90 earned-run average for the Toledo Sox, which earned him the American Association's MVP Award at the end of the season.[65]

Milwaukee had plans to move the gangly pitcher up to the big club in 1954, but first they extracted a promise from him that he would discontinue his basketball career for as long as he wore a Braves uniform. Conley sustained a back injury at the end of the 1953 baseball season, and Braves management was concerned he would cause further damage to his back or his pitching arm if he continued to play professional basketball. Conley reluctantly agreed and in exchange they issued him a contract with additional money to off-set what he would lose by not playing for the Celtics.[66]

The Braves were quite excited about their unusual rookie. "I've never seen a finer pitching prospect in all my years in baseball," crowed Travis Jackson, Conley's manager in Hartford. Braves general manager John Quinn referred to him as "our right-handed Warren Spahn." He had great control to go along with an outstanding fastball and had a whole repertoire of other pitches that he delivered either overhand or sidearm depending on what he wanted the ball to do. "He could deal it any way you liked," said one observer. "From his towering but athletic height of 6–8, Conley could come straight overhand and deliver a fast ball that dropped off an invisible table. He could deliver both pitches off a three-quarter overhand delivery as well, and he could 'take a little off' for a change-of-pace that made even the wiliest hitters lunge and flail."[67]

"The sidearm fast ball is still his best pitch," argued another commentator, "but his assortment has developed considerably. During his first two years in the minors he acquired a pretty fair change-up, and beginning at Toledo in 1953 he perfected both a sidearm and an overhand curve ball. Now he can throw his fast ball overhand too." On top of that, his stride, which included a high leg kick done "partly for psychological effect," was incredibly intimidating. "No wonder that guy is so tough," joked a Washington Senators batter. "When he throws that big shoe of his up there in his pitching motion, you think you're going to get kicked in the chin." The downside to his delivery, though, was that he "uses less body motion than most pitchers; as a result, Gene puts great strain on his arm and shoulder." It was a style of pitching that eventually caused irreparable damage.[68]

Conley had a stellar rookie season, winning 14 and losing nine while maintaining a 2.96 ERA. Appearing in 28 games, all but one as a starter, he came in third behind established stars Lou Burdette and Warren Spahn in total wins and surpassed Burdette in winning percentage. He was chosen as one of the pitchers to participate in the mid-summer All-Star game and came in third in the Rookie of the Year voting, one notch above teammate Hank Aaron. Conley might have produced an even better season, but he was shut down in mid–September because his back began bothering him again, an ailment that flared up throughout his baseball career.[69]

He pitched well in the first half of the 1955 campaign before developing shoulder problems that led to him being sidelined from late July to the end of the season. From 1956 through 1958, he pitched mostly from the bullpen, an arrangement that did not work well for him. The 1958 season in particular was disastrous. He failed to win a single game while losing six in 26 appearances that comprised a total of 72 innings of play.

He claimed that his poor performance "wasn't a matter of arm trouble, it was just that I started off poorly and never got the chance to get squared away. You see, we had a very strong staff and once I was dropped from the rotation I couldn't get back in.... So they put me in the bull pen and forgot about me. I got lost down there." At the end of the summer he was informed that his salary was to be cut 25 percent, which prompted him to again play basketball with the Celtics to supplement his income. That, of course, did not sit well with Braves management. "I'm sure he could be a winner again," admitted Braves manager Fred Haney. "But after going out and playing basketball against orders, he had to go." Then when he showed up late to spring training in 1959, he was told to "forget it. You've been traded to the Phillies."[70]

Conley continued to play professional basketball in the winter during his two years with Philadelphia and later in Boston when he was traded to the Red Sox. He saw no problem engaging in both sports at their highest levels, convinced that doing so kept him in condition. "Basketball helps me in three ways," he argued. "It gives me stamina, strengthens my legs and helps my wind." In addition, he found the two sports challenged him in different ways.

> In baseball there's much more individual responsibility, especially if you're a pitcher. You're alone out there on the mound, really isolated, and nobody can help you throw the ball over the plate. The only comparable moment in basketball is the free throw; that's when you're really on the spot. Otherwise you're always working as part of a unit every moment, hitting the open man, looking for an opening, always playing together.

He thought basketball to be the more forgiving of the two because "there's more room for error in basketball, more room for making a mistake and getting away with it." He did admit that "since the seasons overlapped by three weeks at each end I used to get the feeling I was playing some kind of ball for thirteen months each year." It is highly likely, though, that instead of keeping him "in top condition," this constant pounding to his body without a period of rest and recuperation caused the reoccurring back, arm, and shoulder problems that prematurely ended his career in both sports.[71]

His first season with the Phillies seemed to revive him. He was again made a starter and the regularity of that role resulted in a 12–7 season and another trip to the All-Star game. In fact, had he not broken his hand in mid–August, he might have approached the 20-game mark. While initially tolerating his basketball activities, by the beginning of 1960 Phillies management had had their fill of it, too, and insisted he focus on baseball alone. He refused and, after finishing at 8–14, he became one half of a "giant" trade: Philadelphia shipped him to the Red Sox in exchange for 6-foot-7 right-hander Frank Sullivan, the second tallest man in the majors.[72]

Conley loved playing in Boston where he was already known for his basketball capers. And the Red Sox front office seemed accepting of his winter activities. Clearly, though, his career was in decline. His first season with the Sox was less than outstanding. He won 11 while losing 14 and his earned-run average ballooned to an unacceptable 4.91. On top of that, his 33 home runs allowed were second most in the American League. His

1962 season was only marginally better. He won more games (15) than he lost (14) and his ERA dropped below 4.00, but his arm was gone.

In addition, his behavior, which in times past crossed the line, became increasingly erratic. In mid-September he disappeared for several days only to be discovered in a New York airport intending to fly to Israel, but he failed to bring along his passport. "I had my fun," he said years later. "I was no lily on the pond. I know I was nuts sometimes, but why not? I had to be a little crazy to play both sports." At the age of 32, Conley's baseball and basketball adventures came to a sad end. He developed severe shoulder problems and in 1963 pitched just a little over 40 innings, going 3–4 with a 6.64 earned-run average, the second highest of his career. Conley was devastated when he failed to make a comeback pitching for the Burlington Indians in the Class A Carolina League in the spring of 1964. He was found later that day crying in the pews of a local church. When asked by a congregant if his mother had died, Conley responded dejectedly, "No, sir. I lost my fastball." The right-hander, however, had no reason to be ashamed. Over 11 major league seasons, he compiled a 91–96 record with a respectable 3.82 ERA, decent numbers for someone who wore himself down "playing some kind of ball for thirteen months each year."[73]

Conley's initial season with the Red Sox started with promise. After completing his Celtics duties that winter, he had just a couple of weeks to get ready for baseball. His initial start on April 25 against the Washington Senators was a gem. He pitched eight solid innings, giving up just one earned run and winning, 6–1, for his first victory of the year. By the time he faced the Yankees for the first time in his career, he had a 2–3 record with a 2.84 earned-run average. While Conley never did have much success against the Bombers, losing seven straight games to New York over a two-year period, he did pitch well on the afternoon of May 24. The problem that day was Roger Maris.[74]

While the Bosox entered the game with a below-.500 record, more than half of their games were won or lost by a single run. Even Yankee manager Ralph Houk admitted that Boston was a tough team to play regardless of how many wins or losses they had. The game that day proved his point. For the initial three innings, Conley limited the Bombers to just two meaningless singles. He retired Maris on a popout to third. In the fourth, Boston was the first to strike, plating a run on a Russ Nixon sacrifice fly. But in the bottom of that frame, Conley ran into his first spot of trouble. After walking Hector Lopez to start the second half, his only free pass of the game, Johnny Blanchard grounded into a force out at second base.

With one gone and Blanchard on first, Maris faced Conley for the second time that afternoon. After offering up a ball, the pitcher, trying to keep the ball away from Maris' power, delivered a fastball right over the heart of the plate, his only mistake in an otherwise fine outing. Maris, who rarely missed errant pitches, connected, sending the ball straight down the right field line. It struck high on the right side of the foul pole 296 feet away, a foot or two below the third level roof. Because the ball ricocheted off the pole into foul territory, Maris was unsure if it was fair or not. He stood briefly at the plate until the umpire signaled a home run. "Truly, the ball was belted," commented one Boston sportswriter. "It might have traveled all the way over the roof at Fenway Park." Afterwards, Conley bemoaned how close the ball came to being foul. "This is a game of inches," he said. "If I made that pitch an inch better it would have been a foul ball. I didn't take the inch on Maris but he took it on me." In fact, Houk thought it probably would have been declared foul if it had been hit elsewhere.[75]

The never-say-die Sox tied the game in the top of the eighth on a Gary Geiger solo-shot off of starter Ralph Terry. Chet Nichols replaced Conley in the bottom of that inning and held the Yankees scoreless. Going into the ninth knotted at two each, Terry shut down the Sox in their half of that inning. Then the Yankees five o'clock lightning struck once again. After Nichols retired Yogi Berra on a fly ball to right, he surrendered a triple to Moose Skowron, who was benched for several games due to his lack of offensive production. Tracy Stallard relieved Nichols, and proceeded to load the bases on two walks, one intentional, the other not. At that point, Mickey Mantle, who did not start because of a groin injury, made his dramatic entrance into the game. Stallard, however, was able to retire Mantle on a full-count strikeout. But the Yankees prevailed when Tony Kubek, who was hitless in four previous plate appearances, followed with a single to center-right, giving New York a much-needed 3–2 victory.[76]

Home Run # 9—Game 38—May 28—Day Game

Roger Maris was not the only one feeling good about the way his hitting was going. Ralph Houk was positively ecstatic about the recent revival of the Yankee offense. Much to his relief, the Yankees were "starting to come around at the plate and probably will show more offense from here on.... I'd say we've definitely been improving in recent games. We're getting a few more runs now that [Roger] Maris had started hitting for us. [Tony] Kubek has started hitting better, too, and so has [Cletis] Boyer." His only real concern at the point was the starting pitching, especially the failure of Bob Turley and Art Ditmar to perform as they did in seasons past. Houk would soon have to address that particular problem.[77]

While Maris failed to homer—he did hit a ball some 344 feet to right that was hauled in at the warning track—or drive in any runs in the May 25 game, he did score a run after he walked in his first plate appearance of the night. He also contributed with his glove in top of the ninth when he raced from his center-field position (Mantle was still out of the lineup) to make a last-second, one-handed snag of a 400-foot drive off the bat of Red Sox third baseman Frank Malzone. The real heroes that evening were Johnny Blanchard, who hit a two-run dinger in the first inning, and Tony Kubek, who did the same in the second stanza. In spite of a 6–4 win, however, the Yanks gained little ground against front-running Detroit. But things were definitely improving.[78]

A steady rain over the next couple of days postponed two games against the visiting White Sox. During the interim before a doubleheader scheduled for May 28, Houk made an important decision that had a profound impact on Whitey Ford. In the past the ace of the Yankee pitching staff had taken the mound every fifth day. Houk approached the left-hander about starting every fourth day, which Ford readily agreed to do. "Right now Ford is our most reliable starter.... He thinks he can get his best results on such a program and I'm going along with it." Not only did this move help shore-up the problematic pitching staff, it meant Ford would appear in enough additional games that he stood a real chance of winning 20 games for the first time in his career.[79]

The May 28 daylight doubleheader was the first meeting of the Yankees and the White Sox that season. Chicago was experiencing a miserable spring with a 14–24 record that left them languishing in last place, but they certainly did not play like bottom feeders in the first half of the twin bill. Starter Bob Turley, who clearly was in decline, lasted only three innings, giving up five runs, all but one earned. The five Yankee pitchers who replaced him did little better. In all they allowed 14 runs on three homers, including Wes Covington's third inning grand slam off of Turley. New York made a valiant attempt to come back. They scored six runs in the sixth, including a Bob Cerv grand slam off of starter Early Wynn, and three more in the seventh to put them temporarily ahead. The Sox, however, added four runs in both the eighth and ninth innings to club the Bombers into submission, thus breaking a six-game losing streak. It was a truly ugly affair. Maris went hitless in five plate appearances although he did walk twice and score a run.

The late afternoon contest had a completely different result. The White Sox starter was a veteran right-hander with the improbable name of Calvin Coolidge Julius Caesar Tuskahoma McLish, a former Indians teammate of Maris. Cal, as he was more commonly called, began his major league career with the Brooklyn Dodgers in 1944 at the tender age of 18. He went 3–10 in 23 games that season before spending 1945 in military service.

He played for three different clubs (the Dodgers, Pirates, and Cubs) over the next ten years, mostly in the minor leagues. When he was traded to Cleveland in 1956, his career finally took a turn for the better. He pitched mainly from the bullpen his first two seasons with the Indians, but when manager Joe Gordon began using him as a starter in 1958, he came into his own. That season he was 16–8, leading the starting staff in wins, ERA, innings pitched, and complete games. He won 19 and lost 8 the following year, the best record of his career, while again leading all starters in wins, innings pitched, and complete games.

Unquestionably, pitching consistently in that role had a profoundly positive impact on the then 32-year-old hurler. As he acknowledged, "Only one thing made me successful and that was the chance to pitch. Every time I got a good starting shot I did well." For reasons known only to Indians general manager Frank Lane, at the end of the 1959 season McLish became just one more victim of Lane's uncontrollable trading impulse in spite of winning 35 games in two years. "I should have known I was going to be traded somewhere," McLish disclosed. "I never could please him. And I don't understand why." He was part of a four-player deal that sent him and two others to Cincinnati for second baseman Johnny Temple, a local favorite.[80]

It was not a good move for either the Reds or the right-hander. He had a horrendous year in which he won only four while losing 14. McLish, who preferred pitching to contact, did not perform well in the cozy confines of Crosley Field. "I think the park in Cincinnati bothered him," speculated his soon-to-be White Sox manager Al Lopez. "Cal is a low ball pitcher who doesn't strike out many. He makes them hit the ball. Our bigger park [Comiskey Park] is better suited to his style of pitching." In addition, McLish believed his bad year with the Reds was due in part to the performance pressures he felt from the club's management and "the reaction of the fans and the press in Cincinnati to the deal which sent Johnny Temple to Cleveland for me. They were critical of the club for getting rid of Temple." On top of all that, he was unfamiliar with the batters in the National League. "The kind of pitcher I was, for me to have an advantage I had to know hitters very well and pitch accordingly," he explained. Whatever the cause for his off-year in 1960, he was excited to be back in the American League in 1961.[81]

One of the unique things about McLish (other than his name) was that he was ambidextrous. While he never pitched with his left hand in a regulation major league game, he apparently tried it at least once in spring training according to Phillies manager

Gene Mauch's recollection in 1964. "I remember McLish … switching the glove from one hand to another after he got two strikes on Dixie Walker in a squad game. Dixie wasn't looking. All of a sudden there is McLish throwing a lefthanded fastball and Dixie was so shocked that he broke everybody up." McLish claimed to have pitched a doubleheader in winter ball, one game right-handed, the other with his left, but that sounds more apocryphal than true.[82]

McLish was not a dominating pitcher with a blazing fastball. Instead he relied on a changeup (he was referred to as "a change-up master"), a slider, a sinking fastball, a curve, and a screwball. "It is the completeness of his game that makes him effective," according to sportswriter Irv Goodman. "He throws a fast ball that is not as fast as it was in 1944, but which moves downward, as Bob Lemon's once did, and becomes a sinker. He throws a workable slider, a combination of curves, an effective screwball … and an excellent change of pace. Putting all this together into a worthwhile repertoire is Cal's exceptional control. He can put the ball where he wants it." He was a thinking-man's pitcher, one who relied on wile over speed. "Pitching is personal," he asserted. "It's a lot like a game of chess." Since he did not have overpowering stuff, he had "to study the hitter's style and his habits."

> Then you often can anticipate him in my way of pitching. That's my big thrill—surprising 'em. If I am sure a man expects a curve, I give him the fast ball. I like to see them look up in amazement as if to say, "Where did that old buzzard get the nerve to throw me one through the middle?" Most hitters guess with you and if you can figure what they want and give 'em something different, they never are ready to hit it.[83]

As it turned out, McLish had a mediocre season with Chicago, winning 10 while losing 13, and although he started 27 of his 31 games, he pitched just a little over 162 innings. Unknown to anyone but himself, McLish was suffering from a double hernia that was the root cause of his poor performance in both Cincinnati and Chicago. "My strength was sapped. Always felt groggy. I pitched two years needing an operation, which really set me back. But when you were a pitcher like I was, you don't like to give up what chance you might have. So I didn't tell anybody." Surgery at the end of the season took care of that problem. "I'm feeling so goddamn good I'm like a racehorse again," he said when fully healed.[84]

In late March 1962, the 36-year-old righty was traded to the Phillies as a replacement for third baseman Andy Carey, who refused to report to Philadelphia. Manager Gene Mauch, who was a teammate of McLish on three occasions, believed the aging pitcher "should be pretty good insurance in case some of our kids get off badly." Indeed, Mauch's expectations were more than fulfilled.[85]

In his inaugural season with the Phillies, McLish went 11–5, followed by a 13–11 record in 1963, pretty impressive numbers for a pitcher considered to be past his prime. His pitching career came to a halt in mid–July 1964 because of a rotator cuff injury in his right shoulder. He had experienced it late in the summer of 1963 and the problem persisted into the following year. He appeared in only two games that season. McLish ended his 15-year major league career with a 92–92 record, pitching over 1,600 innings in 352 games. He remained in baseball as a pitching coach.

The second half of the May 28 doubleheader began at 6:00 p.m. that evening. Mantle, who was still recovering from a pulled groin muscle, was benched and Maris started the game in center field. For the first time that season, he batted in the fourth spot. He found that opposing pitchers were being more careful pitching to him now that he had his stroke back. "After I hit my eighth homer, I was walked twice in the final game against Boston and twice more in the opener against Chicago the next series," he noted.[86]

Apparently McLish did not get the memo, because in Maris' first plate appearance, he parked his ninth home run, a solo shot, into the right-field seats to open the second inning. McLish recalled long after the event, "I tried to throw him a cross-seam fastball on the outside part of [the] plate figuring if he did hit it, it would be on the ground. But I got it up a little bit and he hit it to deep right-center field." After the Chisox scored three runs on two dingers off the struggling Art Ditmar in the third inning, New York came back to tie it at three in the bottom of that same frame. They then added two more runs in the bottom of the next inning, which was all they would need. Jim Coates replaced Ditmar, holding the visitors scoreless over the next six innings for a 5–3 victory and a split in the doubleheader. The Bombers were now in third place, four and a half games behind Detroit with Cleveland one game in front of them.[87]

That home run was the only hit Maris had in four plate appearances, which left him with a less-than-spectacular .238 batting average, but at least it was moving in the right direction. In the 10 games since hitting the first of the four homers over four consecutive games, he was batting a cool .333 with six round-trippers and 12 RBIs. "I had all but forgotten the dreary days at the start of the '61 season," Maris declared later. "I had picked up almost fifty points in my batting average and, more important, had been hitting home runs with some frequency. I was beginning to make it interesting for Mickey Mantle, who was defending the home-run title." In fact, the right fielder was just one behind Mantle, who had not hit a home run since May 16. What neither of them knew at the time was that they were about to go on a home-run-hitting binge that would entrance the nation all summer long.[88]

Home Runs # 10 and 11—Game 40—May 30—Day Game

On May 29 the Yankees traveled to Boston to take on the eighth-place Red Sox in four games at Fenway Park, a series which marked the real beginning of the Maris-Mantle home run race. New York ended up losing a 2–1 squeaker in that opening game, a night affair played in a cold drizzle after the start time was delayed nearly an hour and a half because of rain. Whitey Ford suffered his second defeat of the year after giving up a solo homer to Jackie Jensen in the bottom of the second and another run on a Vic Wertz single in the bottom of the seventh. The only bright spot for the visitors was Mickey Mantle's blast into the right-field bullpen in the top of the seventh inning, his eleventh of the year. With the Tigers idle, the Yankee loss dropped them another half-game behind the league leaders. Maris failed to reach base and, in the ninth, struck out with one on and one gone. The game ended when another Mantle drive to right was captured just in front of the bullpen.

After the game, Ralph Houk announced he was demoting Art Ditmar to bullpen duties because of his poor performance as a starter. "I don't know just where Art has gone astray," he said, "but it is obvious he is not pitching the way we know he can. So maybe a couple of weeks in the bullpen as middle reliever will help straighten him out." Ditmar never did make another start for New York. Just before the trading deadline in mid–June, the big right-hander was sent to Kansas City along with Deron Johnson for southpaw Bud Daley. Bob Turley, too, was dropped from the regular pitching rotation and, after a June 1 start in which he lasted only two innings, he appeared in just six more games the rest of that summer. Rookie Rollie Sheldon and reliever Bill Stafford were selected to replace them as part of the starting staff that now included Whitey Ford, Ralph Terry, and the newly-acquired Daley. It was a good decision on Houk's part as both performed well in their new roles. The pitching staff was at long last stabilized.[89]

The second game of the series on the afternoon of May 30 was one for the record books in which the Yankees demonstrated to all concerned why they were known as the Bronx Bombers. New York clubbed seven home runs, just one shy of the major league record, including two each from Maris, Mantle, and Moose Skowron to tie another big league feat. The wild affair was punctuated by a throwing incident that resulted in a Boston reliever being tagged with a $50 fine. Said *Boston American* columnist Austen Lake after three Boston "clay pigeons" gave up 12 runs in all, "It was a generosity which the visiting marksmen accepted by belting SEVEN high octane shots ... clear out of the park to drive in eleven of the Yankees 12 runs. And all solid muscle drives too, which would've been legitimate homers in any major league park. Nothing pop-flyish about those pokes, six of which caught westerly tail winds to reach the distant right field steerage section, and one that flew high into the nets above Lansdown St."[90]

Red Sox starter Gene Conley, who served up Maris' eighth round-tripper a week earlier, was the first to sample the might of the Yankees. In the opening inning, Mickey Mantle, facing a full count, smashed the first homer of the game some 380 feet into the visitor's bullpen with Clete Boyer and Maris aboard after they had singled. It all went downhill from there. Having retired the side in order in the top of the second inning, in the following stanza Conley ceded Maris his tenth dinger of the year, a rocket that traveled about 400 feet into the right-field stands. Yankee starter Ralph Terry and reliever Bill Stafford then combined to allow three Sox runs in the bottom half of the third, but that was the extent of the Boston offense the rest of the day. Conley then opened the fourth inning with a Moose Skowron blast over the Green Monster in left, the only one of the seven Yankee homers hit in that direction. When Yogi Berra took Conley deep to open the sixth frame, the beleaguered starter was lifted for reliever Dave Hillman. He promptly surrendered Skowron's second homer of the afternoon, this time off the roof of the Sox bullpen. Hillman allowed another run on a Tony Kubek single before retiring Maris on a pop fly to left to end the inning. The next victim of the Yankee barrage was veteran reliever Mike Fornieles, who replaced Hillman to open the eighth inning.[91]

Cuban-born Jose Miquel "Mike" Fornieles had been in the major leagues nine seasons, mostly from the bullpen, when he entered the game in relief of Dave Hillman. His first appearance in the big leagues, though, was as a starter with the Washington Senators in 1952. The 20-year-old September call-up was quite impressive, pitching a complete-game, one-hit shutout of the Philadelphia Athletics. He made one more start and two relief appearances that month to end his inaugural year with a 2–2 won-loss record and an impressive 1.37 ERA.

In December he was traded to the Chicago White Sox in exchange for southpaw Chuck Stobbs. In a little over three seasons there, he went 15–13 pitching mainly in relief. In May 1956 he was traded to the Baltimore Orioles as part of a six-player deal. In the middle of the 1957 season he once more had to pack his bags, this time making the journey to Boston. He continued to alternate between starting and relieving until the Red Sox discovered that his real talent was as a closer.

From 1958 through 1962, the stalwart righty appeared in 252 games, but in only 10 as an opener. It was in the closer's role that he fully blossomed as a major league pitcher. He compiled a 31–28 record that included 46 saves in 148 games finished over that period. His best season was in 1960 when he was first among American League pitchers in game appearances (70, a new league record) and games finished and second in saves. His 10 wins and 5 losses were the best won-loss record of his career and his sterling 2.64 earned-run average was the lowest since his brief 1952 call-up. In recognition of that outstanding season, Fornieles was selected as the first-ever American League recipient of *The Sporting News*' Fireman of the Year Award.[92]

Fornieles owed his success to his ability to throw five different pitches, depending on the need at any given moment. A fastball, a curve, a slider, a screwball, and a knuckleball were all a part of his arsenal. "The pitch which is working best for him on a particular day is the one he keeps throwing," according to his regular catcher, Russ Nixon. "Sometimes it's a fast ball; sometimes it's the curve or the knuckler. You can't tell what it's going to be on any day until he starts throwing to hitters. Because it could be a different pitch every day, he became very effective." Interestingly, Fornieles preferred to start, but "if I'm going to help the club by pitching relief, I'll help myself, too," he commented upon accepting the *TSN* award.[93]

Boston's star closer often played winter ball in his native Cuba. By 1961, though, the country was firmly under Fidel Castro's control and relations between the United States and its island neighbor had grown decidedly worse. As a result, Fornieles had great difficulty returning to the States after he was done playing ball there. The Red Sox front office, with good reason as it turned out, was very concerned that the Cuban government would not allow him or any of the dozens of other Cuban-born players to leave the country. It was not until early January that an official with the Cuban Foreign Ministry announced that all players would be allowed to resume their major league careers. What was not publicly known at the time, however, was that Fornieles and the others had to commit to return to Cuba, which he promised, but did not do. Since he was allowed to take only the equivalent of $5.00 out of Cuba, the crafty right-hander circumvented that restriction by hiding $200 in the fingers of his baseball glove. He was not permitted to leave Cuba until late February and then was late showing up for spring training in Arizona because an airline strike left him stuck in Miami once he did return to U.S. soil.[94]

Fornieles had been struggling the early part of the season when he entered the game in relief of Hillman. From April 11 to May 25, he pitched a little over 20 innings, compiling a 1–2 record with three saves and a dreadful 8.71 earned-run average. Part of his problem was that he had already given up seven home runs, way too many for a closer. He had also walked more (11) than he struck out (9). There did not seem to be anything physically wrong with him, so perhaps it was the struggle he had getting out of Cuba and the resulting delay in his spring training preparation that were at the root of his poor performance. Whatever the reason, he was not the same pitcher he was the summer before.

The eighth inning started off well enough for the right-hander. He retired Bobby Richardson on a groundout and struck out pitcher Jim Coates before giving up consecutive singles to Clete Boyer and Tony Kubek. Then he had to face Roger Maris. After going 3–1 on the Yankee slugger, Fornieles threw a curveball that Maris parked some 450 feet away, a dozen rows deep into the right-field stands for his eleventh home run of the year. "Mike's curve ball wasn't behaving for him," Maris said later, "but it was for us. He got one down my alley, and I sent it flying into the wide open spaces of right field for number eleven." Adding insult to injury, after tying Mantle up with two quick strikes, the switch hitter plastered a knee-high pitch into the center field stands, that one also traveling about 450 feet, for his thirteenth round-tripper. It was the first time that season Maris and Mantle had homered back-to-back. The M and M Boys had arrived at last.[95]

Oddly, that lousy outing by Fornieles marked the turning point in his season. He was given his first start of the year—and his first in three seasons—on June 5, pitching a complete game 6–2 victory. Over the next 43 appearances, he won eight and lost six while saving 12 games. His ERA during that period was a respectable 3.55. And he did not give up another dinger after that May 30 game.

Manager Pinky Higgins felt his pitcher's improvement was due to two reasons: "No. 1, he has corrected a fault in his style and No. 2, he has regained his confidence." Red Sox catcher Jim Pagliaroni noted that Fornieles' "curve ball was flattening out. He was getting creamed. Now he's got the curve breaking down again." Fornieles ended the summer with nine wins, eight losses, and 15 saves, lowering his earned-run average to 4.69, a considerable drop from its high of 9.53 after the May 30 contest. The Cuban national was never the same pitcher after the 1961 season, however. He pitched two more years, ending his major league career in mid–July 1963 at the age of 31 as a reliever for the Twins. His career totals included 63 wins and 64 losses with a 3.96 ERA in a little over 1156 innings pitched.[96]

Home Run # 12—Game 41—May 31—Night Game

The following night saw the Yankees and Red Sox go at it once again in a back-and-forth contest that was not decided until the final out. Rookie Rollie Sheldon was making just his third start of the season for New York while Tom Brewer, fresh off a two-week stay on the disabled list with a sore arm, was toeing the rubber for Boston. It was clear from the start that Brewer was not his usual self. In the first inning he gave up a double to Clete Boyer, walked both Maris and Mantle, and allowed a run to score on a Yogi Berra groundout. When he opened the second inning by surrendering a single to Elston Howard and a double to Bobby Richardson, he was lifted for journeyman reliever/starter Billy Muffett.

The 30-year-old right-hander began his major league career in the National League after laboring nearly seven seasons in the bush leagues. Beginning at the age of 18 in 1949, Muffett played for six different minor league teams ranging from Class C Helena to Triple-A Omaha over a nine-year stretch. His best season was in 1951 when he compiled a 22–9 record with an accompanying 2.25 earned-run average playing for the Class C Monroe Sports. As a result of his superlative performance, he was voted Most Valuable Player in the Cotton States League. After spending the next two years in military service, Muffett split time between starting and relieving for Double-A Shreveport, a season in which an arm injury resulted in a 5–11 won-loss record and a 4.83 ERA. The next two summers witnessed a decided improvement as he pitched for four different teams while amassing an overall record of 27–18.

The 1957 season was the turning point in his career. He started the year pitching for the Houston Buffaloes in the Texas League where he won 14 while losing only 6 with an outstanding 2.20 earned-run average. Then in early August he got his big break when he was called up by the St. Louis Cardinals. Over the next two months he relieved in 23 games, ending with a 3–2 record that included eight saves and a 2.25 ERA.

The one blemish on this otherwise stellar record came on September 23 when Hank Aaron took the right-hander deep in the eleventh inning with a walk-off two-run homer to clinch the National League pennant for Milwaukee, the only dinger Muffett allowed that season. That one pitch to the Hammer—a hanging curveball—would haunt him for the next several years as he was traded to the Giants at the end of the 1958 season, then to the Red Sox in the middle of 1959 after going 0–0 with a 5.40 ERA in five games for San Francisco. "I haven't been able to live that pitch down yet," he said in 1960. "It was my seventh game in seven days and that guy Aaron has to pick on me to clinch the pennant. I'll bet I've been asked about that pitch 9,000 times since then."[97]

The Red Sox acquired Muffett on July 26, 1959, in a trade with the Giants. He was sent to Boston's Triple-A team in Minneapolis where he was 4–4 with a 3.44 ERA in 20 games, pitching mostly out of the bullpen. He was invited to the Red Sox's spring training camp the following season. It was there that Boston pitching coach Sal Maglie, who was a Cardinal teammate of his in 1958, grew to admire his determination almost as much as his pitching. "Muffett has the right attitude and that covers a lot," proclaimed the Barber. "You can do a lot with a guy with the right attitude who wants to work and learn." Maglie added that Muffett "gives you everything he has. That's what I liked about him."[98]

The right-hander had an average fastball as well as an excellent curve and knuckleball, all delivered without a windup. He credited his Houston manager Harry Walker with converting him to the Don Larsen–style of pitching. "I was tipping off my pitches when I wound up," he said. "When I was going to throw a fast ball I'd raise my glove over my head. For a curve I'd keep the glove in front of my face. Walker told me to pitch without a windup and it worked." It was Maglie, though, who helped him develop an improved curveball to go along with his no-windup delivery. "I have a curve now that I didn't have when I was with St. Louis. Maglie showed me how to do it. I had a relaxed curve. I wasn't snapping my wrists like I should to make the ball break right."[99]

The Boston pitching coach dearly wanted to keep Muffett with the Red Sox when they broke camp, but he was overruled. Thus the righty began the 1960 season back in Minneapolis where he appeared in 17 games, 11 of those as a starter. Finally in mid–June he got the call to join the big club, and he made the most of the opportunity. He was used in relief in his first six games and was not particularly impressive in those initial outings. In just 11⅔ innings pitched, he was 0–1 with an inflated 7.71 earned-run average. Then he was called upon to start the second game of a July 7 doubleheader against Washington and he turned in a gem of a performance, a complete-game 4–2 victory in which he allowed just four hits. "He goes right into rotation as my No. 5 starter," proclaimed Red Sox manager Pinky Higgins after the game. From then until the end of the season, Muffett appeared in 16 more games, 13 of those as a starter. He was 5–3 with a 2.93 ERA during that time, ending the summer with a cumulative record of six wins against four losses and a very respectable 3.24 earned-run average.[100]

In 1960 when his stuff was working, Muffett was particularly tough on Maris and Mantle. The right fielder had just one hit in 11 plate appearances against the right-hander while Mantle was two for 11, one of the hits a solo shot, for a .182 batting average. In fact, Muffett struck out the Mick looking with two curves and a knuckleball the first time ever the two faced each other. Wrote one wag about that initial confrontation, "Little Billy Muffett/Stood on a tuffet/Making Yanks eat his curves—and hey!/Instead of a slider/He knuckled a glider/To frighten Mr. Mantle away." But that was in 1960. In 1961 it was an entirely different story.[101]

In his first 10 outings of the season, six of those as a starter, he compiled a losing record of no wins and four losses and his ERA was an inferior 6.75 in less than 33 innings pitched. He had also become homer-prone. By the time he entered the May 31 contest in relief of Brewer, he had already allowed six round-trippers. Part of his poor record may have been due to a sore shoulder he suffered during spring training which caused him to miss three weeks of preparation for the upcoming season. Apparently Muffett had unknowingly changed his delivery from full overhand to three quarters and it had aggravated the muscles in the front part of his right shoulder. While the pain ceased once his motion was corrected, this earlier injury was at play in his sub-standard performance in 1961. On top of that, the right-hander had problems controlling his weight. The extra pounds, Muffett contended, were behind his pitching woes in 1961. "I was too full around the shoulders and mid-section from too much eating on the banquet circuit. I found the extra poundage hindered my delivery. This I think brought on my arm trouble."[102]

Whatever the cause of Muffett's ineffectiveness on the mound, he definitely was not the pitcher he was at the end of the 1960 season. The righty completed the inning that Brewer began, retiring the next three Yankee batters on two strikeouts and a lineout. In the top of the third, though, he faced Roger Maris for the first time that day. After the Bosox tied the score at one all in the bottom of second inning, Maris put the Yanks back in front with "a prodigious 440-foot poke high up in the rightfield bleachers" off of Muffett. Then in the top of the fourth, all hell broke loose when the Yankees plated five runs, including Mickey Mantle's fourteenth homer of the season, a two-run jack with Maris aboard. That was all the scoring for New York that night. Boston made a valiant attempt to come back, but the game ended with a 7–6 Yankee victory. It was Sheldon's first win of the season and a combined 26 homers for Maris and Mantle, one more than the entire Red Sox team. The Yankees gained a game on Detroit, but were still in third place, a game and a half behind Cleveland and three and a half back of the Tigers.[103]

As for Muffett, he got his first win of the season in his next outing, but added only two more after that, ending the summer with a 3–11 record and a 5.67 ERA. It was the only time in his career that he spent an entire season in the major leagues. After a hideous outing in his first start in 1962 in which he gave up four earned runs in four innings, the righty was cut from the major league roster and sent back to the minors. He spent the next four years attempting to make it back to the bigs, but was never able to do so. After appearing in eight games for Double-A Tulsa at the beginning of 1965, Muffett called it quits on his pitching career. Over six major league seasons, he compiled a record of 16 wins and 23 losses on a cumulative 4.23 earned-run average in 125 games, a fourth of those as a starter. He did not leave baseball entirely, however. He spent 18 summers as a pitching coach for the Cardinals, Angels, and Tigers before retiring after the 1994 season.

4

June

Home Run # 13—Game 43—June 2—Night Game

From May 17, when his home run streak began, to the end of the month, Maris hammered nine dingers while driving in 19. At the same time, he batted an impressive .326, raising his overall batting average to .245. During those same two weeks, Mantle batted an equally impressive .343 while adding four more homers to his total and driving in seven. And the press was beginning to take notice. Stories about the "professional rivalry" between the two started appearing in the newspapers for the first time. "No question about it," one unidentified teammate was quoted as saying. "It figures. Both of them are proud guys and both of them have the talent. Call it competition or call it whatever you want, but whatever it is it's good for this ball team and good for them."[1]

Other teams were now aware of what the power of Mantle and Maris meant to them. "I wish I could say I'm glad to see them both hitting home runs," Red Sox manager Pinky Higgins said. "All I can say is when they're hitting together you've got a problem, especially if you're a pitcher." In the next month, the two collectively added another 26 homers with Maris more than doubling his output. The Yankee juggernaut was gathering steam and the fight for the pennant would be between New York and Detroit alone as the others dropped further back in the pack.[2]

Maris was anticipating a productive June. "I really felt that things were looking up and perhaps began to feel that, if lucky, I could come close to equaling last season's home-run total [39]." As he wrestled with the idea of repeating his output from June of 1960 (14 home runs, 34 runs batted in), he reflected on how difficult it was for a power hitter to be successful. "A home-run hitter is a strange type of hitter," he noted. "There are times when he is hitting everything into the air and it goes into the seats, then again he might be just a little off and everything is a line-drive single." What was it that made one hit a homer, the other not? "I really believe that the difference between a home run and a single on a hard hit ball is one-eighth inch. If you hit a ball hard on the under part of it, you have a home run. Hit the ball one-eighth inch higher up on the ball and it is a line drive. There is no way a hitter can adjust to hit one-eighth inch lower … it just happens."[3]

June, however, had a rocky beginning for Maris and the Yankees. In the fourth and final game of the Boston series, the Yankees got behind early and were never able to recover. Starter Bob Turley lasted only two innings before being lifted in the top of the third after he gave up three runs. Art Ditmar replaced the ineffective right-hander, but he, too, could not get the job done. By the end of that inning, the Bombers were down five to one. The Bosox added two more runs to make it 7–1 through the first seven innings. Though New York plated two in the eighth and two more in the ninth, it was not enough to overcome the Red Sox lead. For his part, Maris contributed nothing but a walk in five plate appearances.

The Yankees traveled next to Chicago to take on the last-place White Sox in a three-game stand. Maris was not looking forward to playing in Comiskey Park. Even though he hit four of his six homers there in 1960, he believed "the Chicago pitchers have been tough for me, especially in their own park. It wasn't the spot I would have picked for starting off the month of June, which I was hoping would be a good one." He was about to discover that 1961 was an entirely different year for him when it came to the White Sox pitching staff.[4]

In the earlier two games against Chicago, Maris had one home run, but that was his only hit in nine plate appearances, leaving him with a pathetic .143 batting average. That was not the case over the next three games, nor would it be for the season as a whole. The White Sox starter in that first of the three contests was Cal McLish, who Maris had taken deep at Yankee Stadium in the second half of the doubleheader on May 28. Opposing him was Yankee ace Whitey Ford going for his seventh win against two losses.

Ford got off to a poor start, giving up a two-run dinger to Al Smith in the bottom of the first inning. He settled down after that, holding the White Sox to those two runs. McLish retired the side in order to open the game, which ended with Maris hitting a grounder back to the mound for the third out of the inning. The right-hander allowed the Bombers to inch back when he surrendered a solo shot to Yogi Berra in the top of the second. Then they took the lead for good in the third on a Tony Kubek sacrifice fly and Maris' lucky number 13 bomb with Ford aboard. While Maris later admitted that he could not recall the details of this second home run off of McLish "for love nor money," it was a monster blast to right which careened off an advertising sign for a local television station that hung from the railing in the upper deck of the stadium. After that, reliever Russ Kemmerer held Maris hitless the rest of the game. The Yankees added single runs in the fourth and sixth innings to secure for Ford his fourth complete-game victory of the young season. For McLish, who was lifted after three innings, it was his sixth defeat of the year. After the game Ralph Houk announced that Bob Turley was consigned to the bullpen and Jim Coates was his replacement as a starter.[5]

Home Run # 14—Game 44—June 3—Day Game

The game the following afternoon was one of those designed to drive a manager insane. You think you have the game in the bag until the home team ties it in the bottom of the eighth, then goes on to win it with a walk-off home run in extra innings. The Sox starter was Bob Shaw, a key member of the Go-Go Sox pitching staff that led Chicago to the 1959 American League championship. That June 3 contest, however, was his second to last appearance in a White Sox uniform.

Shaw made his first major league appearance for the Detroit Tigers on August 11, 1957, pitching three innings of relief in which he gave up four earned runs to his future team, the Chicago White Sox. He appeared in six more games for the Tigers that season, all from the bullpen. The following year he pitched in eleven games for Detroit, two of them as a starter, before being traded along with Ray Boone to the White Sox for Bill

Fisher and Tito Francona. Shaw left the club to return home a couple of weeks before the trade because he knew he would be sent back to the minors. He called that move "the greatest decision I ever made in my life. My whole career turned around." It was a fortunate transaction for him because he finally got the opportunity to demonstrate his pitching ability, especially when he became a starter in early May 1959.[6]

Usually pitching behind 39-year-old Early Wynn, he compiled an unexpected 18–6 record with an outstanding 2.69 ERA. His winning percentage was the best in the American League and he placed in the top 10 in ERA, wins, innings pitched, games played, shutouts, and fewest home runs allowed per nine innings pitched. At the end of the season, he came in third for the Cy Young Award (won by teammate Wynn) and even received consideration as the American League MVP. The Go-Go Sox won the American League pennant that year thanks in large part to the pitching of Wynn and Shaw. In fact, the two combined to clinch the pennant on September 22 when Shaw relieved Wynn to preserve a 4–2 victory over the Cleveland Indians. In the World Series Shaw started two of the games against the Los Angeles Dodgers, losing Game 2, 4–3, but winning the crucial fifth game, 1–0, when the Sox were down three games to one. Although the Chisox ended up losing the Series to Los Angeles, the 26-year-old righty could take great pride in his performance that year.

The brilliance of the right-hander's 1959 pitching made his 1960 campaign look mediocre in comparison. His record was an uninspired 13–13 and his earned-run average mushroomed to 4.06 while pitching for a third-place club that finished 10 games behind the Yankees. With the exception of Billy Pierce (14–7), none of the starters were particularly effective that summer. Even Early Wynn barely had a winning season after going 13–12. The only reason Chicago won 90 games and stayed in contention until late in the season was because of the relief corps of five pitchers who won 40 games while losing only 21. In comparison, the four starters lost nearly as many (42) as they won (45).

When Bob Shaw was on, though, he was nearly unhittable. He did not have a dominating fastball, but did have an outstanding sinker to go along with his curve and changeup. His mentor was Early Wynn, with whom he roomed while pitching for Chicago. "I had a slightly open stance as did Wynn," he noted in his 1972 instructional manual on pitching. "We both had three-quarter-arm deliveries," he added. White Sox manager Al Lopez loved his youthful hurler. "He has all the makings. A good sinker ball, a good motion, free and easy with no strain, and what I like most of all is that he listens to instruction. You don't have to repeat yourself when you're talking to him," proclaimed El Senor.[7]

Shaw's most notorious pitch, though, was his spitball, something he resorted to later in his career. He consistently denied he used the wet one, but legendary grease-ball pitcher Gaylord Perry confirmed it in his 1974 autobiography, claiming that Shaw taught him how to throw one. Still a youngster when Shaw joined the Giants in 1964, Perry timidly approached his more experienced teammate to ask him what he was doing to make his sinker "[arrive] at the plate in a very unnatural way, shooting in about thigh-high, then dipping to the ankles." At first Shaw insisted, "It's just a natural sinker," before demonstrating how he caused the ball to plunge so drastically.

> He wet his two fingers, placed them on top of the ball, wound and fired. And down it went. "This is all there is to it, Gaylord," he said. "But it takes a lot of work. You got to know how much to apply, where, how to hold the ball and control it, and, most important, how to load it up without anybody seeing you. It's a dangerous pitch. You can hurt your arm. If you get caught, you can get into trouble. And it'll take a long time to master it. But, if you can learn it, it'll make you a lot of money."

And indeed, Shaw worked with Perry that summer helping him develop what became his bread-and-butter pitch.[8]

His 1961 season started out decently enough. By the end of May he had a 3–4 record with a 3.08 ERA, although he did blow two save opportunities and had given up nine homers, which was not typical of him. The June 3 game was his first appearance of the season against the Yankees. Maris faced Shaw 30 times over the previous three seasons, but never hit a home run off of him. Shaw was particularly effective against the Yankee right-fielder during the 1960 campaign, keeping him hitless in nine plate appearances.

So when Maris stepped in against his White Sox opponent in the first inning, it looked like history was repeating itself when he hit into a ground-ball double play. Shaw was cruising along when Maris walked to the plate with one on in the fourth inning. Again the pitcher came out on top, inducing the red-hot Maris to fly out to right field. In the sixth Maris did plate a run when Wes Covington "made an inelegant muff" of the slugger's fly ball down the right-field line, allowing Clete Boyer, who had driven in Bobby Richardson with a single earlier in the inning, to score all the way from second base on the error. Yankee starter Ralph Terry, however, allowed the Sox to tie the game at two each in the bottom half of that inning on a run-scoring groundout by Nellie Fox and a single by the "inelegant" Wes Covington.[9]

Shaw was still in charge until the eighth inning. With one out, the White Sox pitcher walked Boyer, then gave up a double to Tony Kubek, leaving runners on second and third for Maris. This time the Yankee slugger took full advantage of the weakening hurler by driving the ball deep into the right-field seats, putting New York ahead, 5–2. But the Chisox came roaring back with three runs of their own in the bottom of the eighth.

And so the game went into extra innings with the score knotted at five each. Then in the bottom of the thirteenth, Art Ditmar, recently demoted to the Yankee bullpen when he failed as a starter, delivered a first-pitch shoulder-high fastball to lead-off batter Roy Sievers, who promptly parked it into the left-field stands for a hard-fought Chicago victory. While it may have been the "most painful defeat to date" for the Yankees, for Maris it was another step closer to the Babe. His three-run blast in the eighth was his eleventh homer since May 17, and one that tied him with Mickey Mantle in the home-run race. "It was the first time all season that I had caught up to him and it felt good, but it would have felt even better had it been the pay-off," he admitted.[10]

June 9 saw Shaw's tenure with the White Sox come to an end after a two-inning start in which he allowed five earned runs. The following day he was part of an eight-player trade that sent him to Kansas City. Although he went 9–10 the rest of the season with a 4.31 ERA, it was not a bad record for a club that won only 61 games, leaving them tied for last place with the Washington Senators. He surrendered 25 four-baggers that season, the most of his career, but 11 of those were in the 14 games he played for Chicago. In his 26 Kansas City appearances, he allowed 14 more. The following summer he bounced back, winning 15 while losing nine with a 2.80 ERA for the Milwaukee Braves, the lowest among the starting staff. While he had a losing record with Milwaukee the next year (7–11), his earned-run average dropped to 2.61.

It was during this season that he set a new major league record that he undoubtedly did not want. In a May 4 contest against the Cubs, he balked five times, including three in the third inning alone, and was fined $250 as a result of this dubious accomplishment. Shaw said afterwards, "I actually never came to a dead stop while slowing up and checking the runner. Now I know you've got to bring your hands together quick, jam them against your body, and then check the runner." Why a pitcher in his seventh major league season did not know that already was never explained.[11]

Shaw next moved to the Giants in 1964 and in two full seasons there compiled a winning record. His second year with San Francisco saw him triumph in 16 outings against just nine losses while maintaining a 2.64 ERA, the lowest of his major league career. After going 1–4 with San Francisco at the beginning of the 1966 campaign, he was traded to the Mets where he again won more than he lost (11–10, 3.92 ERA). The 34-year-old right-hander's big league career came to an abrupt end in mid–September 1967 after appearing in 32 games split between the Mets and the Cubs. He had a dismal 3–11 cumulative record when he received his unconditional release by Chicago while he was at home in Florida during two consecutive open dates. He spent 11 seasons in the majors, compiling an admirable record of 108 wins against 98 losses with a cumulative 3.52 ERA in 430 game appearances, more than half of them as a starter.[12]

Home Run # 15—Game 45—June 4—Day Game

Maris passed Mantle for the first time that season in the following afternoon's game in Comiskey. The White Sox starter that day was Billy Pierce, who generally pitched well for Chicago. But after he gave up four runs with two away in the top of the first on three walks, a wild pitch, an error, and a three-run double to Elston Howard with the bases full, he was lifted for relief-specialist Russ Kemmerer.

Dutch, as Kemmerer was sometimes called, had already appeared in nearly 200 games in the majors, mostly as a starter, when he stepped in to rescue the struggling Pierce that day. The right-hander came up with Boston in 1954 where he managed to have one of his few winning seasons, going 5–3 with a 3.82 ERA after his call-up in late June. After relieving in his initial five appearances, he got his first start on July 18, an impressive outing in which he pitched a complete-game, one-hit shutout against Baltimore.

After such a promising start to his big league career, he struggled in the early part of the 1955 season with Boston and was sent back down to their Double-A affiliate in Louisville, Kentucky. His problems continued there, however, and he ended the season with three wins and eight losses to go along with his 4.96 earned-run average. Consequently Kemmerer spent the entire 1956 season pitching for Triple-A San Francisco in the Pacific Coast League where he showed considerable improvement. While he had a losing record (12–14), his ERA (3.48) declined significantly over the previous year.

One roadblock to success that Kemmerer had to overcome was obsessing about his performance from game to game, worrying that he was not good enough. "Not only did I worry about the batters, but I'd even worry about the pitcher for the other club. I'd worry through the night. I'd have trouble falling asleep. I'd wake up tired and frayed. I never could relax. After one game I'd start worrying about the next." He credited San Francisco Seals manager Joe Gordon with helping him overcome his anxiety. Gordon told the youngster that he would "get knocked out of the box some time or another. It happens to the best of them.... You have everything you need to be a winner. You don't have to win every game." Gordon's advice worked. "He managed to get over the message to me. Don't ask me how. But as I listened to him I began to calm down. I began to enjoy myself. I'd be ready all the time."[13]

And sure enough, Kemmerer was recalled to the big club in 1957. But the right-hander was traded to Washington after just one outing with the Red Sox. He injured his arm playing winter ball and Boston management was not convinced he would recover. "One morning, I got up and couldn't raise my arm," he explained to one interviewer. "You didn't want to tell anybody you were hurt because they had so many guys waiting. They didn't fool with you, send you to the doctor or do anything; they would just call somebody else. They thought I had lost my fastball. So I was available to be traded to the Senators at that time. They called me in and told me I was traded."[14]

The change of scenery, though, did not enhance his pitching. After spending a little over three seasons with the perennial cellar-dwelling Senators in which he compiled a losing record (21–45) primarily as a starter, his contract was purchased by the White Sox in early 1960. That move turned his career around. After he arrived in Chicago, he went 6–3 with a 2.98 earned-run average, the lowest of his major league career. The White Sox used him almost exclusively out of the bullpen, usually as a middle reliever. He had found his true calling. The following summer he was 3–3 with a 4.38 ERA in 47 games. "Hardly the number I expected or wanted," he admitted years later, "but that was a lot of outings in those days."[15]

The reliever spent the first half of the 1962 season in Chicago, but after appearing in 20 games, he was traded to the newly-formed Houston Colt .45's for southpaw Dean Stone. He appeared in 36 games there, two of those as a starter, for a cumulative total of 56 appearances, the most in his career. He ended that season with seven wins, four losses, three saves, and a 4.03 earned-run average.

The 32-year-old's major league career came to an end with Houston in late June 1963 when he was sent down to Triple-A Oklahoma City after pitching in 17 games with no decisions and a 5.65 earned-run average. He spent the following summer with the 89ers as well; although he was 8–6 with a 2.70 earned-run average there, he called it quits at the end of the season. He compiled a 43–59 record with a cumulative 4.46 ERA in 302 games, two-thirds of them as a reliever, over his nine years in the big leagues. He left professional baseball to be the pitching coach at Indiana University where he earned a degree in parks and recreation in 1977.[16]

Bob Swift, the Senators' pitching coach in 1960, said that although the righty was "streaky," he "has everything to win, a good fast ball and a good curve and control, too." Kemmerer himself thought his best pitch was his "good sinking fastball that dived in hard toward a right-handed hitter and broke down and away from a left-handed batter. This movement of my fastball resembled the action of a spitball." Although at times he "was accused of throwing the wet one," he denied ever doing so. "For one reason or another whenever I tried it [the spitball], the pitch straightened out!" He tried to keep the ball low because it "usually resulted in a high percentage of ground balls being hit when I pitched." According to him, the other pitches in his repertoire included a curve, a changeup, a slider, and a slip pitch (a type of changeup).[17]

Although Kemmerer was 0–2 when he relieved Billy Pierce with two gone in the top of the first inning in that June 4 contest, he maintained a superb 1.89 earned-run average in the 38 innings he pitched to date. More importantly, he surrendered only two home runs in those 16 games. But the righty was one of Maris' favorite targets. In the four previous seasons the two confronted one another, the Yankee slugger managed to hit four round-trippers off the hurler, including a game in 1958 in which Maris hit an inside-the-park homer in one inning followed by a triple and a grand slam in another inning. Even though Maris failed to park any off of Kemmerer in 1960, he did bat .429 against him that season. It was no surprise to either of them when Maris once again went deep on the reliever.

After getting that final out of the first inning with no further damage, Kemmerer retired the Yankees in order in the second. Then Maris stepped up to the plate to open the third frame. Kemmerer handled the right fielder quite effectively on May 28 and June 2, inducing him to pop out each of the three times they faced each other. In this at-bat, however, the advantage went to Maris who got every bit of that one-eighth inch necessary to rocket the ball deep into the right-field seats. It was Maris' third homer of the series and his fifteenth of the season, moving him ahead of Mantle for the first time. "It was a great feeling I took out of Chicago with me," he acknowledged. "Hitting a home run in each of the three games gave me a big lift. I began to wonder if I was really going to have another good June. Certainly I couldn't have asked for a better start."[18]

Kemmerer ran into deeper trouble the next inning, allowing singles to the first two batters before committing a fatal fielding error that loaded the bases. By the time the inning was done, he was gone and the Yankees had added four more runs for a 10–1 rout of the struggling White Sox. Ralph Houk was quite pleased with the results, noting that it gave "a lift to a team that's been battling to the wire game after game." The manager's enthusiasm, though, was tempered by the tough decisions he had to make soon regarding the Yankee pitching staff.[19]

The first move was to bring up Hal Reniff from Richmond. The rookie reliever made his first appearance for New York on June 8, pitching 1⅔ innings of one-hit ball. By the end of the season, Reniff was 2–0 with two saves and a fine 2.58 ERA in over 45 innings pitched. Then on June 14, Art Ditmar was traded along with Deron Johnson to Kansas City for seven-year veteran southpaw Bud Daley who was to be used as a fifth starter and occasional reliever. He went 8–9 with a 3.96 earned-run average, a considerable improvement over the ineffective Ditmar. With Ditmar gone and Bob Turley effectively benched, the starting staff now consisted of ace Whitey Ford, right-hander Ralph Terry, youngsters Bill Stafford and Rollie Sheldon, and the newly-acquired Daley. Closer Luis Arroyo was having a career year in which he led the American League in saves (29) and game appearances (65) while compiling 15–5 record and a 2.19 ERA. The Puerto Rican left-hander, along with Jim Coates, Hal Reniff, and Tex Clevenger, comprised a bullpen that was one of the best in the American League. They collectively combined for a 29–11 record by season's end.

"The nice thing about the new four-man rotation was that it worked," the delighted manager said. "We were playing superior ball. Mantle and Maris saved one game by picture-book catches.... Our infield was reeling off lightning double plays. Ellie Howard seemed to dominate each game he caught." The struggles of the early spring were gone at last. The Yankees could now focus on catching the Tigers and winning the pennant.[20]

Home Run # 16—Game 48—June 6—Night Game

The following day the Yankees hosted the Minnesota Twins in a twi-night doubleheader. Maris had a particular dislike for double affairs, especially those that began in the early evening and did not end until nearly midnight. Historically, he did not perform well in these situations. As he explained it, "I would try to bear down in the first game in an effort to insure not having a bad day. It didn't help. Perhaps it was a case of bearing down too hard, or trying too hard to get over this hurdle. Perhaps it was because I don't relish playing two games in a day in the first place."[21]

Whatever the reasons were for his offensive failures in doubleheaders, the June 5 contests were no exception to the rule. While New York won both halves by comfortable margins, the Yankee right fielder contributed nothing to the outcome. He went 0-for-3 in the first game and 0-for-2 in the second, although he did score a run in the sixth inning of that game after he was hit by a pitch to open the frame. His teammates, though, continued to blast homers at a record pace, including number 15 off the bat of Mickey Mantle, a 420-foot clout into the right-center field seats that again tied him with Maris for the home run lead. The Bombers combined for 28 round-trippers in 14 consecutive games. For the Twins, who were battling with Los Angeles and Chicago for the distinction of holding last place, it was their tenth and eleventh straight defeats. The Yankees were still in third place, but cut the Tiger lead to four games.[22]

The Yankee onslaught continued in the third face-off of their four-game series with Minnesota, a night affair that saw Whitey Ford go for his eighth victory of the season. Facing him was left-hander Jack Kralick, who remarkably enough had a winning record (4–3) and an excellent ERA (3.14) for a team that had won only one out of their previous 17 games. Maris put the Yankees on the board first with a sacrifice fly to left field that plated Clete Boyer from third. Kralick struck out the slugger in the third and retired him on a fly ball in the fourth, before he was lifted at the end of the fifth inning with the Yankees up, 3–0. Replacing him was little-known rookie right-hander Ed Palmquist, who pitched briefly for the Los Angeles Dodgers in 1960 before being traded to Minnesota in early May 1961.

The 6-foot-3, 195-pound righty had languished in the Dodgers organization since 1951 with two years out for military service. He began his professional career as a starter, but by the time he was promoted to Triple-A in 1958, he was used primarily in relief. He had decent, if not outstanding, numbers in the minors (his best season was 1958 in which he compiled a 9–12 record with a 2.09 in 59 games), before he was brought up to the big club in early June 1960. A scouting report at that time described him thus: "Throws good sinker. Fast ball is alive. Ordinary control. Very mediocre curve. Needs pitch to fool left-handed hitters. Has chance to be relief pitcher on major league club." He showed some promise after his call-up that summer, appearing in 22 games as a reliever. He ended with a 0–1 record and a team-best 2.54 ERA for the fourth-place Dodgers. That was the highpoint of his career. After running up a 6.23 earned-run average in five appearances with Los Angeles in early 1961, the Twins picked him up on waivers for $20,000.[23]

Minnesota had high hopes for their new acquisition. In his inaugural outing on May 13 in relief of starter Jim Kaat, he won his first—and only—major league game. Relying on a sinking fastball, which he considered "my best pitch," along with his questionable curve and a screwball, the 28-year-old allowed only one run on a sacrifice fly in 2⅔ innings pitched. Manager Cookie Lavagetto had nothing but praise for Palmquist after the game. "He looks mean on the mound. I think he has the heart for relief pitching. He certainly pitched out of a couple of tight spots the first time out." But sadly his pitching performance declined precipitously after that. Eight games later his ERA exploded to 9.43 and his major league career came to an abrupt end. He pitched in just three games for the Triple-A Vancouver Mounties in 1962 before he was released, then in nine games for the Daimai Orions in the Japan Pacific League in 1963, finally calling it quits at the age of 30.[24]

When Maris stepped to the plate to confront Palmquist in the bottom of the sixth, it was the first—and only—time the two faced off against each other. "After the homerless double-header, things began to pick up again," Maris said about that game. "In the first inning I had 'gone' with a pitch from a left-hander [Kralick] and got a sacrifice fly to left to knock in our first run. Then in the sixth inning I came up with two men on base and reached the stands with number sixteen." It was a line shot into the right-field bleachers that gave him the home-run lead once more. The Yankee win combined with a Detroit loss moved the Bombers to within three games of the Bengals.[25]

Home Run # 17—Game 49—June 7—Day Game

Maris continued his torrid home-run pace in the fourth contest against the Twins the following afternoon. Toeing the rubber for Minnesota was "The Cuban Cowboy," Pedro Ramos, who Maris took deep on May 3 for his second homer of the season. The erratic right-hander was well on his way to leading all American League pitchers in losses for the fourth straight season and in home runs for the third time in his major league career. Coming into the game, he sported a 3–6 record and had already surrendered 13 four-baggers in his 13 game appearances.

That day's game began well for Ramos, however. The only Yankee to reach base in the first two innings was Clete Boyer on a fielding error by the Twins' shortstop. He even handled Maris well, retiring him on a fly ball to center in the first inning. Holding a one-run lead when he strode to the mound to open the third frame, it looked like he was headed for a good outing. After inducing Bobby Richardson to ground out to short to open the inning, he allowed the good-hitting pitcher Ralph Terry to reach first on a blooper to right. Boyer flew out to left, followed by a Tony Kubek single to center. With two gone, Ramos might be able to get out of the inning without damage, but first he had to retire Maris. Interestingly, the Yankee slugger had not batted particularly well against the right-hander that season. Maris had only one hit against him in eight previous plate-appearances, and that was his three-run shot on May 3. But Ramos was prone to over-confidence, particularly on his ability to throw his fastball past good hitters.

"I knew that Ramos had a good curve, a change, and a fine fast ball," Maris recalled about that at-bat. "I was trying to guess with him as he started to work on me. He was trying to get out of a jam. There are times when Pedro almost dares a hitter.... This was one of those times. He tried to throw a two-strike fast ball past me." Maris had guessed correctly. "I can still see that pitch. It was a beauty. Fast and down the middle and right in my power range. Don't think it wasn't a thrill to see number seventeen fly into the stands to put us ahead ... to stay."[26]

Maris' "tremendous drive deep into the upper right-field deck" put the Yanks up, 3–1. When Mickey Mantle followed with a single and Yogi Berra with his ninth homer of the year, the game was all but over. Ramos settled down after that, pitching through the seventh inning without allowing another run, but Ralph Terry was having one of his best outings of the season. Ramos shut Maris down following that disastrous third inning. He retired the slugger on a fly out to right to open the fifth inning and on a pop fly to second base to end the seventh, but by then it was far too late.[27]

Maris was especially delighted about that homer off of Ramos. "I am proud of all my home runs," he admitted, "but when they come with men on base they are gilt-edged.

When you get a big tonk [home run] that ties the game, puts your club back into the game or puts it ahead it is a real thrill. I always get special satisfaction when I know one of my homers had a big hand in winning a game. This one did, and it was a great feeling." As for Ramos, he maintained a humorous perspective on his tendency to pitch longballs. When later in the season he was asked about the probability of someone breaking Ruth's record, he replied, "I think I have a better chance of breaking it myself.... The way everybody has been hitting homers off me, I'm a chinch to give up more than 60!" While he never quite reached that height, he did allow 39 that year.[28]

Home Run # 18—Game 52—June 9—Night Game

On June 8, the Yankees played their second twi-night doubleheader in four days. They ended up splitting the twin affair with the visiting Kansas City Athletics, winning the first game, 6–1, but losing the nightcap, 9–6. It was a typical doubleheader outing for Maris, who failed to get a hit in nine plate-appearances. He did score one run after he was walked to open the third inning of the first game, but that was his total offensive contribution; his batting average declined to .226.

The game the following night was one of those messy affairs that saw four rain-delays, including one in the seventh inning that lasted nearly an hour and a half. With over two hours of weather-related halts in the game, the final out was not made until well after midnight. "It was one of those games a ballplayer sees in his nightmares," Maris commented, "and [it] began to feel as if we had been in the park all day." By the time Hank Bauer grounded out to end the prolonged contest, however, Maris was glad the game had not been called before he had a chance to bat in the bottom of the seventh inning.[29]

The skies were threatening when Jim Coates delivered his first pitch at 8:13 p.m. Opposing him was 31-year-old veteran right-hander Ray Herbert, a native of Detroit who began his professional career in 1949 as a starter for the Tigers' Triple-A affiliate, the Toledo Mud Hens. While it was not unheard of for an inexperienced player to start at such a high level of play, in Herbert's case it was probably a mistake. He started out well enough, pitching a shutout in his first outing, but then lost his next two assignments by the scores of 10–6 and 7–4. By the end of his first season he won six while losing 17 with a 5.80 earned-run average over 35 games, hardly an auspicious beginning for the 19-year-old. Herbert was pitching for the worst team in the American Association, which in part accounted for his unsuccessful season, but the underlying problem was his lack of control. In 163 innings pitched, he walked 120 batters while striking out just 76. This issue haunted him until late in his career.[30]

The following year he showed considerable improvement. While he was still walking more than he struck out, he did compile an 11–12 record and lowered his ERA to 3.69 pitching for the Mud Hens. In late August he was called up by the big club, making his first appearance in a Tigers uniform on August 27 against the Philadelphia Athletics, a complete-game, 4–3 loss. He won one game while losing another in his next seven outings, mostly in relief, ending with a very respectable 3.63 ERA. He remained with the Tigers through the beginning of the 1951 season, which started off with a bang: by May 8 he had a perfect 4–0 record with a minuscule 1.42 earned-run average in 12⅔ innings of relief work. Then, like so many of his generation, his baseball career was put on hold while he met his military obligations.

Whether it was due to the interruption of military service, the fact that Detroit had decidedly mediocre teams in 1953 and 1954, his continuing tendency to issue too many free passes, his still limited pitching experience, or a combination of these factors, Herbert's final two seasons with Detroit were decidedly undistinguished. Used almost entirely in relief, the right hander's overall performance (4–6, 5.24 ERA in 1953; 3–6, 5.87 ERA in 1954) heralded the end of his tenure with Detroit. Labeled by *The Sporting News* a "problem right-hander" who "never has prospered" working out of the Bengal's bullpen, the vastly improved Tigers were more than happy to see him go. On May 11, 1955, he was purchased by the Kansas City Athletics. A's manager Lou Boudreau was delighted by Herbert's arrival, telling one commentator that he had been after the youngster for the past several years, even as manager of the Red Sox. "We're beginning to jell now as far as our pitching staff is concerned," he added.[31]

Herbert's first year with the Athletics was less than impressive. Apparently jelling was not in his immediate future. He lost six games, including five starts in a row, before he won his first one. He struggled throughout the season, ending it with eight losses to go along with that lone victory while producing a horrendous 6.24 earned-run average for his efforts, by far the worst of his career. He was still walking too many, but a sore arm followed by a viral infection impacted his performance as well. In addition, Kansas City continued to shunt him between starting and relieving, which could not help but be a factor. As time demonstrated, Herbert was more suited to starting games than relieving them.[32]

Kansas City made a smart move at the end of the 1955 season: they sent their struggling right-hander to their Triple-A affiliate for further development. Over the next two seasons, he pitched solely at the minor league level, first at Columbus, then at Buffalo. In that first summer, all of his 26 appearances were as a starter. He ended the campaign at 9–9 and his 4.44 ERA, while still high, was moving in the right direction. In 1957 he did even better In 38 games (19 as a starter) he won 13 and lost only 8 and his 3.52 ERA was one of his best in years. Perhaps more importantly, his strikeouts were finally exceeding his walks, a sure sign he was gaining control over his pitches. He finally seemed ready to perform consistently at the major league level.

Herbert was one of the mainstays of the Kansas City pitching staff over the next three seasons. From 1958 through 1960 he appeared in 116 games, 75 of them starts. Had he been hurling for a better team, he might have compiled a much better record. As it was, he won 33 while losing 34 with a decent 3.81 earned-run average in a little over 611 innings pitched. He definitely had established control over his pitches; his 329 strikeouts far exceeded his 189 walks in those outings.

Better command of his pitches was one reason for his success on the mound. The other was confidence. "Ray has taken some time to find himself," noted one critic, but he "is moving up as a possible No. 1 starter after many years in the sport." As Kansas City manager Harry Craft observed, "He pitches with authority now." The right-hander always had a good sinking fastball, the speed of which was once compared to that of Bob Feller. But he often over-relied on "the big one," as he called it, because he had difficulty getting his curve over the plate. A's pitching coach Johnny Sain worked with him on that problem as well as helping him develop a better change-of-pace to use as the third pitch in his repertoire. "Herbert is the most improved pitcher I've seen," commented Sain. The pitcher had nothing but praise for his coach in return. "He has good ideas about pitching and I've always liked to talk with him," explained the righty. "The big thing he did for me was to talk me into throwing my curve more. Before I didn't use the curve much. Now I throw it about a third of the time. He also showed me how to throw my fast ball so it would take off. Before, about all I threw was a sinker."[33]

The latter half of the 1960 season was his breakthrough period. He had a losing record the first part of the summer, but maintained a good 3.80 ERA. The problem was two-fold: his teammates did not give him much run-support and he was dealing with a bad back that hindered his follow-through, thus preventing him from "getting as much on the ball as I should have." In the second half, however, he went on a tear, winning 11, losing six, and posting an outstanding 2.83 earned-run average, for a season record of 14–15 and a 3.28 ERA. Together he and Bud Daley produced 30 of the Athletics' 58 wins that year. One sportswriter considered him to be "one of the two or three top pitchers in the American League" during that period, primarily due to his "perserverance [sic]" and "an improved curve ball and better control." Reflecting on the upcoming 1961 campaign, the reporter contended that "no one knows what the A's rebuilding plans will be for next season but any plans for improving the pitching staff will have to center around Ray Herbert."[34]

Making Herbert the core of a rebuild in 1961 was doomed when Frank Lane became general manager of the Athletics. Initially, he thought Herbert and Bud Daley to be "a pair of outstanding pitchers," but Herbert made the fatal mistake of taking Lane at his word. He immediately got into a salary dispute with the notoriously cheap and thin-skinned general manager and became a holdout in the spring of 1961. As the disagreement dragged on, Lane became less and less enamored with his "outstanding" pitcher. By the end of February the back-and-forth had turned nasty. Lane sent Herbert a contract which the pitcher quickly returned unsigned. "Finally he [Lane] sent it back again and this time he said it was the last one I'd get and I could 'sign it, hang it on the wall or tear it up,'" claimed Herbert. "So I wrote him an answer saying, 'I won't sign it, the figures are too much of a disgrace to hang it on the wall, so here it is and you know what you can do with it.' I had torn the contract into a thousand little pieces and put them into a brown manila envelope along with my letter."[35]

Naturally Lane went ballistic, but eventually the two met face-to-face with Herbert getting about twice what Lane had originally offered. It was the perfect example of winning the battle only to lose the war, however. Suddenly Lane found that "pitching represents the A's most obvious weakness and … is making every effort to strengthen the staff." The obvious translation was that Trader Lane was about to put troublemakers like Herbert on the trading block. It took a few weeks, but by early summer Herbert, along with Bud Daley, found themselves pitching in different uniforms.[36]

Perhaps the ugliness surrounding the contract dispute and the swirling trade rumors unsettled Herbert as he started the 1961 season. On April 11, he opened for Kansas City in Boston, winning it, 5–2, after pitching six innings of one-run ball. His second start was the home opener on April 21. Although he suffered a 5–3 loss, he pitched well, giving up two runs over seven innings. After that outing, though, things began to deteriorate. By the time of that June 9 game against the Yankees, his record was 3–5 and his ERA a bloated 5.10. Control appeared to be a problem again and he was allowing more home runs than was typically the case. What Herbert did not know when he took the mound to open that night's contest was that it was to be his last appearance for the Athletics. The following day he was part of an eight-player deal that sent him and three teammates to the Chicago White Sox in exchange for Bob Shaw and three of his compatriots.

Kansas City was the first to score in that June 9 contest. With two away, Yankee starter Jim Coates allowed center fielder Gene Stephens to slam his first homer of the season off the upper-deck façade in right. Herbert then retired the Yankee batters in order in the bottom of that inning, including getting Roger Maris to ground back to first. The Yanks tied the score at one-all when Stephens mishandled an Elston Howard fly ball to center in the bottom of the second inning. Herbert ran into his first real trouble in the next inning. After getting the first two outs, he gave up singles to Tony Kubek and Maris. Mickey Mantle then launched his sixteenth homer deep into the left field seats, putting the Bombers up, 4–1. The Yanks added another run while the A's produced four of their own to tie the game at five apiece going into the seventh inning.

With a downpour threatening, Kubek opened the top half of the inning with a double off of Herbert. Then Maris made his way to the batter's box. The slugger had some success facing his former teammate the previous two seasons. Although he was 0-for-2 against him in 1959, his four hits in 18 at-bats in 1960 included two dingers. He was about to add a third. "Ray had been pitching me outside all day," the slugger recalled. "This time he tried to sneak a fast ball past me on the inside corner. Fortunately I wasn't fooled and was able to get good wood on the ball. I can almost still hear the ring of bat meeting ball as I drove it into the [right field] seats." Maris' homer put the Yankees ahead to stay. After Herbert walked Mantle, the skies opened up and the game was delayed for nearly an hour and a half. By the time play resumed, Herbert was gone, his final outing for Kansas City ending in an 8–5 Yankee victory. When he and Maris met again later that season, Herbert was donning a White Sox uniform and Maris was well on his way to catching the Babe.[37]

The trade to Chicago proved to be a propitious one for Herbert. He won his first three starts with the White Sox, including a one-run, complete-game victory in his first outing for his new team. By the end of the summer, he won nine more games while losing six and his earned-run average (4.05) was over a run lower (5.38) than it was earlier in the season with Kansas City. Although he did give up an additional 15 homers (25 in all—the most in his career), his 36–50 walks-to-strikeouts ratio showed improvement.

The 1962 season was his career-year. The 32-year-old right hander won 20 games while losing nine. His ERA dropped to 3.27 and he surrendered only13 homers that entire summer. This stellar performance earned him his first, and only, All-Star appearance and some consideration for the American League MVP Award. He attributed this sudden improvement to the tutoring of Chicago manager Al Lopez and pitching coach Ray Berres. Together they worked with him on improving control of his curveball. Eventually "it began paying off," Lopez said. "By last season [1962], he was getting it over consistently. Mixing it with his fast ball and a slider made him a tremendous pitcher." This enhanced pitching continued into the 1963 season, but by then 33-year-old was rapidly approaching the end of his major league career. He pitched one more season with the White Sox, then was traded to the Philadelphia Phillies at the end of 1964. He performed two summers there (7–13, 3.98 ERA) before hanging up his spikes. Herbert ended his 14-year career having won 104 games against 107 losses with a cumulative 4.01 earned-run average.[38]

Home Runs # 19 and 20—Game 55—June 11—Day Game/ Second Game of Doubleheader

The Yankees faced veteran southpaw Joe Nuxhall the following afternoon to complete the four-game home stand against the Athletics. "The Ol' Left-Hander," who had the distinction of pitching his first major league game in 1944 at the age of 15, had no problems with Maris that day. The Yankee slugger, swinging a cold bat, was 0-for-4 against the 32-year-old lefty. He did reach base in the third inning, but that was due to an error on the part of the A's right fielder. Mantle, however, had a more successful outing, a 2-for-3 day that included a triple and his seventeenth homer of the year off of reliever Bill Kunkel. He was now one behind Maris in that department. Whitey Ford pitched a complete-game for his ninth victory of the season, giving up three earned runs on two third-inning homers. One of those was a solo shot by Nuxhall, the other an inside-the-park, two-run, 461-foot monster drive off the bat of 38-year-old Hank Bauer that saw the ball role beyond the center-field monuments.

The win left New York in third place, but just two games behind the surprising league-leading Cleveland Indians with Detroit between the two. It was the Bombers ninth win in 12 games going back to June 1. "The Yankees, it may be safe to report, are definitely beginning to roll," crowed the *New York Times*. "If the two front-runners are beginning to cast some anxious glances to the rear, it could be with reason."[39]

The following day saw another doubleheader, the third such since the first of the month. Maris, of course, was not looking forward to it at all. "It had reached a point where I was conscious of the many bad days I had had when we were playing a so-called bargain bill," he recollected. "I had hit six homers in twelve June games, but in the two double-headers we had played [in June] I had an 0 for 12 [actually 0-for-13] horse collar. It was weighing me down, preying on my mind as we took the field for the first game." He had every right to expect the worst. In the eight doubleheaders the Yankees played since the beginning of the season, Maris was a cumulative 9-for-57 for a .158 batting average. He did park two homers in those games, but that hardly made up for so dismal a record.[40]

In the first half of the twin bill against the visiting Los Angeles Angels, it certainly looked like Maris was staying true to form. He managed a single in four at-bats, but it came to naught. Yankee starter Ralph Terry eked out a 2–1 complete-game victory, thanks to Yogi Berra's two dingers and the fine fielding of Maris and Mickey Mantle.

New York was clinging to a 1–0 lead in the sixth inning when Angels third baseman Eddie Yost slammed a long fly ball into deep left-center field. It "looked good for extra bases. But Mantle, tearing at top speed, collared this one with a backhand catch." Then in the seventh center fielder Ken Hunt blasted one Maris' way. "It appeared to have just enough steam to carry into the lower stand. But Roger timed his leap perfectly, caught the ball and went head over heels into the seats." Maris said afterwards, "I could have been hurt, but was lucky. I landed in a lady's lap in the first row of the stands, and we were still ahead." In the ninth with the score 2–0, Maris again robbed an Angel of a home run when he leaned backwards over the Yankee bullpen railing to snag a drive by Ted Kluszewski, the muscular first baseman. While Hunt, the next batter up, was finally able to reach the left-field seats for his eleventh homer of the year, it was not enough to overcome the Yankee two-run lead.[41]

The second game of the afternoon was an entirely different affair when it came to Maris' bat. His victims in that contest were two former Yankee teammates, Eli Grba and Johnny James. The game was decided early on when the Yankees' "Thunder and Lightning"—Grba's moniker for Mantle and Maris—lowered the boom on the Los Angeles starter before he had completed even three innings of work. Errors by the Angels' first and third basemen to open the bottom of the first allowed Clete Boyer and Tony Kubek to reach base in front of the M and M Boys. While Maris failed to deliver, popping out to third, Mantle did not. His three-run bomb into the right-field bleachers gave him his eighteenth homer and the Yankees an early lead that they would not lose. The unfortunate right-hander, who pitched well for the bottom-dwelling Angels during the early part of the season, then retired the next two batters to end the inning.[42]

Grba got through the second allowing just a single to Bobby Richardson, but was not so lucky in the following inning when he faced Maris again. "My old friend Grba was pitching when I came up in the third to end my double-header jinx.... Number nineteen soared into the [right field] stands as Eli's new found curve lost its wrinkle," Maris said. The shell-shocked righty labored through the remainder of that stanza without further damage, but that was the end of the day for him. When the fourth frame opened, reliever Johnny James was standing on the mound.[43]

The right-hand hurling James lingered in the Yankee farm system for six years before making a one-time relief appearance for the Bombers in early September 1958, pitching three innings of scoreless ball. He returned to Triple-A Richmond in 1959. Although he began his professional career as a starter, he was converted to a reliever early on. While he produced winning records in all but one of his eight minor league seasons, he often performed badly in spring training games, which may have been why he was not called up sooner than he was. "For some reason, he has been ineffective in camp through the years—prejudicing [Yankee manager] Casey Stengel's critical eye from the start," suggested one New York sportswriter. "It became almost a neurosis with James."[44]

Then things turned around for the 26-year-old as the Yankees were preparing for the 1960 season. "I felt I could get my ball over for the first time," James said. "Even with a 3–0 count, I was confident I could get my curve across." Deron Johnson, his regular catcher in Richmond, was one who believed James would be successful in the big leagues. "He has all the equipment—sinker, slider, curve and good fast ball. He certainly is ready for the majors—but he needs work to stay sharp." New York catcher Yogi Berra concurred. "He has more stuff than any other young pitcher we have had in my time," the Yankee great asserted. "He has a sinker and a slider, a fast ball and a curve, and a letup. His control is great. He has stuff and he ain't afraid of nobody."[45]

James, who won the James P. Dawson Award as the Yankee rookie with the best performance in training camp and who was pronounced the American League's best rookie pitching prospect by *The Sporting News* at the start of the season, lived up to these glowing recommendations during the first half of the 1960 campaign. In 43⅓ innings of relief work from late April through the end of July, he won five games, lost one—due to a fielding error by Maris in the bottom of the ninth inning of a game against Cleveland on June 26—and saved two others. He did this while maintaining a 4.36 earned-run average, a somewhat inflated figure because of four poor outings in those 28 game appearances. Then out of the blue Stengel sent him back to Richmond. "I wasn't shocked," claimed James, "but I was disappointed. Stengel told me that he was looking for a pitcher who had not run out of his options to send to Richmond." The Yankee manager instructed his pitcher to develop a screwball or forkball to add to his basic four, after which he would be recalled to New York.[46]

"I went to Richmond and worked on those new pitches. But they gave me nothing but trouble. I did no better than 3–2 in the International League [in 1960]. I have abandoned my effort to develop these new deliveries. I have four pitches, and need no more." James used his sinker and slider as his go-to pitches. Despite Stengel's promise, James remained in Richmond the rest of the season, never returning to New York until the following year when the aging Yankee skipper was no longer at the helm.[47]

One of the things that may have prevented James from advancing through the minors more quickly and sticking in the big leagues when he did make it was his size. At 5-foot-10 and 160 pounds, he was one of the smaller pitchers in the game. Although he "was not a sought after prospect" because of his comparatively small stature, James always felt he had a good fastball.

> I think anybody who saw me play back in those days, if you were to ask them, would say that I threw really hard for a person my size. I had a good arm. My fastball ran in to right-handed hitters, with sink. After playing three or four years, I picked up a slider, which gave me a breaking pitch I could throw for strikes. I couldn't consistently throw my curveball for strikes.

When an interviewer years later asked him what he would do differently, he replied, "I would work on a change up more as well as control. Lift weights. Think more about how to pitch. For the most part I was a 'thrower' not a pitcher." Indeed, control was a major problem for him as evidenced by the fact that he often walked more batters than he struck out. He issued 84 free passes against 73 strikeouts in 119 innings of major league relief work, not good numbers for someone whose primary task was to stop the bleeding or hold on to a lead.[48]

James made it back to the Yankees in 1961 for one game of relief work before Ryne Duren, Lee Thomas, and he were shipped off to the Angels on May 8 for Bob Cerv and Tex Clevenger. In what was his final season in the majors, he appeared in 36 games for Los Angeles, including three starts, before ending the summer with a combined record of 0–2 and a 5.20 ERA. He spent the entire 1962 season toiling in the minors for three different teams before calling it quits for good.

James and Maris had never faced each other before that June 11 game. It was also the only game he would ever pitch against the Yankees. The right-hander started off with good control, retiring the side in order after relieving Grba to open the fourth inning. In the fifth, he walked Kubek, eliminated Maris on a popout to third, struck out Mantle looking, and induced Yogi Berra to fly out to the center fielder.

James continued to pitch effectively until the bottom of the seventh. After striking out both Boyer and Kubek, he only had to get through Maris to end the inning. Wanting to get ahead of the Yankee slugger, he delivered a first-pitch fastball. "He [James] must have been really mad at us [for trading him] for he really bore down and did a great job of relief," Maris acknowledged. "He gave up only two hits over the last five innings, but one of them made me a happy guy. It was my twentieth home run and came in the seventh inning to put a period to one of the best double-headers of my life."[49]

After the Maris home run, James struck out Mantle for the second time that day. The center fielder threw his helmet down and, as he walked back to the dugout, jokingly said to James, "If you had pitched like that when you were with us you'd still be here." Maris' second homer of the day put him two up on Mantle. With that doubleheader sweep, the Yankees were still in third place, but just a half game behind Detroit and two out of first.[50]

Home Run # 21—Game 57—June 13—Night Game

It was around this time that sportswriters really began to take notice of the home run battle that was raging between Maris and Mantle. As a consequence, both came under greater scrutiny, much to the chagrin of the Yankee right fielder. Maris loved the fact that he and Mantle were having this back-and-forth contest between them. "It was becoming pretty obvious that Mickey and I were helping each other to hit home runs," he said. "We were actually challenging each other, but also pacing each other. It is hard to say just how much we helped each other, but definitely the way we were going after home runs made each of us try that much harder."[51]

What he did not like was being the focus of so much press attention. He politely answered their questions, but was blunt and direct as always. At times his frustration and irritation with all the queries, especially those he answered multiple times before, became apparent. That, combined with the reputation he earned early in his career for being obstinate, resulted in terms like "angry," "red-necked," "malcontent," and "surly" being used by some reporters to describe his personality. "Roger the red-necked Yankee" was what one commentator called him. "Maris doesn't take surly pills. He only acts that way. The Yankee slugger is really a nice man," the reporter admitted. "It's just that he's perpetually sore." Of course, Maris did not help matters much when he would respond to these characterizations with comments like "I was born red-necked—guess I'll stay that way."[52]

The spectre of Babe Ruth also made an appearance in mid–June. Suddenly there were comparisons between his home-run pace and that of Maris and Mantle. It was still too early in the summer to take that comparison too seriously (Maris and Mantle certainly did not), but now the M and M Boys found themselves competing with the Babe as well as each other. That was one battle they could not win. In the eyes of the Ruth partisans, they would never top the mighty Babe, even though, according to them, the two Yankee pretenders were given advantages that Ruth was not.

"This is the time of year when someone is always going to tie, or beat Babe Ruth's major league record," snidely wrote one sports editor. "Beat Babe Ruth? Huh! Not even with all the souping up of baseballs and continuous tinkering with the rules to favor the hitter, no one will—certainly not the likes of Mickey Mantle or Roger Maris. Why won't they? Principally because they lack what it takes in those final August-September days." Maris, in particular, was held up to scorn because of his batting average. He was "just a now-and-then long fly belter" according to them. "So even if someone should by hook or crook tie the Ruth homer mark Babe sill would have him beaten 500 miles on all-around team value. Nor was he a grumpy bat thrower if he didn't hit one well, or sullen grouser, moaning and groaning that the scorers 'beat me out' of a close hit!" Of course, these naysayers failed to recognize Maris' excellent fielding or that he was one of the league leaders in runs driven in. Such acknowledgment did not fit with their storyline.[53]

Mantle handled these disparaging remarks better than Maris, perhaps because he had been the target for so long he was used to it. Having Maris take some of the heat also helped him to better compartmentalize this hyperbolic criticism. Maris, on the other hand, tended to take such nasty commentary to heart, which made him angry. He hated the sudden barrage of publicity anyway. Personal attacks like these only made matters worse. While he continued to talk with the press as the focus on him grew ever more intense, he did become increasingly leery as he began to perceive some sportswriters as being out to get him.

While neither Maris nor Mantle nor any of the other Yankees hit a home run in the June 12 contest, New York won it anyway behind the four-hit pitching of Bill Stafford for a three-game sweep of the cellar-mired Angels. The victory moved the Yankees into second place, percentage points ahead of Detroit and just a game behind the Indians. After the final out, the team caught a chartered flight to Cleveland for an important three-game series against the league-leaders. It marked the beginning of a 16-day road trip with stops in Detroit, Kansas City, Minnesota, and Los Angeles before returning home the last day of the month.

All three games with the Tribe were night affairs, which usually meant few, if any, homers for Maris. This time it was different. He was in a hitting groove and he knew it. Like many ballplayers, he had his rituals to follow when things were going well. For some, it was not washing their socks or not changing their undershirts. Others carried charms or went through a set of motions before entering the batter's box. For the Yankee bomber, it was eating breakfast with his friend Big Julie Isaacson at New York's Stage Deli before every home game. But most importantly, they both had to eat the same meal every time: baloney and eggs. "I used to say, 'Rog, you're going to kill this Jew,'" Isaacson told Tony Kubek. "He said he didn't care. He was hitting and as long as he was hitting, we were going to eat baloney and eggs every morning at the Stage."[54]

In the first game of the series, Jim Perry got the call for the Indians while Jim Coates toed the rubber for the Yankees. The game was all but decided in the first two innings when Cleveland jumped on the New York starter for six earned runs. A two-run blast by catcher John Romano topped off the four-run first inning while a lead-off homer by third baseman Bubba Phillips and a run-scoring single by left fielder Tito Francona created a hole so deep that not even the power-laden Bombers could club their way out of it. The big right-hander was on his game, holding New York scoreless until the sixth inning when Maris came up to bat with the bases empty and one away.

Perry overpowered the Yankee slugger in his first two appearances that night. In the first inning with Clete Boyer on base, Maris drove the ball to deep right, but it was snagged by Willie Kirkland just before it entered the stands. Then in the third with two on and two gone, he induced Maris to pop out to the catcher. Not hitting in those potential run-scoring situations frustrated him to no end. Always the consummate team-player, the right fielder's preference was for plating runs over hitting homers. Although the third time around he parked his twenty-first homer into the right-field seats, it did nothing to change the outcome of the game; the Yankees lost, 7–2.

Maris was irritated with himself that the dinger came with the bases empty. "Even as you trot around the bases at a time like that you think about the time before," he said. "You are wishing that you might have gotten the home run when it could have helped the ball club. This was another homer for me, but meant nothing to the team as we lost the game. The real thrill is gone from those losing-game homers."[55]

Home Run # 22—Game 58—June 14—Night Game

It was chilly and windy when the two teams met the following night. Whitey Ford was going for his tenth victory; right-hander Gary Bell, with his 4–5 record and a good 3.38 ERA, was hoping to go the distance for Cleveland. He started off in top form, eliminating the first three Yankee batters, when Maris ground into a double play to end the inning. He cruised through the next two innings as well. Then in the fourth things began to unravel for the Cleveland starter.

Tony Kubek was credited with a leadoff double when Chuck Essegian misjudged his fly ball to right. That set the stage for Maris who was appearing for the second time that night. As he did in the two games on May 19 and May 20 when he hit number five off of Perry in the first game and number six off of Bell in the second, the slugger was about to repeat the pattern. He homered off of Perry the previous night, now it was Bell's turn. And like he did with Perry, Maris blasted his twenty-second of the year (his tenth since the first of June) deep into the right-field stands.

Maris, never one to forget a perceived slight, took particular delight in going deep against the Indians. "Any home run I hit against Cleveland has a sweet taste," he gloated. "I had come up to the majors with the Indians, had a few disagreements, and had been traded off. Each time you come back and help beat a team that traded you, it gives you a feeling of great satisfaction."[56]

It was also Maris' forty-ninth and fiftieth runs batted in of the season, giving him the team lead in that category as well. Cleveland manager Jimmy Dykes was less than pleased that Bell had tried to get Maris out on a fastball. "He's a guy you never should give that fast ball [to] unless it's in tight. I don't know when they'll learn," he complained. "Sure he's a good fast ball hit[ter] but look at his average. Somebody's getting him out."[57]

Maris' dinger opened the flood gates for the Yankees. The Bombers added three runs in the sixth and another four in the seventh (including Bobby Richardson's three-run shot, his first home run of the year) to give Ford a comfortable 9–2 lead going into the seventh. After he surrendered three runs to the Indians in the bottom half of that inning, Ford was lifted for phenomenal closer Louis Arroyo. The screwball-hurling lefty held the Indians scoreless over the final two innings, giving the Yankees an 11–5 victory, Ford his tenth win, and himself his eleventh save.[58]

Earlier that afternoon, the Yankees made the trade for southpaw Bud Daley. Shortly after that, ineffective left-handed reliever Danny McDevitt was sent to Minnesota for veteran infielder Billy Gardner. Although it was general manager Roy Hamey who finalized these trades, Ralph Houk was quite pleased with the results. "I think we're now set for the big drive," he announced to the press. "Barring injuries, the team will stay intact until September." Years later, Houk expressed his belief that the Ditmar-Daley deal was key to the Yankee's success in 1961. Referring to Daley as "a poor man's Whitey Ford," the Major asserted that "it turned out to be a hell of a trade for us. We could go either way with Daley; he could pitch long relief or he could start. And he'd take the ball any time. Bud did a great job for us. I don't think we would have won the pennant without him."[59]

In an event of lesser import, Whitey Ford was elected the Yankees' player representative that same day. Ever the jokester, Ford cracked to the press after his election, "If Jack Kennedy has a cabinet, why not me? I'm naming Mickey Secretary of the Bubble Gum Department. Roger always has a chip on his shoulder so he'll be Secretary of Grievances. Yogi'll be my elder statesman, like this here Barney Baruch. Bob Turley's so smart that he can take charge of everything anyone else can't do." The mood in the clubhouse had clearly improved from earlier that season.[60]

Home Run # 23—Game 61—June 17—Night Game

June 15 saw another night game and while Maris was 2-for-5, both of those were singles off of Jim "Mudcat" Grant that did not result in any runs. Mantle, however, blasted his nineteenth of the year into the left-field stands leading off the seventh inning. It had the added benefit of tying the score at one apiece. When Elston Howard plated a second run three batters later, it put the Yanks ahead until the bottom of the ninth when John Romano managed to tie it up with a run-scoring single of his own. It was the excellent pitching of Ralph Terry, not the Yankee bats, which made the difference that night. He hurled a complete-game, 11-inning masterpiece, winning it after John Blanchard added a third run to the Yankee total with a single that scored Bob Cerv in the top of the eleventh. After the 25-year-old right-hander got the final out in the bottom of that inning for his fifth win with no losses, the Yankees suddenly found themselves in first place for the first time that season, but by only a few percentage points.

New York did not remain league-leaders for long, however. The next night found them facing their season nemesis, the Detroit Tigers. For Maris and the Yankees, it was a miserable outing. The slugging right-fielder made four trips to the plate without a thing to show for it. He even began to wonder if he was headed into one of his all-too-familiar slumps. "Things had been going too good," he thought, "maybe it was time for a dive."[61]

Adding to his woes, Maris committed two of the Yankees' three errors in the first inning, which resulted in two Bengal runs. With a man on first, Bill Bruton singled to right. In what should have been a routine job of fielding, Maris misplayed the ball. He compounded that mistake by throwing the ball past everyone, allowing the runner on first to score. Clete Boyer then committed the third error of the inning for the second run. The Tigers plated two more that night, eventually defeating the Yankees, 4–2. The loss dropped New York back into third place a game behind both Detroit and Cleveland after the Indians were victorious that same evening.[62]

The next night saw one of those bizarre contests in which pitching collapsed on both sides and no lead was safe. A total of six home runs flew over the outfield walls of Tiger Stadium, two by the home team, four by the visitors. Starting for the Bombers that evening was the newly-acquired Bud Daley, making his first appearance in a Yankee uniform. Opposing him was veteran southpaw Don Mossi, another former Cleveland teammate of Maris, who became a regular starter two seasons earlier when he was traded by the Cleveland Indians to Detroit during the winter of 1958. The baseball gods were not kind to either pitcher that day: Daley never made it out of the second inning, Mossi was removed in the fourth.

With his prominent ears and rather large proboscis, the fastball-hurling southpaw was one of the most recognizable players in the major leagues. Mossi, who carried the unfortunate monikers of "Ears" or "The Sphinx," seemingly came out of nowhere when he joined the World Series–bound pitching staff of the Cleveland Indians in 1954. In fact, though, he toiled in the Cleveland farm system for five years before joining the big club. Because baseball rules at the time dictated that a player with five years of minor league experience must either be promoted or put on waivers, the Indians decided that Mossi was too valuable an asset to let go to another team.

The left-handed Californian began his professional career in 1949 with the Cleveland's Class C affiliate, the Bakersfield Indians. His two seasons there were decent, but he had a tendency to walk too many batters which resulted in ERAs well above 4.00. His control showed steady improvement over the next four seasons to the point that he was consistently striking out far more than he walked. The 1953 season was pivotal to his development as a major league pitcher. Playing for Double-A Tulsa in the Texas League, he got the chance to start on a regular basis, pitching 201 innings in which he went

Left-handed Don Mossi of the Detroit Tigers and right-handed Bennie Daniels of the Washington Senators provided two of Maris' homers in 1961. Maris blasted number 23 off of Mossi in Detroit on June 17 and number 44 off of Daniels in Washington, D.C., on August 13. Maris hammered four homers in total during that four-game August stand in Griffith Stadium, finally solving the problem he had going deep in the Senators' home field.

12–12 with an excellent 2.91 earned-run average. Most importantly, he walked only 90 while striking out 145.

Mossi faced a daunting task when he arrived at the Indians 1954 spring training camp. He was trying to make a pitching staff that was one of the best in the majors, going up against the likes of Bob Feller, Mike Garcia, Early Wynn, and Bob Lemon. It quickly became apparent, though, that he had the stuff needed to stay with the club when it left for Cleveland. Manager Al Lopez commented to that effect after a particularly good outing against the New York Giants in which he faced 10 batters in three innings of relief, allowing just a walk while punching out four others. "The kid's got something," stated Lopez who was unfamiliar with Mossi before he came to Phoenix. "I can't understand why he wasn't a big winner in the minors. He has a sneaky fast ball, a good curve and good control." The only problems the Indians' skipper saw was that "he hasn't been hiding his curve very well" and that "he has to develop a change-up."[63]

Mossi thought that part of his success was due to a "locked" left elbow that prevented him from fully straightening out his pitching arm. It was discovered during a physical exam for military service. "The doctor noticed that my arm was a little bent and took an X-ray. It showed that my forearm doesn't fit into the socket properly," a condition that was likely due to a childhood injury. "It hurts once in a while now," he admitted, "but nothing serious. If anything, it makes me a little wild. There's never been a time when I couldn't pitch because of my elbow and they say it won't give me any trouble later on."[64]

Make the club he did, but as a reliever, not a starter. He, along with his roommate Ray Narleski and future Hall-of-Famer Hal Newhouser, made up the core of a relief staff that won 16 while saving 29 others. They were central to Cleveland's success that season. As one commentator noted, "Without them, the Indians wouldn't be in first place today." Cleveland pitching coach Mel Harder singled out Mossi and Narleski in particular for possessing the two essential ingredients that made up an outstanding relief pitcher—control and temperament. "Those two fellows don't let anyone scare them. When they have to go in, they are the calmest guys in the park. They just walk out to the hill and say, 'Gimme that ball.'"[65]

Relying primarily on his outstanding fastball and an excellent curve, Mossi produced one of the best rookie seasons he could ever have imagined. None other than Ted Williams sang the praises of the 25-year-old southpaw. The first time the two faced each other, Mossi retired "The Splendid Splinter" on three consecutive groundouts. Said Williams after the game, "The kid has a real good fast ball. It moves so much you have trouble pulling it." By season's end, Mossi was sporting a 6–1 record with seven saves and an incredible 1.94 ERA, the best among both starters and relievers. His 93 innings pitched was the most among the relief staff. Probably his most consequential outing was his last when he got one of his rare starting assignments. On September 22 he hurled a complete game 3–1 victory over the Chicago White Sox to give the Indians 110 wins, tying them with the 1927 Yankees for the American League record. And while Cleveland with its 111–43 regular season was swept in four games by the New York Giants in the World Series that year, Mossi performed well, allowing no runs in four innings of work.[66]

The 1955 season again saw Mossi pitching almost exclusively out of the bullpen. While he had fewer wins and more losses and a few less innings pitched because he did not get as many starts, he appeared in more games than in his rookie year and had more saves as well. His earned-run average increased slightly (2.42), but it proved to be the second lowest of his major league career. Most significantly, he had only 18 walks in those 57 games. He continued to perform well the following year. Despite the fact that his earned-run average grew by over a run, his won-loss record was basically the same and he added two more saves to his total.

In 1957 with Al Lopez gone and Kerby Farrell as his replacement, Mossi saw a significant change in how he was used. Although he was still designated a relief pitcher, nearly two-thirds of his 36 appearances that season were in the starter's role. Both he and his roommate Ray Narleski actually preferred starting to relieving, in large part because there was a greater financial reward going to those who opened games. They also found relieving "to be quite a grind," as Narleski expressed it. "Weeks have gone by when Don and I warmed up every day. They say a relief pitcher lasts longer, but I can't believe it." Both knew that it was a difficult task switching back and forth between the two types of assignments, but they wanted the chance to start when the need arose. Looking to the future, Mossi added, "Someday I'd like to come to spring training knowing I'll be a starting pitcher and pace myself accordingly."[67]

Mossi got his first opportunity to open a game on May 28 after having been out of the lineup nearly two weeks with back trouble. He had a remarkable outing that day, pitching eight innings of three-run ball for a 4–3 victory. On June 12 he pitched his first complete game in three years, whipping the Boston Red Sox, 6–1, and striking out Ted Williams twice. By early July he was 6–2 with a 2.87 earned-run average, good enough that Yankee manager Casey Stengel selected him for the American League All-Star team. Mossi was not as successful the second half of the season, in part because of a shoulder injury he suffered on August 24. In 13 starts between July 13 and September 27, he won five and lost seven. He ended up opening 22 games in all, compiling a 10–9 record with a 4.08 ERA in that capacity, whereas he was 1–1 with a 4.43 earned-run average in 14 games as a reliever.[68]

The 1958 campaign was Mossi's last in a Cleveland uniform. Frank Lane replaced Hank Greenberg as general manager and Kerby Farrell was gone as well, succeeded in turn by Bobby Bragan and Joe Gordon. Chaos ruled as Lane established his usual revolving door, trading players hither and yon before, during, and after the season, including the likes of Roger Maris, Early Wynn, Bob Lemon, Mike Garcia, Bud Daley, Hoyt Wilhelm, and Hank Aguirre. Mossi was one who remained until the end, finally being sent to the Tigers along with his friend Narleski and rookie infielder Ossie Alvarez in exchange for Billy Martin and pitcher Al Cicotte on November 20.

The even-tempered southpaw took it all in stride when the ax finally fell. "I kind of expected it," he commented upon hearing about the trade. "Of all the towns in the league, Detroit would have been my preference. It's a good club to play for, a good town and a good ballpark." In the meantime, he was consigned back to the bullpen. He ended the 1958 season with a losing record for the first time in his professional career, but his 3.90 ERA was an improvement over the year before.[69]

Mossi found new life in a Tigers uniform. Detroit management made a smart decision by moving him into the starting rotation on a fulltime basis after his first month with the team. The savvy left-hander responded well to this more structured role, joining Frank Lary, future Hall-of-Famer Jim Bunning, and six-year Tiger veteran Paul Foytack as Detroit's front four. In his first season with a team that ended in fourth place, he had the best won-loss record (17–9) and the lowest earned-run average (3.36) among all the starters. He was fourth in the American League in wins, ninth in innings pitched, ninth in games started, eighth in strikeouts, second in complete games, and fourth in shutouts. To top it all off, he nearly stole the mantel of "Yankee Killer" from Frank Lary: he was 6–2 with a 2.08 ERA in eight games against New York while Lary was 5–1 with a 3.16 ERA in seven games. Clearly he enjoyed the change in scenery.

By this point in his career, Mossi had lost a little on his fastball. His curve became his go-to pitch and he began developing "a change-of-pace pitch that fades" like a screwball. "Now he throws junk, mostly," observed sportswriter Dan Daniel. "He sliders and he sinkers, and he lets up, and now and then he will even offer a knuckler. This startling and radical change in style has enabled Mossi to organize a fresh career." He was most effective against power hitters like Mantle and Maris. "The Yankees cannot time Mossi," continued Daniel. "He makes them furnish all the power." Indeed, Maris managed just two home runs off of him in 73 career plate appearances, Mantle three in 137 trips to the plate.[70]

Mossi suffered from arm problems throughout the 1960 season, which negatively impacted his effectiveness on the mound. He managed a winning record and a decent ERA, but made only three starts in August. His season came to an abrupt end after a five-inning victory over the Yankees on August 28. He was again dominant against the Bombers, winning four, losing two while maintaining a 2.96 earned-run average. Mantle did park one off of him, but Maris had a measly single in 17 at-bats for a miserable .059

batting average. And in spite of his physical ailments, Mossi maintained his fine control, placing second in the American League in fewest walks per nine innings pitched.[71]

The stalwart southpaw made a complete recovery for the 1961 season. He remained healthy, which showed in his season record of 15 wins against seven losses with a 2.96 ERA (best among the starting staff). He placed sixth in the American League in wins, first in fewest walks per nine innings pitched, tenth in innings pitched, seventh in games started, and fourth in complete games. The one knock against him that year was the number of homers allowed. He surrendered 29 dingers for fifth most in the American League, a figure that was partially inflated due to one game against Cleveland in which he offered up five gopher balls, all solo shots, three of them in one inning alone. It was an uncharacteristic outing which he won in spite of setting the team record for the most homers in one game.

Mossi came into that June 17 game against the Yankees with an outstanding 7–1 record and a minuscule 2.02 earned-run average. He had faced the Bombers twice that season already, but without a decision. They were not particularly noteworthy outings, either. On April 26, he allowed seven runs over four innings, including a home run to Tony Kubek. On May 14, he lasted seven innings, giving up four earned runs on two-run shots by Bob Cerv and Moose Skowron.

When it came to Roger Maris, it was a different story entirely. The lefty owned the Yankee slugger. In the three previous seasons, Maris managed only two singles in 33 plate appearances, never once coming close to a homer. Mossi's plan for that evening was one which worked well for him in the past. "I keep it away as much as I can. Then brush him back. Fast balls and sliders outside and then two or three fast balls inside."[72]

Mossi sailed through the first three innings with very little difficulty. He issued a walk to Mickey Mantle and a single to Moose Skowron in the second inning, but neither crossed the plate. In the first inning he pitched Maris outside, which resulted in a fly out to left field. Bud Daley, on the other hand, ran into trouble from the very beginning. Perhaps he was nervous pitching his first game for the Yankees or maybe he just did not have his stuff that day, but whatever the cause, he immediately loaded the bases to open the frame. When Clete Boyer then booted a groundball that should have been a sure double play, it all went downhill from there. Two batters later the Yankees were down four runs. Daley allowed two more runners to come home in the second before he was lifted for Rollie Sheldon. The young right-hander was equally ineffective, permitting a third run that inning and another on a home run in the third. With an 8–0 lead going into the fourth, it looked as if Mossi was home free. Roger Maris, though, decided that the Yankees had had enough humiliation that day.

Mossi made some adjustments to his pitching pattern to Maris in that second at-bat. Instead of relying on his fastball to get the right fielder out, he decided that a crooked pitch would do the trick; Maris thought otherwise. "I guess I had been expecting a curve because I was ready," explained the slugger. "There was no doubt about this one once it was hit. It went deep into the [right-field] upper deck and had that good solid ring to it." As he circled the bases, Maris felt a special thrill taking the southpaw deep. "It was a great satisfaction for me to hit one off Mossi, especially since it was the first one I had ever hit off him." (It was the only one he would hit off of Mossi in the seven seasons he faced him.) Apparently Mossi was rattled by the blast, for he proceeded to walk Mantle then give up four singles and a double which led to four more runs. When Maris came to bat the second time that frame with two on and two gone, his twenty-third home run victim was in the showers and right-hander Paul Foytack was on the mound.[73]

Seeing a righty and not a lefty surprised Maris a little since he hit right-handed pitching considerably better. But that was not the case this time around. "I guess I was trying too hard or Foytack was too smart for me," he admitted later. "He pitched me tight, and I hit a ball on the handle and rolled out to first base." Maris, ever his own harshest critic, was more upset that he had ended the Yankee rally than pleased that he had parked one. "Once again I was mad at myself for hitting the homer with none on, then flopping with two men on base and a chance to put us ahead."[74]

Over the next five innings, two Yankee relievers allowed four more runs to score, providing the Tigers with a 12–5 advantage going into the ninth. With two gone, Detroit seemed to have the game well in hand, but then all hell broke loose. Clete Boyer hit a solo round-tripper to left that was followed by a Tony Kubek single and a Maris double. Mantle added three more runs with his twentieth homer of the year, a monster blast into the right-field upper deck that "surely periled the citizens cowering out there." Elston Howard plated one more with a dinger to left before Moose Skowron hit a screamer to the shortstop for the third out, giving Detroit a hard-fought 12–10 victory and a two-game lead over the Yankees.[75]

That June 17 game proved to be psychologically significant for Maris, something that restored his self-confidence in ways he had not expected. He called the home run off Mossi "a real shot in the arm to me" because he finally believed he was past his early-season struggles. "I was beginning to feel that I was in for a really good year. Only a month earlier I was worried about getting twenty-five [homers] for the year, yet now I was ready to pass that."[76]

It was especially encouraging because it came off a difficult left-handed pitcher. Not surprisingly, he hit right-handers better than southpaws. In his career he batted .274 with a home run every 17.50 at-bats against righties while hitting .218 with a homer every 22.57 at-bats against southpaws. In 1961, his production against left-handers was clearly better, as it was against right-handers. He batted .232 with a home run every 14.75 at-bats; for right-handed pitching it was every 8.43 at-bats.

Don Mossi's productivity declined after the 1961 season. In 1962 he experienced the second losing season of his career, ending the year with an 11–13 record on a 4.19 earned-run average in 35 games, eight of those in relief. There was a slight improvement the following summer, his final one in a Tiger uniform. After producing a 7–7 record with a 3.74 ERA in 1963, pitching in just a little over 122 innings mixed between starts and relief, the Chicago White Sox purchased his contract in the spring of 1964. Although the 35-year-old lefty still maintained his remarkable control, the end was clearly approaching. Even though he was again dealing with arm problems, Mossi nonetheless worked 40 innings of relief for the Sox, ending the summer at 3–1 and a 2.93 ERA before he was released by Chicago. Kansas City gave him one more season under the sun, picking him up as a free agent for the 1965 campaign. There he went 5–8 with seven saves on a 3.74 ERA in 51 games as a reliever before retiring. In his 12 seasons in the major leagues, he established a very fine record of 101 wins, 80 losses, and 50 saves with a cumulative 3.43 earned-run average.

Home Run # 24—Game 62—June 18—Day Game

The Yankees were in real danger of being swept by the Tigers, which would drop them even further behind the league-leaders. Frank Lary, who dominated the Bombers like no other pitcher, was the starter on that June 18 afternoon. "The Yankee Killer" conquered them twice already that season and came into the contest with a 10–3 record. But the Yankees had their own ace-in-the-hole, Whitey Ford, taking the ball for them. Although he faced Detroit twice earlier without a decision, including a wild late–April outing in which he gave up 10 runs, he was always best when the game was on the line.

It became clear early on that Lary was not on his game. He got out of the first inning without damage in spite of giving up two singles and a walk to Maris. In the second frame, though, everything imploded. Back-to-back gopher balls from Moose Skowron and Johnny Blanchard quickly gave the Yankees a two-run lead. Those homers were followed by two singles, the second off the bat of Ford. After a sacrifice bunt by Bobby Richardson loaded the bases, Clete Boyer knocked a sacrifice fly to right to drive in the runner from third. Maris followed with a single that again filled the bases. Mickey Mantle then produced his own sacrifice fly to score Ford from third. By the time the inning ended, New York was up 4–0, giving the left-hander all the runs he needed to do the job. When Lary allowed another run in the third inning, recently-acquired right-hander Jerry Casale was brought in to relieve the beleaguered starter. He had no better luck than did the Tiger ace.

The Red Sox signed the hard-throwing pitcher right out of high school in 1952 for a bonus of over $30,000 (nearly $300,000 in 2018 dollars). He was one of several hurlers seen to be the future of the Boston pitching staff. His winning record in five years of minor league ball indicated he had a bright future ahead of him. Boston scout/pitching instructor Charlie Wagner stated categorically that Casale "has a better arm than any pitcher I saw in the minor leagues all last season [1955]," adding that "he's a better pitcher than some of the fellows we saw pitch in the [1946] World Series." Although lacking experience, "He's got the equipment to be a big winner," Wagner concluded. "I don't think there's a better pitching prospect in the minors than Casale." Another observer noted that "this big fellow from Brooklyn throws bullets and the only thing he needs is a little more polish on his curve ball."[77]

While having some control problems early in his professional career, by the time he reached the Triple-A level he was striking out far more than he walked. In fact, with the Louisville Colonels in 1955, he ranked first in the American Association in strikeouts and sixth in earned-run average and his 17–11 record was best on the team. He felt he had a real shot at making the big club in 1956, but was sent back to the minors instead, this time assigned to the San Francisco Seals in the Pacific Coast League. He initially indicated some unhappiness at being cut from the opening day roster, but soon got over that. "What'd be the sense of going up to the Red Sox if I didn't pitch? The best thing that could have happened to me was getting in another season in the minors, in a strong league like the PCL. The jump to the majors doesn't look so big to me now," he indicated later in the season.[78]

Casale used that season to his full advantage. He again had the best record on the team and while his ERA increased to 4.10, he still struck out more than he walked. Even though his best pitch continued to be a fastball "with a hop on it," he worked on improving his curve and developing a slider and on following through on his pitches better. "I've quit just trying to see how hard I can throw the ball," he said. "In the small minors I found a fast ball alone would get you by. But I soon learned when you get up to the high minors you can't always throw it by the hitters, or if that's your only pitch they'll tee off on it." He also found out that when pitching to batters with major league experience,

"You've got to give them something besides one pitch to look at. Now I try to let 'em hit that first pitch, with something on it."[79]

It appeared that Casale was now ready for his shot at the big time. At the end of the 1956 season, Red Sox veteran scout Neil Mahoney stated, "There's no question about Casale's arm. It's big league.... Now, it's a question as to whether he has enough experience to pitch in the big leagues. Control comes with experience and if Casale has those now, he could step in and take a regular turn on the mound." Joe Cronin, then general manager of the Red Sox, was high on the youngster, considering him to be one of the hardest throwers in the league. Unfortunately, the young hurler did not get the chance to show what he could do with the Bosox in 1957. Uncle Sam intervened and Casale was inducted into the Army in late 1956, delaying his major league debut until after he was discharged, allowing him to appear in three innings of relief in late September 1958.[80]

It seemed that the disruption to his career did not hurt him any. After tuning up by playing winter ball in Venezuela, the right-hander was primed and ready to begin his rookie season in 1959. On his very first outing on April 15, he pitched a complete game victory over the Washington Senators, contributing to his own cause by hitting a three-run homer deep into the left-center field stands in the sixth inning. He was not so fortunate after that, losing four games in a combination of starts and relief work before winning again on May 30. From that point on, though, he turned his season around. By the end of June he was 6–5 with a 3.84 ERA, ending the season with five consecutive victories and a team-best 13–8 record. He was seen as one of the few bright spots on an otherwise mediocre pitching crew, "the strong-armed young giant who someday will become a mainstay on the Sox staff." But there were warning signs that things were not as good as they seemed. For one thing, he issued nearly as many walks as he did strikeouts. Equally concerning, he offered up 20 dingers in 179⅔ innings pitched, just three short of landing him in the top 10 in that category as well.[81]

Red Sox manager Billy Jurges had high hopes for the sophomore in 1960, indicating that Casale was one of three starters expected to be the core of an improved pitching staff. Sadly, the hurler's second season turned into a complete disaster. After winning his first two starts, all appeared right with the world. Then he started losing. Those two victories were his sum total for the season. By mid-season he was relegated to bullpen duties "until he could get over his mound troubles." He never did. He ended the season with nine losses to go along with those two early wins and a grotesque 6.19 earned-run average. What happened? Red Sox pitching coach Sal Maglie believed his problems stemmed from "tipping his pitches" by where he placed his hands at rest before delivering the ball. That being the case, what advice did management give the struggling pitcher? Go home over the winter and practice his delivery in front of a mirror until he used the same motion on every pitch, regardless of what it was. One Boston scribe referred to this rather dismissive attitude on the part of the team as "still another reprehensible reflection on the Boston brass."[82]

Casale stated years later that a painful arm was the root cause of his difficulties. He continued to pitch in spite of it because he did not want to be removed from the lineup. "I went to the bullpen when I should have gone to see a doctor," he admitted. Whatever was behind his sudden decline, the Red Sox saw him as expendable and left him exposed to the 1960 expansion draft, just another part of American League president Joe Cronin's "'used carcass lot' auction." Although Boston manager Pinky Higgins thought the right-hander "may come back to haunt us," he let him go anyway because "something has gone from his fast ball. And he's got a lot of confidence to get back."[83]

The Los Angeles Angels became Casale's new home. Manager Bill Rigney had "high hopes" that he and the other pitchers selected would "do better than people expect." The right-hander did get his chance to prove he could still pitch effectively but was unable to deliver. He lost his first three starts and in two of those assignments did not make it past the fifth inning before being removed. He appeared in ten more games as a starter or reliever, winning just one and saving another. His tenure with the Angels ended after a June 4 start in which he was taken out in the third inning after surrendering four earned runs. Even though he was 1–5 with a 6.54 ERA in a little over 42 innings pitched, the Tigers were willing to take a chance on him. On June 7 he was sent to Detroit in exchange for Jim Donohue, a right-handed rookie pitcher.[84]

When he took the ball in relief of Frank Lary on June 18, it was just his second appearance in a Detroit uniform. His first was on June 11 when he pitched two scoreless innings of relief against the Indians, striking out three of their batters. That was a very promising start. Although Casale had become prone to offering up long balls, he seemed to have Maris' number. The two faced off thirteen times previously and all the Yankee slugger could manage to get off of him were two singles and a lone RBI. Their encounter that day was their first of the season

After taking the mound in the third inning with a runner on and one away, Casale retired Whitey Ford and Bobby Richardson on fly balls to staunch the bleeding. He was equally effective the next inning, including getting Maris out on a grounder back to the mound. He allowed his first run in the fifth, but that was unearned because of a throwing error on the part of Ozzie Virgil, the Tiger third baseman. After Clete Boyer singled to open the sixth frame, Casale retired Maris on a popout to second and Mickey Mantle and Yogi Berra on fly balls to center. The righty ran into his first bit of real trouble in the seventh inning when Johnny Blanchard parked one with the bases empty into the right-field stands. Then in the eighth he faced Maris for the third time, which turned out not to be the charm.

The inning opened with Richardson grounding out to short and Boyer slapping a single to left. Then Maris followed with a two-run blast into the right-field balcony that "closed out the carnage," a 9–0 shellacking of first-place Detroit. The Tigers could console themselves that they took two out of the three contests, but the Yankees were still breathing down their necks, only one game out. The Indians separated the two by half a game after they split a doubleheader that same day. Later when Maris attempted to recall any of the details about that at-bat, the only thing which came to mind was that it was his twenty-fourth homer of the season. It was "strictly a help to my average and a boost to my pride for the club had already won the game. It didn't win a ball game, but I was glad to get it."[85]

Although that homer was the last hit Maris ever get off of him, for Casale it was one step closer to ending his major league career. After giving up another four-bagger nine days later in a rare start that lasted five innings, he was sent to the Tigers Triple-A affiliate in Denver to see if he could straighten himself out. He did pitch adequately there the remainder of the summer, good enough to give him a final opportunity to produce at the big league level when he made Detroit's opening-day roster in 1962. "He has been a good pitcher," Tiger manager Kerby Farrell noted, "and there's no reason why he can't be good again." Casale was used in 18 games, all but one from the bullpen, before he was sent back to Denver with one win, two losses, and a 4.66 earned-run average. That marked the end of his tenure in the big leagues. The following summer he pitched 39 innings of mostly relief work for the New York Mets minor league club in Buffalo before receiving his release in June. Over parts of five seasons in the majors, he compiled a 17–24 record with a 5.08 cumulative earned-run average.[86]

Home Run # 25—Game 63—June 19—Night Game

Immediately after the game, the Yankees boarded a chartered flight to Kansas City for a series of four night games against the sixth-place Athletics. For New York it meant three more wins; for Maris it resulted in another three added to the homer column. And he was headed home to be with his family, which made him happier and more relaxed. Any lingering concerns he had about his wife and unborn child dissipated upon his arrival. "I found that my wife's health was fine and there were no doubts about having the baby."[87]

First up was 29-year-old rookie Jim Archer. One Kansas City sportswriter compared him to "Joe Btfsplk," the hard-luck character from the Li'l Abner comic strip who was always depicted with a black raincloud hovering over his head. Indeed, it seemed like the left-handed pitcher would never get his shot at the big time. Originally signed by the Yankees in 1951, he spent parts of two seasons toiling in their Class D clubs before spending the next three years in semipro ball and military service. He returned to the minors in 1955, this time as part of the Orioles organization. He then spent the next six seasons slowly climbing the minor league ladder from Class B to Triple-A without even a single sip of coffee in The Show.[88]

His lack of opportunity to demonstrate at the major league level what he had to offer was through no fault of his own, however. He could point to excellent seasons with outstanding walks-to-strikeouts ratios, even at the highest levels of the minors. With the Triple-A Miami Marlins in 1959, for example, he compiled a record of 13 wins against 11 losses with a praiseworthy 2.81 earned-run average for a team that finished seventh in the International League. He thought for sure he would finally make the Orioles after that, but when spring training camp broke, manager Paul Richards told him he was going back to Miami. There he posted an 11–12 record with a 3.33 ERA, which on the surface appeared mediocre, but in fact made him one of the best pitchers on a team that again finished in seventh place.

So why then did the Orioles not call him up? The problem was that he did not have an overpowering fastball, which put him at a distinct disadvantage when competing for a spot on the big league roster with fireballers like Milt Pappas, Steve Barber, and Chuck Estrada. What he did have was outstanding control and excellent curves and off-speed pitches. Apparently Baltimore management was not impressed with that pitch repertoire (one Baltimore sportswriter labeled him "a Triple-A player at best") and in late January 1961 he was traded to the Athletics along with a slew of other players for outfielders Russ Snyder and Whitey Herzog. Although Archer was disappointed that he did not make it with the Orioles, he was happy about the trade. "I think I would have made the staff this season [1961] if I had stayed with Baltimore, but I was glad when they traded me to the A's because I knew I'd have more of an opportunity." It turned out to be the best thing that could have happened to him.[89]

The long-suffering southpaw made it at last. When the A's broke camp in early April, Archer finally was part of a major league pitching staff. But that little dark cloud continued to follow him. Once he got to Kansas City, he was consigned to the bullpen where he sat, and sat, and sat before he got his first call nearly three weeks into the season. On April 30, he was given the ball to start the second half of a doubleheader against the Los Angeles Angels. It was the A's thirteenth game of the season, but it turned out to be Archer's lucky number. For eight solid innings he blanked the Angels while the Athletics held on to a three run lead. Then in the ninth, after striking out Albie Pearson to open the inning, the Kansas City third baseman booted the ball, an error which led to two unearned runs. Archer was lifted after the first Angel crossed the plate, but his relief allowed just that second run to score, giving the left-hander his first major league victory.

Had that little black cloud finally dissipated? Unfortunately, no, it had not. In spite of being considered by manager Joe Gordon as having "made the best showing of any member of the staff," Archer was again sent back to the bullpen where he sat for another week. Then on May 6 he made his second appearance, this time in relief of A's starter Ken Johnson who never even made it out of the first inning. Entering with a 3–0 deficit, Archer proceeded to battle Baltimore's Steve Barber for six and a third innings, allowing just one unearned run while striking out eight and walking one. Although the Athletics lost the contest, Gordon had nothing but praise for his reliever. "Archer kept stride with Barber, and if Jim continues his fine pitching, he could develop into one of the best southpaws in the majors," the manager contended.[90]

The lefty demonstrated in two appearances that he had the stuff to open games, so what happened next? He was sent back to the bullpen. He made six more relief appearances from May 9 through May 20, earning three saves (one of those against the Yankees) while maintaining a 1.29 ERA. Fate in the guise of team owner Charles Finley then stepped in. Typically owners do not insert themselves into on-field management decisions, but "Charlie O" was not your typical boss. He called general manager Frank Lane and told him to begin using Archer as a starter. Naturally that irritated Lane, but he told Joe Gordon to do so nonetheless. While feelings may have been bruised, Finley made the right call. On May 24 Archer started for the second time that season. He pitched seven strong innings and, while he was not credited with the win, he had proven to all and sundry that he could toe the rubber with the best of them. He pitched in 30 more games that season, 25 of them as a starter. He added two more saves to that column and though he lost 15 games against nine victories, almost all them were due to a lack of run support from his teammates. By the end of the season, he sported a nifty 3.20 earned-run average, considerably below the league average of 4.02.[91]

Ernest Mehl, the dean of Kansas City sportswriters, declared Archer to be "the leading pitcher on the A's staff." He praised the southpaw for the very thing that others in the past discounted—his fastball. "Although Archer's fast ball never would be timed for its speed," he wrote, "it has been the excellent use of this pitch which has improved the caliber of his pitching this year." Archer used his best pitch, a screwball according to Mehl, and "three curves of varying speed" to set up his fastball. "When a batter expects some sort of a curve he is not prepared for the fast ball and Jim has been throwing it quite often as his payoff pitch. It's fast enough except when the hitter is looking for it and Jim tries to make sure he isn't looking." Another observer noted that "Archer is not the overpowering type hurler, but he pitches with a purpose. He employs an assortment of pitches to foil rival batters. On occasion Archer will slip over a fast ball which makes his slider, sinker and knuckler more effective. The uncanny A's southpaw has the knack of setting up a hitter. His control is exceptionally good." And *The Sporting News* called him "the bright spot in the otherwise dismal Kansas City picture."[92]

According to Mehl, the Yankees "admitted themselves that of all the pitchers they faced, none gave them more trouble than this left-hander." Indeed, Archer generally handled the Yankee big boppers well. Yankee manager Ralph Houk saw the southpaw as someone "who could trouble our big bats if he had control. He was not a thrower. He mixed speeds; when he pinpointed the ball he was tough for any club."[93]

His June 19 start was his fourth time facing the powerful New York lineup. One good sign for him that day was that in the 16 games (61 innings) he had pitched thus far, he allowed just one home run. In fact, he was home-run-stingy with all the other clubs as well, allowing only .482 home runs per nine innings pitched, third fewest in the American League that year.

That evening's game opened with some dramatic news. Joe Gordon was fired as manager and veteran outfielder Hank Bauer appointed to the role of player/manager, which came as quite a surprise to the Kansas City players. It turned out to be an eventful night for the first-time skipper. Perhaps Archer was still adjusting to the news when he opened the top of the first by surrendering a double to Bobby Richardson. A groundout by Clete Boyer moved Richardson to third, while a walk to Maris put runners on the corners for Mickey Mantle. The Yankee center fielder was greeted with a wild pitch that plated Richardson. At that point, Archer settled down. He struck out Mantle then Elston Howard to end what could have been a disastrous inning.

The A's southpaw cruised along until the fourth when Moose Skowron parked one with two gone. The Athletics finally answered with a run of their own in the bottom of that frame, then tied it at two in the seventh. In the ninth inning it was lefty versus lefty when Maris stepped into the batter's box to open it for his fourth plate appearance of the day.

Maris had not done well against Archer up to that point. Back in early May, the Yankee slugger did manage a run-scoring single off of the left-hander, but that was his only hit over their next eight confrontations. The future homer king was in the zone, though, and left-handed pitching, no matter how good, was not a problem for him when he was locked in. "Jim Archer, a tough left-hander, was working for the Athletics," Maris explained. "He had given me a lot of headaches in the earlier games, but I guess at this point I was just rolling too good to be stopped by anyone. He was giving us the usual tough battle, but I managed to get hold of one and sent it over the right-field wall for number twenty-five to put the Yankees ahead."[94]

Nearly 50 years later, Archer could still vividly see that home run. "I remember it like it was yesterday," he recalled. "It was the sound of the bat. I struck him out the first time with my fastball [which occurred during Maris' second plate appearance of the day to end the third inning] and I thought I set him up. I made a mistake." The sound of bat meeting ball was so solid that the pitcher did not even turn around; he knew it was gone.[95]

If the blow rattled Archer, he did not show it. Mantle followed with a single, but Howard grounded into a double play and Skowron fouled out to limit the damage to just that Maris run. The game was not done yet, however. With the score 3–2 in favor of the Yankees, the A's made a dramatic comeback in the bottom of the ninth. After Norm Siebern hit an inside-the-park home run which was followed by a Wes Covington blast that came to rest on the right-field berm, Archer had his fifth win and Bauer his first managerial victory.[96]

Jim Archer lost his next two outings against the Bombers, but allowed just one earned run in each of them. Maris managed only an insignificant single in nine trips to the plate in those two games. The right fielder ended up having more plate appearances (21) against Archer than any other batter in the pitcher's career. Maris batted an anemic .167 over the two seasons Archer played and that June 19 dinger was the only one he ever hit off of him.

It looked like Jim Archer was facing a golden future. He was expected to be an integral part of the Athletics' pitching staff in 1962, but then that foreboding thunderhead appeared once again. He pulled a leg muscle while running in the early part of spring training. That injury resulted in a change to his gait which in turn caused him to strain his pitching arm. Tendonitis then developed in his shoulder, which led to him being shut down until late April. It was thought the problem would clear by then, but it did not. Although he appeared periodically, he was never able to get beyond his arm problems. To top it all off, he was struck on the right knee by a line shot off the bat of Clete Boyer during a game in mid-July after he had been out of the lineup for a couple of weeks. That injury set him back another two weeks. When he returned, he did pitch relief in ten more games, but by then it was all but over. By season's end his record was 0–1 with a horrendous 9.43 earned-run average.

The unlucky left-hander attempted a comeback the following year pitching in the minor leagues, but he never made it back to the majors. That little black cloud had done him in. In two seasons pitching in the big leagues he compiled a 9–16 record with a decent 3.94 earned-run average. One can only speculate as to how well he would have done had he been given an opportunity earlier in his career or had he not suffered such debilitating injuries following his rookie season.[97]

Home Run # 26—Game 64—June 20—Night Game

If it seemed like Joe Nuxhall had been around forever when he stepped to the mound to open the June 20 contest against the Yankees, it was because he had. "The Ol' Left-hander," as he was sometimes called, had the distinction of being the youngest player ever to appear in a major league game. On June 10, 1944, at the ripe old age of 15 years, 10 months, and 11 days, the Cincinnati Reds called upon him to pitch the ninth inning of a game in which they were being trounced 13–0 by the visiting St. Louis Cardinals. After getting two quick outs with a walk in between, the floodgates opened and the terrified teenage hurler was pounded for five runs on a wild pitch, four more walks, and a couple of singles, straddling him with a 67.50 earned-run average in his debut outing.

How in the world did a junior high school student, big though he was at 6-foot-3 and 190 pounds, come to pitch in a major league game against the best team in the National League? The Second World War depleted the big league rosters so badly that scouts wandered the hinterlands hunting for anyone who could field, hit, or pitch without looking the complete fool. One of these bird dogs was in Hamilton, Ohio, observing Nuxhall's father pitch in a Sunday league game when he spotted Joe, a left-hander whose fastball topped out at 85 mph. That was 1943 and his parents would not let him sign with the Reds. The following year, though, they did and once school was out, he joined the team.

He mostly rode the pine, nothing more than a fan observing from the dugout. Then on June 10 as the Reds were getting the tar beat out of them by the World Series–bound Red Birds, manager Bill McKechnie decided it was time to see what the youngster had to offer. "I was just sitting there watching the Cardinals beat up on the Reds when, geez, all of a sudden McKechnie yells at me to warm up. I was scared to death," he recalled years later. "I got all shook up and tripped over the top step and fell flat on my face in the dirt. It was embarrassing." Nonetheless, he did as instructed and when the ninth inning opened, he found himself standing on the mound. "Probably two weeks prior to that, I was pitching against seventh-, eighth- and ninth-graders, kids 13 and 14 years old. All of a sudden, I look up and there's Stan Musial and the likes. It was a scary situation." Indeed. He started well enough, but then he glanced at the on-deck circle where "Stan the Man" was awaiting his turn to bat. "That must have been when I realized where I was at," he remembered. The rest, as they say, is history. At least he could take some pride in the fact that Musial, the 1943 National League Most Valuable Player, only hit a single off of him.[98]

After that dramatic introduction to the majors, Nuxhall spent the rest of that summer and the next six seasons honing his craft in the minors. Then in 1952 he again made the big league squad, this time for good. It took him a couple of seasons to get it all together, but by 1954 he was fast becoming one of the better pitchers in the National League. The following season was his break-out year. With his 17–12 record and a 3.47 earned-run average, he was the best hurler on a Cincinnati team that finished in fifth place. Among all National League pitchers, he was seventh in ERA, third in wins, tenth in fewest walks per nine innings pitched, sixth in games played, second in innings pitched, fourth in complete games, first in shutouts, and, while tied for ninth in home runs allowed (25), he was ninth in fewest home runs per nine innings pitched. He tossed more innings than any other National League lefty and tied Warren Spahn for the most wins by a southpaw in the league. And he appeared in his first All-Star game, pitching 3⅓ innings of scoreless relief to help the National League preserve its 6–5 victory over the American League.[99]

Nuxhall really began to come into his own once he learned to control his fastball, rated one of the fastest among left-handed pitchers, and after he added a second pitch—a slider—to go along with it. The left-hander had a reputation for wildness when he first came up to the show, often walking more than he struck out. He credited a minor league manager with helping him understand what he was doing wrong. Nuxhall had a temper which he often directed at himself. "I'd be wild," he said, "then I'd get mad at myself. The wilder I got, the madder I'd get. So one day [Tulsa manager Al] Vincent told me that if he ever saw me getting mad out on the mound, he would yank me out of the game even if I was leading 20 to 0. After that, if I got wild, I'd just slow down between pitches. You know, like counting ten." But it was not until he added a slider to his pitch selection that he started to win more consistently. "Some people think a slider is just a nickel curve ball, but it's altogether a different pitch," Nuxhall contended. "A curve ball breaks sharply and usually down and away. A slider moves in on a batter."[100]

The left-hander was one of those pitchers who was a slow starter, someone whose second half of the season was often far superior to his first half. That was the case in 1956 when he was 1–5 with a 4.91 ERA during the first two months of summer, then began to win on a regular basis, ending with a 13–11 record and a 3.72 ERA. He also seemed to be both injury-prone and subject to periodic arm problems, especially in the early spring, which certainly limited his effectiveness. Twice that season he was struck on the leg by a line drive and suffered a third injury in August when he pulled a side muscle while batting. That pattern repeated itself in 1957. On July 1 he was 2–5 with a 6.22 earned-run average; by season's end his record improved to 10–10 and his ERA dropped to 4.75.

Though nether season was a disaster, they were disappointing, especially when compared to his stellar 1955 campaign. Reds general manager Gabe Paul thought he had hit on a solution to Nuxhall's early season woes: have him start working on getting his arm in shape before spring training began. That was exactly what Paul did early in 1958. He sent Nuxhall to a rookie pitching camp in Plant City, Florida, two weeks before reporting to the Reds' regular training camp so that he could "work the soreness out of his arm." That move certainly seemed to help. Instead of a losing record early in the season as he had in the past, Nuxhall was 5–3 with a 3.04 earned-run average at the end of June. While his pitching was not as sharp in the latter half of the season, he still managed to win 12 games while losing 11 (six of the losses were by one run) and had decreased his earned-run average to 3.79, nearly a full point from the year before.[101]

The Reds' GM was so pleased with Nuxhall's 1958 performance that he intended to send him to winter ball in Cuba to strengthen his arm and to get in shape, but Fidel Castro's revolution put the kibosh on that plan. As an alternative, he enrolled the pitcher in a Tampa, Florida, pitching school that was held a month before spring training began. This time the extra conditioning did not help. As late as July 25, the 30-year-old southpaw was 3–9 with a 5.03 ERA, hampered in part by a sore arm that cropped up in mid–May which kept him sidelined for two weeks. Then he suddenly began to win again. He pitched three complete-game victories in a row and never lost another game that year. He even had the distinction of tying a major league record by striking out four batters in one inning during an August 11 game against the Milwaukee Braves.

Nuxhall attributed his sudden turn-around to better control. "I'm just getting the ball where I want it now," he explained. Then the injury bug raised its head once again. In an August 19 outing against the Los Angeles Dodgers, Nuxhall injured his right knee sliding into second base and on August 24 had to be hospitalized when it became infected. In spite of being out of the lineup for a month, the veteran left-hander was able to salvage the rest of the summer, ending with a 9–9 record and a 4.24 ERA.[102]

Nuxhall's tenure with Cincinnati came to an abrupt finish at the end of the 1960 season, the worst campaign in his long career. Relegated primarily to the bullpen, he managed just one win against eight losses. He became more and more frustrated as the season wore on, and the fans began to boo him every time he appeared. In a late July game his anger was so out of control that he pushed rookie umpire Eddie Vargo to the ground after he called a runner safe in a close play at first. It took two teammates—including the notoriously hot-headed Billy Martin—to wrestle the pitcher to the ground to prevent him from further assaulting Vargo. He was fined $250 (a little over $2,000 in 2018 dollars) and suspended for five days because of his behavior. By September the Reds made it known they were willing to trade him. Even Nuxhall himself thought that would be the best for all concerned. "I have loved it in Cincinnati and it would be tough to go," he announced in October. "I hate to say it, but I hope I'm traded." The big southpaw got his wish. After 10 seasons in a Reds uniform, he was sent to the Kansas City Athletics for pitchers John Briggs and John Tsitouris on January 25, 1961.[103]

His 1961 season started out in untypical fashion. Instead of an early losing record, he was red hot in spite of limited pitching appearances. In his first six starts through June 5, he was 4–1 with a 3.43 earned-run average. One of those was a complete game victory over the Washington Senators. His performance came as somewhat of a surprise to both the pitcher and the front office. "For a while, Joe must have wondered about himself, but the doubts are disappearing as he takes a regular turn on the hill and succeeds with more *eclat* than anyone else on the staff," wrote Ernest Mehl in *The Sporting News*.[104]

But then things began to go badly. He lost four of his next six starts and his ERA exploded to 4.97. From mid–July on he pitched exclusively from the bullpen. While he occasionally showed flashes of pitching brilliance, for the most part he struggled. By the end of the season, he was 5–8 with an unacceptable 5.34 ERA. In his defense, he was pitching to batters he had never faced before for a team that ended in ninth place after losing 100 games. Even at that, it was at best another disappointing season for him.

Nuxhall pitched against the Bombers just twice prior to the June 20 contest. On April 17, he opened the eighth inning in relief with the A's down, 3–0, but faced only two batters after giving up a single and a walk before he was lifted. Then on June 10, he started against them, surrendering four runs (three earned) in seven innings of work. Although it resulted in his second loss of the season, he did pitch effectively against the powerful Yankee lineup. Maris, in particular, had difficulty with the left-hander, failing to hit safely in four trips to the plate.

The southpaw was dominating over the first two innings of the June 20 start. He retired the first three Yankee batters he faced, including Maris who grounded out to end the inning. In the top of the second, he struck out Mickey Mantle before Elston Howard singled. Nuxhall then retired the next two batters to hold New York scoreless. In the bottom of that inning, the lefty aided his own cause when he tripled off of Yankee starter Bill Stafford, scoring Jerry Lumpe from first base.

But in the third it turned sour, in part because of the poor play of his teammates, but also because of his own wildness. The first four batsmen reached base on a double, two walks, and an error by the left fielder. Two runs crossed the plate, one on a passed ball, the other on the error. Nuxhall then retired Maris on a fly to right before Mantle singled to drive in the third run of the inning. After walking Howard to again fill the bases, he struck out Moose Skowron and induced Bob Cerv to ground out to end the inning. The lefty seemed to calm down after that. He got through the fourth with only a harmless single to Bobby Richardson, then added a run to the Athletics column when he doubled home Lumpe who had doubled to open the inning. His two RBIs were the only runs Kansas City scored that evening.

Perhaps the 32-year-old pitcher was exhausted from all the base running he had to do, because in the fifth inning he was lifted after he allowed three runs to cross the plate. It was Maris who started the Yankee onslaught. He opened that frame and made short work of it by blasting his twenty-sixth home run, which nearly left the park, hitting just a foot below the top of the 40-foot high outer wall after passing over the outfield barrier. (Municipal Stadium had the typical outfield walls, but they were encased by a high outer wall that ran parallel to the streets outside the stadium.) It "was the longest to right field at the stadium this season," stated one observer. It was Maris' fourth homer in four consecutive games and his eighth in the last ten.[105]

That blast off of Nuxhall was the second round-tripper Maris hit off of left-handed pitching in two days, and he was "sitting on top of the world. I felt that I was in the sort of streak that all home-run hitters dream of. I was getting that good loft to the ball with enough power to scale the walls. Not even left-handers were stopping me, and that made it extra special in my mind."[106]

The Bombers added two more runs that inning when Skowron doubled home Mantle and Howard after both singled off of Nuxhall. That made the score 6–2 in favor of New York, which was the final outcome of the game. With the win, the Yankees moved into second place behind Detroit and percentage points ahead of Cleveland. The Indians' loss to the White Sox that day marked the beginning of an extended losing streak for them, ending their run for the title. From that point forward, the race was strictly between the Yankees and the Tigers.

In late November Nuxhall was cut from the Kansas City roster. Within a week, he was signed as a free agent by the Baltimore Orioles. In April 1962 the Los Angeles Angels acquired him from Baltimore. He appeared in only five games for the Angels, pitching a little over five innings of relief with no won-loss record, but an outrageous 10.13 ERA.

On April 27 he made his last appearance in an Angels uniform, opening the sixth inning of a game in Detroit with the Tigers already up 10–4. After giving up three runs when two were out, Nuxhall's frustration—probably building for the past two seasons—came to a head. With Al Kaline standing on third having driven in two runs on a triple, the veteran lefty plunked Norm Cash, the next batter up, on the back. Umpire Ed Runge immediately fined Nuxhall $50 (slightly over $400 in 2018 dollars) for intentionally striking Cash. Then as the umpire turned his back to return to home plate, Nuxhall hurled the ball into the stands. That action naturally resulted in him being tossed from the game. It marked the end of his very brief tenure in Los Angeles. His American League adventure came to an end in mid–May when he was given his unconditional release.[107]

Then the miracle of miracles happened: the Cincinnati Reds decided to bring him back home. Before adding him to their big league roster, however, management sent Nuxhall to their Triple-A team in San Diego for rejuvenation. He appeared in 15 games for the Padres, 11 of them starts, winning nine while losing only two on a fantastic 3.21 earned-run average. He tossed seven complete games and three shutouts in 84 innings pitched. He even won a July 12 outing against the Hawaii Islanders with a walk-off home run in the tenth inning. The "slightly over the hill" southpaw clearly demonstrated that he had a few miles left in his arm—and his bat.[108]

In late July Nuxhall was called up to Cincinnati. "There have been some nice memories and great breaks for me in this game," Nuxhall reminisced years later, "but if I had to pick one thing it would be coming back to the Reds in 1962. When I left, got sent down, I never dreamed that I'd be back here. So when I got the call from the Reds, it was very special." The grateful 33-year-old got his first chance at showing his appreciation when he entered a July 22 game in the fifth inning against the Mets with New York up, 4–1. He pitched 3⅓ innings of scoreless ball and, when Cincinnati scored six runs in the sixth inning, two of which he drove in with a double, he got credit for the win. After three more relief appearances, the veteran was moved back into the starting rotation. He won four of those nine starts (one of them a complete game) to end his first season back at 5–0 with a 3.03 earned-run average.

Nuxhall attributed his successful comeback to two things: controlling his temper when things started going badly and regaining confidence in his pitching. "I used to get so mad I'd just fire the ball through there and the batters would hit it. Now I'm more relaxed." The fact that he was receiving vocal support from the fans must have been a big help as well. Instead of all of nasty catcalls he heard in 1960, he was instead receiving cheers. "That really took a big load off of me, relaxed me and consequently I did well." In addition, he became more self-assured about his pitch selection and pitch location. "I had lost confidence in pitching to certain areas, like pitching inside," he said. Prior to his returning to the Reds, "it seemed like [batters] would hit the ball a hundred miles" whenever he tried to come inside on them. Working on both issues during his minor league stay helped him recover the form that worked so well for him earlier in his career.[109]

The 1963 season was arguably the second best of his career. At the age of 34, he won 15, lost eight, and maintained an outstanding 2.61 ERA over 35 games (29 starts). He continued to throw for the Reds for three more seasons, compiling a fine 26–20 record and a 3.99 earned-run average in 99 game appearances, more than half as a starter. Over 16 seasons in the major leagues, he could point with pride to a cumulative 135–117 won-loss record and a decent 3.90 earned-run average achieved in 526 games. After putting away his glove in early 1967, he joined the Reds broadcast team where he remained until 2004, retiring 60 years after his major league debut. He had come a long way from that frightened boy who stood on the mound in the summer of 1944 staring into the eyes of Stan Musial.

Home Run # 27—Game 66—June 22—Night Game

Maris failed to homer in the third outing against the Athletics on the night of June 21, but he was 2-for-4 and scored two runs in the Yankees' 5–3 win. The big bat that evening was Mickey Mantle who clouted two monster shots, one of which landed on the street outside Municipal Stadium. Maris was on base for both of those rockets. The first struck the scoreboard estimated at 425 feet distant, the second careened off of Brooklyn Avenue some 475 feet away. The "Commerce Comet" now had 22 four-baggers to Maris' 26, leaving them in first and second place in both leagues, and tied at 55 RBIs apiece, just three behind Norm Cash with 58.[110]

Maris went on a tear in the following night's game against Kansas City, going 4-for-5 with four runs batted in on a single, two doubles, and his twenty-seventh home run. By the end of his rampage against four different A's pitchers, he had raised his batting average to .258, helping Whitey Ford win his twelfth game in the process. His first victim of the game was rookie right-hander Norm Bass.

The 22-year-old Bass, younger brother of Los Angeles Rams running back Dick Bass, was a product of the Kansas City farm system. The 6-foot-3, 205-pound 19-year-old right-hander began his professional career with the Class C Pocatello A's in 1958. With his 11–9 record and 5.67 earned-run average, one of the lowest on the team, he was considered a good pitching prospect still in need of development. He continued to progress through the minor league system and in 1960 he moved from Class B to Triple-A all in that single season. With his cumulative record that year of six wins, 12 losses, and a 5.12 ERA, there was some question as to whether he was ready to make the jump to the big leagues.

Kansas City, desperate for decent pitching, gave the youngster a fair shot at it during spring training in 1961 and he rose to the occasion. Bass, with his "overpowering fastball, a good curve and an effective changeup," was evaluated as "the most impressive of all the young pitchers" trying to make the Athletics' roster. "Bass is an imposing sight on the mound," noted one sportswriter, "and he is equally as awesome when he throws." Manager Joe Gordon liked what he saw, but was somewhat reluctant to commit to giving Bass a spot on the pitching staff because of his mediocre record in the minors the year before. The youngster tried to assuage that concern by arguing he had changed his pitching style to address his control issues. "I'm getting the ball over much better," he claimed. "My control was bad last year [1960] but I was still throwing sidearm then. Now I'm throwing overhand, which is my natural motion, and I haven't had any trouble with control."[111]

Bass indicated that he started using a sidearm delivery on the advice of a physician after he began experiencing severe arm problems. It turned out that the cause of his pain was a hernia of which he was not aware. Once it was repaired, he was advised to start with a sidearm delivery to give his arm time to recover, then to gradually raise it as the arm got stronger. "I was still throwing sidearm through most of last season, and I had a lot of control trouble. The ball would sail and take off and I didn't know where it was going. Now I'm throwing overhand. My arm is fine and I have the feeling I know where the ball is going." At the same time, he found that his curveball improved considerably with this overhand motion. "Now I come over and down with the ball and I can get it down where the batter isn't so likely to hit it." This change in delivery did indeed appear to be the reason for his good showing that spring. In his first 10 innings of pitching duty, he allowed just one run and issued only three walks.[112]

Bass' outstanding spring did win him a spot on the team. He made his first major league pitching appearance on April 23, inducing the Indians' Jimmy Piersall to fly out to end the ninth inning in a 10–8 loss. Two days later, he got his first start, going all nine innings in a complete game 20–2 victory. He allowed just two earned runs, but he did walk nine batters, which was troublesome. He then threw three innings of scoreless relief on April 30, ending the month with a 1.46 earned-run average.

In spite of his good showings, there was still some doubt in the minds of manager Joe Gordon and general manager Frank Lane as to whether or not to keep him on the team or send him back to the minors. Three players needed to be cut in order to reduce the roster size, and the two felt they would rather keep outfielder Leo Posada than Bass. But then team owner Charles Finley intervened as he did in the case of Jim Archer and ordered Gordon and Lane to give Bass another start. While they chaffed at Finley's "interference," they did as instructed. Bass took the mound against the White Sox on May 12. While he went seven strong innings allowing just two runs, only one of them earned, he ended up losing, 2–1. He won three of his next four starting assignments, two of which were complete games.[113]

On June 3 he blanked the Washington Senators, the first shutout of the season for Kansas City. "Throughout spring training and the early stages of the season, Norm Bass was rigid with tension," wrote Joe McGuff of the *Kansas City Star* after that game. "He never smiled and seldom spoke. He conducted himself as if at any moment he expected to have a one-way ticket to Shreveport [the A's Double-A affiliate] shoved in his hand. As Bass established himself more firmly with the Athletics he began to relax and gain confidence. Today he unwound sufficiently to pitch the first shutout of the season." There was no more talk of the rookie being cut from the roster.[114]

His next three starts were not nearly as impressive, though. In fact he lost all of them, giving him a losing record and raising his earned-run average from 2.77 on June 3 to 3.56 after an 11-inning complete-game loss to the Angels on June 18. Clearly in a downward spiral, his June 22 outing against the Yankees was the worst of his young major league career.

The rookie hurler first faced the Yankees just 10 days earlier, going seven innings, but losing, 4–3. Maris and Mantle failed to get a hit off of him that day, but both scored after they were walked. His undoing came in the second inning when he gave up two earned runs while confronting eight New York batters. He settled down after that, yielding just two more runs over the next five innings. All in all, it was not a bad outing for someone battling the mighty Bomber lineup for the first time.

Perhaps he was not fully recovered from pitching an 11-inning game just four days earlier, because Bass got into trouble early on that June 22 evening. Clete Boyer opened the game with a single, followed by a Maris double after Tony Kubek struck out. But Bass was able to pull himself together, striking out Mantle and retiring Yogi Berra on a fly to leave both baserunners stranded. In the second he was not nearly that fortunate. After Moose Skowron flied out, Johnny Blanchard and Bobby Richardson singled and Whitey Ford walked to load the bases. Boyer then doubled to drive in two runs, leaving Ford on third and himself on second. When Bass got Kubek to ground to third for the second out of the inning, it looked like he might be able to close out that frame without further damage. But then Maris took his turn at bat.

The Yankee right fielder blistered a Bass fastball, sending it screaming over the right-field wall. Just as it had two days earlier, the ball crashed into the tall outer wall just short of the top. That marked the end of Bass' outing. After walking Mantle, he was lifted for former-Yankee hurler, Art Ditmar. Maris went on to hit another double and a single for another RBI, giving him four for the night and tying him with Norm Cash for the league-lead in runs batted in.[115]

After Bass had another poor start on June 27, he was sent to the bullpen to see if he could regain his earlier success. While he struggled at times, there were games when he pitched brilliantly. He threw well enough that the A's decided to give him another shot at starting. On August 4 he tossed a 5-0 shutout of the Boston Red Sox, thus confirming that he had gotten his act together. He continued to show progress so that by the end of the season he was 11–11 with a 4.69 ERA. It was the best won-loss record among the starting staff and, though his earned-run average was high, it was still among the lowest of all the Kansas City pitchers.

He was seen by many as a star of the future, a "bright ray in the Kaycee Clouds" as one sportswriter put it. His 11 victories "were quite an impressive total considering the fact that this was his first season in the majors and he was pitching for a club which had less run-producing power than any other in the league," remarked another observer. "Possibly Bass exceeded expectations more than anyone else on the roster, and there is good reason to believe that he will become one of the league's better pitchers in years to come." If there were any real concerns, it was his inconsistent control—he walked 82, struck out 74—and his overreliance on his fastball. In that August 4 shutout, he threw just one changeup and six curves; the rest were all fastballs. As everyone knew, a starting pitcher cannot rely on heat alone.[116]

The sophomore pitcher worked assiduously on developing an effective curve and changeup during spring training in 1962, but to little effect. He lost five of his first seven starts, again walking far more than he struck out. He won his first game on May 19 pitching in relief and his second two starts later, but that was his total for the season. By mid-July he was 2–6 with a 6.09 earned-run average, a very disappointing record that resulted in him being sent back to the minors for the rest of the summer. While he pitched decently enough in Portland, something was obviously wrong with him.[117]

The root cause of his difficulties was arm and shoulder pain. It got so bad that he had to be shut down at times. Even cortisone shots provided only temporary relief. He lost speed on his fastball and there were frequent occasions when his elbow would lock up on him. He attempted a comeback in 1963, but that fizzled. After appearing in just three games in April without a won-loss record but a horrendous 11.74 earned-run average, he returned to the minors. Over the next three summers he attempted to regain his form, but the pain was just too great. He made one last try in 1965, pitching and winning one game with the Double-A El Paso Sun Kings before he called it quits.

Unknown to him at the time, he was a victim of insipient rheumatoid arthritis. The doctor who diagnosed it told Bass that he was playing at only 60 percent efficiency for a long time due to his medical condition. "It about killed me," Bass said about the diagnosis. "Reading that doctor's report, it about killed me." The former A's pitcher, who played football in college, decided to try making it in professional football like his brother in spite of his physical problems. Oddly enough, he was selected by the Denver Broncos in 1964 as a starting safety, but lasted only four games before he had to give that up as well. A once-promising athletic career came to a sad end.[118]

After hitting four homers in four consecutive games and another on June 22, Maris was feeling confident about his chances of breaking his own record of 39 home runs established the year before. "It was one of my high spots of the season," he noted. "The pressure that was to come hadn't hit me yet. I was riding high, going good in all departments." That was not his assessment of how he felt then, but one made after the season was over. In reality, though, he was already feeling increased pressure to perform, it was just not yet at the height it became in August and September. First, there were those pesky comparisons with Ruth and the endless questions about whether he thought he could break the Babe's record or not. While he attempted to deflect those queries by saying it was too early to even think about that, in fact he was. When pressed further, he would say that no one would break the record.[119]

Most immediately in front of him, however, was the record for the most homers hit in a month set by Tigers rookie Rudy York. In August 1937 the infielder/catcher belted 18 round-trippers on his way to 35 for the season. With his home run on June 22, Maris' total for the month stood at 15, leaving him seven more games to catch or surpass York. Naturally, the press began asking him about his chances of beating that record as well.

The York accomplishment was clearly on his mind, with the result that he began to intentionally swing for the fences in an attempt to better York. "For the first time I was playing under the pressure of trying to attain something," he realized. "Each time I went to bat it was with the thought of that monthly record somewhere in my mind. That was bad. Once you start consciously trying for home runs, you've had it." And that was what happened. Maris failed to hit another one during those remaining seven games. "I know I was conscious of the record. I know that there was pressure on me, but I didn't realize until later how much I had let the effort bother me. I was trying too hard. In trying too hard I lost my normal swing and the home runs suddenly stopped. It had been so easy, but now it became so hard. It proved to be a good lesson to me."[120]

Interestingly, if one were to ignore the arbitrary measurement of "month" and instead look at the number of home runs hit in a 31-day period, Maris did indeed surpass the York record. From May 17 when his offensive barrage started through June 20, he exploded with an incredible 23 home runs, nearly two-thirds of his 36 hits in that stretch. To be fair to York, he played in only 30 games in August. Maris appeared in 36 from May 17 through June 20. But even if one were to give York six additional games before or after August, Maris still surpassed him. From July 19 through August 31, York hit 20 homers; from August 1 through September 6, 19.

And though his batting average was still a low .258, it began to climb steadily from that point on until it reached its height of .288 in mid–July. Even at that, Maris continued to come under scathing criticism. Many felt that batting below .300 made one an inferior hitter. They resented Maris, who never hit above .300 in his career, for his audacity in challenging the great Babe Ruth. The belief that batting average was the only measure of hitting excellence was so ingrained in most players' psyches that even Maris himself was conflicted about it. On some occasions he would make statements like "I'm more concerned with my batting average. That's the thing that figures to help the team more than anything else I can do." At other times he insisted he was "satisfied" because "you're most valuable to your team with the home runs and the RBI." It was only later in the season when he began to perceive the constant criticism of his batting average as a personal attack instead of just a comparison between ballplayers that he grew angry when questioned about it.[121]

What his critics refused to give him credit for was how many runs he drove in and how much better he hit when the game was on the line. There are "soft" .300 hitters, those who hit in situations when the bases were empty or regularly failed to do so with runners in scoring position or when there were runners on and two out. Maris' batting average actually increased in those situations. With bases empty, he batted .241 (316 at-bats). With runners on, it was .303 (274 at-bats). When it came to runners in scoring position (128 at-bats), he maintained a .328 batting average. And with runners on and two away, he hit .333 in 87 at-bats. Not too shabby for someone widely berated for being a mediocre hitter.[122]

Despite the fact that Maris' home run production hit a brief dry spell at the end of the month, as Tony Kubek said, "June belonged to Roger." Mickey Mantle, though, suddenly kicked into high gear. He blasted three more dingers those next seven games, raising his total to 25, just two behind his teammate. The home run race was definitely still on.[123]

Maris was not unproductive during that temporary lull in his home-run assault. He batted .273, hit three doubles, drove in six runs, scored another seven, and walked nine times while striking out on just three trips to the plate. He had hoped to do better since they were playing six of those contests with the Twins and Angels, both venues that were home-run friendly. But Maris was trying too hard to park a few, with the unsurprising result that he did not. In Minnesota, "I ran into bad luck. I hit a lot of balls well, but that one-eighth inch was no longer on my side. Every ball I hit solid was a line drive, not a long fly that might go over a fence." That did seem to be the case. In the first game he was 0–4, but two of those outs were on a fly ball and a line drive. In the second contest, he was 1–2 with two walks, a double to right, and a fly out to center and was also hit by a pitch. In the third and final game in the series, he was 1–3 with two walks, two ground-outs, and a double to right. Mantle did not hit a homer in any of those contests.[124]

The Yankees then flew to Los Angeles for a three game series. Wrigley Field (home to television's *Home Run Derby*) should have been ideal for a long-ball hitter like Maris, but it was not. "The park has nice friendly fences, but they didn't help me. I was still trying too hard, still pressing too much." Mantle, however, certainly took advantage of the setting, hitting a solo shot in the first game and a two-run blast with Maris aboard in the ninth inning of the final contest. Maris had two lonely singles in ten at-bats in those three games.[125]

Because they dropped two out of three against the last-place Angels, the Bombers failed to gain ground on the Tigers. "When you lose to a tailender that's playing his worst, it pains. And when you lose two in a row to the same tailender, it's like losing a leg," grumbled Ralph Houk. But the long road trip was not a total disaster by any means. Perhaps they should have won more, but taking nine of the contests was not bad for 16 grueling days on the road without a break.[126]

Just before heading out on the trip out west, Maris and Bob Cerv rented an apartment in Queens to give them some privacy from the hoards that seemed to be everywhere. It was especially important to Maris that he have a refuge away from the crowds. Mantle soon joined them. It is quite likely that had Maris not made "the smartest move I made all summer," the lack of a quiet place that he could use as a retreat in order to recharge his batteries would have negatively impacted his performance that summer. It clearly was beneficial to Mantle as well. "Now we were able to relax completely away from the park," Maris said. "It was great to be able to come 'home' after a ball game and just sit around…. There were many times late in August, and before, that I thanked my lucky stars that we had made the move."[127]

Long-ball fever was in full swing by the time the Yankees returned to New York on June 30. While others were also belting homers at a record pace, by July Maris and Mantle had become *the* poster boys for home-run-hitting prowess. Baseball's bible, *The Sporting News*, gave them its official *imprimatur* on the front page of the June 28 issue with a large drawing entitled "Dial Double M for Murder and Mayhem." It depicted the two Yankee sluggers belting home runs while the spectral images of Babe Ruth and Lou Gehrig look on, a downcast Ruth saying, "Hey, Lou, these kids might make us look like pikers."[128]

It seemed like everyone wanted to see Mantle and Maris hammer the ball, even if it meant a loss for the local favorites. Cleveland drew over 70,000 fans for their three-game series. In Detroit it was nearly 148,000. Kansas City saw crowds of over 73,000 attend the four games there. Over 100,000 fans passed through the Twins' turnstiles for those three battles. And tiny Wrigley Field in Los Angeles witnessed nearly 50,000 Angelinos come to those three night contests. "The M and M thing began to get to me," Ralph Houk confessed. It was beginning to get to Roger Maris as well.[129]

5

JULY

Home Run # 28—Game 74—July 1—Day Game

The Yankees jetted home after the final game with the Angels, landing that evening after an exhausting road trip. They were scheduled to play the Senators the following afternoon, which should have been pretty much of a cakewalk, but their fortunes thus far against the lowly Nats gave one pause for concern: in the four games played to date, the Bombers lost three of them. With Maris "cooled off" a bit, manager Ralph Houk was hoping the return to Yankee Stadium would "restore Roger Maris to slugging vigor." And, in fact, it did.[1]

Whitey Ford was going for his fourteenth win when he opened that first of three contests against the Senators on the afternoon of June 30. At first it appeared that the Yankees might be headed for another loss to Washington after Ford allowed an unearned run to score in the first inning and his opponent, Dick Donovan, held the Bombers scoreless for the first five. Then the twin killing machine kicked into action.

With Bobby Richardson on second in the sixth, Maris hit a ground-rule-double that plated the first Yankee run. That was followed by a mammoth blast from Mantle "that sailed and sailed and sailed" before striking the top of the center-field wall some 460 feet distant. The ball struck with such force that it bounced back over the head of center fielder Willie Tasby. As it rolled toward the infield, Mantle crossed home plate with Maris in front of him before any of the Washington outfielders were able to run it down. It was the Mick's twenty-fifth homer of the season, leaving him just two behind his partner in crime. Maris added the icing to Ford's victory cake when he plated another two runs in the eighth inning with a single that scored Richardson and Tony Kubek from third and second respectively. Ford's win was his eighth straight in June, tying him with Rube Marquard for the most wins by a left-hander in that month.[2]

If the Yankee manager had any concerns that Maris was in a prolonged homer drought, those fears were laid to rest during the first five games in July when the right fielder added five home runs to his total, putting him more than halfway along the road to conquering the Babe. Not to be outdone, Mantle produced three of his own to keep him within striking distance of his teammate.

Bill Stafford opened the first game of July. His opponent was little-known and little-used southpaw Carl Mathias. Neither made it past the third inning. Stafford was the first to get into trouble. In the second inning he surrendered a three-run inside-the-park homer to left fielder Marty Keough. Mickey Mantle got one of those runs back with a 450-foot jack into the left-field seats to open the bottom of the second. In the third,

Stafford added to his miseries by surrendering a two-run dinger to catcher Gene Green, this one clearing the right-field wall, putting the Senators up, 5–1. Then in the bottom of that inning, Mantle smacked his second homer of the day, this time with Bobby Richardson and Maris aboard after they had singled. Both starters were gone when the fourth inning opened.

Relievers Rollie Sheldon for the Yankees and Joe McClain for Washington battled neck-and-neck over the next four innings. McClain was the first to crack. After walking Mantle with two out in the seventh, the Senators' rookie right-hander gave up a single to Elston Howard. That safety scored Mantle, who had stolen second in spite of a pitchout, to tie the game at five. But that did not last long. Jim Coates relieved Sheldon to open the ninth and promptly grooved a pitch to first baseman Dale Long, who proceeded to park it in the right field stands. With Washington ahead by one, veteran relief-specialist Dave Sisler was called upon to seal the deal.

The bespectacled right-hander seemed destined to play baseball from the moment of his birth. Son of Hall-of-Fame first baseman George Sisler and kid brother to outfielder/first baseman Dick Sisler, the younger Sisler grew up immersed in the world of America's Pastime. He played baseball throughout his growing years and, by the time he entered Princeton University (where he graduated magna cum laude with a degree in engineering), the 6-foot-4, 200-pound athlete was engaged in both baseball and basketball.

He signed his first professional contract with the Boston Red Sox in the spring of 1953 while he was finishing up his college work. Upon graduation, he was sent to the club's Single-A affiliate in Albany, New York. He appeared in 21 games for the Senators, compiling a very handsome record of 12 wins against 7 losses with a 2.60 earned-run average. The future Red Sox hurler then spent the next two years in military service. Sisler developed his craft while stationed at Fort Meade in Maryland. He reportedly went 13–2 while hurling for the base team. One of his opponents from a rival Army team said of Sisler, "He has a great curve ball, good fast ball and very good control."[3]

In the spring of 1955, he was granted leave to pitch for the Red Sox against the New York Giants in a charity game on May 23 at Fenway Park to raise money for hospitalized veterans. His performance that night was so good he even "dazzled" Giants manager Leo Durocher, who referred to Sisler as "a great prospect." Red Sox skipper Pinky Higgins was particularly taken by Sisler's mound presence. "There were 34,000 people in the ball park that night, and they didn't bother him a bit. He was like an icicle out there."[4]

As the young right-hander was awaiting his official discharge from the Army in early 1956, he was sent to the Red Sox's rookie pitching school in Sarasota, Florida. After three weeks there, Higgins was sufficiently impressed with "Sisler's poise, pretty good curve, and mound savvy" that he extended him an invitation to try out for the big club. His excellent performance over those next few weeks, aided by the fact that baseball rules at the time allowed him to remain as an extra player on the roster all season long because he was a recently discharged veteran, convinced Higgins to bring him to Boston as a reliever.[5]

Sisler's baptism under fire occurred on the afternoon of April 21 when he was sent in as relief in the sixth inning with the Sox down 8–3 against the Yankees. While he did give up an unearned run and struck Andy Carey with a pitch, he contained the powerful Yankee lineup without further damage. Then on April 28, he faced the Yankees for the second time that season. He entered the game in the seventh inning with one on and the game tied at two. He allowed one run that inning and another on a Mickey Mantle triple in the eighth, but his teammates backed him up with four runs of their own. When Sisler retired the side in the top of the ninth—including striking out Hank Bauer on three fastballs—he had secured his first major league victory.

After the game, Higgins sang Sisler's praises. "He doesn't choke under the gun," he said. "He proved that. Did you see those three pitches he threw Hank Bauer? He just fired them past Hank." The manager also indicated that his young charge was gradually working his way into the starting rotation. "But Dave won't always be a reliever. He has the ability to be a starter. He's young and strong and he's learning all the time." Red Sox pitching coach Dave Ferriss called Sisler "a real take-charge guy. Why, he's even better when there are men on bases. He hides the ball good and his speed fools you. Actually he's much faster than he looks. Got a good fast ball which does a lot of things…. He hasn't got a big curve. It's more a quick curve. But we're working on the curve, and it's coming along great." The rookie added a changeup to his pitch selection as the summer wore on.[6]

Sisler continued to pitch well in relief and was happy to do so even though it was new to him. "I rather like it," he admitted. "When I joined this club and saw the pitching staff, I feared that I would be a bench warmer, but relief pitching has enabled me to see plenty of action." One thing he knew he had to do as a starter was to pace himself better. "I just get in there and fire with everything I've got." Oddly, when asked the secret to his success, he pointed to his glasses. He acquired new, form-fitting ones on the recommendation of former Red Sox player and current San Francisco Seals manager Eddie Joost. "I feel comfortable and I know it has helped me," Sisler proclaimed.[7]

He finally got a chance to start, opening on the road against the Kansas City Athletics on the afternoon of June 24 with the temperature hovering near 100 degrees. It was a rocky, but not disastrous, outing, hampered in part by the heat and the fact that he had not started a game in months. He gave up five earned runs over seven innings, but in spite of a 5–2 loss, the manager was happy with his performance. "But Sisler showed me something," Higgins said after the game. "He came off two relief jobs that were long and rough. Still, beyond that bad first inning against the A's he had a well-pitched game."[8]

Sisler made 13 more starts in his next 19 game appearances. He had three complete-game victories to end his rookie season at 9–8 with a 4.62 ERA. His final outing of the summer was a 10-inning, complete-game, 7–4, victory over the Yankees on September 30. He walked only one batter while striking out seven. As a result of his performance that summer, Sisler was named to *The Sporting News*' "Rookie All-Star Team" and Boston-area sportswriters selected him as their "Rookie of the Year."[9]

Sisler's sophomore season in 1957 began with a bang. His first two starts were against the Yankees, hurling complete-game victories on both occasions while running his record to 4–0 against the Bombers. Some commentators noted that he seemed to perform best under pressure. "Put him on the mound with runners on first and second, none out, and a Berra, Mantle or Bauer menacing at the plate, and he displays courage, determination, craftiness and guile," declared one sportswriter. Sisler believed it was his "developing confidence in certain pitches and knowing when you can get them over when you need them" that was the basis of his ability to perform in those situations. More than anything, it was this tenacity that impressed many who observed him. As Red Sox coach Mickey Owen once humorously said of him, "He looks like a scholar from M.I.T. but plays like a footballer from Notre Dame."[10]

The 25-year-old right-hander beat the Yankees again on July 4 to make it five consecutive wins over them, but then developed back and arm problems that saw him miss several starts and limited his effectiveness on the mound. He was out of the lineup for most of July and all of August and when he returned he was never quite able to get back on track. He was 0–4—including back-to-back losses to the Yankees in his last two starts—with a 7.27 ERA during that period. He ended the season with a disappointing seven wins, eight losses and a 4.71 earned-run average in 19 game starts and three relief appearances.[11]

The 1958 season began in excellent fashion, but then deteriorated after mid–June. In his first 12 games, Sisler was 6–2 with four complete games and a 3.95 earned-run average. From that point on, though, he did not complete another game, going 2–7 with a 5.78 ERA in 18 outings. He ended the year winning eight and losing nine on a 4.94 earned-run average, pretty much a repeat of the season before. No one seemed to be able to account for his "mysterious failures." Perhaps Sisler summed it up best when he told one interviewer, "I was just a 50–50 pitcher. I had some good games and some bad games."[12]

Sisler started the 1959 season in the Boston bullpen, but it was clear by now that the Red Sox were shopping him around. The front office announced in early May that he was traded to Detroit for southpaw Billy Hoeft. One reason the Tigers went with Sisler even though he was prone to periodic arm troubles was that he generally pitched outstanding ball when facing the Yankees. They felt by adding him to a staff that included Frank Lary and Jim Bunning, two other pitchers with winning records against New York, they now had a "Yankee-Tormenting Trio" that might finally help them overcome the perennial league champions.[13]

And Sisler did live up to his billing as far as the Yankees were concerned. Limited strictly to relief appearances for the Tigers, the right-hander entered four games against the Bombers without giving up a run. He pitched effectively most of the other times as well. His record that season was one win, three defeats, seven saves, three blown saves, four holds, and a 4.01 earned-run average. He did even better in 1960. In fact, it was his best performance since his rookie year. He appeared in 41 games, nearly half of them as the closer, winning seven, losing five, and saving five others. His ERA was an astounding 2.48, lowest of his career and first among all the Tiger pitchers.

Clearly the righty had proven that he had the ability and drive to pitch with the best of them. His 1960 performance ranked him as one of the elite relievers in the American League. By all accounts he was to be an essential part of the Tigers' plans for the future. For some inexplicable reason, though, the Detroit front office left him exposed to the American League expansion draft. He, along with teammate Pete Burnside, were the only pitchers in the available talent pool who won as many as seven games in 1960, so they were prime targets for selection. To no one's surprise, both he and Burnside were snapped up by the new Senators, the second and fourth pitchers respectively selected by Washington.[14]

The Senators were quite pleased with their acquisition of Sisler and he seemed happy—but perhaps a little surprised—to be with them. Manager Mickey Vernon "rate[d] him now as the absolute best [reliever] in the American League. He'd have been one of the good relief pitchers in any era." Vernon noted that the 29-year-old was outstanding "in tight, late-inning situations with the opposition on base. It is then that [he] shows his hard low one, the sinker-ball pitch that has been inviting the double-play grounders."

Sisler quickly proved his worth to his new team. In his first 25 game appearances through the end of June, he was 1–2 with nine saves on a 2.48 earned-run average. "I like being a relief pitcher," he admitted. "It best suits my type. I'm not suited for nine innings of pitching."[15]

Sisler continued his good work against the Yankees. He faced them in both ends of a doubleheader on April 30 without surrendering a run. He confronted them for the third time on May 16, hurling 2⅓ innings of scoreless relief to earn his fifth save of the season. So he seemed primed and ready for another good outing against the Bombers on July 1, hoping to chalk up his tenth save when he opened the ninth inning with a one-run lead.

Roger Maris had other plans for that inning, however. It was not that the Yankee slugger had a particularly good record batting against Sisler and was feeling confident because of that. In fact, he had never homered off of him in 20 trips to the plate going back to 1957 and had grounded out twice in two earlier appearances that season. But as Maris himself acknowledged, when he was in the zone he could handle anybody. Although he had not hit a home run since June 22, he had two clean knocks the first game home from the long road trip. It convinced him that he was "getting back into my stride" after pulling both to right field. All that was lacking, he thought to himself, was that "eighth inch" difference between a line drive and a four-bagger. So as he kneeled in the on-deck circle awaiting his turn to bat, he knew his home-run stroke was back.[16]

Tony Kubek opened the frame with a single to right on the very first pitch Sisler threw him. Maris did not waste any time, either. He came to the plate "hoping to get a single that could push Tony around to third with the tying run. If I could do that, then our chances for at least a tie would be good." Instead, Sisler's first pitch to him "came wrapped for delivery to some kid in the right-field stands. It was right down my alley." The ball flew into the right-field seats just a little to the left of the foul pole 296 feet away, giving the Yankees a 6–5 walk-off victory and Maris number 28. The game-winning clout moved him back into the home-run lead after Mantle's two earlier in the game had tied it up temporarily.[17]

Maris commented later that "Dave had made a mistake because it was a hitter's pitch. I don't think he expected me to sacrifice. If I had, then Mickey would have been walked and therefore there was no point in my sacrificing. Mistake or not, it was a pitch I would love to see more often…. Those are the homers that really give you a glow." Undoubtedly his "glow" increased when he learned that same day that he and Mantle were both elected to the American League All-Star team, with the first game slated for San Francisco on July 11 and the second in Boston on July 31.[18]

The loss of that game marked a decided downturn in Sisler's pitching and the beginning of the end to his time with the Senators. From that day on, he won only one game while losing five others. In addition, he saved just two more games while failing to preserve another two. He ended the summer at 2–8 with eleven saves, six blown saves, and a 4.18 earned-run average. In mid–September Sisler became "the player to be named later" in a deal that sent him and $75,000 in cash to Cincinnati in exchange for pitcher Claude Osteen.

"Despite our thinness in pitching, it was my belief that we could afford to unload Sisler," commented Washington general manager Ed Doherty upon announcing the deal. "He was not helping us, which is the best index I know for selling a player." Adding his two cents' worth, D.C.-based sportswriter Shirley Povich declared Sisler to be "perhaps the biggest disappointment of the Senators last season after a brilliant start as a relief pitcher." Of course, as Senators manager Mickey Vernon noted, although Sisler's pitching deteriorated in the second half of the season, it was a team effort that led to the loss of 100 games and a tie for last place with the other expansion franchise.[19]

Reds general manager Bill DeWitt, who was GM for the Tigers when Sisler pitched for them, was delighted with the trade. He believed that the acquisition of the 30-year-old right-hander, along with that of two other pitchers, put the pitching staff "on a near even par with that of last year" which led the Reds to the 1961 National League championship. Sisler was happy with the move as well. He knew and liked DeWitt and Dick Sisler, his brother, was a coach for the Reds. And his career was indeed rejuvenated pitching for a club that ended up winning 98 games. He made 35 relief appearances, winning four, losing three, and saving another while maintaining a 3.92 earned-run average.[20]

Therefore it must have come as somewhat of a surprise to him when he was told early in 1963 that he was to be cut from the big club's roster and sent down to the minor leagues. The problem was that he was a 31-year-old reliever who was competing with nearly a dozen others, many younger than him, for a handful of open slots on the Reds' pitching staff. He spent 1963 with the San Diego Padres in the Pacific Coast League attempting to make it back to the big club, but by the end of the season he realized that was not going to happen and decided to retire. While he may not have lived up to the expectations some had of him, he had nothing of which to be ashamed. In seven major league seasons, he won 38, lost 44, and saved 28 on a cumulative 4.33 ERA, toiling away for clubs that never finished above third place, three of which had losing records.

Home Runs # 29 and 30—Game 75—July 2—Day Game

Maris was one of those streaky power hitters who clumped home runs in bunches. He would hit four or five in that same number of games, then cool off for a bit before going on another rampage. That was certainly the case in early July. He hit one on July 1 after a week of not doing so, and was about to launch another cluster of dingers starting with the July 2 afternoon game against the hapless Senators.

Washington came into the contest having lost not only the first two to the Yankees, but 13 of their last 16 games going back to June 16, so the outcome of that day's affair came as no surprise to anyone. Starting pitcher for the Senators was Pete Burnside who, after his first 13 appearances that season, was sporting a 1–4 record with an inferior 5.73 earned-run average. Interestingly, though, he surrendered only four round-trippers in those games, including number four to Maris on May 17. The southpaw's underlying problem was one of control and hits allowed. Thus he was a prime target for a big bopper like Maris.

Burnside looked like he was having one of his better days when he started the game. He retired the side in order in the first inning, which ended with Maris popping out to short. In the second he made the mistake of walking Mickey Mantle in front of Elston Howard, who promptly parked one into the left-field seats. His opponent, Bud Daley, however, gave up a couple of runs as well, so the game was tied at two when Burnside's day collapsed in ruin during the third inning.

When a pitcher opens a frame by walking his mound opponent, the outcome cannot be anything but bad. After Daley got that initial free pass and Bobby Richardson popped out, Burnside then proceeded to walk Tony Kubek, putting two runners on for Maris. The Yankee slugger, realizing that Burnside was struggling with his control, knew the pitcher would not want to load the bases with another walk, thus setting up a potential grand slam by Mantle. "By now Pete was trying to aim the ball as he tried to get it over the plate," Maris noted. "He aimed one too well [probably one of his fastballs], and it became number twenty-nine." It was "a towering poke that glanced off the screen affixed to the right-field foul pole." Burnside was removed after he walked Mantle. Right-hander Johnny Klippstein was his replacement. The reliever first walked Howard before striking out Moose Skowron and Bob Cerv to end the inning. Maris' blast put the Yankees ahead to stay.[21]

Klippstein, a 6-foot-1 right-hander, first started playing professional ball as a 16-year-old minor leaguer in 1944. His initial assignment was to the Class B Allentown Cardinals where he pitched six games before being sent to the Class D Lima Red Birds for another seven outings. He remained a member of the Cardinals organization for four seasons (with 1946 spent in the military), a period he found distressing because he kept being moved up and down the minor league ladder. "I was getting discouraged because I felt like I was failing," he said years later. "Every time I would move a step, it seemed like I would go a step back. I didn't think about quitting because I was still very young. But the Cardinals didn't have me in their plans."[22]

Clearly they did not because St. Louis allowed him to be drafted by the Brooklyn Dodgers at the end of 1948. The Bums sent him to their Double-A Mobile affiliate where he went 15–8 with a 2.95 earned-run average in 33 game starts. It was there that he got somewhat of a reputation as a troublemaker because he dared asked for a salary increase in the middle of the season. He received a three-day suspension for his efforts. The Dodgers intended to promote him to Montreal the following season, but the Chicago Cubs intervened and acquired him in late 1949 under the rule 5 draft regulations. It was with the Cubs that he made his major league debut in 1950.[23]

The 22-year-old wowed Cubs manager Frankie Frisch during spring training with his fastball. "Brother, that boy can throw," exclaimed "The Fordham Flash." "He's just the fastest fellow we have in camp right now. Some of the [St. Louis] Browns admitted he was throwing the ball right past them." Although he knew Klippstein was still "just a baby" who "needs more experience," he planned to start him once the regular season began. "I don't care if he gets his ears knocked off. I'll start him 30 or 40 times. The way he can fire the ball he'll win eventually." On a more realistic note, pitching coach Spud Davis was concerned about his young charge's problems with control. Apparently, Klippstein looked at the ground instead of the plate when going into his windup, which Davis thought to be the basic flaw in his delivery. They worked on that and on occasion there were good results. In one practice session, the pitcher threw a dozen or so fastballs and an equal number of curves in the strike zone. A pleased Davis proclaimed, "Now if we can help him develop a good change-up pitch, we'll have something."[24]

The promise, however, did not prove to be the fact. The rookie was roughed up early on and never really recovered. He made 33 game appearances in 1950, but only a third of those were starts, many of them very short outings. He managed three complete games, but ended the year at 2–9 with an ugly 5.25 earned-run average. The fact that he gave up 64 free passes against 51 strikeouts was a strong indication that control was still a big issue with him, as it would be throughout most of his career.

Known as "The Wild Man of Borneo" because of his lack of control, Klippstein remained with the Cubs for five seasons never once having a winning record. His cumulative totals for Chicago were 31 wins and 51 losses with a 4.79 ERA in 193 games, a little less than half of which were starts. He also walked more than he struck out. He was very much a work-in-progress during those years.

Part of the problem during his time with the Cubs, Klippstein believed, was that various managers insisted he throw more fastballs than his other pitches. "We played all day games and it would get shadowy in the sixth or seventh inning and they figured it would be hard for batters to pick up fastballs," he explained. "The result is that I never got confidence in my curveball because I wasn't throwing it when I needed a strike. At 3 and 1, there was no way I'd throw a curveball. My curve wasn't bad and I wish I could have thrown it more because I could have been a better pitcher." Cubs pitching coach Charlie Root determined that Klippstein's problems stemmed from him continuing to look down at the ground when in his pitching motion and the fact that he "was pitching out in the open far away from his body. The batter could follow the ball too easily." He worked with the young pitcher in addressing those issues, which helped somewhat.[25]

When Klippstein ended the 1954 campaign with a 4–11 record on a 5.29 ERA, the Cubs decided it was time to let him go. On October 1, he was part of a five-player swap that sent him to Cincinnati. "I hated to give him up because he's young and I still think he'll be a good pitcher," said Wid Matthews, the Cubs director of player personnel, "but I feel we made a good deal [for outfielders]." The Reds also thought they had made a good trade. "Birdie [Tebbetts, Reds manager] thinks Klippstein can become a capable pitcher and that's why we took him, despite his poor record with the Cubs the last three seasons," said Gabe Paul, Cincinnati general manager.[26]

And the change of scenery did in fact improve Klippstein's fortunes. In his first season with the Reds, he had a losing record, but an excellent 3.39 earned-run average in 39 game appearances. Then in 1956 he experienced his first winning season in the majors with 12 victories and 11 losses on a 4.09 ERA in 211 innings pitched, mostly as a starter.

He attributed his new found success to the development of a slider to use along with his fastball and curve. One advantage the new pitch had over the curve was that he could throw it consistently for a strike. "It gives me the breaking ball I've needed," he asserted, "and you don't have the same wear and tear on your arm that you get when you throw a curve." His delivery of the pitch was three-quarters rather than overhand. "That way the ball breaks on the same plane instead of down and away. It's mistaken frequently for a fast ball when coming plateward."[27]

He was still wild, though, walking 82 while striking out 86 and led the American League in hit batsmen with 10. In addition, he was in the top 10 among American League pitchers in earned runs, hits allowed, and home runs, which was unusual for him. His inconsistent performances were confounding to the pitcher and management alike. GM Paul thought his ups-and-downs were because he was "trying to experiment with trick stuff." He told his pitcher, "We've watched you closely and noted that if you are getting some fellow out with your fast ball, you switch away from that and try to trick him with curves or soft stuff, only to get belted plenty. And when your curve is getting them out, you try to switch to fast balls and generally get slammed."[28]

The 1957 season was not nearly as productive as the previous two. His won-loss record fell to 8–11 and his earned-run average swelled to 5.05, nearly a run higher than in 1956. He was used mainly as a reliever with only 18 starts in his 46 appearances. Manager Birdie Tebbetts expressed disappointment in Klippstein's development, so it was just a matter of time before he was traded away. That occurred mid-way through the 1958 season. On June 15 he and three other players were sent to the Los Angeles Dodgers for Don Newcombe.

The Reds used him mainly from the bullpen in 1957 and 1958. The Dodgers planned to continue that practice when he arrived there. Klippstein was pleased with the move. "I credit Tebbetts for being the one to move me to the bullpen for a purpose, not as a demotion," he said. "I had already considered that I might be able to prolong my career as a reliever." And that was exactly what Dodgers manager Walt Alston did. Klippstein appeared in 45 games from June 17 until the end of the season without a single start and it agreed with him. He went 3–5 with nine saves and a much improved 3.80 earned-run average in those outings.[29]

"I learned I could pitch quite often," he acknowledged years after his retirement. "That was the biggest break I could have had because I'd stick around for another nine years as a reliever. I walked too many batters to be a successful starter. As a reliever, I worked more often and gained better control—I got more confidence in my breaking pitches and batters couldn't always expect the fastball when I needed a strike." He did walk 44 batters, but he also struck out 73 for a much better walk-hit ratio.[30]

It looked like the right-handed reliever was headed for another good season in 1959 when he suddenly developed back problems a third of the way through the summer, which limited his appearances and decreased his effectiveness when he did pitch. He appeared in 17 games in April and May, producing a 4–0 record with one save on a 4.60 earned-run average. Shortly thereafter, he began having muscle spasms in his back and was fitted with a corset while taking shots to relieve the pain, but that did not do much to help him overcome his difficulties. He was able to pitch in just 11 more games the last three months of the season, which saw his ERA explode to 8.79. He appeared in the first game of the 1959 World Series, however. With the Dodgers being blown out by the Chicago White Sox, 11–0, he entered the game in the seventh, allowing just a meaningless hit over two innings of work. Although he was still suffering from back pain, "it was a real thrill to play in the Series.... It was enjoyable." That, though, marked the end of his tenure with Los Angeles.[31]

The Dodgers decided that they had no further need for a 32-year-old reliever with back problems and on April 11, 1960, sold him to the Cleveland Indians for $25,000. Although he was in a new league with a whole new set of batters he had never faced before, Klippstein had one of the best seasons of his career. He appeared in 49 games solely as a reliever, most often in the role of closer. He won five, lost five, and led the American League in saves with 14. Perhaps most remarkable of all, his earned-run average dropped below 3.00 (2.91) for the first time in his career. "I had one of my best years," he recalled. He was no longer bothered by his back, but in the last month of the season he suffered some arm problems. "I got a lot of work. When Jimmy Dykes became manager [after both Joe Gordon and Jo-Jo White were terminated], I pitched several games in a brief period and my arm went dead. Jimmy asked me if I could pitch if he needed me. I told him honestly that I couldn't—the only time in my career when I refused to take the ball."[32]

One of his biggest thrills that summer was getting the chance to face Ted Williams four times before the Splinter's retirement. The first two times he was able to get Williams out to end the games, but on the third occasion Williams parked one. On August 10 in the top of the ninth inning with one on and two gone, "I made up my mind to throw him all breaking balls and change-ups, except for a first-pitch fastball for a strike. He hit the first pitch out of the ballpark. Sometimes the hitter is a helluva lot smarter than the pitcher."[33]

In spite of his outstanding season with the Indians, they left him exposed to the expansion draft and he was the third pitcher selected by the Washington Senators. Ed Doherty, the Nats' general manager, was expecting a lot out of his corps of relievers. "We didn't get a lot of solid starting pitchers from the other clubs in the player pool," he acknowledged, "and that was to be expected." But he was not upset by the lack of starting depth. "If we are a little short on starters, we are fortunate to have good relievers around." Noting that "no club has too many relief men," Doherty added, "[Dave] Sisler, Klippstein and [Pete] Burnside would be strong relief men on any club. Allowing for any disappointment in our starters, we will have men in the bull pen to take up a lot of slack."[34]

And relieve, Klippstein did. He appeared in 42 games, over half as the closer, ending the season with a respectable 2–2 record but an awful 6.78 earned-run average. Control was again a problem: he walked 43 while striking out 41 and uncorked 10 wild pitches to lead the American League in that unwanted category. He was also eminently hittable, allowing 83 safeties in 71⅔ innings pitched. He admitted later, "I had a terrible year, which I didn't like in front of all the people I grew up with [in Silver Spring, Maryland]. I didn't know what was wrong. It got so bad that I went up to the manager, Mickey Vernon, in the middle of the year, prior to the trading deadline, to get his assurance that I could bring my family to Washington from Chicago. He said okay."[35]

Interestingly, though, when Klippstein appeared in that July 2 game, he had given up only four home runs in his previous 17 outings. After entering in relief of Pete Burnside to successfully close out the third inning, he pitched the next four without allowing a run. But then with one gone in the bottom of the seventh, Maris strode to the plate to start a home run barrage.

The Yankee slugger faced his opponent five times previously in 1960, striking out twice, grounding out twice, and hitting a single the fifth time. This day, though, he had Klippstein's number. In the fifth inning, Maris hit an infield single, but the righty was able to close out that frame without a run scoring. As Maris recalled, "I knew I was back in one of my streaks" when he entered the batter's box in the seventh. "It didn't make much difference who was pitching. My swing was in the groove, my timing was on the beam, and the eighth inch was back on my side. I hit number thirty to account for my fourth RBI [and second homer] of the day." He did not just "hit" it, he plastered it. The ball was a rocket that struck the base of the upper deck in right field.[36]

That knock demoralized Klippstein. He allowed three more runs before the inning was done. Then in the eighth gave up an even bigger blast to Mantle, who parked the ball halfway up into the top deck seats in right with one aboard. Moose Skowron jacked the third homer off of the beleaguered pitcher that afternoon, this one into the left-field seats. By the time it was over, the Bombers had destroyed "the shell-shocked Senators," 13–4, leaving them one game behind Detroit, who lost to the Orioles. In the home-run race, Maris had 30, Mantle 28.[37]

At the end of the season, the roaming pitcher got his walking papers once again, returning to the National League. The Reds got him back in mid–December as part of a four-player trade with the Senators. He appeared in 40 games for them, seven of them starts, and closed 16 others. He was still walking about as many as he struck out and gave up a hit plus per inning pitched, but ended with a 7–6 record and a much-improved 4.47 earned-run average, more than two runs better than the season before.

His most memorable game occurred on August 6 against the Houston Colt .45's when he relieved in the eleventh inning with no score on either side. He held Houston scoreless in the next two innings, then in the top of the thirteenth with two out and nobody on, he smacked his first and only home run of the year, putting the Reds up a run. In the bottom of the inning, he prevented Houston from scoring, becoming just the third pitcher in major league history to win 1–0 by hitting a home run in extra innings. The 34-year-old hurler said after the game, "that trip around the bases seemed like two miles. I felt so tired I could hardly lift my legs."[38]

Klippstein's stay in Cincinnati was a brief one. On March 25, 1963, he was purchased by the Philadelphia Phillies. Manager Gene Mauch was quite pleased by the acquisition. "He can still throw hard and we think he can help us," he said. And, in fact, he did. He made 48 relief appearances, closing 23 of those for eight saves. He ended the season with a 5–6 record and his minuscule 1.93 earned-run average was the best of his career. By this point, the right-hander was relying much less on his fastball and much more on breaking stuff. "I threw more change-ups, curves, and sliders. I still had a good fastball," he insisted, "but didn't throw it as much. I was better because I could mix up my pitches."[39]

Klippstein was still with the Phillies at the beginning of the 1964 season, but was used sparingly, appearing in only 11 games as a reliever. He continued to perform well, though, going 2–1 with a save in those few outings. But at the end of June he was sold to the Minnesota Twins. Although he failed to win a game and lost four, he did maintain an outstanding 1.94 earned-run average in the 46⅓ innings he worked for them.

In 1965 Klippstein, at the age of 37, had his best season ever. He won nine games while losing three in 56 relief appearances, 24 of which he closed, all the while maintaining a 2.24 ERA. The main reason for his success was a new pitch which he learned from Twins pitching coach Johnny Sain. Klippstein described it as "throwing a curve like a fast ball with a side spin. I had never seen it before. It has worked very well for me. It helps me set up my fast ball." It also improved his control. He struck out nearly twice as many batters as he walked. He made two appearances in the 1965 World Series against the Dodgers, pitching a scoreless ninth inning in Game 3 and two more shutout innings in the deciding Game 7, a 2–0 Minnesota loss.[40]

He again played for the Twins in 1966, but by now he was showing the signs of age. Used in only 26 games, 16 as the closer, he ended the summer with a 1–1 record, three saves, and a 3.40 earned-run average. Minnesota released him at the end of the season. In spite of being 39 years old, he made one last attempt to remain in the majors. The Detroit Tigers signed him as a free agent in the spring of 1967, but he appeared in just five games before he was dropped by them in early June.

Johnny Klippstein, "the poor man's Marco Polo," had quite an amazing career that stretched over 18 seasons with eight different teams. He ended with 101 wins, 118 losses, and 65 saves on a 4.24 ERA in 711 games. Reflecting on his career, the pitcher whose fastball was once referred to as "electric," expressed disappointment that he had not had a better winning record. "I don't know the answers," he said when asked what he believed was the problem. "I think I fooled around with too many offbeat pitches, the knuckler and scroogie and slider, when I should have known the fast ball was my bread-and-butter. I must have walked 800 guys [in actuality, 978] and 500 of them scored."[41]

Home Run # 31—Game 77—July 4—Day Game/ Second Game of Doubleheader

After a day off, the Yankees had an important Fourth of July doubleheader with the visiting Detroit Tigers. Both teams knew the stakes were high. If New York could take both halves, they would be in first place; if they lost both, they would be three games back. To add to the tension, Yankee manager Ralph Houk and Detroit's skipper Bob Scheffing engaged in some psychological gamesmanship before the games, naming who their starters were—Whitey Ford and Bob Turley for the Yanks, Don Mossi and Frank Lary for the Tigers—but refusing to announce who would start which game. "I'm not saying," commented Houk, "whether I intend to pitch Ford in the first or second game. I don't see any reason why I should give away anything." When Houk was told Scheffing would match Mossi with Ford regardless of which game it was, Houk retorted, "Well, he can just bring them both to the ball park and let them wait until I hand my lineup to the plate umpire just before the start of the first game. Then he can find out our rotation."[42]

Nearly 75,000 fans—the largest crowd since 1947—crammed into Yankee Stadium to see the epic battle between the two league leaders. As it turned out, Ford did start the first game and, as the Tiger manager had promised, Mossi faced off against him. The Yankee southpaw was going for his fifteenth victory, Detroit's counterpart for his tenth.

It turned out to be somewhat anticlimactic. Ford was on his game while Mossi was done in by errors that appeared to unnerve him. The Tigers struck first with a solo home run off of Ford in the top of the sixth inning. But then two Detroit errors and a series of timely hits in the bottom of that frame led to six Yankee runs and the Tiger starter being lifted before the inning was over. Although Maris did not homer, he contributed to one of those runs with a single then scored one on an Elston Howard bases-loaded triple that ended Mossi's day. By the time the conflict ended, Ford had a complete-game 6–2 victory and the Yankees were tied for first place.

The second half of the twin-bill pitted struggling Bob Turley against the formidable Frank Lary, Detroit's ace right-hander. He entered the contest with a remarkable 25–9 record against the Bombers over six seasons, including two complete-game victories in the current one. It was the best winning record of all the teams he faced. In fact, with the exception of the Minnesota Twins (18–15) and the Los Angeles Angels (5–3), Lary had a career losing or break-even record against every other team in the American League. There was no obvious explanation as to why he dominated such a perennial winner. Even Lary himself did not know exactly. It was not that he had the good fortune to be pitching for an equally powerful team. From 1954, the year he began his major league career with the Tigers, through 1960, Detroit finished no higher than fourth place in the American League. They had losing records in three of those years and a 77–77 record in another.

So why was he so successful against New York? One possible answer was that it was "his ability to deliver all his pitches at varying speeds, ranging from fast to floating. This keeps batters off balance, especially the Yanks." Lary acknowledged as much when he told one reporter, "I move the ball in and out and try to make the Yankees, as well as all others, hit my pitch. Against Maris and Mantle I use a lot of breaking stuff. The idea is to throw them close, away from their power. In general I mix up the pitches a lot and I like to know early in each game which pitch is doing the best." In addition, he claimed, "Control and confidence are my main assets. I pitch to the Yankees the same as any other club." He admitted that in 1961, "I haven't been using my knuckler as much as usual" because he was experiencing some arm pain. But he did use his fastball and "the usual curves and change-up."[43]

One sportswriter observed a slight change in Lary's pitching pattern that summer. "Instead of trying to overpower the hitters, Lary is getting them out with his assortment of curves and sliders. The results are unbelievable." Tigers pitching coach Tom Ferrick added, "Lary is pitching better than ever before because he is keeping his stuff low. He's less vulnerable than when he keeps blazing away with his fast ball. They can hit the high fast ball out of the park. Lary has curves, sliders and sinkers to do the job."[44]

Pitch selection and plate location were only part of the reason as to why the Yankees consistently failed against him, however. He had a career losing record (13–14) against the lowly Kansas City Athletics, for example, so the explanation must include something else. The answer lay in his self-confidence, especially when playing New York. Bill Norman, one of his managers in 1959 when he whipped the Bombers five times with only one defeat, stated, "The only explanation I can think of is that Frank knows he can beat the Yankees—and they know it, too. It's more a psychological factor than anything else. Frank is one of those loosey-goosey types who drips with confidence whether he's pitching or playing checkers. From the dugout, he looks like he's daring batters to hit him. And against the Yankees, it almost seems like child's play." It put the Yankee batters back on their heels, expecting to lose no matter what. "I didn't have any trouble hitting him," Yankee catcher Elston Howard once stated. "Yogi and Mantle [and Maris] hit him pretty good, too. But we couldn't beat him. He'd beat us 3–2, then the next time we'd hit him but the Tigers would win 7–6. That Lary just had a curse on us, I guess."[45]

Detroit ace Frank Lary was known as "The Yankee Killer" for his years-long dominance over the Bronx Bombers. The right-hander was having a career-year in 1961 (23–9) and would have won the Cy Young Award that season had Whitey Ford not had an even better year (25–4). While most Yankees found the Tiger hurler difficult to hit, Maris had no problems with him, jacking three four-baggers off of him that summer (numbers 31, 52, and 57).

Although Lary was having a career-year in 1961, he had his ups-and-downs as a pitcher. He first took the mound for Detroit in 1954, appearing in three games in September. The following year as a rookie, he won 14 while losing 15 with a good 3.10 earned-run average. His sophomore summer was one for the record books. He won 21 games, lost 13, had 20 complete outings, and led American League pitchers in wins, games started, innings pitched, and batters faced. The season did not start out that way, however. In the first half, he was a miserable 4–10 with an earned-run average near 4.00. Then from July 5 to the end of the year, he won 19 while losing just four and maintaining a 2.60 ERA.

The reason for this incredible turnaround was the effective use of a knuckleball he had developed but not used. "He'd been fooling around with it, but not with a mind toward using it in a game," recalled Detroit bullpen coach Jack Tighe. "I recommended it. It gave him another pitch to go with his curve, fastball and slider. It made him tough." Lary began throwing it about eight or so times in a game. "I found myself striking out hitters with good eyes, using my knuckler. I made Ted Williams mad with it. I tried it on Mickey Mantle, and he didn't get a hit off it." He often used the knuckleball to "keep hitters off balance and set them up for my good pitch. That's usually my overhand curve, especially against a lefthanded hitter. I think an overhand curve is the toughest pitch in baseball."[46]

Lary experienced a significant drop-off in 1957. He won 11 games, but lost 16, and his earned-run average was 3.98. He had almost as many game starts as he did the previous summer, but nearly half the number of complete games. In 10 of those outings he lasted five or fewer innings. He just was not the pitcher he was in 1956. He did bounce back in 1958, however. Although his won-loss record was close to even, his earned-run average decreased by over a run to 2.90 and he completed 19 games, most in the American League.

His performance that season was particularly enhanced by his outings against the Yankees. He won seven games—almost half his total that year—while losing just one and his ERA was an incredible 1.86. It was the best season he would ever have facing New York. "When the history of the 1958 Tigers is written," noted one Detroit sportswriter, "it will be a drama based on their success against the Yankees. The hero will be Frank Lary, hard-throwing knuckleball ace, who now 'owns' the Yankees—lock, stock and barrel." The Tigers finished in fifth place (the Yankees in first) at an even 77 wins, 77 losses, with the 28-year-old right-hander as their ace.[47]

Lary had another good season in 1959, going 17–10, which tied him with Jim Bunning and Don Mossi in the number of victories. His earned-run average rose slightly to 3.55, but he appeared in fewer games and managed only 11 complete games because he suffered elbow problems late in the season. The 5-foot-11 hurler appeared in just three contests in September, two of those for a loss, before calling it quits for the rest of the summer.

He had a slight falloff in the 1960 campaign, in part because he was playing for a team that finished in sixth place with an inferior 71–83 record. He did win a team-best 15 games, but lost an equal amount. His elbow seemed not to bother him. He led the league in games started, innings pitched, and complete games as well as hits allowed and hit batsmen. It was one of those "win a few, lose a few" sorts of years, probably best exemplified by the fact that he was 2–2 against the Bombers with a 4.23 ERA. His season, in fact, was salvaged only by winning four of his last five starts.[48]

The 1961 campaign was the best in the 31-year-old pitcher's career. The Tigers had one of their strongest lineups in years and Lary started like a house afire. Often he began slowly, then gained steam as the season wore on. In 1961 he was hot from the very beginning. He had four straight victories, the first three complete games, before suffering his first defeat on May 3. By the end of June he was 11–4 and showed no signs of slowing down. "He's strong and has good stuff," commented Tiger manager Bob Scheffing. "But that's only part of it. He does everything well—pitching, hitting, fielding, holding runners on base, base running." His 3.66 earned-run average was a tad high, but as his skipper noted, "in the case of Lary, he knows when to bear down when he has to. He has the heart and stuff to win."[49]

The fact that he had the likes of Al Kaline, Norm Cash, and Rocky Colavito for offensive support did not hurt either. When he entered that July 4 affair, he was 11–4 in 17 games, including 11 complete ones, with a 3.66 ERA. He had already beaten the Yankees twice, going all nine innings on both occasions, while losing on June 18 when he gave up five earned runs in the first three innings. No matter the loss, though, he knew, as did New York, he could conquer them almost at will.

Lary's performance in that crucial second game of the doubleheader proved what a masterful hold he had over the Yankees. The Tiger ace and Bob Turley appeared to be evenly matched for the first two innings, but then the tide began to turn in Detroit's favor in the third frame. "Bullet Bob," who because of arm problems was not the dominate pitcher he was in the past, loaded the bases on two walks and a single. Then when he walked Norm Cash for the first Tiger run, he was removed for Jim Coates, who was able to get out of Turley's mess without allowing another run.

It stayed a one-run game until the fifth when a Tony Kubek error, a walk, and a Rocky Colavito single off of Coates gave Detroit a 2–0 lead. Lary, in the meantime, blanked the Bombers through the first seven innings, walking just three batters while giving up harmless singles to three others. Maris, in three trips to the plate thus far, walked once, but grounded out and popped out the other two times.

Maris generally had good success against the Tiger right-hander. In his first season with the Yankees, for example, he was seven for 17 (.412), including two doubles, a triple, and two homers. In 14 plate appearances in 1961 thus far, the Yankee slugger had managed just three singles and three walks that did not amount to anything. His fifteenth face-off against Lary had an entirely different result.

In the bottom of the eighth, the Tiger starter quickly dispatched the first two Yankee batters. But then he made two fatal mistakes: he surrendered a double to Tony Kubek and threw a curveball to Maris. "There were two out when Kubek doubled to right to give me a chance," Maris recalled. "As usual in a double-header I hadn't done much, and it was getting late." Then came that curve. "This time I managed to connect.... It had just enough carry to get it over Al Kaline's leaping grab." Yankee skipper Ralph Houk was anxiously viewing from the dugout when Maris' bat connected with the ball. "I nearly fell off the dugout steps when Roger's low line drive took off for the right field corner," he recalled. "Kaline raced after it. He'll get it—he's diving into the stand! He's—. The ball struck a seat in the first row, bounced back on the field. Umpire [Red] Flaherty stood on the right field foul line. He turned, raised his arm in the home-run sign. Oh, how I loved that Flaherty just then!"[50]

As the Detroit right-fielder tumbled into the seats in his vain attempt to collar the ball, Maris circled the bases a very happy camper. "That's one of the homers I hit in 1961 that I circled in my memory," he stated after the season. "It gave me a great feeling to step up in the clutch of one of the most important games of the year and tie the score with a home run. I'm always tickled to get a home run in that situation, especially when I'm having a good year." In addition, Maris saw it as his answer to critics who argued that he only parked the ball "when they didn't mean anything: that I didn't hit homers in clutch situations. Here was one crucial situation where I delivered and it felt great."[51]

The game was far from over, however. In the top of the ninth, Yankee reliever Rollie

Sheldon opened by allowing a single to pinch-hitter Bobo Osborne, who was then replaced by pinch-runner Chico Fernandez. Lary sacrificed Fernandez to second, after which Sheldon retired shortstop Dick McAuliffe on a pop fly. With first base open, Sheldon intentionally walked Kaline to face the less-potent bat of Bill Bruton. It would have been a great move had Sheldon not unintentionally walked the replacement center fielder. Now with two out, the bases loaded, and the power-hitting right-handed Rocky Colavito at bat, Detroit manager Bob Scheffing made a bold move: he called for a triple steal. By the time the Yankee pitcher realized what was happening, it was too late to tag Fernandez as he slid across home plate.

Manager Houk was as shocked as everyone else on the Yankee bench. He was not even aware of what was happening until coach Frank Crosetti yelled, "There he goes!" "A triple steal—a rarity these days—and I'm on the dirty end of it, for it was as unexpected to me as Rollie," Houk bitterly recollected. Sheldon did manage to retire Colavito on a fly to short, but by then the Tigers were up by a run. But turnabout is fair play, as they say. In the bottom of that inning, Lary gave up singles to Moose Skowron and Johnny Blanchard. With runners on first and third and two away, pinch-hitter Hector Lopez then hit a slow-roller to third base that scored Skowron and tied the game again, sending it into extra innings.[52]

With Bill Stafford now toeing the rubber in the tenth, pinch-hitter Dick Brown socked a ground-rule double with Steve Boros on and two away to put runners on second and third. All Stafford had to do was retire the next batter, the Detroit pitcher, to end the threat. That was easier said than done. Maris called Lary "one of the greatest competitors I have ever faced. He can beat you with his bat as well as his arm. Here he used his bat with surprising and devastating effect."[53]

Indeed he did. "In no time there were two strikes against Lary," wrote John Drebinger in the *New York Times*. "Then he brazenly bunted the next pitch down the third-base line. Stafford tore in, scooped up the ball and tossed it to [catcher Johnny] Blanchard at the plate. But [Steve] Boros slid safely home. The Tigers for the third time were in front, and this time they made it stick." Lary, naturally, was elated. "I knew I had a heads-up guy in Boros down at third. I figured if I could lay it down he could score. I wouldn't have tried the bunt with one out. The pitch was high, and good for bunting." When Lary gave up a single to open the bottom of the inning, he was lifted for two relievers who managed to prevent the Yankees from scoring. Thus the crucial two-game set to decide first place ended with the standings as they were.[54]

Lary did not face the Yankees again until a championship-deciding three-game series in New York two months later. In between the two outings, he won seven more games while losing three. By season's end, he was exhausted. He pitched more than 275 innings in 36 game-starts and threw a league-leading 22 complete contests. It came as no surprise to anyone when he remarked in late September, ""My arm is awful tired." He ended the season at 23–9, second to Whitey Ford for the best record in the American League. He came in third in the Cy Young Award voting behind Ford, the winner, and Warren Spahn of the Milwaukee Braves.[55]

The fierce competitor developed shoulder and arm problems early in the 1962 season and never fully recovered. In his first outing on April 13, he beat the Yankees, but it was all downhill after that. It was not until mid–June that he won his second game, which was his last victory that year. He suffered six losses, including one to New York, and finished a miserable season at 2–6 with a 5.74 earned-run average.

The following summer was not much better. He managed to lower his ERA to 3.27, but made only 14 starts in 16 games, winning just four of them with losing nine. Two of those defeats were back-to-back starts against the Yankees in early September. He was no longer "The Yankee Killer." His troubles continued over the next two seasons. After six games for Detroit in which he went 0–2, he was sold to the New York Mets in late May 1964. He made 13 appearances with them before they traded him to the Milwaukee Braves.

The Braves used him as both a starter and reliever in five games before they sold him back to the Mets in early 1965. He actually pitched quite well for New York. His 1–2 won-loss record was not impressive, but his 2.98 earned-run average certainly was. But after 14 outings, the Mets traded him to the Chicago White Sox in early July. He made another 14 appearances for the Sox, winning one and losing none, but his ERA jumped to 4.05. Now 35 and still suffering from arm troubles, Chicago released him at the end of the season. Ironically, the one game he did win for the Sox was a July 31 affair against the Detroit Tigers. It was his last major league victory. Lary retired after 12 major league seasons with a winning record (128–116) and a good 3.49 earned-run average. It was his 28–13 lifetime record against the Bronx Bombers, however, that will always be his claim-to-fame. He tried coaching for a while, but did not enjoy it. "I missed not being a player," he told one interviewer. "Hanging around as a coach made it more difficult. Baseball was great to me, but I knew when I was finished."[56]

Home Run # 32—Game 78—July 5—Day Game

With less than half the season over, Maris was well on his way to catching Babe Ruth with Mickey Mantle in close pursuit. "It was around here that things started to close in on me as well as Mickey," Maris realized. The press and public's obsession with the home-run race, almost to the exclusion of all else, kicked up a notch and Maris, who hated the attention, really began to feel the pressure for the first time. Mantle, he commented, had been through it before and was better equipped to deal with the hubbub, "but it was something new to me."[57]

One of the changes that became more apparent was how he was treated by the media. "I liked to kid around with several of the writers who travel with the Yankees all the time. I felt at ease with them and free to say whatever came into my mind." Now, he believed, he had to be more cautious with them—which he failed to do more often than not—because "I never knew when something I would say as a gag would get into the papers as if I meant it." Thus, his relationship with reporters, especially ones he did not know and was not comfortable around, began to sour. "There was always the chance that some writer, who didn't know I was kidding, would wander by and hear something that made him think he had a scoop. It was the beginning of my going on the defensive when writers were around me." This distrustful attitude was exacerbated by his belief that he was being intentionally baited. "I had to watch for the loaded questions," he asserted.[58]

As Maris and Mantle continued to pound out homers at a record pace, the defenders of the Ruth legend began to gather their forces. Sports columnists started raising the issue of the longer schedule giving an unfair advantage to the two Yankee sluggers. Pressure began to mount on baseball commissioner Ford Frick to make some sort of "ruling" on whether Ruth's single-season record had to be broken in the same number of games

Ruth played for it to be "official" or not. Frick, as Ruth's friend and ghostwriter, needed little prompting to take such action. "Commissioner Ford C. Frick, normally calm and relaxed, is apprehensive," wrote Dan Daniel, dean of the New York–based sportswriters, in his nationally syndicated column in early July. "His fears have to do with the obvious threat to Babe Ruth's home run record of 60, set in 1927."[59]

After acknowledging Frick's close friendship with Ruth, Daniel went on to explain, "What bothers Frick is not so much the possibility of a new record but the chance that it will be set with the help of the new 10-club schedule.... The commissioner is opposed to acceptance in such circumstances." According to Daniel, Frick was especially concerned that Maris might be the one to break the record. "Frick is in an uncomfortable sweat. His temperature rises five degrees every time Maris, in particular, who has hit 32 homers in 78 contests, with 85 more in which to explode 29 for the record, once again reaches the stands." One can easily understand how Maris, with his no-nonsense personality and his hypersensitivity to criticism he deemed unfair, would take offense at being singled out like that.[60]

The length of the schedule was not the only issue being raised to disparage those chasing the Ruth record. The ball is "a souped up onion," the bats are livelier with "terrific driving power," the parks are smaller, the pitching "is both inadequate and spread woefully thin," were all used to explain away the torrid pace Maris and Mantle were on. Even the Yankee batting order was employed as a way of belittling Maris in particular. Critics argued that he was getting the breaks over Mantle because he batted in front of his teammate. "Who would ever walk Maris to get to Mantle?" they asked. Maris got fatter pitches to hit because of the fear of Mantle, the argument went. Plus Maris had more at-bats than Mantle because he batted third. Few ever mentioned the fact that as a switch-hitter, Mantle might be the one with an advantage.[61]

As if being criticized by the Ruth supporters were not enough, Maris was subjected to the growing wrath of the boo-birds, not just on the road, but at home as well. "You can't print some of the names they call me when I'm out there [in right field]," he told one reporter. "They're always yelling at me, telling me I'm going to be traded back to Kansas City, that I'm a bum, that I'm lousy." Mantle, too, received his share of heckling. "I can't help it if they boo," he conceded. "They expect me to hit a home run every time I come to bat. I got a good start this year and they cheered. But let me strike out a few times and they'll boo worse than ever." And, like Maris, he was often accused of being cold and churlish toward the press. This perception of Mantle changed as the summer wore on, however. As the two battled back and forth for the home-run lead, Mantle began to be viewed as the "true" Yankee and as the underdog in the race, Maris as the interloper who was undeserving of the title.[62]

A slumping Cleveland team opened a two-game series against the Yankees in an afternoon contest on July 5. The Indians, in the thick of things with Detroit and New York in the early part of the season, suddenly started to run out of gas in mid–June. In the 21 games they played between June 15 and July 4, they had lost 14 of them, leaving them 5½ games behind the Tigers. By the time they finished their brief stay in New York, they were no longer serious contenders for the league championship.

Rollie Sheldon, who was caught flatfooted the day before when Detroit's Chico Fernandez stole home to tie up the game in the top of the ninth, got the call for New York. Cleveland gave the ball to Gary Bell. Sheldon was sharp from the beginning, which was not the case with the Tribe's right-hander. He was basically singled to death: Yogi Berra hit a run-scoring single in the first inning, Maris and Mickey Mantle added two more runs on singles in the third, and Bobby Richardson and Tony Kubek ended Bell's day in the fourth with a pair of singles of their own. With the Yankees up, 5–0, and Sheldon cruising along, the outcome was readily apparent to the 24,000 spectators looking on. Bob Allen was called in to replace Bell and threw perfect ball over the next two innings. Then Frank Funk, Cleveland's brilliant rookie relief artist, was sent to the mound to pitch the final two innings of a lost cause.

The 25-year-old right-hander was a product of the Giants farm system. He was a workhorse who showed great promise from the very beginning. He spent five years pitching outstanding ball in the minors, starting at the age of 18 in 1954. He was 14–11 with a 3.86 earned-run average his first year at the Class D level, then 18–7 with an even better 3.34 ERA after moving up to Class C ball the following season. He pitched over 200 innings in both summers. By the time he made it to the Triple-A level in 1958, he was used almost exclusively as a reliever. In a season split between Double-and Triple-A, he won 14 games, lost nine, and maintained an excellent 2.60 earned-run average while appearing in 56 games.

Then in April of 1959, the Giants optioned him to the Toronto Maple Leafs in the International League, an independent club not affiliated with any of the major league teams. It was there that he ran into his first serious arm problems. In late May, he appeared in five successive games, pitching over 14 innings of relief. As a result of this overuse, he had to be shut down for over a week to give his aching arm a rest. The condition resurfaced in late June, which ended in another period of pitching inactivity. He ended the summer with six wins, 10 losses, and a 3.71 ERA, decent numbers for a pitcher bothered by arm troubles.[63]

The Giants for some reason never gave Funk his shot at the major leagues no matter how well he performed. That was about to change. Toronto became affiliated with the Cleveland Indians in the fall of 1959, ending seven seasons of independence. It was a good move on the part of the Leafs' owner, Jack Cooke. Toronto, consigned to last place in the International League in 1959, won it all in 1960. The decision to join up with Cleveland, however, meant the Indians had first dibs on any player they wanted at a cost of $15,000 each. They chose to exercise that privilege at the end of August when they purchased Funk's contract.

The right-hander was fully recovered from his wing miseries experienced the summer before. He did contract the mumps in the middle of July, but that did not prevent him from having a successful campaign in 1960. He appeared in 32 games, seven as a starter, ending with a 6–3 record and an outstanding 2.10 earned-run average. Funk even added a no-hitter to his resume. In the first game of a June 16 twin affair against the Havana Sugar Kings, he hurled seven innings of hitless ball to secure a 1–0 victory. Interestingly, Funk pitched a seven-inning, four-hit shutout in the opening half of a doubleheader just two days earlier and then two more innings of scoreless ball to close out the second game as well. He relied mainly on his fastball for the earlier two outings and his slider and curve for the no-hit game. "I have better control of my breaking pitches when I'm slightly tired," he commented afterwards. If any pitcher was primed for the big time, it was Frank Funk.[64]

When Gary Bell went down with a sore shoulder at the end of August, Funk was called up from Toronto to take his place. And the right-hander took every advantage of this long-awaited opportunity to show that he belonged there. He made his major league debut on September 3 when he relieved in the seventh inning with the Tribe down, 5–2, to the Kansas City Athletics. Funk held the A's scoreless for the next two innings and when his teammates plated four runs in the top of the ninth, he secured his first major league victory. He appeared the second time on September 6 and again on September 10, pitching four innings of relief in each and winning both when the Indians again came from behind in the late innings. By the time the season was done, Funk could point to an excellent 4–2 record and a minuscule 1.99 earned-run average over nine games. Cleveland management and fans alike were ecstatic with their latest find. The *Plain Dealer's* Jimmy Doyle, in his unique poetic way, expressed the hopes of all when he wrote, "Toronto prophets said Frank Funk/Would help the Tribe a lot/And what they said was not the bunk/A bullpen ace we've got." The future looked bright indeed.[65]

Just before the start of the 1961 season, *The Sporting News* predicted Funk would be the American League Rookie Pitcher of the Year. With the way he performed that spring, however, it looked like the prognosticator had missed the mark. The 25-year-old hurler was plagued by a sore elbow early on and never really had time to get in shape. His performance was so bad that even the normally self-assured hurler had his doubts. "I really was worried," he admitted. "In fact, I was about ready to take the gas pipe, figuratively speaking, of course." He even resorted to using a nerve-stimulator called the "Dyna-Wave" on his pitching arm.[66]

And it seemed to help: Funk started the season like gangbusters. He made his first outing on April 14 in the ninth inning against the Senators and struck out the side. The following day he pitched two innings of scoreless relief to earn his first save. Although the third time out was not the charm—he gave up four earned runs in 1⅔ innings—by the end of June he was 8–6 with seven saves and a 2.21 earned-run average. He had also worked 53 innings, which was quite a lot for so early in the season. He paid the price for that over-use later in the summer.

Funk's go-to pitches were his low fastball and slider. But he acquired a pretty good curve over the winter, and began using that as well. The problem, though, was that he had yet to develop confidence in his crooked pitch. When he found that he could not throw it for strikes, he resorted to overusing his fastball. That often got him into trouble, which was what happened to him in his third outing. Pitching in the eighth against the Detroit Tigers with the Indians up, 2–1, he walked the first two batters then intentionally walked a third with one out to load the bases. Since he did not have good control of his curve, he started using the fastball with Tiger third baseman Steve Boros at the plate. "I tried my curve and I couldn't get it over," he explained after the loss. "That meant I had to use my fast ball and I tried to keep it low and outside and I just missed. The hitters knew that's what I was going to throw and I was afraid they'd be ready for it." And Boros was, hitting it to left field for a three-run double. Such are the travails of a rookie pitcher.[67]

"The trademark of the Frank Funk personality is confidence," observed Bob Dolgan in the *Cleveland Plain Dealer*. "He is so confident that he would probably work a crossword with an ink pen." Some would go a bit further and call him cocky. "I feel that I'm going to get the batter out," he proclaimed. "I don't care who it is. I feel I'll get him. They've got to hit you sometime, naturally, but over a full season I don't think there's a batter in the league who could do .300 against me." That was quite a bold claim from someone in their first full major league season. He was also prone to moodiness and anger when riled and was not afraid to pitch inside when he believed he was being challenged by a hitter.

> I used it on [Minnesota Twins shortstop] Zorro Versalles [on May 22]. And he glared at me. That got me mad. Here's this little guy [5-foot-10] giving me the business, as though he's about to knock the next pitch out. I made up my mind to throw the next one right down the middle, putting all I had on it. My thinking was: "All right. You think you're strong enough to hit this fast ball, go on." I know I shouldn't have gotten mad. But I wasn't thinking about that. I poured it over and he bailed out and just waved at the ball.

This strikeout was in the late innings of a tied game that went fifteen. Funk got away with it that time—he ended up as the winner—but that would not always be the case.[68]

So when Funk took the mound in the seventh inning of that July 5 contest against the Yankees, he was filled with self-confidence, convinced he could get anyone out. That did prove to be spot on with Tony Kubek, the first Bomber up that inning. Funk induced a groundout to second, thus leaving the bases empty for Roger Maris. The two had confronted each other just once before when Funk retired Maris on a pop out to third in a June 15 game. The pitcher knew Maris was a "dangerous" hitter, but believed he was having a "freak" season and would be no more of a problem than the first time the two faced off. "No .260 hitter should ever hit that many homers," he complained after the season. He was about to learn a very valuable lesson, to wit, ".240 and .250 hitters" were "major leaguers just like the .300 hitters are."[69]

According to John Romano, Funk's battery mate that game, the righty must have thrown "something like 29 curveballs" to set Maris up, but the slugger kept fouling them off. Then, as he had in the past when his curve was not working the way he wanted, he tried to sneak a fastball past the Yankee right fielder. Romano knew it was a mistake because "Maris was a good fastball hitter" and this time it was not Zorro Versalles at the plate.[70]

Maris, naturally, was tickled pink. Funk "likes to throw the fast ball, and usually puts it where he wants it," Maris recalled. "This time he put one where I wanted it, and I was able to get it into the seats for number thirty-two. I remember it for only one reason. Funk had come into the league late last season, and I hadn't hit a homer off him." Maris' self-proclaimed goal was to hit a home run off of every pitcher in the American League. "I don't mean all in one season," he clarified, "but as long as there are pitchers you haven't hit for a home run they stand as a challenge to you. With this homer I was able to cross Funk off my list of 'untouchables.'"[71]

Maris ended that game with three hits total to raise his batting average to .278, which pleased him mightily. "Perhaps, if I tell the truth, I was prouder of my climbing batting average than anything else at that point," he acknowledged. Why, especially since Yankee management was more concerned with home runs and RBIs than his batting average? It was because of the continual criticism he endured for his failure to hit for average.

> There had been a whisper here and there that I was lucky. People were asking how I could hit home runs and only be hitting around .250. It was getting under my skin. I didn't like it, not a little bit. I think it was somewhere around here where I began to be called red-necked Roger or the Last Angry Man…. When my batting average moved up and the whispers died out, I think my disposition improved too. No one likes to be called a lucky hitter.

The "whisper here and there" was really quite a bit more than that. In fact, it was something his critics raised frequently all season long. Even though he may have been feeling better about that at this point in the battle, the whispers became a roar as he got closer to Babe Ruth.[72]

In retrospect, it was a foolish decision to use Funk in a game when the Indians were down five runs in the late innings and the opposing pitcher was having one of his best games ever. It was Funk's thirtieth appearance of the season and his fifty-ninth inning pitched, so his arm was tired. The Maris homer was only the fifth he surrendered to that point, but over the next four outings Funk allowed three more, all in successive games. Not surprisingly, it got to the pitcher, a rookie who was not used to hitting a wall like that. "This is a nightmare," he admitted after that third homer in mid-July. "I'll have to get me a new batch of tranquilizers if this keeps up. My luck had better change soon."[73]

Things began to improve somewhat once management realized they were over-utilizing the young pitcher. As one observer noted toward the end of the summer, "Frank Funk was good in the bull pen but may have been overworked." From mid-July until the end of the season, Funk hurled only 33⅓ more innings, about a third as many as in the first half of the season. It was a wise move on the part of the Indians, especially reducing the number of back-to-back outings that was the case previously. In spite of the late pitching slump, Funk did manage to compile a respectable record of 11 wins, 11 loses, and 11 saves (and 11 blown saves) with a decent 3.31 ERA. He was sixth among American League pitchers in both saves and games played and second in games finished. He and the Indians were looking forward to the 1962 campaign.[74]

There was a new manager when Funk came to spring training in 1962, someone he knew quite well. Jimmy Dykes was replaced by 35-year-old Mel McGaha, who managed the Toronto Maple Leafs in 1960 when Funk was pitching for them. He was one of those no-nonsense managers who did not hesitate to confront a player he thought was not giving his all or who tried to buck him. Funk, however, was very complimentary about the in-coming skipper. "I never saw a manager who could get the players' respect so easily. He wouldn't even seem to work at it, but you knew he was boss. When he sees fit, he really can chew out a guy—in private." Funk's positive opinion changed drastically before the end of the summer.[75]

Funk's performance that season was not nearly as sharp as the year before. He was elevating his pitches with the result that home runs became an issue. At the end of July when he had worked 58 innings of relief, he had already surrendered 10 dingers, twice the number he did in the same number of innings in 1961. He did get a handle on it after that, allowing just one more round-tripper the rest of the season, but by then McGaha was using him less. That infuriated Funk

In mid-August the manager sent him back to the minors, which caused the pitcher to explode. "He's the worst manager I ever saw," Funk grumbled publicly. "And I'm not the only guy on the club who feels that way. Almost everybody does. That's why we're going so bad. He told me he was sending me down because I lost my confidence. What's he know about my confidence? I haven't lost it. He lost confidence in me a long time ago. I know that." Funk was probably just letting off steam because of his disappointment with how the season was going for him, but it set the stage for his later departure from Cleveland. He returned in mid-September with much improved pitching control, but by then it was too late. No player, especially one who was less productive than in the past, rages to the press like he did and not pay the price. In spite of a relatively good year in which he was 2–1 with six saves and a 3.24 earned-run average, he did not figure "strongly in the Tribe's plans" for the future. On November 27, he was part of a five-player trade that sent him to the Milwaukee Braves.[76]

Milwaukee management was enthusiastic about their acquisition of Funk. Manager Bobby Bragan proclaimed, "Funk will be our No. 1 reliever." That may have been his plans, but the pitcher injured his back in spring training and never fully recovered. Then a sore finger added to his miseries. He had a rough—and late—start to the season and by August was used very little. He was able to pitch just over 43 innings, less than half of what he was able to do in each of the two previous seasons. Although he managed a 3–3 record with no saves and a great 2.68 earned-run average, his major league career was over. Funk was optioned back to the Braves' Triple-A affiliate in Denver at the end of spring training in 1964. He then spent five seasons trying to make a comeback, but that was not to be. Funk's final summer as a professional pitcher was in 1969, but he did not leave baseball entirely. He managed in the minors for several years and was pitching coach for a number of major league teams before calling it quits for good.[77]

Home Run # 33—Game 82—July 9—Day Game

Although Maris did not hit a home run in the next three games, he swung the bat well, going 3-for-10 with a double and four runs batted in. More importantly, the Yankees continued their winning ways. After beating Cleveland on July 6, the Bombers then took the next two games over Boston to recapture first place by half a game. Mantle added his twenty-ninth homer on July 8 to help his buddy Whitey Ford win his tenth consecutive game, giving him 16 in all. Maris was pleased in spite of going homerless. "I was still getting my hits and I knew a home run would come along. My swing was still in the groove, and, sooner or later, I would get a ball into the air and hit it hard enough to go out." His four RBIs left him just two behind league-leader Jim Gentile, Baltimore's big first baseman. He managed to raise his batting average up some 75 points (.279) from where it was after the first month of the season. He could finally put those awful days behind him.[78]

New York had a daytime doubleheader against fourth-place Boston on July 9 to wrap up a four-game series before the first All-Star game on July 11 at Candlestick Park in San Francisco. Whitey Ford, Tony Kubek, Mickey Mantle, and Maris were among the players scheduled to start for the American League. First, though, if they could take those two games against Boston, they would solidify their tenuous hold on first place.

Starting for New York in the first game was Rollie Sheldon, who had shutout the Indians on just four hits in his last outing. Facing him was 24-year-old right-hander Bill Monbouquette, in his fourth season with the Red Sox, already one of the mainstays of their starting staff. Monbo (occasionally Mombo), as he was commonly known, spent four years in the Boston farm system until his major league debut in 1958. As a native of Medford, Massachusetts, just a stone's throw from Boston, Monbouquette was delighted to be drafted by the Red Sox as an 18-year-old just out of high school. "I signed with the Sox because it meant if I did make the grade I'd be pitching back in my home town. A lot of baseball players don't like to play at home, but I feel different about it."[79]

In many ways, his attitude and personality were similar to Maris. The Yankee slugger also enjoyed playing before the hometown folks. In fact, he demanded that he begin his professional career in his boyhood home of Fargo, North Dakota, or he would walk. Both were determined, assertive and self-confident individuals who had no difficulty standing up for themselves. "I know how I am when I get mad," Monbouquette told one interviewer late in his retirement. "I don't like to tell people I'm uncontrollable, but I don't take crap from anybody." Maris could not have said it better.[80]

He spent his first three seasons working his way up from Class D to Class A ball where he compiled a winning record, 17–11 at the D level, 12–7 split between B and A. In 1958, he jumped to the Triple-A level, playing most of that season for the Minneapolis Millers of the American Association. Monbouquette had an 8–9 record with a 3.16 earned-run average when he was called up to the big club in mid–July. His first appearance was as a starter on July 18, a game in which he lasted just five innings, giving up five runs. He suffered his first loss five days later, again lasting just five innings. He pitched his first major league complete game, another loss, in his third start. Then on August 5 he won his first game in the majors, another complete contest in which he allowed a single run over nine innings of work. Manager Pinky Higgins was delighted with the young pitcher's progress. "I like what I saw," he said after that first outing. "He'll work into our pitching rotation. He was ahead of the batters, he didn't scare, he had good control." Monbouquette continued to improve as the season came to an end, even winning his last two starts for a 3–4 record and a 3.31 ERA. The 21-year-old had made his presence known.[81]

Monbouquette came into the big leagues with a good, but not overpowering, fastball and an adequate curve. He had been pitching with a sidearm delivery, but a Red Sox scout early on convinced him to use an overhand motion. "From then on my fast ball picked up. It's by far my best pitch now." A few years later Red Sox pitching coach Sal Maglie worked with him on improving his "breaking stuff. I usually throw a lot of sliders, but I found that my curve ball was working better than ever." His ability to hide the ball aided his pitching immensely. "I was the type of guy who had a good arc. My arm came up and stayed behind my head so it made it tough to pick up the ball; it's called deception of your motion. Then you don't have to throw 100 miles per hour."[82]

One thing he was never obsessed with was striking out hitters, although he did do a lot of that. "On some days I struck out a lot of batters," he recalled, "but I preferred not throwing a lot of pitches to get a batter out, especially at Fenway where batters didn't go to the plate taking pitches. I wanted them to make outs swinging at first and second pitches outside the strike zone." Key to his success was his great control. He was among the top ten American League pitchers in the strikeouts-per-walks ratio in five of those six seasons from 1960 through 1965. "Monbo has an edge on most pitchers in that he has such excellent control he rarely throws more than three or four pitches to a hitter. In fact, control is his No. 1 weapon," wrote Larry Claflin in *The Sporting News*. In addition, he was one of the best conditioned pitchers in the majors, staying in shape during the off-season primarily by running. Red Sox manager Johnny Pesky ranked him with Bob Feller in terms of their conditioning. "Bill punishes himself like Feller used to with his constant running and calisthenics. They both have pride in their work and don't get out of shape."[83]

No one had to convince him to throw high and tight to a batter. Monbouquette, much like Early Wynn, saw home plate as his territory and did not hesitate to move a batter back or even hit him if he thought the hitter deserved it. "Even as a rookie I wasn't leery about throwing inside—it didn't matter if I hit the batter because it was his job to get out of the way," Monbouquette asserted. "I was a very feisty pitcher, one of the last who would charge off the mound and get into the umpire's face to argue a call."[84]

The perfect example of his combativeness occurred in his first outing of the 1959 season. Monbouquette was called in during the sixth inning of a game against the Yankees in which the Bombers were slaughtering the Red Sox. The right-hander got through the first two innings without incident, but then in the eighth he allowed three earned runs on a double to Mickey Mantle and a triple to Moose Skowron. With Skowron on third and Gil McDougald at the plate, he unleashed a pitch that struck the Yankee second baseman on the hands.

> As [McDougald] stood at the plate wringing his hands in pain, the Boston hurler rushed in, protesting to [home plate umpire Ed] Runge that the ball had struck Gil's bat. He brushed past McDougald, jostling him slightly, and when Gil made an angry remark, Monbouquette whirled from Runge and was about to charge the Yankee star when the arbiter grabbed him and stepped between the two, averting a possible fight.

The Boston hurler claimed that a lecture—which included a threat of being sent down to Minneapolis—by Red Sox general manager Joe Cronin later that season helped him get his anger under control. Perhaps it did somewhat, but he remained a "feisty" player throughout his career.[85]

The 1959 season saw the right-hander pitching mostly out of the bullpen the first half of the season, then as a starter from that point on. He got his first win on May 4 when he relieved in the second inning with the bases full, no outs, and the Kansas City Athletics already ahead, 3–0. Monbouquette came into the game sporting an awful 11.25 earned-run average after his first three appearances of the season and was well aware that he was on the verge of being sent back to the minors. Showing the poise and determination of a grizzled veteran, he struck out the first two A's batters then retired Roger Maris on a groundout to first to end the inning. He pitched one-run ball over the next six frames, and when the Red Sox came through with eight runs of their own, he was credited with the victory.

"He convinced me that he should stay in this league," manager Pinky Higgins proclaimed. "He's going to be a good pitcher. He had his troubles earlier in the season and I thought that maybe he would be better off in Minneapolis. But the last time that we were here [in Kansas City] he showed me that he deserved to stay with us and get more work with us." When Billy Jurges took over the reins in mid-July, he moved Monbouquette into the starting rotation fulltime. In 14 game starts from July 19 through late September, he went 5–4 with four complete games on a 3.57 earned-run average. "He's learning something every time out," commented the Boston skipper. "He's a battler and a good worker. You've got to work and work and work at this game if you want to be successful. And Mombo is the type who wants to be a winner and works at it."[86]

Monbouquette established himself as the ace of the Boston pitching staff during the 1960 season. He had a rocky start, but by May he began to get on track. On May 3 he posted his third win on a one-hit shutout of the Detroit Tigers, the first in his major league career. "It proves that hard work pays off," pronounced Jurges after the game. "Mombo has been as hard a worker as we've got on the club. He hasn't the greatest stuff in the world, but he's got a great heart and a great desire to win." He was elected to the American League All-Star team for the first time, starting the first game on July 11. Unfortunately he took the loss after giving up three runs in the first inning and another run in the second on a Del Crandall solo blast. "It was still a thrill" in spite of the loss, he said. By the end of the summer he had won 14, lost 11, with 12 complete games while pitching over 200 innings for the first time in his professional career. He was seventh in wins among American League pitchers, seventh in strikeouts, fifth in strikeouts per nine innings pitched, eighth in innings pitched, tenth in games started, fifth in compete games, and fourth in shutouts.[87]

Monbouquette continued his excellent work in the 1961 season, although his 14–14 record might at first indicate a middling performance. Lack of run support plagued him throughout the campaign. Indeed, he lost his first three starts, two of those by one run. In fact, six of his defeats were by one run. He might well have been a 20-game winner with just a little more offense on the part of his teammates. Part of the problem, too, was that early in the season he was tipping off his pitches. Once he understood what was happening, he abandoned his windup and went to pitching from the stretch. He also lost confidence in his fastball after batters teed-off on it a few times. "I tried to get cute and I tried to make every pitch a perfect one.... I would try to shave the corners with it [his fastball] or waste it, and then try to get the batters out with my curveball." That was when he got into trouble, either walking a batter or offering up "a fat pitch" that would be hammered. "The curveball just isn't my 'out' pitch," he came to realize. It took manager Pinky Higgins and pitching coach Sal Maglie to convince him to start relying on his heater again.[88]

He and fellow starter Don Schwall were considered the "two stoppers" on a starting staff with no other winning pitchers. The highlight of his season occurred against the Washington Senators on May 12 when he struck out 17 batters, setting a new Red Sox record. He just missed tying the major league record of 18 after catcher Jim Pagliaroni dropped a third-strike foul tip off the bat of Jim King in the eighth inning; on the next pitch, King grounded out, pitcher to first base. "I had the ball in the webbing of my glove," the catcher confessed afterwards. "I felt like digging a hole under home plate and crawling into it."[89]

Monbouquette was 8–6 with a 3.16 earned-run average when he started that first game of the doubleheader in Yankee Stadium on July 9. He was pitching quite well that day, giving up just two earned runs through the first six innings. The problem, though, was that Rollie Sheldon was having another great outing in which he hurled his second consecutive shutout. The only real opportunity the Red Sox had to get to him was in the second inning when back-to-back singles put Boston runners on first and second with one away. That uprising, however, was quashed by the great fielding and throwing arm of Maris. When the next batter hit a single to right, Maris quickly scooped up the ball and hurled a perfect strike to Elston Howard who tagged out the baserunner trying to score from second. Sheldon then got the third out and it was easy sailing from that point on. By the time Maris came to the plate in the seventh inning for his fourth appearance of the day, the Yankees were already up, 2–0, and Sheldon was untouchable.[90]

Maris was quite familiar with Monbouquette and his style of pitching, having faced him 39 times prior to this at-bat. Other than a solo home run in 1959, the Yankee slugger had difficulty with the pitcher the first two seasons they faced off. But by the time he became a Yankee, Maris had Monbouquette's number. In 1960 he batted .353 against the right-hander, going six for 17, including a double, a triple, and a home run. Monbouquette once commented that it was difficult to pitch to Maris with Mickey Mantle on deck, but that he preferred pitching to Mantle because "he was easier to strike out." In 1961 Maris struck out 67 times in 698 plate appearances, Mantle 112 times in 646 plate appearances.[91]

Maris already walked and singled that game, so he was clearly locked in to whatever Monbouquette had to offer up. It was a slider. By the time the ball sailed over the auxiliary scoreboard in right-center field to land some 400 feet into the seats, the game was all but done. Maris now had hit 33 dingers prior to the first All-Star break, putting him well ahead of Ruth's pace. With Mantle four homers behind him, Maris for the first time began to think he might actually beat out his partner in mayhem for the home run title. He realized, though, that there were still plenty of games left in the season for Mantle to surpass him. "I have great respect for Mantle's ability to hit homers and knew that if I slipped just a little he would surely collar me," Maris acknowledged. And he was correct in his assessment.[92]

Monbouquette started another 16 games after that loss, including three more against the Yankees. He won six and lost seven to end the summer at 14–14 with a cumulative 3.39 ERA. The next two seasons were productive ones. On August 1, 1962, he pitched a no-hitter against the Chicago White Sox, which missed being a perfect game by a walk in the second inning. His no-hit feat seemed to inspire his performance the rest of the season. He was 8–10 coming in to the contest, but after losing his next start, he went on to win six of his next eight decisions.

Then in 1963 he won 20 games for the first—and only—time in his professional career. Considering that he was pitching for a seventh place team that lost 85 games that summer, winning over a quarter of them was quite an accomplishment. He still had his great control; in fact, his strikeouts-to-walks ratio was best in the American League. Naturally, the pitcher was expecting a significant raise for his 1963 performance. Pinky Higgins, now the Sox general manager, thought otherwise. Reports were that Monbouquette wanted an increase in the range of $10,000; he was offered a third of that. A nasty contract dispute resulted in hard feelings between the staff ace and the GM. The two even came to blows, "wrestling and throwing punches," before things were settled. "I eventually got the raise I wanted," said Monbouquette, "but it wasn't a comfortable situation."[93]

That was his last winning season for the Red Sox. In 1964 he was 13–14—still the best record among the starting pitchers—with his worst earned-run average (4.04) since 1959. The following year was even worse. Although his ERA dropped to 3.70, he won only 10 and his 18 losses led the American League. No one on the Boston starting staff had a winning record in a season that saw the Red Sox lose 100 games. A shakeup was clearly in the cards, and on October 4 Monbouquette was traded to the Detroit Tigers after eight years with Boston. He was not unhappy about the change of scenery. "Detroit has been one of my favorite towns and favorite ball parks," he announced upon hearing about the move via a telephone call, adding, "I was getting tired of being with a second division team; pitching with a losing ball team. What else can I say?"[94]

Monbouquette lasted just a little over one season with the Tigers. He appeared in 30 games, but more than half of those were out of the bullpen. He had a losing record and an extremely high 4.73 earned-run average, the worst he experienced in his 11 major league seasons. The disgruntled pitcher never found his place with Detroit. He was especially upset about being removed as a starter. "I'm a starter, not a reliever," he complained after the season. Expressing his belief—and hope—that he would be traded, he concluded, "It was a wasted year, the most disgusting I've had in baseball." After just two games with the Tigers in 1967, he was given his unconditional release in mid-May, which came as a shock to him. "I don't believe I ever felt lower or had less confidence in my life than I did the day I was released," he confessed. He tried out for several clubs over the next two weeks before he was signed by the Yankees at the end of the month.[95]

Now 30 and approaching the end of his career, Monbouquette was brought in to replace Jim Bouton, who was afflicted with a sore arm. He appeared in 33 games for the Yanks, only 10 of which were starts. He compiled a 6–5 record with two complete games, a shutout, and a save on a very nice 2.36 earned-run average in a little over 133 innings pitched. "I knew all along I could still pitch successfully in the majors," he said after the season. By this point in his career, his fastball had lost some of its zip, so he resorted to using more breaking pitches. According to one observer, "he has also become an artist in the field of pitching. He moves the ball around, changes speed and keeps the hitters off balance and rarely makes a bad pitch."[96]

The Yankees were so delighted that they gave him another shot at being a starter and through early June he was successful. But then he started to lose regularly and his ERA mushroomed from 3.40 on June 1 to 4.43 a month later. By that point of the season he was consigned back to the bullpen. After losing in a relief appearance on July 1, leaving him with a 5–7 record, he was traded to the San Francisco Giants on July 12 for right-handed reliever Lindy McDaniel. He appeared in just two games before a groin injury sidelined him for two weeks. He relieved in five more games when he returned in mid–August, losing one and saving another in eight plus innings pitched. That marked the end of his playing career. The Houston Astros purchased him on a provisional basis at the end of 1968, but returned him to the Giants in April the following spring; San Francisco released him immediately.

Although his days as a pitcher were over, he spent many seasons as a minor league manager and as a pitching coach. While certainly not Hall-of-Fame statistics, Bill Monbouquette had a very fine career. He won 114, lost 112, and had 78 complete games—including 18 shutouts—with a cumulative 3.68 earned-run average. "I loved what I did," he said long after retirement. "There was nothing bad about being a ballplayer. There's nothing wrong with dreaming and nothing wrong with fulfilling a dream.... Baseball was my life and I owed it everything I had. It was everything I hoped it would be and much more."[97]

Home Run # 34—Game 84—July 13—Night Game

The Yankees lost the second half of that July 9 doubleheader, 9–6, to end up back in second place, but just a half game behind the Tigers. Ralph Houk and the players not participating in the first All-Star game took the opportunity to rest up for the second half of the season that began on July 13 in Chicago. For Maris, Mickey Mantle, Whitey Ford, Tony Kubek, Yogi Berra, and Elston Howard, it meant another trip out west to take on the National League All-Stars. Ford started for the American League, going three innings and giving up one run. The game itself went 10 innings before the National League squeaked out a one-run victory on Roberto Clemente's run-scoring single off of Hoyt Wilhelm. Maris and Kubek played the entire game while Mantle was replaced by Al Kaline in the seventh inning. Berra and Howard got into the game in the later innings as replacement players. Maris was one for four with a single, a walk, and two strikeouts in five plate appearances; Mantle was zero for three with two strikeouts.

Most of the American League players did not enjoy the experience of performing in wind-swept Candlestick Park. "Every time I threw the ball it behaved like Hoyt Wilhelm's knuckler," Tony Kubek said. Another visiting player commented after the game, "No one talked about the ball game. Everyone talked about the damn wind." Maris, in his typical blunt style, groused, "If I had to play here all the time I'd quit. Sure, we play for money but when the fun goes out of it, I don't see how it would be worth it." He admitted later that "I'm afraid that I got a little too frank when asked about the park." But that was just the way he was: ask him a question and he gave an honest, direct, and unvarnished response.[98]

As Maris returned from San Francisco, he could not help but ponder his history of slumping in mid-summer. "Ever since I had been in the league I never put two good halves together," he realized. He tried not to think too much about it, but writers kept bringing it up, which irritated him. He claimed, though, that it did not really bother him because he thought he knew the underlying cause of his downturns—injuries. "Each time I had slumped late in the season it was after an injury had sidelined me for a while. I was never able to get back into stride." He felt that "everyone was waiting for me to start slipping as we moved into the second half of the season, but I was just as determined to fool them. I felt certain that if I could avoid injury, then I could avoid a slump."[99]

Many gave the edge to Mantle because of Maris' tendency to slip into prolonged droughts. Noted sports commentator Dan Daniel argued that "before long Mantle will spurt ahead of Maris, who is addicted by long habit, to drastic slumps." New York journalist Jack Lang claimed to have queried numerous players about who they thought had the best chance of catching Ruth. "It is the opinion of the majority of major league players I polled that while both might hit 60 or more, Mantle is more likely than Maris [who] is prone to long slumps in which he does not hit whereas Mantle is the steady type who doesn't go too many games without hitting at least one." He added that Maris also had a disadvantage being a left-hander who did not hit southpaw pitching well, while the switch-hitting Mantle "isn't apt to be stopped no matter which way the pitcher is throwing."[100]

Some sportswriters thought, though, that even if Maris could avoid slumping, he was not "emotionally equipped to withstand the pressure" as the season wore on and he got closer to Ruth. Baseball sage and former Yankee manager Casey Stengel begged to differ. "I never recall seeing anything excitable about the man," he noted. He also commented that, to his mind, Maris was a great all-round player. Speaking in his usual "Stengelese" style, this astute observer of baseball talent rated the current home-run leader as thus:

> I give the man one point for speed. I do this because he can run fast. I give him another point because he can slide fast. Then I give him a point because he can bunt. I also give him a point because he can field. He is very good around fences. Sometimes even on top of fences.... Next I give him a point because he can throw. A right fielder has to be a thrower, or else he's no right fielder. So I add up my points and I've got five for him even before I come to his hitting. I would say this is a good man, and I would say the same about the fella in center [Mickey Mantle].[101]

On top of this media obsession with Maris' mid-season slumps, stories began circulating that Mantle and Maris were not getting along. That suggestion of hostility between the two simply added to Maris' growing annoyance with the press. Even though he and Mantle both took great pains to point out how absurd those reports of discord were, noting that they voluntarily shared the same apartment and spent considerable time together away from the playing field, "that didn't stop the nasty rumors."[102]

Although stories about his slumps and his relationship with Mantle may have gotten Maris "hot under the collar," they were simply background noise when he was on the field. Nothing but the pressure he put on himself mattered when he was batting or patrolling the outfield. Being in the game was Maris' haven, his escape from the constant questions and commentary that he felt were a slight to him or an invasion of his privacy. "Each time I go out onto the field I am completely wrapped up in the job at hand," he explained. "If things don't go right for me on the field my temper can definitely start to climb pretty quickly. Once I put on my uniform I guess I change. My mind is concerned with baseball, only baseball."[103]

His mind was definitely focused on the job at hand the night of July 13 when he stepped to the plate to face Early Wynn in the first inning with one on and one away as a crowd of nearly 44,000 packed Comiskey Park in anticipation of the battle unfolding before them. The combative, batter-hating 40-year-old right hander, now in his twenty-first season of major league baseball, was not about to give in to this young upstart from North Dakota. In spite of his age, the future Hall-of-Famer still had a great arm and a history of handling Maris effectively. The Yankee slugger managed just one home run (1959) in 43 previous plate appearances against Wynn and had yet to get a hit off of him in 1961.

Wynn, nicknamed Gus by his teammates, began his major league career with the Washington Senators at the ripe old age of 19 back in 1939. Even as a youngster he was considered one of the meanest pitchers in the game. One sportswriter described Wynn as "a man of passive mien with a warm and mature sense of humor" when he was not pitching, but once he stepped on the mound, he "adopts a venomous, tough-minded, heavy-howled demeanor." As he once explained, "That mound out there between the white lines, that's my office. It's were I conduct my business and make my living. There are old roommates of mine all over the league, some of the best friends I have. Not one of them is my friend when he's up there with a bat. He's my mortal enemy."[104]

He had no compunctions at all about hitting a batter if he thought he deserved it, which was always the case when a batter hit a screamer back towards him. "When I knock a man down, I'm never trying to hit him. I'm just trying to set him up for my next pitch. If I really want to hit somebody, I aim at his ribs. There's no danger of injuring him too badly and a fast ball in the ribs hurts bad enough." In an oft-repeated tale, Wynn was once asked by a reporter if he would even throw at his own mother. "Mother was a pretty good curve-ball hitter" was his response. It was only a slight exaggeration. Writer Roger Kahn witnessed Wynn throw batting practice to his own son, Joe, before a game at Yankee Stadium one day. When Joe finally tagged one of his balls for a line drive, Wynn knocked him down on the very next pitch. "You shouldn't crowd me" was all he said to the young man.[105]

While he saw opposing hitters as the enemy, he was very protective of his teammates. Larry Doby, who was called up to the Cleveland Indians in mid–1947 as the first African American player in the American League, was subjected to the same racist animus as was Jackie Robinson. This hostility often took the form of pitchers intentionally throwing at him. One hurler in particular seemed to have it in for Doby and frequently aimed for his head. Wynn, who was traded to the Indians in 1949, took umbrage at this practice and thought it was time to send a message. The next time this pitcher came to the plate after nearly beaning Doby, Wynn knocked him down with a close, inside pitch. When his flattened opponent stood up and stepped back into the box, Wynn did it again. With the pitcher still lying in the dirt, Wynn walked from the mound and calmly told him, "Just remember, Doby is on my side and anybody who has trouble with him has trouble with me."[106]

Wynn was blessed with a blazing fastball, but that was about all he had while pitching for the Washington Senators. In his first two seasons (1939 and 1941) with the perennial losers, he pitched in only eight games, spending the rest of the time in the minors. He became a fulltime starter in 1942, appearing in 30 games for a 10–16 record and a bloated 5.12 earned-run average. He had an about-face the following season, going 18–12 on a 2.91 ERA, then declined to 8–17 in 1944. After spending 1945 in military service, he returned to the Senators, again repeating the pattern of a good season followed by a bad one. After a disastrous 1948 campaign when he won 8 and lost 19 with an awful 5.82 earned-run average, the Senators decided they had seen enough and traded him along with Mickey Vernon to the Cleveland Indians for three other players.

It was a fortuitous move for the pitcher as well as his new team. Wynn had the best nine years of his career pitching for the Indians. Cleveland, in return, developed a pitcher who helped lead them to the 1954 World Series. Wynn was 11–7 with a rather high 4.15 ERA that first summer in Cleveland, but became one of the most dominant pitchers in the game after that. He was 18–8 with the best earned-run average in the league the following year, and in 1951 became a 20-game winner for the first time. He won 20 or more games four times in an Indians uniform and in 1953 led all American League pitchers with 23 victories. From 1949 through 1957, he won 163 games and lost 100, completed 143 of his outings (including 24 shutouts), maintained a cumulative 3.27 ERA, and hurled over 2,231 innings. He received votes for the Most Valuable Player Award on five separate occasions and was on the American League All-Star team three consecutive years.

It was under the tutelage of Indians pitching coach Mel Harder that Wynn finally came into his own. "I could throw the ball when I came here," he recalled toward the end of his career, "but Mel made a pitcher out of me." Harder convinced Wynn to take a little off his heater so the batter's timing would be off. Most importantly, he taught Wynn how to throw a great curveball. "When I came to the Indians in '49 I didn't know how to throw one," he conceded. "Mel improved my curve and slider, and he could watch me and tell the moment my delivery was wrong. He was great at detecting little things." Harder also talked the pitcher into using his knuckleball, which he had when he came to Cleveland, but was afraid to use in a game. "It's a different pitch to keep the batter guessing so he won't be looking for the fast ball or curve all the time," Wynn reasoned.

Enhancing his pitch selection was the consistency of his pitching motion, his ability to throw exactly the same way every time regardless of what he chose to deliver. "All pitchers try to do that," Wynn acknowledged. "With me it's a question of training, of forcing myself to do it. It's tough throwing a change-up with the same motion as a fast ball." The fundamental key to successful pitching, Wynn argued, was "moving the ball around. To keep a batter off stride, you come high inside with one pitch, low outside with another and then back high inside again with the third. No matter who the batter is, you move the ball. You pitch to corners." The right-hander, who tended to add poundage in the off-season, ran as a means of weight control and staying in shape. "I think I run much more than the average pitcher," he contended. It certainly helped, plus it strengthened his legs, which was of great benefit. "If a pitcher keeps his legs in shape his whole body is conditioned," he proclaimed.[107]

After going 20–9 with a 2.72 earned-run average in 1956, Wynn suddenly went into a decline. The following season he was 14–17, his first losing one with Cleveland, and in spite of leading the league in strikeouts, his ERA skyrocketed to 4.31. The great Indians pitching staff of the early 1950s was rapidly aging—Wynn was 37, Bob Lemon, 36, and Mike Garcia, 33—so management decided to make a move to restock with younger players. Consequently, Wynn was traded to the Chicago White Sox, Lemon was released in mid–1958, and Garcia was released a month before Lemon (but resigned as a free agent the following year).

Although it seemed that Wynn was past his prime as a pitcher, that turned out not to be the case. After a mediocre 1958 season in which he was 14–16 with a 4.13 ERA, the

39-year-old right-hander produced the best season of his distinguished career. He led the American League with 22 wins, 37 game starts, 255⅔ innings pitched, and 1,076 batters faced. In addition, he was ninth in earned-run average, fourth in fewest hits per nine innings pitched, fifth in strikeouts per nine innings pitched, third in total strikeouts, fourth in complete games, and second in shutouts.

He was the ace of a pitching staff that produced 94 victories to take the American League pennant by five games over Cleveland, his former team. "Wynn's ability to beat the Indians and the Yankees was a decisive factor in Chicago's first American League flag in 40 years," proclaimed *The Sporting News*, adding that his six wins over the Tribe were "a great thrill for Early, who had been traded away by the Indians two years ago." To top it all off, he won the major league Cy Young Award in a landslide vote, was selected *The Sporting News* Major League Player of the Year, and placed third in the American League Most Valuable Player voting.[108]

In 1960, Wynn's age and physical ailments—he long suffered from gout that often impacted the elbow on his pitching arm—started to come into play. He managed a winning season (13–12) and a good 3.49 earned-run average and led the league in shutouts, but his career was clearly coming to an end. Wynn had his sight set on winning 300 games before retirement. He started the 1961 season with 284, so he was determined to reach his goal before season's end. He was 7–1 coming in to that July 13 contest against the Yankees, leaving him just nine games from the magic number of which all pitchers dream. He did not take a step closer that night, however.

It was clear from the beginning that the right-hander did not have his stuff. Bobby Richardson led off with a single to left, followed by a Tony Kubek sacrifice bunt to move him along to second. Then it was Maris' turn to face the 41-year-old hurler. "Early has a little of everything and is usually tough," commented the Yankee right fielder. "This time, however, he didn't seem to have much. When I saw the pitch I couldn't wait to swing." Maris crushed the ball, which struck a sign between the lower and upper decks in right-center field. Mantle then followed with a monster shot of his own into the center-field upper deck, giving him 30 for the season. When Clete Boyer, the eighth batter of the inning, plated another run, Wynn's day was done. The Bombers went on to win, 6–2, giving starter Bill Stafford his eighth victory and moving the Yankees back into first place temporarily.[109]

Maris was somewhat surprised by the reaction of the Chicago faithful to his and Mantle's homers. "[O]ddly enough, they delighted a crowd of better than 44,000. The home-run excitement was beginning to get even the fans in other cities. They wanted their team to win, but they also came out to see if M and M would hit a homer. When we did, they were happy." Less pleased was baseball commissioner Ford Frick. With both Maris and Mantle well head of Ruth's 1927 pace, he was concerned that one of them might actually surpass his old friend. The commissioner knew the time was nigh to deal with this home run threat. He announced that before the second All-Star break he would make a "ruling" on whether or not Ruth's record was "officially" broken if accomplished in more than 154 games; that pronouncement was set for July 17.[110]

As for Early Wynn, he won his eighth game of the season on his next start, giving him 292 career victories. Sadly, though, that was his last victory of the summer. After a no-decision on July 22, Wynn's arm became so sore he could not even lift it. He was sent to Johns Hopkins Hospital in Baltimore for examination. It came as no surprise to anyone that his persistent gout had once again flared up. The White Sox at first hoped he might recover enough to resume his pitching duties, but that was not to be. After further consultation with his physician, the ailing pitcher decided to shut it down for the summer and returned to his home in Venice, Florida.[111]

Wynn returned to the White Sox the following season, but it was apparent to all that he was not the same pitcher he had been. He did start in 26 of his 27 game appearances, but was only able to secure seven victories against 15 defeats. After pitching a complete-game win on September 8 to reach 299, he failed to secure number 300 in his last three starts, even though in two of them he went the distance. On November 20 he was released by Chicago.

But the burly hurler was not about to call it quits yet. He spent the spring of 1963 trying to stay in shape in the hopes that some team would sign him up. He attempted to make it back with the Sox during spring training, but failed in those efforts in spite of pitching well. Finally in mid–June, Wynn was picked up by his old team, the Cleveland Indians. Their fans and the local press were ecstatic. "The glorious return to Cleveland of Early Wynn provides that team with a real Indian, perhaps one who can inspire his mates to go on the warpath once again," crowed Lee Allen in *The Sporting News*.[112]

He made his first start on June 21, pitching a complete game, but losing, 2–0. He had two more starts and a relief appearance before he accomplished his elusive goal. On July 13, the 43-year-old hurler toed the rubber in the second half of a doubleheader against the Kansas City Athletics. Although he was only able to pitch five innings, he retired to the radio booth with the Indians ahead, 5–4. Jerry Walker relieved him, limiting the A's to just three hits and no runs over the next four innings to give Wynn victory number 300. He was cheered by his teammates when he entered the Cleveland clubhouse after the game. "I'm glad I finally made it," an exhausted Wynn stated. "Every pitch got to be a great effort. I wanted to win so badly I tried to make each pitch perfect." That was the last win ever in his illustrious major league career. When he retired at the end of the season to become a pitching coach with the Indians, he had 300 wins, 244 loses, a 3.54 earned-run average, and 4,564 innings pitched while facing 19,408 batters over 23 seasons with three different American League clubs. He was elected to the Baseball Hall of Fame along with Sandy Koufax and Yogi Berra in 1972.[113]

Home Run # 35—Game 86—July 15—Day Game

After hitting a homer, a double, and a single in the July 13 game, Maris was feeling very good about his chances of a great season. He raised his batting average to .288, the highest it would be that summer. While it gradually went down, especially in September when he began to really press for home runs and found himself swinging at bad pitches, he was well on his way to a career year.

The Yankees were stymied by left-hander Juan Pizarro the following night. It was not surprising that Maris, who did not hit southpaws nearly as well as right-handed hurlers and had faced Pizarro only once before, was blanked in four trips to the plate. "Much of his [Pizarro's] success stemmed from his ability to stop Roger Maris," wrote the *New York Times*. He struck out once, fouled out to the catcher twice, and popped out to first base. The other Yankees had problems with the White Sox pitcher as well. The only run he allowed was an eighth-inning solo homer to Mickey Mantle, a line drive into the lower left-field seats for his thirty-first of the season.[114]

Maris' performance the following afternoon was the difference between night and day. It was not an easy battle for the Bombers, but one in which they finally prevailed in extra innings. It was one of those games which saw seven balls leave the park, but was finally decided on a measly single. The Yankees got on the scoreboard first when Elston Howard jacked one into the left-field seats off of starter Ray Herbert in the second inning. That lead, however, quickly evaporated when Sox catcher Sherm Lollar took Ralph Terry deep with no one aboard in the bottom of the inning.

The Yanks took the lead again in the next frame thanks to Maris' thirty-fifth round-tripper of the year. Two were gone when he stepped into the batter's box to face "my old friend Herbert" for the second time that day. Herbert came to the White Sox on June 10 as part of an eight-player swap with the Athletics. The 31-year-old pitcher, who clashed with Kansas City general manager Frank Lane during salary negotiations in the pre-season, was happy to move to Chicago. He was 3–6 with a 5.38 earned-run average at the time of the exchange, but was 4–2 with a 4.61 ERA since his arrival in the Windy City. He won his first three starts before losing two of his next three outings. He most recently appeared on July 9 in a relief role, scoring a victory after pitching the final two innings against the Cleveland Indians. The Chicago right-hander retired the Yankee slugger on a pop fly in the first inning of the July 15 contest, but Maris, who hit number 18 off of his former Kansas City teammate on June 9 when he was still hurling for the A's, was not fooled this time. The ball landed in the right-field upper deck about 20 feet to the left of the foul pole.[115]

But his thirty-fifth home run was not the only thing that made the game "one of my best days of the season and gave me a great deal of satisfaction." In the second inning, he gunned down J. C. Martin, Chicago first baseman, trying to stretch a single into a double, which was the last out of the inning. In the sixth with the Yankees down, 8–2, he started a four-run rally with a triple off of Herbert—that some said was close to an inside-the-park home run to open the frame. In the bottom of the eighth he prevented the White Sox from adding to their lead when he caught a Jim Landis fly ball for the second out, then hurled a bullet to catcher Johnny Blanchard to nab the fleet-footed Luis Aparicio, who had tagged up and was trying to score from third. Then in the top of the ninth, he hit a double off of left-handed reliever Frank Baumann that scored Bobby Richardson to tie the game at eight all. It was "a dazzling exhibition of all-round play that won over even the 37,730 raucous Chicago partisans at Comiskey Park." The Yankees went ahead in the top of the tenth when a Tony Kubek single scored Clete Boyer from third. Luis Arroyo successfully closed out the bottom of the inning for a hard-fought Yankee victory that kept them in first place by percentage a few points.[116]

Ford Frick's Pronouncement and the Lost Home Run

As Roger Maris was the first to admit, he was "the type of hitter who can get into a rut very easily. Without knowing why, I will suddenly get out of the groove and the base hits will stop." And that was exactly what happened over the next five games. He failed to hit even a lowly single in his next 20 trips to the plate. But two things happened that may have been factors in this sudden dry spell: he and Mantle lost a home run due to a rainout and baseball commissioner Ford Frick decided to throw a protective barrier around his hero, Babe Ruth, both of which occurred on the same day.

While Maris may have experienced a brief lull in his home-run assault, Mickey

Mantle certainly did not. The Yankees caught a flight to Baltimore immediately after their 10-inning victory over the White Sox to take on the third-place Orioles in a three-game series. On July 16, the Mick drove in both runs of a New York 2–1 victory, including his thirty-second dinger to move him to within three of Maris, who was hitless that day. Mantle's solo shot traveled 430 feet, bouncing off a running track behind the center-field wall before striking the scoreboard. That same day, Al Downing became the Yankees' first African American pitcher when he was called up from Single-A Binghamton to shore up a pitching staff hampered by arm problems to Ralph Terry and Bill Stafford. The 20-year-old southpaw appeared in just five games that season, but then went on to a successful 17-year major league career.[117]

New York was scheduled for a twi-night doubleheader on July 17, a rainy Monday evening in Baltimore. Before the start of that contest, Ford Frick made his long-awaited edict about the single-season home run record. In a meeting with a group of sportswriters in his office, he proclaimed,

> Any player who hits more than 60 home runs during the first 154 games of his club's schedule would be recognized as having established a new record. If any player does hit more than 60 home runs in the course of the new 162-game schedule [in the American League], then there would have to be some distinction made in the record books to show that Babe Ruth's record was made in a 154-game schedule and that the total of more than 60 home runs was compiled with a 162-game schedule in effect.

Frank Slocum, Frick's personal assistant, remembered the commissioner being concerned about the bad impression his decision might make. "It bothered him in the sense he felt people would think he would compromise something against another ballplayer to Ruth's advantage," Slocum contended. Contrary to popular belief, Frick did not use the word "asterisk" in relation to a record set after 154 games. That was a suggestion made by Dick Young, one of the reporters in attendance at Frick's press conference.[118]

It was a brazen move on the part of the commissioner. There was no "official" record book maintained by major league baseball, just those produced by private companies like the Elias Sports Bureau, and he had absolutely no authority to dictate to them how baseball records should be recorded. He was "working the ref" and he was very successful in doing so. A poll of the Baseball Writers' Association of America conducted by *The Sporting News* showed that two out of every three sportswriters supported Frick's decision. Even many of the players—at least initially—voiced their agreement with the commissioner. Those individuals who opposed his decree pointed to the fact that he said nothing of other records and that he waited until Ruth's record was under attack before intervening.[119]

Whether intended or not, his statement had the ultimate effect of delegitimizing in the minds of many what Maris and Mantle were doing. "It was clearly a biased decision and any legal test would describe it as a post facto law and clearly unfair in that context," argued writer Maury Allen. "Baseball records are always subject to some interpretation; but in a game which has succeeded because the records are so significant, where past and present can be measured.... Frick's decision was outrageous." As Allen observed, "The ruling would create an awful barrier for Maris and Mantle. They were now faced with a countdown each day that separated them from all other attempts at a baseball record."[120]

Both were immediately put in the uncomfortable position of having to respond to Frick's actions. Not surprisingly, Mantle seemed less disturbed by the announcement than did Maris. In fact, the Mick initially voiced support for the ruling; he would eventually change his views on the matter. Maris was cautious in his response, not wanting to come across as angry. "I think the commissioner shouldn't have made any 154-game ruling when he did," he said. "But if Mick breaks it, I hope he does it in 154. The same goes for me." Later he commented, "That was a debate I wanted no part of at this time.... The Commissioner made the ruling, and there was nothing I could do about it. I was just playing ball, doing the best I could, and hoping for a pennant." Years afterwards, Maury Allen recalled Maris' physical appearance as he talked with reporters. "The muscles on his face were taut. His eyes stared fixedly. His expression could only be described as a sneer. Roger Maris would not have a quiet day the rest of that season."[121]

While acknowledging that "the battle lines were drawn," Maris claimed that Frick's dictate did not increase the pressure on him. "I can't really say that it did. Of course it made everyone more conscious of the record, especially the pitchers. It put the spotlight on the record and, therefore, started more talk about it, more questions." There is no doubt it was always in the back of his mind, no matter what he said publicly. He ruminated over it, eventually seeing it as a dismissal of him personally even though it was aimed at Mantle as well. It was an irritant that reporters always kept fresh. From then until the end of the season, not only was he asked repeatedly if he could beat Ruth's record, but if he could do it within the 154-game limitation established by Frick as well. "What Frick did was take the joy out of the race," Allen contended. "Up to that time, it was a fun competition, but he stepped into the middle of it and made it ugly."[122]

To top it off, the fact that the vast majority of sportswriters verbalized their agreement with Frick made Maris even more suspicious of their motives. It confirmed his belief that he was seen as an interloper and someone not worthy of being mentioned in the same breath as the immortal Babe (or Mantle, for that matter). "Mickey Mantle might not have been the god Ruth was," wrote Maris biographers Tom Clavin and Danny Peary, "but at least he was a Titan. Roger Maris, being a mere mortal, was unacceptable."[123]

Even the weather seemed to be working against the M and M Boys that day. The storm clouds were literally gathering as that evening's twin bill got underway. With Whitey Ford going for his seventeenth victory, rain started falling in the third inning with the Yankees in front, 3–0. It remained that way until the sixth when Mantle led off the inning with his thirty-third homer, leaving him two behind Maris. Ford continued to pitch masterfully as the rain slackened in the sixth, finally ending up with a complete-game shutout, 5–0. Maris' contribution was a run scored after a walk in the first inning.

Rain continued to threaten as the second half of the doubleheader got underway. Starting for the Orioles was Hal "Skinny" Brown, a 36-year-old right-handed knuckleballer who began his major league career with the White Sox in 1951. His two seasons with Chicago were not particularly impressive. Used primarily as a reliever, he was 2–3 with a rather high 4.23 earned-run average in 1952 before being traded to the Boston Red Sox. He assumed the role of starter in his first season with Boston, and although he had an 11–6 record, his 4.65 ERA approached astronomical proportions. Brown spent most of the 1954 season working from the Red Sox bullpen with an occasional start. It was a devastating year for him (1–8, 4.12 ERA), one in which he lost confidence in his ability to pitch because of the continual switching from starting to relieving with long periods of inactivity in between. "I know I can win," he asserted. "But if I knew whether I was a starter or reliever, I'd be better off. You can prime yourself either way. And I'll do either, whichever they want."[124]

Brown spent most of the following summer pitching for the Oakland Oaks in the Pacific Coast League where, with the help of Oaks skipper Lefty O'Doul, he began to regain his self-confidence. He was 9–2 with a 2.95 earned-run average when the baseball gods smiled upon him: on July 14 his contract was picked up by the Baltimore Orioles, reuniting him with his former minor league manager, Paul Richards. The Baltimore pilot, who managed Brown when he was with the Seattle Rainiers in 1950, used him as a reliever and spot starter, but on a more regular basis than what the right-hander experienced in Boston. And Brown responded with renewed vigor in that role. In his first four full seasons with the Orioles (1956–1959), he was 34–29 with a 3.76 earned-run average, a considerable improvement over his Red Sox years.[125]

Baltimore started a youth movement in the late 1950s in an attempt to rebuild a struggling franchise. In 1960 when the Orioles gave the Yankees a run for their money, four of their five starters were 22 or younger. The fifth, Hal Brown, was 35, but he, along with several other oldsters like 37-year-old Hoyt Wilhelm, provided the veteran experience and work ethic needed to successfully develop a group of youngsters. "They help balance the scales and give some maturity and essential experience to the squad, along with dependable professional ability," wrote *The Sporting News*. Brown was the elder statesman of the pitching staff, someone the younger hurlers could turn to for help. A young Billy O'Dell, who roomed with Brown for a while, had nothing but praise for the older player. "[H]e gave me a lot of good advice about playing baseball and about being a major leaguer," O'Dell recalled.[126]

And for two seasons this pairing of older and young players worked. In 1960 when the Orioles finished second, Brown was 12–5 with a 3.06 ERA; in 1961 when the club finished third, he was 10–6 with a 3.19 ERA. Then in 1962 Richards left to become general manager of the new Houston Colt .45's and Baltimore fell to seventh place. Brown still had a winning record that summer, but his earned-run average mushroomed to 4.10. On September 7, the Yankees purchased his contract, using him in only two games before selling his contract to Houston in the spring of 1963. Now 38, he was long past his prime. In two seasons with the cellar-dwelling Colt .45's, his earned-run average was a good 3.62, but his 8–26 won-loss record was hardly one to recommend him for continuation in the major leagues. He was released by Houston in late September 1964, ending his 14-year big league career with 85 wins, 92 losses, and a cumulative 3.81 ERA.

Brown entered that second game of the July 17 doubleheader with a 7–3 record and a 3.75 earned-run average. Both Maris and Mantle were quite familiar with the knuckleball artist, who also threw a "slip pitch," a type of changeup taught to him by Paul Richards. The Yankee right-fielder homered off of him twice prior to 1961, Mantle six times. So it was not a total shock when Maris parked one in the first inning, Mantle in the fourth. At that point in the game, Mother Nature intervened. Just as the fifth inning started with the Bombers leading, 4–1, the heavens opened up. As thunder pealed and lightning struck, the visitors sat in their dugout praying that the storm would subside long enough to complete five innings, thus making the game official. The umpires waited over an hour before calling the game, leaving Maris and Mantle to ponder the significance of a lost homer apiece on the same day that Ford Frick changed the ground rules.[127]

The game was not simply postponed to be picked up at a later date at the point where it was suspended. Instead, it was played from the beginning as the first half of a September 19 doubleheader. Neither of them smacked one in either of those two games. It proved to be a significant event for Maris. Had the home run stood, he would have tied Ruth by Frick's deadline and had 62 total by season's end. Ruth, it should be added, did not lose any home runs to weather or for any other reason in 1927.

Both the players took it all in stride. Mantle had just emerged from the showers when the sportswriters entered the clubhouse. With blood on his neck because he nicked himself while shaving, he joked, "I cut my throat" when asked how he felt about losing a home run. Maris responded, "What are you going to do, fight city hall?" After the season, he claimed, "Even when I did get up into the high numbers I never worried about the 'lost' one. There is no use crying over spilt milk." But a couple of days before game 155, he had a slightly different reaction. With 58 homers to his credit, a weary Maris admitted the lost home run would have taken some of the pressure off of him. "That homer I lost looks bigger every day. That would have given me 59. It would have made it a little less difficult."[128]

Home Run # 36—Game 92—July 21—Night Game

With Maris' mini-slump continuing over the next three games against the Senators in Washington, Mantle used the opportunity to pass his teammate in the home run race. He belted two round-trippers in a night game on July 18 to tie Maris at 35. The first was a two-run shot in the first inning, a "sky-scraping fly to right that struck high up on the light pole above the fence and rebounded on to the field." Then in the eighth he blasted one over the scoreboard in right field. His thirty-sixth came in the second game of a doubleheader on the following night as he launched it over the right-field wall to take a one-homer lead over Maris.[129]

The struggling right-fielder did have a number of hard-hit flies, several of which were to left and center fields, an indication that his swing was just a tad off. He was not too concerned, however. "In my mind," he said, "it was strictly a case of having been too hot not to cool down. I didn't even think that possibly it was the start of a second half slump. I didn't think it, but everyone else did. That became the favorite question." In spite of losing two of three to the Senators, the Yankees held on to first place over the Tigers by a couple of percentage points.[130]

The Bombers had an off-day before heading to Boston to take on the sixth-place Red Sox on the night of July 21. It was one of those games in which neither starter was effective, a ton of runs were scored on both sides—19 in all—and the battle, ending after three and a half hours of play, seemed to last forever. Whitey Ford started for New York, but was removed in the fifth inning after surrendering seven earned runs. Bill Monbouquette got the call for Boston, but he was no more successful than his counterpart. He was relieved in the sixth after giving up six earned runs, including three homers. It was the perfect situation for Maris to get back on track, which he did in his first at-bat.

Maris took Monbouquette deep for number 33 just a week and a half earlier. The Boston right-hander had one other start since that July 9 defeat, but then was out for a week because of the death of his 47-year-old mother. That night's game was his first start since returning to the lineup. It did not take long for Maris and the Yankees to get things started. With two away in the first inning, he got hold of a Monbouquette pitch that he launched into the Red Sox bullpen in right. It was his first hit in his last 19 at-bats. Maris rounded the bases with a sense of relief that he had not fallen into a prolonged slump.

Then just as he sat back down in the dugout, Mantle belted his thirty-seventh deep into the center-field seats to move him back into the lead. It was the third time that season they homered back-to-back, a perfect example of how the two drove each other. Maris claimed not to be worried that his partner was in the home-run lead. "There was plenty of time left in the season, and I thought that I had a good shot at taking the home-run title." At that time, though, both they and most sportswriters thought Mantle stood the better chance of catching the Babe because of his switch-hitting abilities. As Maris himself acknowledged, "Because of the different pitchers and parks, Mantle has the edge. I've always thought he had the edge for those reasons. I have power only one way, to right field."[131]

The New York lead did not last for long, however. The Red Sox tied it up in the bottom of the second with two runs of their own. Then the Yankees went ahead again in the top of the next inning on a Yogi Berra two-run long ball with Maris aboard after he singled. Boston got a run back in the fourth before two more Yankee runs in the fifth put them up, 6–3. At that point, the game collapsed for Ford. In the bottom of the fifth, he surrendered four runs to give the Red Sox their first lead of the game, 7–6. The score remained there until the bottom of the eighth when Boston added an unearned insurance run off of Luis Arroyo to provide them a two-run advantage going into the ninth. That was when the renowned Yankee "five o'clock lightning" struck. After Berra drove in one run, pinch-hitter Johnny Blanchard smashed the first grand slam of his career to put the Bombers ahead permanently, 11–8. "This is one of those games that makes you proud to be a Yankee," proclaimed Maris. "Proud to be part of such a great ball club."[132]

Home Runs # 37 and 38—Game 95—July 25— Night Game/First Game of Doubleheader

Maris' bat remained silent in the final two contests with Boston. He was hitless in six at-bats on July 22, another interminable contest in which both starters failed, a slew of runs were scored (20 total), and the lead went back and forth. Just as in the previous meeting, pinch-hitter Johnny Blanchard was the offensive hero when his ninth inning solo shot tied the game at nine. Bobby Richardson and Tony Kubek then added runs of their own to give the Yankees another come-from-behind victory. Maris did better the following afternoon, hitting a two-run single in the third to put the Yankees ahead by a run. But New York lost the game in the bottom of the ninth after reliever Bud Daley gave up a pair of runs to Boston.

Instead of having an off-day after the Red Sox series, the Yankees traveled back to New York to take on the San Francisco Giants in an exhibition game on the night of July 24. The Giants had not played in New York since 1957, so there was considerable excitement about the battle to come. Nearly 50,000 fans poured into Yankee Stadium to see Mantle and Maris take on Willie Mays. While Maris failed to get a safety, Mantle did not disappoint the Yankee faithful. The Mick blasted a 420-foot rocket into the center-field seats for the only run New York got. Not to be outdone, Mays drove in two runs with a single in the fifth. The Giants picked up a couple of more tallies to give them a 4–1 victory.[133]

Next up for the Yankees was a twi-night doubleheader on July 25 as the start of a four-game series against the visiting Chicago White Sox. Maris hated twin bills, especially those at night, and he had good reason for feeling that way. Doubleheaders—there were

23 of them in 1961—were a distinct disadvantage for him. He typically performed poorly in those situations. He failed to hit in five of them, and had only one safety in each of six others. Although he did hit 13 home runs in those 46 games, the Yankee right fielder batted just .229, 40 points below his season average. He did much better when both games were in the day—a .292 batting average with eight home runs—than when the first game was in the day and the second at night (.212 batting average with one home run) or in twin affairs at night (.152 batting average with four home runs). In fact, his performance when both games were at night would have been much worse had it not been for his uncharacteristically productive performance in that evening's two-for-one contest.

As he, Mantle, and Bob Cerv drove to the Stadium early that day, Maris began to feel physically ill. "Maybe it was the heat [88 degrees at game-time], or something I ate," he told reporters after the game. "I just felt washed out. I didn't want to play." Most likely it was what he recognized months later—his anxiety over playing two games at night during a period in which he was struggling offensively. "If I had to say why I felt off key, then I guess it would be that the double-header was preying on my mind. I never liked two games in one day. I had had so many bad days in bargain bills that it probably was beginning to get to me." Regardless of how he was feeling before game time, Maris did suit-up and take his usual position in right field, which was a fortunate decision. Those two games turned out to be the greatest of his career and key to his incredible season.[134]

Starters in the first game were Whitey Ford, who was trying for his eighteenth win, and left-hander Frank Baumann, who was a product of the Red Sox farm system. The 6-foot, 205-pound southpaw was a stand-out pitcher in high school who was pursued heavily by several clubs when he graduated in 1952. A bidding war broke out among several teams with the Red Sox finally securing his services for $85,000, making him one of the highest paid "bonus babies" of that era.

The 18-year-old began his professional career at the highest level in the minor leagues, making his first start with the Triple-A Louisville Colonels on June 22. Using "his zippy fast ball and his sharp-breaking curve," the teenaged pitcher hurled a seven-inning shutout during which he surrendered just four hits while striking out five. "He looked awfully good to me," proclaimed manager Pinky Higgins. "I was surprised at his poise. You never would have guessed it was his first time out." After that incredible introduction, Baumann pitched more like the typical novice he was, ending the season at 4–6 with a 4.09 earned-run average.[135]

His sophomore minor league season was far more successful. He won 10 games while losing one and maintained an excellent 2.55 earned-run average. Later that fall he was called up for military service which lasted until the middle of 1955. His first major league appearance was on July 31, pitching over five innings of scoreless relief to secure his first big league victory. He was not quite so successful in his first career start on August 11, lasting one inning after giving up four earned runs. He experienced arm problems after that game and did not appear again until August 27. He did have a 2–1 record at the end of the 1955 campaign, but his ERA exploded to 5.82.[136]

The southpaw continued to experience arm difficulties off and on throughout the 1956 season, which limited the number of outings he had. He appeared in just seven games for Boston before being sent down to Single-A Albany in late June. He made one relief appearance for the Senators, but was shut down for the rest of the year because of the discomfort in his pitching arm. Baumann's 1957 season was much better. Having overcome the sore arm, he spent most of the summer pitching for the Double-A

Oklahoma City Indians. After going 10–7 with a 3.80 earned-run average in 26 games, he was recalled to Boston for the final month of the campaign. He got his first start on September 29, hurling seven innings of two-run ball for a win over the first-place Yankees. The Red Sox were thrilled with what they saw. "It's the first time that Baumann looked something like the kid we first had in Louisville back in 1953," crowed manager Pinky Higgins. "I don't think he was quite as fast as he was in '53, but he was fast enough and his fast ball was alive.... He got the ball where he wanted it and was in control all the time."[137]

That great promise demonstrated against New York did not come to fruition in 1958. He pitched well at the start of the season, including tossing his first major league complete game against the Cleveland Indians on May 4, going all 12 innings for a 2–1 victory. But after that things deteriorated. On June 15 he lasted just 1⅓ innings of relief in which he gave up eight earned runs. Boston had seen enough. He was sent down to Double-A Memphis and while he performed well there, the seeds of doubt were now firmly planted. Boston sports columnist Hy Hurwitz suggested that the upcoming campaign might be Baumann's "final test." The highly-paid "bonus talent" had ample opportunities to prove himself, but "has been found lacking." Hurwitz postulated 1959 very well could be the pitcher's final year with the Red Sox.[138]

Baumann was given a chance, spending all of the season with the Red Sox, and while he ended the summer with a winning record, his overall performance was less than inspiring. In the eyes of Boston management, he had failed that "final test." In five seasons with the Bosox, he compiled a 13–8 record on a cumulative 4.32 earned-run average in 54 games, pretty mediocre numbers from someone who was expected to become a dominant pitcher. On November 3, he was traded to the Chicago White Sox for infielder Ron Jackson.

Baumann was not bitter about the trade, but felt that the Red Sox had not given him enough pitching opportunities to become a consistent winner. "I have to work a lot to be effective and I didn't get it," he said. "No, I guess you can't really blame them for giving up on me," he added, "but I wasn't about to give up on myself." His self-assessment appeared to be on the mark. In 47 games for Chicago that season, he won 13, lost 6 and maintained a 2.67 earned-run average, the best in both leagues. He credited Chicago manager Al Lopez and pitching coach Ray Berres with helping him overcome the bad pitching habits he developed over the years to compensate for his sore arm. "It wasn't any one thing you can point to," he explained, "they just showed me how to get back to the kind of pitching that I had started out with, and their patience was the best thing that ever happened to me." Realizing that his fastball had lost some of its speed, he changed his grip on the ball, which resulted in a natural sinking motion on his heater. "The sinker ball became the extra weapon I had needed.... It allowed me to work the hitters low and away much more easily."[139]

Unfortunately, his 1960 success did not repeat itself in 1961. He won his first outing—a three-inning relief appearance against the Washington Senators—but after that, things suddenly worsened. By mid–July he was 6–7 with a horrendous 5.60 earned-run average. Al Lopez began referring to his 27-year-old charge as "our biggest disappointment.... He just hasn't been the same pitcher." Lopez observed that Baumann had fallen back into his bad pitching habits. "He's dropping his shoulder and is coming close to side-arm and his sinking fast ball isn't sinking." His season-long statistics proved how ineffective he became: 10–13 with a 5.61 ERA. His 117 earned runs surrendered tied him for first place in the American League and his 22 homers allowed were twice as many as the previous year. So the pitcher the Yankees faced on July 25 was far from the hurler he was in 1960.[140]

Baumann started that game with a 7–7 record, but his earned-run average of 5.62 indicated that he was eminently hittable. In fact, he had already given up 10 dingers, just one less than in the entire 1960 season. Maris had never homered off of him, although he did hit him well. In 1961 alone, he doubled twice and singled once in six plate appearances. Baumann struck him out in the first inning, but Maris was loaded for bear in the fourth. "Baumann was working carefully," he recalled, "but I got hold of one and it went high into right field." The smash was a screaming line drive that looked like it might go foul. "I stood at the plate, then saw the ball hit the foul screen on the right-field pole. Boy, that couldn't have been closer if I had walked out there and thrown the ball."[141]

With Bobby Richardson aboard on a walk, Ford now had a two-run lead. But moments later it increased a run when Mantle, batting right-handed against the left-handed Baumann, scorched a liner of his own that hit the screen on the left-field foul pole. "Poor Bauman," Maris commiserated. "He was losing 3–0 by inches." Maris now had 37, Mantle 38. "Maybe you think we didn't take a ribbing from the boys on the bench" for the mirror homers. "Imagine each of us, back to back, hitting balls against the opposite foul screens. It was a million to one shot, but it came through." Neither ball traveled great distances, but it was enough to clear both walls. Years later Baumann asserted that "in any other ballpark they'd have been caught or foul balls." Maybe, but as Maris once said, "To me a home run is a home run whether it goes 200 feet or 400 ... over the wall is far enough no matter where the wall might be. I didn't draw the plans for the ball parks, I didn't put the fences where they are. If I hit a ball over a fence it's a home run to me. I don't measure them, I just count them." Baumann faced Maris one more time that day, inducing him to pop up for the final out of the fifth inning. After giving up singles to Mantle and Elston Howard to open the sixth, Baumann was replaced.[142]

Baumann made somewhat of a comeback in 1962, ending the year at 7–6 and a much-improved 3.38 earned-run average. He was used less—just 40 games of which a fourth were starts—which may have been one of the reasons he performed better. He also added a better curve to his pitch selection as well as an improved slider. "The hitters know I have a few more pitches, so they can't lay back for the fast ball anymore," he explained. His arm problems resurfaced midway through the 1963 campaign. It marked the coming end to his career. He missed most of July and August due to a torn bicep tendon, which limited him to just 24 game appearances, all but one as a reliever. When the summer drew to a close, he had won two, lost another, and held a 3.04 earned-run average, his best since the 1960 season.[143]

The 1964 campaign was the worst of his major league career thus far. He was 0–3 with an awful 6.19 ERA, throwing only 32 innings over 22 games. Now considered a "fringe player" by the White Sox, he was traded to the Chicago Cubs at the end of the season for another marginal player, catcher Jimmie Schaffer. The Cubs, desperate for better relief pitching, promised to give Baumann "a full shot in the Cub bull pen." Sadly, things did not turn out as hoped. He made just three appearances in April and another in early May, before he was demoted to the Triple-A Salt Lake City Bees. There he pitched in 11 games before he was released. Over 11 big league seasons, Baumann won 45, lost 38, and saved 14 with a cumulative 4.11 earned-run average.[144]

Veteran right-hander Don Larsen relieved Baumann in the sixth with two on and no outs. One run came in when Moose Skowron grounded out, but Larsen got out of the inning with no further damage. He held the Yankees scoreless in the seventh before starting the eighth with Maris the first batter up.

Most remember Larsen only for his perfect game in the 1956 World Series, but he actually was a pretty decent pitcher in four of his five seasons with the Yankees. He played four years (1947–1950) in the low minors for the St. Louis Browns, then the next two years in military service. "Gooney Bird," as he was sometimes called because of his sometimes-outrageous behavior and love of the nightlife, went straight to the big club in 1953 once his military obligations were met.

His inaugural season with the lowly Browns was one of stark contrasts. He was 2–11 at the end of August, but then pitched two shutouts, two other complete games and a nine-inning start for five consecutive victories, ending the summer at 7–12 with a 4.16 earned-run average. As inconsistent as his performance was that summer, it was absolutely dreadful in 1954 when the franchise was moved to Baltimore to become the Orioles. In 29 game appearances, he won only three while losing a league-high 21. Two of his wins, however, were complete-game victories over the Yankees, which brought him to the attention of New York manager Casey Stengel. In late 1954 he was part of a 17-player swap with the Orioles that brought him and "Bullet Bob" Turley to New York. While some thought Larsen's potential "problematical," in fact his five seasons with the Yankees (1955–1959) were the most productive (45–24, 3.50 ERA) of his 14 years in the majors.[145]

The 6-foot-4, 215-pound right-hander had a reputation as being lackadaisical and lazy. On top of that, he was known as a hard drinker who frequently missed curfew. "The reason Larsen didn't care if he won or lost was that afterward he'd go out and have four or five drinks," recalled former Browns teammate Jim Brosnan. "Twice he took his bottle and disappeared with a woman." Some said that he was not worth the problems he would cause the Yankees. Casey Stengel disagreed. The Yankee skipper called the stories about Larsen "just a lot of hearsay nonsense. In a town like Baltimore, a player seen about after midnight lends himself to rumors. I have a feeling that Larsen will prove himself with us."[146]

Larsen's first season with the Yankees had a rocky beginning, however. He developed a sore shoulder in spring training and his performance and behavior because of it irritated Stengel. "He says he has a bad shoulder and he won't even try to pitch," grumbled the New York skipper, "and he came into camp overweight." Stengel's punishment was to have Larsen work out while wearing a rubber suit. "The only thing I can do with a character like him is to run him and he don't even want to run." Larsen performed so poorly in the early part of the regular season that on May 11 he was sent down to the Yankees' Triple-A affiliate in Denver. New York was even open to trading him. As the big right-hander's arm gradually healed and he got his act together, he started to pitch quite well for the Bears. During one 24-day stretch, he won five consecutive outings.[147]

Larsen already had a great fastball, but he began working more seriously on mixing it with changeups and curves; he even experimented with a screwball. He went 9–1 with a 3.69 earned-run average with Denver and was recalled to the big club as a result. On July 31 he got his first start since returning from the minors, pitching a two-run complete game victory over the Kansas City Athletics. He then won his next four outings, one of which was a shutout, two others complete games, and finished the summer with three wins in his last four outings. By the end of the season he was 9–2 with a 3.06 earned-run average. He performed well enough in the latter half of the regular season that he was given the start in Game 4 of the 1955 World Series against the Brooklyn Dodgers. While it did not go well—four innings pitched, five earned runs for the loss—at least it demonstrated he had regained management's confidence in his abilities. The Yankees were no longer shopping him around.[148]

Casey Stengel expected great things of Larsen for the 1956 season, but it certainly did not start out that way. The right-hander, who had a contract in his clause governing his weight and conduct, wrecked his car in the early hours of the morning on April 3. The miscreant, who had broken curfew, claimed he fell asleep. "It was just a bad day" was all he said. Few, however, had any doubts that drink was involved. Even he admitted years later that he had been "visiting the local waterholes" shortly before the accident. In spite of his misbehavior, the Yankee skipper seemed to take it in stride: "It was his first trip off the reservation this spring and he has done some fine pitching in the 23 innings in which we have used him."[149]

In spite of his shenanigans, Larsen started the 1956 campaign in fine fashion, pitching a complete game victory on April 17. By the end of August he was 7–5 in 33 appearances, 16 of them starts, but his earned-run average was nearly 4.00. Suddenly he discovered what the problem was: he was tipping his pitches. In a game against the Red Sox late in the season, he noticed that Boston's Del Baker, standing in the third base coach's box, was calling every one of his pitches. Larsen used an "elongated and windmill windup," but was experimenting with a no-windup delivery. He quickly conferred with pitching coach Jim Turner, who had been working with him on this different motion, and decided in the middle of the game to switch to it. The first time he employed it in an entire game was on September 3, shutting out the Orioles, 5–0; he won his last three starts of the regular season using it.[150]

He was convinced this new style of delivery was the secret to his incredible perfect Game 5 in the World Series, although he lasted less than two innings using it in Game 2. "The ability to get the ball quickly to the plate, often before the batter is ready for it, is its biggest asset," observed one sportswriter. "The biggest drawback is that you don't hide the ball from the batter." St. Louis Cardinals pitcher Tom Poholsky identified another benefit of this new pitching style, it helped with control. "[I]t enables the pitcher to keep his eye on the target," he surmised. "A fellow with a long windup, including some twisting around, has to take his eye off the plate and that's where he loses control."[151]

More than anything, though, it was a form of pitching that most batters had not seen before and it confounded them. "Every batter swings a little differently and has a different stance," Poholsky explained, "but most batters have one thing in common. They watch the pitcher and his motion." Batters make adjustments to the position of their bats as the pitcher is in his windup. The "trick" in the no-windup delivery, Poholsky postulated, was for the pitcher to deliver the ball before the batter was fully settled. Larsen confirmed Poholsky's assessment. "I felt I had better balance, and somehow that seemed to help my control," he expounded. "Also, the fact that I pitched with no wind-up put the hitters a bit off-guard because they had less time to get set and less time to prepare to hit."[152]

Whatever the advantages or disadvantages of the no-windup style, it certainly worked for Larsen. For nine innings he threw perfect ball, something rarely done at all—there were only six perfect games previously—and never in a World Series game before. It made an instant celebrity out of Larsen and, perhaps in doing so, set expectations so high he could never meet them. "I'm not sure what people expected from me after the perfect game," he reminisced 50 years after the event. "Those who managed me, or coached me, or played with or against me must have had certain expectations, and perhaps I disappointed some of them by not living up to their standards."[153]

The start of the 1957 season was not a good one for Larsen. He was 2–1 by the end of May, but his earned-run average was an unacceptable 6.29. His performance improved as the season wore on—10–4. 3.74 ERA at season's end—but it was a struggle for him. Afflicted with what Casey Stengel termed "a tender arm," he was limited to just 139⅔ innings pitched. He did appear in two games of the World Series against the Milwaukee Braves, winning Game 2 after relieving Bob Turley in the second inning, but losing the deciding Game 7 after he was lifted in the third inning having given up three runs. There were rumors that the Yankees were about to trade him, but by December they decided to hold on to him for at least another season. "The guy has the arm, the size and the power," explained Casey Stengel. "You don't quit cold on a pitcher like that."[154]

The following season was punctuated by arm and shoulder problems, then by synovitis, an inflammation of the synovial membrane in the elbow, that developed in midsummer, limiting him to just 19 starts. On July 1 he was 7–1 with a fantastic 1.77 earned-run average; by the end of the month, he declined to 7–5 with a 2.92 ERA. He ended the season at 9–6 with a 3.07 earned-run average, but there were growing concerns that his arm issues were developing into a chronic problem. Larsen recovered in time to appear in two games of the 1958 World Series, again against the Braves. He pitched a seven-inning shutout in Game 3 to win it, 4–0, but got a no-decision in Game 7 when he was lifted in the third inning with two on and New York up, 2–1. The Yankees decided to stick with him for another season.[155]

The 1959 campaign was a disaster for all concerned. Larsen ended with a losing season and a high 4.33 earned-run average. The Yankees landed in third place just four games above .500. Changes had to be made and Larsen became a key part of it. On December 11 he was included in a multi-player trade with the Kansas City Athletics that brought Roger Maris to the Yankees. New York was most decidedly the winner in that deal. Larsen was 1–10 with a 5.38 earned-run average caused, in part, by a sore arm. Maris slammed 39 home runs and won the American League Most Valuable Player Award. The following season Larsen appeared in eight games for the A's (all but one in relief) with a 1–0 record on a 4.20 ERA before he became part of another multi-player swap on June 10 that sent him to the Chicago White Sox.

Larsen appeared in 25 games for the White Sox in 1961, almost entirely as a reliever. He was able to turn his career around there, ending his summer at 7–2 with two saves and a rather high 4.12 earned-run average. Now 32, Larsen again had to pack his bags, this time journeying to the West Coast as part of a trade with the San Francisco Giants on November 30. The Giants used him strictly as a reliever over the next two seasons. He performed well in that role, winning 12, losing 11, and saving 14 while maintaining a 3.82 ERA.

The right-hander demonstrated that he could still produce under pressure. When the Giants and Los Angeles Dodgers ended the 1962 season in a tie for first place, a three-game playoff series was required to determine who would be the National League champions. In the second game, Larsen relieved in the sixth with the Dodgers up, 6–5, and a runner on third and one away. An error on the part of the catcher allowed a run to score, but Larsen got the next two outs to prevent any additional tallies. He then pitched a scoreless one-hit eighth before handing the ball to Bobby Bolin; Los Angeles ended up winning, 8–7. Then in the deciding third game, he relieved Juan Marichal in the eighth with one on and none gone and the Dodgers up, 4–2. He completed that inning without allowing a run and was credited with the win after the Giants staged a rally in the top of the ninth to take it all, 6–4. He made three relief appearances in the World Series against the Yankees, getting credit for winning Game 4 after pitching a third of an inning in the bottom of the sixth.

Larsen spent one more full season in San Francisco before being purchased by the Houston Colt .45's on May 20, 1964. He went 4–8 with an outstanding 2.26 earned-run average for the ninth place club before he was traded to the Baltimore Orioles on April 24, 1965. Now 35, the aging hurler appeared in 27 games for Baltimore, ending with a 1–2 record and another outstanding 2.67 ERA. He spent all of 1966 toiling in the minors after the Orioles released him at the start of the season. The Chicago Cubs signed him as a free agent at the start of the 1967 campaign. He was called up in early July, but was sent down to the minors after just three games. Larsen's professional career came to an end in 1968 after spending much of that summer in the minor leagues attempting to make a comeback with the Cubs. In his 14 major league seasons, he won 81, lost 91, and saved 23 on a 3.78 earned-run average in 412 games. He remains to this day the only one ever to pitch a perfect game in the World Series. "Baseball was an incredible experience for me, and I cherish its memories to this day," he said late in life. "God gave me the talent to pitch in the major leagues, and to pitch a perfect game, and I know in my heart that I gave baseball every ounce of effort I had every time I went between the lines."[156]

When Larsen entered in relief of Frank Baumann in the sixth inning of the first game of the July 25 doubleheader, he had already appeared in 10 games, one as a starter and five as the closer. He pitched well since arriving in Chicago, hurling 29⅓ innings for a 2–1 record and a save on a 3.38 earned-run average. With two on and no outs, he induced Bill Skowron to groundout to the second baseman, which allowed Mickey Mantle to score from third, but then ended the inning by getting Bob Cerv and Clete Boyer to fly out to center. He allowed a single in the following inning but no additional runs, leaving the Yankees up, 4–0, going into the bottom of the eighth. First up was Roger Maris.

The Yankee right fielder had not had many opportunities to face Larsen in the past. He did hit a home run off of him in 1959, but that was pretty much the extent of his offensive production in 13 previous plate appearances. On July 15 Larsen got Maris out on a long fly ball to right that fell just short of a homer, but that was their only confrontation so far in the 1961 season.

Interestingly, when Larsen came in to this game, Maris claimed to have turned to Bob Cerv and said he felt he would hit a home run off of him if Larsen were still around when he next came to bat. "It is hard to explain the feeling, but a hitter gets it once in a while," he maintained. And sure enough, Maris connected on Larsen's first pitch, lifting "a lofty shot" into the right-center field seats behind the scoreboard there; he was again tied with Mantle. "I hope no one saw me chuckling as I went around the bases, but it was a big thrill" after his earlier prediction. Maris faced Larsen again in the eighth inning of the second game, but the battle went to the pitcher that time; Maris grounded out to second base. Luis Arroyo, who relieved Ford in the eighth, did give up a run in the top of the ninth, but that was not nearly enough to overcome the Yanks' five-run lead. Whitey Ford now had 18 victories against two defeats.[157]

Home Runs # 39 and 40—Game 96—July 25— Night Game/Second Game of Doubleheader

Maris, who arrived at the Stadium dreading a night doubleheader, was now feeling pretty good. "I had forgotten how lousy I had felt when I came to the park," he commented. He would be feeling even better by the time the second game of the twin bill came to a conclusion.[158]

Chicago starter Juan Pizarro, who pitched a complete game victory against the Bombers on July 14, was not the same pitcher this time out. He got though the first inning without incident, but the flood gates opened wide in the second. Clete Boyer hit a home run with one aboard for two runs, Tony Kubek singled with two on for another run, and Maris knocked in a fourth run with a single of his own. After Elston Howard and Moose Skowron singled to open the third, Pizarro was lifted for reliever Russ Kemmerer. The right-hander limited the damage to one more tally and then had two out in the bottom of the fourth when Maris came to the plate. The Yankee slugger homered off of Kemmerer on June 4 for number 15, so it was not much of a surprise when he took him deep again for number 39. Oddly, it was a dinger that led to the ejection of White Sox manager Al Lopez.

Maris' knock was a low, vicious line drive that right-fielder Floyd Robinson nearly snagged. After the ball entered the stands just a couple of rows deep, it bounced back onto the field. Lopez flew out of the dugout as Maris rounded the bases, yelling at first base umpire Frank Umont. The frustrated manager was convinced the ball had not gone into the stands at all, but instead had bounced off Robinson's glove. Umont, however, insisted the ball did indeed cross over the low outfield wall only to land back on the field after striking a spectator who was trying to catch it. When Lopez persisted in his angry protest, arguing that Umont had not made it down the line far enough to see where the ball went, the umpire tossed him from the game. At that point, umpire Charlie Berry intervened, calmed Lopez down, and escorted him off the field.[159]

Kemmerer finished that inning by getting Mantle to ground back to the first baseman, then was lifted at the start of the sixth for Warren Hacker. The 36-year-old right-hander began his professional career in 1946 with the independent Pampa Oilers of the Class C West Texas-New Mexico League. He was 20–4 with a 3.68 earned-run average that summer, making the jump to Class B ball the next year, pitching for the Texarkana Bears in the Big State League. He established a 9–5 record with a high 4.99 ERA for the Bears, but on September 15 pitched a shutout over the Greenville Majors to break a tie for first place in the league. He then helped Texarkana win the league championship by hurling two of the four victories over Wichita Falls.

Hacker performed so well in spring training in 1948 that he earned himself an unexpected promotion to the Shreveport Sports in the Double-A Texas League. He had a standout season with the Sports, compiling a record of 17 wins, 14 losses, and a respectable 3.18 earned-run average in 45 games. The pitcher was praised for his "durability [249 innings pitched for the Sports] and control" and for "his rubber right arm." He pitched to contact rather than attempting to rack up strikeouts. "Hacker does not make a practice of trying to blow down the opposition with his fast ball," wrote *The Sporting News*. "A tireless workman, Hacker sees action whenever the occasion demands thread-needle control." In late September the Chicago Cubs purchased his contract from the unaffiliated Sports, where he appeared in three games for Chicago before the season ended.[160]

Hacker spent the next three summers bouncing back and forth between the Cubs and the minor leagues while he matured as a pitcher. He played most of the 1951 season with the Los Angeles Angels in the Pacific Coast League. While he was 8–15 with the Angels, his pitching was actually much better than his won-loss record might indicate. Five of his victories were shutouts; on August 30 he lost 1–0 in spite of retiring 25 Hollywood Stars batters in a row, and on September 7 he tossed a no-hitter against the Seattle Rainiers, which missed being a perfect game by one walk in the fourth inning.

"I never pay any attention to the won and loss record anyway," remarked Wid Matthews, the Cubs director of personnel. Instead, he judged pitching potential on the "essential features of pitching averages" such as "innings pitched, hits allowed, and strikeouts and walks.... On that pitching yardstick Hacker certainly measures up well." Hacker's 3.87 earned-run average, 28 game appearances, 193 innings pitched, 161 hits allowed, and 54 walks against 100 strikeouts were what impressed Matthews. He had a lively fastball as his basic pitch. In addition, "Hacker has a wonderful knuckleball and, what's more important, can get it over," continued the Cubs official. "Hacker's curve is just average, but it is good enough the way he mixes it in with his fast ball, sinker and knuckleball. He's rough on righthanders because of his side-arm delivery and he has become more successful against lefthanded swingers because he has perfected a three-quarter delivery."[161]

Matthews' faith in Hacker was more than fulfilled in his 1952 campaign with the Cubs. He ended that summer with 15 wins, nine losses, and a stellar 2.58 earned-run average in 33 games. He was also third in shutouts and second in the strikeouts per walks ratio. His rookie performance was good enough for him to receive consideration for the National League Most Valuable Player Award. "Warren Hacker ... has soared to major league stardom from minor league uncertainty with supersonic speed," wrote journalist Ed Burns. "[H]e suddenly has become one of the National League's most brilliant righthanders."[162]

Unfortunately, his success in 1952 did not continue into the 1953 season. That summer he led the league in losses with 19 while winning just 12, his 4.38 ERA was nearly two runs higher than the year before, and he led the league with 35 home runs surrendered. Part of the problem was that he was not given much run support. By mid–June he lost 10 games, five of them on shutouts, two more by one run. He soon earned the moniker "Hard-Luck Hacker." He was also "hard-luck" when it came to physical ailments. He suffered a series of blisters on his fingers over a six-week period that certainly hampered his pitching ability. The bottom line, though, was that the 28-year-old right-hander was giving up far more hits than he was in 1952.[163]

Hacker spent three more full seasons for the Cubs, but was never able to repeat anything like his 1952 performance. He was 20–41 with a 4.39 earned-run average in nearly 540 innings pitched from 1954 through 1956, and his cumulative 94 homers those three years again placed him among the top 10 in the American League. His strikeouts to walks ratio was still among the best, so control was not the issue. Stan Hack, his manager those three seasons, thought the problem lay in him trying too hard to stay in shape. "He's still a Boy Scout at heart," Hack suggested. "He worries so much about staying in condition that he wears himself out working. That's his only trouble."[164]

It was actually more than that. For one thing, his knuckleball had so much movement on it that it was occasionally difficult for his catchers to contain; at other times it was creamed. He lost a no-hit bid in the ninth inning of a game against the Milwaukee Braves on May 21, 1955, because his knuckler "took a queer bend." He planned using it to strike out George Crowe, a utility infielder who was pinch-hitting for the pitcher, "[b]ut the pitch didn't do what he [Hacker] hoped. It broke down across the plate, belt high, and Crowe took a vicious swing. The ball sailed into the right field bleacher about ten rows up." But Hacker thought his sinker was the real problem when it came to gopher balls and stopped using it for a while. The fact that finger blisters continued to be an ongoing issue for him those three seasons were a factor in his pitching woes as well.[165]

After going 3–13 with a 4.66 ERA in 1956, the Cubs decided the time had come to get rid of him. On November 13 he was part of a five-player trade with the Cincinnati Reds. Redlegs manager Birdie Tebbetts was in love with Hacker's sinker and good control. "I want to work with Hacker, and believe he can be converted into a winning hurler, especially for a club like the Reds which can give him better support in all respects than the losing Cub teams of recent years can afford him," Tebbetts declared. The first thing the manager did was to discourage Hacker from using his knuckleball. "The knuckleball is only a crutch for a pitcher to lean on when he's trying to stay in the major leagues," he said, adding that he had "enough to win without it." Even though Hacker pitched well enough that Tebbetts considered him still to be a "formidable performer," the Reds decided in mid–June to put him on waivers.

At age 32, he was picked up by the Philadelphia Phillies on June 26 and two days later was pitching relief against his former team. He won his first three starts before losing the next three. By summer's end he was 4–4 with a 4.50 earned-run average in 20 games, half of them as a starter. Hacker pitched so poorly the first part of the 1958 season that the Phillies sent him down to their Triple-A affiliate in Miami. He stayed in the Philadelphia farm system for the next three years trying to work his way back to the majors. On June 1, 1961, the Chicago White Sox purchased his contract, bringing him back up the next day to be used primarily as a closer. He did quite well in that capacity. He was 2–2 with five saves and a good 3.45 earned-run average in 20 games at the time of his appearance in the second game of the July 25 twin contest with the Yankees.[166]

Maris was facing Hacker for just the third time ever when he stepped in against him in the sixth inning. On the two previous occasions, the right-hander retired Maris on a pop fly to the shortstop and a fly ball to the right fielder. Maris already had three home runs under his belt, so the likelihood of a fourth was pretty remote. The slugger again called his shot when he saw Hacker enter the game in the fifth inning. "This doesn't happen often to me, but here for the second time in one night I just seemed to feel a home run. Once again I told [Bob] Cerv how I felt," he remembered. Cerv was incredulous. "Why don't you quit while you're ahead," the big reserve outfielder responded.[167]

Hacker cruised through the fifth, retiring the side in order, but suddenly lost his stuff in the sixth. Clete Boyer led off with a homer to left. After retiring pitcher Bill Stafford on a ground out, Bobby Richardson hit a single and Tony Kubek followed with a double to put runners on second and third in front of Maris. There "would be no point in walking me," Maris thought as he strode to the plate, not with Mantle next up. "Because of the feeling I had confided to Cerv, I faced Hacker full of confidence.... I don't know if one of Hacker's knuckle balls didn't dance or a curve didn't curve, but I remember how it felt as I hit it. It felt great. I knew it was gone."[168]

So did everyone else in the Stadium. There was no doubt about this one. "Maris sent the ball, on a first pitch, soaring over the 407-foot marker in right center, protected by a screen on top of the high back wall." Some estimated the ball traveled at least 450 feet into the seats. "It probably was the longest homer Maris has hit as a Yankee," speculated the Associated Press. Number 40 was now in the books, leaving him two up on Mantle, while surpassing his 1960 home run total. After Mantle walked and Elston Howard homered, Hacker was able to get the final two outs of the inning. Don Larsen relieved for the last two innings with no additional Yankee runs. The Bombers had indeed bombed the White Sox, 12–0, putting them back into first place a half-game ahead of the Tigers.[169]

That game was Hacker's worst outing of the 1961 season by far. He got back on track after that, closing out the summer with three wins, three losses and eight saves on a 3.77 ERA. It marked the end of his 12-year journey in the major leagues. He spent the next five seasons at the Triple-A level for the White Sox, but never made it back to the big club. Now 41, he threw in the towel at the end of the 1966 season. He spent the next few years managing in the minor leagues before leaving the game for good.

There was a telling incident that happened in Maris' first at-bat in the second contest that demonstrated the intensity of his approach to the game. Juan Pizarro, a tough left-hander who retired Maris on three consecutive pop ups in a game two weeks earlier, got him to do so again in that initial plate appearance. Even though he had just completed a game in which he had two homers and three RBIs, Maris was infuriated that he failed to deliver, especially since there was a runner on base. "Roger was mad as hell," one of his teammates revealed. "Roger doesn't kid around too much," commented Joe DeMaestri, a Yankee utility infielder. "He takes the game more seriously than lots of other guys," which was why manager Ralph Houk respected his right fielder so much. "Maris is the ideal bear down ballplayer. Always out to win. A real pro."[170]

Maris was hypercritical of himself, a character trait that sometimes made him appear angry immediately after a game. He admitted that he could be "a hot-headed, red-necked, miserable guy" when he failed to live up to his own expectations. Those reporters who followed the Yankees on a regular basis knew Maris had a playful side as well, but came to expect "occasional temper tantrums" from him and did not take it personally. That was not the case with those in the press who did not know him well. All they saw was a highly-paid, angry young player who appeared to be ungrateful for the spectacular season he was having. Unfortunately, that perception became the one most commonly portrayed in newspapers across the country, a one-dimensional portrait that haunted him the last two months of the season as the pressure on him mounted to levels most other players never experienced.[171]

Mantle, of course, had his angry side, too. His was demonstrated by throwing his bat or kicking something in the dugout and then sulking at his locker after the game. But sportswriters were used to this behavior from him, so it surprised no one when he engaged in it. Interestingly, they tended to forgive him his transgressions when they did not do so for Maris. Partly it was because Mantle, who was in his eleventh season with New York, was now viewed as the heart and soul of the Yankees, and thus the more deserving of the two. Maris, on the other hand, had spent just one season in Yankee pinstripes. In addition, Mantle was seen as the underdog to that upstart Maris, and who doesn't love an underdog? So Mantle's angry outbursts were overshadowed by his "fine, ribald humor" and "his inherent class." Maris was found wanting in comparison.[172]

Reporters swarmed around Maris immediately after the game, asking question after question as they surrounded him in the clubhouse. "Newsmen knocked each other over for standing room at Roger's locker after the game," recalled Ralph Houk. "What kind of pitches did he hit? Did he favor Wheaties, the breakfast of champions? Did he eat two steaks for dinner? Rog' was snapped, taped, quizzed until after midnight." It was a pattern that repeated itself time and again as the season wore on. "This was one night I didn't care what they asked," Maris stated later.[173]

He was relaxed as he answered the barrage of questions hurled at him and, as always, was direct and frank in his responses. When asked for the umpteenth time if he thought he would break Ruth's record, his inevitable response was that he was "just wheeling the bat on every swing and trying to ignore the record. I don't read the papers enough to have all the talk about Ruth's record put any pressure on me." Was he concerned that Mantle might surpass him? "Boy, I just want him to keep hitting 'em, too. The way he's going, they've got to pitch to me first." What about his sub-.300 batting average? "Listen, you can forget about batting averages. There are two things a player never forgets—his home runs and runs-batted-in totals." Was the ball juiced? "I didn't know if the ball was a 'rabbit,' but it was okay with me as long as they were jumping off my bat." Then why so many home runs compared to Ruth's day? "I told the writers that I didn't think it was the ball, but the hitters. To me the old-timers were a bunch of Punch-and-Judy hitters. Any time I saw pictures of the old-timers I noticed they choked the bat. They were just trying to meet the ball and drive it past the infielders. They didn't swing from the end the way I, and most of today's players, swing."[174]

For Maris being regularly subjected to this type of grilling by the media quickly became a living hell. As Maury Allen, who covered the Yankees for the *New York Post*, remembered it, "there were anywhere from twenty to forty members of the press, radio, and television around Maris or Mantle or both." It was something Maris, even more than Mantle, had to confront after every game from late July until the final game. Allen described the pure pandemonium that erupted during the final two months of the season:

> Magazine writers began collecting. More and more newspapers were sending two, three or four sportswriters to cover the Yankees, one to watch the game and two or three more to write about Roger. They approached him immediately as he entered the clubhouse, dogged his steps, hounded him for reaction to quotes and interviews about him appearing around the country, followed him to the batting cage, studied his hitting style, watch the game, and repeated the cycle after the game. He found no rest until he entered his car at home and drove off with Cerv or Mantle or Julie Isaacson or some other friend.

Babe Ruth never had to endure this type of frenzy, Allen pointed out. He "never saw press after a game because sportswriters only started visiting baseball clubhouses for postgame quotes after World War II. When Ruth chased the home run record in 1927, it was his own mark of 59 in 1921 he was chasing. Maris and Mantle were chasing history."[175]

Phil Pepe, who began covering the Yankees for the *New York World-Telegram and Sun* on a fulltime basis in early August, arrived on the scene just at the point where the stress on Maris was really beginning to show.

> At first, I found him [Maris] to be Jolly Roger, mostly cordial, cooperative, approachable, and relatively at ease. At the same time, he spoke in a dull monotone, with platitudes and clichés. He had very little to offer, but there was rarely an edge in his voice. He didn't smile often, but when he did it was a warm, welcoming smile that brightened a pleasant, handsome face that was crowned by a blond crew cut. As time went on and the criticism piled up along with the incessant, inane questioning, Maris became less approachable, more difficult to interview, and less quotable....
>
> Occasionally he answered questions curtly. It was not out of malice or lack of cooperation. In retrospect, I believe it was simply Maris being Maris. He got no enjoyment out of being the center of

attention. He didn't play for records [or] for personal glory. His priorities were family, country, team. He was among the most humble of stars.[176]

This frenetic and agonizing scrutiny was not confined to the clubhouse alone. He was hounded and followed by groupies and autograph seekers wherever he went. One of the reasons he, Mantle, and Cerv rented an apartment in New York rather than live out of local hotel rooms as many of their teammates did was because they could not cross a lobby or even rest peacefully in their accommodations without a gaggle of fans chasing them. Maury Allen observed how, when traveling, Maris "hid in his room or in a teammate's room. The phone never stopped ringing. The lobbies of the hotels were being inundated with fans. People were constantly knocking at Maris's hotel door at all hours. Young fans seemed to have a knack for discovery, always finding Maris's room."[177]

He told of an incident that occurred one night after a late-ending away game. Around 2:00 in the morning someone started pounding on his door. He opened it only to find a young woman standing there. "Mr. Maris?" "No," Allen responded. "Aren't you Roger Maris?" "I'm not that lucky," he said. "I was told he was in room 679," she explained. "Might be," Allen told her. "This is 697." At that point she took off in hot pursuit of her quarry. Allen did not indicate what happened after she left, but Maris would have been horrified if she did find his room. Unlike some players, he was devoted to his wife and children and did not play around on the road. Incidents like this one just added fuel to his intense dislike of all the hype surrounding him that summer. "I couldn't go anywhere," Maris complained. "If I went out to dinner a crowd would collect. I had to stay in my room all the time. I hated it. I really like to be around people. I like to be able to sit around with my friends and shoot the breeze. I like to be free to do anything I want. Now I wasn't free to do anything or go anywhere."[178]

Sadly, there was no one there to help guide or shelter Maris from the onslaught of press and public. Bob Fishel, who handled press relations for the Yankees during that period, admitted years later that the organization made a mistake leaving Maris to fend for himself. "Maybe we didn't do as good a job of protecting Roger as we could have. We should have done something like the Reds did with [Pete] Rose. An organized postgame press conference each day as he chased the [Ty] Cobb [all-time hits] record. That was it. But who knew? The record chase got too big too fast."[179]

As if the increasingly bright spotlight of celebrity was not pressure enough for him to endure, it was around this time he began to sense a decided fan preference for Mantle to break the record rather than him. Ralph Houk started receiving letters insisting he bat Mantle ahead of Maris because many fans—as did some in the press—believed Maris had the advantage batting in front of Mantle. Houk, of course, was having none of it. "I have the batting order set up this way for a reason," he stated. "I'm not getting involved in the home-run race. I'm only interested in the pennant race and for that I believe the present batting order is my best. I want Mickey in between Rog and Yogi."[180]

That preference was often expressed in boos for Maris and cheers for Mantle. Although Mantle had been heckled frequently in the past, now Maris was more the focus of fan ire. "Mick and I were going good and had a home-run race going. The fans began to get behind Mickey," he soon realized. "Now he would be cheered all the time, while the fans began to get on me. It wasn't vicious, but they got off Mickey and on me." Even Mantle noticed how he was cheered much more often than in the past. "Hey, Rog," he ribbed Maris one day, "it's nice to have you around. You seem to be taking over the boo-birds. It's nice to see them on somebody else for a change." An informal poll of 50 Yankee partisans standing in line to buy tickets for an early August game confirmed the shift in favor of Mantle. While some stated they did not want either of them surpassing Ruth, most others indicated they "wouldn't mind if Mantle, a .326 hitter, broke Ruth's record, but would be disappointed if Maris, batting .276, did so."[181]

Maris and, to a lesser extent, Mantle, began receiving angry letters from those who did not want him to become the new single-season home run king. "From the way my mail reads, I gather that most people are rooting against me, rather than for me," he told one sportswriter. "Naturally, some of the letters are friendly. But the majority of people who write me are pretty rough. It seems most of them want to tell me I'm a bum." Mantle got his share of abusive letters, too, but, as the reporter noted, "Maris is annoyed by the public's hostility. Mantle, who has been hooted for years at Yankee Stadium, takes the criticism in stride." Maris, though, had "become the principal target of the public's wrath," which was hard for him to handle. It became even more distressing for him as the letters grew increasing hateful—including death threats—the closer he got to the record.[182]

6

AUGUST

Home Run # 41—Game 106—August 4—Night Game

Ray Herbert, one of Maris' favorite victims in 1961, was pitching for Chicago the next afternoon. The Yankee slugger took the right-hander deep twice already that season for numbers 18 and 35, but he had no luck against him that day. He went zero for three in three plate appearances, including two groundouts and a fly to right. "I figured that perhaps I was tired from all the excitement of the night before. It is tough to play the afternoon following a twi-night double-header," he noted. That must indeed have been the case because none of the other Yankees had any difficulty with Herbert. Mantle hit number 39 with one on in the first inning, launching one deep into the right-center field seats, "scattering a covey of shirtless sunbathers." Johnny Blanchard immediately followed with a solo shot of his own into the right-field stands. In the fourth, Blanchard again parked one off of Herbert, giving him four homers in four consecutive at bats which tied a major league record. Two outs later, the light-hitting Clete Boyer rapped the fourth homer that day off of the unlucky pitcher. The Bombers won, 5–2, keeping them in first place by half a game.[1]

The Yankees made it a clean, four-game sweep the next night, defeating the White Sox, 4–3. Maris hit a single in the first inning and contributed a run in the fourth with a double. As he was coming into second, though, he felt something pop in his left thigh. He was able to score on a Mantle single, which proved to be the deciding run, but was hobbling so badly he had to be removed from the game. It was nothing season-ending—a pulled hamstring—but Maris immediately became concerned that his "second-half injury jinx" had reared its ugly head once again. He was especially fearful he would be benched for an extended period. "That had happened before," he recalled, "and, each time, got me off timing and out of the groove." And, naturally, the press speculated that Maris' pursuit of Ruth might come up short because of it. "Injury Hoodoo Hits Maris for Third Straight Season," screamed a caption in *The Sporting News*. After recounting how his injuries in 1959 (appendicitis) and 1960 (bruised ribs) had seriously disrupted his offensive production those two seasons, the article described how "the hamstring muscle ... has much to do with holding the athlete together." Because of the affliction, "his advantage over Ruth, and fine chance to go into September with 50 or more homers, was fading."[2]

Adding insult to injury, some in the press were critical of how Maris was responding to his bum leg. "[A]lthough Roger's a fine fellow, he's a bit of a worrier," wrote John Drebinger of the *New York Times* a bit snidely. "He frets no end when the slightest muscle twinge throws off the delicate mechanism of his perfect timing. On the other hand, Mantle, though far more prone to injury, seems impervious to pain." In other words, Maris was a whiner who gave in to pain, Mantle a stoic who played through it.[3]

There was no doubt the injury limited his playing time and most likely slowed his home-run onslaught, but fortunately it was only a bump in the road. With his thigh tightly bandaged, he was able to play in the afternoon contest on July 28, the first of three games with the visiting Baltimore Orioles. He managed a single in four plate appearances, but Baltimore skunked the Yanks, 4–0. He was held out of the lineup the following afternoon because it had rained all night and Ralph Houk was afraid Maris might slip on the wet grass, causing even greater injury to his leg. Yogi Berra, who was playing right for the hobbled Maris, hit an eighth inning homer to give Whitey Ford his nineteenth victory. With a twin bill on July 30, Houk decided to keep Maris on the bench for the first game. He did appear as a pinch-hitter in the ninth, but grounded out to end the game, a 4–0 loss. Maris had a hit and a walk in the second game, but was removed in the eighth for a pinch-runner.[4]

The Orioles went on to win, 2–1, but not without some post-game fireworks. When the Yankees loaded the bases with no outs in the bottom of the ninth, it seemed a cinch the Bombers would bring in at least one run to tie the game. Fortune, however, was not smiling on them that day. Standing at the plate with a 3–2 count, Clete Boyer started to first when the next pitch appeared to be low and outside. Home plate umpire Ed Hurley saw it differently and called Boyer out. The Yankee dugout stirred in disgust at the call, but that was just the first out and the bases were still loaded. But then Hector Lopez, who pinch-hit, swung at the first pitch, grounding into a classic 6–4–3 double play. Game over. Houk, still steaming from the called third strike to Boyer, rushed Hurley and, in the course of a vociferous exchange, made physical contact with the umpire. According to Hurley, "He definitely bumped me. I'll have to report it to the league." Houk did not recall touching Hurley, but he did admit to shoving and being shoved. Johnny Blanchard had to grab the enraged manager from behind and drag him from the field. The next day Houk was fined $250 and suspended for five days.[5]

On July 31, the second All-Star game was held, this time in Boston. Still concerned about his leg, Maris did pinch-hit—unsuccessfully—but otherwise did not appear in the game. Not having homered since the July 25 doubleheader, he was somewhat concerned that he had lost his home-run stroke. "I was off just enough so that I stopped hitting the ball in the air. Suddenly home runs would be few and far between." On top of that, his leg still bothered him and would until mid–August, which may explain why he had only one homer over the next 11 games. Mantle, as well, did not hit a dinger in the final five games of July, but his homer drought did not last as long.[6]

When play resumed on August 2, home-run fever was in full swing. The *New York Times*, as well as many papers across the country, began publishing daily graphics depicting how the two Yankee boppers were doing in comparison to Ruth. The tight pennant race between New York and Detroit took a backseat to the daily exploits of the M and M Boys. The second half of the season opened at home with a doubleheader against the Kansas City Athletics. Amazingly, New York was still in first place despite losing all three contests to the Orioles. Ralph Houk could only watch from the sidelines as the Bombers renewed their push for the league championship.

With Frank Crosetti managing from the third base coach's box, the Yankees were able to pull off a twin victory. Whitey Ford was going for his twentieth win in the first game, but had to resign himself to a no-decision when the A's tied it up at five in the top of the ninth inning. Fortunately, the Yanks were able to win it on an error by the Kansas City catcher as Maris crossed the plate on a fielder's choice off the bat of Bob Cerv. Luis Arroyo, after relieving Ford in the ninth, was credited with the victory. New York had an easier time in the second game, winning it, 12–5. Maris did not homer, but did drive in the first New York run on a double to left. Mantle then blasted a ball into the upper right-field deck with Maris aboard, tying him with his compatriot at 40 each. Maris was hit on the right leg by an Art Ditmar fastball to open the third. A ground-rule double by Yogi Berra moved him to third, which was followed by a Johnny Blanchard single that plated both of them. Maris was removed at that point as a precaution so that he could ice down the area struck by the pitch. He was back in the lineup the next night, but it was for naught. The A's jumped on starter Bud Daley for three runs in the first inning and never looked back, winning it, 6–1, behind the masterful pitching of Bob Shaw. Maris scored the lone Yankee run on a Yogi Berra double in the sixth inning.[7]

The Minnesota Twins came into town for a four-game set beginning with a single contest the night of August 4. Starting for the Twins was right-hander Camilo Pascual, a product of the Washington Senators organization. Cuban-born "Little Potato"—his older brother, Carlos, was called "Potato"—pitching in his eighth major league season, became one of the most dominant hurlers in the American League in spite of playing for some very weak teams. Maris was once asked which pitcher gave him the most difficulty. Without hesitation he named the Twins' righty, stating that he was "the pitcher I'd like most to see out of the league." Indeed, in 51 at-bats from 1957 through 1960, Maris hit a pathetic .137 with just one home run (1958) among his seven safeties. Even in the current campaign when the Yankee slugger handled most pitchers well, he had only a double in nine plate appearances against Pascual.[8]

Based on his performance during his first four years with the Washington Senators (1954–1957), few would have guessed that the 5-foot-11, 170-pound right-hander would end up pitching 18 seasons in the major leagues. Part of the problem was that the Senators could not decide if he was better as a starter or a reliever and kept alternating him between the two. As a result, he won just 20 games while losing 54 with an awful cumulative 5.10 earned-run average over those four summers. The 1955 campaign was particularly torturous for the young hurler as he appeared in 43 games, mostly in relief, ending at 2–12 with a 6.14 ERA. He blamed manager Chuck Dressen for not using him enough and made it known that he preferred to be traded rather than continue under Dressen's stewardship. But the Washington front office had no intentions of getting rid of a pitcher who showed great promise in spite of what his won-loss record indicated. For his part, the Senators' skipper stated, "I like Pascual and his chances of being a big winner. I'd be a fool to alienate a fellow with so much potential."[9]

Although 1956 was not a stellar year for Pascual (6–18, 5.87 ERA), there were signs that things were turning around. For one thing, the 22-year-old was learning to control his temper, which Dressen identified as one of his biggest problems. "He doesn't get mad anymore when a ball is booted behind him. Last year he'd get sore and try to ram his fast ball past the batter and they'd ram it back at him even faster." One indication of his improvement was his strikeouts-to-walks ratio. In 1955 he walked 70 while striking out 82. In 1956 it was 89 walks to 162 strikeouts, tying him with Walter Johnson for the Senators' season strikeout record, which he broke in 1959. The fact that he was being used more as a starter was also a factor in his turnaround.[10]

One issue he definitely had to overcome was his propensity for giving up gopher balls. He led the American League with 33 that season, which was one reason he lost so many games. "He's his own worst handicap," argued Dressen. "He acts as if nobody is supposed to get a hit off his fast ball. When it does, he gets mad and wants to strike the next eight guys out. By that time a lot of stuff has come off his fast ball and he's throwing fat ones up there." The manager did comment, though, that he thought Pascual to be "the best six-inning pitcher in baseball." The righty admitted as much late in his career. "I used to throw as hard as I could for almost six innings. I would strike out everybody. But I couldn't go nine innings and win games."[11]

Pascual had losing records in 1957 (8–17) and 1958 (8–12), but it was clear by now that he was on the cusp of a great career. He got a handle on his home-run problem, allowing just 11 in 1957 and 14 in 1958, and his earned-run average steadily declined over those two summers, 4.10 and 3.15, respectively. He continued to strike out far more than he walked. In fact, he led the American League in strikeouts per nine innings pitched in 1958. His big breakthrough came in 1959 when he finally reached his full potential. He started off by losing his first two starts, but then pitched lights out after that. By the end of the summer he won 17 and lost 10 for a team that finished last with a 63–91 record. His 2.64 earned-run average was the second best among American League pitchers and he placed fourth in wins. He also led the league in complete games and shutouts while coming in second in strikeouts and fewest home runs in nine innings pitched.

He was elected to the American League All-Star team for the first time and was in contention for the Most Valuable Player Award. Suddenly, other teams were anxious to acquire Pascal, as well as Harmon Killebrew, with the Cincinnati Reds offering as much as $500,000 apiece for them. Senators owner Cal Griffith, though, refused to part with either the 25-year-old hurler or his slugger. "[Reds vice-president] Gabe Paul doesn't have to prove to me Pascual is the best pitcher in the majors," declared Griffith. "That was the boast I was making all last season [1958] and Pascual proved me to be right."[12]

What was the secret to Pascual's growing success? First, it was his wicked curveball—what he referred to as "my big curve" as opposed to his "slow curve"—that many considered among the finest in the game. He used to deliver it sidearm until Hall-of-Fame pitcher Dolf Luque taught him to throw it overhand. He acknowledged that before converting to that delivery, he "never really had control of my curve. It wasn't sharp." Making the adjustment was the key to its effectiveness. "Without a doubt the Cuban [Pascual] had the most feared curveball in the American League for 18 years," contended Russ Kemmerer, a former teammate. "Camilo had a direct overhand delivery and a high leg kick that shielded the ball from the hitter until the last possible moment. To make it more deceptive he twisted his body around almost to second base before delivering the ball to the plate." It "would spin madly toward the batter, and then, at the last second, would break away with a huge, round-house arc."[13]

The right-hander had an outstanding fastball to complement his curve. "Pascual had a blazing fastball that he kept high in the strike zone," continued Kemmerer. "His curve started out at the same level and broke straight down ending up about knee high," he added. Pascual clarified, though, that "it wasn't until I learned to throw my fast ball low as well as high that I became a big winner." Long-time infielder Pete Runnels believed Pascual's fastball to be as overpowering as that of Sandy Koufax. "Koufax? He's fast, but how can anybody hum 'em in there faster than Camilo Pascual of the Twins?" Phil Rizzuto, one-time Yankee shortstop, recalled, "When I was hitting against him, I couldn't get a foul. He has as good a curve as anybody in the business and his fast ball sings." It was the combination of the two pitches that made Pascual such a domineering pitcher. As Ted Williams once observed, "I've seen guys with better curves, and some with better fast balls. But I've never seen a pitcher who could throw both as well as Pascual." And he had great control to go along with this pitching arsenal. From 1961 through 1963, he led the league in strikeouts (629) while issuing very few walks in comparison (240); his 3.49 strikeouts-to-walks ratio in 1962 was tops in the American League.[14]

Pascual's final season in Washington was hampered by a sore arm that kept him out of the lineup all of September, but he still managed a 12–8 record with a great 3.03 earned-run average. In 1961 the franchise was relocated to Minnesota to become the Twins and it was there that Pascual pitched the best ball of his career. He went 88–57 with a cumulative 3.31 ERA from 1961 through 1966 before being traded back to the new Senators. He led the league in strikeouts three times, twice in complete games and shutouts, and won 20 or more games in two consecutive seasons (1962–1963). Pascual was plagued with arm and shoulder problems off and on throughout his career and in 1965 missed all of August as he underwent surgery to repair muscle damage near his right armpit. He recovered sufficiently to start Game 3 of the 1965 World Series, but suffered the loss after giving up three runs in five innings of work.[15]

The 1966 campaign was Pascual's last with the Twins. He had a great beginning to the season—he was 6–1 with a 2.52 earned-run average by mid–May—but then began experiencing arm difficulties once again. He made only four appearances in August and September, ending the season at 8–6 with a very swollen 4.89 ERA. The time had come for him to leave the Twin Cities and on December 3 he was traded back to the Washington Senators. Now 33 years old with his glory days behind him, nonetheless he was the best pitcher on the second-division Senators for the next two seasons. By 1969, however, it was readily apparent that the veteran right-hander was fast approaching the end. After managing only two wins against five defeats on an awful 6.83 earned-run average through early July, he was picked up by the Cincinnati Reds. Sadly, he made just five appearances for them before further arm problems put him on the disabled list in early August.

After being released by Cincinnati on April 13, 1970, he was signed by the Los Angeles Dodgers that same day. He appeared in 10 games as a reliever then was released in late August. He pitched briefly for the Cleveland Indians in early 1971 before his professional career came to an end at the age of 37. Had Pascual been pitching for better teams earlier on, it is quite possible he would have been elected to the Hall of Fame. As it was, he won 174 games, lost 170 with a cumulative 3.63 earned-run average in 529 game appearances over 18 major league seasons. Most impressive were his 2,167 strikeouts, ranking him sixty-eighth on the all-time list in that category.

The right-handed curveball artist was 8–12 at the start of the August 4 contest at Yankee Stadium. His earned-run average was a decent 3.67, but his home-run numbers were up, 19 to that point. Part of the reason for his losing record was that he was still adjusting to pitching in Metropolitan Stadium, a hitter-friendly park, as opposed to the more-cavernous venue of Griffith Stadium. "Is very hard to pitch here," he explained to one interviewer. Yankee Stadium also seemed to give him fits in the home-run department. In fact, he surrendered more career homers in New York—26 in 32 games—than in any other away-park. That pattern was about to repeat itself.[16]

Had it not been for a rough start, Pascual could have been victorious that day. He allowed four earned runs in the first two innings, but only one more after that. But he was doomed from the very beginning. After giving up singles to Bobby Richardson and Tony Kubek to open the bottom of the first, he then had to face Maris. The Yankee right fielder did not homer in his previous eight games, but he did bat .364 during that stretch, so he was not in a hitting slump. Maris found Pascual to be "the toughest right-hand pitcher in the league for me." So far in 1961, he had only one hit in nine plate appearances against his tormentor.[17]

But Pascual did not have his usual control that night and Maris connected on a fat pitch, launching a rocket down the line that struck the right-field foul pole, giving him number 41, one more than Mantle. "[T]his wasn't the pitcher I would have picked to try and end that streak against me," he commented later. What made Maris especially proud was that those three RBIs made it 101 for the year, surpassing the goal of 100 he set for himself early in the spring. "From now on each RBI I got would be 'gravy,' and maybe I could get enough 'gravy' to slip into the RBI title."[18]

Pascual gave up another run in the second inning on a Richardson double, but then settled down until the sixth when Elston Howard hit a solo shot off of him. He was replaced in the eighth with the Twins down, 5–2, but was not collared with the loss when Minnesota tied it up on a three-run dinger by Harmon Killebrew off of Luis Arroyo in the top of the eighth. The game went into extra innings before Johnny Blanchard gave the Yankees a hard-fought victory on a three-run blast of his own with two gone in the bottom of the tenth.

The Bunt Heard Around the World

Maris did not hit another homer until a week later, a seven-game drought during which his bat cooled off in other ways as well. The Yankees, however, continued to win without him, taking eight consecutive contests to put them ahead of Detroit by four games. It was also during this stretch that Mantle retook the home run lead.

The Yankees won the following afternoon, 2–1, with Maris scoring what proved to be the winning run in the eighth after he singled and Mantle tripled him home. The doubleheader starting the afternoon of August 6 was all Mantle. Whitey Ford was again going for his twentieth victory, but got into trouble early, giving up five earned runs in the first three innings alone. Mantle, in the meantime, did his best to keep the game close. He belted a two-run homer in the first inning and solo a round-tripper in the third to make it 5–3 in favor of the Twins. Those two shots gave him 42 for the season, one better than Maris. The Yanks tied it up in the fifth and there it remained until the tenth when Ford gave up another run on a solo homer, his third gopher ball of the day. Fortunately, Johnny Blanchard tied it back up with a jack of his own to open the bottom of the tenth. It was not until the fifteenth inning that New York secured the victory on a Yogi Berra force out at second that scored Bobby Richardson from third. Hal Reniff got the win in relief. Mantle homered for the third time that day leading off the second inning of the second game, giving him 43. It was the first of three runs the Bombers scored that game, but it was enough to beat the Twins who managed just two runs of their own. Maris had two singles in 12 at-bats, but nether contributed to New York's twin victories.

The Los Angeles Angels arrived in town the next day to begin a four-game series starting with a single contest that night. It was an ordinary game other than for what Maris did in his second at-bat of the evening. With the Angels up, 1–0, he stepped to the plate in the third inning with Bobby Richardson on third and two away. Noticing that the infielders were playing back because everyone expected him to swing for the fences, Maris signaled to Richardson that he had something else in mind. When Angels starter Ken McBride delivered the pitch, Maris laid down a perfect bunt along the third-base line. "The surprised Angels were caught flat footed," he recalled. "I had no trouble beating it out for a hit and got the tying run home. The fans were shocked."[19]

"Shocked," to say the least; there were even some boos when he did it instead of swinging away. But it was not only the spectators who were stunned. Sportswriters across the country were incredulous. How could a player who had a good shot of surpassing Babe Ruth dare laydown a bunt instead of trying to hit one out? The very audacity of it all! Since the Yankees ended up winning, 4–1, the press was even more critical of his decision than they might ordinarily have been.

When reporters entered the clubhouse after the game, the only thing they wanted to ask about was the Maris bunt. "Pencils were poised and reporters were elbowing each other in the approved manner as they jockeyed for position, the better to capture the pearls that tumbled from Maris' lips." Yes, he told the scribes, it was his decision to bunt in that situation. "What I was interested in at the time was getting the run in," he explained. But you sacrificed an at-bat to drive in a run that ultimately was not needed, they argued. "We might not have got another one," he responded. "I've told you guys the game wasn't all home runs. Other runs count, too." When one of the writers challenged Maris, calling his response "bull," he became angry. "I told them that if we went on to win the pennant, I didn't care if I didn't hit another home run all season," he said afterwards. "I would gladly settle for my forty-one as long as I could get hits that helped win the flag. I admitted that I liked to hit homers, but insisted that I wasn't always swinging for them." While some writers might not have believed he was being completely honest with them, it was not the last time he bunted that season, further proof that he meant what he said. He did so again in the first inning of a game against the Indians on September 7 when he had 54 homers and his opportunities for catching Ruth were dwindling rapidly.[20]

Mantle leapt to his teammate's defense. "It was a big league play by a big league ballplayer," he proclaimed. "Home runs are great, but the idea in this clubhouse is to win the pennant. That ought to prove home runs don't win 'em all. It was a helluva play." Mantle noted that he bunted often as well, and would have done so in that same situation. "I bunt a lot, and sometimes I get criticized for not swinging and maybe hitting one into the seats. I say they're wrong. I try to play baseball to win. Just like Roger did in this case. Sometimes a bunt is better than a home run. Sometimes it's a much better gamble." Ralph Houk, managing for the first time since serving out his five-game suspension, gave his full support to Maris' decision. "That was a hell of a play," to told the assembled press. "It proves that Maris puts winning ahead of home runs.... It was clever baseball."[21]

Home Run # 42—Game 114—August 11—Night Game

Although Maris batted a meager .091 over the next three games against the Angels, he did not believe he was in a real batting slump. "It had now been some sixteen games in which I had hit only one home run," he said. "I wasn't in a slump for in twelve of the sixteen games I had had one or more hits. I had been doing my job. I was getting hits and knocking in runs to help the club keep winning." In fact, during that homerless period he drove in seven runs, scored eight, and walked nine times while striking out on three occasions, so he was not that far off his usual level of offensive production. Ralph Houk agreed. "Maris is not in trouble," the Yankee manager insisted. "There are certain pitchers who make trouble for you as you go along. But Maris isn't in trouble. Not by any means."[22]

Maris, though, began to feel a little concerned after going hitless against the Angels the last two games of the series. "I began to wonder if something had gone wrong with my swing," he confessed. The Yankees boarded a train to Washington after the August 10 game for a four-game series with the Senators. Griffith Stadium was not his favorite venue, mainly because of the 30-foot tall right-field wall that stopped many a ball from leaving the park. In his last visit there in mid–July, he failed to get even one hit in 12 trips to the plate, which added to his anxiety. "In the back of my mind I think I had an idea that this series might well tell the story as far as my home-run championship hopes were concerned."[23]

Fortunately, as the team slowly made its way to D.C., he had a lengthy conversation with Wally Moses, the Yankee hitting coach, about his recent hitting difficulties, especially his lack of home runs. As Moses related it, "I ran into Roger in the men's room on the train, and we started talking about hitting. I know it's hard to believe, but we spent four hours in the men's room talking hitting. Roger was worried about losing his confidence and didn't want to fall off down the stretch like he had in 1960. He also had a mental block about the Washington ballpark. He kept telling me he couldn't hit there." Moses thought Maris' problem was that he had begun to swing too hard, getting away from his shorter, more compact stroke. Whatever advice Moses imparted, it seemed to work, because Maris went on a tear in Griffith Stadium.[24]

The clouds did not part for Maris immediately, however. In that first contest on the night of August 11, he popped out his first two times at bat and flew out to center with runners on the corners his second time at the plate in the third inning to bring it to a close. Other than a sacrifice fly in the first to plate a run, Mantle did not do much either. Not so the other Yankee batsmen. They scored eight runs in the first three innings, bringing an early end to starter Joe McClain's evening. Fortunately for Maris, McClain was replaced by Pete Burnside, one of Maris' most accommodating left-handers. He hit numbers four and 29 off of him earlier in the season, but he was self-admittedly "a little homer hungry" as he approached the plate with two gone in the fifth inning for his fourth at-bat of the day.[25]

Burnside quickly induced Maris to pop the ball up into foul territory about 10 feet behind the first-base bag. Bud Zipfel, the Senators' first baseman, and Chuck Cottier, the second baseman, both rushed toward the ball. "This, surely, was the meekest of flies, one that any Little Leaguer could have gathered in with ease and grace," wrote the *New York Times* sarcastically. "However, the big leaguers on defense for the Senators did nothing of the kind. They permitted the ball to fall safely between them, as both backed off." Surely it was a sign from the baseball gods that Maris had suffered long enough. The misplayed ball "dropped on the grass and sat there fat and saucy, grinning evilly. Everybody in the ball park could feel it was a terrible mistake. You don't give a slugger like Maris two outs in the same time at bat. Burnside, who had already headed for the dugout, trudged back to the mound."[26]

Sure enough, on the very next pitch Maris was off to the races once again. "Pete came in with a fast ball," he said. "He was trying to jam me; trying to make me hit the ball on the fists and bounce it to the infield. This time, however, he didn't get it tight enough. It was over the plate, and I connected." Maris knew he had hit the ball well, but he was not sure if the ball was high enough to clear the imposing right-field wall. "High enough? It was one of the highest drives I had ever hit. It not only went over the fence, but went halfway up the light tower in back of the fence." The ball bounced back onto the field after striking the tower. Maris was delighted not only for finally getting his home-run swing back, but also because this four-bagger was his first that summer at Griffith Stadium. He had a personal goal of hitting a homer in all ten American League ballparks that season and now only Baltimore's Memorial Stadium was left to be conquered. Not to be outdone, Mantle, with two outs and one on in the seventh inning, greeted Burnside with a 400-foot line-drive blast into the center-field stands, giving him 44 for the year. The race for the record was most definitely back on. Although the Senators staged a small rally, the game ended in a 12–5 Yankee victory, their ninth consecutive triumph.[27]

Home Run # 43—Game 115—August 12—Day Game

The Yankees and Senators clashed again the following afternoon with young Bill Stafford facing the 6-foot-3 veteran right-hander Dick Donovan who, at the age of 33, was pitching in his eleventh major league season. His road to the show was not an easy one. The Boston Braves signed him in 1947 and for the first three summers he knocked around in the minors before getting his call-up to the big club in 1950. He pitched well enough for their farm teams, but for some reason the Braves gave him few opportunities to toe the rubber when he was with the parent club. As a result, he was 0–4 with a huge 6.87 earned-run average in 25 game appearances with the Braves from 1950 through 1952. "I just never did get the opportunity to work and I have to do a lot of pitching to remain sharp," he explained. "The pattern usually was to let me pitch an inning or two, then I wouldn't work again for ten days. When I was tossed into a game again after that layoff, I pitched sloppily and then I'd be on the way back to the minors."[28]

Donovan, though, was not one to give up. When he was informed that he was to be shipped to the Toledo Mud Hens, the Braves Triple-A affiliate, for the 1953 season, he rebelled. "I demanded to be traded, because I knew if I went back to Toledo, I'd simply be buried in their organization and never again would get a chance," he said. "I believed I could win in the major leagues and I wanted a chance to prove it." The Braves refused to trade Donovan, but eventually did allow him to report to the Atlanta Crackers in the Southern Association, an independently-owned club which had a working relationship with the Braves.[29]

The manager there was Gene Mauch, a former roommate, who encouraged Donovan to make the move to Atlanta. "[I]t turned out to be the best thing that ever happened to me," he said later. It brought him into contact with Atlanta pitching coach Whit Wyatt, who took the right-hander under his wing. "I can't praise Wyatt enough. He showed me how to throw the slider [which became Donovan's dominant pitch], taught me pitching savvy and also gave me a new business interest [selling insurance] on the side." He was 11–8 with the Crackers that season, which drew the interest of the Detroit Tigers. The Bengels, however, gave him just a look-see at the beginning of the 1954 campaign before returning him to the Crackers. He was thrilled to be going back to Atlanta. "I would rather pitch in the minor leagues any day than sit around on the bench in the major leagues when you know they are not going to use you." He called it "the most important year of my pitching career." He continued to work with Wyatt, who was now managing the Crackers, in developing his wicked slider to go along with his sinking fastball and curve. The proof was in the pudding: Donovan had a break-out season in 1954, going 18–8 with an outstanding 2.69 earned-run average in 27 game-starts with the Crackers. On September 7, the Chicago White Sox purchased his contract from the Braves, which proved to be the turning point in his career.[30]

Although Donovan exceeded his rookie status three years earlier, it was not until his 1955 season in Chicago that he truly became a major leaguer. Finally given the chance to pitch regularly at the big-league level, he won 15, lost nine, and maintained a good 3.32 ERA in 29 games. He most likely would have had an even better season had it not been interrupted by an appendectomy that laid him up for three weeks in late July. Prior to that, he was 13–4 with a remarkable 2.70 earned-run average. The illness knocked him off his stride. From his return on August 21 through the end of the season, he won only two games while losing five with a 5.17 ERA, nearly twice what it had been.

His outstanding performance that summer led to his selection to the American League All-Star team. He became one of the mainstays of the Chicago starting rotation over the next four seasons, going 52–40 with a cumulative 3.25 ERA during that four-year span. The 1957 season was an especially successful one for Donovan. His .727 winning percentage among American League pitchers and his 16 complete games were the most in the league. He came in second in Cy Young Award voting—losing out to Warren Spahn—and even received consideration for the American League Most Valuable Player Award. Perhaps the highest praise of all came from Harry Craft, manager of the Kansas City Athletics, who said, "If I knew my life depended on winning one ball game, I'd want Dick Donovan to pitch it for me."[31]

His maturity as a pitcher, the development of a variety of pitches, and his great control—263 walks versus 494 strikeouts from 1955 through 1959—were the basis of his success. His most effective pitch was the slider he learned from Whit Wyatt. "I learned to throw it off my fast ball motion and make it break away from right-handed hitters," he expounded. "It was equally good breaking in on left-handers." Chuck Dressen, manager of the Washington Senators, said that Donovan "drives you crazy with those sliders." Donovan claimed it was the slider "that made my career. The slider gave me the third pitch I needed to be a winner." White Sox catcher Sherm Lollar thought it was when he learned to throw his fastball so that it broke in on right-handers that he began to win consistently. "Previous to that, everything I saw—his curve and slider—broke away from a righthander, and they'd soon catch up with him if he didn't have a variation." Ray Berres, the Chicago pitching coach, agreed with Lollar's observation. "It is his fastball breaking in on the fists [of the right-handed batter] that is the perfect complement to the slider. They make each other effective. And now he's adding a slip pitch [a type of changeup] to his assortment of stuff."[32]

The 1959 season saw a downturn for the Chicago ace. It was the year of the "Go-Go Sox" when Chicago won the American League championship behind the stellar pitching of 22-game winner Early Wynn and 18-game winner Bob Shaw. Donovan was hampered by a sore elbow that limited his pitching to some 180 innings, resulting in his first losing season in the majors. Although he was the loser in Game 3 of the World Series against the Los Angeles Dodgers, he did redeem himself in Game 5 when he relieved in the eighth inning with the bases loaded and only one away. After inducing Carl Furillo to pop out to third and Don Zimmer to fly out to left to end the Dodger threat, he then retired the side in order in the ninth to preserve a 1–0 Chicago victory, using just 11 pitches in all to do so. *The Sporting News* called it "one of the finest stands in World's Series annals."[33]

A sore shoulder plagued the now 32-year-old right-hander throughout the 1960 campaign. He began the season as a starter, but was sent to the bullpen when it became apparent that he was unable to finish any of his games. While he did have a 6–1 record, his earned-run average mushroomed to 5.38 in a little less than 79 innings pitched. The Sox concluded that his best days were over and left him exposed to the expansion draft; the new Washington Senators selected him, convinced that he still had a lot to offer. "I know Dick can pitch," proclaimed manager Mickey Vernon. "I'm glad he's with us."[34]

As for Donovan, he was motivated to prove that he suffered from no lingering arm or shoulder problems. "[White Sox manager Al] Lopez was under the impression I had a sore arm, but that is not true. I did have a lame shoulder for a while, but it healed quickly and I was ready when I was being bypassed." He and Lopez had not gotten along, so he was not unhappy about the move. "I felt like I'd been paroled from prison," he told one sportswriter. Donovan reported to spring training camp early, determined to get into shape so that he could pitch the season opener against his old team. "I want to win for Washington, but I also want to show Al Lopez he should have used me more last season."[35]

Donovan did indeed take the ball for the inaugural game of the 1961 season, pitching a complete game, but losing to the White Sox by a single run, 4–3. He was a victim of bad luck in the early part of the season, losing his next four starts, all of them by a lone run. He was also out for several weeks after colliding with Yankee second baseman Bobby Richardson in a game against New York on April 30. He then won his next three starts before losing three more. On July 6, though, he got hot and won his next six outings. By the end of the season he was 10–10 with a remarkable 2.40 earned-run average, best in the league. "I've never pitched better in my life," he said later. He was fourth among American League pitchers in fewest home runs allowed per nine innings pitched and his walks and hits per innings pitched topped all other hurlers. He was benched three separate times due to injuries, but bounced back after each incident. Manager Mickey Vernon referred to Donovan as "'the stopper' on our staff, the guarantee that we are going to have no long losing streaks. He not only wins but is a big morale factor on our ball club."[36]

Since he was the Senators' most effective pitcher, it came as somewhat of a jolt when he and two other players were traded to the Cleveland Indians on October 6 for good-hitting, but troubled, outfielder Jimmy Piersall. Washington scored the fewest runs in the American League in 1961, and the front office felt they needed an offensive leader more than an established pitcher who was fast approaching his mid–30s. "It is imperative that we get the Piersall type of player, not alone for his ability, but to enliven the Washington club," stated team general manager Ed Doherty. "We had too many unexciting players last season." The trade did not work out well for the Senators. They lost 101 games in 1962, one more than the year before, and Piersall's batting average fell nearly 80 points, from .322 in 1961 to .244 in 1962. The Indians, on the other hand, got a real bargain in Donovan.[37]

The 1962 season was the best in Donovan's long career. He won eight of his first nine starts and did not lose his first game until May 28. By the end of August he was 18–7, leaving him within striking distance of achieving what all pitchers want, a 20-win season. Although he showed signs of weakening the final month, he did manage to tack on those elusive two wins for a 20–10 record with a 3.59 earned-run average; it was one-fourth of the Indians' total victories that summer. He was second among American League pitchers in wins, second in complete games, first in shutouts, first in fewest walks per nine innings pitched, and sixth in innings pitched. In addition to him being selected to the American League All-Star team and receiving consideration for the Most Valuable Player Award, *The Sporting News* voted him the American League Pitcher of the Year.

At 35, there was no way Donovan could top, or even come close to, what he did in 1962. In 1963, he ended at 11–13 with a 4.24 earned-run average. The following season was even less productive. He pitched in only 158⅓ innings, ending the year with a 7–9 record on a 4.55 ERA. The end came on June 15, 1965, when the Indians released him after he appeared in just 12 games, compiling a losing record and his worst earned-run average (5.96) since the 1955 campaign when he made it to the majors to stay. His major league lifetime record of 122 wins, 99 losses, and a cumulative 3.67 ERA over 15 seasons was one he could look back on with pride. "I figure baseball was good to me," he said at the time of his release. "So many big leaguers refuse to accept the fact they are through. These fellows think the game owes them a permanent living." That was certainly not the case with Dick Donovan, a man of great dignity and determination. He knew the time had come to put away the glove and spikes.[38]

When Donovan entered the August 12 contest against the Yankees, it was the first time he had pitched in over two weeks because of a pulled muscle in his right arm. But he was "a real professional," as Senators manager Mickey Vernon observed, who always "gives you an all-out effort." He was not about to bow down to the Yankee juggernaut just because he had not taken the mound since July 25. While he lost to the Yankees the first two times he faced them earlier in the season, he hurled a complete game victory over them on July 19, winning 12–2. He respected both Maris and Mantle, but was not intimidated by their power, even though he knew full well that "[n]either is easy to pitch to because you can't make a mistake. Maris has that pure home-run swing. Mantle will bunt occasionally, but you can't underestimate his power."[39]

Mantle homered off of Donovan five times between 1955 and 1960 and did so twice more earlier in the 1961 season, but that was not the case this time around, hitting just a single in four trips to the plate. Maris, on the other hand, was less successful in the home run department. He had just one off of Donovan (1960) in four previous summers and managed only a lowly single in 10 plate-appearances against Donovan so far in the current season. The Yankee slugger found his opponent to be a tricky moundsman. "When Dick is right he is one of the toughest pitchers in the league to hit for a home run," he conceded. "He throws everything low and has great control. A pull hitter has to be right in the groove to loft one of Donovan's sinkers." But Maris was in the groove that game as evidenced by him hitting a double off the right-field wall his first time up to bat.[40]

Then in the fourth inning with the Senators up, 1–0, Maris got the "loft" he failed to get in that first at-bat, sending a full-count pitch high over the 30-foot wall in right field. "I guess Dick got one of his pitches higher than he wanted to," Maris said later. That homer left him one behind Mantle at 44. But that was it for the Yankee scoring. When pinch-hitter Gene Green smashed a grand slam off of reliever Luis Arroyo in the seventh inning, the Bombers' nine-game winning streak came to an end and Donovan secured his fifth win in a row and his fifth consecutive complete game.[41]

Home Run # 44—Game 116—August 13—Day Game/ First Game of Doubleheader

Maris was relieved after hitting home runs in two successive games at Griffith Stadium, his most frustrating venue. In the four previous seasons, he had only two homers in 33 plate appearances there. Having matched that output in just two games, he hoped that the "jinx" of Griffith Stadium had ended at last. Ever the worrier, though, he was concerned about how he would perform in the following afternoon's doubleheader. In addition to his well-founded dread of twin bills, he went hitless in 12 trips to the plate the last time the Yankees visited Washington on July 18–19. But that was then and this was now.

In the first game that afternoon, Bud Daley got the call for the Yankees, right-hander Bennie Daniels for the Senators. A product of the Pittsburgh Pirates organization, the 6-foot-1 hurler began his professional career in 1951 at the age of 19. He spent the first two seasons in Class C ball, followed by two years of military service. After his discharge in 1955, he spent the first part of the season back in the low minors pitching for the Billings Mustangs in the Pioneer League. His good performance there—10–6, 2.96 ERA—earned him a promotion to the Class A Lincoln Chiefs where he went 4–4 with a 4.33 earned-run average in 14 games. Daniels remained with the Chiefs for the entire 1956 campaign, winning his first 10 games before suffering a loss on July 21. By the end of the season he compiled an excellent record of 15 wins and three loses on a 4.08 ERA. The Pirates were so impressed with his performance that summer that he was assigned to the Hollywood Stars in the Pacific Coast League the following year.[42]

While some players might have been intimidated by the jump from Single-A to the top rung of the minor league ladder, that was not the case for the 25-year-old Daniels. He came on like a house afire and did not slow down. He won his first game on April 14, 3–2, on a home run he hit in the final inning. "He is off to one of the best starts for a young pitcher I've ever seen," proclaimed manager Clyde King manager of the Stars. "And he'll continue to improve because he is learning control." In early July he became the league's first 10-game winner, at one point winning six games in a row. He also started for the southern division of the PCL on July 2 in its annual All-Star game, hurling three innings of no-hit ball, although a run scored when his teammates committed two errors behind him. When the season came to an end, he had compiled the second best record on the team (17–8, 2.95 ERA), resulting in a call-up to the parent club. On September 24, Daniels pitched his first major league game, tossing seven innings of two-run ball against the Brooklyn Dodgers in the last game ever to be played at Ebbets Field. Although he lost, 2–0, the future looked bright for the Pirates' prospect.[43]

Daniels performed so well in the 1958 spring training camp that Pirates manager Danny Murtaugh made him the team's fifth starter. But things did not turn out as hoped. By the end of May, Daniels was 0–2 with a horrendous 9.95 ERA in six game appearances, in large part because of control issues. Pittsburgh brass decided he needed more seasoning and sent him down to the Columbus Jets, the club's Triple-A affiliate in the International League. He was 4–1 with a 2.31 earned-run average in his first five starts for the Jets and by season's end he had a 14–6 record on a 3.09 ERA. He also seemed to have conquered his control problem; he walked 56 while striking out 112 in 160 innings pitched for Columbus. He was recalled to Pittsburgh in late September where he appeared in two games.

In this first outing back, he pitched the first complete game of his major league career, losing 1–0.[44]

Daniels' primary pitch was a fastball that had a lot of movement on it, so much so that it sometimes took off in unexpected directions. Dick Rand, his catcher in Columbus, was the recipient of a broken finger on his glove hand because of how difficult it was to judge the flight of his heater. "When he lets the fast one go, nobody—including Bennie, the catcher and the hitter—knows how it's going to move," he said. Daniels agreed with his catcher: "I can't be sure myself what it's going to do." The pitch also had a lot of sinking action to it. Clyde King, now managing the Jets, proclaimed it "one of the best sinking fast balls in the game." His sinker when kept low was very difficult to hit because it "comes up like a grapefruit and fades like an aspirin dissolved in water," according veteran sportswriter Bob Addie. Ben Wade, who pitched for the Hollywood Stars the year Daniels was with them, commented, "Bennie's not the fastest, but his ball moves more—real good breaking stuff. They don't hit him much. When he's in trouble, it's because he's wild." But as Rand noted, "the ball moves and it moves different ways at different times. I suppose you could call it 'wildness,' but it's the kind a lot of pitchers wish they had."[45]

Daniels stayed with the Pirates for the entire 1959 campaign, making him a rookie at the age of 27. He appeared in 34 games, only 12 of which were starts. Alternating between starting and relieving may have been the underlying cause for his mediocre performance that summer (7–9, 5.45). In April he relieved, in May started, from June through early August he mostly relieved, then started four games before being moved back to the bullpen.

There was an ugly incident with racial overtones in a game against the St. Louis Cardinals on May 3 that underscored the problems he—and other African American players—faced at the big-league level during that time. Daniels struck Cardinals player/manager Solly Hemus on the leg in his first at-bat of the game. Most believed Hemus intentionally stuck his leg out to be hit. As Hemus walked toward first, he called Daniels a "black bastard," causing both benches to empty. Then in the sixth, Daniels' first pitch came close to hitting Hemus again. When the pitcher delivered the ball the second time, Hemus intentionally let go of the bat as he viciously swung before the ball even arrived, sending the bat flying toward the mound. Daniels charged Hemus, both benches again cleared, and several punches were thrown. Hemus snarked later, "The bat slipped out of my hand. I was trying to hit to left field. I guess the ball slipped out of Daniels' hand when he conked me [in the first inning]." Hemus claimed later he was just trying to fire up his team. He praised Daniels as a player, but no one—including Daniels and most of the black players with the Cardinals—believed he was sincere. Daniels took to referring to Hemus as "Little Faubus," an epithet derived from Orval Faubus, the racist governor of Arkansas in the 1950s.[46]

Although the Pirates were disappointed with Daniels' 1959 performance, they kept him on the team during the early part of the 1960 season. Danny Murtaugh felt his right-hander was about to "blossom out," so he remained in the starting rotation. Daniels had three starts in April and another two in May, but he was unable to go the distance in any of them. He was relegated back to the bullpen in June, but that did not go well either. At the end of the month he was 1–3 with a 7.81 earned-run average. Having failed to develop in the way the Pirates hoped, they decided to send him down to the Columbus Jets once again. Although he started out well there, winning his first four outings, he then lost nine in a row to end the season at 4–9 with a 3.08 earned-run average. Pittsburgh decided it was time to cut their ties with the struggling pitcher and on December 16 he and two other players were traded to the Washington Senators for veteran pitcher Bobby Schantz. It turned out to be just what Daniels needed.[47]

Daniels found new life with the Nats in 1961. He came to camp willing to be either a starter or reliever. "I don't care," he announced, "as long as I get to pitch." Management believed Daniels' basic problem was a lack of self-confidence. "We think he found himself overshadowed and discouraged by [Bob] Friend, Vern Law, Harvey Haddix and Vinegar Bend Mizell," speculated Ed Doherty, Washington's general manager. One the smartest moves the Senators made was to use Daniels as a starter consistently rather than switch him back and forth between starting and relieving. Daniels responded well to his role as one of the anchors in the Washington starting rotation. "I won't make any predictions about how many games I'll win or lose," he said at the end of spring training, "but I've never felt better."[48]

Daniels had a rough beginning to the season, losing three of his first four starts and not making it past the third inning for a no-decision in the other. The weather may have been a factor in the early goings. Although he said cold weather did not bother him much, "I like it hot. I pitch well in warm weather." As the weather warmed, the 29-year-old began winning. He won three consecutive starts—including his first complete game of the season—in May before hitting a rough patch in June after pulling a muscle in his leg. After spending most of the month in the bullpen, he pitched his second complete game of the season on June 28. From then on, he got back on track, ending the season with the best won-loss record (12–11) on the team and the second best earned-run average (3.44) behind Dick Donovan's league-leading 2.40.

And, like Donovan, he was a victim of the Senators' poor offense, losing eight of his games by two or fewer runs. In fact, the Senators plated only 17 runs total in his 11 defeats. His 12 complete games were fourth best in the American League and, again like Donovan, he was home-run stingy. He allowed just 14 dingers in 212 innings pitched, placing him sixth among American League pitchers for fewest homers per nine innings pitched. Manager Mickey Vernon was ecstatic about Daniels' performance. "Bennie has more confidence now, that's the big thing," Vernon concluded. "After all, he had been shuffled around quite a bit before and now he knows he's a starting pitcher with a big league club. He realizes it's a break for him and he shows it every time he goes out there."[49]

Unfortunately, though, 1961 was the pinnacle of Daniels' career. After winning the opening day game in the new D.C. Stadium—making him the first African American pitcher to ever open the season for the Senators—against the Detroit Tigers on April 9, he then lost 10 before winning another game. By the end of the season he was 7–16 with a 4.85 earned-run average. Arm problems and a sore elbow that cropped up early in the season never really cleared up. It knocked him off his stride and he was never able to get back into the groove after that. He was so ineffective that by mid–May on he was used mainly in relief; less than half of his 44 game appearances were as a starter. Rollie Hemsley, third base coach with the Nats in 1962, asserted that management mishandled Daniels that season. "They had Bennie Daniels all fouled up," he asserted. "They pitched him 11 times with a sore arm. He never knew whether he was a starter or a reliever. Bennie needed a little help. A pat on the back once in a while doesn't hurt."[50]

Daniels struggled from then until the end of his major league career. He remained in a Senators uniform for three more seasons (1963–1965), never once coming close to his 1961 achievement. From 1962 through 1965, he was 25–49 on a cumulative 4.39 earned-run average. Toward the end he became so fearful that he might not make the five-year major league service minimum to receive a pension that his hair started following out. He did meet the base requirement during the 1965 season, an event commemorated by having his head shaved in the Senators' clubhouse. Washington management, though, had pretty much given up on Daniels and at the end of the summer he was sent back to the minors. Now 34, he spent the 1966 season pitching for the Hawaii Islanders in the Pacific Coast League before ending his professional baseball career. He pitched nine years in the majors, compiling a record of 45 wins and 76 losses on a cumulative 4.44 ERA.

Chuck Hinton, Daniels' roommate during his Washington years, praised Daniels as "the kindest, most helpful, best-liked, most down-to-earth guy on those teams.... He was a big, gutty guy, always pitching in pain, getting no support and losing. He was an inspiration to me, a big brother. He made no bones, no excuses when he lost. Just took his lumps."[51]

Daniels was 6–6 with a 3.60 earned-run average when he strode to the mound to open that first game of the August 13 doubleheader against the visiting Bombers. He was new to the American League, so Maris and Mantle had limited experience facing the tall right-hander. On July 19 in New York, Mantle singled, struck out twice, and flew out to left in four plate appearances. Maris was equally unsuccessful against Daniels' sinking fastball, flying out twice, grounding out to first, and walking in his fourth at-bat of the day. Daniels' only difficulty that night was allowing four runs off the bats of Clete Boyer, batting eighth, and pitcher Bud Daley. Other than that, the Yankee power hitters could not touch him, resulting in a complete 8–4 game victory over the mighty Bombers.

With the largest crowd of the season—27,368—cheering on their local favorites, Daniels did not disappoint the Washington loyalists, handily defeating the Yankees, 12–2, in his fifth complete game of the summer. But the crowd, many of whom hoped to see the M and M Boys launch a few long balls, was not disappointed in that respect either. Maris singled with two out in his first at-bat of the game, but was stranded when Mantle struck out. The Senators plated a run in the bottom of the first on a Chuck Hinton dinger off of starter Bud Daley.

The score remained 1–0 in favor of Washington until the fourth inning when Maris opened the frame in his second plate appearance of the day. Daniels made the mistake of going full on Maris before trying to sneak a fastball past the lefty. As Maris recalled, Daniels "was throwing hard and with perfect control," but then on the sixth pitch he "got one in my alley." It was another monster blast, hitting the outfield wall before landing in the Senators' bullpen in right-center field some 450 away. "Nothing like this had ever happened to me before," Maris recalled. "I really felt good as I circled the bases with number forty-four chalked up to my record.... It seemed odd that, on the last time I would be playing here before they 'salted' the old ballpark away, I was having a good series."[52]

The game remained tied at one until the Senators drove in six runs in the sixth inning and another four in the seventh, giving them a 10-run lead. Another Washington run in the bottom of the eighth was simply icing on the cake. All that was left was to give Maris and Mantle one more opportunity to park one. Maris struck out against Daniels to open the ninth inning, but Mantle took full advantage of this fourth at-bat of the day, blasting a 1–1 pitch into the same spot as Maris did in the fourth for his forty-fifth of the season. "Roger Maris and Mickey Mantle," wrote Bill Fuchs in the *Evening Star*, "the guys who produce more big hits than Rogers and Hammerstein, have left Washington after another smash show that's got almost everybody wishing for more." The Maris-Mantle home-run race became the biggest draw of the season in the American League with sellout crowds for nearly every game the Yankees played. As *The Sporting News* was later to note, "The only thing that saved the American League from financial disaster in September was the home-run drive of Roger Maris and Mickey Mantle."[53]

Home Run # 45—Game 117—August 13—Day Game/ Second Game of Doubleheader

Maris may have been a little dazed from his three home runs in three successive games at Griffith Stadium, but his pyrotechnics were far from over. In the second game that afternoon, Senators relief ace Marty Kutyna was handed the ball for a rare start that summer. The side-arming right-hander had relieved in games, over half as the closer, before he was given his first major league starting assignment ever on July 28 due to a variety of injuries to the regular staff. Although he pitched well in that outing, he was ill-equipped to handle starting duties and the Yankees benefited from his unfamiliarity with pitching more than a few innings in a time.

The 6-foot, 190-pound righty's road to the show was a long and varied one. He was originally signed by the St. Louis Cardinals, making his debut in professional ball in 1953 hurling for the Class D Paducah Chiefs in the Kentucky-Illinois-Tennessee League at the age of 20. He showed great promise, appearing in 34 games primarily as a starter and compiling a 17–7 record with a 2.89 earned-run average, best on the team. He spent most of the following summer starting for the Class D Hamilton Cardinals before being moved up a step to the Fresno Cardinals where he appeared in 11 games, used mainly in relief for the first time.

The Cardinals seemed uncertain whether he was better as a starter or a reliever. As he advanced from Single-A to Triple-A over the next three seasons, he switched back and forth between the two roles. On December 5, 1957, St. Louis decided to part ways with their 24-year-old hurler, trading him with two other pitchers to the Cincinnati Reds, an exchange that brought center fielder Curt Flood to the Red Birds. Although he had five years of minor league experience, Reds general manager Gabe Paul said, "we're gambling in acquiring kids like Kutyna.... All our scouting reports say he's a fine major league prospect."[54]

The Reds felt, though, that Kutyna had "been around long enough to acquire the poise that is necessary in the major leagues" and planned to give him serious consideration for inclusion on their roster at the end of spring training. It was not until the final days of camp that he was cut from the pitching squad and sent to play for the Seattle Rainiers, the club's Triple-A affiliate in the Pacific Coast League. Although he posted an 8–10 record on a 4.17 ERA in 36 game appearances, Kutyna was one of the better pitchers on a team that won just 68 games. Apparently the Reds felt their "fine major league prospect" was expendable and on March 31, 1959, traded him to the Kansas City Athletics.[55]

Whitey Herzog, the A's young outfielder, was quite pleased when he heard about the swap, noting he had played against the pitcher while in the International League. "He has a good fast ball and an effective curve," Herzog said. Kutyna spent most of 1959 back in the Pacific Coast League, this time pitching for the Portland Beavers. Used primarily as a starter, he won 14 and lost 10 on a fine 3.34 earned-run average, which included a shutout among his 12 complete games. Late in the summer he developed a reputation as the club's "stopper" after securing the only two wins in 12 games played at the end of August. He was the "lone bright spot during the disastrous fortnight." He finally made the jump to the big leagues when he was called up in late September, appearing in four games while earning one save without giving up a single run in 7⅓ innings of relief. He had arrived at last.[56]

The right-hander came to the majors with a variety of pitches, all tossed side-arm, a "delivery that bothers righthanded hitters." A former minor league teammate claimed Kutyna "has one of the best sliders I've seen and he knows how to mix up his pitches. He's a real student of pitching, too." He had a good fastball and changeup and a pretty decent curve as well. "I [throw] a lot of junk there," he stated. He was not in the least concerned about his pitching assignments, just as long as he was given the opportunity to play. "I'm not worried about how I'm used. Reliever or starter, it doesn't make any difference [to me]," he announced. So reliever it was. He started just six times in 159 game appearances over his four seasons in the major leagues.[57]

The Athletics were thrilled with Kutyna's performance after his September call-up and expected great things from him in the 1960 campaign. "It seems Marty gets overlooked a lot but just you wait and see," argued teammate Russ Snyder. "He was effective late last season [1959] when we brought him up and I think he can help us a lot." The outfielder's prophecy turned out to be right on the money. He appeared in 51 games, 30 of them as the closer. He ended the year with a 3–2 record that included four saves on a 3.94 earned-run average in 61⅔ innings pitched. The Athletics had every intention of keeping him in that position for the 1961 season, but they were in desperate need of a frontline catcher and on December 29 sent him and $25,000 in cash to the new Washington Senators in exchange for Haywood Sullivan, a catcher the Nats acquired a few weeks earlier.[58]

It may have been a change of team, but it was not a change in role. Kutyna was pleased with the move. "I've got more confidence than I ever had before by being with this new ball club," he crowed. "These guys want to win." He went on to acknowledge the help Washington pitching coach Sid Hudson gave him during spring training. "Hudson really taught me a few things [this] spring. He opened me up and got me to throw a sinker." Kutyna proved his value to the team in his very first outing, a 6⅓ relief gem against the Chicago White Sox in which he gave up no runs on four hits for the win. "It took me a year and two months of pitching to go more than three innings," explained the right-hander after the game. "I never went more than three innings last year with Kansas City."[59]

Kutyna continued to excel from that point until the last third of the season. He was 3–0 with two saves before suffering his first loss on May 31. By the end of July he was 6–2 with a 3.35 earned-run average in 34 games. That sixth win came in a rare start on July 28, his first since pitching for Portland in 1959. The reliever expressed some trepidation before the game, but was more than willing to take on the task assigned him. "Don't misunderstand me," he said to the press, "[manager] Mickey Vernon has asked me to start and I'll do anything to help the team. But.... I've gotten so I like relieving." He performed so well in that outing—beating his former team, 10–6, with four earned runs in seven innings of work—that Vernon kept him in the starting rotation in four of his next five appearances. That proved to be a mistake, however. From August 2 until the end of the season, a two-month stretch that included five starts in 16 games, he was 0–6 with a 4.76

earned-run average. Clearly Vernon should have left well enough alone. In spite of his late-season slump, Kutyna ended the year at 6–8 with a 3.97 ERA, respectable numbers for a team that finished tied for last place after losing 100 games. He was also below the league average in home runs allowed per nine innings pitched.[60]

The Senators were so pleased with their "No. 1 relief pitcher" that they gave Kutyna a pay raise for 1962. It was an up-and-down season for the 29-year-old reliever. By the end of April, he had appeared in six games, surrendering just one earned run for a loss in nine innings pitched. Then he began to struggle. By the end of July he was 3–6 with four blown saves and his ERA climbed to 3.24. Because of his penchant for giving up home runs in the month of July—three in nine games after just three in the previous 26 games—he was tagged with the nickname "Boom-Boom." He had periods when he was pitching like he did in 1961, but overall his 1962 performance was mediocre at best. By season's end he was 5–6 with five blown saves on an earned-run average of 4.04 in 54 games. Washington management found his pitching to be "unimpressive" and in December his contract was sold to the Buffalo Bisons, the New York Mets Triple-A club in the International League, in order to make room on the roster for trades and new signings. He appeared in only 10 games there before he was released in mid–May, bringing his 11 season professional baseball career to a close. He ended his four summers in the majors with a record of 14 wins, 16 losses, and eight saves on a cumulative 3.88 earned-run average in 159 game appearances.[61]

Kutyna was making his fourth start of the summer when he opened the second half of that August 13 doubleheader. Had it not been for the rough first inning, he would have had an excellent outing. As it was, though, he began the game by giving up a single to Bobby Richardson. After retiring Tony Kubek on a fly ball to left, he next faced Maris who was on a home-run hitting spree. As Maris himself said, "when a home-run hitter gets into his groove it is difficult to stop him." But the Yankee right fielder had only limited success against the Senators' main reliever. He was hitless against him in three appearances during the 1960 season, but had one single for two runs out of two matchups earlier in 1961. Kutyna, therefore, believed he could handle Maris and started the slugger off with his money pitch, a slider. Unfortunately for him, it did not break like it was supposed to do and Maris hammered it for a two-run homer that sailed high over the right-field wall.[62]

"I could hardly believe it as I saw the ball disappear over the 31-foot fence," Maris commented on his fourth homer in four consecutive games. "This can't be Washington I thought to myself." He was again tied with Mantle for the home-run lead at 45. The rattled pitcher was not out of the woods yet. After inducing a groundout from Mantle, Johnny Blanchard tripled and then scored on Elston Howard's single. Kutyna got the next two outs to stop the bleeding, but by then it was too late. In four of the next five innings, he retired the Yankees in order, including Maris twice on fly balls. After giving up another run in the seventh, Kutyna was replaced by Mike Garcia. Maris greeted him with a single to open the eighth, scoring after Mantle walked and Blanchard singled. The Yankees plated four more runs that inning, ending the day with a 9–4 victory which left them 3½ games in front of second-place Detroit.[63]

Home Run # 46—Game 118—August 15—Night Game

It was pure pandemonium in the clubhouse afterwards. Maris was elated after finally conquering Griffith Stadium, thus bringing an end to his two-week home run slump in which he parked only one prior to the Washington series. He was expansive in his responses to the press, perhaps too much so. First, he expounded on what he felt to be the cause of his lack of home runs in the previous 16 games. He was getting set in the box during a recent game when he noticed that his right foot was turned in too much. As a result, "I couldn't handle that stuff they were throwing me inside. They were jamming me and I couldn't do anything about it. That pitch handcuffed me until we started the series in Washington. That's when I got the right toe pointed the other way."[64]

The assembled press asked him for the umpteenth time if he thought he could break the Ruth record. For the first time he openly admitted that he was thinking about it in addition to his first priority, helping the Yankees win the pennant. When asked about his back-and-forth battle for the lead with Mantle, he said he hoped "Mickey would hit eighty ... and that I would finish with eighty-one." He stated his belief that Mantle had the advantage over him. "He is stronger than I am and can hit balls out of any park in any direction. I had to hit mine out of right field, except by accident, because I had to pull the ball to get full power." Del Webb, Yankee co-owner, agreed with Maris' assessment. "Mantle, of course, has more power, and hits to all fields. Most of the time, Maris is strictly a pull hitter to right field.... It stands to reason that I would have to pick Mantle over Maris."[65]

Maris became noticeably agitated when asked for his reaction to Ruth-era players claiming they had it harder in their day. "That's a lot of bull," he responded vehemently. "I don't think there is any comparison between baseball today and in the old days," he continued. "It is much tougher now for many reasons. I know that real good hitters of olden days would still be good hitters today, but I doubt if there would be any .400 hitters. Not only is the defense better, but there is a big difference in the schedule and playing conditions." He went on to say that the earlier generation played only day games and did not have to contend with night games or twi-night doubleheaders. In addition, they did not have to travel from coast-to-coast. "How about the different time zones we play in now," he asked. "Do you realize that when we take the field at 8 o'clock in Los Angeles, it is actually 11 o'clock to our bodies? Our reflexes are tired when we start a game. All players going into L. A. feel the difference in time. It also upsets our normal eating and sleeping habits." While it was an honest response, it did not win any converts among the "old-timers," nor did it persuade the Ruth loyalists. All it did was further irritate his critics.[66]

Maris, always sensitive to perceived slights, lashed out at those who believed a sub-.300 hitter was a "bum" who was undeserving of being mentioned in the same breath as Ruth. "What am I supposed to do," he inquired. "I admire Ruth. He was the greatest. But they make it sound like I'd be doing something sacrilegious if I broke the record." Not only did such criticism hurt his pride, but it called into question his professionalism. "Who sets these people up as judges? What makes them think they are capable of deciding whether someone is lousy or not when he's doing a good job? How can anyone who knows nothing about the profession decide whether a person is good, bad, or lousy?" That angry rejoinder was not designed to win friends or influence people, as Maris knew all too well. Acknowledging that he "was just in a mood to get it all out of my system," Maris realized that such unvarnished honesty would likely get him into trouble, but he did not really care if it did because he was staying true to himself. It was simply a case of Maris being Maris.[67]

The slugger did have his defenders among the press who found suggestions that he was somehow unworthy to be unfair. Veteran New York journalist Jimmy Cannon argued that both Maris and Mantle's pursuit of the Babe was entirely appropriate. They were "only attempting to hit as many home runs as Ruth," he wrote. "They aren't trying to deface his memory. But I find animosity in people of Ruth's age. It is as though Maris and Mantle were not entitled to challenge Ruth's achievement." That, he said bluntly, was "a mean and silly theory…. If Mantle and Maris are able to hit 61 home runs, I want them to. Such competition is the only reason for baseball." Arthur Daley of the *New York Times* agreed, referring to the intractable Ruth supporters as "wild-eyed zealots…. Fierce has been their resentment of the false gods who have arisen from time to time and attempted to replace their idol atop the pedestal. These are the worshipers of Babe Ruth." Daley called upon Ruth's "idolators" to "reconcile themselves to the fact that the mark that had seemed so untouchable for so long is doomed for erasure eventually." Even when it was broken, however, that did not reduce the Babe's stature one iota.[68]

The Yankees had an off-day as they returned to New York to host the Chicago White Sox for three contests before heading out on a grueling 14-day, 13-game road trip to Cleveland, Los Angeles, Kansas City, and Minnesota. "It's a long season by August," Ralph Houk once commented. "The sun seems hotter than in any other month. The humidity hangs around after dark. Even sleeping in an air-conditioned room doesn't restore your energy. Ballplayers begin to long for October, lazy days and cool nights." It is during the dog days of summer when many players begin to fade and playing seems a chore. "I'm tired all the time," Maris confessed to sportswriter Phil Pepe. "The bat gets heavier this time of year. I can't wait for the season to end." But as exhausted as he may have been, Maris was never one to quit. Carry on he would, especially with the pennant still undecided and the Ruth record seemingly within his grasp.[69]

Left-hander Juan Pizarro, ace of the Chicago White Sox's pitching staff, tossed a complete-game victory over the Yankees on August 15, beating Whitey Ford, 2–1. The only run he allowed was Maris' forty-sixth home run to open the bottom of the fourth inning.

It was the battle of the left-handers the night of August 15. Whitey Ford, who crossed the 20-games-won threshold on August 10, was facing flame-throwing southpaw Juan Pizarro, new to the American League after four seasons with the Milwaukee Braves. His rise to the major leagues was meteoric to say the least. The 5-foot-11, 170-pound phenom from Puerto Rico was pitching for his hometown team in Santurce when the Braves acquired the 19-year-old in early 1956 for a reported $35,000 (over $300,000 in 2018 dollars). He was sent to the Jacksonville Braves in the Class A South Atlantic League where he performed beyond all expectations, winning 23 and losing six on a fantastic 1.77

earned-run average. Most impressive was his 274 innings pitched in which he struck out 318 while walking 149.[70]

Labeled from the start as "the next Warren Spahn," a very heavy burden to bear for someone so untested, he was put on the big league roster in 1957 even though he had just one year of experience in organized ball. According to Braves scout Ted McGrew, Pizarro "has a major league fast ball [estimated at 95-miles-per-hour] and a major league curve…. He has extraordinary stuff as it is, and as soon as he gains poise he'll be a lulu. That will come with experience." He also had a screwball which he used mostly with right-handed batters.[71]

One thing he did not lack was self-confidence. When asked in spring training what he needed to improve upon to make it in the majors, he responded with just one word: "Nothing." Some expressed concern that he was being rushed to the big leagues before he had the chance to fully develop. The fact that the Braves already had a strong pitching staff meant that there were long periods when the youngster would not be used. "Will he pitch often enough … to warrant being brought all the way up to the major leagues instead of going to Wichita [the Braves Triple-A affiliate] for another season of minor league seasoning," asked sports columnist Bob Wolf. Although manager Fred Haney insisted that would not be a problem, in fact it was.[72]

The young left-hander began the season as a starter, but did not make his first appearance in that role until May 4, losing, 1–0, in seven innings of work. He opened eight more times over the next six weeks, but was then relegated to the bullpen. He spent most of July pitching for the Wichita Braves before being called back up to Milwaukee. He started one game and relieved in nine others, ending with a 5–6 record on a high 4.62 ERA. Wolf declared Pizarro's first season to be a "disappointment" which he blamed on inexperience. "Had he been able to spend the entire campaign at Wichita, pitching every fourth or fifth day, instead of rusting away in the Braves' bull pen, he might have been ready for stardom in 1958."[73]

After pitching spectacularly in the Puerto Rican League over the winter—including a no-hitter and another game in which he struck out 19—he seemed better prepared for the major leagues. Recognizing that their novice hurler "undoubtedly was under pressure in attempting to live up to his advance billing" as a "can't miss star" when he was put on the Braves' roster in 1957, he was sent back to Wichita to start the season, a wise move on the part of Milwaukee. He was recalled in late July, appearing in 16 games where he pitched seven complete games and ended with a 6–4 record and a great 2.70 earned-run average. Pizarro spent two more seasons with the Braves, but was never able to achieve the superstar status that was unreasonably expected of him. In 1959, he was 6–2 with a 3.77 earned-run average in 29 games, half of them starts, and in 1960 he posted a 6–7 record with a 4.55 ERA in 21 games.[74]

Unfortunately, by this time the 23-year-old had earned a reputation as someone hard to handle and resistant to instruction. Chuck Dressen, Braves manager in 1960, said his charge lacked the desire to win. "Desire means a lot, but this man doesn't have it," he proclaimed. Pizarro was the first to admit that he could be a handful at times. "I enjoy life," he said. "I don't do anything half-assed, even if that means raising a lot of hell. I like the track, the casino, every day I have my drinks." But he was also the victim of the stereotypic views then prevalent in baseball about Latino players being wild and uncontrollable. The fact that he was of African descent added to the prejudices that confronted him. "I just never got a chance in Milwaukee. Because I was Latin they thought I was a troublemaker," he contended. "I had my moments, everyone does. But my pitching, that was *mucho* okay."[75]

On December 15 he and Joey Jay were sent to the Cincinnati Reds for Roy McMillan. The Reds immediately sent him and Cal McLish to the Chicago White Sox for Gene Freese. While White Sox president Bill Veeck was excited about the acquisition of Pizarro, even he, who was one of the most racially progressive officials in professional baseball, could not help but reflect the biases of the times. "In the case of Pizarro, who supposedly lacks the drive and aggressiveness to win, if anyone can put a fire under him it is [manager Al] Lopez," he asserted. "After all, he has one big advantage with the players from the Caribbean area—he speaks the language. And he has a better psychological understanding of them than any other manager."[76]

At first angry about the trade, Pizarro came to realize that it worked out for the best in the long run. "The White Sox didn't give up on me, they didn't punish me, and I pitched my ass off for them," he remarked years later about the five seasons he pitched for Chicago. For the first time, Pizarro was given a real opportunity to demonstrate what he was capable of doing and he responded to the confidence placed in him by becoming the best pitcher on the White Sox staff. The 1961 campaign was his breakthrough season. When the summer began, though, it appeared that he was headed for the same outcome as in his Braves period. He performed poorly during spring training and, as a consequence, was consigned to the bullpen because manager Al Lopez did not quite trust him to handle a starter's duties effectively. And his relief activity—0–0, 4.97 ERA in 12 games—did not do anything to convince the Chicago skipper to think differently. In fact, there were even rumors that he was on the trading block.[77]

But the ineffectiveness of left-handed starter Billy Pierce followed by a sore arm for Early Wynn opened the door for Pizarro to enter the starting rotation. He took full advantage of the opportunity presented him. On June 10 he tossed seven innings without giving up an earned run and on his next start went eight to earn his first win of the season. That was followed by three more victories—including two complete games—before he hit a brief skid in early July, losing three games in a row. Then he beat the Yankees, 6–1, in a complete-game outing on July 14. From that point until the end of the season he was 9–4 with two saves and a 3.08 earned-run average. He finished with 14 wins, seven losses, 188 strikeouts and a 3.05 earned-run average, making him the ace of the starting staff.[78]

The 1962 campaign started off well with two complete-game victories, but then he hit an inexplicable rough patch, losing four of his next five outings and failing to go past the fourth inning in three others. Lopez thought his left-hander might have a sore arm, but Pizarro denied it. Some suggested he was tired after pitching winter ball, but he claimed that was not the case either. Suddenly, things turned around. On June 2 he won for the third time, pitching all nine innings. July saw him win six of nine games before entering a period of alternating winning with losing. By summer's end he was 12–14 with a 3.81 earned-run average. Pizarro was out from late August through early September after he suffered an injury to his pitching hand from a line drive off the bat of Al Kaline, but that did not explain his inconsistent performance. More than likely it was his personal behavior, including late-night partying and missed practices, that was the main cause of his erratic pitching.[79]

The disappointment of the 1962 season was followed by the two best years of his career. In 1963 he went 16–8 with an incredible 2.39 ERA followed by a 19–9 record on a 2.56 earned-run average, giving him a cumulative 35–17 record and a 2.48 ERA in 65 games. His control was beyond reproach. He had 325 strikeouts with only 118 walks in some 454 innings pitched. He was a two-time All-Star and in 1964 was considered for the Most Valuable Player Award. In those two summers, he was in the top 10 among American League pitchers in earned-run average, wins, fewest hits per nine innings pitched, and shutouts.

One of the reasons for this turnaround was his use of a slow curve to go along with his fastball, changeup, and slider. When asked what his best pitch was, Pizarro could not say with any certainty. "I don't know," he responded. "I think it's my slow curve. I get a lot of strikeouts with the slow curve." Another was because he pitched regularly without long periods of inactivity. Billy Herman, a coach during the Milwaukee years, was convinced that was the primary reason for his improvement. With the Braves, "he had it tough, pitching once a week or pitching every ten days. He never really had a chance to get in the groove. One bad game and he was back in the bull pen." Al Lopez thought he started to win consistently once he started to believe he could do so. "Now he knows he's a winner. It was a matter of proving it to himself."[80]

Pizarro started the 1965 season with a sore arm, a condition he did not tell the Sox about until June. He was late getting into condition because he was a holdout for more salary, then was unable to go the distance in any game from late April until August. His earned-run average was a horrendous 7.32 at the end of June before it was discovered he had torn the triceps tendon in his left shoulder. He was placed on the disabled list at that point and did not resume pitching until August 4. From that point on, he won five while losing just one on a 2.60 earned-run average, allowing him to finish the season at 6–3 with a 3.43 ERA.

Although he continued to pitch in the major leagues through 1974, he was not the same pitcher he had been before his injury and was used primarily as a reliever. He made just 58 starts in 240 game appearances for a 41–45 record and a cumulative 3.76 ERA. The White Sox traded him to the Pittsburgh Pirates at the end of 1966, starting a pattern in which he moved from team to team, going from the Pirates to the Boston Red Sox to the Cleveland Indians to the Oakland Athletics to the California Angels to the Chicago Cubs to the Houston Astros to the Pirates again, either as part of a trade or as a free agent. When he failed to make the Pirates' 1975 roster, he continued to play ball in Mexico and in Puerto Rico for the next few years. In 18 major-league seasons, Pizarro compiled a 131–105 record and a fine 3.43 earned-run average in 488 games, 245 of which was as a starter.[81]

Yankee sluggers feasted off of White Sox pitchers in 1961, hitting more homers off of their staff than that of any other team. At the time of the August 15 contest, the Bombers had a combined 25 home runs playing the White Sox; Maris had 10 of them, Mantle four. In spite of his success with Chisox hurlers, however, Maris found Pizarro to be "one of the toughest pitchers in the league." He certainly had reason to feel that way. He managed only two singles in seven previous face-offs against the southpaw. In the other five trips to the plate, he popped out four times and struck out once. Interestingly, though, Pizarro actually handled right-handed hitters better than he did lefties; they batted just .216 against him while left-handers batted .261.[82]

But the White Sox hurler was at the top of his game that evening. He started off a little shaky, giving up a single to Tony Kubek and a walk to Maris, but got out of the inning without any damage. Whitey Ford had his problems early on as well, allowing the Sox to plate two runs in the second inning. After that it was a pitching duel between the two left-handers. Pizarro retired the side in order in both the second and third innings, leaving Maris to open the fourth in his second appearance of the day.

Pizarro, who was relying on his heater to tame the Yanks early in the game, thought he could do the same to Maris. This time, though, instead of walking the right fielder, he delivered his fastball right into Maris' happy zone. Number 46 was not his typical line-drive rocket, but a skyscraper that "traveled higher than the light tower atop the right-field roof. It was a long time in coming down into the stands—as if reluctant to face the problems of re-entry." And that was it for the Yankee offense. Maris just missed a homer in the eighth when the ball flew into the stands about a foot foul, but he did hit a double on the next pitch. Luis Arroyo replaced Ford in the eighth and held the Sox scoreless over the next two innings, but New York's failure to plate another run resulted in an agonizing 2–1 loss. In addition to reducing the Yankees' lead over Detroit to two games—the Tigers won both games of a doubleheader against Baltimore that day—it ended Ford's 14-game winning streak. Maris was now a homer up on Mantle, giving him the lead in the home-run race that he did not relinquish for the rest of the season.[83]

Home Runs # 47 and 48—Game 119—August 16— Day Game

In spite of the Yankee loss, Maris admitted he felt good after the game. He had gotten two of the four Yankee hits, he had homered off a left-hander he found difficult to hit— it was the only home run Maris ever slugged off of Pizarro over eight seasons—and he saw it as putting his critics in their place. "[L]ousy hitters," he argued, "don't get a double and homer off a good pitcher when he has had a hot night." That response showed how truly disturbed he was by those who dismissed him as unworthy of wearing the home-run crown. He was never really able to let go of such criticism because he internalized it. It was something that dogged him throughout his career.[84]

The White Sox threw another left-hander at the Yankees the following afternoon. This time it was Chicago stalwart Billy Pierce, who had been with the team since he was acquired from Detroit after the 1948 season. The durable southpaw first entered professional ball in 1945 as an 18-year-old Tiger prospect. He spent the first part of the season riding the pine with the big club, appearing in just three June games, before being sent down to the Double-A Buffalo Bisons. He was recalled for two more games in September, ending with a 0–0 record and a minuscule 1.80 earned-run average in a total of 10 innings of relief work. Although he did not appear in the 1945 World Series, he was given a ring when the Tigers beat the Chicago Cubs in seven games. As he remarked years later, "I didn't know it would be my only world title."[85]

Pierce spent the next two seasons pitching for the Bisons, now a Triple-A club. He hurt his back midway through the 1946 campaign, which limited his pitching to just 10 games. He was healthy the following year, but because there was concern his back was not fully healed, he appear in only 28 games. He did pitch well, though—14–8, 3.87 ERA— and his performance that summer earned him a spot on the Detroit roster for the entire 1948 season. He never again pitched in the minor leagues.

At 5-foot-10 and 160 pounds, Pierce was one of the smaller players in the game. In spite of his rather diminutive size, he had a great fastball that he relied on almost exclusively. His main problem was one of control. In the 55⅓ innings he pitched in 1948, he walked 51 batters while striking out only 38. He was 3–0 his first full major league season, but his 6.34 earned-run average meant that he was not fooling many hitters. As Tigers manager Steve O'Neill commented during spring training, "He has wonderful stuff, but he can't get the ball over. He's probably a Lefty Grove or Hal Newhouser case—it's going to take time for him to find the strike zone." He eventually found his control, but it would not be with the Tigers. Shortly after the season ended, he, along with $10,000 cash, was traded to the Chicago White Sox for catcher Aaron Robinson. Initially upset about the swap—he heard about it on the radio—before long he came to see it as "a good break."[86]

His first two seasons with the Sox were somewhat less than impressive. His 3.94 earned-run average was at the high end of acceptable, but his 19–31 won-loss record was nothing to crow about. His problem remained one of delivering the ball in the strike zone. In 65 games, mostly as a starter, he walked 249 and struck out 213 in 391 innings of work. Then good fortune smiled upon the 24-year-old fastballer: Paul Richards, who was his player/manager with the Buffalo Bisons in 1947, was selected as the new skipper of the White Sox for 1951. Richards had worked closely with Pierce in Buffalo and, as his catcher on the days the youngster pitched, helped him develop better control. "Pierce was well neigh invincible for the Bisons whenever Richards' leg would permit the Bison manager to catch the wild young lefthander during the 1947 season," observed *The Sporting News*. Under Richards' renewed tutelage, Pierce became one of the best pitchers of the 1950s.[87]

Richards believed that in order to gain control, a pitcher had to "take stuff off" his pitches, especially fastballs and curves. He also knew that successful hurlers did not rely on fastballs alone, they used a variety of pitches to work off of their fast one. And that is exactly what he taught Pierce. "Paul always kept telling me that I needed more than just a fast ball and a curve.... I found that the fast ball was fine to set the hitters up with, but it can blow up in your face if you try to get them out with it regularly." Long after his retirement, Pierce praised Richards for helping him develop a slider that he could use alongside of his heater and crooked pitch. "I learned to control my fastball better and, at Richards' request, learned a third pitch to go with my fastball and curve—a slider," explained Pierce. "Developing the slider helped me tremendously because it gave me a third out pitch. I threw it almost as hard as my fastball, but I could throw it for strikes better than the fast ball or good curve.... Richards made me work on it, and it took me about two years before it was consistent." It was at that point when Pierce felt he became a "pitcher" rather than just a "thrower."[88]

Richards' work with his young left-hander paid dividends almost immediately. He hurled complete-game victories his first two starts of the 1951 season, walking six while striking out 12. By early June he was 7–2 with 30 walks and 42 strikeouts. Like most young pitchers, he was not able to keep up that pace all season long, but he did end the summer with a 15–14 record—eight of the losses by two or fewer runs—on an excellent 3.03 earned-run average. Most importantly, he definitely learned to control his pitches, issuing 73 walks while striking out 113. Pierce showed even more improvement in 1952. At 15–12 on a remarkable 2.57 earned-run average, he clearly had become the ace of the Chicago staff. Even general manager Frank Lane, who traded players at the drop of a hat, declared Pierce to be "untouchable."[89]

The 1953 season was when everything finally came into alignment for Pierce. Not only did he nearly become the first White Sox pitcher since 1941 to win twenty games—18–12, 2.72 ERA—but his 186 strikeouts and fewest hits per nine innings pitched were best in the American League. He was also among the top 10 American League pitchers in wins, earned-run average, innings pitched, games started, complete games, and shutouts. In addition, he had the honor of starting the 1953 All-Star game, tossing three innings of one-hit ball. Pierce attributed his success to "greater confidence and more work." Paul Richards thought it was because "he has learned to mix speed with curves and an occasional slider."[90]

Pierce's 1954 season was hampered by an adhesion in his pitching arm—which bothered him the rest of his career—that hurt until he could "tear it" free. It kept him out of the lineup from late May through mid–June. He had a little difficulty getting back on track when he did return. In July he pitched four consecutive complete games, including two shutouts, winning two and losing two. He ended the summer with a 9–10 record and a higher ERA than the season before (3.48), but his 148 strikeouts-to-86 walks ratio was still excellent. After that off-year, Pierce established himself as one of the best pitchers in all of baseball. From 1955 through 1958, he won 72 games while losing only 42 on a cumulative earned-run average of 2.86. He won twenty games in two consecutive seasons (1956–1957) and led the American League with a 1.97 earned-run average and strikeouts per walks in 1955, complete games in 1956, wins and complete games in 1957, and complete games in 1958. He was an All-Star in all four of those seasons and was considered for the Most Valuable Player Award in 1955, 1956, and 1957.

Perhaps the highlight of this four-year period occurred on June 27, 1958, in a game against the Washington Senators. He was just one out away from becoming the eighth pitcher—and first left-hander—to toss a perfect game. Although pinch-hitter Ed Fitz Gerald laced a double down the first-base line to end Pierce's historic bid, he, in keeping with his even-tempered disposition, was not undone by what had occurred. He struck out Albie Pearson on three pitches to end the game. In the clubhouse later he praised shortstop Luis Aparicio for his fine glove-work and catcher Sherm Lollar for how he called the game, concluding, "The big thing is that we won."[91]

His 1959 season was marked by periods of excellence followed by those of mediocrity. He pitched a six-hit shutout victory in his second start of the year followed by a loss in his next outing that saw him last just two innings. And that was the way the season went, winning a couple then losing a couple. In mid–August he sustained a pulled muscle in his hip that kept him out of the lineup for three weeks. He returned in early September to help the Sox take the American League flag, but did not start a game in the World Series. Instead he relieved in three of the six games, pitching scoreless ball in the four innings he worked. His regular season ended with a 14–15 record and a 3.62 ERA, nearly a run higher than the year before. Pierce bounced back in 1960, again winning 14 but with half the number of losses. It was the best won-loss percentage on the team. His hip injury resurfaced late in the summer, which limited his work to fewer than 200 innings for the first time since his injury-plagued 1954 campaign. He saw a steady decline in innings pitched from that point on.[92]

Pierce's 1961 season was disappointing by his standards. He was 1–5 in early June before he started winning more consistently. He was able to fashion a 10–9 record, but his 3.80 earned-run average was relatively high and he pitched fewer innings, in part because he was used more often than in the past as a reliever. He still had his great control, but at age 34 with periodic arm and hip problems he was past his prime, or so the White Sox thought. After 13 seasons in a Chicago uniform, he—along with Don Larsen—was traded to the San Francisco Giants for four other players. He ended his tenure with Chicago having won 186 games against 152 losses on a fine cumulative 3.19 earned-run average, and his 1,796 strikeouts were the most of any Sox hurler at that time.

The Giants were quite anxious to add the veteran left-hander to their staff. Owner Horace Stoneman acknowledged, "When we started our negotiations, Pierce was our primary objective.... We were told Pierce may tire after six or seven innings, but [manager] Alvin Dark plans to space his starts, and our San Francisco climate, which I understand Billy is delighted with, should also help his stamina." He saw Pierce "as a classy veteran who can win that big game in a pennant fight."[93]

Although Stoneman's prediction ultimately turned out to be on the money, at first it did not appear that way. To say that Pierce had a mediocre spring would be a gross understatement; he was nothing short of horrible. In his first four exhibition games, he was hammered for 32 hits and 27 earned runs in 13⅔ innings worked. The Giants expressed their confidence in him despite his poor showing. Their only concern was about how often to use him. "We know Billy can pitch," said pitching coach Larry Jansen. "What we don't know is how much he needs in between."[94]

When the regular season started, however, it was an entirely different Billy Pierce who took the mound. He opened his first game on April 13, going over seven innings to win it, 7–2. The fans were so excited they gave him a standing ovation when he left the field. "The cheers really got to me inside," he said after the game. "Fans nowhere have been more wonderful. I felt it way down deep." And that great outing was just the beginning. He won his next start, and the one after that, and the one after that until he had strung together eight victories in eight consecutive games, including one shutout and two other complete games.[95]

No pitcher could keep up a torrid pace like that, not even a 35-year-old veteran who was pitching like a 25-year-old. He lost his next two starting assignments, the second one because he gave up a double, then was spiked covering first base by the second batter he faced. Reliever Don Larsen allowed the run to score, leaving Pierce a one-run deficit that the Giants were not able to overcome. The spiking tore a huge gash in his heel that required 14 stitches. It knocked him out of the lineup for the next four weeks. It took him awhile to get back to his winning ways once he returned, but by August he was his old self.

His true value to the Giants was amply demonstrated in the three-game playoff series with the Los Angeles Dodgers to decide the National League Championship. On October 1, Pierce was given the ball for the first game of the series. His opponent was Sandy Koufax, who was 14–6 with a 2.41 earned-run average coming into the contest. San Francisco jumped on the Dodger left-hander for two runs in the first inning and another to open the second, at which point Koufax was yanked. Pierce, on the other hand, dominated the Los Angeles hitters from the get-go. He allowed the Dodgers just three meaningless hits over nine innings that included six strikeouts and a single walk. By the time the dust had settled, Pierce was the victor in a complete game shutout. After the Dodgers took the second game, the Giants were facing elimination in the third contest until they scored four runs in the top of the ninth to take a 6–4 lead. Pierce was called in to close it out, which he did in fine fashion, retiring the side in order. In the World Series against the Yankees, he lost the third game to Bill Stafford, 3–2, but then went the distance in Game 6 to defeat Whitey Ford, 5–2. He was in the bullpen warming up in the ninth inning of Game 7 when Willie McCovey lined out to Bobby Richardson to end the game with the Yanks up, 1–0. The aging southpaw ended the year at 16–6 on a 3.49 earned-run average, going 12–0 at Candlestick.

But that was it. Used primarily as a reliever in 1963, he showed that age had caught up with him at last. He started off as he ended the season before, pitching a complete game shutout at Candlestick. But it was all downhill after that. By summer's end he won just three games while losing 11 others and his 4.27 ERA was his worst since his rookie season in 1948. He remained with the Giants the following year, appearing in 34 games, to end at 3–0 with an exceptional 2.20 earned-run average. On the last day of the season, he announced his retirement, bringing to an end a stellar 18-year major league career in which he won 211 games and lost 169 while compiling a cumulative 3.27 ERA with 1,999 strikeouts. *The Sporting News* called him "one of the game's gentlemen and top pitchers," saying that baseball was "a little poorer" with his exit from the game. "I leave without a regret and with only fine memories," he said in his announcement. "I've gotten more out of baseball than most men ever get because of the cards sometimes turning up the wrong way for them. For me, they've invariably been in my favor."[96]

Although the 1961 campaign did not start out very well for him, by the time of the August 16 game against the Yankees, he had turned a 1–5 start to 7–7, lowering his earned-run average from 4.47 to 3.54. His two previous starts were complete game victories, the second one a shutout over the Kansas City Athletics. While he often struggled when facing the Yankees—25–37 lifetime—the current season was a particularly difficult one for him. He did have a save against the Bombers on May 28, but then suffered a loss on June 4 and another on July 27.

When it came to Maris, however, he was much more successful. The Yankee slugger had just one homer off of him (1960) over the four seasons prior to 1961 and his batting average was never greater than .176 in any of those years. But the present season was entirely different. Not only was Maris in a hot streak, but he was hitting southpaws much better than ever before. "It so happened that at this point of the season, I felt just as confident facing a left-hander as I did facing a right-hander; in fact, even more so," he stated. "For some reason I was following the pitches of southpaws better than the right-handers at this time." As for Pierce, he typically pitched Maris inside, but when he did go outside, it was "way outside. And of course, one never walked Roger to get to Mantle."[97]

Ironically, August 16 was also "Babe Ruth Day" at Yankee Stadium, a fact that Maris did not realize until a reporter told him after the game. More than 1,000 Babe Ruth League players were among the nearly 30,000 in attendance celebrating the thirteenth anniversary of Ruth's passing. It was likely not a very happy day for the Babe's acolytes amongst the crowd. Pierce barely had a chance to settle in before Maris took him deep in the first inning with Bobby Richardson aboard. Rather than attempting to tie up Maris with an inside fastball, he tried to hurl one past him on the outside part of the plate. Apparently it was not outside far enough, because Maris blasted it into the second row of the upper right-field deck for his sixth homer in as many games.

The Maris homer express continued to roll onward in the fourth inning. Pierce retired the side in order in the second and two were gone with Richardson again on base when Maris stepped into the box for his second at-bat of the afternoon. Realizing that his heater had not worked, Pierce resorted to his crooked pitch. "I looked at a couple of curves," Maris recalled, "then found one that I liked. Again the bat had that certain ring." This time the ball traveled a little farther, landing three rows back in the upper deck in right for number 48. That made it seven dingers in six straight games, a new American League record previously held by Lou Gehrig and two other players, and one that tied the National League record. That ended Pierce's day. The White Sox tied the game up in the sixth, but the Yankees finally won when Bob Cerv was struck by a pitch in the bottom of the ninth with the bases loaded.[98]

Claire Ruth, the Bambino's widow, was at that game and posed for pictures with the M and M Boys. They were all smiles, but Mrs. Ruth made it clear that she did not want to see the record broken by either of them. When Maris was asked after the game about her sentiments, he said that he was not offended by her remarks, that he thought it only natural she should feel that way. He jokingly said he hoped his wife would be as protective of him if he were to set a new record. He again insisted he was not dwelling on Ruth or his 60 homers. In fact, he commented, "What I want is the dough, not the record. I don't intend to keep making $8,000 a year the rest of life." While the financial security of his family was always uppermost in his mind, this response was meant as a joke more than anything else. He was making around $32,000 a year, not $8,000, as the assembled press well knew. There had been a lot of talk about how he and/or Mantle stood to make a bundle of money if they broke Ruth's record. But oftentimes, reporters took such injudicious remarks too seriously, casting him in a bad light.[99]

Joe Reichler of the Associated Press reported a comment Maris made in that postgame interview in which he referred to himself as being "born surly and I'm going to stay that way. Everything in life is tough." While that may have been an accurate quote—it was not the first time he said something along those lines—it was the way in which it was framed that made the remark even more damaging. This statement, Reichler wrote, was said "through thin lips that always seem to be snarling." But as Dan Daniel, veteran sportswriter for the *New York World Telegram*, explained, "Maris has been taken at his word by reporters on the road. He is indulging in self-indictment founded on a phony statement. Roger is not surly. He may be bewildered. Possibly he is scared.... Maris' description of himself as surly is a defensive hoax. Besieged by newspaper and magazine writers, reinforced by television and radio men, Maris and Mantle, neither voluble, are at a loss for words."[100]

It was those who did not follow the Yankees or Maris regularly who tended to take such comments literally since they were unfamiliar with the Maris personality and his intense dislike of being the focus of so much attention. Always his own worst enemy, he would sometimes call reporters' questions "silly," especially the most oft-asked one: did he think he would break the record? "How the heck would I know whether I'll break Babe Ruth's record," he said at that mass interview session around his locker. "Besides, you're the only guys thinking about it. I don't. All I'm interested in is having a good season and winning the pennant." Maris, of course, was indeed thinking about the record now that he was approaching 50 home runs, but his response was a typical one designed to deflect such "silly" questions.[101]

It was exactly that type of retort that his critics latched onto. Emil Tagliabue, sports columnist for the *Corpus Christi Times*, jumped all over Maris for his denials that the record was on his mind. The writer, who was not even at that August 16 game in New York, referred to Maris as "Roger the Red Neck," stating his belief that the slugger was "not now the world's greatest exponent of the truth.... Either Maris is an out-an-out prevaricator or his ideas of success and ours are as far apart as Eddie Fisher and Debbie Reynolds [Hollywood stars who had recently gone through a nasty divorce]." Maris would have been far better served had he not been so blunt, but he simply was incapable of being otherwise.[102]

Home Run # 49—Game 123—August 20—Day Game/ First Game of Doubleheader

All good things must eventually come to an end, which they did for the Yankee right fielder. New York hosted the White Sox for the final game of their series on the afternoon of August 17. Chicago again sent a left-hander to the mound, Frank Baumann, who Maris had taken deep for number 37 on July 25. This time he was not as fortunate. Baumann struck out Maris in the first inning, then retired him on groundouts in the third, fourth, and sixth to bring an inglorious end to Maris' consecutive home-run streak. The Yankees won without his assistance, 5–3, moving them up four games over the Tigers who lost two successive games against the Orioles. Then it was time to hit the road to Cleveland, the start of a 13-game journey that would end with a return home on September 1 to take on Detroit in a pennant-deciding three-game series.

It was during the latter part of August that the "lively ball" debate reached a crescendo. With many fans, some journalists, and a score of players arguing that the ball was juiced, the *New York Times* and *Sports Illustrated* had the ball tested separately by outside research firms. The *Times* conclusion: "maybe it is, and maybe it isn't." The researchers for *Sports Illustrated* reached the "tentative engineering conclusion" that it was compared to the balls from 1952, but just slightly more so to those used in 1953. Sportswriter Dan Daniel and many others refuted these findings. "It is futile to rip up a ball ten to 15 years old and compare its innards with those of the 1961 leather," he reasonably argued. "Baseballs suffer a drying up process through time." There was no definitive answer one way or the other, so the argument continued unabated.[103]

Disputes over the nature of the modern bat arose around this same time as well. Some contended that it was not the ball that was lively, it was the bat. "A second go-round on a pioneer research tour taken several years ago has strengthened the conviction that the current rash of homer hitting is attributable to revised qualities of the bat, rather than the ball," contended Joseph Sheehan in the *New York Times*. Why, he asked, were the likes of Maris and Mantle and a handful of other players hitting so many home runs? "Simply because most of today's players are taking heavier swings with lighter bats at more or less the same old ball," he concluded.[104]

The implication, of course, was that it was somehow cheating to use a bat significantly lighter than the ones used by Ruth and his contemporaries. What Sheehan and those who agreed with him failed to mention was that lighter bats were in vogue at least a decade before the 1961. Yes, there was an increase in home runs during the ten plus years lighter bats had become the standard, because a lighter bat can be swung faster and it is bat speed more than bat weight that effects how far a ball travels. But if it was the type of bat being used that accounted for the homers Maris and Mantle were hitting, why then was 1961 the exception and not the rule? If the cause was lighter bats, would not there have been summers prior to 1961 where Ruth's record was seriously threatened? The fact that there were not indicated that the home run pace Maris and Mantle were setting could not be explained away by any single factor like the weight of the bat.

Maris' next two games were not any better than the last one. On the night of August

18, 37,840 fans, the largest crowd of the summer, came to Cleveland Stadium hoping to see the Indians win and Maris and Mantle homer. They got their first wish, but not their second. Jim "Mudcat" Grant pitched a gem, a three-hit, one-run game to beat the mighty Bombers, 5–1. Not only did Maris and Mantle fail to hit even a single, but they were the last two outs of the ninth, Maris striking out, Mantle flying out to left. The two Yankee powerhouses had nothing but praise for Grant after the game. "That's the best I've ever seen him," proclaimed Maris, who was fed a steady diet of curves. "I never did hit him," said Mantle, who saw nothing but fastballs. "He's got the edge on me." Detroit beat Boston to reduce their deficit to three games.[105]

The game on the following afternoon ended pretty much the same for the M and M Boys. Whitey Ford did win his twenty-first, 3–2, but Mantle managed a lowly single in the eighth inning while Maris was hitless in five trips to the plate, making him 0–13 in his last three games. Ever the professional, however, he did not allow his recent struggles at the plate to effect his fielding. In the seventh inning he took what appeared to be a sure home run away from Willie Kirkland, Cleveland right fielder, by jumping high in the air to snag the ball just as it was crossing the fence.[106]

The tonic for Maris' hitting woes arrived in the form of Jim Perry during the first game of a Sunday afternoon twin bill the next day. The tall right-hander, who surrendered numbers five and 21 to Maris earlier in the season, was not having a good summer at all. He had a 9–10 record and a high 4.20 earned-run average, in large part because he had already surrendered 21 home runs in his 26 starts to date. He ended the season first among American League pitchers in earned runs allowed and sixth in homers surrendered.

The game got off to an inauspicious beginning for the beleaguered hurler. After Bobby Richardson singled to open the game and Maris walked with one away, Mantle hammered his forty-sixth homer into the right-field seats to give the Yanks an instant 3–0 lead. Then in the third with Billy Gardner on with a single, Maris, on a full count, pounded his forty-ninth into the same general area as did his partner in crime. Maris' blast landed further into the stands than did Mantle's, which "barely cleared the rail fence near the 365-foot marker." Later, Maris said "Perry didn't have his real live fast ball" that day, but he "knew Perry would come in with his best pitch—the fast ball. He would try to put everything he had on it, aiming for a corner. Now he goes into his wind-up; the pitch comes down the pike. I had guessed right! It was a Perry fast ball. I was ready, I had it timed, and it was well hit." Mantle plated another run in the sixth. With Ralph Terry pitching a shutout, it was all the Yankees needed to claim their eighty-first victory of the year.[107]

Maris failed to get a safety in the second game, but he did reach base in the sixth after he was struck by a pitch, and scored in the eighth after walking. Mantle was responsible for two of the Yankees' five runs, including a walk in the sixth with the bases loaded and a single in the eighth that drove in another run. The Yankees won, 5–2, which was fortunate because the Tigers won their doubleheader as well, leaving them three games behind the league-leaders.

In spite of his forty-ninth dinger, Maris had only that one hit in his last 22 plate appearances. Some in the press began to wonder if he had it in him to stay the course. "[I]t's beginning to look now as though the immortal shadow of Babe Ruth may yet withstand this latest siege at the most glamorous record in the book.... Maris came into this set 14 games ahead of the pace and he leaves it 10 ahead, but Ruth's gait gets hotter and hotter from here on in." Even Maris was having his doubts. "Hitting-wise it was one of my low points of the season," he acknowledged. "In fact, I was feeling worse about my hitting than at any time since the slump early in May. There were to be more low spots later on, but from a different cause. It was at this point that my batting average started to slip down from its peak. Unfortunately, I would not be able to reverse the trend very much from here on out." Maris was batting .288 on August 16, his highest average of the summer. By the end of the road trip, it declined to .271, remaining in that general neighborhood for the rest of the season.[108]

Home Run # 50—Game 125—August 22—Night Game

After the second game on August 20 in Cleveland, the Yankees caught a four-hour overnight flight to the west coast to take on the Angels for three games. With no contest scheduled for August 21, Maris, Mantle, and Yogi Berra traveled to Universal Studios to film a scene for *That Touch of Mink*, a romantic comedy starring Doris Day and Cary Grant. In it, Day and Grant are sitting in a replica of the home dugout at Yankee Stadium while a game is in progress. Seated with them are the three Yankees. Mantle and Maris are tossed by the home plate umpire because they supported Day as she argues about an outside pitch he called a strike. Berra is then bounced after the umpire accuses him of being sarcastic for supporting his call. Even in the confines of a film lot, however, they could not escape the pursuit of fans. Movie crews and their families surrounded them as they toured the studio before filming began. "It was quite an experience," Maris stated, "and we enjoyed it. We toured the studio, met several stars, and for a while were able to get our minds off baseball."[109]

Maris had a surprise awaiting him when the three returned to their hotel after the shoot. The front desk clerk handed him a message as he walked in informing him that his fourth child—and third son—had arrived a month earlier than expected. He was much relieved, though, in spite of not being by his wife's side. (There was no paternity leave for players back then.) "All the worries [about the health of his wife and unborn child] of the spring had proved unfounded. Pat and the baby were both fine, and I was a happy, relaxed man that night."[110]

The August 22 game was an evening contest that pitted Bill Stafford against the Angels' ace, rookie Ken McBride. For some reason, Maris had problems hitting home runs at L.A.'s Wrigley Field, a long-ball hitter's park. He did blast number 5 there on May 6, but had failed to do so since then. So the chances of him hitting another, especially while mired in a batting slump, did not look good as the game began. The fact that Maris was relatively unfamiliar with McBride's stuff—managing two singles and three walks in 11 previous plate appearances—did not bode well for the slugger either.

The 6-foot-1, 190-pound right-hander began his professional career in 1954 pitching for the Bluefield Blue-Grays, the Boston Red Sox Class D affiliate. The 18-year-old compiled the second best record for a team that finished first in the Appalachian League. He spent the next three seasons working his way up in the Red Sox organization, putting together a 30–29 record as he moved steadily from Class D to Double-A. McBride showed signs of brilliance during his minor-league apprenticeship, hurling back-to-back one-hitters for Bluefield in 1954 and a no-hitter for the Class B Greensboro Patriots on August 30, 1956.[111]

McBride's full potential came to the forefront during the 1959 season pitching for the Triple-A Indianapolis Indians. By early June he was 7–1, making him the first seven-game winner in the American Association that season. He injured his non-pitching shoulder in late June, but returned after two weeks on the disabled list to win his eleventh game, a five-hit, 2–1 victory on July 17. In spite of his excellent campaign—11–5, 2.79 ERA—with Indianapolis, though, Boston sold him to the pennant-bound Chicago White Sox on August 1. McBride was immediately called up to the big club and on August 4 made his major league career debut, losing, 3–2, after an error to open the eighth resulted in two unearned runs. The young hurler got his second start on August 9, then relieved in nine more games to end the season at 0–1 with a decent 3.18 earned-run average.[112]

McBride spent most of the following season with the Triple-A San Diego Padres and, even though he had an 11–14 record, he maintained a good 3.23 earned-run average, making him one of the better pitchers on a mediocre team. He was brought back up to the White Sox in mid–September, appearing in five games as a reliever. The Sox planned on retaining him for use as a reliever, but left him exposed to the expansion draft instead. He was snapped up by the Los Angeles Angels, a move that was the real start of his major league career.[113]

The right-hander's money pitch was his sinker which, when he was on, resulted in a lot of groundball outs. "McBride offers no testimony that the sinker is the greatest thing since Hungarian meat balls," quipped sportswriter Melvin Durslag, but "he sticks with the pitch, as often as 90 percent of the time." McBride admitted he did not have a strong enough arm to live off his fastball alone and his curveball was "not good enough. So the most effective thing I can do is use the sinker with control." Therein lay the problem, as Jack Spring, a fellow pitcher with the Angels, noted. Observing that McBride "had probably the best sinkerball that I've ever seen outside of Mel Stottlemyre—but if his mechanics weren't just perfect he would lose his sinker, or it wouldn't be as good some days…. But he was a fine pitcher and, ooh, when he had his sinker going, there wasn't anybody that could beat him…. That sinkerball was his bread-and-butter."[114]

McBride quickly established himself as the anchor of the Angels starting staff. He was 5–2 at the end of May, a nine-game stretch that included three complete games. His May 23 shutout was the first such scoreless affair in Los Angeles history. He did have three straight losses in mid–June, primarily because his teammates plated just one run total in those games. He was victimized again by lackluster hitting, losing four straight starts in August because of poor run support. Although he ended the season with a 12–15 record, his 3.65 earned-run average was good and he did pitch 11 complete games in over 240 innings of work, ninth most among American League pitchers. He was fourth in strikeouts per nine innings pitched, fifth in strikeouts, third in games started, and ninth in complete games. His 28 home runs allowed were sixth most in the league, but 19 of those came while pitching at home in the dinger-friendly confines of Wrigley Field. Considering that the Angels lost 91 games, those were not bad numbers for the rookie pitcher.

The Angel ace appeared to be on his way to a 20-win season in 1962 when he sustained a cracked rib in late July. He was 11–3 with a 3.25 earned-run average at the time he went down. He had hurled two consecutive shutouts at home in the new Dodger Stadium before suffering the injury, which he believed occurred during that second shutout. "My side started hurting during the night of that July 21 win over Cleveland," he said. "It hurt so bad I couldn't even sleep." He tried to come back on August 3, but left the game in the seventh after giving up four earned runs to the Orioles in Baltimore. He attempted one last start on September 16 at home, but was again ineffective because of his ailments. As it was, he ended the season at 11–5 with a 3.50 ERA. "I don't think I'm exaggerating when I say McBride would have won 20 games during 1962 if he hadn't been injured," Angels manager Bill Rigney contended. McBride agreed. "I know I was putting the ball where I wanted it and I know that teams were having a lot of trouble getting runs off of me" before the injury occurred. "I don't see why I couldn't expect to maintain that pace."[115]

Although he was healthy at the start of the 1963 campaign, at first it did not appear that way. He was 3–6 at the end of May before he got back on the winning track. He went 9–1 with a minuscule 2.02 earned-run average from June 1 through July 30, but then he seemed to run out of gas. He was 1–5 the rest of the season with a gigantic 5.81 ERA, ending the summer with 13 wins and 12 losses on a 3.26 earned-run average in 251 innings pitched, a club record at the time. He was first in the league in hit batsmen with 14, a record few pitchers point to with pride; he had no hesitation pitching inside and would occasionally plunk a batter if need be.

After winning his first start of the 1964 season, his production declined from there. He lost 10 of his next 12 starts and his earned-run average exploded to 4.70. He claimed that his arm was not bothering him, but that turned out to be less than truthful. He confessed to an interviewer much later that he felt something "pop" in his second start of the season and he was never the same after that. His control was gone and his sinker became eminently hittable. By summer's end he was 4–13 with a humongous 5.26 ERA in just 161⅓ innings pitched; his major league career was all but done.[116]

McBride never recovered after that disastrous 1964 campaign. His arm continued to bother him, which limited his appearances. He pitched in only eight games for three losses before the club sent him down to their Single-A affiliate in San Jose. He made just three starts for the Bees before calling it quits. One can only speculate as to what he might have achieved had he not been so seriously injured in 1964 at the age of 28. As it was, he compiled a 40–50 record on a cumulative 3.79 earned-run average over eight major league seasons.[117]

The Angels hurler had lost four straight games—two of them by one run—when he started against the Yankees on August 22. It was not that he was pitching badly, it was that he was given no run support; the Angels scored a total of five runs in those four games. And while he had surrendered 21 home runs that season already, only one of those was in those four outings. In fact, had he not been shelled in a game at home on August 31 when four dingers left the stadium, he was actually doing quite well in preventing the long ball at home.

A record crowd of nearly 20,000 spectators packed Wrigley Field that night. Everyone, it seemed, wanted to witness the historic home run race that overshadowed everything else going on in baseball. The Angel batters gave him an early lead for a change, taking Bill Stafford deep back-to-back for three runs in the first inning. McBride, in the meantime, held the Bombers scoreless for the first five innings. Maris got on in the first inning with a single, then McBride got him on a pop fly in the third. The right-hander retired the first Yankee batter in the sixth before giving up a single to Billy Gardner.

McBride was pitching the slugger on the outside of the plate in an attempt to keep him from successfully pulling the ball. Maris, at some point in this third at-bat, decided to go with the pitch, something he rarely did. Perhaps he should have tried that more often that season, because he smashed the ball to the deepest part of park, straightaway center field some 412 feet distant. "It was one of my best shots of the season," he said. Number 50 not only put Maris up four on Mantle, it also set a new major league record for most home runs before September. Fortunately for McBride, Earl Averill homered off of reliever Luis Arroyo in the bottom of the eighth to give the pitcher a two-run cushion going into the final inning. As it turned out, it was a needed run because Yogi Berra greeted McBride with a homer to open the ninth. And that was the way the game ended, a 4–3 Angels victory. The Yankee loss coupled with a Detroit win over Cleveland left New York two up on the pesky Tigers.[118]

Home Run # 51—Game 129—August 26—Day Game

Maris had now entered territory known by just a handful of other players. He was only the ninth man in major league history to hit 50 or more home runs in a season, and with more than a month left, he stood a good chance of going far beyond that. Crossing that line meant the obsessive public scrutiny of his every move—autograph seekers even began following him into church—and the resulting pressure on him increased exponentially from that point on. Despite his best attempts to keep the homer record at the back of his mind, he was now completely aware of it each time he came to bat. No one was counting Mantle out, not with his experience, power, switch-hitting ability, and home run prowess, but being four back of Maris meant the press and public focused almost entirely on the right fielder alone. He lived under a microscope from then on, never finding a moments peace until the final out of the final game of the season.

Maris did not park one the following night, but his nearly-a-homer triple in the tenth inning produced the winning run. Whitey Ford started, but was removed after giving up six earned runs in the first four innings. Maris scored the first Yankee tally in the fourth and the second in the sixth after he was walked to open both frames. With the score tied at six, Maris came up in the tenth inning with one on and two gone for his sixth plate appearance of the game. By this point in the season, many pitchers, not wanting to be the one who went down in history as the deliverer of the record-breaking homer, "adopted the don't-give-him-anything-good [to hit] pitching policy."[119]

As a subscriber to that very sensible approach, rookie right-handed reliever Jim Donohue "started working on me to keep his pitches low and away. I was feeling disgusted by this time. The two strike-outs [earlier in the game] had annoyed me, but the three walks were even more annoying. I wanted at least to get a chance to swing. I hadn't yet reached the point where I was going for bad pitches. That would come later." Then Donohue made a mistake, leaving the ball up in the zone. "This time Roger took full advantage of his opportunity, clobber[ing] a Jim Donohue pitch against the 412-foot sign high on the wall in dead center for a triple." The blast, which hit two inches from the top of the fence, scored Billy Gardner from first, giving the Bombers a lead they did not surrender. A wild pitch to Yogi Berra a batter later allowed Maris to cross the plate, putting the Yanks up, 8–6. Luis Arroyo shutdown the Angels in the bottom of the inning for a come-from-behind New York victory, one that expanded their league-lead to three games after Detroit lost to Cleveland.[120]

The Yankees lost the third game of the series the following night, 6–4. Maris was hitless in five trips to the plate, although a sacrifice fly in the third scored a run. Mantle managed a single in the fifth for his only hit of the game. The Yankees flew to Kansas

City immediately after the contest, giving Maris the chance to visit his wife and family for three days. He found little peace there, however. Some thoughtless reporter on the Raytown newspaper listed the Maris' home address in his son's birth announcement, resulting in a mass of strangers driving by their home, intruding on their privacy. People even came to the door demanding autographs.

"My feeling of relaxation and contentment melted away in the fire of my suddenly exploding temper," Maris acknowledged. "This was going too far.... I don't think I have ever been more angry in my life than I was at that moment. This was an unthinking, uncalled for invasion of my privacy." One can fully appreciate the fury Maris must have felt. Incidents like this one made his life a living hell the last few weeks of the season. He stayed behind when the Yankees flew to Minnesota following the conclusion of the August 27 game. The crowds dissipated when the Yanks left town, giving the Maris family at least one day of peace and quiet before he hit the road again.[121]

Nearly 31,000 fans, the largest crowd of the season, packed Municipal Stadium the night of August 25 to see the Yankees take on the Athletics. Maris and Mantle both failed to homer, but the right fielder did score the first run of the game after he was hit on the head by a Jim Archer pitch to open the fourth inning. Two batters later, Moose Skowron singled, scoring Maris from second. The Yankees won, 3–0, on Ralph Terry's second consecutive shutout.

A throng of over 32,000 hurried through the turnstiles the following afternoon for the second game of the series. The city assigned an additional 30 police officers to the stadium to help with crowd control and to prevent the "over-enthusiastic" from jumping onto the field. Typical of the many fans there that day was 25-year-old Lori Beth Zumbrun who was attending her first major league game, along with her mother, Patricia, and father, Forrest. Mr. Zumbrun announced with pride, "I sold Maris a set of tires and I'd like to see him hit a home run." The family was there solely to witness the former Kansas City outfielder park one, which he did. Unfortunately for Mrs. Zumbrun, she missed it because she was off buying potato chips at the time.[122]

Getting the call for the Athletics was 22-year-old Jerry Walker, a sometimes starter, sometimes reliever who was obtained from the Baltimore Orioles just prior to the start of the season. The 6-foot-1, 195-pound right-hander was signed by Baltimore directly out of high school in 1957. His school pitching record of 52 wins against just one loss made him much sought after by several major league teams. The Birds won the bidding contest, signing the 18-year-old for over $5,000 (not $60,000 as reported by some sources). Under baseball's Bonus Rule then in effect, Baltimore had to keep him on their roster for a year without sending the player to the minor leagues. Those players, known as "bonus babies," often spent the time riding the pine, but that was not the case with Walker. He appeared in 13 games from early July to the end of the season. One of his three starts was a ten-inning shutout of the Washington Senators in which he allowed only four hits while striking out three and walking one. He ended the season at 1–0 with a great 2.93 earned-run average in 27⅔ innings of work.[123]

The Orioles' hot prospect began the 1958 season with the team, but it quickly became apparent that he was not ready for the big time. He relieved in three games before management decided he would be better off developing his pitch selection by playing regularly with one of their minor league affiliates. In early May he was sent to the Single-A Knoxville Smokies in the South Atlantic League where his 18–4 won-loss record and outstanding 2.61 ERA made him the best pitcher in the league. He also swung a pretty good bat. In a game on August 19 with the score tied a two in the bottom of the ninth, Walker, who was making his first start after being out a week with a throat infection, announced, "I'm tired! Somebody get on and I'll get this thing over with." That was precisely what he did. With two on, he lined the first pitch he saw into center field to win the game, 3–2, his sixteenth victory of the season. He was recalled to Baltimore in September, again pitching from the bullpen in three games.[124]

With his superb 1958 minor league season, it was all but certain that he would stick with Baltimore all of 1959. Using great control while mixing up his pitches consisting of a "sneaky" fastball, a sharp curve, and a good slider, he quickly established himself as an essential member of Baltimore's outstanding starting rotation. "He's mighty quick," said Harry Brecheen, the Orioles pitching coach, "and has such a deceptively smooth motion he can throw the ball by a batter when he decides to reach back and put a little mustard on it." Baltimore catcher Gus Triandos noted that Walker's fastball "doesn't move as much [as that of teammate Milt Pappas], but he's so sneaky the ball's hard to time. He changes speeds good, too, to keep them [batters] off balance."[125]

As a proud member of the Birds' famed "Kiddie Korps"—comprised of Walker, Milt Pappas, and Jack Fisher, all of them 20 years old—he won his first start of the season, 6–1, a complete-game gem in which he limited the Washington Senators to eight hits. His second victory came on May 7, another complete-game outing against the Senators. Then on May 24, he went the distance against the New York Yankees, striking out Mickey Mantle three times to defeat them, 2–1. "I'd like to have ten percent of him," proclaimed manager Paul Richards after that performance. "If I did, I wouldn't have to worry about finances. This young man has a lot of savvy. He's going to be around for a long time."[126]

By early August he was 8–5 with three saves and a spectacular 2.62 earned-run average. Yankee skipper Casey Stengel, who managed the American League All-Star team, was so impressed with the rookie hurler—he had beaten the Yankees twice already that season—that he chose him to start the second All-Star game on August 3. After allowing a run in the first inning, he held the National League scoreless over the next two, and when the American League grabbed the lead in the third inning and held on to it to the end, he was credited with the victory. It made him the youngest pitcher—20 years, six months—ever to win an All-Star game.[127]

Walker's most impressive outing came against the Chicago White Sox in the second game of a doubleheader on September 11. He held the Sox scoreless for 16 innings on 188 pitches, finally winning it when Baltimore third baseman Brooks Robinson singled home the winning run with two out in the bottom of the sixteenth. "One of the best efforts I can remember," proclaimed Paul Richards. "And I qualify it only because I saw the great Carl Hubbell of the Giants beat the Cardinals, 1–0, in 18 innings in 1933." His season record of 11 wins and 10 losses on a 2.92 earned-run average was one of the best on the staff.[128]

The Orioles expected big things from Walker the following season, but it did not turn out as planned. He was hampered by a number of physical ailments that limited his effectiveness, including arm problems and, oddly, severe allergic reactions to grass and the ingredients in his wife's talcum powder, which were not identified until tests were run late in the season. As a result, he pitched over 60 fewer innings that he did in 1959, and his 3–4 record on a 3.74 earned-run average resulted in a late-spring trade the following season with the Kansas City Athletics.[129]

As it turned out, Walker's 1961 campaign did not show much improvement. While his allergies were under control, his best pitch, the slider, suddenly deserted him and he had trouble finding the plate with it. "In my case my slider just stopped breaking," he explained. "Besides that, I was having trouble getting it over." One of his problems was that he had gotten out of his natural rhythm. "When things aren't going right you have to think about your stride and where you release the ball and a lot of other things. Then you really have trouble because it's hard to think about all those things and throw naturally."[130]

Toward the end of the season he resorted to using a no-windup delivery on some pitches because he thought he was tipping them off. "I had the same problem last year [1960], but I thought I had it licked. After being told again this season, I started practicing the new delivery in the bull-pen." While that may have helped a little—he was 4–6 with a 3.78 ERA in his last ten games—ultimately his season was less than a brilliant one (8–14, 4.82 ERA) in which he was tenth among American League pitchers in walks, fourth in wild pitches, and second in hit batsmen.[131]

Walker was hoping for a fresh start in 1962 and at first it looked like he was going to have a good season. Although he hurt his back during spring training, he recovered in time to pitch his first game of the summer on April 14, a 7–3 win over Chicago in which he was able to go eight innings. He tossed his first complete game on May 1 and his first shutout on May 31, for a 6–2 record and a 4.44 earned-run average. Then things began to turn for the worse. He was 2–4 in June and his ERA mushroomed to 5.18.

Normally an even-tempered individual, his frustration with his up-and-down pitching was beginning to show. In a game against the Los Angeles Angels on June 20, Walker unintentionally struck Leon Wagner with a pitch. Wagner, angered by being hit, threw his bat at Walker. The pitcher, now furious, threw the ball at Wagner and plunked him again as he was walking to first base, causing the benches to empty. Both were fined for their actions. And so it went. In a game on August 1, he strained a muscle in his shoulder and missed over two weeks as a result. He was consigned to bullpen duty when he did return, and while he did not lose a game, his 9.60 ERA in those final eight appearances probably sealed his fate. After ending the year at 8–9 with a high 5.90 earned-run average, Walker was traded to the Cleveland Indians in late February 1963 for Chuck Essegian.[132]

Cleveland general manager Gabe Paul admitted that "the deal is a gamble." They were trading away a popular outfielder who hit 21 homers and drove in 50 for a struggling 24-year-old right-hander who managed only one winning season in six years. That move did not play out as hoped. All but two of Walker's 39 game appearances were in relief and his 6–6 record with a 4.91 earned-run average did not bode well for a long-term relationship with the Indians.

He had his moments, however. Future Hall-of-Famer Early Wynn ended his tenure with the Chicago White Sox in 1962 having won 299 games over 22 major league seasons. Desperate for number 300, he signed with the Cleveland Indians in the latter part of June. On July 13 the 43-year-old started the second game of a doubleheader against the Kansas City Athletics. After surrendering one earned run in the fourth and three more in the fifth, he was relieved by Walker to start the sixth inning with the Indians leading, 5–4. The right-hander held the A's scoreless over the next four innings while Cleveland added two insurance runs to secure Wynn's three-hundredth victory, the final one of his long and storied career. Wynn was effusive in his praise of Walker, his roommate, in the clubhouse after the game. "I felt better with Jerry out there, better than if I was still in. Jerry and I are going to have a party. I'm going to buy him the biggest steak he's ever had."[133]

Walker made three game appearances at the start of the 1964 campaign, but after going 0–1 with a 5.68 ERA in 6⅓ innings of relief, Cleveland optioned him to Triple-A Jacksonville. Used primarily as a starter with the Suns, he compiled a 10–9 record, but his earned-run average was a mediocre 4.20. Although still inconsistent, he had the occasional great outing when he showed flashes of his old self. On August 26, he hurled a near no-hitter—a single in the seventh ruined it—over the Richmond Virginians. His performance for the Suns led to his recall by the Indians in mid–September where he appeared as a reliever in three games.[134]

Walker spent the entire 1965 season relieving for the Portland Beavers in the Pacific Coast League before the Indians released him. He was a non-roster invitee to the Yankees' spring training camp in 1966. New York picked up his contract and sent him to its Triple-A affiliate, the Toledo Mud Hens. In spite of a hand injury suffered in June, Walker appeared in 39 games, mostly as a reliever, where he ended the season with a 1–6 record, but on a decent 3.43 earned-run average. The following summer the Yankees sent the now 28-year-old former major leaguer to Double-A Binghamton in the Eastern League where he was used primarily as a coach. He did relieve in five games and start another that summer, however. After his playing days were done, Walker remained in organized ball as a manager, scout, coach, front office executive, and general manager until his retirement in 2014. He pitched in eight major league seasons, ending with 37 wins and 44 losses on a cumulative 4.36 earned-run average in 190 games, 90 of them as a starter.

Walker had lost three of his four previous starts before taking the mound on that August 26 contest against the Yankees. He was 5–10 with a 5.11 earned-run average at that point in the season. Interestingly, Maris generally handled Walker well—.429 batting average in 1959, .500 in 1960—but he had never taken the pitcher deep in 25 plate appearances from 1958 through the first half of 1961. In fact, the Yankee slugger had failed to hit Walker at all in the current season, and his first three at-bats—a strikeout, a pop out, and a walk—in the August 26 game indicated that he was struggling against the right-hander.

With the Yankees up, 3–0, going into the sixth, it was clear Walker did not have his best stuff that day. Tony Kubek greeted him with a homer to open the inning before Maris stepped to the plate for his fourth time that day. Walker started the right fielder off with a series of changeups down and away. With the count 3–2, the pitcher decided he could sneak a fastball past the slugger for a strikeout. Although the pitch to Maris was low and outside, it caught just enough of the plate for him to reach it with the fat part of the bat. The ball took off on a line shot to right-center field, clearing the fence at the 378 foot mark. "I was worried at first," Maris said after the game. "I didn't think it … was going to carry. I hit a low ball. It wasn't a good pitch, but I got a good piece of it." He now led Mantle by five home runs. In his final at-bat of the day, Maris came close to parking another one, but it fell short by about five feet.[135]

By this point of the season, both Maris and Mantle were feeling the debilitating effects of the long season. With his typical bluntness, Maris stated after the game, "I'm tired, and I'll be glad when this season is over. I've only missed one game this season. It's been a long grind, and I'm still not thinking about records." Mantle, more circumspect, did not openly admit he was exhausted, but he did comment on his position in the homer race. "I've got a long way to go," he noted. "He's [Maris] got it going pretty good. It's been a week [six games] since I hit one." But whatever pressure they were feeling and no matter how "tired" either of them felt, it did not create any acrimony between them as some in the press suggested. "Neither he [Mantle] nor Roger mulled around about things that don't exist," Ralph Houk stated. "No ballplayer alive could take our normal daily routine and survive, if he started dramatizing himself. Mickey and Roger were playing team-ball; they weren't in a contest to see who could hit the most home runs."[136]

Some writers jumped all over Maris for his open admission of feeling fatigued. Houk was quick to come to his defense. "Roger was tired physically," he agreed. "He was answering a thousand questions a day. Smart alecks were putting answers in his mouth by asking him trick questions, giving misleading twists to his polite replies, calling him 'an angry young man, a psychological case.'" Houk contended it was the "hit-or-miss scribblers," those who did not cover the Yankees regularly, who were the most critical of Maris and, to a lesser extent, Mantle. He called them "pests, like mosquitoes" while "New York writers understood them—they were presenting a fair picture of their personalities, temperaments, and problems."[137]

Houk realized that Maris, who was the most stressed, was the one least equipped to handle it. He encouraged his right fielder to mollify the press with pat answers and to avoid them if at all possible when he was feeling particularly weary. "Figure out your answers and stick to them," he told his right fielder. "Talk baseball. Talk about winning the flag. Tell the exact truth as you see it. When you feel tired, excuse yourself. Go to the shower room. They can't follow you there. By the time you've showered, they'll be gone." The problem with these suggestions, though, was that the press was not satisfied with rote responses and kept badgering Maris until he said something that they could sink their teeth into. And avoiding reporters by going to the showers might have been good practical advice, but when Maris tried exactly that toward the end of the season, he was vilified for doing so. It seemed as if there was nothing he could do or say that would please those who saw him as somehow wanting or lacking or less than heroic.[138]

7

SEPTEMBER

Home Runs # 52 and 53—Game 135—September 2— Day Game

And just like that Maris' bat went cold. Not only did he fail to homer over the next five games, he barely hit at all. In the August 27 game against the A's, he walked one time in five trips to the plate in an 8–7 Yankee victory. After an off-day, the Yankees flew to Minnesota to take on the Twins in a three-game series. They ended up losing two out of the three. Maris' only offensive contribution came in the August 30 game, a single that plated a run in the eighth inning to help Bill Stafford achieve a four-run shutout; other than that he was hitless. Mantle did get things going again, however. He hit a home run on August 30 and another on August 31 to give him 48 for the year. More importantly, he was swinging a hot bat again, hitting .417 in the Twins' series.

Maris was in a low mood as the Yankees flew home after the final game with the Twins to take on the Detroit Tigers, now just a game and a half back, for three of the most important battles of the season. "I had a lot of thinking to do on that plane ride," Maris said. "The way I had flopped in Minneapolis and the fact that I was in a terrible slump bothered me. On the road trip I had dropped nineteen points in my batting average [actually 12 points, down to .271]. I knew we were going into a sink or swim, do or die series with Detroit and I wanted to be at my peak." He certainly had cause for concern. He batted just .133 on the road, managing only six hits—three of them homers—in 60 plate-appearances. It only added to the pressure on him as he headed down the home stretch. In fact, he became so stressed that in early September he developed a rash and small patches of his hair began to fall out. Bob Cerv claimed he was the first to notice his apartment-mate's hair loss. Maris, on the other hand, said it was a barber who first spotted it. Regardless of how it came to his attention, it was a clear indication that the strain was taking a physical toll on him.[1]

"This Is It! Yanks vs. Tigers," screamed a headline in the *New York Post*. Accompanying the article was a comic illustration of a generic Yankee player standing on the back of a tiger as he reached for the championship flag. The more sedate *New York Times* said simply, "Tigers Are Coming; So Are 180,000 Customers." No matter how it was stated, everyone knew it was the epic battle for the American League pennant. If the Yankees swept, they would be well on their way to their twenty-sixth postseason appearance. If they lost all three or even two out of the three, the Tigers stood a good chance of taking it all.[2]

The first game of the series on the first of September was everything a true baseball fan could hope for, minus the home runs. Over 65,000 spectators filed into Yankee Stadium on a sweltering summer evening to witness what turned out to be a pitchers' duel to the very end. Tensions were running high as Whitey Ford, going for his twenty-third victory, took the mound to start the festivities. He was a little shaky at first, giving up a triple to Al Kaline after two were gone, but got out of the jam by eliminating Rocky Colavito on a ground ball to short. Lefty Don Mossi was even sharper. After surrendering a single to Tony Kubek with one out, he struck out Maris and Mantle to serve notice that he was not the least bit intimidated by the powerful Yankee lineup. And that was the way it went over the next four innings.

After Mossi retired Kubek and Maris on fly balls in the bottom of the fourth, he struck out Mantle swinging. Ford was rocking along in the top of the fifth when suddenly he strained a muscle in his hip and had to be replaced by Bud Daley with one on and two gone. Fortunately for the Bombers, the southpaw was on his game and eliminated Jake Wood on a groundout. Mossi continued to pitch the game of his life. In the sixth he got Maris on an inning-ending double-play groundout and induced Mantle to pop out to open the seventh. In the top of the eighth, Yogi Berra made the defensive play of the game. With a runner on and one away, Al Kaline smashed a rocket down the third base line that ricocheted off the left-field wall, rebounding directly back to the waiting glove of Berra, who was patrolling the outfield that game. Berra pivoted and made a perfect throw, nailing Kaline at second base while holding the runner at third. "If I didn't go to second on that play, I'd have been loafing," the Tiger right fielder explained after the game. "I didn't see the ball come off the fence, but when I saw Berra pick it up, I wondered how he got it so quick. Give him credit. He made a great play." The sagacious Yankee catcher had his own explanation. "If I'd throwed like an outfielder I prob'ly wouldn't have got the man. But I throwed like a catcher, without taking a step, so my throw was in time to nail him." And there you have it.[3]

There was still no score going into the ninth. In the top of the inning, closer Luis Arroyo retired the Tigers in order. Maris opened the bottom half of the frame by flying out to right. Mantle then struck out for the third time and, before returning to the dugout, confronted home plate umpire Art Paparella about his strike-calling ability. Elston Howard followed with a single on the first pitch he saw. Yogi Berra did likewise, smacking a single into deep right-center field that moved Howard along to third.

The stage was now set for a dramatic ending. The Yankee faithful stood in anticipation as Bill Skowron, who had yet to get a hit, approached the plate. Mossi had the Moose at one and two when he decided to waste a pitch hoping Skowron would go fishing. "A curve ball, a lousy curve ball" was what he offered up. "He bites at the bad curve, but this one I got high," Mossi groaned. "[I]t was right down the middle. If it was low, I'd have gotten him out. He swings and misses at those all night." But this time the first baseman did not miss. He connected and sent the ball bouncing past the third baseman to score Howard. Game over. The win expanded New York's lead to two and a half games. Perhaps as important, it lowered the pressure on the Bombers while increasing it exponentially on the Tigers. As Murray Robinson wrote the following day, "It served notice on the Detroiters that the Yanks, cucumber-cool in the stifling heat, could win with both Roger Maris and Mickey Mantle handcuffed."[4]

It was all Roger Maris the following afternoon, a scorcher of a day with over 50,000 fans wilting in temperatures that reached the mid–90s. Young Ralph Terry was given the call for the Yankees while Frank Lary was handed the ball for Detroit. The Tiger righty had faced the Yankees on four previous occasions that season, beating them three times while suffering one loss. At 19–7 coming in to the game, he was second only to Whitey Ford in wins among all major league pitchers. Maris did homer off of him on July 4, but other than that, the pitcher limited the Yankee slugger to three singles in 15 trips to the plate. And with Maris mired in a deep slump, the advantage appeared to be all Lary's.

It was a rough beginning for Ralph Terry. With two away in the first, Al Kaline singled to left to set the stage for Rocky Colavito, the Tiger's big bopper. With one mighty swing of his bat, the Rock parked his fortieth round-tripper of the year, giving Detroit an early two-run lead. But then Terry settled down. He held the Tigers scoreless until he ran into trouble with two gone in the eighth, at which point Luis Arroyo was called in to put down the Bengal uprising. Meanwhile, the Yankees started their comeback in the bottom of the second. Mantle walked to start the inning, and with two out, scored the first Yankee run when Moose Skowron, hero of the previous night's contest, doubled him home. With the score 2–1 in favor the Detroit, Maris led off the fourth with a double to center. A passed ball to Mantle moved him to third, and when the Mick laid down a sacrifice bunt to second, Maris scored the tying run.

The score remained that way until the sixth when Maris came to the plate after two were gone. Everyone in the stadium knew how important this at-bat was. As Maris said, "Every pitch could mean the ball game here." Lary ran the count full, then delivered the ball right into Maris' wheelhouse. "I knew it was gone as soon as I hit it. That old sweet ring of a hard-hit drive was there." The homer was not a cheap shot; it landed deep into the right-field lower deck some six rows back, putting the Yankees up to stay. Maris called it "one of the sweetest home runs I've ever hit. It came in a clutch spot in a very crucial series and just when I was anxious to do something to help the ball club win this big one.... Getting that home run against Detroit, and also off the Tigers' toughest pitcher, at this point of the season certainly meant a great deal to me." Lary, though, was less than gracious when asked about that homer after the game. "Maris should hit a 100 in this ball park," he moaned. "He hits pop fly balls and they fall for home runs."[5]

Perhaps the Detroit pitcher had reason to complain, because the roof fell in on him during the eighth inning. After getting Clete Boyer to fly out to open the frame, he gave up a well-hit single to Luis Arroyo, the Yankee reliever. Although the screwball artist swung a pretty good bat for a pitcher—he was hitting a little over .300 at the time—it should have been a warning that Lary had hit the wall. But Tiger manager Bob Scheffing ignored it and allowed his ace to remain in the game. When Bobby Richardson followed with a single of his own, Arroyo raced around second and slid face-first into third just ahead of Al Kaline's throw. Richardson, reading the play expertly, raced to second on the throw. Time was called as Scheffing strolled to the mound to talk to his pitcher. Apparently Lary convinced the Tiger skipper that he could handle Tony Kubek because he was not replaced. With the infield drawn in in an attempt of prevent a run, the Yankee shortstop swung at the first pitch, smacking the ball into left field, scoring both Arroyo and Richardson. And that ended Frank Lary's day.

As Maris stood on deck, Scheffing finally made his move, calling in left-handed relief artist Hank Aguirre to face the Yankee slugger. It seemed like a good idea at the time. Although Maris had hit two homers off of Aguirre over the three previous seasons, the southpaw generally had the right fielder's number. Maris had not gotten a safety off of him in four at-bats earlier in the season, including the most recent faceoff on July 4 when he popped out in the tenth inning with a runner on first and the Yankees down a run. But as Maris noted, "just because a man gets me out once, that is no reason to think he'll do it again. He has to get me out again, here and now, last time doesn't count." Still, the percentages were on Aguirre's side.[6]

The tall, lanky California native was a product of the Cleveland Indians farm system. He first entered professional baseball in 1951 at the age of 20 and for the next three seasons performed in the lower minors, mainly as a starter. He won 36 games while losing 28 from 1952 through 1954 before the Indians moved him up to their Double-A franchise in Indianapolis. He quickly established himself as the team's ace, compiling an 11–9 record on a 3.24 earned-run average in 33 games.

In early September he was called up to the big club and on September 10 made his major league debut relieving in the sixth inning of a game against the Boston Red Sox in which Cleveland was losing, 7–4. He retired the side in order, including striking out Ted Williams to end the inning. When the Indians scored five runs in the next frame, the 6-foot-4, 193-pound novice big-leaguer was credited with the win. The Splinter complimented the youngster after the game, saying, "The kid is so tall and skinny, all I saw was arms and legs." According to a story Aguirre told for years afterwards, he approached Williams in the locker room to get his autograph on the ball he struck him out on. A few games later, as the tale goes, Williams parked one off of Aguirre and, as he circled the bases, supposedly said, "Hey, kid! If you find that one, I'll autograph it, too!" While probably apocryphal, there was a basis of fact to the story. In a game on July 19, 1958, Williams did indeed homer off of Aguirre, who was pitching for Detroit, a two-run walk-off shot in the bottom the twelfth inning to defeat the Tigers, 7–6. Whether he said anything to the pitcher was never mentioned at the time.[7]

Aguirre ended his first major league adventure in fine fashion. On September 20, he shut out the Detroit Tigers, limiting them to three hits, for a 2–0 record and a 1.46 earned-run average in four game appearances. He began the 1956 season back with Indianapolis where he compiled a 10–6 record with a fine 2.50 ERA in 16 games as a starter. The Indians called him back up in July, during which he started nine of his 16 games. He had two complete outings, one of them a shutout, to finish with three wins and five losses.

Aguirre's performance the following season failed to impress the Cleveland brass. After beginning the year with the San Diego Padres in the Pacific Coast League, he returned to the Indians in early June after Bob Lemon suffered an injury. When he ran up a huge 8.31 earned-run average in six games as a reliever, he was returned to the Padres. The southpaw was recalled at the end of the season, appearing in four more games for the Tribe, ending the summer at 1–1 with a rather large 5.75 ERA. The Indians saw him as expendable and on February 18, 1958, he was traded to the Detroit Tigers as part of a four-player deal. While Cleveland general manager Frank Lane declared that Aguirre had "yet to prove [he] can pitch major league ball," the Tigers believed he could and over the next 10 seasons he was to prove them correct in their assessment of his abilities.[8]

Detroit decided he was at his best as a reliever and used him almost exclusively in that capacity. In 44 game appearances, he managed to compile a 3–4 record with five saves while maintaining a 3.75 earned-run average in 69⅔ innings pitched. In spite of a so-so season, Detroit still liked what they saw in Aguirre. Opponents failed to score off of him in 30 of his 41 relief appearances, including one stretch of 10 games in which he did not allow a run, so the potential was there.

It was his consistency that was the problem. "We like Aguirre's attitude and also his arm," commented John McHale, the Tigers' general manager. "He's ready to come in everyday, if needed." The southpaw certainly had a vast repertoire of pitches from which he could draw. He had a great fastball, a "so-so" curve, a slider "that looked like a sinker," and a variety of off-speed pitches to confound hitters. He also developed an outstanding screwball that he used effectively with right-handed batters. "The fast ball is my primary pitch," Aguirre acknowledged. "When I use the fast ball more, it makes my breaking stuff better." Tigers manager Chuck Dressen thought he depended too much on his heater at times. "Hank's pretty fast and when he keeps his screwball (reverse curve) low, they don't hit it. Sometimes he gets in the habit of holding back on his curve."[9]

Aguirre was optioned to the Charleston Senators in the American Association after three relief appearances for Detroit early in the 1959 season. He became part of Cleveland manager Bill Norman's "Lost Legion," a group of players—including Tito Francona and Maury Wills—the manager decided did not fit with his plans for the coming season. "The Tigers are going with their power instead of pitching," he was told. He played well for Charleston in spite of being ignored and by the time the 1960 season rolled around, Detroit had a different manager, Jimmy Dykes, and a general manager, Rick Ferrell, who believed he deserved another "major league shot. He had a good season for us in 1958." And Aguirre rose to the occasion. "I still think I can win in the big leagues," he said, and he did.[10]

It was during the 1960 season that Aguirre established himself as one of the best relievers in the league. He appeared in 37 games, mostly in the closer's position, and completed the summer at 5–3 with 10 saves and a fantastic 2.85 earned-run average in 94⅔ innings pitched. "Hank means as much to the club as any starting pitcher," contended Joe Gordon, Detroit manager. Tiger pitching coach Tom Ferrick noted that "Hank's got the desire and right attitude" to go with his pitch selection and great control. The Tigers' great 1961 campaign, though, was an off-year for their relief ace. Aguirre became ill early in the season, which caused him to lose weight and struggle at times, especially with his control. He was suffering from periodic chest pains and though three different physicians told him it was not heart-related, he was certain that it was. Finally, the team physician convinced him that "a quirk in his pitching motion" was the cause of his discomfort and once he corrected that, the pain subsided. He still managed to appear in more games than any other reliever, but he lacked the stamina he displayed the year before, down nearly half the innings pitched from 1960. His record of four wins and four losses with eight saves and a 3.25 ERA was not awful, it was just not what he and the team had come to expect from him.[11]

Then came the 1962 campaign, which turned out to be the lefty's greatest season. He was healthy now and had regained the weight he had lost the previous year. As was the pattern, he began the summer in the bullpen, relieving primarily as the closer. Once manager Bob Scheffing became convinced Aguirre was back to form, he gave him his first start in two years, a May 24 outing against the Yankees. All he did was pitch a 2–1 complete game victory over the reigning World Series champions. He made his second start in mid–June, and then on June 29 he hurled a 1–0 shutout of the Baltimore Orioles. From that point forward, the 31-year-old appeared primarily as a starter. By season's end, he compiled a 16–8 record with a league-best 2.21 earned-run average, the lowest in the American League since 1945.

He also led the league in fewest walks and hits per innings pitched and fewest hits per nine innings pitched while finishing in the top 10 in wins, strikeouts per nine innings pitched, total strikeouts, complete games, and fewest home runs allowed per nine innings pitched. Pitching coach Tom Ferrick attributed Aguirre's success to his ability to change speeds and "get[ting]his breaking stuff over [the plate]." He was a reserve in both All-Star games and was credited with a hold in the second one. At the end of the season, he received consideration for the American League Most Valuable Player award in recognition of his pitching accomplishments.[12]

Although he never came close to duplicating that outstanding performance, he remained in the Tigers starting rotation for the next three seasons. In spite of occasional arm, elbow, and shoulder troubles, he compiled a 33–35 record with a decent cumulative 3.67 earned-run average in 102 games, 92 of them as the opener. He had a terrible season in 1964, going 5–10, largely due to conflicts with manager Chuck Dressen, who other players found difficult as well. But he bounced back in 1965, winning 14 while losing 10.

Now 35, the southpaw realized that he would have a difficult time competing against younger pitchers. "A pitcher goes on a year-to-year basis, especially at my age," he admitted early in the 1966 season. "But I want to stay in this as long as I can." Dressen planned to use his pitcher every five or six days with some relief appearances in between, which was exactly what he did. "That's the best way for an older pitcher to stay sharp," the Detroit skipper maintained. Aguirre was not opposed to that plan. As the season wore on, though, it was obvious that the left-hander was well past his prime. He appeared in 30 games, half of them as a starter, ending the summer at 3–9 with a 3.82 ERA. That marked the end of days as a regular in the starting rotation.[13]

The 1967 campaign was Aguirre's last in a Tiger uniform. Except for one start, he spent the entire season in the bullpen. He did pitch well when he got the chance and maintained an excellent 2.40 earned-run average. He was called upon so infrequently, he told one sports columnist, "You could hear my elbow creaking clear up to the upper deck." His one start was in the second game of a doubleheader against the Yankees on June 5, a no-decision in which he went 4⅓ innings. To the utter astonishment of all, he hit a bases-loaded triple in the second inning with two out and the outfield drawn in for the notoriously poor-hitting pitcher. Tiger announcer Ernie Harwell claimed years later that as Aguirre took a lead from third, he told the Tigers third base coach, "I think I can steal home." The astonished coach allegedly responded, "Hank, it took you twelve years to get here—don't screw it up now!"[14]

In early April 1968, Detroit traded their 37-year-old reliever to the Los Angeles Dodgers to clear their roster for younger players. Los Angeles wanted to bolster its bullpen with more left-handed pitching and Aguirre fit the bill. He again was used sparingly, but he performed quite well in spite of long periods of inactivity. In fact, he maintained an amazing 0.69 earned-run average in the 25 games in which he appeared. The Dodgers, though, released him late in the year and he remained a free agent until the Chicago Cubs signed him in March the following spring.

"I should have plenty left," he said at the time of his signing. He relieved in 41 games that season, going 1–0 with an excellent 2.60 earned-run average in 45 innings of work. He stayed with Chicago for the first half of the 1970 season, managing to win three games with no defeats, but his ERA jumped to 4.50. In early July he was released by the Cubs after they acquired Milt Pappas from the Atlanta Braves, bringing an end to a 16-year major league career in which he won 75, lost 72, and saved 33 on a cumulative 3.25

earned-run average in 447 games, a third of them as the starter. He stayed in baseball for a few years as a pitching coach for the Cubs before starting Mexican Industries, a specialty business in Detroit that supplied parts for Volkswagens. It ended up growing from nine to 900 employees before his premature death from prostate cancer in 1994. "He was a real part of the Detroit community," Ernie Harwell said upon learning of his passing. "He's the kind of fellow we all took to."[15]

When Detroit's closer entered in the eighth inning of that September 2 contest against the Yankees, he had a record of three wins, four losses, and eight saves on a 3.50 earned-run average. Like many before him, he was quite aware that Mantle was on deck, so as Maris began his at-bat, Aguirre was cautious in how he pitched to the slugger since he did not want to face the Mick with two runners on. The Yankee switch hitter generally feasted off of the southpaw's offerings, as he had in late April when he took him deep and on May 14 when he scored the winning run after singling to open the eleventh inning. The idea of facing him was not one he relished. What the pitcher did not know was that Mantle was incapable of swinging the bat because of a muscle pull in his left arm he sustained batting in the sixth inning; he remained in the game strictly for his defense. Mantle promised Houk he would bunt "every time if I would let him stay in for defensive purposes in center field." Houk relented in spite of his better judgment. "He had no business staying in the game, but I let him. The team needed a leader, didn't it?"[16]

Aguirre, working carefully, ran the count full on Maris. Then he tried to slip a fastball past the Yankee right fielder. "This time he failed," commented Maris. "I got good wood on it, and number fifty-three went into the seats." The ball followed the same trajectory as his fifty-second in the sixth inning. What he did not realize at the time was that he now had hit more homers in a season than any other Yankee except Babe Ruth. Maris noted that he was "feeling a great glow" after that dinger because it came off of a left-hander. He was somewhat defensive about critics questioning his ability to hit southpaws, so whenever he took one deep, it was a special pleasure to him. That blow pretty much ended the game. Mantle followed with a bunt single, receiving a scattering of boos for not swinging away. The fans, like everyone else except Houk, did not know Mantle was physically incapable of doing anything else.[17]

There was a lot of excitement in the Yankee clubhouse after the game. The victory moved them 3½ games up on the Tigers and there was the real possibility of a sweep that would give them a commanding lead that the Tigers would find difficult to overcome. The one concern was Mantle; would he be able to play in the third game of the series and, if so, would he be able to swing? As it turned out, those concerns proved groundless.

Naturally, Maris was the focus of the press' attention, answering the same questions over and over again. Once more he claimed not to obsess about the Ruth record, but did admit to thinking about the number of homers he had hit "when I settle down ... after a couple of batters go by, maybe." When asked why he had not hit a homer in the week prior to this game, he responded, "If I could hit a home run every time I came up, there would be nothing to this game. And you know something? It may be October 1st before I hit another one."[18]

Maris went out of his way to praise Mantle for his bunt in the fourth inning that allowed Maris to score the tying run. "He easily could have gone for the fence and gotten himself a sacrifice fly. But he didn't.... He bunted hard to make sure I got home all right. Now, if he were hoggish about home runs, would he have done that? Hell, no." Maris may have had his game-tying bunt in a game a month earlier at the back of his mind when he made those comments. After all, he took so much guff for doing so then that he wanted to defend Mantle before he was subjected to similar criticism. It was also his way of dispelling the unfounded rumors that he and Mantle were feuding. "Mantle may hit more [home runs] than I do yet," he stated. "Don't count him out or me in."[19]

Mantle's arm felt much better the following afternoon, so he remained in the lineup for the third game of the series. And what a game it was for him. He smashed his forty-ninth home run in the first inning, a two-run shot with Maris aboard, into the lower right-field seats that gave the Yankees a temporary lead. Then in the bottom of the ninth with the Yankees down a run, he opened that frame by blasting his fiftieth into the right-field stands close to the bullpen to tie it up at five all. Then with two on and two out, Elston Howard parked one in the left-field seats for a 8–5 come-from-behind Yankee victory.

And just like that the Tigers were done. It sent them into a tailspin in which they lost their next five games to leave them 10 behind the Yankees, who won their next 10 games. It was a nearly-insurmountable lead that, for all intents and purposes, marked the end of the American League pennant race. Lyall Smith, sports editor for the *Detroit Free Press*, labeled it "the biggest, fastest and most disastrous skid in Detroit diamond history. Until somebody comes up with a quicker one, it could be the fastest nose dive in big league history." Manager Bob Scheffing summed it up the best. "We didn't fold," he said. "We merely bowed to the most powerful team in the majors."[20]

Home Run # 54—Game 140—September 6—Day Game

With the championship race all but over, the home run competition between Maris and Mantle became the sole focus of everyone's attention. "The Mantle-Maris clouting overshadowed games and scores," Houk recalled. "Fans cheered their long drives, fair or foul, jeered at pitchers who walked 'em. Police set up barricades at the players' entrance to hold back thousands who tried to catch a glimpse of them. Strangers, including many foreigners with perfectly good credentials, invaded our quarters.... Even New York writers forgot everything but the home-run race." It got so bad that Houk was forced to clear the clubhouse of reporters a half hour before the games. The pandemonium only increased as Maris got closer to the record.[21]

Mantle's two-homer day came at a price; his arm was so swollen after that game that he was out of the lineup for a doubleheader against the Senators on September 4. He did come in during the ninth inning of the first game in order to cover center field, but that was it. Fortunately, the Yankees did not need his bat as they won the first game, 5–3, and then the second one, 3–2. Maris did not aid the cause either, failing to get a hit in eight at-bats. He was furious at himself, and when he entered the locker room after the second game, he was in a sour mood as the assembled reporters began to bombard him with questions.

"I had done nothing [offensively]," he said, so why did they insist on interviewing him and not those of his teammates who contributed to the twin victories? Although the other players understood that he did not ask to be the center of so much attention and that, in fact, he hated it, he was embarrassed nonetheless and it added to his growing irritation as the questioning droned on. Then, according to him, "some of them started to get a little raw in their questions, and I got hot under the collar. For some reason I started to put the rap on the fans," some of whom had booed him after each failure at the plate. "They are a lousy bunch of front runners, that's what they are," he declared. "Hit a home run and they love you, but make out and they start booing." He stated his preference for the fans in Kansas City, a comment that was sure to irritate the New York fan base even further. When reminded that the spectators had paid good money to get in, he angrily replied, "I didn't ask them to come." He was just letting off steam, not unlike Mantle and many other players who have had a bad game, but unfortunately he did it in front of the media. He was mortified the next morning when he read the interview in the papers and wished he could apologize to the fans for his unwarranted retorts. He tried to clarify his comments by saying he meant just those few who booed him at every opportunity, not the majority of fans, but by then it was too late, the damage was done.[22]

One of the things Maris acknowledged in that postgame interview was that he was "swinging at pitches I should never swing at. I wasn't before, but the last couple of weeks I've been trying to pull balls I shouldn't. I know I shouldn't, and should wait for my pitch to hit, but I've been doing it anyhow." That pattern continued the following night when he again went hitless in four at-bats, dropping his batting average to .266. Not so Mantle. In that September 5 contest against the Senators, he led off the second inning with his fifty-first homer, a monster blast that landed deep into the right-field upper deck to tie the score at one apiece. In the fifth inning, Elston Howard put the Yankees ahead to stay with his sixteenth jack of the year. With four additional runs in the seventh, the Bombers swept Washington, making it six consecutive victories to start the month of September. Even though New York now held a commanding 7½ game lead over the Tigers, "that doesn't mean we can take anything for granted," said Ralph Houk. "Baseball history is full of examples that show what can happen to a first-place team in a few days. I don't think there's any danger of a so-called letdown, but there's always the so-called danger of losing ball games."[23]

After his 0–12 performance in three games against Washington, the press made much of the fact that Maris was only five games ahead of Ruth's 1927 homer pace. He was to expand that lead, though, the following afternoon when the Yankees took on the Senators for their fourth contest of the series and their final meeting of the year. Whitey Ford took the mound going for his twenty-third win of the season while newly-acquired right-hander Tom Cheney was given the ball for Washington.

The 5-foot-11 starter had languished in the minor leagues with the St. Louis Cardinals and the Pittsburgh Pirates since 1952 with only brief appearances in the majors until the Pirates traded him to the Senators at the end of June. He was 1–2 with a humongous 8.84 earned-run average since coming to Washington and his five home runs surrendered in his six games to date did not bode well for that September 6 afternoon contest with the Yankees. He showed considerable improvement pitching for the Senators over the next three seasons, but in 1961 he was still basically a struggling minor leaguer trying to stick with a big league club.

Cheney began his professional career in 1952, signing for $1,500 at the age of 17 to play in the St. Louis Cardinals organization. He spent his first two seasons hurling for the Albany Cardinals in the Class D Georgia-Florida League before moving up to Class C ball in 1954. It was while playing for the Fresno Cardinals in the California League that he experienced his first winning season. More than half of his starts were complete games and four of those were shutouts. "I think the Cards considered me a good prospect by this time," he recalled years later, "but I didn't expect to be in the majors for a while. In the St. Louis system, they didn't figure you'd reach Triple A or the big leagues for 5 to 7 years."[24]

He did make the move to Single-A the following summer, however, and again demonstrated that he could win at that higher level. His 14–12 record and 3.25 earned-run average were best among all pitchers on the Columbus Cardinals staff, which earned him a brief promotion to the Triple-A Omaha Cardinals, appearing in one game. He stayed with that club in 1956 where he continued his winning ways by compiling a 10–5 record and an excellent 2.93 ERA in 29 games, including 10 complete games with three shutouts among them. In mid-season, Cardinals general manager Frank Lane paid a visit to Omaha to watch Cheney and outfield prospect Charlie Peete specifically and came away impressed by what he saw. "But we've got no plans to bring them up at this time," he said. He thought both needed further development to become true big league players. "[W]e'd want to be certain they'd get to play enough to justify joining us," he explained. Cheney did get an invitation to join the Cardinals 1957 spring training camp, however, the first time he was extended that honor.[25]

The 170-pound right-hander came to camp after hurling excellent ball over the winter. Future Yankee manager Ralph Houk, who had plenty of opportunities to observe the pitching prospect in winter league competition, said Cheney "looked ready [for the majors] to me. Yes, I'd say he's an excellent prospect." And the 22-year-old went about proving Houk correct. Using his "good curve and fast ball," he produced one good outing after another. "Even the hitters say he's got good stuff," commented Johnny Keane, Cheney's manager in Omaha, "and when they tell you that, you know the pitcher has it. They're reluctant with praise most of the time, you know." By the time training camp broke, the young pitcher had won a spot on the big club's pitching staff.[26]

Cheney made his major league debut on April 21, pitching four innings of scoreless relief facing the Chicago Cubs. "[T]he ... kid does have a good arm, good stuff, good control and a good attitude," proclaimed sportswriter Bob Broeg, "a combination that could make him an early success." But success was a while in coming. On April 28 he made his first start, and though he did not allow a run in four innings of work, he did walk six while striking out half that many, a warning sign that he was not quite ready for the big time. On May 3, he got another start, but this time he lasted just a third of an inning, giving up three runs on three walks and a triple. After going two thirds of an inning in a May 8 start, he was sent back to Omaha once again. "At the time, I could throw hard but my control was off and on, like it would be my entire career," he noted years later. "I couldn't tell when warming up how it would be in the game. I was taught that if you were wild to be wild throwing hard and not aim the ball because that's when you got hurt." He went on to explain his pitching style. "Out of 10 pitches, I'd throw 7 or 8 fastballs. My strikeout pitch was a high fastball. On a 2–2, I figured the hitter was anxious so I usually went with the fastball but I had a good curve."[27]

Interestingly, he preferred pitching to left-handed batters rather than righties. The reason was that "my fastball ran. They call it a cut fastball. I could jam a left-hander but had trouble pitching a right-handed hitter inside." He added a knuckleball to his pitch selection, learned courtesy of Hoyt Wilhelm, who was his roommate for a time. He admitted it did not hold a candle to those tossed by Wilhelm, "but it was good at times." And he eventually developed a slider and a screwball to include with his arsenal. "I'll throw a screwball to left-handed hitters but it's more of a change than a real scroojie."[28]

He got himself straightened out back in Triple-A, ending the season at 14–8 on a great 2.62 earned-run average. He also regained his control, walking 61 while striking out 175 in 182 innings pitched. But then the draft came a-knocking at the end of the season and he spent the next two years in military service where he continued to play ball. Cheney immediately rejoined the Cardinals after his discharge from the Army in May 1959, but he was totally unprepared for the majors after being out so long. It was not until he had appeared in 11 games for a 0–1 record and an awful 6.94 earned-run average that St. Louis realized his time would be better spent back in the minors. He managed to go 5–6 with a 4.38 ERA in 14 games for Omaha, and at the end of the season he was sent to Cuba to continue playing winter ball. It was while there that he learned he was traded to the Pittsburgh Pirates, just another pawn in one of general manager Frank Lane's many trading frenzies. "I thought of all the years I had spent in the Cardinals organization and how when I was on the brink of making it in the majors, they traded me," he later reminisced. "But I wasn't bitter."[29]

He ended up on a team that went on to win the World Series over the Yankees, a seven-game contest that ended in dramatic fashion on a game-ending home run by the light-hitting Bill Mazeroski. "When I got to Pittsburgh, I discovered I wasn't just on a great team but got to play with a great bunch of guys," he fondly recalled. But first he had to pay his dues. He began the season with the Triple-A Columbus Jets, a team that finished in the second division of the International League. He was 4–8 with a 3.16 ERA when the Bucs called him up at the end of June. What was not readily apparent in his record was that his 115 strikeouts were the most in the International League at the time of his call-up. That combined with his 47 walks were a clear indication that he had regained his control.[30]

Cheney made his first appearance for the Pirates on July 2, a start in which he lasted 3⅔ innings for a loss. But then on July 6 he went seven innings to beat the Cincinnati Reds, 5–2, for his first major league win. He topped that outing on his next start, beating the Reds again, this time achieving his first major league shutout by a score of 5–0. By season's end, the 25-year-old rookie was owner of a 2–2 record (3.98 ERA) and was headed to the World Series with the National League champions.

He found himself relieving in three of the games. In Game 2 with the Bombers up 15–1, he closed out the Yankees final inning, striking out Roger Maris, but allowing Mickey Mantle to score on a wild pitch to Moose Skowron. Then in Game 3, another Yankee blowout, he relieved for two innings, ending the seventh frame by striking out Mantle looking. He replaced starter Bob Friend in the third inning of Game 6 with runners on first and third and New York up, 3–0. He allowed three more runs to score before closing out the inning in what turned out to be another trouncing by the Yankees, 12–0. But he and his teammates ended up with World Series rings after the Yanks lost Game 7, 10–9. "I was in only 11 games, 8 as a starter," Cheney noted later. "Yet this team was so tight that I was voted a full World Series share. They accepted me."[31]

Cheney was looking forward to spending all of 1961 with the Pirates, but it did not turn out that way. He made his first appearance on April 16, entering the game to open the eighth inning with Pittsburgh down, 8–4, to the Los Angeles Dodgers. He was hammered, giving up five runs on four walks and a homer without recording a single out before he was yanked. Shortly after that, he received a word that his father had died unexpectedly, requiring him to return home to help out his mother. He knew he was on the verge of being cut from the team, so he spoke with Joe Brown, the Pirates' general manager, asking if he was to be sent down. Brown assured him that he was not going back to Columbus. When the grieving pitcher returned, however, he was informed that he was indeed returning to the minors.

Infuriated at what he viewed as a broken promise, he cursed the general manager and told him to arrange a trade, "because I'll never play for *you* again"; that was exactly what happened. He pitched nine games for Columbus going 6–2 on a fine 3.20 ERA before he was sent to the Washington Senators at the end of June for pitcher Tom Sturdivant. Bad luck seemed to follow him there. After a rough beginning with his new team, he pulled the muscles around his ribcage in a July 22 game against the Los Angeles Angels and was out of action for the next month and a half. He was ineffective when he did return. In his first game back, he lasted just two-thirds of an inning after giving up five earned runs on a hit, five walks, and two wild pitches, ending his horrible summer at 1–3 on an 8.80 earned-run average.[32]

Cheney was not guaranteed to make the club out of spring training in 1962 after his less than auspicious half-season debut with the Senators. Even though he pitched just 10 innings total prior to the beginning of the regular season, the Senators decided to include him on the roster when the team broke camp. He was assigned to the bullpen initially. He did well in his first appearance, but then struggled in the next two before settling down. He started his first game on May 15 and though he ended up losing it by a run, he managed over seven innings of work, walking four while striking out six. At least he was headed in the right direction.

When he was on, he was difficult to hit, but he had periods of wildness that saw him knocked out of the box early in games. He ascribed his problems as psychological in nature. "I was overanalyzing everything and was unable to relax. They gave me little pills to help relax my nerves." He tried those on several occasions before the start of a game, but found they did not help. "My problem was that I was paranoid about the first inning," he admitted. "I tended to overthrow in the first inning and was wild.... If I got past the third or fourth inning, I was usually home free and got increasingly stronger."[33]

Such was the case on September 12 when he faced the Orioles in Baltimore. He had three shutouts already that season, so he knew he could go deep into a game when he had his control, but no one expected him to do what he did in that game against the Birds. He started out giving up two singles in the first inning, but he did not walk anyone and did not allow a run. At that point the cosmic tumblers clicked into place and he began pitching like he never had before. Over the next 15 innings he held the Orioles scoreless, racking up 21 strikeouts in the process. In fact, he struck out every player in the starting lineup at least once except for left fielder Boog Powell. After the Senators' first baseman Bud Zipfel hit a home run in the top of the sixteenth inning to put Washington up, 2–1, Cheney simply had to get through the bottom of that frame, which he did in fine fashion, striking out pinch-hitter Dick Williams looking to end the game.[34]

He set a new major league record for strikeouts in an extra-inning game, using an incredible 228 pitches to do so. "In the bottom of the 16th, I just wanted to get it over with," Cheney said. "They had curfew in Baltimore and I knew that would be the last inning. I was still concerned about winning the ball game. Wins were few and far between in those days." By the end of the summer, the 27-year-old right-hander finally became an established pitcher. His 1962 campaign was his best ever, ending with a 7–9 record and a good 3.17 earned-run average in 173⅓ innings of work, over 120 more than he ever hurled before. His performance that season was one of the best on a team that ended in last place after losing 101 games. He was seventh in the league in earned-run average, second in fewest hits per nine innings pitched, second in strikeouts per nine innings pitched, sixth in shutouts, and fifth in fewest home runs per nine innings pitched.[35]

Cheney began the 1963 season by winning his first four starts, all of them complete games, two of them shutouts. Then he hit the skids, losing six straight before righting the ship in June. His earned-run average remain a low 2.62 during that period, however, so it was not that he had suddenly lost his ability to pitch. He went through June and early July winning one, then losing the next. Part of the problem may have been due to a personality conflict with manger Gil Hodges, who took over as skipper in mid-season. "I wasn't his favorite person and he wasn't mine," Cheney commented. "I wouldn't let Hodges or anyone else tell me how to pitch." He was 8–9 with an excellent 2.88 ERA when he injured his arm during a July 11 outing against the Orioles. "I knew something had happened. I threw a pitch and it felt like someone had a knife and ripped me down the forearm." He took cortisone shots to help with the pain, but he was unable to pitch more than three innings in a game from that point on. The Senators shut him down completely in late August. What they did not know at the time was that he had damaged a tendon in his elbow. It led to an early end to his career.[36]

Cheney seemed to be over his arm problems by the time spring training in 1964 rolled around. The team physician examined him and when X-rays showed nothing untoward, he concluded that Cheney suffered from "tennis elbow" the previous season, and declared him fit to begin pitching again. But things were not as they first appeared. He had some tenderness early in training camp, but the pain receded. Then early on in the regular season, he began experiencing elbow discomfort again. He had difficulty going deep into games, but on June 9 he hurled a complete game against the Kansas City Athletics, beating them, 5–1, for his first win of the summer.[37]

But that victory came at a very high cost; he damaged his elbow so severely that he made just one more start before he was shut down as he had been the previous summer. An examination at the Mayo Clinic several days later revealed he had torn muscles in his elbow and was not suffering from "tennis elbow" as originally thought. His elbow felt better later that year, giving him hope that he would return in 1965, but early that spring he decided to retire. After staying out a year, he attempted a comeback in 1966, but after a May 9 start in which he lasted just a little over two innings, he was cut from the team. He spent the next few months in the minors hoping to keep pitching by becoming a knuckleballer, but that, too, failed; his baseball career had come to an end. He spent eight years in the majors, ending with 19 wins and 29 losses with a 3.77 earned-run average in 115 games, 71 of them as a starter.[38]

"I didn't like how my baseball career ended, particularly because I was so young [he was 31]," he said years later. "But I realized how fortunate I was to have made it to the majors. Not many make it.... I also cherished the togetherness of players in an era when we didn't make enough money for money to matter. So I got about as much out of the game as a person could ask for."[39]

Cheney appeared to be on top of his game when he opened the September 6 outing against the Yankees. He retired the side in order in the first three innings, including inducing Maris to pop out to third base in the first inning and striking out Mantle, Johnny Blanchard, and Elston Howard in the second frame. He began the fourth inning as he did other first three, eliminating Bobby Richardson and Tony Kubek before Maris came to the plate for the second time that day.

It was only the third time in his major league career that Maris faced Cheney. The setting of their first confrontation was in the second game of the 1960 World Series; Cheney struck him out on that occasion. They battled some in the minor leagues when Maris was with Indianapolis, so Cheney, who had retired the first 11 batters the Yankees sent to the plate that afternoon, was convinced he could handle the Yankee slugger for the third out of the inning. "I knew how to pitch him," he declared later.[40]

Maris, too, was beginning to doubt he would ever get another hit, let alone a dinger. "I hadn't had a hit for the entire series and was beginning to wonder if I was going into a September dive like the one I had two years earlier. I still refused to let it get me but, aside from the Detroit series, I had done nothing in almost three weeks." When Maris stepped into the box, Cheney knew "it was a situation where I didn't want to walk him. He wasn't going to beat me that way.... His success didn't surprise me in Yankee Stadium. Hitting that many [homer runs], yes, but he was strictly a pull hitter and had that short porch in right field to shoot for. Roger couldn't handle the ball too well away from him, but in 1961, if he got the ball from the center of the plate in, he didn't miss it. He didn't miss my pitch."[41]

Indeed, he did not. The ball landed in the Yankee bullpen in right field, giving the Bombers a lead they did not lose. After walking Mantle, Blanchard parked one for his seventeenth of the season. Howard singled to center, followed by Moose Skowron's blast to right to put New York up, 5–0, ending Cheney's day. Blanchard hit another in the sixth inning off of Johnny Klippstein and reserve infielder Bob Hale hit his first as a Yankee in the eighth, setting a new American League record of 210 team home runs; Maris and Mantle had exactly half of those.[42]

In the clubhouse after the game, Maris acknowledged he was now completely conscious of the Ruth record each time he came to bat. In fact, he started collecting each home run ball he could after he had hit more than forty. "When I reached that point," he explained, "I began to think that perhaps I would never hit that many again. Each one might be the last, so I wanted to get that one." He wrote the number and date on those he got back, some of which he then gave to his friends. The inevitable question about his batting average came up in the interview as well. Commenting on Maris' relatively low .271 average at the time, a young reporter from Texas asked Maris if he would rather hit 60 home runs or bat over .300. The player was polite in his response, asking his inquisitor what he would rather do. Replying that he would choose to hit .300, something many players have done, than break a long-established record, Maris replied, "To each his own." The Yankee right fielder, irritated by the implied slight on his batting ability, commented later to *New York Post* columnist Leonard Shecter, "Anybody who asks that is an idiot. What's average got to do with home runs?"[43]

Home Run # 55—Game 141—September 7—Night Game

The following evening the Yankees played host to the Cleveland Indians in the first game of a five-game series. It was the final face-off of the season between the longtime rivals. Taking the mound for the Tribe was 6-foot-3, 200-pound southpaw Dick Stigman pitching in his second major league season. The left-hander battled the Bombers twice earlier that season, the most recent outing on August 20, hurling the final six innings in which he gave up one run after the Indians starter surrendered five over the first four frames. His opponent this game was Ralph Terry, going for his thirteenth win with just two losses.

Stigman was signed by Cleveland in 1954 several days after graduating high school in rural Minnesota. He spent the next six summers perfecting his craft in the minor leagues. He struggled his first two seasons, but then in 1956 everything seemed to fall into place. He was the best pitcher on the Class D Vidalia Indians and his 1.44 earned-run average was the lowest in the entire Georgia State League. He jumped to the Double-A level the following year where he went 8–14 for the Mobile Bears; many of those losses were due to a lack of run support. Although he had a losing record, his earned-run average was a good 3.81 and he pitched nine complete games, two of those shutouts. After starting the 1958 campaign with the Triple-A San Diego Padres, Cleveland management decided he needed further seasoning and sent him back to Mobile. He quickly established himself as one of the best pitchers in the Southern Association, ending with 15 wins, seven losses, and an outstanding 2.44 ERA.

The "brilliant prospect," as *The Sporting News* labeled him, was called up for military duty at the end of the season, but was given his release before the start of spring training the following year because it was discovered he suffered from Raynaud's syndrome. It was a condition in which he experienced blood vessel spasms at the tip of his left index finger, causing the finger to go numb. Fortunately, though, medication and warm weather returned feeling to the finger so that it did not adversely affect his pitching career.[44]

Stigman spent all of the 1959 season pitching for the San Diego Padres. While his 9–17 record was the worst in the Pacific Coast League, he actually pitched much better than it appeared. He struck out 181 batters in 191 innings pitched to lead the league in that category. At times he was absolutely brilliant. On May 26, the same day that Harvey Haddix tossed 12 perfect innings against the Milwaukee Braves before losing in the thirteenth, Stigman experienced similar heartbreak. He hurled 10 hitless innings against the Salt Lake City Bees before a two-out single in the eleventh ended his bid for a no-hitter. He was lifted in the twelfth for a pinch-hitter before the Padres scored a run in the thirteen for a win, leaving Stigman with a no-decision.[45]

Despite his losing record in 1959, he performed so well in winter ball and during spring training that Cleveland manager Joe Gordon decided to give him a shot with the big league club. The skipper was desperate for a left-hander he could use as a reliever and a fifth starter. "Maybe I'll use him a few more times in relief to let him get his feet on the ground," Gordon proclaimed at the start of the season, "but I'll start him before long." Even though his young pitcher had problems with control from time to time, Gordon knew "Dick's got real good stuff" and "if he got the ball over they wouldn't hit him."[46]

Stigman came into the league with "a fast ball that crackled like summer lightning and a popping curve ball." What he lacked was self-confidence, something he gained over time. Commenting on his mediocre performance the previous summer, Stigman admitted that he was "pressing.... I tried so hard there were times I'd shake all over." His performance in Nicaragua that winter and in training camp calmed him down considerably. In addition, pitching coach Mel Harder helped him improve his curveball. "I had trouble getting it over until Mel advised me to pitch from the left side of the rubber." The pitcher used a "knuckle curve where you fold your index finger back and your fingernail goes on top of the ball to get it out of the way so more pressure is on the middle finger." He delivered it in a variety of ways depending on the situation. One he threw "as though I was using a fast ball more like a slider with a sharp break, [which] would go down. The other curve was more over the top with a bigger break and sometimes three quarters more to lefties. The latter was easier to vary the speed."[47]

Although Gordon initially planned to use Stigman in relief situations where there were no runners on base because of his concern over the rookie's control, his first appearance came in the third inning of an April 22 contest against the Kansas City Athletics with two runners on and two away. Stigman induced a groundout to end the threat, then pitched two more innings of hitless ball. The manager later admitted he "was taking a chance by bringing him in with men on base," but was so pleased with Stigman's performance that he started him against the A's on May 1. He allowed just one run over nine innings for his first major league victory. "I found a fifth starter in Stigman," Gordon announced after the game. "There's no doubt about his having a big league arm."[48]

And that was the way it went for the first half of the season. He won his second game in relief against the Yankees on May 10, then secured his first save on May 17, coming in to get the final out after Mickey Mantle hit a grand slam off of starter Gary Bell. By the end of June he was 4–4 with six saves, three complete games, and a fine 3.32 earned-run average. To the youngster's surprise, he was picked by Al Lopez, skipper of the American League All-Star team, as a reserve on the pitching staff. Although he did not appear in either game, it was quite an honor for the novice pitcher.

But then the reality of a long season set in. Stigman began to struggle; by season's end he was 5–11 with nine saves and a high 4.51 ERA. Joe Gordon was replaced as manager in mid-season, which may have been part of his problem. The left-hander prospered under Gordon's guidance, knowing he had the manager's confidence, but was less comfortable around replacement manager Jimmy Dykes. "Dick Stigman has the earmarks of a good pitcher," Dykes declared at the end of the summer. "His only trouble so far is that he gets upset easily. I've been talking to him." Then in early September, Stigman began to experience pain in his pitching elbow during his wind-ups, something that surely hampered his delivery.[49]

In spite of his disappointing second half in 1960, Cleveland still had confidence in their young southpaw. Stigman came to spring training in 1961 determined to improve his control and regain his form. He blamed the difficulties he encountered the year before on a weary arm. "I just got tired," the 25-year-old pitcher explained. "I was working in and out of the rotation and toward the end I lost something extra. My arm is not strong enough to stand irregular duty. My body wasn't tired, my arm was." Sadly, though, Stigman tore a muscle in his pitching elbow in training camp and was placed on the disabled list until early June. He looked good his first two outings back, winning consecutive relief appearances, but then experienced a frustrating decline after that. He ended with two wins and five losses and a bloated 4.62 earned-run average in some 64 innings pitched.[50]

He ascribed his problems, though, not to his earlier elbow injury, but on his lack of use. "Maybe I'm prejudiced, but I can't help feeling that if [manager Jimmy] Dykes had given me the same chance he gave [roommate] Barry [Latman]—I mean the chance to start regularly—my troubles would be mostly behind me." Pitching coach Mel Harder disagreed, pointing to Stigman's "lack of concentration" and his need "to be more aggressive," especially after "a club comes up with a key hit." Whatever the cause of his woes, they were not addressed with the Indians. On April 2, 1962, he and first baseman Vic Power were traded to the Minnesota Twins for Pedro Ramos. It proved to be a fortuitous event for Stigman.[51]

It was while pitching for the Twins that Stigman had his first winning major league season. He pitched out of the bullpen the first half of the summer. He indicated a preference for starting, but as long as he was used regularly, he was happy to be a reliever. "The only thing I want is steady work," he said. And that he got. He appeared in 23 games through the end of June, 13 of those as the closer, compiling a 3–2 record with three saves and a 3.54 earned-run average over 28 innings of work. After the lefty allowed just one hit with four strikeouts in two innings of relief against the Yankees on July 6, Twins manager Sam Mele decided to give his hurler a chance to start a game. On July 18 he pitched a complete game victory over his old team, lowering his ERA to 3.07 while demonstrating to all he had the ability to go the distance. To top it off, he struck out 11 of his former teammates. His cause was helped by Bob Allison and Harmon Killebrew both hitting grand slams in the opening inning, the first time that had been done in a single frame in the major leagues.[52]

He followed that start with another complete-game win, this one over the Detroit Tigers, limiting them to a single run while whiffing eight; he now had 57 strikeouts in 50 innings of work. *The Sporting News* declared him "the brightest light of the week on the pitching staff." He continued to pitch well as a starter, ending the season with a flourish by winning his last three starts, two of those complete games. His 12–5 cumulative record was the best winning percentage in the American League and his 3.66 ERA was third best among Minnesota's regular pitching staff. The 26-year-old, who was considered a throw-in player in the trade that brought him to Minnesota, had established himself as a solid major league pitcher at last.[53]

The 1963 campaign turned out to be the highlight of his career. He indicated early on his desire to be a starter, mainly because pitching regularly in that capacity allowed him to "settle down to more of a routine and better prepare himself"; he got his wish. He appeared in 33 games, all as an opener, for a 15–15 record with 15 complete games, three of those shutouts. He may have been a 20-game winner had he received better run support. Nine of his losses were by two or fewer runs, including four in his first six starts by a single run; the Twins were shut out in four of his losses. He sported a good 3.25 earned-run average in 241 innings pitched and placed third among American League pitchers in total strikeouts and fourth in strikeouts per nine innings pitched. He was also eighth in total walks and fourth in home runs allowed.[54]

Stigman entered the 1964 season excited about his progress as a starter. "I've still got to improve on getting ahead of the batter," he said. "I made a great stride in this direction last year, but I don't think I have conquered it. I don't think of myself as having problems. I just think in terms of trying to get better at everything, including fielding." Twins pitching coach Gordon Maltzberger concurred, adding that the pitcher was past thinking like a reliever. "Now Stigman realizes he must go into each game with the idea of pitching a full nine innings and taking the victory or loss. He does not try to strike out every batter. He has learned to take something off his curve ball once in a while and that he does not have to throw his Sunday curve every time." Most importantly, the southpaw "learn[ed] to control his curve and get ahead of the batter.... He learned it so well that he could even throw his curve when he was behind the batter. So the batter could no longer wait for his fast ball when he was ahead of Stigman."[55]

In spite of such enthusiasm, however, the season started off poorly for the 28-year-old. In his first game, he was blasted for five earned runs in five innings. He did not win his first outing until May 27, at which time he was 1–3 with a huge 5.72 ERA. Things improved somewhat after that. He pitched his first complete game in his next assignment and his first shutout a month later. On July 3, he hurled his best game of the year, a 10-inning shutout of the Yankees. By the end of the month he was 5–9 with a much-improved 3.82 earned-run average. His early-season struggles were due in part to his curveball. "I couldn't get my curve over the plate. And the batters were just waiting for my fast ball," he admitted. But even though he gained control over his curve, he continued to lose, going just 1–6 over his final 10 starts to end the season at 6–15 with a 4.03 ERA. Again, a lack of offensive production by his teammates hurt him; eight of his losses were by two runs or less and four of his wins were by a single run. But so did his propensity for offering up gopher balls. He surrendered 31 in all, sixth most in the American League.[56]

After such a lackluster season, it was only natural that he would be one of the players Twins owner Cal Griffith dangled as bait in a possible trade. But Minnesota decided to give the left-hander a chance to turn things around. Stigman acknowledged he failed to deliver the previous summer. "I fell into too many bad habits—made the wrong pitch too often. A lot of things went wrong—with the club and with me." The pitcher added a slip pitch to use alongside of his fastball and curve. "If I can work more often early, I can use [it] more, and I won't be reduced to two pitches in tight situations," he commented.[57]

After failing to perform effectively in his first five starts, he was moved back into the bullpen, making very few starts after that. He got his first win on June 11, then his second one on June 29 after he blew the lead in relief. The lack of regular work hurt him. "All you can do is keep throwing and hope you will be ready," he said. But he did not complain about working from the bullpen. "I'm happy to have a job and to get a chance to help the team," he told the press. It was an up-and-down season for the southpaw. His performance was not improved by a foot injury in early September that shut him down the last three weeks of the season. He was 4–2 with four saves on a rather large 4.37 ERA, his worst with Minnesota. The Twins won the American League pennant that summer, but Stigman did not appear in any of the seven World Series games. The club planned to use him as a reliever in 1966, but on April 6 he was traded to the Boston Red Sox.[58]

He was used primarily as a starter the first two months of the season with his new team, but then was consigned mostly to relief work from June to the end of the summer. Even at that, he was used sparingly from July on, sometimes having to sit for more than a week between appearances. He was not called upon at all after a two-inning relief outing against the Yankees on September 10. Ending the season at 2–1 on a 5.44 earned-run average, the highest of his big league career, his pitching days were numbered. On December 15 he was traded to the Cincinnati Reds. They assigned him to Triple-A Buffalo for the 1967 campaign where he went 7–12 with a 4.36 ERA in 21 games as a starter. He was 7–2 through mid-June, but after he lost his next nine decisions, he was sold to San Diego, the Philadelphia Phillies Triple-A franchise. He opened two games for the Padres, who then sold him to the Pittsburgh Pirates. He refused to report, bringing an end to a 14-year professional pitching career. Over seven major league seasons, he won 46, lost 54, and saved 16 on a cumulative 4.03 earned-run average in 235 games, half of those as a starter.[59]

Although Stigman was just coming back from a serious elbow injury at the time of his September 7 outing against the Yankees, Maris still considered him to be "a tough customer," someone he had difficulty hitting. Based on his 19 plate appearances against the left-hander prior to that night's contest, that was indeed the case. He batted just .182 in 14 trips to the plate in 1960 and had one single in five at-bats so far in the current season; he had yet to drive in a run off the southpaw.[60]

But Stigman was not having a good season and was not on top of his game. He started off well enough after he recovered from his early-season elbow problems, winning in relief in his first appearances of the season on June 11and again on June 16 in a rare start. After those two victories, though, he failed to deliver consistently. Part of the problem was that he did not get along with manager Jimmy Dykes. He was convinced Dykes did not believe in his abilities and thus used him sparingly, mostly in situations where the game was already lost. "That's all I'm getting," he complained. "Mop-ups. The only games I get into, they're gone.... I don't think Dykes likes me. [Joe] Gordon [his manager the first half of 1960] liked me and I pitched a lot." The pitcher claimed a few days later he was misquoted about his feelings toward Dykes, but did reiterate that he wanted more pitching assignments. Whether his perception was accurate or not, the fact that he felt that way undoubtedly affected his pitching. He asserted, however, that he was not concerned about Maris. "Look, he's a left-handed hitter. I got confidence against left-handed hitters." The Cleveland manager advised his pitcher before the game, "Don't be afraid to let 'em know you're out there. You can give it to 'em high and inside once in a while. If they glare at you, you're set. All you got to do then is curve 'em." Stigman did just that to Maris in the third inning with disastrous results.[61]

First, however, the Yankee slugger surprised everyone in the stadium in the opening inning by laying down a perfect drag bunt to score Tony Kubek, who had tripled, giving the Yankees an immediate lead. When he pulled that same play a month earlier, he was booed by many for not swinging for the fences. This time he was cheered by the Yankee faithful for this selfless act. "It's better 1–0 than 0–0," he commented after the game. "As long as we're fighting for the pennant, what the hell?" Then he added, "Well, if we had the pennant clinched I guess I'd have been swinging for the home runs." His actions certainly pleased the Yankee manager. "It was a very smart play by Roger," Ralph Houk said in praise of his right fielder. "That ought to prove we're playing to win."[62]

No one was more taken aback by Maris' bunt than the Indians hurler. "None of us were ready for it," he admitted afterwards. If Stigman was rattled, it did not seem to affect his pitching. He retired Mantle and Elston Howard to end the inning and in the second was the victim of sloppy fielding for an unearned run, making the score 2–0 going into the third frame. That was when Maris came to the plate for the second time that evening.[63]

When Maris stepped into the box with two away, it was obvious that he was not going to bunt again. Stigman's first pitch was a high, inside curve that moved Maris back from the plate. (Maris did not believe it was intentional.) But then he delivered another crooked pitch because "you're supposed to throw him curves," he explained. "Last year, this year, probably next year. You don't change much on hitters. But I didn't have a good curve tonight. It was so bad I almost hit him with that first one. The next one was lousy, too. It hung." It was a fatal mistake. By the time the ball crashed into the right-center field seats, it had traveled some 400 feet to give Maris his fifty-fifth of the year, putting him four up on Mantle and eight games ahead of the Babe's pace. "Maybe that was his mistake [going with the curve] because Maris wound up chopping him up like hamburger," wrote columnist Leonard Shecter. "He left the kid bleeding out there like a calf in a veal factory."[64]

Maris had one more shot at Stigman, this time in the sixth with the score tied at three. Kubek opened with a double, followed by a Maris single. When Mantle then doubled to score Kubek, Stigman was lifted for reliever Bobby Locke. Maris plated his third run of the day off of Locke in the seventh on a sacrifice fly to give him one of his best outings in weeks. The Bombers won, 7–3, moving them nine games up on the Tigers.

In the clubhouse after the game, Mantle all but conceded the home run race to Maris. "Roger is a cinch to do it," he said. "He ought to make it with plenty to spare. He's almost there. He's got 55 now and he's got time." When the interviewer stated that it would be nice to see Maris break the record, Mantle responded, "You're damn right. I say good luck to him. He's hitting them out of the park better than anyone else and he deserves credit. He's the guy doing it."[65]

Maris admitted that he now had "a burning desire to break the record." Recognizing that the pennant race was all but over, "I began to feel that, since I was this close with so much time left, I really had a good shot at the record." He also was motivated by his desire to show his critics just how good a hitter he was. "I was tired of hearing and reading that I was a lousy hitter, that I wasn't in Ruth's class and didn't deserve to have so many homers…. I became so irked with the whole situation that I just felt I'd like to break the record just to hear them squeal louder." Perhaps his wanting to stick it to his detractors was not the most noble of sentiments, but it was one that was perfectly understandable.[66]

Home Run # 56—Game 143—September 9—Day Game

Maris failed to hit in the evening contest with the Indians on September 8, but he did bring Bobby Richardson home on a groundout in the opening inning for the first of nine runs the Yankees scored that night. Mickey Mantle, however, tightened the home run race slightly when he launched his fifty-second homer into the right-field seats in the fifth inning. The Yankees went on to pound Cleveland, 9–1, for their ninth consecutive victory. Mantle's dinger gave the two sluggers 107 home runs, tying them with the mark Babe Ruth and Lou Gehrig set in 1927. It also tied his personal season record of 52 round-trippers which he produced during his 1956 Triple-Crown season. Maris and Mantle now had one more home run than all the other Yankee players combined. With Detroit's eighth straight loss, the Bombers stretched their lead over the second-place Tigers to 10 games.

Right-hander Jim Grant took the ball

Jim "Mudcat" Grant was the only winning pitcher (15-9) on the Cleveland Indians starting staff in 1961. He defeated the Yankees, 5–1, on August 18 with Maris going 0-for-4, including two strikeouts. On September 9, though, the right-hander surrendered home runs to Johnny Blanchard, Elston Howard, and Maris (number 56) for a no-decision.

for the Indians the following afternoon in the third game of the five-game series. The 6-foot-1, 200-pound hurler was more popularly known as Mudcat, a sobriquet bestowed upon him by a veteran teammate in his first year of organized ball. He and the other new players were assigned nicknames "as part of a rookie initiation. Because I was black and my spikes and pants were so raggedy they assumed I was from the rural South and they guessed it was Mississippi," Grant clarified years later. "Leroy Irby, a first baseman, started getting on me saying I was as ugly as a Mississippi Mudcat, the mudcat being the biggest, ugliest of all catfish." Thus he became Mudcat from that day forth.[67]

Grant was signed by the Cleveland Indians at the age of 18 in 1954. Beginning his professional career with the Fargo-Moorhead Twins, the same franchise Maris played for a year earlier, he won 21 games while losing five. And, just like Maris before him, he won the Northern League's Rookie of the Year Award for his outstanding performance that summer.

Grant steadily worked his way through the minor league system, pitching outstanding ball as he rose up the organizational ladder. He was 19–3 with Class B Keokuk in 1955, 12–13 with Class A Reading the following summer, and 18–7 with a 2.32 ERA playing for the San Diego Padres in the Pacific Coast League in 1957. Ralph Kiner, Padres general manager, thought Grant was a sure major leaguer. "I've never seen a young pitcher come along as fast as he has. He wants to learn and is willing to take advice. That is a big point in his favor."[68]

Like Satchel Paige before him, Grant took to naming his pitches. One he used on occasion was his "Cloud Ball," "which contained a little moisture." His dominant pitch was his "Comet Ball," a "sizzling" fastball that he used to great advantage. In a June 6 outing he struck out 14 batters in 15 innings, then six days later fanned 13 in a nine-inning contest. By season's end, he led the PCL in complete games with 18 and strikeouts with 178. What he lacked for success in the big leagues was a decent curveball, according to club officials. They were so anxious to move him up that they sent Mel Harder, Cleveland pitching coach, to work with their prospect while he pitched winter ball in Cuba.[69]

Grant progressed to the point that the Indians took him with them when they moved north after spring training in 1958. The 22-year-old debuted on April 17, beating the Kansas City Athletics, 3–2, in a complete-game effort. After a no-decision on his next start, he pitched two consecutive complete-game victories, giving him a 3–0 record on a 1.85 earned-run average. As the league got used to the youngster, though, realty set in and he began to lose as often as he won. And when Joe Gordon replaced Bobby Bragan as manager midway through the season, he was used more often out of the bullpen. He completed the year at 10–11 with a respectable 3.84 earned-run average in 204 innings pitched. One problem that plagued him was his control. While he led all Cleveland pitchers in strikeouts with 111, he also outpaced them with 104 free passes. It was a pattern that haunted him throughout his tenure with the team.

One of the things that helped Grant in his rookie season was his friendship with Larry Doby, who he called "my greatest hero." Baseball was still rife with the underlying racism that was an inherent part of the sport since its beginnings and, although it was over a decade since the color line was broken, black players still faced discrimination and hostility from white teammates, officials, and fans. As the first African American in the American League, Doby had long dealt with this ugly side of the game for years and helped Grant, who certainly confronted his own share of racism playing in the minors, adjust to the realities of life in the big leagues for players of color. "The most I ever learned about the game was from him," Grant said years later. "He taught me everything from how to dress and mix colors to how to become part of the [black] community."[70]

Life was no bed of roses for African American and black Latino players in the 1960s. "The feeling among many people is that after Jackie Robinson and Larry Doby integrated baseball, it was easy for the black players that followed," Grant commented. "That's bullshit.... A lot of us who came along after Jackie and Larry broke in were justifiably angry at our treatment. We had to go along with much that was humiliating. For instance, because I was black, it was generally accepted by the powers that be that I wasn't smart enough to both pitch and call my own game—it was infuriating that the white manager and his white catcher called my games." In spite of "the constant pain and aggravation of being dehumanized," Grant came to realize, with Doby's guidance, that "you can only take your anger to a certain level or you can't compete. You have to be able to kick out your anger until after the game." It was a tough lesson to learn. "Believe me, the racial thing was a brutal psychological war between me and the people out to bury me.... I could've wound up pacing the floor like a lot of players, but I didn't let anyone destroy me. I waged that psychological war successfully."[71]

The next two seasons with Cleveland were adequate, but not great. He had a winning record of 19–15, but his cumulative 4.26 ERA was high, his control was still an issue, and he had a propensity for giving up home runs. In fact, he placed in the top 10 in that category both of those seasons and in five of the following six. He continued to shuttle back and forth between the bullpen and starting, which may have been a factor. The 1960 campaign was a particularly troublesome one for him. He suffered from a sore shoulder at the beginning of spring and did not make his first start until late May.

As if that were not enough, his summer ended abruptly on a very sour note. At the beginning of a game on September 16 as some of the pitchers stood in the bullpen while the National Anthem was being sung, Grant changed the lyrics "the land of the free and the home of the brave" to "this land is not so free, I can't even go to Mississippi." Bullpen coach Ted Wilks, who was from Texas, overheard him and responded angrily, "If you don't like our country, why in the hell don't you get out?" Grant replied to the effect that if he wanted to leave the country, "all I have to do is go to Texas." Wilks screamed back, "Well, if we catch your black nigger ass in Texas, we're going to hang you from the nearest tree." At that point Grant "threw a punch upside his jaw and down he went." He then stormed into the clubhouse, changed clothes, and left the stadium without informing manager Jimmy Dykes of the incident. "As soon as I left I knew I was doing the wrong thing," Grant said the following day. "I was going to turn around and come back, but didn't." He called Dykes after the game to apologize for leaving, but the manager felt he had no recourse but to suspend his pitcher—with pay—for the rest of the season. As for Wilks, he was coaching for the Athletics the following season.[72]

The 1961 season was when Grant began to settle in as frontline hurler. Jimmy Dykes made the decision to use the right-hander strictly as a starter, a move that profoundly impacted Grant's development. "If they started me as much as some of the other pitchers, I'd win more," Grant predicted in training camp that spring. His prognostication proved to be right on the money. He was given his first start on April 15, beating the Washington Senators, his favorite victim—he was 16–2 over three seasons going into the game—before a four-game stretch with no decisions. Then he won his next six starts, hurling four complete games with two shutouts in the process.[73]

He ended the summer as the team's ace, compiling the best record at 15–9, lowest earned-run average at 3.86, and most shutouts among all the starters. He was sixth among American League pitchers in wins, seventh in innings pitched, fifth in games started, ninth in complete games, sixth in shutouts, but also sixth in earned runs allowed, fifth in walks, and third in home runs allowed with 32. (Three Cleveland pitchers—Grant, Gary Bell, and Jim Perry—were among the top 10 in home runs allowed in 1961; Maris hit six off the trio.) Joe Gordon, Grant's former manager, praised the 25-year-old. "Grant is an entirely different pitcher now. He concentrates on every pitch.... He had to grow up. But not everybody grows up as fast as Mud did." Cleveland pitching coach Mel Harder agreed, stating, "He should get better and better."[74]

And then the military intervened. Grant, a member of the Army Reserve, was called up for active duty in early November. He spent the next nine months managing and pitching for his base team. The Army, though, did give him passes to pitch for the Indians on the weekends, and in May 1962 granted him 30-day leave before his release in mid-July. Despite the erratic scheduling, Grant handled it all as well as could be expected. He relieved in two games in April, then started six in May, winning three of them. After going 1–3 for the month of June, Grant finally received his discharge. In his first game back, though, he hurt his arm, which may have been a factor in his 3–7 record and 4.90 after his return. Grant pointed to the disruption caused by his military duty as the basis of his losing season. "I didn't have any spring training, and that hurt me the most," he explained. "Then I'd join the club each week-end and that didn't give me a chance to get into a routine. The periods of inactivity made it hard for me to get going during the last half [of the season]."[75]

Grant started 1963 on a winning note, pitching a complete-game victory over the Minnesota Twins in his first start of the summer, but then lost two of his next three. And that was the way the year went for him. He would win a few then lose a few to end the season at 13–14 with a good 3.69 earned-run average for a fifth place team that lost 83 of its games. His control showed a marked improvement; while he walked 87, he fanned 157, the most in his major league career. Grant entered spring training in 1964 with the hopes of becoming a consistent winner once again. Manager Birdie Tebbetts had nothing but praise for his charge. "One of these days everything will fall in place and he'll be a twenty-game winner," the skipper asserted. "A pitcher needs a little luck to win 20 games," Grant responded, "but I don't see any reason why I can't reach that figure with the team we'll have behind us this year." That was indeed the case, but not in 1964 and not in a Cleveland uniform.[76]

Grant got off to a poor start in 1964, and at the end of May was 3–4 with a humongous 6.13 earned-run average. The Indians used him as a reliever for three games in early June before trading him to the Minnesota Twins for two other players. General manager Gabe Paul expressed his reluctance of letting Grant go. "He has been a good pitcher and a credit to our organization," he stated, but "I think the trade will help both clubs." Grant's response was more than gracious. "I hate to leave Cleveland. I started here and wanted to finish here. But ballplayers are like street-cars—we come and we go. I was always proud to be an Indian."[77]

While Grant may have been saddened by his departure from Cleveland, it turned out to be a fortuitous move. He turned things around there, going 11–9 with an outstanding 2.82 ERA in 26 games. He compiled his first winning record in three seasons at 14–13, and while he surrendered 32 dingers, he struck out 118 while walking 61. "The Twins [who finished in sixth place] will be better next season, mark my word," he proclaimed that winter. "Everybody says our pitching wasn't good enough, but who can say we don't have four good starters in Camilo Pascual, Dick Stigman, Jim Kaat and that guy Grant?" Little did he know how prescient he was.[78]

There was no indication at the beginning of the 1965 campaign that Grant was about to have the best season of his career. He hurled just three innings in his first start and did not even make it out of the first inning in his second appearance, leaving him with an enormous 18.90 ERA. Then he began to win. He pitched a shutout in his third start, followed by complete-game wins in his next two. At the end of May he was 5–0 and his earned-run average had dropped to 4.04. He did not sustain his first loss until June 7, an eight-inning, two-run affair against the Boston Red Sox. On September 25, he shut out the Washington Senators on one hit, making him the first African American pitcher in the major leagues to win 20 games in a season.

Grant, who had to wrap his knees for two months in the middle of the season because of tendonitis, won his final start on September 29, making him the winningest pitcher in the American League at 21–7. He led the league in shutouts and winning percentage while placing third in innings pitched, second in games started, and second in complete games. Still dinger prone, he led the league in home runs allowed with 34 as well. Twins manager Sam Mele noted how Grant stepped up time and again as the team's "stopper" in their drive toward their first American League pennant. "Jim has won our big games for us all season," he said. "He has stopped our losing slide streaks and beaten the tough clubs." Although Sandy Koufax won the Cy Young Award—there was only one award for both leagues at that time—Grant was named Pitcher of the Year by *The Sporting News* and came in sixth in the American League Most Valuable Player Award voting.[79]

Grant attributed much of his success that season to pitching coach Johnny Sain, who worked with the right-hander in developing a "fast curve" to go along with his slow breaking pitch. "I've never had a real good fast curve before," he admitted. "I've always had a good fast ball, a change of pace and a slow curve.... They said I needed to change speeds. I've always been able to change off my fast ball—throw a straight slow ball up there. But, until this year, I never thought in terms of spinning the ball. That's where Sain helped me." Earl Battey, who caught for Grant, said the change in Grant's curveball was noticeable. "Last year [1964], Jim's slow curve used to start breaking up closer to his hand. The batter could pick it up sooner. This year, it breaks later and he can keep it down better. The batter gives up on it, and then it breaks over the plate."[80]

Grant's superior pitching carried over into the Twins' first World Series appearance in which he went 2–1 in the seven-game contest against the Los Angeles Dodgers. He beat Don Drysdale handily in the first game, 8–2, but lost to him, 7–2, in Game 4. With the Twins facing elimination in Game 6, Grant, on two-days rest and suffering from a cold, pitched one of the best games of his career, defeating Claude Osteen, 5–1, in nine innings while contributing to his own cause by belting a three-run homer in the sixth inning. That four-bagger was the first time since 1920 an American League pitcher had done that in the World Series. After the game when the big right-hander was asked if he felt any pressure pitching in front of the home crowd in such a crucial game, quipped, "What's pressure? Some new kind of dance?" Although Sandy Koufax blanked the Twins, 2–0, the following day to secure the Series for the Dodgers, Grant could look back with pride at his outstanding season.[81]

Grant's 1966 campaign paled in comparison to the previous summer, but his 13–13 record was much better than it seemed. He was 6–12 at the end of July, but eight of those defeats were by two runs or less and his 3.38 ERA was similar to the year before. "Last year I pitched well in tough games until the late innings," he said after the All-Star break. "Then a lot of times our guys would come along and score. This year I've been pitching well until late innings and losing. Maybe I hadn't been concentrating hard enough. I'm not saying I wasn't. I don't know. But I'm going to make certain there is no problem like that in the second half." One change he made was in his delivery, using more of an overhand motion rather than his typical three-quarters style. "I had good stuff pitching three-quarter," he explained, "but if I can get even better stuff pitching more overhand, fine." Whether that was the reason for his second-half improvement is open to argument, but whatever it was, he won seven while losing just one in August and September.[82]

The pitching gods were not smiling on the 31-year-old hurler at all during the 1967 campaign, his last with the Twins. First he was struck on his pitching arm the last week of spring training and got off to a slow start to begin the regular season. He was 0–3 with a large 5.82 earned-run average before he started to put together a winning season. He compiled a 4–2 record with a 2.21 ERA in May, but then aggravated his left knee in June, causing him to miss two weeks. He attempted to come back in July, but after a complete-game victory on July 4, he made only two more appearances that month. He had just one start after that, pitching from the bullpen the rest of the season. Grant was not a happy camper and indicated his desire to be traded. He got his wish; on November 28 he and teammate Zoilo Versalles were traded to the Los Angeles Dodgers for Bob Miller, Ron Perranoski, and John Roseboro.[83]

"I had no intention of coming back," he responded upon hearing about the trade. "It's best they traded me." Stating his displeasure as to how he was treated by manager Cal Ermer because of his lingering knee problem (it was rumored that management thought he was exaggerating the extent of his pain), he also indicated that there was a racial undertone to how he and the other African American players were perceived by the manager and the front office. "It was never there before," he indicated, "but it was this year. It cropped up in the bus incident [a racially-charged 'hassle' that occurred in mid-summer on a trip to Detroit] and those guys don't forget it."[84]

Grant was used as both a starter and reliever to begin the season with the Dodgers, but after he pulled a muscle in his side that caused him to miss two weeks at the end of May, he pitched mainly from the bullpen. Grant performed well in that capacity, going 4–1 with two saves on an excellent 1.74 earned-run average to end the summer at 6–4 with a 2.08 ERA. Although he was considered "one of the club's most consistent and convincing performers," the Dodgers left him exposed to that year's expansion draft and he was selected by the newly-formed Montreal Expos.[85]

Thus began his late-career role as a relief artist. The Expos, though, thought he still had the potential to be a starter and used him in that capacity to begin the 1969 campaign. He opened 10 for Montreal through the end of May and although he had games in which he was his old self, his starting days were behind him. After he compiled a losing record (1–6, 4.89 ERA), the Expos traded him to the St. Louis Cardinals in early June. Disappointed when the Cards informed him that he was to be used primarily as a reliever, he nevertheless pitched well in that role, compiling a record of seven wins, five losses, and seven saves the rest of the summer. On December 5, the Oakland Athletics purchased his contract, bringing him back to the American League.

While he still had dreams of being a starter, the 34-year-old right-hander found new life with the A's as their bullpen ace. By the end of July, he had won four games while saving 18 others, all with a 0.95 earned-run average. In fact, he and teammate Catfish Hunter were considered the anchors on the Oakland pitching staff, the one-two punch that "helped keep the A's heads above water in this might-have-been season." Grant ran his record up to six wins, two losses, and 24 saves on a 1.82 ERA in 72 games when the Pittsburgh Pirates, fighting for the National League East flag, acquired Grant from Oakland in mid–September to help in their stretch drive. Grant was upset by the move. "Everything I did was for the Oakland A's," he said. "You join the club, you put your worth into the club, you hurt for the club, you have an outstanding year for the club, and two weeks before the end of the season, someone [owner Charlie Finley] phones you that you've been sold.... This really hurt." Ever the professional, Grant did his best for the Pirates, winning two, losing one and helping them secure the NL East flag. Pittsburgh was swept by the Cincinnati Reds in three games; Grant did not make an appearance in those contests.[86]

The 1971 season was Grant's last campaign. The 35-year-old hurler appeared in 42 games with the Pirates (5–3, seven saves, 3.60 ERA) before Oakland brought him back on August 10 to help out with their own pennant drive. Grant again was not pleased with this sudden change in venues. Although he was acquired by a contending club, "I'm upset over the fact, I'm just being shuttled," he told the press. Despite his personal feelings, however, Grant performed at his best (1–0, three saves, 1.98 ERA) the last six weeks of the season to help the A's win the NL West division. In spite of Oakland losing all three games to the Baltimore Orioles, Grant did his part to help the club, pitching a scoreless final two innings of Game 3. On November 30, he was released by the Athletics, bringing an end to a fine 14-year major league career. His cumulative record over those summers was 145 wins, 119 losses, 54 saves, and a 3.63 earned-run average in 571 games, over half of them as a starter. Grant, who for years was a professional singer in the off-season, continued his music career after retirement. In addition, he worked for the Cleveland Indians and the Oakland A's as a broadcaster and as a pitching coach in the Carolina League in the 1980s.[87]

Grant was 14–8 with a good 3.60 earned-run average at the time he opened the September 9 contest with the Yankees. He had faced New York twice already that season, including a complete-game victory on August 18 in which he limited the Bombers to three hits, none of them by Maris or Mantle. He had given up 27 homers so far, but Maris had yet to take him deep. In fact, the Yankee slugger had yet to plate a run off of Grant even though he generally hit well against him. Grant considered Maris and teammate Moose Skowron as batters who consistently gave him "the most trouble. I used to think I'd give them my best pitch and this should do it. That best pitch isn't enough. You have to think, too." He struck out New York's slugger in the first inning and induced a force out in the third. Maris began to show signs of life in the fifth with a single to right, but it came to naught. By the time he came up in the seventh frame, the Yankees were down, 7–3. Grant retired Tony Kubek on a fly to left to open that inning, so when Maris stepped to the plate there was no one on.[88]

"Nobody wants to be a member of the Mantle-Maris home run club," asserted Indians pitcher Gary Bell, who was victimized twice by Maris earlier that summer. "Every pitcher in the league is bearing down extra hard on them." Maris agreed with that assessment. "They move me back with the fast ball and try to hit the outside corner with the garbage. The big question is still the same. Are you going to get the good pitch? Are you going to do it when you get the good pitch or foul it off?" Grant's approach that day was to throw Maris "nothing but curves and change-ups and [make] sure he had to supply his own power."[89]

Maris stepped into the box "aiming for the seats. Grant has a whistling fast ball and he works with an unusual delivery. Sometimes it is difficult to time his pitches." Maris took a couple of pitches in an attempt to "gauge" Grant. The count stood at 2–1 when the right-hander delivered what Maris later claimed "wasn't a good pitch. He should have got me out on that one." But he did not. Maris "got a good cut and met the ball solidly," sending it hurling deep into the right field seats for his fifty-sixth. That round-tripper gave Maris and Mantle 108, breaking the two-teammate record set by Ruth and Gehrig in 1927.[90]

The Yankees were still down three runs going into the bottom of the ninth. Hector Lopez opened with a triple off of Grant, scoring when Bobby Richardson successfully bunted behind him. The starter was lifted at that point and Dick Stigman replaced him. The reliever promptly tossed a wild pitch with Tony Kubek at the plate, advancing Richardson to second. Then he ended up walking Kubek to put runners on first and second. Frank Funk was brought in to face Maris. The Yankee right fielder grounded back to the pitcher, but it was enough to move Richardson and Kubek up a base. Manager Jimmy Dykes wanted no part of Mantle and instructed Funk to intentionally walk the switch-hitter. That brought Johnny Blanchard to the plate. The Yankee left fielder, who homered off of Grant earlier in the game, hit a ground-rule double, scoring Richardson and Kubek to tie the game. With Mantle on third, Funk intentionally walked catcher Elston Howard, the league's leading hitter at .362, hoping to prevent any further damage. But first baseman Moose Skowron spoiled all that by stroking a sacrifice fly to right to plate Mantle, giving New York ten consecutive victories.

And just like that the home runs stopped coming for Maris. Over the following week, he got his share of hits—batting .269 during that period—and drove in three runs, but he failed to park one in the next seven games. The problem was that he was pressing, trying to intentionally hit homers, which disrupted his rhythm and altered his natural batting style. "It wasn't long before I began to realize that my desire to really topple the home-run record had changed me.... Now I was swinging at pitches I normally wouldn't go after." The pitchers, of course, sensed his growing desperation and tempted him with balls outside his happy zone. "They started to get me to swing at bad pitches. I was helping them. Walks wouldn't do me any good, so I was up there swinging." Usually a disciplined hitter, he was now striking out as much as he walked.[91]

Maris readily acknowledged the physical and psychological toll the pursuit of Ruth was taking on him. "It's hard," he told New York sportswriter Milton Gross. "You can't know how rough it gets. It's a long year, a tough one. It gets you down." He admitted that "the closer I get [to the record] the more I want it, but the more I wish the year was over." He knew there would be no respite from the mounting pressure and unrelenting public obsession with him until the season ended. "No matter what, you won't be able to get away from it. You won't be able to get away from it.... It's the price you must pay for what you're doing." As he was soon to learn, the intensity of the situation would grow exponentially the final three weeks of the summer.[92]

For Mantle, it was just the opposite. For one thing, the fans began to cheer him each time he strode to the plate or took his position on the field. "They've been like that for about the last week," he said in early September. "I think it's because I'm like an underdog. People all go for the guy that's behind." Maris reportedly responded, "Wish I was. Come on, Mick, hit a few more so I can get a little rest." As one reporter described this recent adulation, "the people regard Maris as a usurper and they're trying to show Mantle they really loved him all the time." With Maris so far ahead in the homer count and so few games left to catch him, Mantle, though he continued to "try like hell" to win the race, knew deep down it was unlikely he would surpass his partner and, as a result, he began to relax. He told Maris after he had belted his forty-eighth homer to best Lou Gehrig's total in 1927, "The pressure is off me. I already beat my guy."[93]

As if to prove his point, the Mick hit his fifty-third home run in the second game of a September 10 doubleheader with the Indians, their final meeting of the year. Maris was 1-for-3 with two RBIs in the first game and 1-for-3 with two runs scored in the second on what was his twenty-seventh birthday. The Yankees won both contests, extending their winning streak to 12 games, while Cleveland's twin defeats extended their losing streak at the Stadium to 18 games over two seasons.

The only real excitement in the first game occurred in the seventh inning when two young men jumped onto the field and charged Cleveland's Jimmy Piersall. The quick-tempered center fielder wasted little time in dispatching his would-be assailants, knocking one down with a punch to his eye, then halting the advance of the other with a kick as his teammates and stadium security rushed the field to corral the miscreant youths. "I'm no Floyd Patterson," he said afterwards, "but I can defend myself alright." Then in the sixth inning of the second contest, a minor kerfuffle broke out when Clete Boyer was the victim of mixed signals on the part of two of the umpires. With two on, the Yankees third baseman hit a ball into the left-field corner. One umpire signaled it was a home run that bounced back onto the field, while the other indicated that it was just a fair ball that hit the fence railing. Boyer, thinking he had homered, slowed down and was tagged out as he reached third. That caused both the player and the fans to protest vigorously—spectators waved handkerchiefs and threw trash onto the field in a demonstration that went on into the eighth inning—but the ruling stood, giving Boyer two RBIs but no home run.[94]

The following day the Yankees headed off on their final road trip of the season, a 13-game affair in which they would play the White Sox, the Tigers, the Orioles, and the Red Sox before returning home for four games to end the season. They were close to clinching the pennant as they boarded the train for Chicago (Maris and Mantle had a television commitment and would fly to Chicago early the next day), needing a combination of eight New York wins and Detroit losses to secure the American League flag. As for the home-run chase, the two Yankee sluggers would hit Ford Frick's arbitrary 154-game limit to "officially" break the record in Baltimore on September 20.

"That day off we had yesterday [September 11] did me a whole lot of good," Maris said upon arrival in the Windy City. "Whatever happens, though, I'll have no excuse if I don't make it. I'll admit I'm going to be leveling for those fences when I get the pitch that suits me. I can tell you that." Mantle expressed confidence in his chances to break the record although he was behind both the Maris and Ruth paces. "I think I've got an edge on the kind of trip we're taking," he proclaimed. Explaining that "a lot of my power hitting both sides of the plate is to the opposite field," he believed he had the advantage over Maris in Comiskey Park and Tiger Stadium. His contention was more wishful thinking than fact. He hit two homers in Comiskey Park and three at Tiger Stadium while Maris had five each in those two stadiums.[95]

Neither Maris nor Mantle hit home runs in the rain-shortened opening contest against the White Sox that night, a 4–3 victory for the Bombers, their thirteenth in a row. Overshadowing that win, though, was a controversy that erupted when Maris criticized home-plate umpire Hank Soar as the players sat in a steamy clubhouse waiting for the game to be called. In the second inning with runners on second and third and one away, Maris, with two strikes, was called out swinging on the next pitch. The right fielder, convinced he had checked his swing—"My body moved, but the bat didn't"—had a few choice words for the umpire as he walked back to the dugout. Then in the sixth with the Yankees up, 4–3, and runners on first and third, Maris squared to bunt in a run. "I was going to bunt, but the pitch was high and unbuntable, but he [Soar] called that a strike, too." He then fouled out to first on the next pitch. "You really stuck it to me that time," he supposedly said to Soar as he stalked away.[96]

Maris exploded in front of the assembled reporters. "I didn't get too many strikes, yet they were being called strikes," he complained. "I was swinging in self-defense. Soar is usually a good umpire, but he was off tonight." Several of the scribes scurried to the umpire to get his reaction to Maris' criticism, and they got exactly what they wanted. "I have no intention of getting into an argument with Maris, but I certainly am not going to let him put the blame on me," he responded. "Maris seems to think every pitch he doesn't swing at is a ball," Soar added. "He's a nice kid, but he's under terrific pressure now.... He is so tight up there he can hardly breathe." Soar felt compelled to add a zinger to his comments. "What's he doing up there trying to bunt?" he asked. "He's after the home run record, isn't he?"[97]

These were typical comments a frustrated player makes when he underperforms, but this was Roger Maris, not just any player, and the press blew it all out of proportion. When Mantle demonstrated his anger after striking out in the first inning, however, no one made much of that. Even though he and Soar talked the next day and straightened out any misunderstandings—according to Maris, both stated they were misquoted—his outburst further cemented his image as a complainer and whiner, someone surly and perpetually angry.

The game scheduled for the following night was called because of rain in the third inning with the Yankees leading, 2–1. That necessitated a doubleheader the next day, September 14. Things did not go the Yankees' way. They lost both halves of the twin bill, 8–3 in the first game, 4–3 in the second. Neither Maris nor Mantle was able to add to his respective home run total. Maris was 3-for-8 with an RBI in the two contests, but Mantle, suffering from a persistent head cold, was 0-for-7. Feeling physically exhausted and totally frustrated, Mantle openly expressed his belief that he would not break Ruth's record. "I can't make it, not even in 162 games," he gloomily stated. Buying in to Ford Frick's 154-game deadline, Mantle added, "It really doesn't matter to me, although all along I've said only 154 games should be recognized." Maris, still feeling upbeat about his chances, refused to concede the record if he broke it in more games than Ruth had to set it. "If you hit 60 home runs it's 60 home runs, not 59. I don't care how many games it takes."[98]

Home Run # 57—Game 151—September 16—Day Game

The Yankees flew to Detroit immediately after the game to take on the Tigers in a twi-night doubleheader the following evening. The Bengals were on the verge of elimination, but that did not mean they were not up for a little revenge for what the Yankees did to them in early September. The Yanks pounded Detroit, 11–1, in the first game, giving Whitey Ford his twenty-fourth victory of the year. Yogi Berra and Moose Skowron each homered for a team total of 222, a new major league record. Maris was 0-for-5 with two strikeouts while Mantle managed one hit with two runs scored and one driven in on a sacrifice fly in the ninth. The two were equally ineffective in the second contest, a 4–2 loss. They did manage back-to-back singles in the eighth with Maris scoring on a fielding error, but that was their total offensive production that evening.

After the game, Maris headed directly to the trainer's room, an off-limits area to the press. By way of explanation, he claimed it was always his practice to do so while in Detroit. "It's just a habit," he said. In addition, his brother was there, and he used the time to talk with him about personal and business matters. Besides, he had contributed nothing offensively that night, so "what could they [the press] want of a guy who had one single in nine trips when there were so many other things to write about?" In fact, though, he was tired and frustrated and had been subjected to vulgar taunts and jeers by Detroit fans during both games. He wanted a halt to the constant questioning for just one night, not an unreasonable desire, but one which he handled in a way certain to irritate those with looming deadlines to report on the home run leader. Instead of asking them to give him a break, which most likely would have fallen on deaf ears, he marched past them saying, "Go talk with someone who had something to do with the game."[99]

His refusal to meet with reporters, especially in contrast to Mantle who made himself available, infuriated the large gaggle of writers used to having Maris ready and willing to answer—albeit sometimes irritably—any questions tossed his way. Even members of the New York contingent, usually supportive of him, denounced his avoidance of the press. They accused him of sulking, of hiding, of acting like a child. They pressured Bob Fishel, the Yankees' public relations spokesperson, into entering the trainer's room to convince Maris to come out. When he returned to announce that Maris refused to talk because he was tired of "being ripped by writers in every city"—he did not mean those in New York, Fishel quickly added—that simply added fuel to the flames. Some even jumped on Ralph Houk, complaining about the policy of players-only in the room. Houk refused to budge, saying Maris had the right to visit with his brother, and when they continued to badger him, the manager, who had a bit of a temper himself, erupted. "You mean his brother shouldn't be allowed to go in and talk to him? Don't tell me who can go in and who can't. Isn't that a great damn thing to be arguing about?"[100]

Some of the reporters hung around until Maris eventually emerged from the showers. When several shouted questions as he walked to his locker, he was abrupt and sarcastic in his response. Do you think you still have a shot at breaking the record, one scribe wanted to know. "What record?" he responded. The Babe Ruth record, the reporter clarified. "Am I close to it? I don't want to talk about it. If you want me to concede, I'll concede." And with that, he turned his back on them, refusing to answer any more questions. "That was red-assed Roger at his best," Maury Allen wrote years afterwards. "This was the essence of so much of the bad publicity that Maris would have to deal with throughout his career. He had been approachable through 149 games of that season. That one game in Detroit, with the press held at bay, did severe damage to his image."[101]

With seven straight homerless games, it looked to most that Maris had hit a wall. He was no longer ahead of Ruth's pace and, based on Frick's proscribed deadline, had just five more games to catch the Babe. Few thought he stood a chance. One critic began referring to him as "Rigor Mortis," a truly nasty and unwarranted epithet. But Maris, a proud and persistent man, was determined to prove his detractors wrong.[102]

Frank Lary, equally determined to make the Yankees pay for his crucial loss to them on September 2, was going for his twenty-first victory. Opposing him was 14-game winner Ralph Terry. It was all Lary and the Tigers from the first inning on. Detroit jumped on Terry for two runs in the first inning. He settled down in the second, but then gave up two more runs in the third and another couple in the fourth before he was lifted with the Tigers in front, 6–2. Detroit plated another run off of reliever Jim Coates, providing them a commanding advantage that the Yankees could not overcome. The game ended with the Tigers winning, 10–4.

The only excitement for New York occurred in the third inning when Maris came to bat for the second time that game. Lary, who gave up two dingers to Maris already that summer, pitched the right fielder carefully, not wanting to add a third round-tripper to his resume. Maris had other plans. With two out and Tony Kubek standing on first, he connected with a Lary fastball "going away" from him. Maris said he "got good wood on it." Lary, damning with faint praise, said the slugger "stuck out his bat and was able to reach it." Maris did more than just "reach it." He launched a rocket that traveled over 360 feet before striking the upper-deck facing on the lower right-center field roof some 82 feet high; he came close to hitting it out of the stadium. The ball careened off the facing and bounced back onto the field where right fielder Al Kaline grabbed it and tossed it to the Yankee dugout.[103]

"This was a big homer for him," Ralph Houk said after the game. "He sure needed it. It will give him a big lift. It he hadn't hit one, he could have been in trouble." Maris attempted to patch up his relationship with the press damaged by his avoidance behavior the night before. He explained that he was angry at the verbal abuse he suffered from fans during those two games, and thus decided to seclude himself in the trainer's room because "I was afraid I might pop off and say something that would only get them [the writers] down on me even more." That explanation seemed to help. "At least Maris was talking again," wrote Louis Effrat in the *New York Times*. "He wasn't saying too much and he could hardly be described as a chatterbox, but he was talking."[104]

Some among the Detroit press criticized him for his response to a question about Al Kaline retrieving the home-run ball for him. "It was nice for Al to have done that," he responded, "but I guess anyone would have done it." It was a less-than-artful statement of appreciation that was blown all out of proportion by the local newspapers who acted as if Maris were slighting Kaline, a very popular player in the city. "I certainly didn't mean it that way," he said afterwards. "I thought it was very thoughtful of Kaline, who has always been a great guy. I wasn't trying to take anything away from him." Clearly some sportswriters and columnists were looking for anything they could use to further bash Maris.[105]

Home Run # 58—Game 152—September 17—Day Game

On the afternoon of September 17, some 44,000 fans crowded into Tiger Stadium to see the final game of the season between the hometown favorites and the hated Yankees. New York needed just four games to grab the American League flag, so a win that day would close the gap to two. With Detroit all but eliminated, the only thing they fought for was their pride and the hope they could delay the Yankees' conquest. Bill Stafford took the mound for the Bombers while future Hall-of-Famer Jim Bunning opened for the Bengals.

The Tigers were the first to draw blood. After Bunning held the Yankees scoreless in the first inning, Norm Cash singled with two on in the bottom of that frame to plate the first run. Moose Skowron tied it up in the second inning with his twenty-sixth homer of the season. Detroit pulled ahead again when Stafford issued a bases-loaded walk to Steve Boros, Detroit third baseman, in the bottom of the third. Then in the top of the fourth, Clete Boyer homered with Skowron on first to put the Yankees ahead for the first time, 3–2.

There the score remained until the seventh when Maris came to the plate with two out and Tony Kubek standing on first. Bunning had walked Maris twice and struck him out once in his three earlier plate appearances, but this time the slugger was not fooled. He smashed a ball to right-center field that looked certain to be his fifty-eighth dinger of the season. Instead it struck a foot below the top of the screen some 370 feet distant for a triple, providing the Yankees with an insurance run. In the bottom of the eighth, though, fate intervened when the Tigers tied it up on a run-scoring single by Jake Wood, who proceeded to score the second run on a three-base throwing error on the part of Skowron, the Yankee first baseman. It turned out to be a gift for Maris.

With the score tied at four, rookie right-hander Terry Fox was brought in to relieve Bunning to open the ninth frame. The 24-year-old relief specialist began his career in 1954 as a starter for the New Iberia Pelicans of the Class C Evangeline League. That first season he went 13–4 with a 3.39 earned-run average followed by an even better summer in 1955. Not only was he the best pitcher on the team, but he ended that campaign with 21wins—tying him for most in the league—and a 2.95 ERA.[106]

The Milwaukee Braves took an interest in the youngster and acquired him at the end of the season. He stumbled the following summer as he was shuttled back and forth among three of the Braves' minor league affiliates where he compiled a less than stellar record of five wins and 14 losses on a large 4.77 earned-run average. Although he had an 11–14 record in 1957 playing for the Double-A Austin Senators, his 3.49 ERA showed a marked improvement and his eight complete games with five shutouts placed him among the league leaders. He started 1958 pitching for the Double-A Atlanta Crackers where he struggled, so was sent back to Austin, using that opportunity to get back on track with a 9–6 record on a 2.62 ERA.

Milwaukee believed enough in their prospect to assign him to the Triple-A Sacramento Solons in the Pacific Coast League in 1959. It was there that his career trajectory changed for the better. Solons manager Bob Elliott thought Fox would be better suited as a reliever and assigned him to full-time bullpen duties. The skipper's assessment was right on the mark. In 42 games of relief, he managed a 9–3 record on an exceptional 2.70 earned-run average. *The Sporting News* called him "the Coast league's most reliable fireman." His future was set.[107]

Fox continued his good work with Sacramento the following summer, going 12–9 with a 3.07 earned-run average before being called up to the big club in September. He relieved in five games and, except for a pounding on September 20 in which he surrendered four earned runs in a third of an inning, turned in excellent work. In spite of his developing talent, however, the Braves parted ways with Fox, making him part of a six-player trade that sent him to the Detroit Tigers at the end of 1960.

Relying on his excellent fastball and sharp curve with an occasional changeup, which he believed was all he needed for relief work, the 6-foot, 175-pound right-hander quickly became the ace of the bullpen staff. His first appearance in a Detroit uniform occurred on April 15 where he earned his first major league save, pitching 3⅓ innings of one-hit relief. He followed that in his second assignment with his first win, this time hurling three innings of scoreless relief that included four strikeouts. He was 3–0 with seven saves and an unbelievable 0.79 earned-run average before he suffered his first loss, a two-inning outing against the Los Angeles Angels on July 7. He ended the 1961 season with five wins, two losses, and 12 saves—fifth most in the American League—on a fantastic 1.41 earned-run average in 39 games, 25 as the closer.[108]

He undoubtedly would have had an even more impressive record had he not suffered from persistent shoulder and elbow pain that cropped up several times during the season, and for most of his career. (He first injured his arm one day in the mid–1950s while polishing his car.) He was out several times during that summer, including a full month from July 20 to August 20 when the Tigers were making their stretch drive. He continued to pitch well in spite of the pain, though. Manager Bob Scheffing firmly believed that had Fox been healthy all season, the Tigers would have gone into September leading the Yankees by at least seven games.[109]

Fox came to training camp the next spring feeling upbeat about his future. Unfortunately, his arm problems flared up again and he spent the early part of the season removed from pitching duties while undergoing cortisone injections. Before returning to the rotation, he was sent to Denver to try out his arm hurling relief for the Bears in five games. Recalled at the end of the month, he made his first appearance on May 30, a two-inning affair in which he gave up two earned runs. From that rough beginning, however, he steadily improved until he again became the best reliever on the team.

Although the manager planned to use Fox sparingly at first, it quickly became apparent that he was so pain-free that he appeared in back-to-back outings on several occasions. On June 24 he pitched eight-scoreless innings in a 22-inning battle with the Yankees, which New York won in the twenty-second inning. "When he's sound of limb, he's the best finishing relief pitcher Detroit has seen since Al Benton in the mid–'40s," proclaimed *The Sporting News*. He ended the summer having relieved in 44 games while compiling a record of three wins, one loss, and 16 saves on an outstanding 1.71 earned-run average. On top of that, he joined the team in a 21-day post-season tour of Japan.[110]

Unlike the previous two summers, Fox pitched the entire 1963 season without pain. "This is the first time in two years that I've been able to bend my elbow without it hurting," he said. In spite of being without arm discomfort, his 1963 output was not at the same levels as in the past. He started off well enough, but then struggled in June and July before turning things around the last two months of the summer. He ended at 8–6 with 11 saves on a respectable 3.59 ERA in a little over 80 innings pitched, the most in his career. Fox was "instrumental in the Tigers' surge from ninth to seventh place [they ended in fifth place]," noted *The Sporting News*.[111]

Fox arrived at spring training early in 1964 to get into shape. Manager Charlie Dressen, who took on the skipper's role in the middle of the previous campaign, was talking about using two other pitchers as his primary relievers. Fox wanted to make sure his arm was strong enough to help him "stand his ground against all invaders." His plan worked. By the end of training camp, Dressen intended to use Fox and the newly-acquired Larry Sherry as his one-two punch out of the bullpen. But unfortunately Fox developed shoulder problems just before the season began and was out until June. After getting in shape pitching briefly with the Knoxville Smokies, he returned to the Tigers, tossing two scoreless innings in his first outing back on June 5. He recorded his first two saves pitching both halves of a doubleheader against the Los Angeles Angels on June 14, going 2⅔ innings in total without allowing a run. "Pitching in both games was no trouble," he said. "I just poured in the fast balls and depended on my fielders." He finished the summer at 4–3 with five saves and a good 3.39 ERA.[112]

Fox turned in a productive season in 1965, winning six, losing four, and saving 10 while lowering his earned-run average to 2.78 in 77⅔ innings of work. Even though he had a good year, there were indications that his tenure with Detroit was about to come to a close. Dressen made it known at the end of the year that he preferred a reliever he could call upon more often. He was particularly concerned about Fox's history of arm problems. "Our relief pitching wasn't right last year," the Detroit pilot commented. "Nobody stayed good the whole time."[113]

It was clear early on in 1966 that Fox was on his way out. Management was looking for a trade, about which the pitcher was quite aware. "If I can't pitch here, I know I can pitch some place," he told the press that spring. And that was exactly what happened. After four game appearances in which he had one save and one loss on an awful 6.30 earned-run average, he was sold to the Philadelphia Phillies for cash and a player to be named later. He had a mediocre season with his new team. He first appeared on May 11, a one-inning affair in which he surrendered two earned runs. Though he began to improve after that, he finished with a 3–3 record, five saves, and a bloated 4.80 ERA. And that marked the finish of his big league career.

Now 31, he relieved for the Phillies' Triple-A franchise in San Diego in 1967. Although he compiled a 3–0 record in 28 games, his earned-run average was an extremely high 5.23. His baseball dreams had come to an end. In seven major league seasons, he won 29 while losing another 19, saved 59, and compiled a cumulative ERA of 2.99 while relieving in 248 games, over half of them as the closer, making him one of the most effective relievers of his generation. One can only speculate as to how much more he could have accomplished had it not been for persistent elbow and shoulder problems.[114]

The rookie right-hander dominated the Yankees throughout the 1961 season. Fox did not allow a run in his four appearances against them prior to the September 17 contest. In his most recent confrontation with the league leaders on September 3, he pitched two solid innings in which he struck out three—Moose Skowron, Elston Howard, and Roger Maris—of the six batters he faced.

Fox quickly dispatched the Yankee batters, allowing just a meaningless single to Bobby Richardson, when he opened the ninth frame that afternoon. After Yankee reliever Luis Arroyo ended the bottom of that inning by striking out Mike Roarke with the bases loaded, the game went into extra innings.

In the tenth, Fox retired Tony Kubek on a groundout, Maris on a fly ball, and Mantle on a pop fly while his counterpart did much the same in the bottom half of that frame. Fox continued to cruise along in the eleventh, allowing just a single to Skowron. Arroyo gave up a safety to open the bottom of that inning, but then retired the next three batters he faced. Fox opened the twelfth by striking out Arroyo, following that up by inducing Richardson to line out to left field. But then he surrendered a single to Kubek, bringing Maris to the plate with one on and two gone.

Although Maris did not hit Fox in two previous at-bats earlier that summer, he seemed primed to do so that day. He homered the day before and hit a triple off of Jim Bunning in the sixth inning of this game, so his swing was back in the groove. Fox ran the count to 2–1 before delivering a curve that did not break as well as he would have liked. It was low and on the outside part of the plate, but "I got a little too much of the plate with it," Fox admitted. "You don't want it to hurt you, but if he breaks the record, fine. That's what the game is." Maris jumped all over it. "I knew it was the one I had been waiting for all day," he said. "The swing … the good swing. The crack of bat against ball. Then the ball sailing far out toward the outfield," Maris reminisced. "I heard that sharp ping of ball on bat," Ralph Houk said. "The drive seemed to shoot out of a gun barrel."[115]

Like the earlier triple, the ball traveled in the same direction, right-center field. Maris noticed right fielder Al Kaline and center fielder Bill Bruton both racing after it as he rounded first not sure if either was going to catch up with it. When he saw it strike the façade between the first and second decks 400 feet away, he knew number 58 was in the books, tying him with Jimmie Foxx and Hank Greenberg. And after Arroyo shut the Tigers down in the bottom of that inning for a win, the Yankees had just two more victories to go before becoming league champions.

Unlike after the doubleheader two days earlier, Maris sat in front of his locker as two dozen reporters hurled questions at him. Yes, he said, "It's the greatest thrill I've ever had in baseball…. I thought I'd have some pretty good seasons but never anything like this. If I never hit another home run, I'll always remember this one." When reminded that he had only three more games to catch Ruth in the limit dictated by Ford Frick, he responded, "I think it ought to count no matter how many games I have to play. It's a season, isn't it? If I get to 61, that'll be more than anybody else." He even joked around with his teammates. Moose Skowron, author of the throwing error that sent the game into extra innings, yelled to Maris in the clubhouse, "Hey, where would you be without me? You'd be a nothin' … a big nothin'." Maris gave him his due, noting that it was "the most beautiful error" he ever saw. And when Luis Arroyo said to him, "I got my sixty [relief appearances], let's see you get yours," all Maris could do was laugh.[116]

Home Run # 59—Game 155—September 20—Night Game

The Yankees had a day off to travel to Baltimore, Babe Ruth's birthplace, to take on the Orioles for four games starting with a doubleheader on September 19. In the clubhouse after the September 17 game, Maris, feeling like he was almost at the breaking point, suggested to Mantle and Bob Cerv that he might ask Ralph Houk if he could sit out one of the games. He thought he would be better off remaining on the bench than slogging through back-to-back games in which he was likely to contribute nothing. His teammates immediately argued he would be making a big mistake to do so. "Rogge," Mantle said, "you can't sit out any games now. As long as this thing is going on, you have to play…. People would really wonder what you were thinking." Cerv told Maris, "I want you to play every game at least until you pass 154. You don't need a day off that badly. We have an off day tomorrow [September 18]." Maris relented. "In the circumstances I guess it would have looked pretty silly for me to stay out for no reason." Besides, he reasoned, Houk would not allow him to miss a game since the Yankees still had not captured the pennant. There were press rumors that Maris did ask Houk to sit out the first game because Steve Barber, a left-hander he had great difficulty hitting, was pitching; Maris hotly denied that was true. "I certainly will face Barber tomorrow," he categorically stated when asked. It was a clear indication, though, that the pressure on him was to the point that he wanted to get away from it all.[117]

Baltimore's Memorial Stadium was one of Maris' two least favorite venues, the other being Griffith Stadium. The only homer he hit there that season so far was the one off of Skinny Brown on July 17 that did not count because the game was called due to rain before the fifth inning was completed. Coming into the doubleheader, Maris had just two hits in 18 at-bats in the Baltimore stadium. On top of that, he had difficulty hitting any of the Orioles' pitchers, regardless of where he faced them. He managed just 11 safeties—including three home runs, the fewest among all the teams—in 53 at-bats in 1961. Yankees catcher Elston Howard knew how problematic it would be for Maris to smack any homers in Baltimore, let alone two to tie and three to break the record. "It's going to be no picnic for Roger," he said. "All I'm saying is that he's got a tough job. It's not only those pitchers. It's the ball park. You've got to pull the ball good and sharp or you're swinging for the long fences in right center and dead center." And if that were not enough, Hurricane Esther was making its way up the Atlantic coast, with forecasts for rising winds and rain in the Baltimore area. No one knew how it would affect the games, let alone if they would even get the four in.[118]

The Orioles were primed and ready for Maris. Steve Barber and Skinny Brown both hoped Maris would break the record, but not off of them. According to Baltimore catcher Gus Triandos, "Steve will pitch him tough. He'll pitch his slider on the outside—up a little. And he'll hope to get his sinker down and in close to Maris." Brown said, "I'll start him off with knuckle balls ... after Barber faces him. If I don't get the knuckle ball over, I'll try a change of pace. I don't want him hitting my fast ball. Let him hit junk, and if he can get that out of the park in Baltimore, good luck to him." Milt Pappas, scheduled to start the third game, planned to pitch Maris away with his fastball, in with his slider, and with "junk" over the plate. "And let him jump at that," he said. But then Pappas added a curious statement. Claiming that Maris was going "to get our best," if he did park one off of him, "I not going to be broken hearted."[119]

Before the two games that night, Whitey Herzog, Maris' friend and former teammate now playing for Baltimore, contacted Maris and asked if he would accompany him to a local hospital to visit a four-year-old boy dying of leukemia. Maris agreed, but only if the press were not informed about it, a policy he followed whenever he visited children in a hospital. Someone did find out about it and brief accounts of his visit appeared in several newspapers and *The Sporting News* a few days later.[120]

Maris was shaken when he saw how gravely ill the youngster was; he died a few days later. "[I]t took my mind completely off my problems and the ball game," he acknowledged. "I hated to see the little fellow lying there with so many big problems." By visiting the child, though, Maris was missing a previously-arranged interview with Milton Gross, sportswriter for the *New York Post*. By all accounts, Gross, not knowing where Maris was, exploded at the perceived slight. He told the Yankee front office that he would "destroy" Maris for standing him up. In the movie *61**, the character Milton Khan is a thinly-disguised depiction of Gross. Khan was portrayed as being angry at Maris for not showing up, "but not as wild-eyed as my father would have been," according to Gross' daughter, Jane.[121]

If Gross was that furious at Maris, he must have gotten over it quickly, for it did not show in any of his columns written at the time. In fact, he met with Maris several times during those days after the incident, including joining him and his wife for dinner the evening of October 1 after Maris had hit his record-breaking sixty-first. The only thing that could possibly be construed as negative was in his column on September 22 when he expressed his opinion that Mantle was more deserving than Maris of the American League Most Valuable Player Award, a feeling shared by many other columnists.[122]

It was a complete circus when Maris arrived at the ballpark. Reporters and photographers followed him everywhere he went, and he did his best to answer questions and pause for photos. "This is the darnedest thing I've ever been connected with," joked one New York scribe. "This guy hasn't been able to do anything like a normal human being for two months. If he hasn't got ulcers by now, he'll never get them." Baltimore manager Luman Harris informed the press that he was going to meet with his pitchers before the games to remind them not to go easy on Maris. The Orioles still had a shot at second place and he wanted to win. "I'm going to tell them to pitch Maris the same way we've always pitched him. He never has hurt us too much."[123]

Mantle was unable to start either of the two games because he was suffering from what he thought was the flu and, with his temperature over 100, was simply too weak to play. He did pinch-hit in the bottom of the ninth in the first game, striking out with two away to end the contest. For Maris, it went the way he feared. Steve Barber was dominant in the first game, surrendering just four hits, none of them to hm. He walked in the first, popped out to first to end the third, grounded to first to open the sixth, and flew out to right in the eighth. The Orioles managed a run off of Whitey Ford in the first inning, which was all they needed with Barber's masterful performance.

It was pretty much the same for Maris facing Skinny Brown in the second game. Unlike the rained out affair on July 17, he had a difficult time getting much off of Brown's knucklers and changeups. He did hit an infield single in the third to put Tony Kubek into scoring position, but popped out, grounded out, and flew out in his other trips to the plate. In his final at-bat, Hoyt Wilhelm struck him out to open the ninth frame. The slugger brought the crowd to its feet in the seventh when he tattooed a Brown slip pitch, but with a strong wind blowing in, it curved foul just as it approached the right-field foul pole. On the next pitch, he flew out to center. Fortunately, though, the other Yankees did get to Brown, driving in three runs before he was lifted after eight. With Bud Daley pitching a complete one-run game, New York reduced its magic number to a single game.[124]

Maris was stoic in the post-game interview, responding calmly to queries hurled at him. He made no excuses for his performance that night. "The wind, of course, didn't help any, but I didn't hit many balls very good either." To the question of whether he could hit three homers in the next game to surpass the Babe, Maris rejoined, "You'd have to be almost a Houdini to hit three in one game, especially in this ball park." He again expressed his irritation at Ford Frick for his edict. "Physically, I've got nine more games before the season ends," he explained. "But as far as Mr. Frick is concerned, I've got one more to go."[125]

Right-hander Milt Pappas was slated to open for the Orioles the night of September 20. His rise to the big leagues was nothing short of meteoric. He was signed by the Orioles out of high school as a pitching phenom pursued by a number of clubs, including his hometown Tigers, but chose Baltimore because they promised him a major league contract. The 6-foot-3, 190-pound non-bonus player was immediately added to the Baltimore roster, but in mid–July was placed on the disabled list on the recommendation of a physician who believed "the lad's bone structure was 'not sufficiently matured to stand the stress of major league pitching.'" The Orioles kept him around, however, to pitch batting practice. When commissioner Ford Frick found out about it, he ordered Pappas be reactivated, thus requiring the team to send another player down to the minors. After pitching two games in relief, giving up one earned run in three innings, the 18-year-old was sent to the team's affiliate in Knoxville. But Pappas was recalled to the Orioles in September after only a few appearances with the Smokies; he never again played in a minor league game. He relieved in two games upon his return, ending his first major league experience with a 1.00 ERA over nine innings of work.[126]

The teenager was fortunate in that he came under the tutelage of manager Paul Richards, who had a knack for developing young moundsmen. Pappas came in to the league with an "overpowering" fastball which "jumps and moves all over the place," but Richards and his staff worked with him on adding a curve, a "wicked-breaking slider," and a "palm pitch" which he threw with the same motion as his fastball, but without snapping his wrist. Harry Brecheen, Baltimore's pitching coach, described him as "a real power pitcher. In fact, I think he's got more

On September 20 the "brash, cocky and bullheaded" Milt Pappas was the starting pitcher in game 155 with Maris needing two home runs to "officially" tie Babe Ruth for the home-run record. The Orioles right-hander claimed years later that he informed Maris the night before the big game that he was going to serve up nothing but fastballs because he wanted him to have a chance at the record in the timeframe dictated by Ford Frick. In the fourth inning, Maris hit number 59 off the unpredictable pitcher.

hard stuff than anyone in the league. He can use his fast ball more than most pitchers, since he has one that sinks and one that rises, and the batters don't get used to it as quickly."[127]

Pappas quickly demonstrated that he had the stuff and the poise to become an excellent major league pitcher. He made his first start of the 1958 season on April 17, tossing 3⅓ innings without allowing a run. He secured his first major league victory on May 4, defeating the Tigers in a seven-inning outing in which he gave up one run while striking out six and walking three. His first complete game occurred on June 6, a 3–1 whipping of the Kansas City Athletics. By the end of the summer he compiled a respectable 10–10 record with three complete games on a 4.06 earned-run average.

Pappas started the 1959 season in fine form, pitching all nine innings to defeat the Washington Senators, 4–3, in his first start. He then struggled a bit before hitting his stride again in July, finishing the month with an 11–5 record and two saves on a 3.71 ERA. He added four more wins—and four more losses—and lowered his ERA to 3.27 by season's end, making him and veteran knuckleballer Hoyt Wilhelm the two best pitchers on the Orioles staff. His 15 complete games were second most in the American League while his four shutouts came in third. He, along with his 20-year-old teammates Jerry Walker and Jack Fisher, were "among the most brilliant hill prospects in the American League." His 15 wins against 9 losses marked the first of nine consecutive seasons in which he posted a winning record.[128]

Along with his obvious pitching abilities, Pappas early on developed a reputation for brashness and extreme self-confidence that bordered on arrogance. Even he admitted as much. "I've had the reputation of being brash, cocky and bullheaded," he announced with some pride. "I'm probably the worst that's ever been." Paul Richards told the story of when he first met Pappas while trying to sign him. Halfway through the skipper's "sales talk," the 18-year-old high schooler stopped him, saying, "You don't have to give me all this bull, Mr. Richards. I'm going to sign with Baltimore anyway." Richards said later, "I thought at the time he needed a trip to the woodshed, but I was glad to get him on my side and there has certainly been no cause for regrets since then."

He became known for his grousing and carping and his complaining about his aches and pains. He often irritated his managers by talking back and by verbalizing his grievances to the press when he felt wronged, and he angered umpires by arguing with them from the mound if he believed they had made a bad call. He even challenged the official scorer at the end of one game by calling the press box to debate a scoring decision. Many front office personnel considered him a troublemaker, especially during his 10 years as a player representative. "Anger engulfs the Orioles' sometime pitching star and sometime problem child like a huge wave, momentarily blinding his judgment," wrote *The Sporting News*. "But there is no undertow, no grudge. And there is always remorse, and a humble, logical self-analysis." Naturally reporters loved him because he was so approachable and outspoken. "Pappas, a personable sort, is so friendly and articulate that his cockiness is by no mean obnoxious," commented one sportswriter. "He's a newspaperman's delight, always affable and willing to answer questions. He has poise beyond his years, and if he knows it, so what?"[129]

Pappas remained one of the best pitchers in the American League over the following six seasons (1960–1965). He compiled an 85–55 record with 64 complete games and 22 shutouts on a cumulative 3.16 earned-run average. His best season was in 1964 with his 16 wins and seven losses and an excellent 2.97 ERA. Of his 13 complete games, seven were shutouts, including three consecutive no-run games late in the season. He was an All-Star in 1962 and again in 1965, his final summer with the Orioles. And he consistently placed among the top 10 pitchers in the American League in earned-run average, complete games, and shutouts during this period.[130]

In December 1965 Pappas became part of what many consider to be one of the worst trades in baseball history. He, along with reliever Jack Baldschun and journeyman outfielder Dick Simpson, were sent to the Cincinnati Reds for future Hall-of-Fame outfielder/first baseman Frank Robinson. It turned out to be a lopsided deal in favor of the Orioles. In his first season with the Baltimore, Robinson won the Triple Crown, the American League Most Valuable Player Award, and the Hickok Belt as the professional athlete of the year and led the Orioles to a four-game sweep of the Dodgers in the World Series. Pappas, on the other hand, barely managed a 12–11 season and his earned-run average jumped from 2.60 in 1965 to 4.29 in 1966. At the time, though, it did not appear to be that bad of a swap. Pappas was considered one of the best right-handers in the American League. He never had a losing season and held the all-time team record for wins, shutouts, complete games, and innings pitched. The pitcher was stunned when he was informed of his trade. "I have no bitterness, though," he said. "I've been paid well here and I've produced, I think."[131]

Cincinnati fans, angered at the loss of Robby, never really embraced their new pitcher, which may account for his mediocre first summer with the team in 1966. The fact that he had arm and knee problems added to his ineffectiveness that season. He was so troubled by his performance—12–11, 4.29 ERA—that he considered retiring at the end of the season. That was just a momentary feeling, for he was back in a Reds uniform the following spring. He bounced back in 1967, winning 16 and losing 13 while lowering his ERA to 3.35. But when he managed only two wins against five losses with a huge 5.60 ERA at the start of the 1968 campaign, he was sent packing as part of a six-player trade with the Atlanta Braves on June 11. The pitcher was in favor of the swap. As the Reds player representative, he often clashed with Bob Howsam, the team's general manager, and felt the change of scenery would do both him and the club good.[132]

Pappas' tenure with the Braves did not last long, however. He did produce a 10–8 record in Atlanta and his 2.37 earned-run average was best on the team. But in "The Year of the Pitcher" when the major league batting average was .237, the lowest ever, it was not necessarily indicative of things to come. In fact, his combined 12 wins against 13 defeats with the Reds and Braves was his first losing season ever. The 1969 campaign was even worse. He struggled through an injury-plagued season in which he managed just six wins as opposed to 10 losses in 144 innings pitched, his fewest since 1958. He managed only one complete game and another outing of 9⅓ innings, but 21 of his 26 game appearances lasted seven or fewer innings. True to his somewhat combative nature, Pappas announced he would retire "before I wear this uniform [Atlanta's] again. Play me or trade me." Paul Richards, now the Braves' vice-president, stated pointedly, "Pappas had better grow up."[133]

Pappas, who sustained a slight fracture in the ring finger on his right hand, spent the first part of 1970 pitching for Atlanta from the bullpen. After an inconsistent first half of the season in which he went 2–2 with an enormous 6.06 ERA, the Braves sold the unhappy and struggling pitcher to the Chicago Cubs where he found new life. The Cubs immediately inserted him into the starting rotation and, though he lost his first outing with them, he then won four straight starts that included three complete games, one of them a shutout.

Suddenly Pappas was "the Cubs' new ace," thus disproving his reputation as being unable to go a full nine innings. "Prior to coming to the Cubs, Pappas had been considered a colossal flop," noted *The Sporting News*. "The Braves, indeed, were so disappointed in him that they might have given him away for a cheese sandwich." Admitting that he had been a "five-inning pitcher" with Atlanta, he explained that his turnaround was due to having the opportunity to go deep into a game. "I haven't been to the seventh, eighth and ninth innings because they [Atlanta] never let me go that far. After a while you begin believing it yourself." Pappas seemed to tire at the end of the season, losing three of his last four starts, but ended with a 10–8 record and an excellent ERA of 2.68 in a Cubs uniform. "I just love this city," he proclaimed after the season. "And I love playing for the Cubs. You know, all that day ball—it's great!" And the fans responded in kind. "I'm very flattered by it all," he said. "I never had anything like this before. I've only been here three months and everyone's treating me fantastically. I just want to stay here forever. I feel like I've finally found a home."[134]

The 32-year-old hurler responded to this positive change by producing two of the best seasons in his 17-year career. In 1971, he pitched over 261 innings, the most by far that he had ever done before. He also won a career-high 17 games while losing 14 with 14 complete games, five of them shutouts, most in the American League. In 1972, Pappas experienced an even better season. Not only did he tie his career high of 17 wins—including all of his last 11 starts—he did it while losing half the number of games he did the summer before. His 2.77 earned-run average was tenth best in the American League and he placed in the top 10 in wins, won-loss percentage, fewest walks and hits per nine innings, and fewest walks per nine innings.

The high—and low—point of that summer occurred in a game on September 2 against the San Diego Padres when he was one out away from a perfect game. Pappas had pinch-hitter Larry Stahl at 1-2 when home plate umpire Bruce Froemming called the next three pitches, sliders on the outside part of the plate, balls. After walking Stahl, the pitcher induced Garry Jestadt to pop out to second for a no-hitter. Pappas was angry at the time, a feeling that grew into fury as the years passed. "I can't fault Froemming," he commented some ten years after the event. "He called a good game. He called them as he saw them. But to this day I think that pitch should have been a strike." Much later he convinced himself that the umpire had it in for him and had intentionally "ruined" his perfect game. "Any one of the four [balls] could've been called a strike and the last two were definitely strikes," he insisted. Froemming's "reaction was a smirk, as if to say, I showed you, didn't I.... I know in my heart until my dying day that Bruce Froemming robbed me of a perfect game, and I believe he did it deliberately." As to why the umpire would do that to him, Pappas never explained.[135]

After an off-year in 1973 in which he was 7–12 with a 4.28 ERA, Pappas was released by the Cubs on April 1, 1974. He compiled a lifetime record of 209 wins—110 in the American League, 99 in the National League—against 164 losses and hurled 129 complete games with 43 shutouts in 3,186 innings pitched while maintaining a cumulative 3.40 earned-run average. "I think I had a helluva career," he said in retrospect. "When I broke in, nobody thought I was going to be around too long. But I was extremely fortunate, especially to last as long as I did, to win that many games and to get a no-hitter."[136]

It was a blustery, rainy morning that greeted Baltimore on September 20. The remnants of Hurricane Esther, with winds expected to gust over 20 miles per hour, did not bode well for the game that night. If cancelled, it would mean a doubleheader the following day. It would also interfere with a nationally televised broadcast planned for that evening. But the rains slackened in early afternoon and the winds, although still blowing in, were not at the level originally feared; the game would go on.

Maris spent the night at the home of Whitey Herzog, his friend from his Kansas City days and the Orioles left fielder. They did not speak of the game, but as they arrived at the ballpark that afternoon, Herzog told Maris, "I hope you hit three homers and we beat you, 4–3." Maris simply smiled and walked away. He found his teammates in a jovial mood when he walked into the clubhouse; they all knew that a win that day would clinch the pennant. As he dressed at his locker, he "felt like everyone was studying me to see how I was reacting, to see if I were cracking up. I felt like a freak in a sideshow." His teammates left him alone. "They knew I was under enough pressure without having to talk about it." Even most of the reporters gave him a break from their endless questioning. "They would come up, mutter a few words of encouragement, and walk away." No one wanted "to break the spell that seemed to be encircling the whole field."[137]

Maris admitted he was "a nervous wreck.... I put on my uniform and started pacing the floor. I was trying to keep my mind clear of the game, trying to think about anything but baseball. I'd walk around, pick up things and study them, trying to find something to do with my hands. I looked at all the newspapers lying around and smoked a few cigarettes. I knew that if I just sat down in front of my locker I'd tighten up in a hundred knots." It rained just before game-time, ending any hope of having batting practice to ease some of the tremendous strain he was under. "It was as if a mysterious pressure was pushing down on the whole park."[138]

At some point, Maris came into Ralph Houk's office "almost in tears." He beseeched the manager to take him out of the lineup. "He said he was tired, worn down, and really didn't want to play," Houk disclosed. "I kept thinking that there was a big crowd, and all the fans wanted to see Roger. And Roger had come so far and gotten so close to the record, that it would be a real shame if he took a day off at this point." The skipper asked Maris to at least start the game and if he still wanted to be benched after a couple of innings, Houk would do so. With that promise, Maris agreed to play. "We talked a little bit more, and he went out and played, and that was the end of it."[139]

At long last it was time to start the show. Teammates wandered by to wish him luck as he sat in the dugout anxiously waiting for the call to play ball. He was so "fogged in.... I don't even remember who said what." Suddenly he found himself kneeling in the on-deck circle while Tony Kubek took his at-bat. Maris noted that Milt Pappas "was getting the ball up a little instead of throwing those grounders he usually pitches. This was good. I figured if he could come over the plate with a couple of strikes I might have a good chance to hit one." Maris had hit a homer off of him in 1959 and again in 1960, but generally batted poorly against the right hander. In the current season, the slugger managed just two walks and a single off the Baltimore pitcher in eight plate appearances. He struck out once and popped out four times in his other trips to the plate. There was no guarantee Maris would be able to take him deep this time even if he did get the pitch he wanted.[140]

But Pappas wanted to see Maris hit one out. He claimed years after the fact that he ran into Maris and Mantle as the three were leaving the stadium after the doubleheader the night before. "I think it's really horse shit the commissioner has to come out and say this with the year you're having," he allegedly told Maris. "I'm going to throw you nothing but fast balls. I want to see you break the damn record." According to him, Maris, stunned by his statement, asked if he were serious. "Damn right, Roger. I want to see you break the record." Pappas supposedly informed him that if he shook his head, he was intending to throw a fastball.[141]

Many question whether Pappas actually told Maris and Mantle about his intentions beforehand; we have only his word for it. But true or not, it would not have been out of character for him to groove pitches to Maris. Indeed, just a few days before the game, he indicated that he would not be "broken hearted" if Maris jacked one off of him. But even if Maris knew what Pappas was going to throw him, it did not make a home run a sure thing. As Baltimore teammate Dick Williams explained, "But knowing what's coming can screw up hitters, which is why most don't want to know."[142]

In any event, Maris did not hit a home run in his first at-bat. As he approached the plate, "I had only one thing on my mind. Whatever happened, I was determined I was going to give it my best shot. I was going down, if I went down, trying my best.... I was going to try for three homers, but three ... two ... one ... or none, I was ready to give it everything I had." With Bobby Richardson on first because of an error, Maris connected with one that shot down the line, but Earl Robinson hauled it in just a few feet from the 14-foot high wall in right. "He nailed it," said Ralph Terry, the Yankees starting pitcher. "But right into the teeth of that wind in right. On a normal day, it's outta there."[143]

Pappas gave up a run in the second on a Clete Boyer single with Moose Skowron on third after hitting a triple. Between innings, Houk glanced at Maris sitting down from him. "Roger had looked paler than usual on the bench. He never said a word to anyone." In the third, Maris came up for the second time ready to swing away. He said something to catcher Gus Triandos, who responded jokingly, "Roger, quit talking to me or people will think I'm getting you good pitches." Maris then "fiddled around, patted the dirt with his shoes, dug in." The first pitch was a ball inside. On the next, Maris swung and missed. The third was another ball. Then on the fourth pitch, Pappas, who claimed he shook his head "a couple of times" to let Maris know what was coming, delivered a fastball right where the slugger liked it, low and outside. "I timed it just right, swung and felt that this time I had connected for one." With a strong wind blowing in from right, Maris was uncertain if it had enough juice to clear the right-field wall. "I was really hoping that it would hit the seats as I neared first base, then I saw it disappear." As he circled the bases to the roar of the crowd and his teammates, "I was only conscious of the fact that, at least, I had come to the end of Mr. Frick's road still battling, still alive."[144]

As he crossed the plate, Maris was greeted by Yogi Berra, who was batting fourth and covering left field because Mantle was still out of the lineup. If Pappas was grooving pitches to Maris, he must have included Berra in his plans as well because the Yankee great parked one in the right-field seats for back-to-back homers. Johnny Blanchard followed with a single, and when Elston Howard doubled to drive him in, Pappas was lifted for 6-foot-6 outfielder-turned-pitcher Dick Hall. Baltimore manager Luman Harris said afterwards, "I think the Yankees were getting Pappas's pitches someway. We tried to find out how they were doing it, but couldn't. I know they swung at Hall a lot different than they did Pappas." He also may have suspected that Pappas was intentionally tossing fat pitches to Maris. "The homer he hit off Pappas was a low fast ball. He'd hit 80 a year if the pitchers put them all there," he commented.[145]

Right-hander Hall was still on the mound when Maris came up in the fourth inning for his third attempt to tie or break Ruth's record. As he stepped into the box with two gone and Kubek on first, he quipped, "Maybe you don't think my tail isn't tight." Fans and players alike were screaming for him to hit another one. "[O]nce he settled into his stance there was utter silence. Some of the fans were holding onto their seats as though they were in a roller coaster which was just approaching the top of the hill before plunging down." He took the first two breaking pitches for strikes before unleashing his powerful swing on the third crooked pitch, smashing a ball that the wind pushed foul as it approached the seats in right. "He was 20 feet short and 20 feet foul of tying Ruth," as one columnist described it. Maris then struck out on a high fastball to end the inning. "I was trying too hard. I wasn't waiting for my pitch."[146]

Baltimore plated a couple off of Ralph Terry in the sixth to close the gap to two runs, 4–2. In the top of the seventh, Maris strode to the plate for the fourth time; Hall was still toeing the rubber. Maris took the first pitch, then hammered the next. "It gave the crowd a thrill but not me—I could see right away it was going to land on the wrong side of the foul pole. Just another loud strike." Maris connected again on the very next pitch. "It was a fast ball, but I wanted to just show it to him outside," explained Hall after the game. "I got it too close to the plate and he almost lost it. I wanted to waste it and come back in with something else.... If he hit that one just a little lower on the bat it was gone for sure." Maris believed he had gotten all of it. "This time I thought I had done it. It was high up towards right field but as I ran toward first I saw the wind catch it and the ball died about 10 feet from the wall in right." As the right-fielder hauled it in, Maris feared that it might be his last at-bat of the game.[147]

But his teammates came to his assistance. Although the Yankees did not score a run in the eighth, they did manage to get two runners on base, thus insuring that Maris would come up third in the ninth inning. At the end of that frame, Luman Harris made a call to the Orioles bullpen to tell knuckleball artist Hoyt Wilhelm to start warming up. The manager knew Maris had one more shot at tying the record and he was determined to prevent him from doing so. "They just didn't want Roger to set [tie] the record in Ruth's hometown," claimed Baltimore left fielder Whitey Herzog. "I'm convinced of that." So was home plate umpire Ed Runge. "We thought Harris had Wes Stock and Billy Hoeft in the bullpen and Maris would have had a chance against either one of those fellows. But Harris made it as tough as possible by going with Wilhelm. It's virtually impossible to hit a homer off those knucklers. Roger's only chance was a pitch that got away from Wilhelm, a pitch that didn't break."[148]

Maris' heart sank when he saw Wilhelm stride to the mound to open the ninth. He had gotten a homer, a double, and two singles off of the pitcher in 1960, but other than that he was 0-for-16, including a strikeout the night before. Maris proclaimed Wilhelm "absolutely the last guy in the world I wanted to see" in that final frame. Before stepping to the plate, he turned to home plate umpire Ed Runge and asked, "Ed, what does this fellow throw?" Maris' humor and calm demeanor in the face of such pressure greatly impressed the arbiter. "I thought that was quite a remark. Here was Maris in his 154th game, with his last chance to tie Ruth's record, and he was cool enough to make a joke."[149]

Wilhelm stared in, resolute in his determination not to give Maris anything but junk to hit. "All I know is that I didn't want him hitting any home run off of me," he declared. "I gave him the best knuckleball I could throw and figured more power to him if he could hit it out." Regardless of the outcome, Maris planned to swing away, even if it meant striking out. He never got the chance, however. The slugger fouled off the first pitch with a half-hearted stroke. On the second, "I started forward with my body, but I didn't let my bat go. I didn't check it. I didn't swing and that last time I wanted to have a full swing." Instead, the ball struck the bat and dribbled back to Wilhelm, who snatched it up and tagged Maris on his way to first base. It was an anticlimactic conclusion to an historic game.[150]

Maris turned and trotted out to his position in center field. As he passed Charlie Berry, the umpire told him, "You gave it a good try, son." Johnny Blanchard, playing right field, caught up to Maris and handed him his glove. "I could see he was disappointed, so I told him how proud I was just to be on the same team with him. Roger smiled at me." When Ralph Terry eliminated all three batters he faced in the bottom of the ninth, the Yankees were American League champions for the twenty-sixth time.[151]

As the winners celebrated in the clubhouse afterwards, Maris stood and faced the media once again. He was both disappointed and elated at the same time. His eyes, wrote one reporter, "told of happiness, of pride, and of a feeling of relief." He said he wanted to do it in 154 games, but was satisfied with what he did accomplish. "I tried hard all night, but I got only one. Now that it's all over, I'm happy with what I got." As far as Ford Frick's pronouncement was concerned, he "makes the rules. If all I will be entitled to will be an asterisk, it will be all right with me." Several months after that game, he reflected on how it was a turning point for him emotionally. "I think it was at a peak that night," he said. "After that I think now that I began to go downhill emotionally."[152]

Maris won over a number of fans and sportswriters by his performance that night. "One thing is certain," wrote Bob Maisel in the Baltimore *Sun*, "nobody will ever be able to accuse Roger Maris of not having the stomach to battle the tensest of situations right down to the end. He proved that last night, earning a standing ovation from the crowd when he trotted from the field." One Baltimore fan in particular was effusive in his praise of the slugger. "I came in here hoping the guy would never hit another home run, and I left pulling for him to tie Ruth. I never would have believed it possible, but he gave it such a try he converted me."[153]

But many others in the press had little praise for Maris, some gloating he had failed to tie Ruth in 154 games, others downright nasty and petty in their criticism of him. Oliver Kuechle, sports editor for the *Milwaukee Journal*, cruelly expressed the contempt for Maris some critics felt. His failure to break Ruth's record "evokes no great regrets here." If Ruth's record were to be broken, "it should be by somebody of greater baseball stature and of greater color and public appeal." Maris, Kuechle asserted, "is not more than a good big league ball player. He is colorless. He has never hit .300 in the majors. He has little of the imposing physique at the plate commonly associated with the true slugger. He has been only average in the field. He is often surly.... There just isn't anything deeply heroic about the man."[154]

In his column for the *Boston Herald*, George Frazier prayed that his sons "never be like Roger Maris. Anything, please, God but that—not even if he were to hit a 100 home runs!" Calling Maris a "whiner" and claiming he lacked "grace under pressure," Frazier compared him unfavorably to teammate Mickey Mantle, "who had been out there day after day through the long season with never a whimper, with only the knifing of the pain inside his body, with only his immense skills and his consummated grace under pressure." Frazier nastily concluded his rant against him by calling on fans to "observe a moment of silence while we burp Roger Maris, home run hitter and endorser of many emoluments, none of them, ironically, a diaper service. Now then, if you will please pass the pablum."[155]

Arthur Daley of the *New York Times*, though far less harsh in his reaction, still referred to Maris as "a glorious failure." Even the generally supportive *New York Post* expressed some pleasure in Maris' failure to break the record by the Frick-

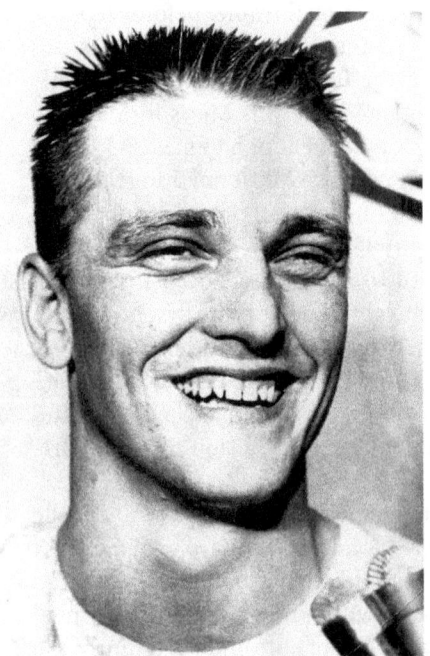

Roger Maris is all smiles after hitting number 59 on September 20. "Now," he mistakenly thought, "it's all over and things will quiet down."

imposed deadline. "Babe Ruth's record stands," trumpeted the paper's editorialist, "and only fools will suggest that any home runs Maris hits in the remaining games of the expanded schedule can be equated with Ruth's achievement."[156]

Home Run # 60—Game 159—September 26—Night Game

If Maris thought the worst was over and he could go about his business without the intrusive gaze of press and public, he was sadly mistaken. While fewer reporters dogged his steps and fan attendance at games in which he played declined, there was still immense public interest in whether or not he could surpass Ruth in what remained of the season. "When I got up the next day, I felt sure that things would quiet down," he recalled. "I hadn't hit sixty in 154 games, things would now start to get normal." Peace he may have wanted, but peace he did not get. "It's worse than ever now," he discovered.[157]

Prior to the game on September 21, Lou Grasmick, a local businessman who pitched five innings in the majors in 1948, drove Maris to a nearby market to see if he could acquire the fifty-ninth home run ball. Bob Reitz, an unemployed laborer, caught the ball, but refused to surrender it the evening before. Maris remained in the car as Grasmick negotiated with Reitz. When Maris was informed Reitz wanted $2,500 for the ball, he responded, "No dice, let's go" and left the area. He also took the opportunity to visit a Baltimore physician about the small patches of hair loss he began experiencing earlier in the month. "I thought I had a disease or something," he said, "but the doctor told me it was a case of nerves from the tension and pressure I've been under." The hair would eventually grow back, he was informed.[158]

He found out very quickly when he arrived at Memorial Stadium that afternoon for the final game with the Orioles that the home run chase was far from over. First, he was informed he was the winner of the Maryland Professional Baseball Players Association's Sultan of Swat Award which would be presented to him at a banquet in the winter. Then to his surprise he was called to the plate prior to the start of the game to receive a special trophy for his "sportsmanship while achieving the ultimate respect and admiration of all Oriole fans." And when the game began, many among the over 22,000 fans in attendance—more even than the night before—were still in a frenzy to see him hit homers.[159]

Young right-hander Jack Fisher was the starter for Baltimore that night. Mantle was still ill, so Maris again took charge of center field. He was the only regular other than Bobby Richardson to take the field that night. Clearly he could have used a break. He was 0-for-4 with a strikeout, hardly the stuff of legend, but he was determined "to play right through. Even if I'm lucky enough to get those two homers, I still won't ask for a day off." Part of the problem, too, was that he continued to swing at bad pitches from hurlers who had no intention of entering the record books as the one who gave up number 60. The Yankees lost, 5–3.[160]

Ralph Houk went out of his way to heap praise on his right fielder after the game. "From the start of the season, Maris' main thoughts were to help the Yankees win the pennant," the manager declared. "Because nobody gave more of himself. Nobody thought more about winning the pennant than Maris. He was strictly unselfish. And he's been through hell." Maris did whatever it took to win a game, explained the manager; he never put the home-run race above team. "The purpose of the game is to win," Houk concluded, "and that's the way Roger played it all the way."[161]

Meanwhile, Ford Frick took the opportunity to reiterate his position on how Maris' accomplishment would be recognized if he tied or broke Ruth's record in the games remaining. He again insisted there would be separate listings, one for the 154-game schedule, the other for the new 162-game schedule. Furthermore, according to him, the same standard would be applied to any other record that happened to be broken. Frick defended his decision by stating his belief that the 162-game model was just a temporary one. "I have every reason to believe that if baseball follows its present trend of expansion we'll be back to 154 games within the next five or six years." Whether Frick actually believed it was just temporary or not only he knew, but it did provide handy cover from some of the harsh criticism he was receiving for making his proclamation in the first place.[162]

The following day the Yankees flew to Boston, so Maris did get a brief respite from his pursuit of Ruth. "It's great to do nothing," he stated. Whitey Ford was trying for his twenty-fifth win when the Yankees took on the Red Sox for a short two-game series in Boston starting the night of September 23. Maris did not homer, but Mickey Mantle, back in the lineup but still feeling weak, hit his fifty-fourth—and final—home run in the first inning to give the Yankees the lead. Ford struggled a bit, but was ahead, 4–3, when he was relieved after five innings of work, enough to give him the victory to end the season with an incredible 25–4 record; not surprisingly, he received the Cy Young Award at the end of the season.[163]

The Bombers played the following afternoon, losing to Bill Monboquette and the Red Sox, 3–1. Mantle, still suffering from a virus, was able to play only six innings, going hitless in three at-bats. Maris again failed to homer, but he did have one single to go along with a walk and two fly outs. The two outs were indicative of the trouble he was having getting his swing back to normal. The first was a fly to center, the second a slicing fly to left, both indicating his inability to pull the ball. On top of that, he was swinging at pitches outside his power zone. "Honest to goodness, a guy could go out of his mind." he confessed. "Every pitch, every ball. You know you're hurting yourself. The average keeps going down. But what good do those bases on balls do? I guess it's my pride—or just plain stubbornness that makes me go after pitches I shouldn't.... But I've got to swing. I've got to give myself a chance. I'd rather go out swinging than go out walking."[164]

But as one reporter noted, much of the growing pressure Maris was experiencing came from him, not from outside factors. "His own anxiety, tension and impatience have been as great a deterrent as have the right arms of pitchers Jack Fisher of Baltimore and Don Schwall and [Bill] Monbouquette for Boston." Feeling especially discouraged after hitting just two singles in the 16 plate appearances since his fifty-ninth homer, Maris feared he might have reached the end of the line. "The way they're pitching me now I'm afraid I'll never get another one. The only way I'll hit one is for the pitcher to make a mistake."[165]

The team had an off-day to travel back to New York on September 25. Pat Maris and Merlyn Mantle were both coming to the city to join their husbands for the final five games of the season. Maris and Mantle had moved from their shared apartment in preparation for their spouses' arrival—Bob Cerv was in the hospital after knee surgery ended his season—which led to a flurry of rumors the two teammates had a major fight and Mantle had moved out as a result. It was a total fabrication, of course, but that type of gossip could not help but raise Maris' irritation level even higher.

After arriving in New York, Mantle visited Dr. Max Jacobson about his lingering illness. "Dr. Feelgood," as he was sometimes called, was recommended by Mel Allen, the

Yankee broadcaster, on the trip home from Boston. "I have a doctor," Allen informed the player. "He'll give you a shot that'll fix you right up." The physician injected Mantle in his hip, striking the bone in the process. "He stuck the needle up too high," Mantle said. "It felt as though he stuck a red hot poker into me. I'm paralyzed." He was able to make it back to his hotel room where he collapsed with a fever. He played the first inning of the game that night, but it marked the end of his regular season. He eventually ended up in an area hospital after the injection site developed a massive infection. The doctors had to lance the wound to let it drain, leaving "a hole so big that you could put a golf ball in it."[166]

Pat Maris arrived the morning of September 26, which gave the couple a chance to visit and relax before the game that night. "I am convinced that having her with me helped relieve a lot of pressure and perhaps made it possible for me to finally reach my goal," he acknowledged.[167]

It was pure bedlam when Maris entered the Yankee clubhouse later that afternoon. Reporters, photographers, and various visitors milled around, all wanting a piece of the slugger. It was so bad that the following day Ralph Houk cleared the clubhouse of all but the players a half hour before the start of the game. Attendance was a third of what it was the last time the Yankees played at home, but the 19,000 fans there that night were just as enthusiastic to see Maris park one.

Taking the ball for Baltimore was 22-year-old right-hander Jack Fisher, part of the corps of fine young pitchers former manager Paul Richards developed. Fisher stymied Maris throughout the season, most recently five days earlier in Baltimore. In fact, Maris managed just two hits off the young hurler in 16 prior plate appearances stretching back to 1959.

Fisher spent just two full seasons in the lower minors before joining the big club in 1959 at the age of 20. The 6-foot-2, 215-pound hurler—nicknamed "Fat Jack" by teammate Hoyt Wilhelm for his tendency to gain weight in the off-season—made his first appearance with the Orioles on April 14, 1959. After the game he was

Right-hander Jack Fisher was pitching for the Baltimore Orioles in 1961 when he faced Maris on the night of September 26. The Yankee slugger, who had difficulty hitting "Fat Jack" during earlier confrontations, had no problems that game, parking this record-tying sixtieth home run deep into the right-field seats at Yankee Stadium in the third inning.

sent to the club's Triple-A affiliate in Miami to hone his skills. He won his first six starts, all complete games, to compile an 8-4 record on a 3.06 earned-run average before being called back up at the end of June. Used mainly in relief the rest of the season, his 1-6 won-loss record was not that impressive, but his 3.05 ERA was excellent. Richards firmly believed that his young protégé "is going to be a great pitcher."[168]

Baltimore gave the Yankees a run for their money in 1960 until New York reeled off 15 straight victories at the end of the season to claim the American League pennant. The Orioles' successful performance that summer was due largely to the team's "Kiddie Korps," a group of five starters and relievers who were 22 years old or younger; Fisher was a key member of that group of infant hurlers. Using a great fastball, an outstanding curve, and an excellent changeup, he fashioned a 12-11 record on a 3.41 ERA in 40 games, half of those in relief. "After facing [Chuck] Estrada, [Steve] Barber, and me, teams hitting against Jack Fisher or Jerry Walker had a tendency to be frustrated at the plate," remembered Milt Pappas about his pitching mate. Although he was inclined to give up too many hits and earned runs—mostly in the latter half of his career—he was stingy in surrendering home runs during his five seasons with Baltimore. In fact, he was third in the American League in fewest home runs per nine innings in 1960, tenth in 1961. While he was not a "mean" pitcher, he was not afraid of throwing inside and hitting a batter on occasion if need be. "I don't enjoy doing it," he admitted, "but I think the point has to be made. It's all part of the game."[169]

The 1960 campaign was Fisher's only winning season in 11 years of major league ball. He was particularly strong at the end of the summer, winning six games in a row, the last three of which were consecutive shutouts. "That season was a lot of fun," Fisher recalled 50 years later. "We were young and dumb enough to think that any time we walked out there, we could beat any team." He became a baseball trivia question after his last appearance of the summer. In a game with the Boston Red Sox on September 28, Fisher took over for Steve Barber with two gone in the first and the Orioles behind, 2-0. He was leading, 4-2, going into the eighth inning when Ted Williams came to the plate for the last at-bat of his career. Fisher delivered a fastball that Williams took deep into the center-field seats for home run number 521. Adding to his miseries, the pitcher gave up two more runs in the bottom of the ninth to lose, 5-4.[170]

Fisher had another solid season in 1961, although his 10-13 record at first blush might indicate otherwise. Part of the problem was that he was a victim of bad fielding behind him. He gave up 104 runs, more than any of the other starters. But 19 of those were unearned, nearly twice as many as Steve Barber, who had 10. He became known as the team's "Hard-Luck Pitcher." On top of that, he seemed to be the unfortunate recipient of bad umpiring in a start on August 30. Although he pitched a complete-game victory, 11-4, he surrendered 12 walks, a club record at the time. Paul Richards believed that home plate umpire Ed Hurley was at fault for the high number of free passes, declaring publicly, "That was Fisher's best game of the year." Hurley, not to be outdone, responded, "Fisher's best game, huh? Well, you can just tell Richards it was my best, too."[171]

A sore shoulder hampered Fisher at the start of the 1962 season. He was placed on the 30-day disabled list during spring training and did not make his first appearance until May 13. And when he did return, he had three good starts, but then struggled after that. Billy Hitchcock, Baltimore's new manager, became irritated with his pitcher's performance, blaming his ineffectiveness on his weight. "If you're too heavy above the waist, you can't keep the ball low for the simple reason that you can't bend during the follow-through," he asserted. "The ball is released high and goes to the hitter the same way." Acting on this belief, Hitchcock assigned Fisher to mostly bullpen duty in the month of June. Naturally, the pitcher resented Hitchcock's contention. "Extra weight doesn't hurt me," he said in response. "I believe it helps."[172]

Fisher did regain his starting position, even managing to toss three complete-game victories in August and September, but his losing record and high 5.09 earned-run average meant his tenure with the Orioles was over. On December 15, he was part of a six-player trade that sent him to the San Francisco Giants, marking the second half of his career as a National League pitcher. "There's a place open on the Giants pitching staff for a No. 4 starter," manager Alvin Dark commented, "and I think Jack Fisher is capable of filling it. Otherwise we wouldn't have made the deal with Baltimore for him."[173]

Fisher's stay with the Giants was short-lived. He was a starter to open the season, but after compiling a 3–7 record with a 4.80 earned-run average, he was relegated to bullpen work. He fit that role well; he made five relief appearances without giving up an earned run before allowing three in a rare start. He relieved in nine more games after that, surrendering just 2 earned runs in those games. By early August he had improved his record to 6–7 and lowered his ERA to 3.58. He stumbled a bit in his next nine games, going 0–3 with a humongous 11.15 earned-run average during that period. After the World Series, the National League held a special draft in an attempt to bring some competitive balance by allowing the Houston Colt .45s and the New York Mets to select a handful of players from the other eight teams; Fisher was chosen by New York.[174]

The now 25-year-old pitcher was not unhappy about the move. The only thing he wanted was to pitch regularly in the starting rotation, which was what he got. "If I get into regular rotation next season [1964], I'll be able to keep my weight down. Nobody says anything about my weight when I win," he noted. Over the next four summers, Fisher became the mainstay of the Mets pitching staff. He hurled over 200 innings in each of those seasons, more than any other of his teammates except for Tom Seaver in 1967. He had an awful 38–73 won-loss record and a less than impressive 4.12 cumulative earned-run average. He led the league in losses with 24 in 1965 and 18 in 1967, placed in the top 10 in home runs allowed in 1966 and 1967, and led the league in earned runs in 1965 and 1967, but for three of those four years, he was the ace of a team that finished no higher than ninth place.[175]

With the Mets moving toward more youthful pitching, Fisher was traded to the Chicago White Sox in mid–December 1967, again as part of a six-player deal. While his final season with the Mets was mediocre at best—9–18, 4.70 ERA—Chicago was convinced he was the missing ingredient they needed for a championship team. "If we'd had Fisher [in 1967], we could have won the pennant," insisted manager Eddie Stanky. After finishing fourth with a winning record in 1967, the White Sox dropped to eighth in 1968 after losing 95 games. The only starter with a record above .500 was Tommy John, who was out much of the previous season. Even though Fisher pitched much better in 1968 than he had the year before—8–13, 2.99 ERA—it was not enough to help a club that scored the fewest runs in the American League. At the end of the year, he was traded to the Cincinnati Reds for two other players, thus beginning his final season in the majors.[176]

Fisher, willing to take the ball in any capacity when asked, moved back and forth between starting and relieving throughout 1969. Try as hard as he might, however, his best days were behind him. He was often knocked out of the box early when he did get a start and managed no more than seven innings in most of the rest. After ending the campaign at 4–4 with a 5.50 earned-run average, the largest of his major league career, his big league days were over. He attempted to make a comeback in 1970 by playing in the minors, but called it quits when the summer ended. Over 11 major league campaigns, he won 86, lost 139, and maintained a 4.06 cumulative ERA in 400 games, 265 as a starter.

Entering that September 26 contest more centered than he had been in weeks, Maris had a premonition he might take one deep. "I feel real good," he proclaimed during batting practice. "This could be the night. I just have a feeling." He was determined to park one for the Yankee faithful. "They had been great to me all season, now perhaps I could give them what they wanted ... if I got lucky," he thought as he waited for the game to begin. In the first inning, he singled to center with two away. Mantle, who played just that first inning because he was still ill, was walked before Fisher got the final out. That was his final at-bat of the regular season. The infection around the site of the shot became so infected that he was hospitalized on September 28.[177]

The Orioles grabbed two runs off of Yankee starter Bud Daley in the second inning, giving them a 2–0 lead when Maris came to the plate in the third with two out. With both Pat Maris and Merlyn Mantle, who were seated side-by-side, and Claire Ruth in the stands, Jack Fisher ran the count to 2–2 before letting lose with the fifth pitch of Maris' at-bat. "I wound up, and in the middle of my delivery, I decided to take a little bit off," the pitcher said nearly 40 years later. "And when I did, all the ball did was just run up there. As soon as I let it go, I knew I was in trouble. It was one of those you'd like to run down there and catch it." The ball came in belt-high over the heart of the plate, the mistake-pitch Maris hoped he would get.[178]

"Fisher was bearing down and trying to get me," Maris recalled. "He was mixing them up, then I saw it coming. It was a high curve. I swung, connected, and heard the roar of the crowd. The ball was high enough and far enough ... but was it foul?" Maris took a few steps toward first, then stood and watched the flight of the ball, still holding onto his bat. As the ball passed into the right-field stands a few feet fair, Maris dropped his bat as he began his home-run trot, head down as usual, lost in a fog. The ball crossed into the upper deck, struck a step near an empty seat six rows back, then rebounded onto the field. Right fielder Earl Robinson retrieved it, gave it to first-base umpire Ed Hurley, who in turn handed it to Yankee first base coach Wally Moses; there would be no fruitless negotiations with a fan for this one.[179]

The over 19,000 spectators in attendance leapt "to its feet and began to roar at the crack of the bat, [and] gave him a standing breath-taking ovation which no one present could ever forget." Maris shook hands with Hector Lopez and the batboys as he crossed home plate before entering the dugout to the congratulations and backslaps of his teammate. "Rog' came back to the bench in a daze," Ralph Houk remembered. "The entire team rose up, cheering him. The crowd was going wild. Rog' tried to sit down in a corner. He was yanked, pushed, shoved up the steps. He acted like a schoolgirl who's just won a knitting prize and has to be pushed on the platform to take a bow." As the crowd continued to cheer and clap, Maris, standing on the top step, removed his cap and waved to the fans in acknowledgment of their support. "I didn't know what to do. Nothing like this had ever happened to me before. I stood and waved my hat, but was in such a daze that I didn't really know what I was doing." In his 684th plate appearance—Ruth hit his sixtieth in plate appearance 687—Maris finally caught that "ghostly sixty," leaving him feeling both relieved and elated. "I couldn't believe I had reached it."[180]

That homer left the Yankees a run behind, but they plated another in the sixth and a third in the seventh to beat the Orioles, 3–2. Maris had two more at-bats, but both of those ended with fly outs. Fisher completed the game and took the loss, which irritated him much more than the home run he surrendered to Maris. "I lost the damn ball game," he said afterwards. "That's the only thing bothering me. What the hell, he never hit one off of me before. I mind every run I give up. I'd rather be the guy who struck him out."[181]

There was pandemonium in the Yankee clubhouse after the game. The Yankee manager described the scene: "Cameramen and newsmen came rushing down to the passageway behind the dugout. They clamored for Roger and the historic ball. Rog' was shot, filmed, interviewed…. I had a mental picture of his being blinded by flash bulbs and beaned the next time he went to bat." Maris and Claire Ruth were interviewed by announcer Red Barber on his postgame television show. After he kissed Mrs. Ruth on her cheek, she told the slugger, "If Babe were here he'd be just as thrilled as I am. Congratulations on a great year and good luck in the Series." Maris, perhaps overly effusive in his response, said, "I'm glad I didn't break Babe Ruth's record. To me this is a record. This is enough for me. It's just as well I didn't do it in 154 games. Don't ask me why. I can't explain it. Just say I'm thrilled with my 60."[182]

He was equally as pleased that the home run ball went deep into the stands. Earlier in the at-bat, he hit a ball off the handle of his bat that landed foul just a couple of rows in. "I'm glad that one didn't make it," he told Mantle. "I'm glad because I didn't hit it good." He did not want anyone disparaging his record-tying homer as a "cheap shot." And, of course, commissioner Ford Frick had to chime in as well. "It's a marvelous thing," said Ruth's acolyte, who was not at the game. "It will go into the books as a record for a 162-game season while Ruth's record stands as the mark for 154 game."[183]

After the interview, Maris came to his locker only to be surrounded by the press. Even though he was anxious to get away because his wife was waiting for him, he stayed and patiently answered all their questions. "First of all," he announced, "I need a beer." After retrieving one from the cooler, he acknowledged that "This is the happiest moment of my life. It's the greatest thing that has happened to me, possibly the greatest thing that will ever happen to me." Always guarded with his emotions, he could not adequately explain to the assembled reporters how he felt as he circled the bases. "I was in a fog. I thought I might feel silly," he said. He admitted how much he wanted to at least tie the record. "Being close, I wanted it. Now I've got it I'm kind of bewildered. I really couldn't say how I feel. Except I feel good." He then added, "I'd like to get one more, just one more." Maris noted, too, the price he paid to get where he was. "I was just thinking what I'd have to put up with from here on in. Let's face it. It hasn't been a picnic." He concluded by holding up the ball, saying, "This is the one I want. The heck with No. 59."[184]

8

OCTOBER

Home Run # 61—Game 163—October 1—Day Game

Maris approached Ralph Houk after the clubhouse was free of reporters to tell the manager he wanted to sit out the game scheduled for the following afternoon. "I know you're tired," Houk responded. "I've known it for a week, but let's talk about it tomorrow morning when you see how you feel." Maris came to the Stadium the following day and told Houk he still wanted a day off; the skipper reluctantly agreed. With just four games left to break the record, some of his teammates and many among the press thought he was making a mistake missing one of them, but as the slugger told one sportswriter, "From up here [tapping his temple] to down here [pointing to his feet], I'm just dead tired. It's been hard, hard not to let this get to me…. I'm shaky. I'm physically tired, but I'm mentally and emotionally tired, too. I just feel done in. There's no point pretending I'm not."[1]

Left-hander Steve Barber was pitching and Maris never did well against him—he did not get a hit off of him at all in 1961—so this game was probably the best of the four to miss. Besides, most of the Yankee regulars were benched as well. Relaxing in the clubhouse, Maris got word around the third inning that Dan Topping, president of the Yankees, wanted to see him. After congratulating the right fielder, Topping suggested Maris ask Houk if he could leave the stadium. The skipper, probably not pleased at the executive's interference, agreed and Maris spent the rest of the day with his wife. With no game scheduled the following day, the break gave him nearly two full days to recuperate. "We really enjoyed this time we had together and never even thought about what might happen the next three days."[2]

Maris came to the ballpark on September 29 rested and ready to play. "I think these two days off have done me a lot of good," he said. "I feel more relaxed than I have been in some time. I'll be swinging freely and if I'm lucky, well, maybe, I'll hit one or two more." He had no safeties, let alone a homer, that night, but he did score the winning run after he was walked in the bottom of the ninth to give the Bombers a victory, 2–1. It was pretty much the same story the following afternoon; he smacked a single in the eighth, but did not come close to parking one. Although he had any number of good pitches to hit, he just was not able to make contact in a way that put the ball in the air. Both Bill Monbouquette and Don Schwall, the Boston starters, said Maris simply failed to take advantage of the opportunities he did have. "The last time up [on September 29], Maris had two pitches that were right down the pipe," Monbouquette claimed. "I was undercutting them," Maris explained. "I gave him six or seven pitches he swung at," noted

280

Schwall about his game on September 30. "That single I gave was the only mistake I made. That pitch was low, as I wanted it, but it was inside where he could hit it." Maris had only one more game to do the seemingly impossible.[3]

Bill Stafford was going for his fourteenth win that final game of the regular season while 23-year-old rookie Tracy Stallard got the assignment for Boston. The 6-foot-5, 200-pound right-hander apprenticed for five years in the Red Sox farm system, including three seasons in the lower minors, before he was promoted to Single-A at the beginning of 1959. He produced a 9–4 record with an outstanding 1.68 earned-run average with the Allentown Red Sox before making the jump to Triple-A later that summer. He appeared in 16 games for the Minneapolis Millers, compiling a losing record but an excellent 2.25 ERA for the American Association team.

Stallard was blessed with an abundance of self-confidence. Shortly before the start of the 1960 campaign when Boston sent him to the minors rather than keep him on the big league roster,

Boston rookie Tracy Stallard became forever associated with Roger Maris when he coughed up number 61 to the new home-run king on October 1, the last game of the season. He said afterwards, "I'm not going to lose any sleep over this. After all, what about the guys who threw the other sixty?"

he announced to all, "Don't forget me. I'll be back with the Red Sox before the season ends. What's more, I'll prove to everyone I can pitch and help this club." Although he did not post a winning record in his repeat stints with Allentown and Minneapolis, there were times when his pitching was absolutely brilliant. In one game at the end of August, he struck out 14 batters in nine innings, leaving him second to Larry Sherry, who fanned 16, but in 11 innings. One Boston sportswriter thought even then "there's a strong possibility that, some day, he might have his name inside, if not on the cover, of many books—baseball's record books, that is." Little did the scribe know at the time how ironically accurate that statement was. The 22-year-old pitcher turned out to be equally prophetic when his early-season prognostication proved to be right on the money. He was called up at the beginning of September, working four innings of relief in an equal number of games without giving up a hit or a run. Perhaps as a sign of things to come, on October 1, his last appearance of the season, he opened the eighth inning of a game against the Yankees by striking out Roger Maris.[4]

The former southpaw, who learned to throw right-handed after a series of youthful accidents degraded his effectiveness in pitching with his left arm, was usually cool and composed when on the mound. He was a fun-loving kid who took things in stride no matter how bad. "That boy has the perfect disposition and arm for a pitcher—free and easy," proclaimed Bosox pitching coach Sal Maglie. "Just needs a proper dose of seriousness."

Manager Billy Jurges said of him, "he's loose, not awkward. He's got rhythm." He came into the majors with a live fastball, often compared in speed to that of Ryne Duren, and a decent curve that Maglie helped him improve. He soon developed a changeup and a slider and added a slip pitch to his assortment of weapons later in his career.[5]

Stallard's best work with the Millers was as a relief pitcher, so when the Red Sox moved north at the end of spring training in 1961, the tall right-hander was assigned to the Boston bullpen. Manager Pinky Higgins was ecstatic at the thought of using Stallard in conjunction with Mike Fornieles, the team's ace closer. "Having Tracy in the bull pen along with Fornieles will solve a problem that gave me many a headache last season [1960]," said the skipper. "He's going to be one of the best in the league."[6]

His rookie season was a rollercoaster ride to say the least; he would pitch well in one game, then get hammered in the next. In 28 game appearances during the first half of the summer, he did manage to save two games and hold three others, but his 4.57 earned-run average was on the high side. After making three consecutive relief outings in early July in which he surrendered just two earned runs in 11⅔ innings of work, the Boston manager decided to give him his first shot at starting a game. On July 16, he managed to go 6⅔ innings against the White Sox while allowing just one run for a no-decision. But then in his next two outings he surrendered 11 earned runs in nine innings of work. He suffered his first loss on August 6; it was an excellent performance in which he allowed just one run in seven innings of work. He finally got his first major league victory in his next start, a game in which he was one out away from a complete contest. But then he lost six of his last eight starts to end the year at 2–7 on a 4.88 earned-run average.

In spite of a rocky rookie season, the Red Sox were still confident in their pitching prospect, believing he "showed signs of becoming a winner" even though he had a losing record. "Stallard already has been named as one of the pitchers Manager Mike Higgins is counting on as a starter this season," wrote *Boston Traveler* columnist Bill Liston. "Tracy, in fact, may be the key to any first-division hopes Higgins is entertaining." He began spring training determined to retain his starting position. Unfortunately, the sophomore pitcher developed shoulder problems early in training camp, a nagging condition that flared up when he rested between innings. "I've had trouble with my shoulder almost every season I've gone to spring training," he said. "Yet, it usually goes away by this time and I'm ready to pitch. I can't understand why it's lingering with me this season."[7]

He was not given his first assignment until May 6, a relief appearance in which he retired the side in order in the ninth inning of a game in Boston. But that was it. The next day he was cut from the roster and sent to the club's Triple-A team in Seattle. Stallard was more or less resigned to the demotion. "I got so far behind and I never caught up," he admitted. The ailing right-hander pitched well enough for the Rainiers that he was recalled in mid–September. He started the second half of a twin bill on September 13, but rain ended the game in the third inning with Stallard pitching scoreless ball. That was the end of his Boston career. In early December, he and Pumpsie Green, Boston's first African American player, were traded to the lowly New York Mets for outfielder Felix Mantilla. To add insult to injury, he was immediately assigned to Buffalo, the Mets' Triple-A affiliate.[8]

There was some advantage for a struggling hurler in becoming a member of a mediocre team like the Mets of the early 1960s. In Stallard's case, he made the club coming out of spring training, again consigned to the bullpen to start the 1963 season. Although he did not perform well in that capacity—0–3 with a horrible 8.25 ERA—he got his first start in the second game of a doubleheader on June 2 out of desperation because the Mets' pitching staff, consisting of nine men total, was worn out. It marked his first starting opportunity since that historic outing on October 1, 1961. He responded like a duck to water, pitching a perfect game through the first four innings, then a no-hitter through the next two until he gave up a run in the seventh. While he did not get a decision that day, he demonstrated that he had the ability to be a starter. He tossed consecutive complete-game victories in his next two starts before hitting the skids in July, losing four out of six games that month. He ended the summer at 6–17, not great, but he cut his earned-run average to 4.71, nearly half of what it was on May 26. And, considering he was playing for a team that lost 111 games and had no pitchers with a winning record, it was not a disastrous season for him.[9]

Stallard remained in the starting lineup at the beginning of 1964. Jack Fisher, author of Maris' record-tying sixtieth home run, joined the Mets that year, making him and Stallard the one-two punch on the starting staff. Though the right-hander still had a losing record—10 wins, 20 losses—with his defeats the most in the American League, he had a very respectable 3.79 earned-run average. Over half of those losses were by two runs or less. One of those defeats was to Jim Bunning on June 21, the day he pitched a perfect game. In addition, his 11 complete games with two shutouts were most in his career.

In a worst-to-first scenario, at the end of 1964 Stallard was traded to the St. Louis Cardinals, champions of the 1964 World Series, making him part of a starting rotation that included Curt Simmons, Ray Sadecki, and future Hall-of-Famer Bob Gibson. "Stallard is a tough competitor and he ought to do a lot better for us because our club can score some runs," manager Red Schoendienst said at the time of the trade. "Our scouts are very high on him" Even though he liked pitching for the Mets, Stallard was delighted with the move. "It's wonderful," he responded upon learning of switch. "It's gotta be, going from a tenth-place club to a World Series winner."[10]

The 27-year-old pitcher took full advantage of the opportunity presented him. While the Cards were not nearly the team they were the year before, Stallard nonetheless produced the second best record on the team behind Gibson and, for the first—and only—time, he ended with a winning record (11–8) on an excellent 3.38 earned-run average.

The 1966 season, his last in the majors, proved to be the polar opposite of the year before. St. Louis had a plethora of pitchers, so he was back in the bullpen to open the season. On top of that, there were days, sometimes even a week or more, between appearances that left him rusty, resulting in erratic pitching. "And there's nothing worse for a ball player than inactivity, no actual game competition," he complained. He got his first start on June 4, an awful outing in which he lasted just three innings. He had three more starts that month, winning one while losing two, and three more in July, all no-decisions, before the Cardinals had seen enough and shipped him to Tulsa in the Pacific Coast League.[11]

He was back in the minors the following year before a season of inactivity in 1968. He tried a comeback in 1969, but to little avail. He was acquired by the Kansas City Royals, who assigned him to the Single-A High Point-Thomasville Royals in the Carolina League as a player/coach, but that was the end of his professional career. He lasted seven seasons in the major leagues, posting a record of 30 wins and 57 losses and a cumulative 4.17 earned-run average, remembered primarily for that one game on October 1, 1961, when he did indeed enter baseball's record book as foretold years earlier.

With so many September calls-ups sitting on the bench, Stallard did not expect to be pitching that final game of the 1961 season. Acting on that assumption, he and Gene Conley, his even taller teammate, decided to visit some of the many nightspots of New York to celebrate the end of a long summer. Sitting in the clubhouse the following morning feeling a little worse for the wear, he was shocked when pitching coach Sal Maglie literally handed him the ball, his signal that the recipient of the horsehide sphere was to start the game. All he could do was look up at Conley and moan, "Oh, shoot."[12]

Maris spent the evening before the final game in the apartment of his friend, Big Julie Isaacson, divvying up World Series tickets he purchased with his own money to give to friends and others who had helped him that summer, such as his barber and the employees of the Stage Deli where he regularly ate breakfast. He then returned to his hotel room. The next morning dawned cool and crisp, perfect weather for baseball. Maris arose early to attend mass with his wife at St. Patrick's Cathedral before Big Julie picked him up for the short ride to the Stadium. "Roger was quiet and nervous," Isaacson recollected. "He didn't say much about wanting to hit that last home run, but I knew that was on his mind."[13]

"When I got to the park for the last game there was one more thing I was certain of—this was the end," Maris noted. "There were no more games, there could be no more excitement about the home runs. Whatever happened today would close the book. That, in itself, was a relief." As in the 154th game when he needed two homers to tie Ruth, he felt everyone was watching him. "I was thinking that I knew now how the monkeys in the zoo must feel." As he dressed, he grew calmer, thinking to himself, "Today I should be on the target. Friday, after the two days of rest, I was under the ball; yesterday I was over it. Today I should be right on it. I just feel it."[14]

A little over 23,000 spectators greeted Maris as he walked onto the field before the start of the game. Because Frick had, in effect, "delegitimized" any homers Maris hit after he imposed his deadline, attendance at Yankee Stadium for the remaining games was well below capacity. Most of the spectators were seated in the right-field sections hoping to catch his final dinger. Sam Gordon, a restaurant owner in Sacramento, California, offered $5,000 (the equivalent of $40,000 in 2018) and other inducements to the fortunate individual who retrieved the ball, which added to the excitement that afternoon.

Bill Stafford opened the game by striking out the side. Then Tracy Stallard took the mound. He retired Bobby Richardson on a grounder back to the box before allowing a single to Tony Kubek, giving Maris his first opportunity of the afternoon. Stallard delivered a low outside fastball on his first pitch, one too tempting for Maris not to take. Instead of pulling the ball, though, he went with the pitch, sending it flying to deep left field where Carl Yastrzemski hauled it in with relative ease. "I found myself wishing I had pulled it," he said. "If I had and it had gone that far to right field it would have been in the seats. At least Stallard was trying to work on me."[15]

The game was still scoreless when Maris came to bat with one gone and nobody on in the fourth inning. There was some commotion in the right-field stands as Maris dug in, but, as he remembered it, the crowd "was so quiet that I almost felt the Stadium was empty." The Yankee pitchers in the bullpen, including Whitey Ford, stood with their gloves on in the hopes of snagging the ball. Stallard's first pitch was high and outside; the crowd booed. Maris stepped back, scratched at the dirt with his right foot, and dug some clay from between the spikes before tapping both feet with his bat, taking a practice swing, and settling back in. The next pitch was the opposite of the first, low and inside, almost striking the ground; the chorus of boos grew in intensity. Maris again lightly knocked his right foot with the bat, pawed at the dirt several times, took three practice swings, and resumed his stance.

Stallard's third delivery was the money ball. Not wanting to walk him in a scoreless game only to face Yogi Berra, the rookie hurled his best fastball, but one that was about waist high and in the heart of the plate. "I was trying to get him out," he said afterwards. "Just like I want to get everyone else out. I got behind Roger and came in with a fast ball. I don't know just where abouts over the plate it was headed, but it would have been a strike if he hadn't hit it." Home plate umpire Bill Kinnamon, who was behind the plate when Maris parked his sixtieth, remembered the pitch as being a slider that broke inside to Maris. Maris jumped all over the pitch. "I was ready and I connected," Maris explained. "As soon as I hit it, I knew it was number sixty-one.... It was the only time that the number of the homer ever flashed into my mind as I hit it. Then I heard the tremendous roar from the crowd. I could see them standing, then my mind went blank again."[16]

Right fielder Lou Clinton raced back to the low outfield wall thinking it was catchable, but the ball soared well beyond his reach, landing some 360 feet distant deep into the lower right-field stands about 10 rows back. There was a wild scramble for the $5,000 prize with 19-year-old Sal Durante, standing on his seat, coming up the winner when he barehanded the ball. Stadium security immediately surrounded the young man and escorted him into the runway while Maris, in a daze, continued his home-run trot. The crowd stood and cheered the new home-run king. One of the few not rising was Pat Maris. "When I saw the ball go into the stands, I couldn't move.... I think I was crying, perhaps saying a little prayer. I had prayed to St. Jude that morning, asking him to help Roger reach his goal, if he thought he deserved it. I felt this was my answer."[17]

After he crossed home and greeted Yogi Berra and the batboy, a fan jumped out of the stands near the Yankee dugout and ran onto the field to shake his hand before climbing back over the railing to disappear into the crowd. Maris briefly entered the dugout, but his teammates pushed him back out, something that was rarely done at the time. "When Roger played, guys never came out of the dugout after a homer to wave at the fans," Yankee third baseman Clete Boyer clarified. With a shy grin on his face, he removed his hat and waived to the fans three times before he was allowed to take his place on the bench. Radio announcer and former Yankee star shortstop Phil Rizzuto called it "one of the greatest things I've ever seen here at Yankee Stadium." As he sat with the back of his head resting against the dugout wall, the exhausted slugger let out a big sigh of relief. Roger Maris had conquered the Babe.[18]

Between innings, Maris met with Durante. The lucky youth attempted to give the ball to him, but the slugger refused. "If they made the offer [of $5,000], then he should get what's coming to him," Maris announced to the assembled media. "I'll even fly out to the coast with him to that restaurant." Maris stated later, "What do you think of that kid? The boy is planning to get married and he can use the money, but he still wanted to give the ball back to me for nothing. It shows there's some good people left in this world after all."[19]

Maris had two more chances to extend the record after that sixty-first blast. In the sixth, he came up for the third time with a runner on and one away. This time the advantage went to Stallard. With the count full, the pitcher hurled a slider; Maris took a mighty cut, but missed it entirely for a strikeout. In the eighth, Chet Nichols was on the mound after Stallard was lifted for a pinch-hitter in the top of that inning. With two away, Maris

Sal Durante, the young fan who caught the historic sixty-first home run, poses with Maris in the clubhouse after the game. He tried to give the ball to the player, but Maris refused, telling him to keep it until he collected the $5,000 offered by a restaurant owner in California. Maris later flew to Sacramento to be with Durante as he received his reward.

popped up to second baseman Chuck Schilling to end the inning, bringing a close to his historic run. Interestingly, with that catch, Schilling set a new American League defensive record for second basemen with fewest errors—eight—in a season; Ford Frick never commented on how that feat should be listed.

In his post-game interview, Stallard was a little defensive when asked about the home run. "People say not to pitch to a guy in a spot like that but I'd rather have him hit a homer than walk him four times. I just can't go out there and try not to get every batter out. That's baseball." He also justified his pitch selection. "He hit what I thought was a perfect pitch from me," he insisted, "and if I had to do it over again, I'd make the same pitch." Denying that he felt badly about the homer, he stated heatedly, "I'm not going to lose any sleep over this. After all, what about the guys who threw the other sixty? That's the first hit he ever got off me. What's all the fuss about. I've thrown 14 other home run balls this season and nobody ever showed up to ask me a lot of silly questions." He then quipped, "I'll tell you this. My price just went up on the banquet circuit." Years later when asked if he grooved the ball to Maris, Stallard responded vehemently, "God no. It was

2–0 and I was just trying to throw a strike. I don't know how anybody could help anybody hit a home run. Even in batting practice. I give him all I got. The fastball was all I had."[20]

Maris was more relaxed and at ease than he had been for weeks as he posed for pictures with Durante and fielded questions from dozens of reporters in front of his locker after the game. "It was a Maris who seemed a foot taller now that a terrible load had been taken off him, now that he had the 61 home runs, now that the season was over," wrote Leonard Shecter in his column the next day. Sipping on a beer, he answered all the usual questions. Was the pressure he was under more physical or mental? "It was more mental than anything else. It was rough. I'm happy it's all over." How was he feeling now that he had broken the record? "Great, great, great. Greatest day of my life." What were his thoughts about the Babe? "Babe Ruth was a big man in baseball and I don't say I'm in his caliber, but naturally I'm happy to go past Ruth's mark." Did he wish he had broken it in the time limit set by Ford Frick? "I would have liked to have done it in 154 games but being as I didn't I'm glad now I didn't and got it when I did…. It gives me a pretty good feeling to know I'm the only man in the history of baseball to hit 61 home runs." Was he trying for another in his last two at-bats? "I didn't care one way or another about a second one today. Sure, I was swinging for another, but I really didn't care."

When asked about Tracy Stallard, he had nothing but praise for the rookie pitcher. "I appreciate the fact that he was man enough to pitch to me and to get me out. When he got behind me he came in with the pitch to try and get me out." What bat did he use to hit the record-setting homer? "I hit 59, 60 and 61 with that bat, my own model. But I must have hit seven other homeruns with Bob Cerv's bat." Was he planning on using it in the upcoming World Series? No, he replied with a smile, "I guess I'll have to retire it." Maris concluded by saying, "I won't consider this 61st homer a great personal achievement unless we beat Cincinnati in the Series. If we do that, I'll really feel we've done something."[21]

Later that night, he and his wife went out for a small celebratory dinner. Joining them were their New York friends, Julie and Selma Isaacson, and Milton Gross, the sportswriter Maris had stood up to visit a dying child in the hospital back in Baltimore. The *Post* columnist wrote about it afterwards. "He had a shrimp cocktail, a steak medium, a mixed salad with French dressing, a baked potato, two glasses of wine, a sliver of cheese cake, two cups of coffee and three cigarettes," according to Gross. "This was the greatest experience of my life," he told his friends. "It had to be, but I wouldn't want to go through it again for anything." Although others in the restaurant stared at him, the party was left alone until the end when a small girl came up to him with a menu in her hand asking for his autograph. He obliged, but when the child asked him to date it as well, he had to ask what day it was. "The date," Isaacson replied, "is the one you did what nobody else ever did."[22]

Following the meal, Maris went to Lenox Hill Hospital to visit Mickey Mantle and Bob Cerv, both still recovering from their respective physical ailments; the two watched the game on television. "I got goose bumps," Mantle said when he saw his friend park sixty-one. As Maris walked into the room, the Mick reportedly yelled, "I hate your guts!" clearly making fun of all those in the press who had spread unfounded rumors that there was a season-long feud between the two Yankee powerhouses. They chatted awhile before Maris headed back to his hotel room for the night. A number of years later, Mantle spoke of his tremendous respect for Maris, especially his grace under pressure. "I'll tell you, he did it like a true champion. He never cracked, not once during the whole ordeal."[23]

There was no game the following day as the Yankees prepared to host the Cincinnati Reds for the first game of the World Series on the afternoon of October 4. Maris arrived at the Stadium thinking it would be quiet, so was a little taken aback to find reporters and photographers milling about. There was a mountain of congratulatory letters and telegrams awaiting him. Among them was one from President John F. Kennedy, reading, "My heartiest congratulations to you on hitting your 61st home run. The American people will always admire a man who overcomes great pressure to achieve an outstanding goal." It was one which Maris framed and treasured the rest of his life. He eventually visited the White House and had his picture taken with JFK. He spent his time in the clubhouse answering the mail and talking with teammates and reporters. While there, Mantle, who was released from the hospital, walked in, his appearance shocking Maris and the other players. "Not only was he pale and sick-looking, but he had a gaping wound high in his right thigh where it had been cut to remove an abscess. He could hardly walk, and running was out of the question." Everyone knew Mantle was determined to play, which he did on a limited basis. More than anything, though, his presence served as an inspiration for the team.[24]

Home Run # 62—Game 3, World Series—October 7— Day Game

Maris expressed some concern about how he would perform in Series with Cincinnati. "I was afraid I wouldn't be of much help," he feared. "I knew that my chase after the home-run record had fouled up my normal swing." He readily admitted that his desire for the record the final few weeks of the season caused him to go for pitches he normally let pass. "I've been trying for just one thing. I didn't give a darn about base hits. There's been only one thing on my mind—home runs." In addition, he knew Mantle would get only limited playing time at best and that it fell upon him to fill the hole in the Yankee offense created by Mantle's absence. "There would be so much more pressure on me," he acknowledged. "I know I've been swinging from the tail and if Mick's not in there I might unconsciously be doing it more than I should."[25]

Although the Yankees were favored to win the Series, no one believed the Reds would be easy to beat. They were a scrappy bunch that had their ups and downs early in the season, but finally put everything together in August to take the National League pennant over the Dodgers by four games. They finished in sixth placed the season before, but a series of good trades in the off-season made the team what it was in 1961. Their offensive strength was built around 25-year-old Frank Robinson who was second in the league in runs batted in, third in home runs, and sixth in batting average. At the end of the season he won his first Most Valuable Player Award. Second to him was Vada Pinson, a speedy 22-year-old outfielder who led the league in hits and placed second in batting average, eighth in runs scored, and second in stolen bases; he came in third in MVP voting that season.

But it was pitching that was the key to the team's success. In fact, most believed the Reds starting staff about equal to that of the Yankees. They had Jim O'Toole, who finished the season at 19–9 with a 3.10 ERA; Joey Jay, one of the players picked up at the end of the previous season, who led the league in wins with 21; and Bob Purkey, at 31 the oldest and most experienced of the three, who ended the season at 16–12 with a 3.73 earned-run average. The trio combined for 56 wins as opposed to 31 losses. The Yankees' top three starters of Whitey Ford, Bill Stafford, and Ralph Terry were 55–16.

If there was any real weakness, it was the propensity of Jay and Purkey to give up home runs. Purkey's 26 was sixth most in the league that summer while Jay's 23 left him just short of the top 10. The Reds had two excellent closers in Jim Brosnan and Bill Henry. Brosnan, the right hander, was 10–4 with 16 saves on an excellent 3.04 earned-run average. Henry, the southpaw, was of equal ability; he, too, saved 16 games, but on an even better 2.19 ERA. "With two relievers like that," wrote Leonard Koppett in the *New York Post*, "the Reds can throw monkey wrenches into budding rallies early in the game, and in every game." The Yankees, of course, had Luis Arroyo, who compiled a 15–5 record with 29 saves on an earned-run average the same as that of Henry.

The Reds scouted the Yankees the last few games of the summer. Indeed, O'Toole and Jay were both present when Maris blasted his sixty-first. They were well aware of Maris' struggles at the plate as he pressed for that elusive record-breaking homer. "[W]hat they've seen hasn't been me," Maris commented before the start of the Series. Reliever Jim Brosnan speculated that Maris "could cave in … if he gets the collar, if we pitch to him real well in the first game, it could kill him." Joey Jay realized that Maris was a good hitter, "but it's entirely possible that what's happened to him could have a bad effect on him. He's built a reputation that now he may have to live up to. He's the greatest home run hitter in history. It may change his swing because he's got to be going for the long ball more than he normally would."[26]

What these pitchers suggested and Maris feared turned out to be the case, at least in the early part of the Series. He sensed from the beginning that he was in trouble. "As I took batting practice before the first game I knew the worst. My normal swing was gone. I was completely off stride. I knew then that I was going to have a rough Series."[27]

It was 25-game winner Whitey Ford versus southpaw Jim O'Toole, who had eight straight victories, in the first game of the Series on October 4 in New York. Mantle was not in the lineup, so Maris patrolled center field and batted third with catcher Elston Howard in the fourth slot. Maris' worst nightmare came true: he popped out to short in the first inning with two runners on, struck out on a full count in the third, grounded back to first to end the fifth, and fouled out to the catcher to bring the seventh to a close. Fortunately Ford, who struggled a bit at the end of the season, was on his game, limiting the Reds to just two hits for a shutout, 2–0. It was his third consecutive shutout in the World Series going back to the year before. O'Toole pitched almost as well, but gave up a fourth-inning homer to Elston Howard and a sixth-inning dinger to Moose Skowron for a tough loss.

The following afternoon was a matchup between two young right-handers, Ralph Terry for the Yankees, Joey Jay for the Reds. If anyone thought Cincinnati would go down easily, they found out differently that day. The game was scoreless the first three innings, but then the Reds jumped in front in the fourth on a two-run homer by first baseman Gordy Coleman. The Yankees tied it up in the bottom of the inning when Yogi Berra parked one with Maris aboard on a walk. After that, though, it was all Cincinnati. The Reds scored the go-ahead run on a passed ball in the fifth and another on a single in the sixth before Terry was lifted at the end of the seventh. Luis Arroyo came on in the eighth and immediately gave up two additional runs for a Reds victory, 6–2. The fact that the Yankees committed three errors on top of the passed ball did not help matters much either.

Maris again had a lousy day at the plate. Other than that walk to open the fourth, he grounded out in the first, struck out with two on to end the fifth, and struck out again in the eighth. He had failed to get a ball out of the infield in eight trips to the plate. He was becoming hesitant and uncertain, having a hard time pulling the trigger even on good pitches. In the post-game interview, Jay said he made just one mistake pitch to Maris, his first delivery in the eighth with Tony Kubek on after a single; it was right in the heart of the plate. "I got away with it because Maris took the pitch. I don't know what might have happened if he had swung." But he did not. "I was quickly learning the price of the first installment I had to pay on the home-run record," Maris said.[28]

With the Series tied at one apiece, the teams had a day off to travel to Cincinnati and hitter-friendly Crosley Field. Maris visited the Reds playpen just once before as part of an exhibition game several years earlier. Most of the other Yankees were unfamiliar with it as well. It was one of the smaller ballparks in the league. The right field foul pole was 366 feet distant, increasing slightly to 383 feet in right-center. It measured 328 feet down the left-field line and only 387 feet to the deepest part of the park in dead center. The only real obstacle was the 70-foot high scoreboard between left and center fields; a ball striking it was still in play. Because of those relatively short distances, there was a fear that the Yankee sluggers would try to overpower the ball, much as they did playing in Los Angeles' homer-prone Wrigley Field where they lost six out of nine games. Mantle, in fact, who missed the first two games, decided to play in the third after parking a number of balls over the right-field fence during batting practice on the day of the game.[29]

Young Bill Stafford started for New York while 31-year-old veteran right-hander Bob Purkey got the call for Cincinnati. The 6-foot-2 hurler was a product of the Pittsburgh Pirates farm system, being signed by his hometown team straight out of high school in 1948 at the age of 18. His minor league record was quite impressive. He was 19–8 with a no-hitter for the Class D Greenville Pirates, then went an even better 17–6 with the Class B Davenport Pirates the next summer. In 1950 he was promoted to Double-A, compiling a 12–12 record for the New Orleans Pelicans. He was just on the cusp of starting his major league career when he was drafted, missing the next two years serving in the Army. He returned to the Pelicans in 1953 after he received his discharge that spring. While he had an 11–13 record for the Southern Association team, he had a decent 3.41 earned-run average. That, combined with his stellar performance in spring training, earned him a position on the big league roster at the start of the 1954 season.

Purkey spent most of that summer assigned to the bullpen. He did start a number of games, some of which were successful, others not so much. In spite of a season-long record of 3–8 with a large 5.07 ERA, the 24-year-old rookie showed a lot of potential. On July 22, for example, he pitched 11 solid innings of a 14-inning game, establishing a new major league record of six putouts by a pitcher in an extra-inning game. He began the 1955 campaign in the starting rotation, losing his first outing, followed by winning back-to-back complete games in the early goings. But then he came down with arm problems, causing him to lose six straight starts as he tried to work through it. He was sent to the bullpen in mid–June before management decided he was better served spending the rest of the season back with the Pelicans. Although it was a slight disruption to his major league career, it was fortunate in one way for it was there that he developed the "dandy" knuckleball which became his signature pitch.[30]

The right-hander had high hopes of making the Pirates' starting roster in 1956, but he tore some ligaments in his right knee at the start of training camp and ended up pitching for the Hollywood Stars, Pittsburgh's Triple-A affiliate. After having the cast removed from his knee in late May, Purkey was able to start 14 of his 20 game appearances, ending that summer with a 6–8 record on a decent 3.36 earned-run average. It was the last time he ever appeared in a minor league uniform.[31]

By this point in his career, Purkey had a vast array of pitches that served him well throughout the next decade in the majors. In addition to a knuckleball, he had a good fastball that moved and broke in sharply on right-handed batters. He called it "my bread-and-butter pitch.... I wouldn't trade my fastball for a lot of others in this league that are thrown faster but straighter." To those two basic pitches he added a slider, a changeup, a slow curve, and a sinker. However, he denied the knuckleball was his primary weapon. "I don't depend mainly on any one pitch," he said. "My knuckler isn't as good as Hoyt Wilhelm's, my fastball not as overpowering as Ryne Duren's, my curve not so sharp as Sad Sam Jones used to throw, and my slider not so effective as Vernon Law's. But put them all together, and they give me a pretty fair repertoire."[32]

Tom Ferrick, his pitching coach after he was traded to Cincinnati, said Purkey did not appear to be very effective at first glance. "You watch Bob warm up and you wouldn't give a plugged nickel for his chances of beating anyone," he said. "He's not the overpowering type of pitcher who catches your eye. He's a cutey. You watch him. His pitches are up and down, in and out. That's why he beats the good clubs. He keeps those hard hitters a little bit off-stride." The great Roberto Clemente found him especially difficult to hit because of his deceptive delivery. "Everything he throws you is the same—same motion, same angle—but you don't know where the ball is going. All you know is it's going to be a strike, so you got to be alive." Ernie Banks was particularly impressed with his sinker. "[It] drops out of sight. I think he could drill for oil with it." And Ron Fairly was taken with the variety of pitches he tossed. "He used to throw everything but the kitchen sink," he commented. "Now he throws the sink, too." He had great poise and control and was not afraid to pitch inside if necessary. According to one sportswriter, though, most batters were not afraid of being brushed back by him. "[H]e throws close to hitters as often as Don Drysdale, but the hitters don't mind because there's plenty of time to get out of the way and they wouldn't get hurt anyhow if they didn't."[33]

The 1957 campaign was Purkey's last as a Pirate. There was some question in spring training about whether he was over his knee injury, but it became apparent early on that he was. He started off in fine fashion, winning two of his first three appearances, but then in August he seemed to run out of gas, losing five while winning just one the last two months of the season. He was pitching for a team that finished in seventh place, so his 11–14 record with a 3.86 earned-run average put him among the top hurlers on the team. But it was not good enough to keep him on the Pirates roster. When he learned in early December he was traded to the Cincinnati Reds for left-handed reliever/occasional starter Don Gross, he was not unhappy about leaving Pittsburgh. "As much as I like to play in my home town, I also like to have some runs scored for me," he commented. "The Pirates didn't score many runs and the Reds scored 'em in droves. This is what I like."[34]

It was with the Reds that Purkey established himself as a top-drawer hurler. "I'm a control pitcher and I need to work regularly to stay sharp," he explained. "The move to Cincinnati gave me that chance." He became the team ace in his very first season with the Reds, ending 1958 with the best record on the team at 17–11 and a good 3.60 earned-run average. Furthermore, 17 of his 34 starts were complete contests, fourth best among National League pitchers. Not only was it his first winning season in the majors, he was selected to the All-Star team for the first time as well. "Sure, some say Purkey's ball looks as big as a grapefruit when it comes up to the plate, but believe me, it's not easy to hit," asserted Tom Ferrick. Calling his pitcher "a real student of the game" who studies the batters at all times, Ferrick said much of his success was due to his great control. "He puts the ball where he wants it. That accounts for much of his effectiveness."[35]

The now 29-year-old hurler stumbled somewhat in 1959 with a 13–18 record on a 4.25 ERA, but bounced back in 1960 with the exact record he had two seasons earlier; he was once again the staff ace. Purkey blamed his off-year n 1959 on pitching coach Clyde King who insisted the pitcher throw harder. "It was a mistake," he said. "I'm not an over-powering pitcher. I never was and never will be. I have to rely upon control and finesse." The Reds made major changes at the end of the season, getting rid of many of their older players while adding younger ones, including Joey Jay. That new mix was what saw the team jump from sixth place in 1960 to the World Series the following year.[36]

After a good winning record of 16–12 and a World Series appearance in 1961, Purkey had the greatest season of his career in 1962. In spite of suffering back spasms in mid-summer that saw him sidelined for nearly two weeks, he fashioned an amazing 23–5 record—the highest winning percentage in the National League—on an excellent 2.81 earned-run average. He also placed fifth in complete games, tenth in shutouts, and second in innings pitched. Now 32, he did all of this by relying more on his knuckleball because there was less strain using it. "The knuckler doesn't take as much out of your arm as the fast ball and slider," he explained. He was selected for both All-Star games and finished third in Cy Young Award voting and eighth for the Most Valuable Player Award.[37]

But that incredible summer marked the zenith of his career. He suffered shoulder problems during spring training in 1963 that plagued him throughout the summer. He did not make his first appearance until May 7 and ceased pitching altogether after September 2, ending the summer at 6–10 in only 137 innings pitched, less than half of what he did the previous year. Relying primarily on his knuckler, he had to alter his delivery because of his shoulder and did not throw as much on the sidelines between starts in order "to protect his arm from strain."[38]

The 34-year-old hurler rested his shoulder over the winter and took it slow and easy in spring training and into the early part of the 1964 campaign. He delivered a complete game in his first outing on April 20, but then spent the first half of the season alternating between winning and losing. In early July he was assigned to the bullpen and did not start again until August. The break from starting seemed to do him good. In the last two months of the season, he won seven and lost three while producing on an outstanding 2.33 earned-run average to end the summer at 11–9 with a cumulative 3.05 ERA. Although he showed considerable improvement, he knew his days in a Reds uniform were over. The inevitable happened in mid–December when he was sent to the St. Louis Cardinals for pitchers Charlie James and an aging Roger Craig. At the time of his departure, Purkey had the third highest winning percentage among all pitchers who had won 80 or more games while with Cincinnati.[39]

Purkey's tenure with the Cards was brief. While he had a winning record at 10–9, his earned-run average exploded to 5.79. In early April of 1966, the Pirates purchased his contract from St. Louis, bringing him back home where it all began. He was used solely as a reliever, appearing in eight games in April and May before missing all of June with a sore arm. He came back for two more appearances in July, but his time had come and he was given his release at the end of the month. "You always worry about this day and no matter what shape you're in, it always takes a little out of you," he said before leaving a major league locker room for the last time. "But I have no regrets and I leave with good feelings all around.... I've taken a great deal out of baseball and I only hope I've given something in return." Over 13 major league seasons, he won 129 games while losing 115 others, all on a cumulative 3.79 earned-run average compiled over 2,114⅔ innings pitched in 386 games, nearly three-fourths of those as a starter.[40]

The third game of the 1961 World Series was the crucial one. If the Yankees won, it was all but over. If the Reds emerged victorious, they had a good chance of going all the way. Cincinnati fans were particularly encouraged by the fact that Mantle, although he was in the lineup for the first time, was still hampered by his recent illness and surgery and Maris had yet to hit a ball to the outfield. Maris took extra batting practice the day before the game, but found little to be happy about. He hit some solid line drives, but also a number of ground balls, all the while failing to put one over the fence in right.[41]

Purkey and Bill Stafford were locked in a real pitchers' duel from the very beginning. The Cincinnati hurler had a no-hitter going until he gave up a harmless double to Elston Howard in the top of the fifth. Stafford did surrender a run-scoring double to Frank Robinson in the third, but was otherwise matching Purkey pitch-for-pitch. Then in the seventh Yogi Berra tied it up with a single that scored Tony Kubek from second. As for Maris and Mantle, they were doing nothing to help the New York cause. The new home-run king popped out to third in the first inning, grounded back to the pitcher in the fourth, and flew out to center in the seventh. The best that could be said to this point was he had at least gotten a ball to the outfield. Mantle was equally ineffective. He flew out to center to open the second inning, did the same to end the fourth, and struck out in the seventh.

"Purkey was pitching as if he could go on forever, mixing sliders and flutterballs [knuckleballs] with fastballs so effectively the Yanks were slamming their bats into the dugout in disgust," wrote author Herb Kamm. But there were signs Purkey was weakening. After the Reds plated a second run to go up, 2–1, in the seventh, the Cincinnati hurler got two quick outs to start the eighth before Johnny Blanchard pinch-hit for Stafford. And, as he had done so often during the regular season, Blanchard came through again. Purkey delivered a first-pitch slider to the reserve catcher, who promptly drove it deep into the right-field bleachers to tie the score at two apiece. Bobby Richardson then singled, but Tony Kubek ended any further threat by flying out to center.[42]

Luis Arroyo came on in relief of Stafford to open the bottom of the eighth, retiring the side in order. Then in the top of the ninth, Maris stepped to the plate for the fourth time that afternoon. "I tried to forget everything that had happened. Tried to forget I was out of tune. I was really concentrating on Purkey," he said. Maris took the first pitch for a strike, then watched two balls sail by. Not wanting to walk Maris only to face Mantle, Purkey made the same mistake he did with Blanchard the inning before, he tried to sneak a slider past the Yankee slugger. "It was low and on the outside corner. Maybe I should have got it inside a bit," he disclosed after the game. "My knuckleball was not working too good and my best pitch was the slider."[43]

Maris did not hesitate this time when he saw the pitch approaching. "I swung and, for the first time since number sixty-one, felt that ringing crack. I knew this one was hit." Right fielder Frank Robinson raced back, but stopped when he saw the ball scream by high overhead to land some 20 rows back in the bleachers. "What a feeling," Maris said later. "Not of exultation, but of relief." Purkey retired the next three batters, including

Mantle on a strikeout, but the damage was done. In the bottom of the inning, Arroyo allowed a one-out double that hit the scoreboard, but retired the next two batters to give the Yankees a crucial victory.[44]

That tough loss broke the back of the Reds' resistance. The Bombers handily won the fourth game behind the pitching of Whitey Ford and Jim Coates, blanking Cincinnati, 7–0. Ford was injured at the start of the sixth inning and was replaced by Coates, but his 32 consecutive scoreless innings stretching back to the 1960 World Series broke Ruth's record of 29⅔ established in 1918 while pitching for the Boston Red Sox. "Poor Babe," Ford wisecracked. "This has been a tough year for him." Maris was hitless, but he was walked to open the fourth inning, advanced to third on a Mantle single, and scored when Elston Howard hit a ground-rule double. Then in the seventh he was intentionally passed—the only one that year for him—and scored along with Bobby Richardson on a Hector Lopez single after advancing to second on a wild pitch.[45]

The Yankees wrapped it all up on the afternoon of October 9, claiming their nineteenth World Series title by defeating the Reds, 13–5. Bud Daley got the win in relief of starter Ralph Terry. Maris doubled in the second inning to score Tony Kubek from first, giving the Yankees a six-run lead after they blew the game open by plating five runs in the opening inning. That and his earlier homer were the extent of his offensive production. Although Maris was disappointed in his Series performance, Cincinnati manager Fred Hutchinson thought his game-winning home run in the third contest was the turning point in the Series. "Even though we played well until today [Game 5] ... Maris' homer was the beginning of the end. We never were the same after that. We had no spark, got no lift and went nowhere after we had evened the series in New York."[46]

Maris did not join in on the clubhouse victory celebration after the game. He was anxious to get back home to his family and a respite from all the pressure he endured for the past seven months. He quickly showered and changed into his street clothes, shouting a few goodbyes to his teammates as he left the clubhouse, refusing to stop for any interviews. He had a plane to catch and he was determined not to miss it. For him the long summer of 1961 was finally over.

Aftermath

Roger Maris' one desire after he arrived home in Raytown, Missouri, was to stay there all winter and to be out of the spotlight. "Being home with the family is the most important thing," he said. "I want to be alone, just with my family. I want to become acquainted with my kids again." But life was never the same after that historic season. He did spend time with his wife and children, but he also was on the road frequently. In October he was part of a five-day home run derby tour of North Carolina with Harmon Killebrew and Jim Gentile. In November he traveled to Sacramento, California, as part of a ceremony in which restaurateur Sam Gordon gave a $5,000 check to Sal Durante for the sixty-first home run ball and then handed it over to Maris. Believing it was to be a private event, the slugger was less than happy to find a small crowd and a television camera there to witness the transaction. "I don't think much of this promotion," he grumbled.[1]

He was also the recipient of a slew of awards that required his attendance at recognition banquets. In addition to being selected the American League's Most Valuable Player for the second straight year, he was presented the Sultan of Swat Award by the Maryland Professional Baseball Players Association, the Player of the Year Award from *The Sporting News*, the Hickok Belt Award as Professional Athlete of the Year, and the Fraternal Order of Eagles-Frederick C. Miller trophy as the Associated Press' Male Athlete of the Year. Sprinter and Olympic gold-medalist Wilma Rudolph won the Female Athlete of the Year Award and was honored at the same event. Maris, kidding on the square, revealed at that particular gathering his true feelings about attending awards events. "The banquet circuit is okay except for four things—speeches, newspapermen, cameramen and traveling." He then added, "One advantage is that the people are usually pleasantly surprised when they actually meet me. They find out I'm not the monster they think I am."[2]

For a man who hated the spotlight, it must have been agonizing, but he did it in spite of wishing he were home. And the press followed him everywhere, many reporting false stories about his behavior at these events. One account of the AP event stated he left the dais immediately after receiving his award to play pool in a backroom. Nothing could have been further from the truth. In fact, he arrived early for a photo shoot, stayed until the end of the program, and then remained afterwards to sign autographs. Another story stated he left a B'nai B'rith dinner in New York early, which was true, but not because he wanted to do so. He was notified just before the ceremony started that he had to take a 10:30 train to Rochester out of Grand Central Station that evening rather than fly the following morning as he was originally told. His hosts were informed of that change as soon as he found out.

Perhaps the story that hurt him the most was one that described how he sign an "X" on a ball for a young boy at a public event during spring training in Ft. Lauderdale. Maris loved children and would never intentionally hurt or dismiss a youngster who approached him. Did he put an "X" on the child's ball? Yes, but only as a joke before signing his real name. In reality, he was at the event with other Yankee players when the boy walked up to him, ball in hand. "I liked his looks and felt he was the type of youngster you could joke with," he said. "As the kid came up, I said to my teammates: 'Watch this.'" He put a small x-mark on the ball and handed it back to the child. The boy walked away a few steps, turned around, and came back to Maris saying, "This isn't your autograph." Maris jokingly responded, "Yes it is, I can't write." The boy started to laugh, saying, "Sure, you can." Maris "took the ball again, signed the autograph and the kid went away happy. It was a case of a reporter seeing only what he wanted to see." This event is still the subject of false mythology. The movie 61* depicts the incident as taking place during the 1961 season with an angry father screaming at Maris for what he did; that was pure Hollywood fiction.[3]

It was clear by early spring 1962 that the vitriol and scorn heaped on him by some in the media in 1961 carried over into the next season. "I found out there were a few out to get me, to downgrade me and run me through the mill," he concluded. "There were a few really giving me the business." Maris became even more reluctant to talk to the press as a result. Things came to a head during spring training. Among other things, he was in a contract tussle with Yankee management over his salary increase. While he finally came to terms with the club, the negotiations stretched out for weeks with the front office implying he was being difficult in his demands, thus painting the portrait of a spoiled prima donna in the process. Then there were several confrontations with the media in March that set the tone for the rest of the season.[4]

First, Maris, chagrined at what he felt was unfair and malicious press coverage over the winter, announced in mid–March that he was going to answer any questions from reporters with the phrase, "No comment. The writers are going to rip me if I talk or if I don't. So I'm not going to say anything and let them write what they please—they're going to write what they want anyway." Admitting that there were writers who treated him fairly, "I can't look at 30 writers and pick out 15 good ones and 15 bad ones. I'm through. No more talking."[5]

That pronouncement, plus the totally distorted report of the "X" incident, prompted Oscar Fraley, sports columnist for United Press International, to pen a blistering commentary about the player. Overreacting to Maris' explanation that he was simply following Ted Williams example of not giving interviews, Fraley wrote,

> [A]ll of a sudden Maris thinks he's another Ted Williams.... [D]espite those 61 home runs last season, anybody in baseball will give you 10-1 Roger is only a fairly faint facsimile of Williams. Williams was a hitter, and you can put that word in capital letters. Maris as a team hitter leaves more than somewhat to be desired.... For a man who belabored the ball at a rather anemic .269 clip, I would have to think Maris has a rather swollen idea of his importance.

Concluding by saying he hoped his two boys chose John Glenn as their hero and not someone like Maris, he stated his reason: "Because guys like Maris bat a round zero with me." Maris, quite understandably, was seething when he next saw Fraley. "Maris, chalk-white in the face with anger, raged at Oscar Fraley." To make matters worse, he did so in front of his teammates and other members of the press. "You hit me where it hurts the most—in my personal life—and you wrote without giving me a chance to explain my side of it," Maris retorted after he was done using expletives.[6]

That was immediately followed by an incident before a game against the New York Mets in St. Petersburg on March 22. A photographer walked up to Maris with Rogers Hornsby in tow in the hopes of getting a picture of the two of them together. The cantankerous Hornsby, a contemporary of Ruth, spent much of the 1961 season belittling Maris at every opportunity as not being worthy of challenging the Babe's home run record. Maris, still brisling over the Hall-of-Famer's dismissive attitude, refused and walked away. Hornsby exploded. "He couldn't carry my bat. He is a little punk ballplayer," the furious Mets coach snapped. "I've posed for pictures with some major league hitters—not bush leaguers like he is."[7]

The *coup de grace* was a blistering two-part column by Jimmy Cannon, noted sportswriter for the *New York Journal-American*, which appeared in newspapers the following week. There are various accounts as to what precipitated Cannon's attack on Maris, but according to Maury Allen, Maris, who was still upset about the two earlier incidents, did not show for a prearranged interview. That perceived slight infuriated the pompous journalist. Cannon was generally supportive of Maris during the home-run chase, but that was no longer the case.[8]

Among other things, Cannon proclaimed Maris was "the most unpopular player on the Yankees." He referred to him as "Roger the Whiner" who "continues to rebuff even his friends among the journalists whose kindness has been rewarded with spiteful denunciations." He claimed many of his teammates hated him, citing anonymous quotes he said came from several of them. Cannon contended Maris was jealous of Mantle because he was "held in awe-tinged affection by the rest of Yankees." Maris, he concluded, "isn't a Ruth or a DiMaggio. He isn't a Mantle either. That's what seems to annoy Roger the Whiner most."[9]

Manager Ralph Houk quickly called a press conference to deny all the allegations made against his player. "Maris is a team player, a good family man and a good man on this baseball club," he said. "Roger is A-1 as far as the players and I are concerned." He also defended Maris over the Hornsby incident. "In my book any man who hits .267 [actually .269], drives in 140 runs [actually 141] and hits 61 home runs is a good hitter.... Some men are not college trained and can't make speeches as easily as others and Roger is one of these." He also disputed that there was any trouble in the Yankee clubhouse. "There isn't any dissension on this club due to Maris or anyone else. Any suggestion that Maris presents a problem to us is false and misleading."[10]

Regardless of Houk's assessment, which many took as something he had to do to try and tamp down all the negative publicity, other columnists unloaded on Maris as well. "Maris has been intolerant, arrogant, short-tempered, inconsiderate," wrote Tommy Devine in the *Miami News*. "He has set himself apart and above the role a star is supposed to play." While some sportswriters, especially those from New York who interacted with him on a regular basis, continued to defend him—though acknowledging he could be quick to take offense at times—the dual columns by Fraley and Cannon were damaging beyond repair. "His image had been locked into the public psyche," contended Maury Allen. "'Red-assed Roger' would be the description heard most often in the ensuing years. He was generally described as an angry young man. Few could penetrate the wall that rose up between Maris and the press as a result of the two scathing assaults by Fraley and Cannon."[11]

Many in the public bought into this image of Maris and let him know it with boos and catcalls when in the field or at bat. Adding to their negative perception was his failure to top his own home run record. Maris knew that 1961 had been a miracle season not ever to be repeated. "Maris will be judged by the past as much as the present," opined Herb Kamm in the *Milwaukee Journal*. "Like it or not, Maris is inescapably wedded to the home run, and his audiences are not likely to be satisfied with less." And that was indeed the case. Although he hit 33 homers in 1962, fifth most in the American League, and drove in 100 runs and helped the Yankees win the World Series in seven games over the San Francisco Giants, many saw him as a failure. "When it became apparent that there would be no repeat of 61 homers, that he'd not even come close, some small minds took parting shots at Maris and when October came, the Idol of 1961 was the Flop of 1962," wrote Bob Stewart in *Baseball's Greatest Players Today*.[12]

Maris suffered a series of injuries over the next four seasons with the Yankees which limited his playing time and hampered his offensive production. The worst of these occurred on June 27, 1965, when he fractured his hand after ramming it against an umpire's shoe while sliding across home plate. He appeared in only four more games—46 in all—before having surgery at the end of the season. The Yankees kept issuing statements that he was day-to-day, leaving the impression that he was malingering. Maris did not know at the time how serious the injury was, he simply knew he could not play because it was agonizing to do so. "All I had to go on was what they told me," he said much later. "I couldn't swing a bat without pain and after a while I couldn't throw the ball without pain, but what could I do? You can't hold your hand out to people who don't believe you and show what pain looks like." It robbed him of all his power. Maris, justifiably, blamed Yankee management for not being straight with him about the extent of his injury and making clear to the public that he was seriously hurt. He played just one more season in Yankee pinstripes, appearing in 119 games, but producing just 13 home runs and 43 RBIs.[13]

He was on the verge of retiring before the Yankees traded him to the St. Louis Cardinals at the end of the year. Cards owner Augie Busch convinced Maris to play for two seasons with the promise of a beer distributorship if he did so. Maris found new life and was much better appreciated than he was in his last few years with the Yankees. He played on a part-time basis, managing 125 games in 1967 and 100 in 1968, his final year. His home run total over those two summers was only 14, but he was a major contributor to the Cardinals' two World Series appearances during that time. In fact, he had the second highest batting average (.385) and the most RBIs (seven) on the team in the 1967 Series.

Maris was proud of his historic accomplishment in 1961, but there were times when he wished it never happened. "Hitting those 61 home runs that year had to be the most important thing I ever did in baseball," he said thinking back to that season of glory, "but it also brought me the most misery." There is no question that Maris brought some of this misery on himself. He could be abrasive, sullen, even "red-assed" as the pressure mounted that long, hot summer of 1961. But the fact that he was not Ruth, not Mantle, not the image of the heroic ballplayer the public seemed to want, hurt him far more than any reaction he had to his sudden fame. The problem, as biographer Maury Allen noted, was that "his values were old-fashioned—hard work, dedication, love of family, pride, loyalty, grace—in a world that exploited pizzazz." But the public and press reaction to him may have been the very thing that helped him achieve what he did. "The more attention he received from the fans and media, the more stubborn he became," wrote teammate Tony Kubek. "Not only was Roger determined to pass Ruth, he was going to prove himself to all the doubters. He did it with incredible single-mindedness and sense of purpose. It was as if he had a vendetta against those who said he couldn't do it. He wasn't malicious, he just wasn't going to let anyone beat him down."[14]

He achieved what many thought was impossible and did it under circumstances no other ballplayer before or since ever experienced. The constant glare of publicity, the negative press, the relentless sniping and criticism of his talent, and the internal pressure he put on himself would have broken a lesser man than Roger Maris. It is testimony to his courage and tenacity that he took all that was thrown at him, never once giving in no matter how bad things got. He had succeeded against all odds.

Appendix: Roger Maris by the Numbers

Roger Maris vs. the Pitchers

Name/Throws	PA		Hits		HRs		RBIs		BA	
	1961	Total	1961	Total	1961	Total	1961	Total	1961	Total
Aguirre, H. (L)	6	53	1	8	1	4	2	10	.200	.170
Archer, J. (L)	19	21	3	3	1	1	2	2	.188	.167
Bass, N. (R)	6	6	2	2	1	1	3	3	.400	.400
Baumann, F. (L)	16	39	5	12	1	2	3	10	.313	.316
Bell, G. (R)	16	84	4	25	2	5	5	14	.400	.347
Brown, H. (R)	10	52	2	12	1*	2	0	5	.222	.245
Burnside, P. (L)	14	40	4	12	3	5	6	10	.286	.316
Casale, J. (R)	3	19	1	3	1	1	2	3	.333	.176
Cheney, T. (R)	2	11	1	2	1	1	1	1	.500	.200
Conley, G. (R)	10	23	4	6	2	2	5	6	.400	.286
Daniels, B. (R)	12	39	2	12	1	1	1	1	.182	.353
Donovan, D. (R)	14	78	4	22	1	4	2	10	.308	.306
Estrada, C. (R)	7	37	4	7	1	1	2	4	.571	.233
Fisher, J. (R)	11	42	2	7	1	1	2	3	.200	.184
Fornieles, M. (R)	2	23	1	6	1	1	3	3	1.000	.333
Fox, T. (R)	3	13	1	6	1	1	2	5	.333	.462
Foytack, P. (R)	4	66	2	13	1	4	1	9	.500	.241
Funk, F. (R)	3	6	1	2	1	1	1	1	.333	.333
Grant, J. (R)	12	60	4	17	1	7	1	12	.333	.315
Grba, E. (R)	17	23	3	5	2	2	3	3	.200	.250
Hacker, W. (R)	3	3	1	1	1	1	3	3	.333	.333
Herbert, R. (R)	17	57	5	12	2	4	3	9	.294	.222
James, J. (R)	2	2	1	1	1	1	1	1	.500	.500
Kemmerer, R. (R)	6	55	3	20	2	6	2	15	.500	.385
Klippstein, J. (R)	5	13	2	3	1	1	1	3	.500	.273
Kutyna, M. (R)	5	11	2	3	1	1	4	5	.400	.300
Larsen, D. (R)	3	16	1	6	1	2	1	4	.333	.429
Lary, F. (R)	22	101	7	31	3	8	5	15	.389	.330

Appendix

Name/Throws	PA		Hits		HRs		RBIs		BA	
	1961	Total	1961	Total	1961	Total	1961	Total	1961	Total
McBride, K. (R)	15	50	4	9	1	1	3	3	.364	.205
McLish, C. (R)	4	25	2	6	2	3	3	6	.500	.250
Monboquette, B. (R)	19	105	5	24	2	7	2	15	.385	.276
Mossi, D. (L)	17	73	4	12	1	2	2	6	.250	.174
Muffett, B. (R)	4	15	1	2	1	1	3	4	.333	.154
Nuxhall, J. (L)	8	8	1	1	1	1	1	1	.125	.125
Palmquist, E. (R)	1	1	1	1	1	1	3	3	1.000	1.000
Pappas, M. (R)	10	95	2	15	1	4	1	14	.250	.169
Pascual, C. (R)	17	125	2	26	1	6	3	18	.154	.234
Perry, J. (R)	15	55	5	16	3	9	7	16	.417	.340
Pierce, B. (L)	8	81	5	15	2	4	6	12	.833	.208
Pizarro, J. (L)	14	57	4	12	1	1	2	6	.308	.235
Purkey, B. (R)	5	5	1	1	1**	1	1	1	.200	.200
Ramos, P. (R)	15	87	3	23	2	7	6	17	.200	.288
Shaw, B. (R)	15	54	5	15	1	1	3	5	.385	.300
Sisler, D. (R)	5	23	1	5	1	1	2	5	.200	.238
Stallard, T. (R)	6	7	1	1	1	1	1	1	.167	.143
Stigman, D. (L)	8	54	4	10	1	3	2	5	.667	.227
Walker, J. (R)	9	40	1	12	1	4	1	8	.143	.375
Wynn, E. (R)	4	48	1	11	1	3	2	8	.500	.275

*HR did not count
**Hit in World Series

Chapter Notes

Chapter 1

1. Roger Maris and Jim Ogle, *Roger Maris at Bat* [hereafter cited as *RMAB*] (Des Moines, IA: Meredith Press, 1962), 173–174.
2. Tom Calvin and Danny Peary, *Roger Maris: Baseball's Reluctant Hero* (New York: Simon & Schuster, 2010), 116.
3. *RMAB*, 134.
4. *RMAB*, 106–107.
5. *RMAB*, 115–116.
6. *RMAB*, 57.
7. *RMAB*, 58, 132–133; Alan Schwarz, "The Man Behind the Myth," *Sport*, October 1998, 80.
8. Harvey Rosenfeld, *Roger Maris*: A Title to Fame* (Fargo, ND: Prairie House, 1991), 58.
9. David Halberstam, *October 1964* (New York: Villard Books, 1994), 162; Ralph Houk and Robert W. Creamer, *Season of Glory: The Amazing Saga of the 1961 New York Yankees* (New York: G. P. Putnam's Sons, 1988), 123–124, 259; *RMAB*, 97.
10. "Angry King of Swat," *New York Times*, October 2, 1961, 38.
11. Jimmy Cannon, "Maris' Side," *New York Journal-American*, September 14, 1961, 26; *RMAB*, 98.
12. *RMAB*, 70.
13. Tom Meany, "Roger Maris: The Man Who Shook Up the Yankees," *Sport*, November 1960, 62–63; Houk, *Season of Glory*, 258–259; Dick Young, "Roomie Cerv 'Amazed' at Rog Maris Patience," *Omaha World Herald*, September 20, 1961, 37.
14. *RMAB*, 116.
15. Halberstam, *October 1964*, 159.
16. Jimmy Cannon, "Roger Maris," *New York Journal-American*, September 3, 1961, 35; Cannon, "Maris' Side."
17. Halberstam, *October 1964*, 159–160.
18. "The Babe Ruth Story," *Time*, August 30, 1948, 46.
19. Mark Inabinett, *Grantland Rice and His Heroes: the Sportswriter as Mythmaker in the 1920s* (Knoxville: University of Tennessee Press, 1994), 5–6; Jon Enriquez, "Coverage of Sports," in *American Journalism: History, Principles, Practices*, edited by W. David Sloan and Lisa Mullikin Parcell (Jefferson, NC: McFarland, 2002), 201.
20. Cannon, "Roger Maris," 35.
21. Enriquez, "Coverage of Sports," 202–203; Alan Schwarz, "The Impartial Press, with an Asterisk," *Inside Sports*, October 1997, 18.
22. *RMAB*, 148; Jimmy Cannon, "Man to Man," *New York Journal-American*, August 9, 1961, 34.
23. Robert L. Teague, "The Not-So-Private Life of the M-Squad," *New York Times*, September 10, 1961, Sec. 5, 2; *RMAB*, 80–81; Houk, *Season of Glory*, 257.
24. Jane Leavy, *The Last Boy: Mickey Mantle and the End of America's Childhood* (New York: HarperCollins, 2010), 234.
25. Schwarz, "Man Behind the Myth," 84.
26. *RMAB*, 146–147; Rick Talley, "Bench Talk," *Rockford (IL) Register Republic*, September 15, 1961, 51.
27. *RMAB*, 147.
28. *RMAB*, 168; Ira Berkow, "Home Run Record a Bitter Memory for Roger Maris," in *The Best of Baseball Digest*, edited by John Kuenster (Chicago: Ivan R. Dee, 2006), 139.
29. *RMAB*, 168–170; Teague, 2.
30. Jack Orr, "Roger Maris," in *My Greatest Day in Baseball*, edited by John P. Carmichael (New York: Grosset and Dunlap, 1968), 109.
31. Leonard Shecter, "Working Press," *New York Post*, September 19, 1961, 48; Sid Gray, "A Man Named Maris," *New York Post*, July 31, 1961, 40.
32. George Frazier, "Maris Talented with Bat but a Champion? Nay!," *Boston Herald*, September 20, 1961, 12.
33. Jim Ogle, "Fact and Legend of Roger Maris," *Sporting News*, January 14, 1967, 25.
34. Halberstam, *October 1964*, 168.
35. "Ruth's Record Can Be Broken Only in 154 Games, Frick Rules," *New York Times*, July 18, 1961, 20; Ford C Frick, *Games, Asterisks, and People: Memoirs of a Lucky Fan* (New York: Crown, 1973), 155; Joseph M. Sheehan, "Yankees Blank Orioles for Ford's 17th Victory," *New York Times*, July 18, 1961, 20.
36. "Lost Home Runs," *Retrosheet*, accessed August 8, 2017, retrosheet.org/losthr.htm.
37. Jack Hand, "Tie Games Won't Count in Bid to Top Ruth's Mark," *Times-Picayune (New Orleans, LA)*, August 11, 1961, 26; Leonard Koppett, "Meanwhile, in Chicago—Another Record?," *New York Post*, September 21, 1961, 70.
38. C. C. Johnson Spink, "Writers Back Frick's Homer Decision," *Sporting News*, August 9, 1961, 4.
39. Arthur Daley, "Protecting the Records," *New York Times*, October 23, 1960, S2; "The 1961 Yankees,"

1991 Elias Baseball Analysist, edited by Seymour Siwoff et al., (New York: Simon & Schuster, 1991), 423.

40. "Koufax Sets Strikeout Record, but Dodgers Lose to Phils, 2–1," *Sun (Baltimore),* September 28, 1961, 29; Shirley Povich, "Morning," *Washington Post,* September 29, 1961, D1; "Gentile's Five Grand-Slams Matched Mark," *Baseball Guide and Record Book 1962,* compiled by J. G. Taylor Spink (St. Louis: Charles Spink and Son, 1962), 111,136.

41. Maury Allen, *Roger Maris: A Man for All Seasons* (New York: Donald I. Fine, 1986), 137–138.

42. Milton Gross, "A Footnote to Frick's *," *New York Post,* September 12, 1961, 57.

43. "Maris, Feeling Fatigued, Wearily Wallops 55th," *Boston Globe,* September 8, 1961, 27; *RMAB,* 199.

44. Joe Trimble, "Group Will Decide on Record If Maris Wallops More Than 60," *Kansas City Star,* September 19, 1961, 12; "Maris Finishes Second to Babe's No. 1," *Sporting News,* September 27, 1961, 10

45. *RMAB,* 196; Ken Rosenthal, "Moments Baseball Would Rather Forget," *Sporting News,* July 29, 2002, 16; "Baseball Drops the Asterisk* from Maris' Record," *Deseret News,* September 5, 1991, accessed January 4, 2018, https://www.deseretnews.com/article/181588/BASEBALL-DROPS-THE-ASTERISK-FROM-MARIS-RECORD.html.

46. Spink, "Writers Back," 1,4.

47. Spink, "Writers Back," 1,4; Eugene Fitzgerald, "Maris Biggest 'Offense' May Be Forthright Honesty," *Fargo (ND) Forum and Moorhead (MN) News,* September 27, 1961, 26.

48. Walter Bingham, "Assault on The Record," *Sports Illustrated,* July 31, 1961, 10.

49. Hy Hurwitz, "Mick 'Wouldn't Want Mark If It Was Set in 155 Games," *Sporting News,* August 9, 1961, 4; Mickey Mantle with Herb Gluck, *The Mick* (Garden City, NY: Doubleday, 1985), 196.

50. Gross, "A Footnote," 57.

51. "Cronin Disputes Frick on HR Mark," *Boston Globe,* September 14, 1961, 41; Bob Holbrook, "Cronin Hails Maris," *Boston Globe,* September 29, 1961, 45; Bob Considine, "Happy Chandler Roots for Mantle and Maris," *Washington Post,* August 22, 1961, A15.

52. Richard J. H. Johnson, "Homer Record After 154 Games Won't Count with Fan on Street," *New York Times,* September 21, 1961, 42.

53. Allen Barra, *Clearing the Bases: The Greatest Baseball Debates of the Last Century* (New York: St. Martin's Press, 2002), 95.

54. "Did Maris Break Ruth HR Record?," *Springfield (MA) Union,* October 3, 1961, 30; Trimble, "Group Will Decide,"12; "Was Frick Out of Bounds in Making Rule? Dan Asks," *Sporting News,* August 9, 1961, 4; John P. Carvalho, *Frick*: Baseball's Third Commissioner* (Jefferson, NC: McFarland, 2016), 12; Oscar Kahan, "Scribes Back Off—Threat to Protest Fades," *Sporting News,* December 13, 1961, 8.

55. Frick, *Games,* 154–155.

56. James Reston, "The Asterisk That Shook the Baseball World," *New York Times,* October 1, 1961, Sec. 4, 8.

57. "Babe Ruth's 60 Home Runs Created No Hysteria in 1927," *Kansas City Times,* September 19, 1961, 12.

58. Povich, "Morning," September 29, 1961, D1; Joe McGuff, "Ruth's 60th Homer Noted Calmly," *Kansas City Star,* August 2, 1961, 37; "Home Run Record Falls as Ruth Hits 60th; Pirates Lose; Giants Out of Race," *New York Times,* October 1, 1927, 12; Bob Considine, "Mantle and Maris Swinging at $-M Rainbow," *New York Journal-American,* August 14, 1961, 24.

59. Jimmy Cannon, "No One Else," *New York Journal-American,* September 18, 1961, 23.

60. Arthur Daley, "Improbable Finish by Foxx Was Strictly in Character," *Milwaukee Journal,* September 18, 1961, 2; Joe King, "Sultan's Big Shadow Starts to Toll 'Ten' Over M-and-M," *Sporting News,* September 6, 1961, 7.

61. Frank Graham, "About Roger Maris," *New York Journal-American,* September 20, 1961, 31; Dan Parker, "Inimitable Bambino Worth 10 Like Mantle, Maris?," *Boston Globe,* September 17, 1961, 69.

62. Roger Kahn, "Pursuit of No. 60: The Ordeal of Roger Maris," *Sports Illustrated,* October 2, 1961, 24; "Immortal Babe Remains 'King,'" *Anderson (IN) Herald Bulletin,* September 21, 1961, 62.

63. "Hornsby-Maris Feud Continues to Grow," *Greeley (CO) Daily Tribune,* March 24, 1962, 11; "Hornsby-Maris Feud Boils," *Joplin (MO) News Herald,* March 24, 1962, 4.

64. "The 1961 Yankees," 432.

65. Arthur Daley, "Sports of the Times," *New York Times,* August 27, 1961, Sec. 5, 2.

66. Jimmy Cannon, "Roger Maris," in *Nobody Asked Me, But...: The World of Jimmy Cannon,* edited by Jack Cannon and Tom Cannon (New York: Holt, Rinehart and Winston, 1978), 50.

67. Ralph Terry with John Wooley, *Right Down the Middle: The Ralph Terry Story* (Tulsa, OK: Mullerhaus, 2016), 127.

68. Bingham, "Assault,"10; Bob Considine, "Maris, Mantle Like Each Other," *Washington Post,* August 16, 1961, C3; Halberstam, 166.

69. *RMAB,* 34–36, 47, 163–164; Larry Stone, "The Quest—Roger Maris," *Seattle Times,* July 6, 1997, accessed January 4, 2018, http://community.seattletimes.nwsource.com/archive/?date=19970706&slug=2548 199; Jimmy Cannon, "Mickey's Story," *New York Journal-American,* September 13, 1961, 34.

70. Cannon, "Mickey's Story," 34; Bob Considine, "Even Amateurs Tip M & M in HR Duel," *New York Journal-American,* August 15, 1961, 22; *RMAB,* 148–149.

71. Considine, "Maris, Mantle," C3; Jack Lang, "Friendly HR Rivalry Keeps Mantle Going," *Long Island Star-Journal,* September 9, 1961, 6; *RMAB,* 79; Tony Kubek and Terry Pluto, *Sixty-One: The Team/The Record/The Men* (New York: Macmillan, 1987), 23.

72. Jimmy Cannon, "The Other Guys," *New York Journal-American,* September 17, 1961, 42.

73. Bobby Richardson with David Thomas, *Impact Player: Leaving a Legacy On and Off the Field* (Carol Stream, IL: Tyndale House, 2012), 116; Kubek, *Sixty-One,* 23; *RMAB,* 157.

74. *RMAB,* 80.

75. Steve Hirdt, "Myths, Misconceptions and Asterisks from '61," *ESPN.com,* 2001, accessed January 19, 2018, https://www.espn.com/page2/s/number/010427.html; "The 1961 Yankees," 425–426.

76. Leonard Koppett, "Mighty Mr. Maris," *Saturday Evening Post,* September 2, 1961, 25; Meany, "Roger Maris," 64.

77. Bingham, "Assault," 10–11.
78. Francis Stann, "Win, Lose or Draw," *Evening Star (Washington, DC)*, December 18, 1961.
79. Hirdt, "Myths."
80. Hirdt, "Myths"; "The 1961 Yankees," 423.
81. Jerry Nason, "Don't Knock '61 Pitching in A. L.," *Boston Globe*, September 7, 1961, 43.
82. Anita Bernstein, "Question Autonomy, with an Asterisk," *Emory Law Journal* 54 (January 15, 2005): 241.
83. "Ball Too Lively Now, Says Early Wynn," *Washington Post*, August 13, 1961, C2; "DiMag Says Psychology Against Topping Ruth," *Fargo (ND) Forum and Moorhead (MN) News*, August 8, 1961, 15.
84. Murray Robinson, "Past Fogs M-Boys' Critics," *New York Journal-American*, August 27, 1961, 37; "Home Runs … 61 in '61?," *Newsweek*, August 14, 1961, 44.
85. Howard M. Tuckner, "'61 Ball May (or May Not) Account for Homers," *New York Times*, August 14, 1961, 1, 19.
86. Robert H. Boyle, "Yes It's Livelier—and Here Is the Proof," *Sports Illustrated*, August 28, 1961, 14–17; Tuckner, "61 Ball," 19.
87. Leonard Koppett, "Working Press," *New York Post*, September 13, 1961, 91.
88. "For the Hot-Stove League: Final Report on Those Baseball Changes," *Popular Mechanics*, December 1961, 84, 210.
89. "For the Hot-Stove League," 84.
90. "For the Hot-Stove League," 212.
91. Joseph M. Sheehan, "The Lively Bat Becomes a Livelier Issue," *New York Times*, August 20, 1961, Sec. 5, 1, 3.
92. "American League Batting Year-by-Year Averages," Baseball-Reference.com, accessed February 14, 2018, https://www.baseball-reference.com/leagues/AL/bat.shtml; "National League Batting Year-by-Year Averages," Baseball-Reference.com, accessed February 20, 2018, https://www.baseball-reference.com/leagues/NL/bat.shtml.
93. "American League Batting Year-by-Year Averages,"; Sheehan, "The Lively Bat," 1, 3.
94. Sheehan, "The Lively Bat," 1, 3; Daniel A. Russell, "Bat Weight, Swing Speed and Ball Velocity," *Physics and Acoustics of Baseball and Softball Bats*, March 27, 2008, accessed February 12, 2018, http://www.acs.psu.edu/drussell/bats/batw8.html; Ben Walker, "Properties of Baseball Bats," *Baseball Research Journal*, Summer 2010, accessed February 13, 2018, http://sabr.org/research/properties-baseball-bats; Davin Coburn, "Baseball Physics: Anatomy of a Home Run," *Popular Mechanics*, December 17, 2009, accessed February 13, 2018, https://www.popularmechanics.com/adventure/sports/a4569/4216783/.
95. Leslie Lieber, "Roger Maris Proves the Old-Timers' Bats Weren't So Bad!," *This Week Magazine*, May 20, 1962, 9–11; Paul Kirkpatrick, "Batting the Ball," *Journal of American Physics* 31 (1963): 611; Sheehan, "The Lively Bat," 1, 3.
96. "The 1961 Yankees," 423–424; Mark Emery, "The Sultan of Swat: 88 Years After Babe Ruth's 60th Blast, a Look at His 1927 Season," *Daily News (New York)*, September 30, 2015, accessed February 20, 2018, http://www.nydailynews.com/sports/baseball/babe-ruth-1927-season-88-years-60th-homer-article-1.2379875.
97. "The 1961 Yankees," 424–425; Barney Kremenke, "New A. L. Parks Stymie Homer Assault," *New York Journal-American*, August 22, 1961, 24; *Baseball Guide and Record Book 1962*, 51; Jim Gordon, "Wrigley Field (Los Angeles)," Society for American Baseball Research, n.d., accessed March 23, 2018, http://sabr.org/bioproj/park/3912a666.
98. Bingham, 11; Philip J. Lowry, *Green Cathedrals: The Ultimate Celebration of Major League and Negro League Ballparks* (New York: Walker, 2006), 71–74; James R. Harrison, "Two Innings Enough for Yankees to Win," *New York Times*, May 23, 1927, 16.
99. Lowry, *Green Cathedrals*, 17, 201–202.
100. *RMAB*, 96; Lowry, *Green Cathedrals*, 111–112, 176; *Baseball Guide and Record Book 1962*, 50.
101. Ernest Mehl, "Sporting Comment," *Kansas City Star*, August 18, 1961, 29.
102. Mehl, "Sporting Comment," 29.
103. Christine Dell'Amore, "Sleep Preferences Predict Baseball Success, Study Says," *National Geographic*, June 16, 2011, accessed February 28, 2018, https://news.nationalgeographic.com/news/2011/06/110615-sleep-major-league-baseball-science/ ; "Sleep Type Predicts Day and Night Batting Averages of Major League Baseball Players," *American Academy of Sleep Medicine*, June 13, 2011, accessed February 26, 2018, https://aasm.org/sleep-type-predicts-day-and-night-batting-averages-of-major-league-baseball-players/. Interestingly, the same trend is seen among pitchers as well. Morning-type pitchers maintained a 3.06 ERA in evening types a 3.49 ERA in games before 7:00 p.m. In games later than that, ERAs increased for both types, but evening types performed slightly better (4.07 ERA) than their morning counterparts (4.15 ERA). See "Sleep Preference Can Predict Performance of Major League Baseball Pitchers," *ScienceDaily*, June 11, 2010, accessed February 26, 2018, https://www.sciencedaily.com/releases/2010/06/100609083223.htm.
104. John Drebinger, "Keeping Up with Cross-Country Slate Is Nightmare of Planes, Trains, Buses," *New York Times*, May 10, 1961, 57; Cleveland Clinic, "Shift Work Sleep Disorder," *My.Clevelandclinic.org*, November 17, 2017, accessed February 22, 2018, https://my.clevelandclinic.org/health/diseases/12146-shift-work-sleep-disorder.
105. C. Cruz, P. Della Rocco, and C. Hackworth, "Effects of Quick Rotating Shift Schedules on the Health and Adjustment of Air Traffic Controllers," *Aviation, Space, and Environmental Medicine* 71 (April 2000): 400–407, accessed February 22, 2018, https://www.ncbi.nlm.nih.gov/pubmed/10766465; James McIntosh, "The Impact of Shift Work on Health," *Medical News Today*, January 11, 2016, accessed February 22, 2018, https://www.medicalnewstoday.com/articles/288310.php.
106. All scheduling and statistical information are from Baseball-Reference.com, accessed February 26, 2018.
107. Drebinger, "Keeping Up," 57.
108. Alex Song, Thomas Severini, and Ravi Allada, "How Jet Lag Impairs Major League Baseball Performance," *Proceedings of the National Academy of Sciences*

114 (February 7, 2017): 1407–1412; Rachael Lallensack, "Jet Lag Puts Baseball Players Off Their Game," *Science*, January 23, 2017, accessed February 22, 2018, http://www.sciencemag.org/news/2017/01/jet-lag-puts-baseball-players-their-game; George Dvorsky, "The Surprising Way Jet Lag Impacts Major League Baseball Games," *Gizmodo*, January 23, 2017, accessed February 28, 2018, https://gizmodo.com/the-surprising-way-jet-lag-impacts-major-league-basebal-1791521616.
  109. Drebinger, "Keeping Up," 57.
  110. Barney Kremenko, "Maris Dreads Tough Schedule," *New York Journal-American*, August 28, 1961, 26; Frazier, "Maris Talented," 12.
  111. American Academy of Sleep Medicine, "Fatigue and Sleep Linked to Major League Baseball Performance and Career Longevity," *ScienceDaily*, May 31, 2013, accessed February 28, 2018, https://www.sciencedaily.com/releases/2013/05/130531105506.htm.
  112. *RMAB*, 201–202.
  113. Houk, *Season of Glory*, 257; Oliver E. Kuechle, "Time Out for Talk," *Milwaukee Journal*, September 22, 1961, Part 2, 11.
  114. Barra, *Clearing the Bases*, 97.
  115. Koppett, "Working Press," September 13, 1961, 91.
  116. George Vecsey, "Roger Maris: No Asterisk," *New York* Times, December 16, 1985, C11; Schwarz, "Man Behind the Myth," 80.
  117. Barra, *Clearing the Bases*, 97–98.

Chapter 2

  1. Roger Maris and Jim Ogle, *Roger Maris at Bat* [hereafter cited as *RMAB*] (Des Moines, IA: Meredith Press, 1962), 100.
  2. Tom Calvin and Danny Peary, *Roger Maris: Baseball's Reluctant Hero* (New York: Simon & Schuster, 2010), 37–38, 46.
  3. Leonard Shecter, *Roger Maris: Home Run Hero* (New York: Bartholomew House, 1961), 42–44.
  4. Shecter, *Roger Maris* 43–44; Leonard Koppett, "Mighty Mr. Maris," *Saturday Evening Post*, September 2, 1961, 24.
  5. Calvin and Peary, *Roger Maris*, 53–59; "Maras Named as Rookie of the Year," *Aberdeen (SD) Daily News*, August 6, 1953, 13; Shecter, 44–45, 49; "Northern League Hurler Wins 5th Game in 8 Days," *Brainerd (MN) Daily Dispatch*, August 5, 1953, 8.
  6. Shecter, *Roger Maris*, 44–45.
  7. *RMAB*, 32; Shecter, *Roger Maris*, 45.
  8. Don Weiskopf, "Batting Style of the Yankees," *Athletic Journal* 41 (January 1961): 16–17; Don Weiskopf, "Hitting the Long Ball," *Athletic Journal* 59 (February 1979): 109.
  9. "Roger Maris: Has He the Stuff for Greatness," *Look*, June 20, 1961, 115.
  10. Lyall Smith, "Swing's Thing in Roger's Record Hop," *Detroit Free Press*, September 19, 1961, 27.
  11. Shecter, *Roger Maris*, 45–46.
  12. *RMAB*, 133; Weiskopf, "Batting Style," 17; Jo-Jo White, "Reading Boss Picks Hardy, Barone," *Brunswick (GA) News*, January 26, 1956, 7; Shecter, *Roger Maris*, 45–46; Koppett, "Mighty Mr. Maris," 54; Sid Gray, "A Man Named Maris," *New York Post*, August 3, 1961, 51.

  13. Shecter, *Roger Maris*, 47–48; "Fortin Tied for Top Mound Mark," *Evansville (IN) Press*, July 11, 1954, 5C; "Keokuk Thumps Indians, 8–5," *Evansville (IN) Courier*, July 12, 1954, 10; "Gott Noses Our Hersh by .003 Point for Three-I League Bat Crown," *Sunday Courier and Press (Evansville, IN)*, September 12, 1954, 4C; "'54 III Batting Averages," *Sunday Courier and Press (Evansville, IN)*, December 12, 1954, 7C.
  14. Shecter, *Roger Maris*, 37–38, 48–49.
  15. Shecter, *Roger Maris*, 37–38, 48–49.
  16. Shecter, *Roger Maris*, 48–49; Calvin and Peary, *Roger Maris*, 72–73; "Hertwick and Dom Minnick '55 Most Valuable in Eastern, *Sporting News*, October 19, 1955, 29; Sid Gray, "A Man Called Maris," *New York Post*, August 1, 1961, 58.
  17. Shecter, *Roger Maris*, 49.
  18. Shecter, *Roger Maris*, 49–50; Gordon Cobbledick, "Plain Dealing," *Cleveland Plain Dealer*, September 14, 1956, 25, and November 29, 1956, 33; "Maris Stops Wings' Rally," *Omaha World Herald*, September 28, 1956, 23; "Indians Win for 2–0 Lead," *Omaha World Herald*, September 29, 1956, 10.
  19. Shecter, *Roger Maris*, 52–56; Harry Jones, "Star Rookies Open Fight for Jobs," *Cleveland Plain Dealer*, February 19, 1957, 26; Harry Jones, "Batting Around," *Cleveland Plain Dealer*, February 25, 1957, 37.
  20. Shecter, *Roger Maris*, 54–56.
  21. Harry Jones, "Can Farrell's Boys Make the Indians," *Cleveland Plain Dealer Pictorial Magazine*, February 17, 1957, 9; James E. Doyle, "The Sport Trail," *Cleveland Plain Dealer*, April 2, 1957, 29; Harry Jones, "Tribe Is Picked to Finish Fourth," *Cleveland Plain Dealer*, April 14, 1957, 3C.
  22. Gordon Cobbledick, "Plain Dealing," *Cleveland Plain* Dealer, April 17, 1957, 27; Harry Jones, "Indians Win in the 11th, 8 to 3," *Cleveland Plain Dealer*, April 19, 1957, 1; James E. Doyle, "The Sport Trail," *Cleveland Plain Dealer*, April 19, 1957, 25; "Good Trick If He Does It at Night," *Cleveland Plain Dealer*, April 19, 1957, 25; Hal Lebovitz, "Maris Always Knew He 'Couldn't Miss,'" *Sporting News*, May 1, 1957, 7.
  23. Harry Jones, "Maris Hikes Sprit of Cleveland Team," *Cleveland Plain Dealer*, April 20, 1957, 25.
  24. "The 1961 Yankees," *1991 Elias Baseball Analysist*, edited by Seymour Siwoff et al. (New York: Simon & Schuster, 1991), 427.
  25. Shecter, *Roger Maris*, 45–47.
  26. Chuck Heaton, "Maris Is Tribe's Newest Casualty," *Cleveland Plain Dealer*, May 11, 1957, 23; "Maris on Shelf for Two Weeks," *Cleveland Plain Dealer*, May 12, 1957, 1C; Harry Jones, "Batting Around," *Cleveland Plain Dealer*, June 30, 1957, 4C; Tom Meany, "Roger Maris: The Man Who Shook Up the Yankees," *Sport*, November 1960, 67.
  27. Harry Jones, "Indians' Bragan Promises He'll Catch Yankees," *Cleveland Plain Dealer*, October 1, 1957, 29; Gordon Cobbledick, "New Tribe Boss Must Rebuild Club," *Cleveland Plain Dealer*, October 17, 1957, 33; Harry Jones, "Frank Lane to Be Indian Boss," *Cleveland Plain Dealer*, November 12, 1957, 1; Gordon Cobbledick, "Plain Dealing," *Cleveland Plain Dealer*, December 3, 1957, 33.
  28. Gray, "Man Called Maris," 58.
  29. Shecter, *Roger Maris*, 58–60, 73–75; Harry Jones, "Batting Around," *Cleveland Plain Dealer*, December

5, 1957, 35; Harry Jones, "Narleski Signs, Gets Pay Boost," *Cleveland Plain Dealer*, January 15, 1958, 25–26; Harry Jones, "Batting Around," *Cleveland Plain Dealer*, May 1, 1958, 30; Bobby Bragan, *You Can't Hit the Ball with the Bat on Your Shoulder: The Baseball Life and Times of Bobby Bragan* (Fort Worth, TX: Summit Group, 1992), 223–225; Harry Jones, "Bragan Out, Joe Gordon Hired," *Cleveland Plain Dealer*, June 27, 1958, 1; J. G. T. Spink, "Looping the Loops," *Sporting News*, May 25, 1960, 6.

30. Ernest Mehl, "Sporting Comment," *Kansas City Star*, June 16, 1958, 10.

31. Shecter, *Roger Maris*, 62; Bill Oliver, "Never!," *Kansas City Star*, September 8, 1958, 22.

32. *RMAB*, 46; Ernest Mehl, "Sporting Comment," *Kansas City* Star, August 14, 1959, 29; Shecter, *Roger Maris*, 67; Joe McDuff, "Baseball Fans Difficult to Figure," *Kansas City Star*, September 4, 1959, 28; Meany, "Roger Maris," 65; Arthur Daley, "The Newest Yankee," *New York Times*, December 15, 1959, 54.

33. Jeff Katz, *The Kansas City A's and the Wrong Half of the Yankees*, Hingham, MA: Maple Street Press, 2007, 4–12, 192–193; Michael Shapiro, "The Del Webb Yankees," *New Yorker*, July 23, 2010, accessed March 9, 2018, https://www.newyorker.com/news/sportingscene/the-del-webb-yankees; Ernest Mehl, "A's Lashed, Lauded for Swapping Maris," *Sporting News*, December 23, 1959, 5–6; "Yanks Get Maris from A's in 7-Player Swap," *Globe-Gazette (Mason City, IA)*, December 12, 1959, 13; Shecter, *Roger Maris*, 83; John Drebinger, "Yanks Trade Bauer, Larsen and Get Maris in 7-Player Deal with Athletics," *New York Times*, December 12, 1959, 27; "Veeck, Lane Blast Yanks Deal," *Philadelphia Inquirer*, December 13, 1959, S2; Milton Gross, "Speaking Out," *New York Post*, July 27, 1961, 56; Gray, "Man Called Maris," 58.

34. Lou O'Neill, "The Yankees Are Our Amigos in Kansas City," *Long Island Star-Journal*, April 7, 1960, 29.

35. Shecter, *Roger Maris*, 86–89; Koppett, "Mighty Mr. Maris," 55; Spink, "Looping," 6.

36. Meany, "Roger Maris," 61.

37. Joe McGuff, "Move to Left Field Difficult for Maris," *Kansas City Star*, February 14, 1960, B1, B4.

38. McGuff, "Move to Left Field " B1, B4; Dan Daniel, "Casey Sees Maris as Right Man to Fill Hole in Left," *Sporting News*, February 3, 1960, 8.

39. Dan Daniel, "Maris Quick to Okay Shift to Left Field," *Sporting News*, March 9, 1960, 9.

40. Meany, "Roger Maris," 62; Shecter, *Roger Maris*, 100–101; "'When I Am Hitting,'" *Time*, August 22, 1960, 43.

41. Meany, "Roger Maris," 63–64.

42. Dan Daniel, "Can Maris Stand the Pressure?," *New York World-Telegram*, October 5, 1960, 49; Shecter, *Roger* Maris, 101.

43. Jane Leavy, *The Last Boy: Mickey Mantle and the End of America's Childhood* (New York: HarperCollins, 2010), 188–189.

44. Leonard Shecter, "Mantle and His Temper," *New York Post*, March 30, 1960, 90; Milton Gross, "'Maris Bat Takes Load Off Mantle,'" *Omaha World Herald*, June 30, 1960, 25.

45. Jack Lang, "MVP 'Jobbing' an Old Story," *Jersey Journal (Jersey City, NJ)*, November 15, 1960, 21S.

46. Arthur Daley, "Mantle or Maris? A Tough Decision," *Richmond (VA) Times-Dispatch*, November 14, 1960, 28.

47. Daley, "Mantle or Maris?," 28; Leonard Shecter, "Maris Isn't the Only Yankee Who's Happy About Award," *New York Post*, November 10, 1960, 96.

48. Oscar Kahan, "MVP Maris Grabs Place on A. L. Glove Team," *Sporting News*, November 30, 1960, 19; "Roger Maris Rules as 'Sultan of Swat,'" *Terre Haute (IN) Star*, January 17, 1961, 7; Al Buck, "Now Maris Is on His Own," *New York Post*, January 30, 1961, 42.

49. Dan Daniel, "Soaring Salaries Heading for New High," *Sporting News*, January 18, 1961, 1–2.

50. Daniel, "Soaring Salaries," 1–2.

51. Salary figures are estimates because they were not publicly disclosed. Figures used are from the "Salaries" category included on each player page in Baseball-Reference.com as well as from the following: Jack Hand, "Roger Maris Questioned About 'Slump' While Signing Estimated $33,000 Pact," *Joplin (MO) News Herald*, January 31, 1961, 6; Dan Daniel, "Homer Duel Cinch to Produce 100-G Pay Check in '62," *Sporting News*, August 30, 1961, 6.

52. Roger Maris and Jim Ogle, *Roger Maris at Bat* [hereafter cited as *RMAB*] (Des Moines, IA: Meredith Press, 1962), 4–7; Pat Maris, "My Husband," *Look*, April 24, 1962, 89–90.

53. *RMAB*, 9.

54. "Chisox Win 3–1," *American-News(Aberdeen, SD)*, March 29, 1961, 19; John Drebinger, "Yanks Beat Cards in 11th and End Long Link with St. Petersburg," *New York Times*, April 6, 1961, 41; John Drebinger, "Houk Says Yanks Will Win Pennant Despite Poor Spring Record," *New York Times*, April 7, 1961, 35; John Drebinger, "Yank Spring Ends in St. Louis Rain," *New York Times*, April 10, 1961, 37.

Chapter 3

1. John Drebinger, "Minnesota Breaks into Majors with a Three-Hit Shutout over Yanks Here," *New York Times*, April 12, 1961, 50.

2. John Drebinger, "Mantle's 4th Homer in 4 Games Helps Yanks Down Orioles, 4–2," *New York Times*, April 22, 1961, 20.

3. Jack Lang, "Yanks Ride on Mick's HR Spree," *Jersey Journal (Jersey City, NJ)*, April 21, 1961, 24S; Charles Feeney, "Mantle Not Likely to Change," *Jersey Journal (Jersey City, NJ)*, April 17, 1961, 17S; John Drebinger, "Houk's Pitching Plans Muddled by Rain that Keeps Yanks Idle," *New York Times*, April 17, 1961, 38c.

4. John Drebinger, "Lary of Tigers Stops Yanks, 4–3, on 7-Hitter," *New York Times*, April 25, 1961, 42; John Drebinger, "Bombers Discuss Trade in Detroit," *New York Times*, April 26, 1961, 46; Ralph Houk, *Ballplayers Are Human, Too* (New York: G. P. Putnam's Sons, 1962), 103; Watson Spoelstra, "Lary Dusts Off Old Hex—Waves Magic Wing as Yanks Wilt," *Sporting News*, May 3, 1961, 4.

5. Tommy Devine, "Up-and-Down Foytack Levels Off as Winner," *Sporting News*, May 7, 1958, 5.

6. Devine, 5.

7. Jerry Nechal, "Paul Foytack," *SABR BioProject*, June 3, 2015, accessed May 21, 2018, https://sabr.org/bio

proj/person/0171793b; "Foytack Bombed as Starter; Assigned to Tiger Bull Pen," *Sporting News*, July 6, 1960, 17.

8. Spoelstra, 5.

9. Joe Falls, "Mantle Goes Pow, Pow—Tigers Bow," *Detroit Free Press*, April 27, 1961, 31.

10. Leonard Koppett, "All Maris Can Do Is to Keep Trying," *New York Post*, May 19, 1961, 92; Leonard Shecter, "Maris Didn't Let the Slump Get Him Down," *New York Post*, April 27, 1961, 76.

11. Dan Daniel, "Yanks Spinning Wheels, Look to Maris for Push," *Sporting News*, May 3, 1961, 12.

12. Houk, *Ballplayers Are Human, Too*, 96–97; Daniel, "Yanks Spinning Wheels," 12.

13. Robert L. Teague, "Yankees Subdue Indians as Mantle's Triple in 7th Delivers Decisive Run," *New York Times*, April 28, 1961, 37; Robert L. Teague, "Fuse of the Bombers," *New York Times*, April 29, 1961, 18.

14. Danny Peary, ed., *We Played the Game: 65 Players Remember Baseball's Greatest Era, 1947–1964* (New York: Hyperion, 1994), 376, 415, 486; Edward Kiersh, *Where Have You Gone, Vince DiMaggio?* (New York: Bantam, 1983), 219; Peter C. Bjarkman, "Pedro Ramos," *SABR BioProject*, August 31, 2011, accessed May 24, 2018, https://sabr.org/bioproj/person/c03a87ec; Tom Briere,"Twins Kick Up Quick Tango for Gay Pedro," *Sporting News*, April 19, 1961, 19; Leonard Koppett, "Lopez Helps Yanks—with His Glove," *New York Post*, May 4, 1961, 70; Herman Weiskopf, "The Infamous Spitter," *Sports Illustrated*, July 30, 1967, accessed September 25, 2018, https://www.si.com/vault/1967/07/31/609382/the-infamous-spitter.

15. "Little Things Do It," *Minneapolis Star*, May 4, 1961, 10; John Drebinger, "Yanks Beat Twins Second Time in Row as Maris' Homer Routs Ramos," *New York Times*, 43; *RMAB*, 9.

16. John Drebinger, "Yanks Beat Twins as Mantle Clouts 9th Homer," *New York Times*, May 5, 1961, 32; John Drebinger, "Boyer's Two-Run Homer in Ninth Enables Yanks to Defeat Angels on Coast," *New York Times*, May 6, 1961, 36.

17. Chuck Johnson and Chuck Boyer, "Eli Grba," *SABR BioProject*, May 4, 2015, accessed May 26, 2018, https://sabr.org/bioproj/person/ea132183; "The 1961 Yankees," *1991 Elias Baseball Analysist*, edited by Seymour Siwoff et al. (New York: Simon & Schuster, 1991), 424–425; Barney Kremenke, "New A. L. Parks Stymie Homer Assault," *New York Journal-American*, August 22, 1961, 24; Jim Gordon, "Wrigley Field (Los Angeles)," *Society for American Baseball Research*, accessed March 23, 2018, http://sabr.org/bioproj/park/3912a666.

18. Johnson and Boyer.

19. John Drebinger, "Angels Topple Bombers on 2 Homers by Wagner," *New York Times*, May 7, 1961, Sec.5, 4.

20. Drebinger,"Angels Topple Bombers," 4; *RMAB*, 9–10.

21. *RMAB*, 9–10.

22. *RMAB*, 10.

23. *RMAB*, 10–11; Houk, *Ballplayers Are Human, Too*, 105; Ralph Houk and Robert W. Creamer, *Season of Glory: The Amazing Saga of the 1961 New York Yankees* (New York: G. P. Putnam's Sons, 1988), 122.

24. *RMAB*, 10–11.

25. *RMAB*, 8, 10.

26. *RMAB*, 13–14; Bob Wolf, "'Poor Start Touched Off Big Four-Bagger Spree,' Rog Reveals," *Sporting News*, January 17, 1962, 16.

27. John Drebinger, "Yankees Trade Duren and Three Others to Angels for Cerv and Clevenger," *New York Times*, May 9, 1961, 47.

28. "Athletics Defeat Yankees 5–4, with Four-Run Rally in Eighth," *New York Times*, May 10, 1961, 56.

29. John Drebinger, "Yankees Top Athletics with Five-Run Eighth as Mantle Ends Batting Slump," *New York Times*, May 11, 1961, 46.

30. Louis Effrat, "Tigers Top Yanks Again, 8–3, and Lead by 4 ½ Games," *New York Times*, May 14, 1961, Sec. 5, 1; "Colavito Says He'd Enter Stands Again to Aid Dad," *New York Times*, May 14, 1961, Sec. 5, 3.

31. Robert L. Teague, "Senators Triumph Over Yankees on a Two-Hitter by Woodeshick and Sisler," *New York Times*, May 17, 1961, 44; Jack Lang, "Houk Stunned by Losses," *Jersey Journal (Jersey City, NJ)*, May 18, 1961, 17S.

32. Charlie Feeney, "Yankees Losing Patience," *Jersey Journal (Jersey City, NJ)*, May 22, 1961, 19S.

33. Bill Rives, "Dallas' Burnside Strikeout King in His First Season," *Sporting News*, July 27, 1955, 36; Joe King, "Seven-Year Trail Brings Burnside to Fling as Giant," *Sporting News*, March 20, 1957, 17; Dick Gordon, "Burnside Blazes as Miller After His Fizzle as Giant," *Sporting News*, August 7, 1957, 37; Leonard Koppett, "The Nats—Cast-Offs with a Sting"' *New York Post*, May 17, 1961, 80.

34. Shirley Povich, "Nats Hurl Roadblock at Bidders—Label Burnside Not Available," *Sporting News*, November 15, 1961, 21.

35. *RMAB*, 12.

36. *RMAB*, 12.

37. Bill Fuchs, "Sizzling Senators Striving to Turn Tables on Orioles," *Evening Star (Washington, DC)*, May 18, 1961, A20; Arthur Daley, "Sports of the Times," *New York Times*, May 18, 1961, 42.

38. "Yanks' Problems: Lack of Key Hits," *New York Times*, May 19, 1961, 35.

39. Hal Lebovitz, "Dazzling Week for Tribe's Jim Perry—Soph of the Year," *Sporting News*, November 9, 1960, 23.

40. Joseph Wancho, "Jim Perry," *SABR BioProject*, October 1, 2015, accessed May 30, 2018, https://sabr.org/bioproj/person/f7911858; John C. Tattersall, "Jim Perry Ties Mark by Giving N.Y. 13 Homers," *Sporting News*, September 7, 1960, 17; James E. Doyle, "The Sport Trail," *Cleveland Plain Dealer*, September 1, 1960, 37; Lebovitz, "Dazzling Week," 42; "Tribe Swap Cooking—Gabe Eyes Lumpe and Socker Siebern," *Sporting News*, December 13, 1961, 21.

41. Wancho, "Jim Perry."

42. John Romano, in telephone interview with the author, July 19, 2017; Chuck Heaton, "Slider Is Perry Special in Opener at Detroit Today," *Cleveland Plain Dealer*, April 11, 1961, 34.

43. Max Nichols, "Perry Patches Twins' Leaking Dike," *Sporting News*, August 14, 1965, 5; Hal Lebovitz, "Peerless Perry Sends Dykes to History Books," *Sporting News*, August 24, 1960, 7.

44. Harry Jones, "Indians' 'Man of the Year' Perry Came Long Way in Two Seasons," *Cleveland Plain*

Dealer, January 22, 1961, 2C; "GI Drills Keep Jim in Shape," *Cleveland Plain Dealer,* January 11, 1960, 29.

45. "Perry in Trouble, 'Thinks too Much,' Skipper Claims," *Sporting News,* September 6, 1961, 13; Lebovitz, "Dazzling Week," 23.

46. *RMAB,* 12.

47. Bob Dolgan, "Indians Five in 8th Stun Yanks, 9–7," *Cleveland Plain Dealer,* May 20, 1961, 29; John Drebinger, "Indians Score Five Runs in Eighth-Inning Rally and Triumph Over Yankees," *New York Times,* May 20, 1961, 16.

48. Cecilia Tan, "Gary Bell," *SABR BioProject,* n.d., accessed June 4, 2018, https://sabr.org/bioproj/person/33810d5c.

49. "Eastern Bat Title by Bartirome by Hairline Margin," *Sporting News,* December 19, 1956, 20; George Leonard, "Don Heffner's Bears Setting Frisky Pace," *Sporting News,* August 7, 1957, 41; "Mobile's Bell Loses One-Hit Game, Then Hurls No-Hitter," *Sporting News,* July 24, 1957, 37.

50. Dan Daniel, "Jensen, Banks Reach for MVP Awards," *Sporting News,* September 10, 1958, 4; Harry Jones, "Timid Rookie Year Ago, Gary Bell Is Now Poised for Stardom," *Cleveland Plain Dealer,* March 15, 1959, 3C.

51. Harry Jones, "Bell Set Goal of 20 Without Aid of 'Duster,'" *Cleveland Plain Dealer,* March 3, 1960, 29.

52. Hal Lebovitz, "Sore Flipper Draws Curtain on Sad Year for Tribe's Gary Bell," *Sporting News,* September 7, 1960, 17.

53. Romano, interview; Hal Lebovitz, "Bell Rated Next Great Tribe Righthander," *Sporting News,* April 15, 1959, 3; Jones, "Bell Sets Goal," 29; Earl Keller, "Padres' Strikeout Ace Bell Tabbed as Sure Major Star," *Sporting News,* May 28, 1958, 29; Bob Dolgan, "3-Hitter by Bell Wins, 3–1," *Cleveland Plain Dealer,* August 10, 1961, 31.

54. Chuck Heaton, "Winning Hit Makes Barger and Nieman's Hand 'Sore,'" *Cleveland Plain Dealer,* June 19, 1961, 27; Gordon Cobbledick, "Plain Dealing," *Cleveland Plain Dealer,* August 8, 1961, 29; Bob Dolgan, "Tribe Is Ranked 3d Best," *Cleveland Plain Dealer,* July 11, 1961, 25; John Drebinger, "Indians Beat Yanks, 4–3," *New York Times,* May 21, 1961, Sec. 5, 1; Bob Dolgan, "Romano's Double Beats Yanks, 4–3," *Cleveland Plain Dealer,* May 21, 1961, 1C.

55. Houk, *Ballplayers Are Human, Too,* 115.

56. Ed Wilks, "Baltimore Pitchers Mowing Down Rivals," *Joplin (MO) News Herald,* June 1, 1960, 2B.

57. Doug Brown, "Orioles Hatching Lofty Hopes for Hill Ace Pappas," *Sporting News,* February 17, 1960, 13; Clancy Loranger, "Mountie Ace Winning Pots with Blazer," *Sporting News,* August 12, 1959, 31.

58. Doug Brown, "Chuck Estrada," *Sporting News,* July 13, 1960, 28.

59. Doug Brown, "Estrada Chases Gloom with Blazing Hummer," *Sporting News,* March 28, 1962, 21; Doug Brown, "Oriole Quiz: Can Estrada Come Back?," *Sporting News,* March 28, 1964, 26.

60. Doug Brown, "'Arm Feels Great' Says Estrada after Tests in Backyard," *Sporting News,* December 21, 1963, 7.

61. John Drebinger, "Yankees Take Opener from Orioles but Bow in Finale before 47,890 Here," *New York Times,* May 22, 1961, 40; "The Old 'College' Try," *Cleveland Plain Dealer,* May 22, 1961, 37.

62. *RMAB,* 13.

63. *RMAB,* 14–15

64. *RMAB,* 14–15; Joe King, "Houk Sees Red at Maris' Trip to Eye Doctor," *Sporting News,* May 31, 1961, 15; Jack Lang, "It Was Ebbets Field at Stadium Last Night," *Jersey Journal (Jersey City, NJ),* May 23, 1961, 19S; Bob Wolf, "'Poor Start Touched Off Big Four-Bagger Spree,' Rog Reveals," *Sporting News,* January 17, 1962, 16; "Eye Drops 'Blind' Maris," *San Antonio (TX) Light,* May 23, 1961, 25; Milton Gross, "Roger Maris: Only Human," *New York Post,* September 25, 1961, 53.

65. "Back Ailment Puts Conley on Shelf Until Next Spring," *Sporting News,* September 30, 1953, 39; Red Thisted, "Braves, Big at Gate, Also Big in Heart," *Sporting News,* October 21, 1953, 17; Gene Conley, in Donald Honig, *Baseball Between the Lines: Baseball in the '40s and '50s as Told by the Men Who Played It* (New York: Coward, McCann and Geoghegan, 1976), 193.

66. Thisted, "Braves, Big at Gate," 17; Conley, 194.

67. Roger Dove, "Conley Tabbed a Major Sure-Shot, *Sporting News,* January 2, 1952, 2; Al Hirshberg, "Big Brave from Milwaukee," *Saturday Evening Post,* March 28, 1955, 106.

68. Emmett Watson, "Almost a Star: The Story of Milwaukee's Gene Conley," *Sport,* March 1957, 53–54; "Bob Addie's Atoms," *Sporting News,* May 10, 1961, 12.

69. Red Thisted, "Injuries Put New Hurdles in Path of Speedster Braves," *Sporting News,* September 15, 1954, 11.

70. Red Thisted, "Second Coin Now Braves' First Thought," *Sporting News,* August 17, 1955, 11; Conley, 199–200; Jack Orr, "Gene Conley: Two-Sport Star," in *Baseball Stars of 1960,* edited by Ray Robinson (New York: Pyramid Books, 1960), 134.

71. Conley, 201–202; Orr, "Gene Conley," 133.

72. "Champ Cager Conley Makes Successful Bow with Bosox,"*Sporting News,* March 3, 1961, 11; Orr, "Gene Conley," 137.

73. Hy Hurwitz, "Jensen, Unlikely to Play, Lands in Hub's Doghouse," *Sporting News,* December 27, 1961, 16; Kiersh, *Were Have You Gone,* 40; Hy Hurwitz, "Sore Shoulder Clouds Conley Future; Surgery Might Finish Hurler's Career," *Sporting News,* July 27, 1963, 8; Conley, 204–205.

74. Tom Monahan, "Conley Gives Credit to Roberts," *Boston Traveler,* April 26, 1961, 37; Hy Hurwitz, "Bosox' Closing Spurt vs. Yanks Gives Big Boost to Future Book," *Sporting News,* September 29, 1962, 14.

75. Joe Cashman, "Sox Lose in 9th, 3–2," *Boston Daily Record,* May 25, 1961, 28; Ed Costello, "Yankees Edge Sox, 3–2," May 25, 1961, 39; Tom Monahan, "Hose Eye Errorless Record," *Boston Traveler,* May 25, 1961, 45; Larry Claflin, "Long Yank Jinx Makes Sox Boil," *Boston American,* May 25, 1961, 8.

76. Robert L. Teague, "Yankees Beat Red Sox on Terry's 3-Hitter and Kubek's 9th Inning Single," *New York Times,* May 25, 1961, 44.

77. Robert L. Teague, "Houk Encouraged by Yankee Hitting," *New York Times,* May 24, 1961, 50; Houk, *Ballplayers Are Human, Too,* 117.

78. Robert L Teague, "Yankees Beat Red Sox; Bombers Sign Gibbs for Bonus of at Least $100,000," *New York Times,* May 26, 1961, 39.

79. John Drebinger, "Rained-Out Yanks Face Long Grind," *New York Times*, May 28, 1961, Sec. 5, 1.
80. "McLish Has New Outlook with Chisox," *Illinois State Journal (Springfield, IL)*, March 10, 1961, 30.
81. "McLish Happy to Be 'Home,'" *Register-Republic (Rockford, IL)*, March 22, 1961, 14B; Hal Lebovitz, "Back-Seat McLish Moves Up as Front-Liner," *Sporting News*, May 13, 1959, 7–8; Cal McLish, in Larry Moffi, *This Side of Cooperstown: An Oral History of Major League Baseball in the 1950s* (Iowa City, IA: University of Iowa Press, 1996), 214; Bob Vanderberg, *Frantic Frank Lane: Baseball's Ultimate Wheeler-Dealer* (Jefferson, NC: McFarland, 2013), 104–105.
82. Al Cartwright, "That First Spring Camp—Big Timers Never Forget," *Sporting News*, February 22, 1964, 17; John Cronley. "Once Over Lightly," *Daily Oklahoman (Oklahoma City, OK)*, August 20, 1959, 21.
83. Irv Goodman, "Cal McLish's Long Haul," *Sport*, September 1959, 37, 75; Joe King, "Clouting 'Em," *Sporting News*, April 5, 1961, 10; Hal Lebovitz, "Perry, Locke Remove Rocks from Injuns' Pennant Trail," *Sporting News*, August 5, 1959, 10.
84. "Medics Give Cheery Report on Chisox' Fox and McLish," *Sporting News*, November 29, 1961, 36; Allen Lewis, "Phils Assault Southpaw Jinx with Dynamite in Stuart Stick," *Sporting News*, December 12, 1964, 10; McLish, *This Side of Cooperstown*, 216.
85. Allen Lewis, "Mauch Sees Mound Vet McLIsh as Valued Starter on Phil Staff," *Sporting News*, April 4, 1962, 32.
86. *RMAB*, 16.
87. John Drebinger, "Yankees Salvage a Split with White Sox in Battle of Home Runs at Stadium," *New York Times*, May 29, 1961, 13; Tom Clavin and Danny Peary, *Roger Maris: Baseball's Reluctant Hero* (New York: Simon & Schuster, 2010), 156–157.
88. *RMAB*, 16.
89. John Drebinger, "Red Sox Beat Yankees in Rain-Delayed Game at Boston," *New York Times*, May 30, 1961, 11; Joe King, "Phenoms Sheldon and Stafford Steady Yanks' Shaky Staff," *Sporting News*, June 14, 1961, 17.
90. Austen Lake, "Spit Is a Nasty Word," *Boston American*, May 31, 1961, 39.
91. John Drebinger, "Yanks Belt 7 Home Runs During 17-Hit Attack that Overwhelms Red Sox," *New York Times*, May 31, 1961, 38; D. Leo Monahan, "7 Yank HR's Rout Sox, 12–3," *Boston Dailey Record*, May 31, 1961, 31, 43; Henry McKenna, "Red Sox Bombed, 12–3," *Boston Herald*, May 31, 1961, 17.
92. Jerry Holtzman, "McDaniel and Fornieles Cop Awards as Majors' Standout Rescue Artists," *Sporting News*, October 12, 1960, 1.
93. Hy Hurwitz, "Relief Star Fornieles Rates Hub's Huzzahs," *Sporting News*, October 12, 1960, 2.
94. Tom Long, "Miguel "Mike" Fornieles, at 66; Left Cuba to Pitch for Red Sox," *Boston Globe*, February 14, 1998; "Cuban Stars Get OK to Play," *Boston Traveler*, January 6, 1961, 39; Milt Greenglass, "Sox Plan(e)s Settled," *Boston Daily Record*, February 24, 1961, 29.
95. Monahan, "7 Yank HR's," 10; McKenna, "Yankees Hit Seven," 18; Drebinger, "Yanks Belt 7," 38; *RMAB*, 17.
96. D. Leo Monahan, "Fornieles Back on Beam," *Boston Daily Record*, June 22, 1961, 28.
97. "Muffett Cotton States' M.V.P.," *Sporting News*, September 12, 1951, 36; "Muffett Wins Job, but Wants to Lose Reputation," *Boston Traveler*, July 8, 1960, 29.
98. Larry Claflin, "Maglie Spotted Muffett Promise," *Boston American*, July 8, 1960, 48; Bub Collins, "Maglie Sold on Muffett," *Boston Herald*, July 11, 1960, 16.
99. Collins, "Maglie Sold," 16.
100. Claflin, "Maglie Spotted," 48.
101. Collins, "Maglie Sold," 16.
102. "Senators-Red Sox Series," *Sporting News*, April 19, 1961, 33; Henry McKenna, "Muffett's Arm Okay Now," *Boston Herald*, April 14, 1961, 35; Ed Costello, "Muffett Arrives 18 Pounds Lighter," *Boston Herald*, February 25, 1962, 57.
103. Joe Cashman, "Yanks Beat Red Sox 7–6 on HRs by Mantle, Maris," *Boston Daily Record*, June 1, 1961, 42; Bill Liston, "Malzone May Change Blue Sox," *Boston Traveler*, June 1, 1961, 43; John Drebinger, "Yanks Beat Red Sox Rally in 19th; Mantle and Maris Connect," *New York Times*, June 1, 1961, 40.

Chapter 4

1. Til Ferdenzi, "Mantle, Maris Give Yanks 1–2 Punch in HR Race," *Boston Daily Record*, June 1, 1961, 20.
2. Ferdenzi, "Mantle, Maris Give Yanks 1–2 Punch," 20.
3. *RMAB*, 18–19.
4. *RMAB*, 19.
5. *RMAB*, 19; Richard Dozer, "Cubs Stop Reds, 7–6; Yanks Rout Sox," *Chicago Daily Tribune*, June 3, 1961, Sec. 5, 1; John Drebinger, "Ford of Yanks Beats White Sox on Two by Berra and One by Maris," *New York Times*, June 3, 1961, 16.
6. Bob Vanderberg, *Sox: From Lane and Fain to Zisk and Fisk*, rev. ed. (Chicago, Chicago Review Press, 1984), 211.
7. Bob Shaw, *Pitching: The Basic Fundamentals and Mechanics of Successful Pitching* (New York: Viking, 1972), 78; Jerry Holtzman, "Shaw Shapes Up as Gee-Whizzer on Chisox Slab," *Sporting News*, August 26, 1959, 4; Barney Kremenko, "Spitter Complaints Delight Mets' Shaw," *Sporting News*, July 30, 1966, 5.
8. Gaylord Perry with Bob Sudyk, *Me and the Spitter: An Autobiographical Confession* (New York: Saturday Review Press, 1974), 130–132.
9. Richard Dozer, "Sox Beat Yanks in 13th; Cubs Roll On," *Chicago Daily Tribune*, June 4, 1961, Sec. 2, 1; John Drebinger, "Homer by Sievers Sends Bombers to 6-to-5 Defeat," *New York Times*, June 4, 1961, Sec. 5; 1, 3.
10. Houk, *Ballplayers Are Human, Too*, 121; *RMAB*, 20.
11. "Five Balks in Game Cost Bob Shaw $250," *Sporting News*, April 29, 1967, 4.
12. Edgar Munzel, "58-Year-Old Cub Wiff Mark Falls to Hill Ace Fergie," *Sporting News*, September 30, 1967, 11.
13. Arthur Siegel, "Unworried Kemmerer Confident," *Boston Traveler*, March 11, 1957, 22.
14. N. Diunte, "Russ Kimmerer, 84, Former Major League Pitcher Was a Master Storyteller," *Baseball Happenings*, December 21, 2014, accessed July 12, 2018,

http://www.baseballhappenings.net/2014/12/russ-kemmerer-84-former-major-league.html?m=1.

15. Russ Kemmerer with W.C. Madden, *Ted Williams: 'Hey, Kid, Just Get It Over the Plate'* (Fishers, IN: Madden Pub., 2002), 91.

16. Don White, "Sore Arm, Blisters Don't Stop IU's Woodward," *Evansville (IN) Courier and Press*, May 29, 1966, 7C.

17. Shirley Povich, "Swift Singles Out Nat Pair for Slab Tips," *Sporting News*, February 3, 1960, 22; Kemmerer, 73, 88.

18. *RMAB*, 20.

19. Houk, *Ballplayers Are Human, Too*, 122.

20. Houk, *Ballplayers Are Human, Too*, 125.

21. *RMAB*, 23–24.

22. Joe King, "Bombers Shatter A. L. Mark with Homer Marathon," *Sporting News*, June 14, 1961, 17; John Drebinger, "Yanks Take Double-Header and Sent Twins to 10th, 11th Straight Defeat," *New York Times*, June 6, 1961, 44.

23. "Scouting Reports on 1960 Major League Rookies—the Cincinnati Reds," *Baseball Digest*, March 1960, 84.

24. Tom Briere, "Twins Sound Siren Over 2 Ace Firemen," *Sporting News*, May 24, 1961, 17.

25. Joseph M. Sheehan, "Yankees Pin 12th Defeat in Row on Twins," *New York Times*, June 7, 1961, 48; *RMAB*, 21.

26. *RMAB*, 21.

27. Joseph M. Sheehan, "Yankees Down Twins with Two Homers in Third for Fifth Straight Win," *New York Times*, June 8, 1961, 41.

28. *RMAB*, 22; Ray Gillespie, "Diamond Facts and Facets," *Sporting News*, August 23, 1961, 16.

29. *RMAB*, 22; Robert L. Teague, "Home Runs by Mantle and Maris Help Yankees Beat Athletics Before 22,418," *New York Times*, June 10, 1961, 15.

30. "American Association," *Sporting News*, May 11, 1949, 42–43.

31. Watson Spoelstra, "J. W. Quickly Carves His Initials on Left Field Post with Tigers," *Sporting News*, March 23, 1955, 11; Ernest Mehl, "Johnson's Bankroll in Turnover Along with Kaycee Talent," *Sporting News*, May 18, 1955, 7; Ernest Mehl, "A's Hopes Rise," *Kansas City Star*, May 16, 1955, 18.

32. Sam Baumgartner, "Waitkus-Torgeson Chess Game Netted $80,000 for Phils," *Sporting News*, August 10, 1955, 14.

33. Ernest Mehl, "A's Pitchers Fail to Keep Step with Craft's Clouters," *Sporting News*, May 20, 1959, 14; Joe McGuff, "Purchases by the A's Are Emergency Steps," *Kansas City Star*, May 12, 1955, 23; Ernest Mehl, "Cerv Swings Pen for $32,500 Setting Salary Mark for Kaycee," *Sporting News*, May 11, 1959, 24; Ernest Mehl, "A's Jell After Skidding Start—Lumpe and Bauer Spark Surge," *Sporting News*, May 4, 1960, 27; Joe McGuff, "Sain Guides Yankee Hurlers," *Kansas City Star*, March 22, 1961, 8C; Barry Gottehrer, "Bud Daley and Ray Herbert," in *Baseball Stars of 1961*, edited by Ray Robinson (New York: Pyramid Books, 1961), 141.

34. Ernest Mehl, "Sporting Comment," *Kansas City Star*, July 22, 1960, 26; Joe McGuff, "Herbert One of Best in League Now," *Kansas City Star*, August 29, 1960, 9; Joe McGuff, "Daley's Hopes of Winning 20 Fade," *Kansas City Star*, August 9, 1960, 11.

35. "A's Not Worst Team Frankie Bossed," *Sporting News*, January 11, 1961, 6; Edgar Munzel,"Late-Bloomer Herbert—Budding Hill Ace," *Sporting News*, May 25, 1963, 3; Joe McGuff, "A's Stalemate with Herbert," *Sporting News*, February 22, 1961, 2C.

36. Joe McGuff, "A's Mound Staff Has Potential, Says Gordon—Lane Disagrees," *Kansas City Star*, March 3, 1961, 23.

37. Joe McGuff, "Homers, Rain Fall on A's," *Kansas City Times*, June 10, 1961, 18; Teague, "Home Runs by Mantle and Maris," 15; *RMAB*, 22–23.

38. Munzel, "Late-Bloomer," 3–4.

39. John Drebinger, "Yanks Beat Athletics," *New York Times*, June 11, 1961, Sec. 5, 1.

40. *RMAB*, 24.

41. John Drebinger, "Yanks, Behind Terry and Sheldon, Take Double-Header from Angels Here," *New York Times*, June 12, 1961, 36; *RMAB*, 24–25.

42. Ray Gillespie, "Diamond Facts and Facets," *Sporting News*, September 27, 1961, 10.

43. *RMAB*, 25. Why Maris referred to Grba's curve as "new found" is a mystery; the pitcher had a good curve that he used long before 1961. See Laurence Leonard, "Ex-Fireman Grba Now Richmond's Standout Starter," *Sporting News*, June 1, 1960, 29.

44. Dick Young, "Bond, Gonzalez Picked as Top Rookies," *Sporting News*, April 27, 1960, 2, 8.

45. "Yogi Calls James the 'Best Yank Rookie in My Time,'" *Sporting News*, April 27, 1960, 2.

46. Dan Daniel, "Cocky Short Staking Quick Claim to Yank Mound Post," *Sporting News*, March 1, 1961, 4; Dick Young, "Bond, Gonzalez Picked as Top Rookies," *Sporting News*, April 27, 1960, 1.

47. Daniel, "Cocky Short," 4; Johnny James, in telephone interview with the author, February 26, 2019.

48. "Catching Up with Johnny James," *Baseball Historian*, December 9, 2011, accessed July 25, 2018, http://baseballhistorian.blogspot.com/2011/12/catching-up-with-johnny-james.html.

49. *RMAB*, 25.

50. James, interview.

51. *RMAB*, 26.

52. Joe Trimble, "'Angry Man' Maris Takes Wrath Out on Poor Ball," *Fort Worth (TX) Star-Telegram*, June 21, 1961, 2; Oscar Fraley, "Maris Shrugs but He Is in Spot to Top Ruth Mark," *Sacramento (CA) Bee*, June 21, 1961, D1–2.

53. L. H. Gregory, "Greg's Gossip," *Oregonian (Portland, OR)*, June 22, 1961, Section 2, 1, 4.

54. Tony Kubek and Terry Pluto, *Sixty-One: The Team, the Record, the Men* (New York: Macmillan, 1987), 87.

55. Bob Dolgan, "Romano Belts 11th; Phillips Also Homers," *Cleveland Plain Dealer*, June 14, 1961, 29; *RMAB*, 26.

56. *RMAB*, 27.

57. Bob Dolgan, "Yanks Drop Tribe into Tie for Top; Rap 2 as Ford Wins 10th, 11–5," *Cleveland Plain Dealer*, June 15, 1961, 33; Chuck Heaton, "Yanks Drop Tribe into Tie for Top; Antonelli Choice Is Debated," *Cleveland Plain Dealer*, June 15, 1961, 34.

58. Heaton, "Yanks Drop," 34.

59. Houk, *Ballplayers Are Human, Too*, 127–129; Houk, *Season of Glory*, 154.

60. Houk, *Ballplayers Are Human, Too*, 127.

61. *RMAB*, 27.
62. John Drebinger, "Tigers Top Yanks with Aid of 5 Errors and Tie Indians for Lead," *New York Times*, June 17, 1961, 16.
63. Harry Jones, "Giants Bounce Garcia, Rout Indians, 13–5," *Cleveland Plain Dealer*, March 13, 1954, 25; "Batting Around," *Cleveland Plain Dealer*, March 14, 1954, 2C.
64. Harry Jones, "Mossi, Rookie Hurler Who Can't Straighten His Left Arm, Is Top Surprise of Tribe Camp," *Cleveland Plain Dealer*, March 21, 1954, 2C.
65. Harry Jones, "Batting Around," *Cleveland Plain Dealer*, July 22, 1954, 21; Dan Cordtz, "Bullpen of Indians Is All Business; That's No Bull," *Cleveland Plain Dealer*, August 22, 1954, 3C.
66. Jones, "Batting Around," July 22, 1954, 21; Harry Jones, "Indians Win 110th to Tie A. L. Record," *Cleveland Plain Dealer*, September 21, 1954, 27.
67. Harry Jones, "Narleski, Mossi Willing to Wait for Starter Role," *Cleveland Plain Dealer*, March 5, 1957, 27.
68. Harry Jones, "Mossi Goes Route, Beats Bosox, 6–1," *Cleveland Plain Dealer*, June 13, 1957, 25; Harry Jones, "Kerby Has Hopes for 4th Place," *Cleveland Plain Dealer*, September 10, 1957, 29.
69. Harry Jones, "Narleski and Martin Happy Over Change," *Cleveland Plain Dealer*, November 21, 1958, 34.
70. Watson Spoelstra, "Bengals Soar on Maxwell's Sunday Punch," *Sporting News*, June 24, 1959, 11; Dan Daniel, "Junk Pitching Taking Heavy Toll of .300 Hitters," *Sporting News*, August 26, 1959, 10.
71. Hal Middlesworth, "Top Tigers Tame Tabbies—Except for Biffer Kuenn," *Sporting News*, April 6, 1960, 14; Watson Spoelstra, "Hill Aces, Farm Phenoms Brighten Bengals Future," *Sporting News*, September 14, 1960, 10.
72. Leonard Shecter, "Mossi Knows How to Pitch Yanks' M&M," *New York Post*, September 3, 1961, 34.
73. *RMAB*, 27.
74. *RMAB*, 28.
75. Joe Falls, "Tigers Stagger by Yanks, 12–10," *Detroit Free Press*, June 18, 1961, 1.
76. *RMAB*, 28.
77. "Bonus Babies on 'Little Millionaires,'" *Sporting News*, August 20, 1952, 13; Hy Hurwitz, "Busy Swap Sessions at Series Show Red Sox Won't Stand Pat," *Sporting News*, October 12, 1955, 16; Bob Holbrook, "Bosox Story a Good One; It's Williams," *Sporting News* April 4, 1956, 8.
78. Hy Hurwitz, "13 Kids Will Dot Boxox Spring Camp," *Sporting News*, January 1, 1956, 6; Holbrook, "Bosox Story," 8; Jack McDonald, "5 Years in Boston Chain—Casale Says He's Lucky," *Sporting News*, June 20, 1956, 25.
79. McDonald, "5 Years," 25.
80. Hy Hurwitz, "Flatbush Flashes—Casale, Aspromonte," *Sporting News*, November 14, 1956, 14; "Casale Called by Army," *Sporting News*, December 5, 1956, 22; Hy Hurwitz, "'Flash Ump's Ruling to Fans After Tricky Play,' Cronin Urges," *Sporting News*, April 29, 1959, 4.
81. Hy Hurwitz, "Rookie Casale Aids in Lightening Load of Bosox Hill Woes," *Sporting News*, June 24, 1959, 14; Alex MacLean, "Casale Once Spurned by 3 N.Y. Ball Clubs," *Boston Advertiser*, July 12, 1959, 36.

82. Hy Hurwitz, "Casale Casts Hopeful Hue on Hub Hose," *Sporting News*, October 7, 1959, 26; Hy Hurwitz, "Geiger's Bat Binge Boosts Hub Attack," *Sporting News*, July 6, 1960, 17.
83. John Gillooly, "Is Casale Loss Another Baumann?," *Boston Daily Record*, March 3, 1961, 64; Tom Larwin, "Jerry Casale," *SABR BioProject*, n.d., accessed August 13, 2018, https://sabr.org/bioproj/person/200 e64f2; "Ted Still Feels Effect of Virus," *Boston Traveler*, September 8, 1959, 46.
84. Braven Dyer, "Nine Working Arms, Angels' Prime Target," *Sporting News*, March 1, 1961, 18.
85. Joe Falls, "Yanks Rout Tigers and Lary, 9–0," *Detroit Free Press*, June 19, 1961, 1; *RMAB*, 28–29.
86. Watson Spoelstra, "Tigers See 20-Win Year Coming Up for Fast-Signer Bunning," *Sporting News*, December 27, 1961, 16.
87. *RMAB*, 30.
88. Joe McGuff, "Archer Finds Luck at New Season Low," *Kansas City Star*, July 16, 1962, 6.
89. Joe McGuff, "Jim Archer Rode Long, Rough Road to Reach Majors," *Kansas City Star*, July 18, 1961, 17; Doug Brown, "Orioles Feather Nest with 2 Newcomers for Picket-Line Duty," *Sporting News*, February 1, 1961, 9.
90. Paul O'Boynick, "No. 13 Brings Luck to Barber," *Kansas City Star*, May 7, 1961, 2B.
91. "Fireworks, and the A's," *Kansas City Star*, May 24, 1961, 1; "Jim Archer Learns Weak Bench Is Costly," *Kansas City Star*, August 31, 1961, 2B.
92. Ernest Mehl, "Sporting Comment," *Kansas City Star*, August 8, 1961, 16; Paul O'Boynick, "Archer Faces Bosox Tonight," *Kansas City Star*, August 30, 1961, 10C; Red Foley, "Ford and Arroyo Spotlight Big Year for Lefty Hurlers," *Sporting News*, August 30, 1961, 9.
93. Ernest Mehl, "Bass Provided Bright Ray in Kaycee Club," *Sporting News*, October 11, 1961, 22; Houk, *Ballplayers Are Human, Too*, 140.
94. *RMAB*, 30–31.
95. Demorris A. Lee, "Jim Archer: A Voice of Integrity for Tarpon Springs," *Tampa Bay Times*, September 10, 2009, NewsBank.
96. Ernest Mehl, "A's Snap Back on Homers," *Kansas City Star*, June 20, 1961, 18; John Drebinger, "Athletics Beat Yanks After Bauer Replaces Gordon as Kansas City Manager," *New York Times*, June 20, 1961, 37.
97. Joe McGuff, "Rotation Shot by Injuries," *Kansas City Star*, March 20, 1962, 20; Ernest Mehl, "Top Crowd Sees A's Hurlers Reel Under Yank Bats," *Sporting News*, July 28, 1962, 30.
98. Joe Kay, "At Age 15, Nuxhall Grew Up in a Hurry: The Youngest-Ever Pitcher in Majors Broke in 50 Years Ago Against Musial," *Los Angeles Times*, June 5, 1994, accessed August 19, 2018, http://articles.latimes.com/1994-06-05/sports/sp-520_1_joe-nuxhall.
99. Tom Swope, "No 20-Win Southpaw in '55 for First Time in 12 Years," *Sporting News*, November 2, 1955, 9.
100. Earl Lawson, "New Nuxhall Nixed His Old 'Wild Man' Rap," *Sporting News*, January 26, 1955, 5; Earl Lawson, "Nuxhall Nixed Temper and Improved Control," *Sporting News*, February 29, 1956, 5; "Flame Throwers of Majors Listed by Sheehan, DeWitt," *Sporting News*, August 29, 1956, 4.

101. Earl Lawson, "Redlegs' Slow-Starting Nuxhall Getting Legs—and Waist—in Trim," *Sporting News*, February 4, 1959, 9; "Nuxhall Rapped on Knee Again," *Sporting News*, August 29, 1956, 23; Tom Swope, "Nuxhall Back on Duty After Injury," *Sporting News*, August 8, 1956, 17; Earl Lawson, "Redlegs Plan Kindergarten for Pitchers," *Sporting News*, November 6, 1957, 17; Tom Swope, "Reds Show They Can Be Toughies Without Big Klu," *Sporting News*, May 15, 1957, 10; Earl Lawson, "Gabe's Yule Gift to Reds' Bailey—Ear-Muffs for Batting Advice," *Sporting News*, December 24, 1958, 23.

102. Lawson, "Redleg's Slow," 9; "Major Flashes," *Sporting News*, June 10, 1959, 35; Earl Lawson, "Reds' Brosnan, Lawrence Torrid Mound Twosome," *Sporting News*, September 23, 1959, 36; "Nuxhall Fourth N. L. Hurler to Wiff Four in One Inning, " *Sporting News*, August 19, 1959, 25; Earl Lawson, "Classy Red Hurlers Stymied by Swatters with Puny Averages," *Sporting News*, August 19, 1959, 19; Earl Lawson, "Red Rappers Knock on Door of Club's Run-Scoring Record," *Sporting News*, September 2, 1959, 19.

103. Earl Lawson, "Walls Using Classy Plate Work to Grab Toehold on First," *Sporting News*, April 6, 1960, 20; "Nuxhall Fined $250, Banned Five Days for Vargo Rhubarb," *Sporting News*, August 3, 1960, 17; "'Love Cincy, but Hope Reds Trade Me,' Nuxhall Declares," *Sporting News*, October 5, 1960, 48; Earl Lawson, "Downhearted Nuxhall Flaps Crying Towel," *Sporting News*, January 11, 1961, 16.

104. Ernest Mehl, "Hellzapoppin in Kaycee—a New Act Every Day," *Sporting News*, May 24, 1961, 4; Ernest Mehl, "A's Douse Front-Office Flames, Fuel Up for Fireworks on Field," *Sporting News*, June 7, 1961, 17."

105. John Drebinger, "Yankees Down Athletics and Gain Second Place as Maris Hits 26th Homer," *New York Times*, June 21, 1961, 41; Joe McGuff, "Yankee Power Jolts A's," *Kansas City Times*, June 21, 1961, 11; Paul O'Boynick, "Daley May Spring 'New Pitch' Tonight in Athletic's Game," *Kansas City Star*, June 21, 1961, 8C.

106. *RMAB*, 31.

107. "Wild Time in Detroit," *Kansas City Star*, May 2, 1962, 14C; "Major Cutdown Deadline Stirs Flurry of Trades, Player Shifts," *Sporting News*, May 16, 1962, 29.

108. Braven Dyer, "Slick DP Combo Throws Lifeline to Angels Hurlers," *Sporting News*, May 23, 1962, 32; "Coast Clipings," *Sporting News*, July 28, 1962, 46.

109. "Nuxhall Pays Quick Return on Red Hill," *Sporting News*, August 4, 1962, 23; Bob Cairns, *Pen Men: Baseball's Greatest Bullpen Stories Told by Men Who Brought the Game Relief* (New York: St. Martin's Press, 1992), 84; "Jeers Turned into Cheers—and Nuxhall Likes Them," *Sporting News*, September 1, 1962, 7; Rick Van Blair, *Dugout to Foxhole: Interviews with Baseball Players Whose Careers Were Affected by World War II* (Jefferson, NC: McFarland, 1994), 153.

110. John Drebinger, "Yanks Sink Athletics as Mantle Drives in All Bombers' Runs with 2 Homers," *New York Times*, June 22, 1961, 39.

111. Joe McGuff, "Norm Bass Is Most Impressive A's Pitcher," *Kansas City Star*, March 24, 1961, 7C.

112. Ernest Mehl, "Sporting Comment," *Kansas City Star*, December 12, 1958, 2D; Joe McGuff, "A's Have New 'Look' Right Now," *Kansas City Star*, March 9, 1961, 14; Joe McGuff, "What Is So Rare as Pitching in Spring," *Kansas City Star*, March 21, 1961, 15; Ernest Mehl, "Sporting Comment," *Kansas City Star*, March 27, 1961, 12.

113. Joe McGuff, "Owner's Order Irks A's Pilot," *Kansas City Star*, May 24, 1961, 10C.

114. Joe McGuff, "A's Stuck with Weird Schedule," *Kansas City Star*, May 1, 1961, 10; Joe McGuff, "Bass Gives A's Shutout," *Kansas City Star*, June 4, 1961, B1.

115. Joe McGuff, "Ford and Maris Rip A's," *Kansas City Star*, June 23, 1961, 22.

116. Mehl, "Bass Provided," 19; "Bass Finds Control," *Kansas City Star*, August 6, 1961, 1B.

117. Ernest Mehl, "A's Confuse Critics, Set Fast Road Clip, Skid in Own Arena," *Sporting News*, May 9, 1962, 18.

118. Joe McGuff, "Between Innings," *Kansas City Star*, March 12, 1963, 12; "Bass Hopes to Be Back in Majors," *Kansas City Star*, January 18, 1963, 14; Bill Richardson, "Norm Bass to Make Pro Football Debut," *Kansas City Star*, August 8, 1964, 6; Diane Pucin, "Arthritis Didn't Rob Bass of Competitive Instincts," *Los Angeles Times*, December 19, 1999, accessed June 1, 2017, http://articles.latimes.com/1999/dec/19/sports/sp-45604.

119. *RMAB*, 29; Oscar Fraley, "Roger Maris Holds 18-Game Bulge on Babe Ruth's Record," *Redlands (CA) Daily Facts*, June 21, 1961, 15; "Slugger Roger Maris Has Singles Allergy," *Springfield (MA) Union*, June 22, 1961, 42.

120. *RMAB*, 33.

121. Fraley, "Roger Maris Holds," 15; "Indians to Toss Mudcat at Yankees," *Newark (OH) Advocate*, June 15, 1961, 24; *RMAB*, 97.

122. "The 1961 Yankees," *1991 Elias Baseball Analysist*, edited by Seymour Siwoff et al. (New York: Simon & Schuster, 1991), 432.

123. Kubek, *Sixty-One*, 88.

124. *RMAB*, 33.

125. *RMAB*, 33.

126. Houk, *Ballplayers Are Human, Too*, 144.

127. *RMAB*, 34–36.

128. "Dial Double M for Murder and Mayhem," *Sporting News*, June 28, 1961, 1.

129. Houk, *Ballplayers Are Human, Too*, 141.

Chapter 5

1. Joseph M. Sheehan, "Yanks Face Senators Tonight, Opening Home Drive for Lead," *New York Times*, June 30, 1961, 17.

2. Joseph M. Sheehan, "Yanks Beat Senators as Ford Gains 8th Victory in Row and 14th of Season," *New York Times*, July 1, 1961, 10.

3. Ralph Wheeler, "Ron Perry Lauds Sisler as Hurler," *Boston Herald*, August 7, 1955, 46.

4. Murray Kramer, "Young Sisler to Hurl Vet's Game," *Boston Daily Record*, May 10, 1955, 25; "Dave Sisler Shows Top Form," *Boston Evening American*, February 13, 1956, 41; Bill Liston, "Sisler Looms Sox Starter," *Boston Traveler*, April 30, 1956, 24D.

5. Ed Costello, "Sisler Earns Red Sox Promotion," *Boston Herald*, February 26, 1956, 41; Liston, "Sisler Looms," 24D.

6. Liston, "Sisler Looms," 24D; Hy Hurwitz, "Bosox Reach into Bull Pen, Find New Starter in Sisler,"

Sporting News September 26, 1956, 9; Oscar Rhul, "From the Ruhl Book," *Sporting News*, June 27, 1956, 14.

7. Murray Kramer, "New Specs Get Assist for Sisler's Success," *Boston Daily Record*, May 11, 1956, 78.

8. Henry McKenna, "A's Curb Sox, 5–2," *Boston Herald*, June 25, 1956, 13; Mike Gillooly, "Sisler Starter Now," *Boston Evening Herald*, June 25, 1956, 49.

9. Hy Hurwitz, "Piersall Wins Writers' Vote as MV Bosox," *Sporting News*, January 23, 1957, 17; Bob Holbrook, "Dave Sisler ... Destined for Stardom?," *Sporting News*, May 8, 1957, 5.

10. Holbrook, "Dave Sisler," 6; D. Leo Monahan, "Sox Eyed Sisler from Early Days," *Boston Daily Record*, April 29, 1957, 57; John Gillooly, "Sisler Top Yank Tamer," *Boston American*, May 12, 1957, 35.

11. Hy Hurwitz, "Stronger Bench Braces Red Sox," *Sporting News*, August 7, 1957, 15.

12. Mike Gillooly, "Strong Hints Sox to Keep Higgins," *Boston American*, September 10, 1958, 5; Rick Huhn, "Dave Sisler," *SABR BioProject*, n.d., accessed August 28, 2018, https://sabr.org/bioproj/person/8057 31ed.

13. "Detroit's Yankee-Killing Trio Now 30–14 Versus Champs," *Sporting News*, May 13, 1959, 5.

14. Holtzman, "McDaniel and Fornieles," 2; "Top Twirlers in Pool Won 7 Games Apiece," *Sporting News*, December 14, 1960, 11; "Data on Draft Choices," *Sporting News*, December 21, 1960, 4.

15. Shirley Povich, "Nats Nab Real Prize in Relief Ace Sisler," *Sporting News*, May 17, 1961, 11; Bill Fuchs," "Sisler's Great Relief Work Proving Boon to Senators," *Evening Star (Washington, DC)*, May 4, 1961, 1D.

16. *RMAB*, 36.

17. *RMAB*, 36–37.

18. Bill Fuchs, "Maris' Blast in 9th Nips Senators," *Evening Star (Washington, DC)*, July 2, 1961, 61; *RMAB*, 36–37.

19. Shirley Povich, "Senators Grab Hamlin to Solve Shortstop Woes," *Sporting News*, December 6, 1961, 23; Mickey Vernon, "Manager's Report in the First Person," *Evening Star (Washington, DC)*, September 22, 1961, A20.

20. "DeWitt Expects New Faces to Spruce Up Red Hill Staff," *Sporting News*, December 27, 1961, 17; Earl Lawson, "Blue-Ribbon Hurlers Spur Hutch to Blueprint Red Flag, *Sporting News*, February 16, 1963, 30.

21. *RMAB*, 37; Joseph M. Sheehan, "Yankees Crush Senators with 5 Homers, Including 2 by Maris," *New York Times*, July 3, 1961, 10.

22. Peary, *We Played the Game*, 61.

23. Peary, *We Played the Game*, 92.

24. Edgar Munzel, "Klippstein Making Cubs Believe They Clipped Rickey for Nugget," *Sporting News*, March 22, 1950, 13.

25. Peary, *We Played the Game*, 250; Edgar Munzel, "Improvement in Cubs' Hurling Stems from Root's Teaching," *Sporting News*, May 21, 1952, 4.

26. John C. Hoffman, "Bruins Turn to Minors for Outfield Aid," *Sporting News*, October 13, 1954, 12; Tom Swope, "'More Deals on Way for Reds'—Gabe," *Sporting News*, October 13, 1954, 12.

27. Earl Lawson, "Hats Off," *Sporting News*, September 21, 1955, 19.

28. Tom Swope, "Reds in Rave Over Curving of Klippstein," *Sporting News*, September 21, 1955, 10.

29. Ed Prell, "Cubs May Make New Pitch for an Old Friend—Bilko," *Sporting News*, November 6, 1957, 16; Peary, *We Played the Game*, 366.

30. Peary, *We Played the Game*, 393–394.

31. Ray Watson, "Craig, Comeback King, Sets Pace in Dodger Drive," *Sporting News*, August 5, 1959, 8; Hal Lebovitz, "Injuns Shake Tepee in Bow to Klippstein," *Sporting News*, May 25, 1960, 8; Peary, *We Played the Game*, 458.

32. Bob Hunter, "Fast-Dealing Bavasi Shuffles Dodgers to Flag-Fighting Size," *Sporting News*, April 20, 1960, 11.

33. Peary, *We Played the Game*, 481–482.

34. Shirley Povich, "Doherty Beams Over Nat Depth of Mound Staff," *Sporting News*, January 18, 1961, 17; Shirley Povich, "Hill Staff Puzzling Nat Wheels," *Sporting News*, February 15, 1961, 18.

35. Peary, *We Played the Game*, 520.

36. *RMAB*, 37.

37. Bill Fuchs, "Shaken Senators Seeking Revenge Against Red Sox," *Evening Star (Washington, DC)*, July 3, 1961, 11; Sheehan, "Yankees Crush Senators, 10.

38. Earl Lawson, "Klippstein Ends 9-Year HR Slump," *Sporting News*, August 18, 1962, 9; John C. Tattersall, "Klippstein Joins Elite Class with 13th Inning HR," *Sporting News*, August 18, 1962, 9.

39. "Klippstein Sold to Phillies; Slated for Duty in Bull Pen," *Sporting News*, April 6, 1963, 32; Peary, *We Played the Game*, 573.

40. Max Nichols, "Old-Dog Klippstein Learning New Hill Tricks," *Sporting News*, July 24, 1965, 7.

41. Sandy Grady, "Modern Marco Polo," *Baseball Digest*, September 1964, 55.

42. Howard M. Tuckner, "Houk Names Ford and Turley to Pitch Here Today for Yanks Against Tigers," *New York Times*, July 4, 1961, 14.

43. "Yanks Will Face Lary at Stadium," *New York Times*, May 12, 1961, 33; Hugh Bradley, "'Breaking Stuff' Stops M & M—Lary," *New York Journal American*, August 31, 1961, 25.

44. Watson Spoelstra, "Lary Dusts Off Old Hex—Waves Magic Wing as Yanks Wilt," *Sporting News*, May 3, 1961, 4.

45. Arthur Richman, "Even Lary Can't Explain How He Hex-Rays Yanks," *Baseball Digest*, June 1959, 57; Moss Klein, "Frank Lary Recalls His Days as a 'Yankee Killer,'" *Baseball Digest*, July 1978, 73.

46. Furman Bisher, "How Frank Lary Learned to Pitch," *Sport*, August 1961, 58.

47. Hal Middlesworth, "Lary Slips Hypo Into Bengels in Star Role as Bomber-Buster," *Sporting News*, July 23, 1958, 8.

48. Hal Middlesworth, "Moves Help Mossi Spot Flaw in Form; Gets Back on Beam," *Sporting News*, September 23, 1959, 15; Watson Spoelstra, "Heat on DeWitt after Gordon Quits Bengals," *Sporting News*, October 12, 1960, 7.

49. Ray Robinson, "Frank Lary: Yankee-Killer," in *Baseball Stars of 1962*, edited. by Ray Robinson (New York: Pyramid Books, 1962), 10.

50. John Drebinger, "Yanks Split with Tigers Before 74,246; Largest Stadium Crowd Since 1947," *New York Times*, July 5, 1961, 38; Houk, *Ballplayers Are Human, Too*, 153.

51. *RMAB*, 40–41.

52. Houk, *Ballplayers Are Human, Too*, 153–154.
53. *RMAB*, 41.
54. Drebinger, "Yanks Split," 38; Robinson, "Frank Lary," 111.
55. Robinson, "Frank Lary," 112.
56. Watson Spoelstra, "Bengals Run Out of Gas in Bumpy Road," *Sporting News*, May 16, 1962, 19; Klein, "Frank Lary Recalls," 74.
57. *RMAB*, 38–39.
58. *RMAB*, 38–39.
59. Dan Daniel, "Babe Ruth's Ghost Begins to Fret," *Evansville (IN) Press*, July 7, 1961, 16.
60. Daniel, "BabeRuth's Ghost," 16.
61. Oscar Fraley, "It's the Bat, Not the Ball That's Causing Big Change," *Redlands (CA) Daily Facts*, June 27, 1961, 8; Oscar Fraley, "Stronger Players, Better Bats Bring Upsurge in Homers, Insists Ball Firm," *Press-Courier (Oxnard, CA)*, July 26, 1961, 26; "Maris Has Edge on Mantle; 27 More At-Bats in 90 Tilts," *Sporting News*, July 26, 1961, 8; Leonard Koppett,"Maris, Ruth HR Duel? No Comparison," *New York Post*, July 6, 1961, 56.
62. "Maris Gets Boos from Home Fans," *Jersey (Jersey City, NJ) Journal*, July 26, 1961, 29; Victor Sebastian, "Mickey Mantle: Baseball's Problem Child," *Family Weekly*, July 29, 1961, 6.
63. "International League," *Sporting News*, June 17, 1959, 36; "International League," *Sporting News*, July 8, 1959, 40.
64. "Swollen with Pride? Nope, Funk Just Has the Mumps," *Sporting* News, July 20, 1960, 32; Neil Mac-Carl, "Flipper Tired, but Funk Fires Leaf No-Hitter," *Sporting News*, June 29, 1960, 31.
65. Harry Jones, "Batting Around," *Cleveland Plain Dealer*, August 30, 1960, 30; James E. Doyle, "The Sport Trail," *Cleveland Plain Dealer*, September 8, 1960, 33.
66. Dan Daniel, "Yastrzemski, Davis Prize Kids of '61," *Sporting News*, April 19, 1961, 1–2; Hal Lebovitz, "Funk's Flinging Puts Feather on Swami's Fedora," *Sporting News*, April 26, 1961, 20.
67. Hal Lebovitz, "Hats Off," *Sporting News*, June 14, 1961, 31; Lebovitz, "Funk's Flinging," 30.
68. Bob Dolgan, "Tribe's Funk Uses Confidence Game to Silence Enemy Bats," *Cleveland Plain Dealer*, May 30, 1961, 37.
69. Bob Dolgan, "'Scribe' Funk Tells Story of Lesson Learned in '61," *Cleveland Plain Dealer*, February 27, 1962, 29; "Maris Just a One-Season Freak to Funk of Indians," *Cleveland Plain Dealer*, February 6, 1962, 25.
70. Romano, interview.
71. *RMAB*, 43.
72. *RMAB*, 44.
73. Hal Lebovitz, "Perry and Funk Seeking Answers," *Cleveland Plain Dealer*, July 16, 1961, 1C.
74. "American League," *Sporting News*, September 27, 1961, 4.
75. Hal Lebovitz, "McGaha to Throw Book at Clubhouse Lawyers," *Sporting News*, October 11, 1961, 13.
76. Bob Dolgan, "Funk Blasts McGaha; Chisox Rout Indians," *Cleveland Plain Dealer*, August 17, 1962, 29; Hal Lebovitz, "Tribe to Mount Big Adcock Bat in Cleanup Spot," *Sporting News*, December 8, 1962, 19.
77. Bob Wolf, "Skipper Bragan Pegs Funk No. 1 Tepee Reliever," *Sporting News*, December 8, 1962, 21; Bob Wolf, "Fire Helmet Fits; Shaw Braces Up Braves' Bull Pen," *Sporting News*, July 27, 1963, 11; Bob Wolf, "Can't Keep Good Man on Bench—Braves' McMillan Proves It," *Sporting News*, April 25, 1964, 19.
78. *RMAB*, 44.
79. Bill Liston, "Monbouquette Sets Deadline," *Boston Traveler*, February 18, 1958, 37.
80. William M Simons, "Pitcher at Twilight: Bill Monbouquette and the American Dream," in *Cooperstown Symposium on Baseball and American Culture, 2002*, ed. by William M. Simons (Jefferson, NC: McFarland, 2003), 44.
81. Mike Gillooly, "'I Liked What I Saw,' Higgins Says of Mombo," *Boston American*, July 19, 1958, 18.
82. Dick Gordon, "Miller Rookies, Ex-Hockey Players, Shine as Hurlers," *Sporting News*, June 11, 1958, 53; Hy Hurwitz, "Barber Tip Helped Mombo Mow Down 17 Nats on Strikes," *Sporting News*, May 24, 1961, 28; Simons, "Pitcher at Twilight," 46.
83. Peary, *We Played the Game*, 412; Larry Claflin, "No Mumbo-Jumbo with Monbo on Hill," *Sporting News*, February 28, 1964, 5; Hy Hurwitz, "Hard-Working Monbo Gets Off to Running Start for Red Sox," *Sporting News*, February 8, 1964, 22.
84. Peary, *We Played the Game*, 412–413.
85. "Runge Nips Rhubarb," *Sporting News*, April 29, 1959, 23.
86. Alex MacLean, "'Monbo' to Face A's," *Boston Daily Record*, June 3, 1959, 27; Hy Hurwitz, "Classy Hurling Duo Heats Up Hub Hopes," *Sporting News*, September 23, 1959, 42.
87. Hy Hurwitz, "Mombo Shows Plenty of Heart, Dinky Curve in One-Hit Dazzler," *Sporting News*, May 18, 1960, 16; Peary, *We Played the Game*, 485.
88. Frank Graham, Jr., "The Education of Bill Monbouquette," *Sport*, August 1962, 69–70.
89. Hy Hurwitz, "Schwall, Mombo Hub Blue-Ribbon Hurlers," *Sporting News*, August 9, 1961, 23; Larry Claflin, "Yanks Covet Sox Monbo," *Boston Record American*, October 27, 1961, 69; Hurwitz, "Barber Tip Helped," 28.
90. Joe Cashman, "Red Sox Beat Yankees, 9–6, Lose Opener, 3–0," *Boston Daily Record*, July 10, 1961, 45.
91. Peary, *We Played the Game*, 519.
92. Clavin and Peary, *Roger Maris*, 171; Cashman, "Red Sox Beat Yankees," 45; *RMAB*, 44–45.
93. Peary, *We Played the Game*, 613; John Gillooly, "Reluctant Sox Give Higgins a Headache," *Boston Record American*, January 30, 1964, 24.
94. "'Happy to Be Going to Detroit'—Monbo," *Boston Record American*, October 5, 1965, 38.
95. Terry Jones, "Disgusted Hurler Monbo Expects Tigers to Trade Him," *Sporting News*, November 26, 1966, 29; Jim Ogle, "Big Payoff for Yanks in Long-Shot Gamble on Monbo," *Sporting News*, September 16, 1967, 22; Jim Ogle, "Washed Up? Yankees' Monbo Proves that All Wrong," *Sporting News*, May 11, 1968, 13.
96. Jim Ogle, "Bouton Sent Off to Syracuse to Revitalize Tender Wing," *Sporting News*, June 17, 1967, 6; Ogle, "Big Payoff," 22.
97. Harry Jupiter, "Hart Beats Hefty Tatoo in Giant Homer Climb," *Sporting News*, August 3, 1968, 7; John Wilson, "Positive Thinking? Big Plus for Astros' Griffin," *Sporting News*, April 12, 1969, 38; Peary, *We Played the Game*, 613.

98. Arthur Daley, "Sports of the Times," *New York Times*, July 13, 1961, 33; *RMAB*, 45; "Wind-Ravaged A. L. Stars Moan," *Boston Evening American*, July 12, 1961, 28.
99. *RMAB*, 46.
100. Dan Daniel, "Maris, Mantle Have Frick Sweating," *Knoxville News-Sentinel*, July 7, 1961, C2; Jack Lang, "Mantle Has Better Chance Than Maris to Beat 60," *Jersey (Jersey City, NJ) Journal*, July 29, 1961, 9.
101. Melvin Durslag, "Prof Talks of 'M' Boys," *Sporting News*, July 26, 1961, 14.
102. *RMAB*, 48.
103. *RMAB*, 47, 57.
104. Bill Furlong, "Early Wynn—Old Meanie," in *Baseball Stars of 1960*, edited by Ray Robinson (New York: Pyramid Books, 1960), 19.
105. Roger Kahn, *Seasons in the Sun* (New York: Harper and Row, 1977), 108.
106. Furlong, "Early Wynn," 20.
107. Hal Lebovitz, "Indians Fanning Camp Fire for Return of Old Gus," *Sporting News*, June 15, 1963, 7; Hal Lebovitz, "Newly-Sharpened Hook Aids Burly Early," *Sporting News*, September 10, 1952, 3; Edgar Munzel, "Ol' Pappy Gus Licked Gout in Greatest Years," *Sporting News*, November 4, 1959, 14: Early Wynn, "The Four Sides of the Beanball Argument," *Sport*, January 1956, 61; Furlong, "Early Wynn," 20–21.
108. Hy Hurwitz, "Wynn Adds Young Award to Laurels List," *Sporting News*, November 4, 1959, 5; Bob Burnes, "Early, Walt, Buzz Best in Big Time," *Sporting News*, December 30, 1959, 1.
109. *RMAB*, 48; Joseph M. Sheehan, "Yanks Beat White Sox and Regain First Place as Maris, Mantle Hit Homers," *New York Times*, July 14, 1961, 15; Edward Prell, "Sox Beaten Early, 6–2; Cubs Lose, 4–3," *Chicago Daily Tribune*, July 14, 1961, Sec. 4, 1.
110. *RMAB*, 48; Dan Daniel, "Babe Ruth's Ghost Begins to Fret," *Evansville (IN) Press*, July 7, 1961, 16.
111. Jerry Holtzman, "Chisox Mound Staff Shaky; Wynn's Sore Flipper Tough Blow," *Sporting News*, August 9, 1961, 18; Jerry Holtzman, "Pale Hose Busting All Their Buttons—It's Wonderful Juan," *Sporting News*, September 6, 1961, 26.
112. Lee Allen, "Cooperstown Corner," *Sporting News*, June 15, 1963, 16.
113. Edgar Munzel, "Wynn Glances for Signal—Sees 'No Vacancy' Sign," *Sporting News*, April 13, 1963, 23; Hal Lebovitz, "Pills Help Early Kill Gout Pain, Then Vet Twirls 300th Victory," *Sporting News*, July 27, 1963, 12.
114. Joseph M. Sheehan, "Yankees Lose to White Sox but Hold First Place as Twins Set Back Tigers," *New York Times*, July 15, 1961, 13.
115. *RMAB*, 49.
116. Joseph M. Sheehan, "Yanks Win," *New York Times*, July 16, 1961, Sec. 5, 1; *RMAB*, 49.
117. Joseph M. Sheehan, "Yankees Turn Back Orioles but Slip to Second Place as Tigers Win Twice," *New York Times*, July 17, 1961, 16; "Yanks Call Up Rookie Southpaw with 9-1 Record at Binghamton," *New York Times*, July 17, 1961, 16.
118. "Ford's Edict May Protect Ruth's Mark," *Boston Evening American*, July 18, 1961, 40; Phil Pepe, *1961: The Inside Story of the Maris-Mantle Home Run Chase* (Chicago: Triumph Books, 2011), 109.

119. Maury Allen, *Roger Maris: A Man for All Seasons* (New York: Donald I. Fine, 1986), 140–141.
120. Allen, *Roger Maris*, 140–141.
121. Hy Hurwitz, "Mick 'Wouldn't Want Mark If It Was Set in 155 Games," *Sporting News*, August 9, 1961, 4; Mickey Mantle with Herb Gluck, *The Mick* (Garden City, NY: Doubleday, 1985), 196; Milton Gross, "A Footnote to Frick's *," *New York Post*, September 12, 1961, 57; *RMAB*, 55; Allen, *Roger Maris*, 141.
122. *RMAB*, 55.
123. Clavin and Peary, *Roger Maris*, 174–175.
124. Mike Gillooly, "Brown Admits Confidence Hurt by Sox," *Boston Evening American*, September 17, 1954, 59.
125. Elton Casey, "Casey at the Bat," *Durham (NC) Sun*, July 15, 1955, 2B.
126. John Steadman, "Richards' Team of Future Arrives Early—Quartet of Slab Starters Only 21 Years Old," *Sporting News*, June 1, 1960, 3; Peary, *We Played the Game*, 373.
127. Pepe, *1961*, 110.
128. *RMAB*, 54; Leonard Shecter, "It Takes Rain to Halt Maris and Mantle," *New York Post*, July 18, 1961, 64; "Roger Maris Bushed, May Ask for Day Off," *Milwaukee Journal*, September 18, 1961, 2.
129. Joseph M. Sheehan, "Yankees Defeat Senators and Take First Place as Tigers Lose to Orioles," *New York Times*, July 19, 1961, 21; Hy Hurwitz, "Red Sox Sniff '58 Dividend on Baumann," *Sporting News*, October 9, 1957, 28.
130. *RMAB*, 58–59.
131. *RMAB*, 58–59; Larry Claflin, "Big Crowd to See Yank Sluggers," *Boston American*, July 21, 1961, 50.
132. *RMAB*, 59.
133. Bob Stevens, "Giants 'Exhibit' Yankees, 4–1," *San Francisco Chronicle*, July 25, 1961, 35–36.
134. *RMAB*, 61; Milton Richman, "Yankees 'M' Boys Clip White Sox in Twin Bill," *Marietta (GA) Journal*, July 26, 1961, 11.
135. Tommy Fitzgerald, "Gold Sox Bonus Kid Glitters in Shutout Debut," *Sporting News*, July 2, 1952, 2.
136. Hy Hurwitz, "Red Sox' Flag Fate Hangs on 16-Game Trip, Mike Admits," *Sporting News*, August 24, 1955, 10.
137. Bob Holbrook, "Lepcio, Taking Over for Goodman, Proves That He's Right Man," *Sporting News*, June 27, 1956, 9; Hy Hurwitz, "Trade Coalition, Cronin Plan for 'Stopping Yankees,'" *Sporting News*, December 12, 1956, 10.
138. Hy Hurwitz, "Some Bosox Bonus Talent in Final Test," *Sporting News*, November 26, 1958, 30.
139. Ed O'Neil, "Baumann New Blueblood of A. L. Hurlers," *Sporting News*, December 21, 1960, 21, 26.
140. Edgar Munzel, "Senor Steaming Up Chisox for Second-Half Flag Dash," *Sporting News*, July 19, 1961, 25.
141. *RMAB*, 64–65.
142. *RMAB*, 64–65; Paul Geisler, Jr., "Frank Baumann," *SABR BioProject*, October 1, 2012, accessed September 27, 2018, https://sabr.org/bioproj/person/df98efc5#sdendnote48anc.
143. "Newly-Developed Curve Ball Has Baumann Back on Beam," *Sporting News*, August 25, 1962, 51; "Buzhardt Replaces Baumann on White Sox Disabled List," *Sporting News*, August 24, 1963, 11.

144. Jerome Holtzman, "Baumann Tapped to Put Some Beef in Cubs' Bull Pen," *Sporting News*, December 12, 1964, 21.
145. "Yanks Got Just What They Needed, Says Greenberg," *Sporting News*, November 24, 1954, 3.
146. Peary, *We Played the Game*, 252; Dan Daniel, "Deadline for Larsen: Must Look Like Real Yankee by June 15," *New York Times*, December 29, 1954, 8.
147. Frank Graham, "Already It's Plain Yankees Pulled No 'Steal' on Richards," *Sporting News*, April 6, 1955, 11; Dan Daniel, "Fold-Up of Larsen Speeds Yanks Hunt for Another Hurler," *Sporting News*, May 18, 1955, 10.
148. "Larsen Wins Five Straight for Denver in 24-Day Span, *Sporting News*, June 29, 1955, 36; J. G. Taylor Spink, "Looping the Loop," *Sporting News*, September 21, 1955, 6.
149. Casey Stengel, "Case Sees Yanks Again Chased by Tribe," *Sporting News*, February 8, 1956, 3; Dan Daniel, "Rangy Rookie Kubek Wins Kudos in Bombers' Camp," *Sporting News*, March 21, 1956, 9; "Don Larsen Overstays Curfew; Wraps His Car Around Pole," *Sporting News*, April 11, 1956, 11; Don Larsen and Mark Shaw, *The Perfect Yankee: The Incredible Story of the Greatest Miracle in Baseball History* (Champaign, IL: Sagamore, 1996), 95–96.
150. Larsen, *The Perfect Yankee*, 98–101.
151. Bob Burnes, "No-Windup Pitch Gains Favor," *Sporting News*, October 31, 1956, 10.
152. Burnes, "No-Windup Pitch," 10; Larsen, *The Perfect Yankee*, 98–101.
153. *The Perfect Yankee*, 222.
154. Dan Daniel, "Bombers Drooling at Vision of Series Gravy with Braves," *Sporting News*, August 21, 1957, 10; Dan Daniel, "Larsen Swap Talk Fades, but He Must Win-or-Else in '58," *Sporting News*, December 11, 1957, 7.
155. Dan Daniel, "Ford and Larsen Shelved, Other Hurlers Keep Yanks on Win Gait," *Sporting News*, September 10, 1958, 7.
156. Larsen, *The Perfect Yankee*, 222.
157. Robert L. Teague, "Maris Hits Four Home Runs as Yanks Beat White Sox Twice and Regain Lead," *New York Times*, July 26, 1961, 23; Edward Prell, "Maris Slams 4 Homers; Sox Lose Pair," *Chicago Daily Tribune*, July 26, 1961, 4; *RMAB*, 65.
158. *RMAB*, 66.
159. Teague, "Maris Hits," 23; Prell, "Maris Slams," 4; *RMAB*, 66.
160. "Two Tie for Lead," *Sporting News*, September 24, 1947, 30; "Big State League," *Sporting News*, October 15, 1947, 27; Otis Harris, "Needle-Threader Hacker Sewing Up Major Trial," *Sporting News*, August 25, 1948, 27.
161. Edgar Munzel, "Up-and-Down Warren Hacker Up with Cubs for Keeps This Time," *Sporting News*, October 31, 1951, 7; "Near-Perfect Game Marked Highlight in Hack's Career," *Sporting News*, November 26, 1952, 5.
162. Ed Burns, "Hats Off," *Sporting News*, August 13, 1952, 17.
163. At McDonough, "Cubs' Hard-Luck Hacker Might Lose 30," *Sporting News*, June 24, 1953, 3; Edgar Munzel, "Cubs Spare Cavvy but Lower Boom on Coaching Staff," *Sporting News*, October 14, 1953, 24.
164. "Hack Diagnosis Hacker's Trouble—He's a Worrier," *Sporting News*, April 14, 1954, 52; John C. Hoffman, "Hack Gets Stylish Results from Cub Patchwork Job," *Sporting News*, June 1, 1955, 10.
165. "Hacker Hurling Sinker Again," *Sporting News*, March 23, 1955, 24.
166. Tom Swope, "Cub-Red Deal Likely Spark to Swap of Cincy Backstop," *Sporting News*, November 21, 1956, 16; "Rookie Kubek Wises Up Quickly," *Sporting News*, April 24, 1957, 17; Dan Daniel, "Where Do Reds Get Their Kick?," *Sporting News*, June 5, 1957, 3.
167. *RMAB*, 67.
168. *RMAB*, 67.
169. Prell, "Maris Slams," 4; "Maris Swat 4 More as Yankees Strut," *Kansas City Times*, July 26, 1961, 12.
170. Sid Gray, "A Man Named Maris," *New York Post*, August 4, 1961, 52.
171. Gray, "A Man," 52.
172. Leonard Shecter, "Mickey Mantle, One Down," *New York Post*, August 6, 1961, 49.
173. *RMAB*, 70–71; Houk, *Ballplayers Are Human, Too*, 172.
174. Jack Hand, "Roger Maris' Four Homers Setting Pace," *Appeal Democrat (Marysville, CA)* July 26, 1961, 16; Robert L. Moore, "Maris Wears Biggest Grin Among Yanks,' *Sedalia (MO) Democrat*, July 26, 1961, 6.
175. Allen, *Roger Maris*, 144–145.
176. Pepe, *1961*, 120, 122.
177. Allen, *Roger Maris*, 143.
178. *RMAB*, 152; Allen, *Roger Maris*, 143.
179. Allen, *Roger Maris*, 145.
180. *RMAB*, 80.
181. *RMAB*, 80–81; Gay Talese, "Fans Want Ruth's Record Broken," *New York Times*, August 11, 1961, 15.
182. Jack Murphy, "Maris, Mantle Wonder If Apology Expected for Spectacular Jobs," *San Diego Union*, August 25, 1961, B4.

Chapter 6

1. *RMAB*, 72; Robert L. Teague, "Blanchard Hits 2 Homers and Mantle Poles No. 39 as Yanks Beat White Sox," *New York Times*, July 27, 1961, 27.
2. *RMAB*, 72–73; Joe King, "Injury Hoodoo Strikes Maris for Third Straight Season," *Sporting News*, August 9, 1961, 13.
3. John Drebinger, "Sports of the Times," *New York Times*, August 2, 1961, 20.
4. Howard M. Tuckner, "Yankees Loss Twice to Orioles," *New York Times*, July 31, 1961, 23.
5. Houk, *Ballplayers Are Human, Too*, 179–181.
6. *RMAB*, 76.
7. Gordon S. White Jr., "Mantle's 40th Homer Highlights Double Victory Over Athletics," *New York Times*, August 3, 1961, 16.
8. Bob Wolf, "'Poor Start Touched Off Big Four-Bagger Spree,' Rog Reveals," *Sporting News*, January 17, 1962, 16.
9. Shirley Povich, "Dressen's Stronger Hand Seen in Shakeup of Nats," *Sporting News*, November 23, 1955, 8; Shirley Povich, "Dressen's Biggest Problem," *Sporting News*, February 29, 1956, 22.
10. Shirley Povich, "Cuban Mound Pair Pegged as Nat Nifties," *Sporting News*, May 9, 1956, 6.

11. Shirley Povich, "Better than '21' Quiz? Pascual Loses 18 and Wins $1,000 Pay Hike," *Sporting News*, March 13, 1957, 8; Max Nichols, "Camilo's Curve Sharper Than Ever," *Sporting News*, April 2, 1966, 4.

12. Shirley Povich, "Reds' Million Offer for Pair Nixed by Nats," *Sporting News*, December 23, 1959, 22.

13. Kemmerer, *Ted Williams*, 139; Don Wise, *1964 Official Baseball Almanac* (Greenwich, CT: Fawcett, 1964), 73; Shirley Povich, "Camilo Pascual," *Sporting News*, May 21, 1958, 21; Jack McDonald, "Mound Magician Pierce Crowned Candlestick King," *Sporting News*, April 27, 1963, 11; Nichols, "Camilo's Curve," 4; Rich Westcott, *Diamond Greats: Profiles and Interviews with 65 of Baseball's History Makers* (Westport, CT: Meckler Books, 1988), 312.

14. Max Nichols, "Camilo's Fast Ball Crackles—Back Surgery a Huge Success," *Sporting News*, October 2, 1965, 9; Nichols, "Camilo's Curve," 4; Westcott, *Diamond Greats*, 312.

15. Max Nichols, "Needlers Jab Twins, Ease Pennant Pressure," *Sporting News*, October 2, 1965, 9.

16. Leonard Shecter, "Pascual Considers Himself Lucky," *New York Post*, June 25, 1961, 44.

17. Robert L. Teague, "Yanks Beat Twins on Blanchard's 3-Run Homer in the 10th; Maris His No. 41," *New York Times*, August 5, 1961, 10; *RMAB*, 79.

18. *RMAB*, 79.

19. *RMAB*, 84.

20. Til Ferdenzi, "'Big League Play by Big Leaguer,'" *New York Journal-American*, August 8, 1961, 20; *RMAB*, 85.

21. Ferdenzi, "Big League," 20; Houk, *Ballplayers are Human, Too*, 189.

22. *RMAB*, 86–87; Ferdenzi, "Big League," 20.

23. *RMAB*, 87–88.

24. Kubek, *Sixty-One*, 93–94.

25. *RMAB*, 89.

26. Louis Effrat, "Yankees Rout Senators for Ninth in Row as Mantle and Maris Hit Homers," *New York Times*, August 12, 1961, 10;.

27. Effrat, "Yankees Rout Senators," 10; *RMAB*, 89; Leonard Shecter, *Roger Maris: Home Run Hero* (New York: Bartholomew House, 1961), 131.

28. Edgar Munzel, "Marty Calls Chisox Better Than His '51 Star-Studded Cards," *Sporting News*, March 9, 1955, 16.

29. Edgar Munzel, "Donovan Winner on Addition of Slider," *Sporting News*, July 6, 1955, 3–4.

30. Munzel, "Donovan Winner," *Sporting News*, 3–4.

31. John C. Hoffman, "Chisox' Spirit Stays High Although Ace Is Laid Low," *Sporting News*, August 10, 1955, 9; Lee Greene, "Dick Donovan: Spunky Vet," in *Baseball Stars of 1963*, edited by Ray Robinson (New York: Pyramid Books, 1963), 147.

32. "Lollar Declares 'Swift One' Sold Him on Righthander," *Sporting News*, July 6, 1955, 3; Munzel, "Donovan Winner," 4; Lee Greene, "Dick Donovan: Comeback Story," in *Baseball Stars of 1962*, edited by Ray Robinson (New York: Pyramid Books, 1962), 148; Bob Addie, "'More Good Pitchers in American,' Claims N. L. 'Traitor' Chuck," *Sporting News*, June 8, 1955, 7; Vanderberg, *Sox*, 173.

33. Frederick G. Lieb, "Donovan's Dandy Deed," *Sporting News*, December 30, 1959, Sec. 2, 8.

34. Shirley Povich, "Donovan Aching to 'Show Lopez' in Nats' Opener," *Sporting News*, March 1, 1961, 14.

35. Povich, "Donovan Aching," 14; Green, "Dick Donovan: Spunky Vet," 148.

36. Greene, "Dick Donovan: Spunky Veteran," 148; Shirley Povich, "Kutyna Chucks Role as Reliever, Shines in Nat Starting Job," *Sporting News*, August 9, 1961, 24.

37. Shirley Povich, "Nats Booming Fiery Piersall as Sparkplug," *Sporting News*, October 18, 1961, 10.

38. "Bob Addie's Atoms," *Sporting News*, July 3, 1965, 14.

39. Bob Addie, "Dick Donovan," *Sporting News*, August 9, 1961, 27; Dave Anderson, "Top Hill Foes Agree M & M Will Snap HR Mark," *New York Journal-American*, August 22, 1961, 24.

40. *RMAB*, 90.

41. *RMAB*, 90; Bob Addie, "Green's Homer Slams Yanks," *Washington Post and Times Herald*, August 13, 1961, C1.

42. "Daniels' Win Streak Snapped," *Sporting News*, August 1, 1956, 33.

43. "Pacific Coast League," *Sporting News*, July 10, 1957, 41; "Pacific Coast League," *Sporting News*, August 7, 1957, 42; Rube Samuelsen, "6,417 See North All-Stars Win as Hurlers Sparkle," *Sporting News*, July 10, 1957, 41; Frank Finch, "Daniels Follows '56 Script in Fast Start at Hollywood," *Sporting News*, May 29, 1957, 29.

44. "Danny High on Daniels," *Sporting News*, March 26, 1958, 31; "Columbus," *Sporting News*, July 2, 1958, 32.

45. Finch, "Daniels Follows '56 Script," 29; Brad Wilson, "Daniels' Fast One Bust Rival Hitters' Hearts, and Catcher's Finger," *Sporting News*, July 23, 1958, 35; Bob Addie, "Bennie Daniels Surprise Whiz of Nat Hill Staff," *Sporting News*, August 23, 1961, 36.

46. Ralph Ray, "Hemus Plunked, Lets Bat Sail in Fracas with Bucs," *Sporting News*, May 13, 1959, 23; Jim Brosnan, *The Long Season* (New York: Harper, 1960), 115; David Halberstam, *October 1964* (New York: Open Road Integrated Media, 2012), 224–225.

47. Les Biederman, "Collapsible Corsairs Battle Old Bugaboo—Breakdown on the Road," *Sporting News*, April 20, 1960, 26; "Jets' Daniels Back on Beam," *Sporting News*, July 27, 1960, 30.

48. Bill Fuchs, "Daniels, a Trade Toss-In, Happy at Chance to Pitch," *Evening Star (Washington, DC)*, February 22, 1961, C9; Bill Fuchs, "Daniels Proves Readiness to Go Route for Senators," *Evening Star (Washington, DC)*, March 30, 1961, A1.

49. Bill Fuchs, "Daniels' Sinker Lifts Club, *Evening Star (Washington, DC)*, July 31, 1961, A12; Bill Fuchs, "Overworked Senator Staff Showing Signs of Strain," *Evening Star (Washington, DC)*, June 12, 1961, A16; Bill Fuchs, "Punchless Senators Hurt Daniels Again," *Evening Star (Washington, DC)*, August 23, 1961, F1; Bill Fuchs, "Future Bright for Daniels," *Evening Star (Washington, DC)*, September 16, 1961, A10.

50. Merrell Whittlesey, "Johnson, Daniels Co-Star as Senators Open in Style," *Evening Star (Washington, DC)*, April 10, 1962, A18; "Sore Elbow Forces Daniels to Skip Nat Visit to Chicago," *Sporting News*, May 23, 1962, 31; Shirley Povich, "Hemsley Tosses Barb at Nats for Mound Strategy," *Sporting News*, December 1, 1962, 25.

51. "Ex-Hurler—Ghetto Robin Hood or Con Man?, *Evansville (IN) Courier*, January 25, 1979, 25.
52. Bob Addie, "Maris Hits 2 Homers, Mantle One for Tie at 45 as Yanks, Nats Split," *Washington Post*, August 14, 1961, A13; Bill Fuchs, "Mantle-Maris Home Run Heroics Prove Smash Hit in Washington," *Evening Star (Washington, DC)*, August 14, 1961, 16; *RMAB*, 91.
53. Addie, "Maris Hits 2 Homers," A13; Fuchs, "Maris-Mantle Home Run Heroics," 16; J. G. Taylor Spink, "Sharp Gate Dip Challenges Big Time," *Sporting News*, October 11, 1961, 1.
54. Earl Lawson, "Early Christmas Shopper Gabe Wraps Up Seven New Hurlers," *Sporting News*, December 18, 1957, 11–12.
55. Earl Lawson, "Birdie Bright-Eyed Over Big Hill Squad," *Sporting News*, March 5, 1958, 5.
56. "A's Sell Craddock," *Kansas City Star*, March 31, 1959, 14; "Prospect to Oregon," *Kansas City Star*, April 2, 1959, 19; "Portland," *Sporting News*, September 9, 1959, 28.
57. Joe McGuff, "Depth to Be Big A's Factor," March 8, 1960, 13; Bill Fuchs, "Kutyna's Showing Brings New Respect for Senators," *Evening Star (Washington, DC)*, April 20, 1961, D1; Francis Stann, "Senators Trade Sullivan to A's for Marty Kutyna," *Evening Star (Washington, DC)*, December 29, 1960, C4.
58. McGuff, "Depth to Be," 13; Stann, "Senators Trade Sulliven," C1, C4.
59. Fuchs, "Kutyna's Showing," D1.
60. Bill Fuchs, "Kutyna Makes First Start Tonight," *Evening Star (Washington, DC)*, July 28, 1961, D1.
61. Merrell Whittlesey, "Baseball Beat," *Evening Star (Washington, DC)*, April 10, 1962, A21; Merrell Whittlesey, "Senators Get Another Lift as Rudolph, Johnson Click," *Evening Star (Washington, DC)*, July 17, 1962, A10; "Senators Drop Seven Players," *Evening Star (Washington, DC)*, December 21, 1962, B7.
62. *RMAB*, 92.
63. Francis Stann, "Win, Lose or Draw," *Evening Star (Washington, DC)*, March 6, 1962, A13; Addie, "Maris Hits 2 Homers," A16; *RMAB*, 92.
64. Til Ferdenzi, "Toe Stance Keeps Maris on HR Beam," *New York Journal-American*, August 14, 1961, 24; *RMAB*, 94–95.
65. Braven Dyer, "Webb Fingers Mantle as Best Bet to Top Ruth's Mark," *Sporting News*, August 2, 1961, 14; *RMAB*, 94–95.
66. Pepe, *1961*, 136; *RMAB*, 95–96.
67. Joe Hinton, "Sizing Up Duos," *Sporting News*, August 2, 1961, 14; *RMAB*, 96–98; Pepe, *1961*, 136.
68. Jimmy Cannon, "All by Himself," *New York Journal-American*, August 17, 1961, 18; Arthur Daley, "Consolation for Idolotors," *New York Times*, August 22, 1961, 34.
69. Houk, *Ballplayers Are Human, Too*, 192; Pepe, *1961*, 141.
70. Bob Wolf, "Phenom Pizarro Sure He'll Make Grade as Brave," *Sporting News*, March 13, 1957, 17; "'Pizarro Could Be as Great as Spahn,' Says Bill Terry," *Sporting News*, October 24, 1956, 8.
71. Wolf, "Phenom Pizarro," 17; Bob Wolf, "McGrew's Peepers Pop After Glimpse of Braves' Pizarro," *Sporting News*, January 2, 1957, 18.
72. Bob Wolf, "Kid Pizarro Pitches Way Onto Braves' Bulging Staff," *Sporting News*, April 24, 1957, 9.

73. Bob Wolf, "Pitcher-Wealthy Braves Still Seek Bull-Pen Bracer," *Sporting News*, December 4, 1957, 20; Moffi, *This Side of Cooperstown*, 125.
74. Pito Alvarez de la Vega, "Pizarro Broadens Braves' Grins with Hill Sparklers," *Sporting News*, January 15, 1958, 20; Pito Alvarez de la Vega, "Pizarro Follows 19-Wiff Game with No Hitter," *Sporting News*, December 11, 1957, 29.
75. George Vass, "Problems Worth Having?," *Baseball Digest*, May 1967, 8; Kiersh, *Where Have You Gone*, 132–133, 135.
76. Edgar Munzel, "Senor to Try Magic on Pizarro, McLish," *Sporting News*, December 28, 1960, 15.
77. Kiersh, *Where Have You Gone*, 135.
78. Edgar Munzel, "Super-Duper Hill Staff Spurs Flag Chatter by Senor," *Sporting News*, April 12, 1961, 29; Edgar Munzel, "Chisox Southpaws Skid—Senor Leaning on Three Righthanders," *Sporting News*, May 10, 1961, 20; "American League," *Sporting News*, May 31, 1961, 36; Jerry Holtzman, "Chisox Mound Staff Shaky; Wynn's Sore Flipper Tough Blow," *Sporting News*, August 9, 1961, 24.
79. Jerry Holtzman, "Puzzler Pizarro Snaps Slump—Twirls Gem After Eight Kayoes," *Sporting News*, June 16, 1962, 10; Edgar Munzel, "Late Hill Bloomer Herbert Hypoes Chisox Comeback," *Sporting News*, September 1, 1962, 11; Kiersh, *Where Have You Gone*, 132.
80. Jerome Holtzman, "Pizarro Finds Answer to Victory Puzzle," *Sporting News*, September 21, 1963, 3.
81. Edgar Munzel, "Eddie Fisher Show-Stopper of Chisox," *Sporting News*, July 10, 1965, 3.
82. Jerry Holtzman, "Pizarro, Lown Earn Grade-A Ranking in Chisox Hill Figures," *Sporting News*, November 29, 1961, 36; Howard M. Tuckner, "Mantle, Maris Await Generous White Sox Hurlers," *New York Times*, August 15, 1961 32; *RMAB*, 98.
83. *RMAB*, 98–99; Robert L. Teague, "White Sox Beat Ford of Yanks Despite No. 46 by Maris," *New York Times*, August 16, 1961, 23.
84. *RMAB*, 99.
85. James, Bill, and Rob Neyer, "Billy Pierce," in *The Neyer/James Guide to Pitchers: An Historical Compendium of Pitching, Pitchers, and Pitches* (New York: Simon & Schuster, 2004), 103.
86. Watson Spoelstra, "Two New Hal Newhousers Sighted in Pierce, Gray," *Sporting News*, February 4, 1948, 18; Ed Burns, "Pierce Paces Hose Pitchers on Control," *Sporting News*, June 6, 1951, 3; Vanderberg, *Sox*, 139–140.
87. Cy Kritzer, "Hose Get Tutor-Taskmaster in Red Corriden's Successor," *Sporting News*, October 18, 1950, 5.
88. Milton Richman, "Nobody Wins with a Fast Ball," *Sport*, July 1956, 68; Kritzer, "Hose Get Tutor," 5; James, "Billy Pierce," 104; Vanderberg, *Sox*, 141.
89. Edgar Munzel, "That Sprint-Man Lane, Slowed to a Walk in Swap Circuit, Keeps Eye Glued on Nats," *Sporting News*, November 5, 1952, 17.
90. Edgar Munzel, "Pierce Looming as Chisox' First 20-Game Ace Since '41," *Sporting News*, July 15, 1953, 20; James, "Billy Pierce," 104.
91. Jerry Holtzman, "Billy Pierce," *Sporting News*, July 9, 1958, 37; Vanderberg, *Sox*, 141.
92. Jerry Holtzman, "Hungry Chisox Jump on Nats, Yanks—Stoke Up for Stretch," *Sporting News*, September 2, 1959, 14.

93. Jack McDonald, "Cepeda and Miller in Line for Heftier Pay Envelopes," *Sporting News*, December 20, 1961, 23.
94. Jack McDonald, "Duffalo Elbowing Way into Giants' Starter Rotation," *Sporting News*, April 4, 1962, 6.
95. Jack McDonald, "Pierce Latest Flame of Candlestick Fans," *Sporting News*, April 25, 1962, 19.
96. Bob Stevens, "Pierce Hangs Up Toeplate as Winner and Gentleman," *Sporting News*, October 10, 1964, 24.
97. *RMAB*, 103; Rick Telander, "The Record Almost Broke Him," *Sports Illustrated*, June 20, 1977, 66, 68.
98. *RMAB*, 105; Robert L. Teague, "Maris Poles Two Homers, for Total of 48, in Yanks Victory Over White Sox," *New York Times*, August 17, 1961, 19; Dan Daniel, "Blasé Broadway Buzzing Over Maris, Mantle HRs," *Sporting News*, August 23, 1961, 7.
99. "More Cash, Not Record Goal of Slugging Maris," *Evansville (IN) Courier and Press*, August 17, 1961, 27; *RMAB*, 105–107; Dan Daniel, "Homer Duel Cinch to Produce 100-G Pay Check in '62," *Sporting News*, August 30, 1961, 6.
100. Joe Reichler, "Maris More Interested in Pay Than Record," *Bellingham (WA) Herald*, August 17, 1961, 7; Dan Daniel, "Frugal Roger Maris Will Hit the Jackpot Beyond Wildest Dreams Because of Homers," *Knoxville News-Sentinel*, August 22, 1961, 15.
101. Reichler, "Maris More Interested," 7.
102. Emil Tagliabue, "Roger the Red Neck," *Corpus Christi (TX) Times*, August 22, 1961, 4B.
103. Howard M. Tuckner, "'61 Ball May (or May Not) Account for Homers," *New York Times*, August 14, 1961, 1, 19; Robert H. Boyle, "Yes It's Livelier—and Here Is the Proof," *Sports Illustrated*, August 28, 1961, 14–17; Daniel, "Blasé Broadway, 7; "Satchel Paige, a Lively 52 (?), Says Ball Is 'Livelier, All Right,'" *New York Times*, August 18, 1961, 24.
104. Joseph M. Sheehan, "The Lively Bat Becomes a Livelier Issue," *New York Times*, August 20, 1961, 1, 3.
105. Chuck Such, "Grant Turns Table—He's Hit with Maris, Mantle," *Canton (OH) Repository*, August 19, 1961, 9.
106. Joseph C. Nichols, "Yankees Beat Indians, 3–2, in 10th; Ford Wins 21st," *New York Times* August 20, 1961, 2S.
107. John Drebinger, "Yankees Turn Back Indians Twice as Maris Hits No. 49 and Mantle No. 46," *New York Times*, August 21, 1961, 26; *RMAB*, 110.
108. Bob Dolgan, "Maris Hits 49th as Yanks Win 2," *Cleveland Plain Dealer*, August 21, 1961, 33; *RMAB*, 111.
109. *RMAB*, 114; Murray Schumach, "Yankees Steal a Scene," *San Francisco Chronicle*, August 25, 1961, 41.
110. Pat Maris, "My Husband," 90; *RMAB*, 114.
111. "Shawnee Sets Homer Record," *Sporting News*, August 11, 1954, 37; "Third No-Hitter in Carolina," *Sporting News*, September 5, 1956, 36.
112. "Indianapolis," *Sporting News*, June 3, 1959, 34; "Indianapolis," *Sporting News*, July 29, 1959, 33.
113. Edgar Munzel, "Fast-Baller Peters Blooming as Slab Beaut on Chisox Vine," *Sporting News*, November 30, 1960, 27.
114. Munzel, "Fast-Baller Peters," 27; Melvin Durslag, "For Him the Sinker's the Payoff," *Baseball Digest*, October-November 1962, 50; Brent Kelley, *The San Francisco Seals, 1946–1957: Interviews with 25 Former Baseballers* (Jefferson, NC: McFarland, 2002), 257.
115. Braven Dyer, "Medic Reports Slip Big Hypo to Angels," *Sporting News*, November 24, 1962, 13; Braven Dyer, "'Injury Robbed McBride of 20 Games,' Rig Says," *Sporting News*, November 10, 1962, 9; Braven Dyer, "Angel Ace McBride Eyes 20-Win Trail," *Sporting News*, March 16, 1963, 10.
116. Braven Dyer, "Angels Pegging Clinton as Cure for Bat Anemia," *Sporting News*, June 20, 1964, 15; Peter M. Gordon, "Ken McBride," *SABR BioProject*, n.d., accessed November 12, 2018, https://sabr.org/bioproj/person/721d5411
117. "American League," *Sporting News*, May 22, 1965, 25.
118. *RMAB*, 119–120; John Drebinger, "Maris Clouts 50th Homer but Yankees Lose to Angels in Contest on Coast," *New York Times*, August 23, 1961, 37.
119. Barney Kremenko, "Maris Misses 51st, Triple Wins Game," *New York Journal-American*, August 24, 1961, 23.
120. *RMAB*, 121–122; Kremenko, "Maris Misses 51st," 23.
121. *RMAB*, 125–127.
122. Jim Lapham, "Big Crowd Sees a Maris Homer," *Kansas City Star*, August 27, 1961, 1A; "Extra Police at Games," *Kansas City Star*, August 26, 1961, 1A.
123. Jerry Walker, in telephone interview with the author, March 20, 2019; "Orioles Sign Oklahoma Kid Hurler for Reported 60 Gs," *Sporting News*, July 19, 1957, 32.
124. "Walker Calls Shot, Wins 16th," *Sporting News*, September 3, 1958, 37.
125. Jim Ellis, "Walker Big-Strider on Road to Hill Fame," *Sporting News*, August 12, 1959, 5.
126. Jim Ellis, "Walker Rare Bird in Oriole Bonus Flock," *Sporting News*, June 3, 1959, 11; Doug Brown, "Birds Beam Over Crib-Kid Mound Trio," *Sporting News*, July 29, 1959.
127. Ellis, "Walker Big-Strider," 5.
128. Doug Brown, "Jerry Walker," *Sporting News*, September 23, 1959, 31.
129. Walker, interview; "A's Swap Williams and Hall for Birds' Walker, Essegian," *Sporting News*, April 19, 1961, 18; Joe McGuff, "Frantic Becomes Frustrated," *Kansas City Star*, April 5, 1961, 36; J. G. Taylor-Spink, "Swami Spink Sees Dodger, Oriole Flags," *Sporting News*, 10; Til Ferdenzi, "Mileage Creeps Up, but Ford's Geared for Racy Summer," *Sporting News*, March 19, 1966, 17.
130. Joe McGuff, "Walker Hopes His Slider Is Effective Again," *Kansas City Star*, March 6, 1962, 16.
131. "Walker Shelves Windup to Stop Tips on Tosses," *Kansas City Star*, August 10, 1961, 17.
132. Joe McGuff, "Jerry Walker Finds Weapon Choice Costly," *Kansas City Star*, June 21, 1962, 23; Paul O'Boynick, "A's and Angels Play It Rough," *Kansas City Star*, August 29, 1962, 14C; Joe McGuff, "Injury-Riddled A's Mound Staff Haunting Bauer," *Kansas City Star*, August 3, 1962, 12.
133. "Indians Take Gamble, Land Hurler Walker," *Sporting News*, March 9, 1963, 8; Paul O'Boynick,

"Wynn Finally Wins 300," *Cleveland Plain Dealer*, July 14, 1963, 1B.
  134. "Walker Optioned to Indians' Farm," *Cleveland Plain Dealer*, May 14, 1964, 66; "Suns' Walker Predicts No-Hit Game, Then Hurls One-Hitter," *Sporting News*, September 12, 1964, 32.
  135. Walker, interview; Ernest Mehl, "Maris, 51—Yankees, 5–1," *Kansas City Star*, August 27, 1961, 1B; Paul O'Boynick, "Grind Telling on Weary Rog," *Kansas City Star*, August 27, 1961, 1B.
  136. O'Boynick, "Grind Telling," 1B; Houk, *Ballplayers Are Human, Too*, 196.
  137. Houk, *Ballplayers Are Human, Too*, 196–197.
  138. Houk, *Ballplayers Are Human, Too*, 196–197.

Chapter 7

  1. *RMAB*, 135–136, 153–154; Kubek, *Sixty-One*, 102.
  2. Leonard Koppett, "This Is It! Yanks vs. Tigers," *New York Post*, September 1, 1961, 68; Robert L. Teague, "Tigers Are Coming; So Are 180,000 Customers," *New York Times*, August 31, 1961, 30.
  3. Murray Robinson, "A Night to Remember," *New York Journal-American*, September 2, 1961, 13.
  4. Robinson, "A Night to Remember," 13; Leonard Shecter, "The Lady and the Tigers," *New York Post*, September 3, 1961, 34.
  5. *RMAB*, 140–141; Bob Holbrook, "Maris Raves … About Mantle's Bunt," *Boston Globe*, September 3, 1961, 68.
  6. *RMAB*, 141.
  7. Barry Jones, "Indians' Aguirre Knocks on Majors Door with Handling of Slugger Mays," *Cleveland Plain Dealer*, March 11, 1956, 3C; "Ted Raps Homer to Top Tigers," *Cleveland Plain Dealer*, July 20, 1958, 1C.
  8. Hal Lebovitz, "'We Couldn't Sit on Hands,' Asserts Lane," *Sporting News*, February 26, 1958, 1.
  9. Watson Spoelstra, "Tigers Cool on Hoeft Deal; Billy Could Get Hot in '59," *Sporting News*, January 7, 1959, 9; Hal Lebovitz, "Tepee Again Bulging with Good Hurlers," *Sporting News*, April 10, 1957, 24; Watson Spoelstra, "Bengals' Starters Get Big Lift from Bull-Pen Blazer Aguirre," *Sporting News*, September 7, 1960, 15; Watson Spoelstra, "Hungry Chico Could Beef Up Tigers' Infield," *Sporting News*, February 1, 1961, 13; Watson Spoelstra, "Is He One-Shot Aguirre—or Bengal Ace," *Sporting News*, December 22, 1962, 8; Watson Spoelstra, "Aguirre Gunning for ERA Honors," *Sporting News*, September 1, 1962, 6, 20; Robert E. Copley, *The Tall Mexican: The Life of Hank Aguirre, All-Star Pitcher, Businessman, Humanitarian* (Houston: Arte Publico Press, 1998), 30; Watson Spoelstra, "New-Style Hank Big Roar in Tiger Tank," *Sporting News*, March 5, 1966, 4; Joe Falls, "Out of Obscurity, Hank Aguirre," *Sport*, April 1963, 72.
  10. Hal Middlesworth, "Aguirre Returns from Lost Legion in Comeback Bid," *Sporting News*, March 23, 1960, 19; Sam Greene, "Narleski Fan Club Led by Dykes," *Sporting News*, January 27, 1960, 16.
  11. Spoelstra, "Bengals' Starters," 15; Watson Spoelstra, "Tigers Keep Paws Crossed as ?? Darken Shortstop Pix," *Sporting News*, November 8, 1961, 9; Spoelstra, "Is He One-Shot," 8.
  12. Spoelstra, "Is He One-Shot," 8; Watson Spoelstra, "Hank Aguirre," *Sporting News*, October 6, 1962, 43.
  13. "Aguirre Doesn't Dilly-Dally: 3 Games in Under 2 Hours," *Sporting News*, September 5, 1964; Joe Falls, "Aguirre's Hit It, Takes Plunge Off Mad, Mad World," *Sporting News*, January 9, 1965, 10; Copley, *Tall Mexican*, 36–37; Spoelstra, "New-Style Hank," 4.
  14. Jim Murray, "Swing Is the Thing with Hank," *Sporting News*, May 11, 1968, 34; Watson Spoelstra, "Sparma Reigns Old Yankee-Killer Rep—Bengals Lick Chops," *Sporting News*, June 17, 1967, 9; Copley, *Tall Mexican*, 35.
  15. Jerome Holtzman, "Aguirre Fits Key Niche in Cubs' Bullpen," *Sporting News*, March 15, 1969, 21; "Hank Aguirre, 62, Ex-Pitcher and Enterprising Businessman," *New York Times*, September 6, 1994, accessed August 24, 2017, https://www.nytimes.com/1994/09/06/obituaries/hank-aguirre-62-ex-pitcher-and-enterprising-businessman.html.
  16. John Drebinger, "Yanks Beat Tigers, 7–2, as Maris Hits 52d and 53d," *New York Times*, September 3, 1961, 2S; Houk, *Ballplayers Are Human, Too*, 206.
  17. Til Ferdenzi, "Maris Clouts 52d and 53d as Yanks Win," *New York Journal-American*, September 3, 1961, 1; *RMAB*, 141–142.
  18. Holbrook, "Maris Raves," 68.
  19. Holbrook, "Maris Raves," 68.
  20. Lyall Smith, "Mossi's Loss Regarded as Pivot Point," *Sporting News*, September 27, 1961, 7.
  21. Houk, *Ballplayers Are Human, Too*, 212–213.
  22. *RMAB*, 146–147.
  23. Leonard Koppett, "Maris: There's More to the Game Than HRs," *New York Post*, September 5, 1961, 72; Robert L. Teague, "Mantle Hits 51st Homer and Howard Also Connects as Yanks Beat Senators," *New York Times*, September 6, 1961, 43.
  24. Peary, *We Played the Game*, 249.
  25. "Cards Won't Call Up Omaha Pair at This Time, Lane Explains," *Sporting News*, July 18, 1956, 11.
  26. Jack Herman, "Chucker Cheney Draws Bead on Redbirds' Roost," *Sporting News*, March 27, 1957, 17–18.
  27. Peary, *We Played the Game*, 356–357.
  28. Bob Broeg, "Tom Cheney," *Sporting* News, May 1, 1957, 21; Peary, *We Played the Game*, 356–357; Bob Addie, "Ex-Bucs Cheney, Leppert Fill Bill in Capital," *Sporting News*, April 27, 1963, 9.
  29. Peary, *We Played the Game*, 429.
  30. "Bucs Obtain Francis, Cheney—Option Daniels, Umbricht," *Sporting News*, July 6, 1960, 37.
  31. Peary, *We Played the Game*, 473.
  32. Peary, *We Played the Game*, 509; "Washington at Los Angeles," *Sporting News*, August 2, 1961, 36.
  33. Peary, *We Played the Game*, 555–556.
  34. Robert C. Gallagher, "Tom Cheney: He Fanned 21 Batters in a Single Game," *Baseball Digest*, 91–92.
  35. Peary, *We Played the Game*, 555–556; Gallagher, "Tom Cheney," 91–92.
  36. Peary, *We Played the Game*, 581–582; Gallagher, "Tom Cheney," 92–93.
  37. Shirely Povich, "Medic's Bulletin on Cheney Wing Cheers Up Nats," *Sporting News*, February 1, 1964, 17; Bob Addie, "Capital Quacking Over Duckworth's Fine Relief Wing," *Sporting News*, May 9, 1964,

18; "Hurler Cheney Through for Season," *Sporting News*, July 4, 1964, 18.

38. Bob Addie, "Hodges Turns Orator; Nats Lend an Ear," *Sporting News*, May 28, 1966, 20.

39. Peary, *We Played the Game*, 614.

40. Peary, *We Played the Game*, 527.

41. Peary, *We Played the Game*, 527; *RMAB*, 149.

42. Peary, *We Played the Game*, 527; *RMAB*, 149.

43. *RMAB*, 151; Leonard Shecter, "Maris Is Thinking Ahead—to No. 60...," *New York Post*, September 7, 1961, 53; Pepe, *1961*, 168.

44. Harry Jones, "Ailment Is Break for Tribe Rookie," *Cleveland Plain Dealer*, February 5, 1959, 29; Hal Lebovitz, "Lane Whips Up New Trade Offers in Bid for Whopping Start," *Sporting News*, December 17, 1958, 18.

45. "San Diego," *Sporting News*, September 23, 1959, 42; "Like Haddix, Pards' Stigman Has No-Hit Gem, Fails to Win," *Sporting News*, June 3, 1959, 28.

46. Harry Jones, "Batting Around," *Cleveland Plain Dealer*, April 24, 1960, 3C; Harry Jones, "Slapnicka Uncovered Stigman in Backwoods of Minnesota," *Cleveland Plain Dealer*, May 8, 1960, 2C.

47. Bob Dolgan, "Stigman Bids to Improve Control, Win Starting Job," *Cleveland Plain Dealer*, February 26, 1961, 1C: Dick Stigman, in telephone interview with the author, February 23, 2019.

48. Jones, "Batting Around," 3C; Chuck Heaton, "Rookies Click, Gordon Beams," *Cleveland Plain Dealer*, May 2, 1960, 33.

49. Hal Lebovitz, "Dykes' Smooth Touch with Kid Curvers Earns New Teepee Term," *Sporting News*, September 28, 1960, 21; Harry Jones, "Batting Around," *Cleveland Plain Dealer*, September 5, 1960, 2F.

50. Dolgan, "Stigman Bids," 1C; Bob Dolgan, "Stigman, 3 Other Tribe Hurlers Sign," *Cleveland Plain Dealer*, February 1, 1962, 33.

51. Gordon Cobbledick, "Plain Dealing," February 28, 1962, 25.

52. Tom Briere, "Power, Stigman Stick Feather in Cal's Swap Cap," *Sporting News*, May 2, 1962, 6.

53. Arno Goethel, "Stigman's Strikeout Slants Spur Twins to Winning Splurge," *Sporting News*, August 4, 1962, 14.

54. Glenn Redmann, "Throw-In Stigman Standout as Twin Thrower," *Sporting News*, January 12, 1963, 9.

55. Max Nichols, "Stigman New Big Man of Twin Mound," *Sporting News*, March 28, 1964, 3.

56. Max Nichols, "Stigman, Thinking Positively, Erases Twin Wild-Man Stigma," *Sporting News*, June 20, 1964, 17;

57. Max Nichols, "More Work, Faster Start—Stigman's Double Twin Order," *Sporting News*, February 27, 1965, 13.

58. Max Nichols, "Sam the Sleuth Scours Staff, Seeking Clue to Fourth Starter," *Sporting News*, May 22, 1965, 9; Max Nichols, "Sain System Just What Twin Hurlers Needed," *Sporting News*, July 17, 1965, 10; Max Nichols, "Twins Count on Stigman as Big Man in Long Relief," *Sporting News*, January 29, 1966, 6.

59. "Bisons Sell Stigman," *Sporting News*, September 2, 1967, 42.

60. *RMAB*, 155.

61. Leonard Shecter, "Maris 55th: What It's Like to the Pitcher," *New York Post*, September 8, 1961, 80; Bob Dolgan, "Maris Wallops 55th Home Run," *Cleveland Plain Dealer*, September 8, 1961, 14; Bob Dolgan, "Batting Around," *Cleveland Plain Dealer*, September 9, 1961, 25.

62. Shecter, "Maris 55th," 80; Shecter, *Roger Maris*, 133; Til Ferdenzi, "Maris 'Cinch to Hit 60 or More,'" *New York Journal-American*, September 8, 1961, 30.

63. Shecter, "Maris 55th," 80.

64. Shecter, "Maris 55th," 80.

65. Ferdenzi, "Maris Cinch," 30.

66. *RMAB*, 155–156.

67. Jim "Mudcat" Grant, *The Black Aces: Baseball's Only African-American Twenty-Game Winners* (Farmingdale, NY: Aventine Press, 2006), 202–203.

68. Earl Keller, "'Comet Ball' Carries Grant Near Top of PCL Hurlers," *Sporting News*, August 28, 1957, 31.

69. Hal Lebovitz, "Lane to Send Tutor Harder to Cuba to Polish Hill Rookies," *Sporting News*, December 25, 1957, 20; Grant, *Black Aces*, 212.

70. Peary, *We Played the Game*, 404.

71. Peary, *We Played the Game*, 440; Kiersh, *Where Have You Gone*, 90–91.

72. "Grant Gets Suspension for Season," *Cleveland Plain Dealer*, September 17, 1960, 21–22; Harry Jones, "Batting Around," *Cleveland Plain Dealer*, September 18, 1960, 4C; Grant, *Black Aces*, 219.

73. Bob Dolgan, "Nats' Shift Gives Mudcat Jump on Pitching Rivals," *Cleveland Plain Dealer*, March 6, 1961, 29.

74. Ed McAuley, "Not to Be Taken for Grant-ed," *Baseball Digest*, August 1961, 5; Hal Lebovitz, "Gabe Sizes Up Twirlers—Tabs '61 'Growth Season,'" *Sporting News*, August 16, 1961, 7.

75. "Mudcat Returns to Tribe," *Cleveland Plain Dealer*, July 18, 1962, 27; Hal Lebovitz, "Mudcat's Busy Year-Round as Tribe Pitchman," *Sporting News*, December 22, 1962, 20.

76. Hal Lebovitz, "Mudcat Winter Whiz as Pitchman for Tribe," *Sporting News*, February 1, 1964, 6; Regis McAuley, "Tribe's Big Four—Kralick, Donovan, Ramos and Grant," *Sporting News*, April 18, 1964, 11.

77. Russell Schneider, " Tribe Gets Strange in Grant Deal," *Cleveland Plain Dealer*, June 16, 1964, 33; Regis McAuley, "Mudcat Seeks New Pigeons Following Transfer to Twins," *Sporting News*, June 27, 1964, 17.

78. Russell Schneider, "Mudcat Testing New Song and Dance Act," *Sporting News*, November 21, 1964, 23.

79. Max Nichols, "The Twins Hooked Whopper in Mudcat," *Sporting News*, October 9, 1965, 3.

80. Max Nichols, "Fast Curve Putting Grant on Road to Biggest Season," *Sporting News*, May 22, 1965, 9.

81. "Ailing Mudcat Bad Medicine for Dodgers' Anemic Bats," *Sporting News*, October 23, 1966, 28.

82. Max Nichols, "More Concentration, That's Mudcat Cure for Mound Miseries," *Sporting News*, July 30, 1966, 12.

83. "Grant Out for Two Weeks, but Twins Have Able Subs," *Sporting News*, April 22, 1967, 16; Bob Hunter, "Mudcat Hooks a Big One—No. 4 Dodger Starter Post," *Sporting* News, March 23, 1968, 27; Max Nichols, "Bench Keeps Twins Afloat Despite Waves of Injuries," *Sporting News*, June 24, 1967, 7–8; Max

Nichols, "Griff Wails Minnesota Blues as Kline, Worthington Flounder," *Sporting News*, August 19, 1967, 17.

84. Arno Goethel, "Ermer Engineer of Trade, Says Shook-Up Zoilo," *Sporting News*, December 16, 1967, 36, 44.

85. Bob Hunter, "Bailey's Thumping Wakes Up Dodgers," *Sporting News*, June 8, 1968, 17; Bob Hunter, "With Big D Sidelined, Dodger Hill Staff Shows Extra Sparkle," *Sporting News*, October 5, 1968, 38;

86. Ron Bergman, "Mudcat, Catfish Keep A's Battling Upstream," *Sporting News*, July 4, 1970, 12; Ron Bergman, "Mudcat Is the Comeback King," *Sporting News*, October 3, 1970, 8.

87. "Mudcat Disenchanted," *Sporting News*, September 4, 1971, 33;

88. McAuley, "Not to Be Taken," 6.

89. "'Hot' Maris Gets 56th Off Mudcat," *Fargo (ND) Forum*, September 10, 1961, 1; Jimmy Cannon, "Maris' Side," *New York Journal-American*, September 14, 1961, 26.

90. Cannon, "Maris' Side," 26; *RMAB*, 159.

91. *RMAB*, 157–158.

92. Milton Gross, "Tension Taking Toll on Maris," *Boston Globe*, September 12, 1961, 35, 37.

93. Leonard Koppett, "Jeers Turn to Cheers for Mantle; Dodgers Run Into a Giant Roadblock," *New York Post*, September 10, 1961, 36; Houk, *Ballplayers Are Human, Too*, 213.

94. "Piersall Accused of 'Daring' Fans," *Boston Globe*, September 12, 1961, 35; John Drebinger, "Mantle Hits No. 53 as Yanks Extend Streak to 12 by Beating Indians Twice," *New York Times*, September 11, 1961, 30; Houk, *Ballplayers Are Human, Too*, 214–215.

95. Til Ferdenzi, "No Excuses If I Miss, Maris Says," *New York Journal-American*, September 12, 1961, 24.

96. John Drebinger, "Maris, Mantle Held to Singles as Yanks Beat White Sox in Curtailed Game," *New York Times*, September 13, 1961, 57; "You Can't Break HR Mark Bunting," *New York Journal-American*, September 13, 1961, 34; Til Ferdenzi, "'56' Slugger Raps Ump's Bad Night," *New York Journal-American*, September 13, 1961, 34; *RMAB*, 166–167; Leonard Shecter, "Maris Starting to Feel the Strain," *New York Post*, September 13, 1961, 96.

97. Drebinger, "Maris, Mantle Held to Singles," 57; "You Can't Break HR Mark Bunting," 34; Til Ferdenzi, "'56' Slugger," 34; *RMAB*, 166–167.

98. Louis Effrat, "Mantle Concedes He Can't Beat Ruth Homer Mark in 162 Games," *New York Times*, September 15, 1961, 37; Leonard Shecter, "Time Running Out on the M Boys," *New York Post*, September 15, 1961, 92.

99. *RMAB*, 175–177, 180; Houk, *Season of Glory*, 241.

100. Louis Effrat, "Maris Sulks in Trainer's Room as Futile Night Changes Mood," *New York Time*, September 16, 1961, 13; Houk, *Ballplayers Are Human, Too*, 216–217; Leonard Shecter, "Maris Isn't Talking—About HRs, Anyway," *New York Post*, September 16, 1961, 34.

101. Pepe, *1961*, 179; Allen, *Roger Maris*, 151.

102. Jerry Nason, "Musial 20-Year Man Tomorrow," *Boston Globe*, September 16, 1961, 7.

103. Lyall Smith, "They're Booing Maris," *Detroit Free Press*, September 17, 1961, 1D.

104. Smith, "They're Booing," 1D–2D; Louis Effrat, "Maris' Big Bat Speaks Louder Than He Does," *New York Times*, September 17, 1961, 1.

105. *RMAB*, 181–182.

106. "Class C," *Sporting News*, October 26, 1955, 20.

107. Phill Collier, "Elliott Molded Castoffs Into Standouts," *Sporting News*, December 2, 1959, 13.

108. Watson Spoelstra, "Tigers Show Cheshire-Cat Grin Over Slimmed-Down Gladding," *Sporting News*, March 6, 1966, 10.

109. Jim Sargent, *The Tigers and Yankees in '61: A Pennant Race for the Ages, the Babe's Record Broken and Stormin' Norman's Greatest Season* (Jefferson, NC: McFarland, 2016), 184; Watson Spoelstra, "None Can Beat Tiger's Fox for Doggedness on Mound," *Sporting News*, September 13, 1961, 8; "Doc Greene in the Detroit News," *Sporting News*, November 1, 1961, 14; Terry Fox, in telephone interview with the author, March 5, 2019.

110. "Daily Hot-Water Treatments Provided Cure for Fox' Arm," *Sporting News*, March 14, 1962, 16; "Tiger Tales," *Sporting News*, May 9, 1962, 17; "Tiger Tales," *Sporting News*, June 16, 1962, 15; Watson Spoelstra, "For Regaining Old Ranking as Lion of Tigers' Bull Pen," *Sporting News*, July 14, 1962, 11.

111. Joe Falls, "Healthy Bengals Chase Old Hospital Hoodoo," *Sporting News*, March 2, 1963, 15; Jerome Holtzman, "Neck-and-Neck Battles Feature Fireman Races," *Sporting News*, August 31, 1963, 15.

112. "Fox Requests Early Start in Bid to Hold Relief Job," *Sporting News*, February 1, 1964, 16; "Fox Pours in His Fireball for Two Saves in One Day," *Sporting News*, June 27, 1964, 18; "Sherry to Team with Fox as Bengals' Bull-Pen Duo, *Sporting News*, April 25, 1964, 20.

113. Watson Spoelstra, "Tigers' Rescuers on Hot Seat—Pilot Dressen May Pull Switch," *Sporting News*, December 11, 1965, 22.

114. Watson Spoelstra, "Tigers Boast Lean, Tough Mound Staff," *Sporting News*, January 15, 1966, 12; Spoelstra, "Tigers Show," 10.

115. Joe Falls, "Maris Slams 58th, Ties Foxx, Greenberg," *Detroit Free Press*, September 18, 1961, 6; "Extra Innings Help Maris," *Kansas City Times*, September 18, 1961, 22; *RMAB*, 184–185; Houk, *Ballplayers Are Human, Too*, 217; Leonard Shecter, "Maris Made the Most of Those Extra Abs," *New York Post*, September 18, 1961, 48.

116. Falls, "Maris Slams," 1, 6; *RMAB*, 186.

117. *RMAB*, 186–187; John Drebinger, "Yanks Can Clinch the Pennant Tonight by Sweeping Twin Bill with Orioles," *New York Times*, September 19, 1961, 38.

118. Til Ferdenzi, "Birds Boast Hill Script to Foil Maris," *New York Journal-American*, September 19, 1961, 19; Roger Birtwell, "Ill Wind Esther May Help Maris," *Boston Globe*, September 19, 1961, 23.

119. Clif Keane, "How Oriole Pitchers Will Work on Maris," *Boston Globe*, September 18, 1961, 25–26.

120. *RMAB*, 190–191.

121. Allen, *Roger Maris*, 151–152; Pepe, *1961*, 186–187; Jane Gross, "Baseball Talk; Baseball Film Faithful to My Father's Memory," *New York Times*, April 15, 2001, accessed January 15, 2009, https://www.nytimes.com/2001/04/15/sports/backtalk-baseball-film-faithful-to-father-s-memory.html.

122. Milton Gross, "Houk Draws the Line," *New York Post*, September 22, 1961, 92; Milton Gross, "For Roger Maris, Victory Dinner," *New York Post*, October 2, 1961, 1, 52.
123. Bob Maisel, "The Morning After," *Sun (Baltimore)*, September 20, 1961, 17, 23.
124. Maisel, "Morning After," 23; Lou Hatter, "Bird Hurlers Stop Maris," *Sun (Baltimore)*, September 20, 1961, 17.
125. Til Ferdenzi, "Rog Sees No Record in 154," *New York Journal-American*, September 20, 1961, 30; "Maris Takes Final Shot at HR Mark," *Boston Globe*, September 20, 1961, 49.
126. "'Immature' Kid Hurler Put on Baltimore's Disabled List," *Sporting News*, July 24, 1957, 11; Jesse A. Linthicum, "Orioles Close in on 3 Club Field Marks," *Sporting News*, August 14, 1957, 19; "Bird Bunts," *Sporting News*, September 18, 1957, 14.
127. Hal Schram, "First Major Win Like Dream Come True for Pappas," *Sporting News*, June 11, 1958, 22; Ellis, "Walker Big-Strider," 5; Jim Ellis, "Milt Pappas," *Sporting News*, August 26, 1959, 23; Doug Brown, "Birds Beam Over Crib-Kid Mound Trio," *Sporting News*, July 29, 1959, 3; Milt Pappas, *Out at Home: Triumph and Tragedy in the Life of a Major Leaguer* (Oshkosh, WI: LKP Group, 2000), 27.
128. Doug Brown, "Rivals Drool Over Trio of Oriole Kids," *Sporting News*, September 30, 1959, 41.
129. Brown, "Birds Beam," 3; Ellis, "Milt Pappas," 23; Doug Brown, "Pappas Kicks Up Fuss Over Bull-Pen Rule," *Sporting News*, August 11, 1962, 20; Doug Brown, "Pitcher Pappas: Orioles' Problem Star," *Sporting News*, June 19, 1965, 5; Gilbert Rogin, "'I'm the Worst That's Ever Been,'" *Sports Illustrated*, April 23, 1964, 54.
130. Brown, "Pitcher Pappas," 5.
131. Doug Brown, "Baldshun Still Phil When Talk of Trade Began," *Sporting News*, December 25, 1965, 11.
132. Bob Hunter, "MVP Robby Shooting for Skipper Post," *Sporting News*, November 19, 1966, 29; Earl Lawson, "Forecast by Pappas Comes Oh So True in Six-Player Deal," *Sporting News*, June 22, 1968, 16.
133. "'Play or Trade'—Pappas; 'Grow Up'—Richards," *Sporting News*, November 22, 1969, 38; Milt Pappas, "The Game I'll Never Forget," *Baseball Digest*, February 1977, 64.
134. Jerome Holtzman, "Meet Mr. Pappas, the Cubs' New Ace," *Sporting News*, August 8, 1970, 14, 46; Jerome Holtzman, "Favorite Town? The Windy City Is Milt's Choice," *Sporting News*, November 14, 1970, 55.
135. Bruce Amspacher, "What Really Happened? An Interview with Major League Pitching Great Milt Pappas," *PSA*, April 11, 2003, accessed January 27, 2019, https://www.psacard.com/articles/articleview/3819/what-really-happened-interview-major-league-pitching-great-milt-pappas; Pappas, *Out at Home*, 258–259.
136. Westcott, *Diamond Greats*, 304.
137. Roger Maris, "'I Tried Not to Think About It,'" *Life*, September 29, 1961, 97; *RMAB*, 193; Roger Maris with Jim Ogle, "I Couldn't Go Through It Again," *Look*, April 10, 1962, 46.
138. Maris, "'I Tried,'" 97; *RMAB*, 193.
139. Kubek, *Sixty-One*, 114; Houk, *Season of Glory*, 246.
140. Maris, "'I Tried,'" 97.
141. Pappas, *Out at Home*, 84.
142. Clavan and Peary, *Roger Maris*, 209.
143. *RMAB*, 193–194; Kubek, *Sixty-One*, 116.
144. Maris, "'I Tried,'" 97; *RMAB*, 194; Houk, *Ballplayers Are Human, Too*, 218; Pappas, *Out at Home*, 84.
145. Bob Maisel, "The Morning After," *Sun (Baltimore)*, September 21, 1961, 22.
146. Maisel, "Morning After," 22; Milton Gross, "Maris Glad It's Over," *New York Post*, September 21, 1961, 72; *RMAB*, 195.
147. Maisel, "Morning After," 22.
148. Kubek, *Sixty-One*, 117; Jack Murphy, "Series Umpire Recalls Drama of Maris' Run at Ruth Record," October 18, 1961, *San Diego Union*, B5.
149. Murphy, "Series Umpire Recalls," B5
150. Maisel, "Morning After," 22; Maris, "'I Tried,'" 97; Kubek, *Sixty-One*, 118; Maris, "I Couldn't," 46; Murphy, "Series Umpire Recalls," B5.
151. Maris, "I Couldn't," 46; Kubek, *Sixty-One*, 119.
152. Louis Effrat, "Maris Is Resigned to * in the Record Books," *New York Times*, September 21, 1961, 42; Milton Gross, "No. 59 Maris's Biggest Homer," *Kansas City Star*, December 14, 1961, 38.
153. Maisel, "Morning After," 22.
154. Oliver E. Kuechle, "Time Out for Talk," *Milwaukee Journal*, September 22, 1961, Part 2, 11.
155. George Frazier, "Maris Talented with Bat but a Champion? Nay!," *Boston Herald*, September 20, 1961, 12.
156. Arthur Daily, "Admirable Failure," *New York Times*, September 22, 1961, 38; "59 Is a Big Number," *New York Post*, September 22, 1961, 48.
157. *RMAB*, 200; "Pressure Still Haunts Roger Maris," *Kansas City Star*, September 25, 1961, 12.
158. Earl Shelby, "Mr. Maris Goes 'Shopping' Here," *Sun (Baltimore)*, September 22, 1961, 23; Til Ferdenzi, "Yank Slugger Welcomes End of HR Drive," *New York Journal-American*, September 22, 1961, 34.
159. *RMAB*, 200–201.
160. "Strain of HR Record Quest Caused Maris to Lose Hair," *Boston Globe*, September 22, 1961, 39.
161. "Maris Put Team Play Before HRs, Say Houk," *Boston Globe*, September 23, 1961, 7.
162. "No * Will Mar Homer Records, Says Frick with [daggers] for Critics," *New York Times*, September 22, 1961, 38.
163. "Strain of HR Record," 39.
164. "Pressure Still Haunts," 12.
165. Til Ferdenzi, "Pitchers Have Maris Chasing No. 60," *New York Journal-American*, September 25, 1961, 27.
166. Mantle, *The Mick*, 195–196.
167. *RMAB*, 203.
168. Don Bostrom, "Fisher Is Remembered for Maris' 60th," *Morning Call (Allentown, PA)*, September 6, 1998, accessed January 31, 2019, http://articles.mcall.com/1998-09-06/sports/3209647_1_frick-ruling-roger-maris-fisher; Jimmy Burns, "Fisher of Marlins Wins First Six on Five-Day System," *Sporting News*, June 3, 1959, 29.
169. Pappas, *Out at Home*, 91; Alex Zirin, "Diamond Facts and Facets," *Sporting News*, September 7, 1960, 10; "Batter Up and Down," *Sports Illustrated*, June 13, 1966, 19.

170. Mike Klingaman, "Catching Up with former Oriole Jack Fisher," *Baltimore Sun*, September 17, 2010, accessed January 31, 2019, https://www.baltimoresun.com/bs-mtblog-2010-09-post_30-story.html.
171. "Bird Seed," *Sporting News*, May 31, 1961, 14; "Bird Seed," *Sporting News*, September 13, 1961, 7.
172. "Bird Seed," *Sporting News*, March 21, 1962, 24; "Fisher Ordered to Bull Pen, Warned to Lose Ten Pounds," *Sporting News*, June 30, 1962, 10; Barney Kremenko, "Recipe for Trouble: Tell Met Ace Fisher He Looks Bit Portly," *Sporting News*, July 10, 1965, 21.
173. "Fisher, Ex-Oriole, Tabbed as Fourth Starter by Dark," *Sporting News*, February 9, 1963, 7.
174. Bill Haas, "Special Draft Draws Yawns; Mets Take Two and Colts One," *Sporting News*, October 19, 1963, 6.
175. "Bulky Jack Fisher Says He Wants Steady Pitching Diet," *Sporting News*, October 26, 1963, 16.
176. Jerome Holtzman, "Stanky Fingers Starting to Itch with New Tommy Gun on Hand," *Sporting News*, December 30, 1967, 29.
177. "Maris, Mantle Both Take a Rest," *Boston Globe*, September 27, 1961, 54; *RMAB*, 203; John Drebinger, "Mantle Is Hospitalized, but Yankees Expect Him to Play in World Series," *New York Times*, September 29, 1961, 40.
178. Bostrom, "Fisher Is Remembered."
179. *RMAB*, 204; John Drebinger, "Maris Hits No. 60 as Yankees Win," *New York Times*, September 27, 1961, 45; Jim Elliot, "Maris Blasts 60th Homer as Yanks Edge Orioles, 3–2," *Sun (Baltimore)*, September 27, 1961, 23.
180. Elliot, "Maris Blasts 60th," 23; Houk, *Ballplayers Are Human, Too*, 223; *RMAB*, 205.
181. "Losing the Game Hurt Fisher Most," *New York Post*, September 27, 1961, 91.
182. Til Ferdenzi, "Maris Belted Belt High Curve," *New York Journal-American*, September 27, 1961, 40; "Mrs. Maris Says: 'He Hit 60 for Me,'" *New York Journal-American*, September27, 1961, 40; Houk, *Ballplayers Are Human, Too*, 223.
183. "Mrs. Maris Says," 40.
184. Leonard Shecter, "Now Maris Is Trying for 61," *New York Post*, September 27, 1961, 85, 92; Joe Reichler, "Maris: Glad I Didn't Hit 60 in 154 Games," *Boston Globe*, September 27, 1961, 27.

Chapter 8

1. Milton Gross, "The Tired Young Man," *New York Post*, September 28, 1961, 80; *RMAB*, 207–208; Leonard Shecter, "Roger's Rest Could Cost Him Record," *New York Post*, September 28, 1961, 84.
2. Gross, "Tired Young Man," 207–208; Shecter, "Roger's Rest," 84.
3. Drebinger, "Mantle Is Hospitalized," 40; Bob Holbrook, "Time Running Out as Maris Presses," *Boston Globe*, September 30, 1961, 7; Gordon S. White Jr., "Schwall Solves Maris Problem," *New York Times*, October 1, 1961, S3.
4. John Gillooly, "Stallard May Prove Sox Mound Find," *Boston Daily Record*, March 1, 1960, 30; Ed Costello, "Sox Stallard Former Lefty," *Boston Herald*, September 18, 1960, 61; "Minneapolis," *Sporting News*, September 9, 1959, 34.

5. Gillooly, "Stallard May Prove," 30; Costello, "Sox Stallard," 61.
6. Joe Chashman, "Sox Stallard Tells Perils of Playing Winter Ball," *Boston Daily Record*, March 3, 1961, 64; Larry Claflin, "Stallard Holds Higgins' Eye," *Boston American*, March 8, 1961, 29.
7. Bill Liston, "Stallard, Pender Form Dawn Patrol," *Boston Traveler*, January 16, 1962, 49.
8. Bill Liston, "Pender in Sox' Corner," *Boston Traveler*, April 14, 1962, 4; Larry Claflin, "Tigers Club Sox 14–6," *Boston Record American*, September 14, 1962, 3.
9. Barney Kremenko, "Tracy Solves Case of Winless Hurler—He's Met Hero Now," *Sporting News*, June 29, 1963, 17.
10. Neal Russo, "Tracy Ticketed for Starter Job on Cards' Staff," *Sporting News*, December 19, 1964, 10; "'Mets Great,' Says Stallard—But He's Happy Redbird," *Sporting News*, December 19, 1964, 15.
11. Neal Russo, "'We're Rusting on the Roost,' Idle Hurlers Beef to Becker," *Sporting News*, May 7, 1966, 20; "Stallard Wins First," *Sporting News*, June 28, 1969, 47.
12. George Vecsey, "The Man Who Served Up #61," *Sport*, May 1974, 70, 72, 75.
13. Kubek, *Sixty-One*, 125; Milton Gross, "Maris Clouted 61st on Empty Stomach," *Boston Globe*, October 3, 1961, 37.
14. *RMAB*, 210; Leonard Shecter, "Maris 'Was Trying for It All the Way,'" *New York Post*, October 2, 1961, 52.
15. *RMAB*, 211.
16. John Drebinger, "Maris Hits 61st in Final Game," *New York Times*, October 2, 1961, 38; "Doesn't Feel Bad About Pitch," *Boston Globe*, October 2, 1961, 16; *RMAB*, 211–212; Treavor Parks, "You Are There—October 1, 1961—Roger Maris' 61st Home Run," *Referee*, May 1996, 52.
17. *RMAB*, 214.
18. Kubek, *Sixty-One*, 127–128.
19. Gordon S. White Jr., "Agile Fan Makes a $5,000 Catch," *New York Times*, October 2, 1961, 38.
20. Dan Shaughnessy, "Tracy Stallard: He Yielded No. 61 to Roger Maris," *Baseball Digest*, January 1962, 60; Henry McKenna, "Yanks Win on Maris' 61st," *Boston Herald*, October 2, 1961, 15, 17; "Red Sox Rookie Hailed by Maris as 'Man Enough to Pitch to Me,'" *New York Times*, October 2, 1961, 38; Walter Bingham, "No. 60 ... and 61," *Sports Illustrated*, October 9, 1961, 17.
21. "61st Homer Makes Roger Maris 'Happy,'" *Sun (Baltimore)*, October 2, 1961, 1; Maris Hits 61st as Yanks Top Bosox, 1–0, in Finale," *Sun (Baltimore)*, October 2, 1961, 1; "Red Sox Rookie," 38; Bob Holbrook, "Maris Smashes 61st; Breaks Ruth Mark in Final Game," *Boston Globe*, October 2, 1961, 15, 16; Bill Liston, "One More Maris '61 Goal—THE Series," *Boston Traveler*, October 2, 1961, 15.
22. Gross, "For Roger Maris," 1, 52.
23. Pepe, *1961*, 233; Clavin and Peary, *Roger Maris*, 227; Mantle, *The Mick*, 197.
24. *RMAB*, 218.
25. Milton Gross, "What Next for Maris?" *New York Post*, October 3, 1961, 56.
26. Gross, "What Next," 56.
27. *RMAB*, 219.

28. *RMAB*, 220; Joseph M. Sheehan, "Grim Houk Says Tough Plays Rather Than Sloppiness Led to Yank Defeat," *New York Times*, October 6, 1961, 45; Louis Effrat, "Hutchinson Points to Chacon's Run on Passed Ball as Possible Key Play," *New York Times*, October 6, 1961, 38; Houk, *Ballplayers Are Human, Too*, 230.

29. Jack Lang, "Reds Home 'House of Horrors,'" *Long Island Star-Journal*, October 7, 1961, 16.

30. "Purkey and Skinner Shatter Fielding Marks in Marathon," *Sporting News*, August 4, 1954, 17; Jack Hernon, "Bragan Planning to Add Hollywood Touch to Pirates," *Sporting News*, November 16, 1955, 17.

31. "Hollywood," *Sporting News*, June 13, 1956, 40.

32. Herb Kamm, "Bob Purkey," in *Baseball's Greatest Players Today*, edited by Jack Orr (New York: J. Lowell Pratt, 1963), 57.

33. Dick Kaplan, "Bob Purkey," in *Baseball Stars of 1959*, edited by Ray Robinson (New York: Pyramid Books, 1959), 112; Louis Effrat, "Purkey Rejects 'Knuckler Label,'" *New York Times*, October 7, 1961, 7; Steve Perkins, "Cincinnati's Pitching Con Man," *Sport*, October 1962, 30–31; Kamm, "Bob Purkey," 51, 57; Leonard Koppett, "Pitching—The Yankees' Weak Spot," *New York Post*, September 28, 1961, 88.

34. "Purkey Deal Came to Soon for Aircaster Bob's Program," *Sporting News*, December 18, 1957, 12.

35. Earl Lawson, "Bob Purkey," *Sporting News*, June 18, 1958, 23; Perkins, "Cincinnati's Pitching Con Man," 31.

36. Earl Lawson, "Bob Purkey," *Sporting News*, July 6, 1960, 21.

37. Earl Lawson, "Purkey Soared to Pitching Peak, Aided by Butterflies," *Sporting News*, October 20, 1962, 15.

38. Earl Lawson, "Ex-Ace Purkey at Crossroads—Is Wing Okay?," *Sporting News*, December 7, 1963, 36.

39. Earl Lawson, "Arm Good as New, but Purkey Fears He's on Red Block," *Sporting News*, December 5, 1964, 30.

40. "Purkey, Released, to Turn to Real Estate, Insurance," *Sporting News*, August 13, 1966, 11.

41. John Drebinger, "Mantle Likely to Be on Sidelines Again as World Series Resumes Today," *New York Times*, October 7, 1961, 16.

42. Kamm, "Bob Purkey," 53.

43. Louis Effrat, "Purkey Discounts Pitch to Maris and Recalls Only Two Mistakes in Game," *New York Times*, October 8, 1961, Sec. 5, 3.

44. *RMAB*, 221–222.

45. Kubek, *Sixty-One*, 137.

46. Louis Effrat, "Hutchinson Says Maris' Third-Game Homer Was Turning Point of Series," *New York Times*, October 10, 1961, 49.

Aftermath

1. Sid Bordman, "Maris Stays Home to Enjoy Family and Friends Here," *Kansas City Star*, January 7, 1962, 1B; Wilbur Adams, "Maris Receives Ball He Socked for '61st Homer," *Sporting News*, November 15, 1961, 9; "Maris Wants to Be Alone After Series," *Kansas City Star*, October 9, 1961, 18.

2. Bob Wolf, "Rog Cites Four Drawbacks to Traveling Banquet Circuit," *Sporting News*, January 17, 1962, 16.

3. Jim Ogle, "Sound Off! Roger Maris Talks Back to His Critics," *Sport*, August 1962, 74.

4. Ogle, "Roger Maris Talks," 73.

5. John Crittenden, "Roger Says He'll Follow a Closed-Mouth Policy," *Miami News*, March 14, 1962, 2C.

6. Oscar Fraley, "Claims Maris 'Bigheaded' with Writers," *Daily Courier (Connellsville, PA)*, March 15, 1962, 7; John Crittenden, "Maris Lashes Out at Writer … 'You Didn't Give Me a Chance,'" *Miami News*, March 19, 1962, 2C.

7. "Maris Snubs Hornsby of Hall of Fame," *Sarasota (FL) Herald-Tribune*, March 23, 1962, 28; Allen, *Roger Maris*, 175.

8. Allen, *Roger Maris*, 176.

9. Jimmy Cannon, "Most Unpopular Player," *Las Vegas Sun*, March 26, 1962, 16; Jimmy Cannon, "Majority Is Infuriated," *Las Vegas Sun*, March 27, 1962, 16.

10. "Roger Is A-1 with Me and the Players," *Miami News*, March 25, 1962, 3; "Home Runs Are Maris' Answers," *Miami News*, March 26, 1962, 5C.

11. Tommy Devine, "Maris Could Profit from Hartack Case," *Miami News*, April 1, 1962, 1C; Jack Hand, "Will 'Red Neck' Image Hurt Rog? Writers Disagree," *Arkansas (Little Rock) Gazette*, March 25, 1962, 2B; Allen, *Roger Maris*, 177.

12. Bob Stewart, "Roger Maris," in *Baseball's Greatest Players Today*, edited by Jack Orr (New York: J. Lowell Pratt, 1963), 25; Herbert Kamm, "Warning to Maris: From Top There's No Way to Go but Down," *Milwaukee Journal*, March 21, 1962, 17.

13. Jerry Izenberg, *The Rivals* (New York: Holt, Rinehart, and Winston, 1968), 283.

14. Paul Hemphill, "#61, the Man Who Hit It," *Sport*, May 1974, 75; Allen, *Roger Maris*, 257; Kubek, *Sixty-One*, 131.

Bibliography

Books

Allen, Maury. *Roger Maris: A Man for All Seasons.* New York: Donald J. Fine, 1986.

Allen, Mel, and Ed Fitzgerald. *You Can't Beat the Hours: A Long, Loving Look at Big-League Baseball—Including Some Yankees I Have Known.* New York: Harper and Row, 1964.

Barra, Allen. *Clearing the Bases: The Greatest Baseball Debates of the Last Century.* New York: St. Martin's Press, 2002.

Bragan, Bobby. *You Can't Hit the Ball with the Bat on Your Shoulder: The Baseball Life and Times of Bobby Bragan.* Fort Worth, TX: Summit Group, 1992.

Cairns, Bob. *Pen Men: Baseball's Greatest Bullpen Stories Told by Men Who Brought the Game Relief.* New York: St. Martin's Press, 1992.

Cannon, Jimmy. *Nobody Asked Me, But...: The World of Jimmy Cannon.* Edited by Jack Cannon and Tom Cannon. New York: Holt, Rinehart and Winston, 1978.

Carmichael, John P., ed. *My Greatest Day in Baseball.* New York: Grosset and Dunlap, 1968.

Carvalho, John P. *Frick*: Baseball's Third Commissioner.* Jefferson, NC: McFarland, 2016.

Clavin, Tom, and Danny Peary. *Roger Maris: Baseball's Reluctant Hero.* New York: Simon & Schuster, 2010.

Copley, Robert E. *The Tall Mexican: The Life of Hank Aguirre, All-Star Pitcher, Businessman, Humanitarian.* Houston: Arte Publico Press, 1998.

Frick, Ford C. *Games, Asterisks, and People: Memoirs of a Lucky Fan.* New York: Crown, 1973.

Golenbock, Peter. *Dynasty: The New York Yankees, 1949–1964.* Englewood Cliffs, NJ: Prentice-Hall, 1975.

Grant, Jim "Mudcat." *The Black Aces: Baseball's Only African-American Twenty-Game Winners.* Farmingdale, NY: Aventine Press, 2006.

Halberstam, David. *October 1964.* New York: Villard, 1994.

Honig, Donald. *Baseball Between the Lines: Baseball in the '40s and '50s as Told by the Men Who Played It.* New York: Coward, McCann and Geoghegan, 1976.

Houk, Ralph. *Ballplayers Are Human, Too.* New York: Putnam, 1962.

Houk, Ralph, and Robert W. Creamer. *Season of Glory: The Amazing Saga of the 1961 New York Yankees.* New York: Putnam, 1988.

Inabinett, Mark. *Grantland Rice and His Heroes: The Sportswriter as Mythmaker in the 1920s.* Knoxville: University of Tennessee Press, 1994.

Izenberg, Jerry. *The Rivals.* New York: Holt, Rinehart, and Winston, 1968.

James, Bill, and Rob Neyer. *The Neyer/James Guide to Pitchers: An Historical Compendium of Pitching, Pitchers, and Pitches.* New York: Simon & Schuster, 2004.

Kahn, Roger. *Seasons in the Sun.* New York: Harper and Row, 1977.

Katz, Jeff. *The Kansas City A's and the Wrong Half of the Yankees: How the Yankees Controlled Two of the Eight American League Franchises During the 1950s.* Hingham, MA: Maple Street Press, 2007.

Kelley, Brent. *The San Francisco Seals, 1946–1957: Interviews with 25 Former Baseballers.* Jefferson, NC: McFarland, 2002.

Kemmerer, Russ, with W. C. Madden. *Ted Williams: 'Hey Kid, Just Get It Over the Plate': A Book about Baseball's Golden Age, Its Great Players and Twinkling Stars.* Fishers, IN: Madden, 2002.

Kiersh, Edward. *Where Have You Gone, Vince DiMaggio?* New York: Bantam, 1983.

Kubek, Tony, and Terry Pluto. *Sixty-One: The Team, the Record, the Men.* New York: Macmillan, 1987.

Kuenster, John, ed. *The Best of Baseball Digest.* Chicago: Ivan R. Dee, 2006.

Larsen, Don, with Mark Shaw. *The Perfect Yankee: The Incredible Story of the Greatest Miracle in Baseball History.* Champaign, IL: Sagamore, 1996.

Leavy, Jane. *The Last Boy: Mickey Mantle and the End of America's Childhood.* New York: HarperCollins, 2010.

Lowry, Philip J. *Green Cathedrals: The Ultimate Celebration of Major League and Negro League Ballparks.* New York: Walker, 2006.

Mantle, Mickey, with Herb Gluck. *The Mick.* New York: Doubleday, 1985.

Maris, Roger, and Jim Ogle. *Roger Maris at Bat.* Des Moines, IA: Meredith, 1962.

Moffi, Larry. *This Side of Cooperstown: An Oral History of Major League Baseball in the 1950s.* Iowa City, IA: University of Iowa Press, 1996.

Orr, Jack, ed. *Baseball's Greatest Players Today.* New York: J. Lowell Pratt, 1963.

Pappas, Milt, with Wayne Mausser and Larry Names. *Out at Home: Triumph and Tragedy in the Live of a Major Leaguer.* Oshkosh, WI: LKP Group, 2000.

Peary, Danny, ed. *We Played the Game: 65 Players Remember Baseball's Greatest Era, 1947–1964.* New York: Hyperion, 1994.

Pepe, Phil. *1961*: The Inside Story of the Maris-Mantle Home Run Chase.* Chicago: Triumph Books, 2011.

Perry, Gaylord, with Bob Sudyk. *Me and the Spitter: An Autobiographical Confession.* New York: Saturday Review Press, 1974.

Richardson, Bobby, with David Thomas. *Impact Player: Leaving a Lasting Legacy On and Off the Field.* Carol Stream, IL: Tyndale House, 2012.

Rizzuto, Phil, and Al Silverman. *The "Miracle" New York Yankees.* New York: Coward-McCann, 1962.

Robinson, Ray, ed. *Baseball Stars of 1959.* New York, Pyramid, 1959.

_____. *Baseball Stars of 1960.* New York, Pyramid, 1960.

_____. *Baseball Stars of 1961.* New York, Pyramid, 1961.

_____. *Baseball Stars of 1962.* New York, Pyramid, 1962.

_____. *Baseball Stars of 1963.* New York, Pyramid, 1963.

Rosenfeld, Harvey. *Roger Maris*: A Title to Fame.* Fargo, ND: Prairie House, 1991.

Sargent, Jim. *The Tigers and Yankees in '61: A Pennant Race for the Ages, the Babe's Record Broken and Stormin' Norman's Greatest Season.* Jefferson, NC: McFarland, 2016.

Shatzkin, Mike, ed. *The Ballplayers: Baseball's Ultimate Biographical Reference.* New York: William Morrow, 1990.

Shaw, Bob. *Pitching: The Basic Fundamentals and Mechanics of Successful Pitching.* New York: Viking, 1972.

Shecter, Leonard. *Roger Maris: Home Run Hero.* New York: Bartholomew House, 1961.

Simons, William M., ed. *Cooperstown Symposium on Baseball and American Culture, 2002.* Jefferson, NC: McFarland, 2003.

Siwoff, Seymour, et al, eds. *1991 Elias Baseball Analysist.* New York: Simon & Schuster, 1991.

Sloan, W. David, and Lisa Mullikin Parcell, eds. *American Journalism: History, Principles, Practices.* Jefferson, NC: McFarland, 2002.

Spink, J. G. Taylor, comp. *Baseball Guide and Record Book 1962.* St. Louis: Charles Spink and Son, 1962.

Terry, Ralph, with John Wooley. *Right Down the Middle: The Ralph Terry Story.* Tulas, OK: Mullerhaus, 2016.

Van Blair, Rick. *Dugout to Foxhole: Interviews with Baseball Players Whose Careers Were Affected by World War II.* Jefferson, NC: McFarland, 1994.

Vanderberg, Bob. *Frantic Frank Lane: Baseball's Ultimate Wheeler-Dealer.* Jefferson, NC: McFarland, 2013.

_____ *Sox: From Lane and Fain to Zisk and Fisk,* rev. ed. Chicago: Chicago Review Press, 1984.

Westcott, Rich. *Diamond Greats: Profiles and Interviews with 65 of Baseball's History Makers.* Westport, CT: Meckler Books, 1988.

Wise, Bill. *1964 Official Baseball Almanac.* Greenwich, CT: Fawcett, 1964.

Interviews

Fox, Terry, in telephone interview with the author, March 5, 2019.

James, Johnny, in telephone interview with the author, February 26, 2019.

Romano, John, in telephone interview with the author, July 19, 2017.

Stigman, Dick, in telephone interview with the author, February 23, 2019.

Walker, Jerry, in telephone interview with the author, March 20, 2019.

Print and Online Articles

American Academy of Sleep Medicine. "Fatigue and Sleep Linked to Major League Baseball Performance and Career Longevity." *ScienceDaily,* May 31, 2013, accessed February 28, 2018, https://www.sciencedaily.com/releases/2013/05/130531105506.htm.

Amspacher, Bruce. "What Really Happened? An Interview with Major League Pitching Great Milt Pappas." *PSA,* April 11, 2003, accessed January 27, 2019, https://www.psacard.com/articles/articleview/3819/what-really-happened-interview-major-league-pitching-great-milt-pappas.

"The Babe Ruth Story." *Time,* August 30, 1948, 46–48.

"Batter Up and Down." *Sports Illustrated,* June 13, 1966, 19.

Bernstein, Anita. "Question Autonomy, with an Asterisk." *Emory Law Journal* 54 (January 15, 2005): 239–259.

Bingham, Walter. "Assault on The Record." *Sports Illustrated,* July 31, 1961, 8–11.

Bingham, Walter. "No. 60 … and 61." *Sports Illustrated,* October 9, 1961, 17.

Bisher, Furman. "How Frank Lary Learned to Pitch." *Sport,* August 1961, 28–59.

Bjarkman, Peter C. "Pedro Ramos." *SABR BioProject,* August 31, 2011, accessed May 24, 2018, https://sabr.org/bioproj/person/c03a87ec.

Boyle, Robert H. "Yes It's Livelier—and Here Is the Proof." *Sports Illustrated,* August 28, 1961, 14–17.

"Catching Up with Johnny James." *Baseball Historian,* December 9, 2011, accessed July 25, 2018, http://baseballhistorian.blogspot.com/2011/12/catching-up-with-johnny-james.html.

Cleveland Clinic. "Shift Work Sleep Disorder." *My.Clevelandclinic.org,* November 17, 2017, accessed

February 22, 2018, https://my.clevelandclinic.org/health/diseases/12146-shift-work-sleep-disorder.

Coburn, Davin. "Baseball Physics: Anatomy of a Home Run.'" *Popular Mechanics*, December 17, 2009, accessed February 13, 2018, https://www.popularmechanics.com/adventure/sports/a4569/4216783/.

Cruz, C., P. Della Rocco, and C. Hackworth. "Effects of Quick Rotating Shift Schedules on the Health and Adjustment of Air Traffic Controllers." *Aviation, Space, and Environmental Medicine* 71 (April 2000): 400–407, accessed February 22, 2018, https://www.ncbi.nlm.nih.gov/pubmed/10766465.

Dell'Amore, Christine. "Sleep Preferences Predict Baseball Success, Study Says." *National Geographic*, June 16, 2011, accessed February 28, 2018, https://news.nationalgeographic.com/news/2011/06/110615-sleep-major-league-baseball-science/.

Diunte, N. "Russ Kimmerer, 84, Former Major League Pitcher Was a Master Storyteller." *Baseball Happenings*, December 21, 2014, accessed July 12, 2018, http://www.baseballhappenings.net/2014/12/russ-kemmerer-84-former-major-league.html?m=1.

Durslag, Melvin. "For Him the Sinker's the Payoff." *Baseball Digest*, October-November 1962, 50.

Dvorsky, George. "The Surprising Way Jet Lag Impacts Major League Baseball Games." *Gizmodo*, January 23, 2017, accessed February 28, 2018, https://gizmodo.com/the-surprising-way-jet-lag-impacts-major-league-basebal-1791521616.

"For the Hot-Stove League: Final Report on Those Baseball Changes." *Popular Mechanics*, December 1961, 82–214.

Gallagher, Robert C. "Tom Cheney: He Fanned 21 Batters in a Single Game." *Baseball Digest*, April 1986, 91–93.

Geisler Jr., Paul. "Frank Baumann." *SABR BioProject*, October 1, 2012, accessed September 27, 2018, https://sabr.org/bioproj/person/df98efc5#sdendnote48anc.

Gordon, Jim. "Wrigley Field (Los Angeles)." *Society for American Baseball Research*, n.d., accessed March 23, 2018, http://sabr.org/bioproj/park/3912a666.

Gordon, Peter M. "Ken McBride." *SABR BioProject*, n.d., accessed November 12, 2018, https://sabr.org/bioproj/person/721d5411.

Grady, Sandy. "Modern Marco Polo." *Baseball Digest*, September 1964, 55–56.

Hemphill, Paul. "#61, the Man Who Hit It." *Sport*, May 1974, 63–77.

Hirdt, Steve. "Myths, Misconceptions and Asterisks from '61." ESPN.com, 2001, accessed January 19, 2018, https://www.espn.com/page2/s/number/010427.html.

Hirshberg, Al. "Big Brave from Milwaukee." *Saturday Evening Post*, March 28, 1955, 30–108.

Huhn, Rick. "Dave Sisler." *SABR BioProject*, n.d., accessed August 28, 2018, https://sabr.org/bioproj/person/805731ed.

Johnson, Chuck, and Chuck Boyer. "Eli Grba." *SABR BioProject*, May 4, 2015, accessed May 26, 2018, https://sabr.org/bioproj/person/ea132183.

Kahn, Roger. "Pursuit of No. 60: The Ordeal of Roger Maris." *Sports Illustrated*, October 2, 1961, 22–72.

Kirkpatrick, Paul. "Batting the Ball." *Journal of American Physics* 31 (1963): 606–613.

Klein, Moss. "Frank Lary Recalls His Days as a 'Yankee Killer.'" *Baseball Digest*, July 1978, 72–74.

Koppett, Leonard. "Mighty Mr. Maris." *Saturday Evening Post*, September 2, 1961, 25.

Lallensack, Rachael. "Jet Lag Puts Baseball Players Off Their Game." *Science*, January 23, 2017, accessed February 22, 2018, http://www.sciencemag.org/news/2017/01/jet-lag-puts-baseball-players-their-game.

Larwin, Tom. "Jerry Casale." *SABR BioProject*, n.d., accessed August 13, 2018, https://sabr.org/bioproj/person/200e64f2.

Lieber, Leslie. "Roger Maris Proves the Old-Timers' Bats Weren't So Bad!" *This Week Magazine*, May 20, 1962, 9–11.

Maris, Pat. "My Husband." *Look*, April 24, 1962, 89–100.

Maris, Roger. "'I Tried Not to Think About It.'" *Life*, September 29, 1961, 97.

Maris, Roger, with Jim Ogle. "I Couldn't Go Through It Again." *Look*, April 10, 1962, 39–46.

McAuley, Ed. "Not to Be Taken for Grant-ed." *Baseball Digest*, August 1961, 5.

McIntosh, James. "The Impact of Shift Work on Health." *Medical News Today*, January 11, 2016, accessed February 22, 2018, https://www.medicalnewstoday.com/articles/288310.php.

Meany, Tom. "Roger Maris: The Man Who Shook Up the Yankees." *Sport*, November 1960, 61–68.

Nechal, Jerry. "Paul Foytack." *SABR BioProject*, June 3, 2015, accessed May 21, 2018, https://sabr.org/bioproj/person/0171793b.

Ogle, Jim. "Sound Off! Roger Maris Talks Back to His Critics," *Sport*, August 1962, 16–75.

Pappas, Milt. "The Game I'll Never Forget." *Baseball Digest*, February 1977, 62–64.

Parks, Treavor. "You Are There—October 1, 1961—Roger Maris' 61st Home Run." *Referee*, May 1996, 52–53.

Perkins, Steve. "Cincinnati's Pitching Con Man." *Sport*, October 1962, 30–31.

Richman, Arthur. "Even Lary Can't Explain How He Hex-Rays Yanks." *Baseball Digest*, June 1959, 57–58.

"Roger Maris: Has He the Stuff for Greatness." *Look*, June 20, 1961, 115.

Rogin, Gilbert. "'I'm the Worst That's Ever Been.'" *Sports Illustrated*, April 23, 1964, 54–63.

Russell, Daniel A. "Bat Weight, Swing Speed and Ball Velocity." *Physics and Acoustics of Baseball and Softball Bats*, March 27, 2008, accessed February 12, 2018, http://www.acs.psu.edu/drussell/bats/batw8.html.

Schwarz, Alan. "The Impartial Press, with an Asterisk." *Inside Sports,* October 1997, 18–19.

"Scouting Reports on 1960 Major League Rookies—the Cincinnati Reds." *Baseball Digest,* March 1960, 84.

Shapiro, Michael. "The Del Webb Yankees." *New Yorker,* July 23, 2010, accessed March 9, 2018, https://www.newyorker.com/news/sporting-scene/the-del-webb-yankees.

Shaughnessy, Dan. "Tracy Stallard: He Yielded No. 61 to Roger Maris." *Baseball Digest,* January 1962, 59–60.

"Sleep Preference Can Predict Performance of Major League Baseball Pitchers." *ScienceDaily,* June 11, 2010, accessed February 26, 2018, https://www.sciencedaily.com/releases/2010/06/100609083223.htm.

"Sleep Type Predicts Day and Night Batting Averages of Major League Baseball Players." *American Academy of Sleep Medicine,* June 13, 2011, accessed February 26, 2018, https://aasm.org/sleep-type-predicts-day-and-night-batting-averages-of-major-league-baseball-players/.

Song, Alex, Thomas Severini, and Ravi Allada, "How Jet Lag Impairs Major League Baseball Performance." *Proceedings of the National Academy of Sciences* 114 (February 7, 2017); 1407–1412

Tan, Cecilia. "Gary Bell." *SABR BioProject,* n.d., accessed June 4, 2018, https://sabr.org/bioproj/person/33810d5c.

Telander, Rick. "The Record Almost Broke Him." *Sports Illustrated,* June 20, 1977, 62–70.

Vass, George. "Problems Worth Having?" *Baseball Digest,* May 1967, 5–13.

Vecsey, George. "The Man Who Served Up # 61." *Sport,* May 1974, 63–75.

Walker, Ben. "Properties of Baseball Bats." *Baseball Research Journal,* Summer 2010, accessed February 13, 2018, http://sabr.org/research/properties-baseball-bats.

Wancho, Joseph. "Jim Perry." *SABR BioProject,* October 1, 2015, accessed May 30, 2018, https://sabr.org/bioproj/person/f7911858.

Watson, Emmett. "Almost a Star: The Story of Milwaukee's Gene Conley." *Sport,* March 1957, 53–61.

Weiskopf, Don. "Batting Style of the Yankees." *Athletic Journal* 41 (January 1961): 16–59.

Weiskopf, Don. "Hitting the Long Ball." *Athletic Journal* 59 (February 1979): 66–110.

Weiskopf, Herman. "The Infamous Spitter." *Sports Illustrated,* July 30, 1967, accessed September 25, 2018, https://www.si.com/vault/1967/07/31/609382/the-infamous-spitter.

Newspapers

Aberdeen (SD) Daily News
American-News (Aberdeen, SD)
Appeal Democrat (Marysville, CA)
Arkansas (Little Rock) Gazette
Bellingham (WA) Herald
Boston Advertiser
Boston American
Boston Daily Record
Boston Globe
Boston Herald
Boston Record American
Boston Traveler
Brainerd (MN) Daily Dispatch
Brunswick (GA) News
Canton (OH) Repository
Chicago Daily Tribune
Cleveland Plain Dealer
Corpus Christi (TX) Times
Daily Courier (Connellsville, PA)
Daily News (New York)
Daily Oklahoman (Oklahoma City, OK)
Detroit Free Press
Durham (NC) Sun
Evansville (IN) Courier and Press
Evening Star (Washington, D.C.)
Evening World-Herald (Omaha, NE)
Fargo (ND) Forum
Fargo (ND) Forum and Moorhead (MN) News
Fort Worth (TX) Star-Telegram
Globe-Gazette (Mason City, IA)
Illinois State Journal (Springfield, IL)
Jersey Journal (Jersey City, NJ)
Joplin (MO) News Herald
Kansas City Star
Kansas City Times
Knoxville News-Sentinel
Las Vegas Sun
Long Island Star-Journal
Los Angeles Times
Marietta (GA) Journal
Miami News
Milwaukee Journal
Minneapolis Star
Morning Call (Allentown, PA)
New York Journal-American
New York Post
New York Times
New York World-Telegram
Newark (OH) Advocate
Omaha World Herald
Oregonian (Portland, OR)
Press-Courier (Oxnard, CA)
Redlands (CA) Daily Facts
Register-Republic (Rockford, IL)
Richmond Times-Dispatch
Sacramento Bee
San Antonio Light
San Diego Union
San Francisco Chronicle
Sarasota Herald-Tribune
Sedalia (MO) Democrat
Sporting News
Springfield (MA) Union
Sun (Baltimore, MD)
Tampa Bay Times
Times-Picayune (New Orleans, LA)
Washington Post
Washington Post and Times Herald

Websites

Baseball-Reference.com
GenealogyBank.com
NewspaperArchives.com
Retrosheet.org
SABR BioProject

INDEX

Aaron, Hank 42, 80, 90
Addie, Bob 200
A.G. Spalding and Brothers 27–28, 30
Aguirre, Hank 114, 230–234
Albany Cardinals 236
Albany Senators 135, 173
Allada, Ravi 36
Allen, Bob 73, 152
Allen, Lee 166
Allen, Maury 4, 16, 168–169, 184–185, 257, 297–298
Allen, Mel 274
Allentown Cardinals 140
Allentown Red Sox 281
Allison, Bob 244
Alou, Matty 40
Alston, Walt 142
Alvarez, Ossie 114
American Association 80, 101, 117, 157, 220, 232, 281
American Journal of Physics 31
Aparicio, Luis 44, 167, 213
Archer, Jim 67, 120–123, 129, 223
Armour Research Foundation 29–30
Arroyo, Luis 66–67, 73, 98, 110, 167, 172, 179, 189, 192, 198, 211, 222, 229–230, 261–262, 289, 293–294
Associated Press 19, 37, 183, 216, 295
Athletic Journal 42
Atlanta Braves 233, 267
Atlanta Crackers 195–196, 259
Auerbach, Red 79
Austin Senators 259
Automatic Canteen Company of America 50
Averill, Earl 222

Babe Ruth League 215
Baker, Del 177
Baker, Frank "Home Run" 31
Bakersfield Indians 111
Baldschun, Jack 266

Baltimore Orioles 2, 14–15, 26, 33, 53–54, 59, 64, 69, 74, 76–78, 87, 120–121, 127, 143, 156, 168–170, 176–177, 179, 188, 195, 211, 217, 221, 223–224, 232, 239–240, 253, 255, 262–266, 268–279
Banks, Ernie 15–16, 18, 291
Barber, Steve 76, 120–121, 262–264, 276, 279–280
Barra, Allen 19, 39–40
Baseball Guide and Record Book 16
Baseball Writers' Association of America 17, 19, 45, 56, 71, 168
Bass, Dick 128
Bass, Norm 128–131
batting style/swing 13, 30–32, 38, 42–44, 61, 65, 92, 117, 131, 171, 184, 193–194, 236, 246, 254, 256, 263, 273–274, 288–289
Bauer, Hank 50, 101, 105, 122, 136
Baumann, Frank 167, 173–175, 179, 217
Bell, Gary 74–76, 109–110, 151–152, 243, 250, 253
Benton, Al 260
Bernstein, Anita 27
Berra, Yogi 3, 15, 24, 57, 73, 75, 83, 87, 89, 93, 100, 105–107, 110, 119, 130, 136, 146, 151, 161, 166, 172, 185, 188–189, 192, 219, 222, 229, 257, 270, 285, 289, 293
Berres, Ray 104, 174, 196
Berry, Charlie 180, 271
Big State League 180
Billings Mustangs 199
Bingham, Walter 1, 18, 25, 32
Binghamton Triplets 168, 226
Bishop Stanley High School (Fargo, North Dakota) 41
Blanchard, Johnny 3, 82–83, 111, 117, 119, 130, 149, 167, 172, 187–189, 192, 205, 240–241, 247, 254, 270–271, 293
Bloomington, Minnesota 32

Bluefield Blue-Grays 219
B'nai B'rith 295
Bolin, Bobby 178
Boone, Ray 93
Boros, Steve 149, 153, 259
Boston American 87
Boston Celtics 79–82
Boston Globe 17, 27
Boston Herald 13, 38, 272
Boston Red Sox 2, 18, 26, 35–36, 52, 79, 81–83, 86–93, 96–97, 102–103, 114, 117–118, 130, 135–138, 156–160, 169–174, 177, 188, 195, 210, 218–220, 231, 245, 251, 255, 272, 274–276, 280–282, 294
Boston Traveler 282
Boudreau, Lou 102
Bouton, Jim 160
Boyer, Clete 40, 64, 83, 87–89, 95, 99, 100, 105, 107, 109, 111, 115–117, 119, 122–123, 130, 165, 167, 179–180, 182, 187–188, 202, 230, 255, 259, 270, 285
Bragan, Bobby 48, 74, 114, 155, 248
Brecheen, Harry 77, 224, 265
Brewer, Tom 89, 91
Briggs, John 125
Broeg, Bob 17, 237
Brooklyn Dodgers 15, 84, 117, 140, 177, 199
Brooklyn Tablet 17
Brosnan, Jim 176, 289
Brown, Dick 149
Brown, Hal "Skinny" 169–170, 263–264
Brown, Joe 238–239
Browning, Pete 31
Bruton, Bill 111, 149, 262
Buffalo Bisons 89, 102, 120, 205, 211–212, 245, 282
Bunning, Jim 114, 137, 147, 259, 262, 283
Burdette, Lou 80
Burlington Indians 82

333

Index

Burns, Ed 181
Burnside, Pete 68–70, 137, 139–140, 143, 194–195
Busch, Augie 298
Butler, Jack 17

California League 236
Candlestick Park (San Francisco) 156, 161, 215
Cannon, Jimmy 8–9, 11, 21–24, 207, 297
Carey, Andy 85, 135
Carolina League 82, 283
Carrasquel, Chico 48
Carroll, Parke 50
Casale, Jerry 117–119
Cash, Norm 18, 127–128, 130, 148, 259
Castro, Fidel 88
Cepeda, Orlando 30
Cerv, Bob 8, 23, 67, 75, 84, 107, 111, 115, 126, 133, 140, 173, 179, 182, 184–185, 189, 216, 228, 262, 274, 287
Chandler, Happy 19
Charleston Senators 232
Cheney, Tom 236–241
Chicago Cubs 16, 84, 95–96, 140–141, 175, 179–182, 210–211, 233–234, 237, 267–268
Chicago White Sox 2, 26, 29, 35–36, 46, 50, 52, 54, 75, 83–87, 93–99, 103–104, 113, 116, 127, 129, 140–143, 150, 160–161, 164–169, 172, 174–175, 178, 180, 182–183, 187, 196–197, 204, 207, 209–214, 216–217, 220, 224–225, 255–257, 277, 282
Cicotte, Al 114
Cincinnati Reds 84–85, 123–125, 127–128, 138–139, 141–144, 182, 185, 190–191, 203, 209, 238, 245, 253, 266–267, 277, 287–294
Claflin, Larry 157
Clavin, Tom 1, 169
Clemente, Roberto 161, 291
Cleveland Clinic 34
Cleveland Indians 2, 9, 27, 32–33, 39, 41–42, 45–50, 52, 61, 71–76, 82, 84, 86, 91, 94, 105–106, 109–115, 119, 126, 129, 133, 142–143, 151–156, 163–167, 174, 191, 193, 197–198, 207, 210, 217–222, 225–226, 231–232, 241–243, 246–250, 253, 255
Cleveland News 45
Cleveland Plain Dealer 46, 153
Cleveland Stadium 32–33, 218
Clevenger, Tex 67, 73, 98, 107
Clinton, Lou 285
Coates, Jim 73, 86, 88, 93, 98, 101, 104, 109, 135, 148, 258, 294

Cobb, Ty 11, 31, 185
Colavito, Rocky 47, 49–50, 67, 148–149, 229–230
Coleman, Gordy 289
Columbus Cardinals 237
Columbus Jets 102, 199–200, 238–239
Comiskey Park (Chicago) 32, 84, 93, 96, 163, 167, 255
Conley, Gene 79–83, 87, 284
Considine, Bob 19–20, 23–24
Cooke, Jack 152
Corpus Christi Times 216
Cottier, Chuck 194
Cotton States League 89
Covington, Wes 84, 95, 122
Craft, Harry 102, 196
Craig, Roger 292
Crandall, Del 158
Creamer, Robert 7–8, 12, 38, 66
Cronin, Joe 13, 18–19, 118, 158
Crosetti, Frank 149, 188
Crosley Field (Cincinnati) 84, 290
Crystal, Billy 1
Cuba 19, 88–89, 125, 238, 248
Cy Young Award 72, 76, 94, 146, 149, 165, 196, 251, 274, 292

Daily News (New York) 10, 14, 17, 19
Daimai Orions 99
Daley, Arthur 21, 49, 54–55, 207, 272
Daley, Bud 87, 98, 103, 110–111, 114–115, 139, 172, 189, 199, 202, 229, 264, 278, 294
Dallas Eagles 69
Daniel, Dan 19, 53, 56, 61, 114, 151, 162, 216–217
Daniels, Bennie 27, 112, 199–202
Dark, Alvin 214, 277
Davenport Pirates 290
Davis, Spud 140
Day, Doris 219
Daytona Beach, Florida 41–42
Dean, Dizzy 27
DeMaestri, Joe 50, 183
Denver Bears 119, 156, 176, 260
Denver Broncos 131
Detroit Tigers 2, 12, 26, 33, 36–38, 43–44, 46, 52, 59–60, 62–64, 67–72, 77–78, 83, 86, 91–93, 98, 100–102, 105, 107, 109, 111–112, 114, 116–117, 119, 126–127, 131–133, 137, 139, 143–151, 153, 158, 160–161, 171, 183, 188, 192, 195, 201, 205, 211–212, 217–218, 222–236, 241, 244, 247, 252, 255–262, 264–265
Devine, Tommy 297
DeWitt, Bill 139

DiMaggio, Joe 27, 297
Ditmar, Art 61, 66, 70, 76, 78, 83, 86, 92, 95, 98, 110, 130, 189
Doby, Larry 163, 248–249
Doherty, Ed 138, 143, 197, 201
Dolgan, Bob 153
Dominican Republic 48
Donohue, Jim 119, 222
Donovan, Dick 18, 134, 195–198, 201
Downing, Al 168
Doyle, Jimmy 46, 153
Drebinger, John 19, 37, 149, 187
Dressen, Chuck 189–190, 196, 208, 232–233, 260–261
Drysdale, Don 251, 291
Duffy, Hugh 18–19
Durante, Sal 285–287, 295
Duren, Ryne 67, 77, 107, 282, 291
Durocher, Leo 8, 135
Durslag, Melvin 220
Dykes, Jimmy 72, 110, 142, 155, 232, 243, 246, 249, 254

Eastern League 45, 74, 80, 226
Ebbets Field (Brooklyn) 199
Effrat, Louis 258
El Paso Sun Kings 131
Elias Sports Bureau 19, 24, 26, 32, 47, 168
Ellenbogen, Jeffrey 34
Elliott, Bob 259
Ermer, Cal 252
Essegian, Chuck 109, 225
Estrada, Chuck 76–78, 120, 276
Evangeline League 259
Evans, Hoot 72

Fairly, Ron 291
fans 12, 185, 151, 185–186, 223, 236, 254–255, 258, 272–273, 278, 285
Fargo, North Dakota 3, 9, 12, 24, 41–42, 57, 156
Fargo Central High School (North Dakota) 41
Fargo Forum and Moorhead News 18
Fargo-Moorhead Twins 41–42, 248
Farrell, Kirby 45–48, 113–114, 119
Faubus, Orval 200
Feller, Bob 69, 74, 102, 157
Female Athlete of the Year (Associated Press) 295
Fenway Park (Boston) 32, 82, 86, 135, 157
Fernandez, Chico 59, 149, 151
Ferrell, Rick 232
Ferrick, Tom 146, 232–233, 291–292
Ferriss, Dave 136

Index

Finley, Charles 121, 129, 253
Fireman of the Year Award 88
Fishel, Bob 185, 257
Fisher, Bill 93–94
Fisher, Eddie 216
Fisher, Jack 76, 224, 266, 273–279, 283
Fitz Gerald, Ed 213
Fitzgerald, Eugene 18
Flaherty, Red 148
Flood, Curt 203
Ford, Whitey 7, 18, 52, 58–59, 67–69, 78, 83, 86–87, 93, 98–99, 105, 109–110, 117, 119, 128, 130, 134, 145–146, 149, 156, 161, 169, 171–173, 175, 179, 188–189, 192, 207, 210–211, 214, 218, 222, 229–230, 236, 257, 264, 274, 284, 289, 294
Fornieles, Mike 87–89, 282
Foster, Bill 27
Foster D. Snell, Inc. 27–28
Fox, Nellie 95
Fox, Terry 2, 259–262
Foxx, Jimmie 11, 15, 21, 38–39, 262
Foytack, Paul 59–61, 114–116
Fraley, Oscar 296–297
Francona, Tito 94, 109, 232
Frazier, George 13, 38, 272
Freese, Gene 52, 209
Fresno Cardinals 203, 236
Frick, Ford 1, 5, 10, 14–20, 39, 150–151, 165, 167–171, 255–257, 262, 264–265, 270, 272, 274, 279, 284, 286–287
Friend, Bob 57, 238
Frisch, Frankie 140
Froemming, Bruce 268
Fuchs, Bill 202
Funk, Frank 75–76, 152–156, 254
Furillo, Carl 197

Gallico, Paul 10
Garcia, Mike 74, 112, 114, 164, 205
Gardner, Billy 110, 218, 221–222
Gaston, Milt 27
Gehrig, Lou 11, 23, 25, 133, 216, 247, 254–255
Geiger, Gary 83
Gentile, Jim 15–16, 18, 30, 156, 295
Georgia-Florida League 236
Georgia State League 242
Gibson, Bob 283
Giles, Warren 19
Glenn, John 296
Gold Glove Award 53, 55
Gonder, Jesse 75
Goodman, Irv 85
Gordon, Joe 48, 74, 84, 96, 114, 121–122, 128–129, 142, 232, 242–243, 246, 248, 250

Gordon, Sam 284, 295
Graff, Milt 47
Graham, Frank 21
Grand Forks, North Dakota 41–42
Grand Forks Chiefs 42
Grant, Cary 219
Grant, Jim "Mudcat" 27, 74, 110, 218, 247–254
Grasmick, Lou 273
Gray, Sid 13
Grba, Eli 52, 64–65, 105–107
Green, Gene 135, 198
Green, Pumpsie 282
Greenberg, Hank 15, 21–22, 38, 41, 45–46, 48, 114, 262
Greensboro Patriots 219
Greenville Majors 180
Greenville Pirates 290
Griffith, Cal 190–191, 245
Griffith Stadium (Washington, DC) 32, 112, 191, 194–195, 199, 203, 205, 263
Groat, Dick 50
Gross, Don 291
Gross, Milton 16, 254, 263, 287
Grove, Lefty 212

Hacker, Warren 180–183
Haddix, Harvey 201, 242
Hadley, Kent 50
Halberstam, David 9, 14, 23
Hale, Bob 241
Hall, Dick 270
Hamey, Roy 66, 78, 110
Hamilton Cardinals 203
Haney, Fred 81, 208
Harder, Mel 75, 113, 164, 242–243, 248, 250
Harris, Bucky 59
Harris, Luman 264, 270–271
Harrison, James 33
Harriss, Slim 27
Hartford Chiefs 80
Harwell, Ernie 233–234
Havana Sugar Kings 152
Hawaii Islanders 127, 202
Held, Woodie 73
Hemsley, Rollie 201
Hemus, Solly 200
Herbert, Ray 101–104, 167, 187
Herman, Billy 210
Herzog, Whitey 7, 120, 203, 263, 268, 271
Hibbing, Minnesota 41
Hickok Belt Award (Professional Athlete of the Year) 266, 295
Higgins, Pinky 89–90, 92, 118, 135–136, 157–160, 173–174, 282
High Point-Thomasville Royals 283
Hillerich and Bradsby Company 31

Hillman, Dave 87–88
Hinton, Chuck 202
Hitchcock, Billy 276–277
Hodges, Gil 240
Hoeft, Billy 137, 271
Hollywood Stars 199–200, 291
Holy Cross Cemetery (Fargo, North Dakota) 3
Hornsby, Rogers 21–22, 297
Houk, Ralph 2, 14, 18, 24, 34, 36, 57–59, 61, 64, 66, 68, 70, 76, 78–79, 82–83, 86–87, 93, 98, 110, 122, 132–134, 145, 148–149, 161, 183, 185, 188, 193–194, 207, 227, 234–237, 246, 257–258, 262, 269–270, 273, 275, 278, 280, 297
Houston Astros 161, 210
Houston Buffaloes 89–90
Houston Colt .45's 97, 144, 170, 179, 277
Howard, Elston 40, 60, 70, 89, 96, 98, 104, 111, 116, 122, 126, 135, 139–140, 145–146, 159, 161, 167, 175, 180, 183, 192, 205, 229, 235–236, 240–241, 246–247, 254, 261, 263, 270, 289, 293–294
Howsam, Bob 267
Hubbell, Carl 69, 224
Hudson, Sid 204
Hunt, Ken 105
Hunter, Catfish 253
Hurley, Ed 188, 276, 278
Hurricane Ester 263, 268
Hurwitz, Hy 17, 174
Hutchinson, Fred 294

Indiana University 97
Indianapolis Indians 45–46, 220, 231, 241
injuries 47–50, 53, 78–79; 186–188, 298–299
International League 106, 120, 152, 199, 203, 205, 238
Irby, Leroy 248
Isaacson, Julie "Big Julie" 7, 9, 23, 109 184, 284, 287
Isaacson, Selma 287

Jackson, Ron 174
Jackson, Travis 80
Jacksonville Braves 207
Jacksonville Suns 226
Jacobson, Max 274
James, Charlie 292
James, Johnny 2, 67, 105–107
James P. Dawson Award 106
Jansen, Larry 214
Japan Pacific League 99
Jay, Joey 209, 288–290, 292
John, Tommy 277

Index

Johnson, Arnold 50
Johnson, Deron 86, 98, 106
Johnson, Ken 121
Johnson, Walter 69, 189
Jones, Harry 46
Jones, Sad Sam 291
Joost, Eddie 136
Joseph S. Ward and Associates 28–29
Jurges, Billy 118, 158, 282

Kaat, Jim 64, 99, 251
Kahn, Roger 21, 163
Kaline, Al 18, 39, 127, 148–149, 161, 209, 229–230, 258, 262
Kamm, Herb 293, 298
Kansas City Athletics 2, 5–9, 12, 23, 26 33, 37, 39, 47–51, 67, 74, 78, 86–87, 95, 98, 101–104, 109, 116, 120–123, 125–130, 133, 136, 146, 151, 153, 158, 166–167, 176, 178, 188–189, 196, 203–215, 223–225, 236, 240, 243, 248–249, 265, 268, 283
Kansas City Star 49, 129
Kase, Max 17, 28
Keane, Johnny 237
Kemmerer, Russ 2, 93, 96–98, 180, 190
Kennedy, John F. 110, 288
Kentucky-Illinois-Tennessee League 203
Keokuk Kernels 42, 45, 248
Keough, Marty 134
Kiddie Korps 76, 224, 276
Killebrew, Harmon 30, 63, 190, 192, 244, 295
Kiner, Ralph 39, 248
King, Clyde 199–200, 292
King, Jim 159
King, Joe 17, 21
Kinnamon, Bill 285
Kirkland, Willie 109, 218
Klaus, Billy 70
Klippstein, Johnny 140–144, 241
Kluszewski, Ted 65, 105
Knoxville Smokies 76, 223, 261, 265
Koppett, Leonard 15, 25, 29, 39, 289
Koufax, Sandy 15, 166, 190, 214, 251
Kralick, Jack 99–100
Kubek, Tony 2, 23–24, 63, 73, 75–76, 78, 83, 87–88, 93, 95, 100, 104–105, 107, 109, 115–116, 130, 132, 134, 138, 140, 148, 152, 154, 156, 161, 165, 167, 172, 180, 182, 192, 205, 226, 229–230, 240, 246, 253–254, 258, 261, 264, 269–270, 284, 290, 293–294, 298

Kuechle, Oliver 39, 272
Kunkel, Bill 105
Kutscher, Scott 38
Kutyna, Marty 70, 203–205

Lake, Austen 87
Landis, Jim 167
Lane, Frank "Trader" 48–50, 84, 103, 114, 121, 129, 167, 212, 231, 237–238
Lang, Jack 54, 162
Larsen, Don 50, 90, 175–179, 183, 213–214
Lary, Frank 59, 67, 77, 114–117, 119, 137, 145–150, 230, 258
Latman, Barry 243
Lavagetto, Cookie 99
Law, Vern 201, 291
League Park (Cleveland) 32–33
Lebovitz, Hal 45–46, 71, 73
Lemon, Bob 74, 85, 112, 114, 164, 231
Lenox Hill Hospital 78, 287
Lima Red Birds 140
Lincoln Chiefs 199
Liston, Bill 282
Little Rock Travelers 74
Locke, Bobby 246–247
Lollar, Sherm 167, 196, 213
Long, Dale 135
Long Island Press 54
Look (magazine) 43
Lopez, Al 45–46, 84, 94, 104, 112–113, 174, 180, 197, 209–210, 243
Lopez, Hector 57, 63, 67, 73, 76, 78, 82, 149, 188, 254, 278, 294
Los Angeles Angels 2, 13, 26, 32, 37, 56, 60, 64–67, 77, 91, 99, 105–109, 119, 121, 125, 127, 129, 132–133, 145, 191–193, 206–207, 210, 219–222, 225, 239, 260–261, 290
Los Angeles Angels (PCL) 181
Los Angeles Dodgers 13, 94, 99, 125, 142, 144, 178–179, 191, 196, 214, 233, 238, 251–252, 266, 288
Louisville Colonels 96, 117, 173–174
Luque, Dolf 190

Maglie, Sal 90, 118, 157, 159, 281–282, 284
Mahoney, Neil 118
Maisel, Bob 272
Male Athlete of the Year (Associated Press) 295
Maltzberger, Gordon 244
Malzone, Frank 83
Manager of the Year 53, 76
Mantilla, Felix 282
Mantle, Merlyn 274, 278

Mantle, Mickey 1–4, 8, 10–14, 16, 18–19, 21–25, 30–31, 39–40, 43, 45, 47, 52–62, 64–68, 70, 73, 75–79, 83, 85–87, 89–92, 95–96, 98–100, 104–108, 110, 114–117, 119, 122, 126, 128–130, 132–136, 138–140, 143, 145–147, 150–152, 156–157, 159–162, 165–173, 175, 179–180, 182–189, 192–195, 198, 202–203, 205–207, 210–211, 215–219, 222–223, 226–230, 234–236, 238, 240–241, 243, 246–247, 253–257, 261–262, 264, 269–270, 272–275, 278–279, 287–290, 293–294, 297–298
Marichal, Juan 179
Maris, Pat 6–7, 47, 51, 56–57, 66, 120, 185, 216, 219, 223, 264, 274–275, 278–280, 284, 287, 295
Maris, Rudy (father) 41
Maris, Rudy, Jr., "Bud" (brother) 6, 41, 257
Marquard, Rube 134
Martin, Billy 114, 125
Martin, J.C. 167
Maryland Professional Baseball Players Association 56, 273, 295
Mathewson, Christy 15
Mathias, Carl 134
Matthews, Eddie 18
Matthews, Wid 141, 181
Mauch, Gene 85, 144, 195
Maxwell, Charlie 72
Mays, Willie 26, 40, 172
Mazeroski, Bill 3, 54, 238
McAuliffe, Dick 149
McBride, Ken 193, 219–222
McClain, Joe 135, 194
McCovey, Willie 40, 214
McDaniel, Lindy 161
McDougald, Gil 53, 158
McGaha, Mel 155
McGrew, Ted 208
McGuff, Joe 129
McHale, John 232
McKechnie, Bill 123–124
McLish, Cal 84–86, 93, 209
McMillan, Roy 209
McNally, Mike 41–42
Meany, Tom 8, 25, 49, 51
Mehl, Ernest 49, 121–122, 125
Mele, Sam 244, 251
Memorial Stadium (Baltimore) 32–33, 195, 263, 273
Memphis Chickasaws 174
Metkovich, George 75
Metropolitan Stadium (Minnesota) 32, 63, 191
Mexican Industries 234

Index

Meyer, Dutch 44–45
Miami Marlins (IL) 120, 182, 276
Miami News 297
Milwaukee Braves 18, 90, 95, 125, 149–150, 155, 178, 181, 207–208, 210, 242, 259
Milwaukee Brewers 80
Milwaukee Journal 39, 272
Minneapolis Millers 90, 157–158, 228, 281
Minnesota Twins 2, 26, 32, 37, 58, 62–64, 66, 71–72, 89, 98–100, 109–110, 132–133, 144–145, 154, 189–192, 207, 223, 228, 242–245, 250–252
Mize, Johnny 33–34, 37–38
Mizell, Vinegar Ben 201
Mobile Bears 74, 140, 242
Monbouquette, Bill 156–160, 171, 274, 280
Monroe Sports 89
Montreal Expos 252
Moon, Wally 13
Moses, Wally 194, 278
Mossi, Don 59, 111–116, 145, 147, 229
Most Valuable Player Award 4, 12, 39, 53, 56, 58, 66, 72, 80, 89, 94, 104, 124, 164–165, 178, 181, 190, 196, 198, 210, 213, 233, 251, 264, 266 288, 292, 295
Muffett, Billy 89–91
Municipal Stadium (Kansas City) 32–33, 126, 128, 223
Murtaugh, Danny 199–200
Musial, Stan 18–19, 124, 128

Narleski, Ray 113,-114
Nason, Jerry 27
National Association of Baseball Writers 76
National Basketball Association 79–82
New Iberia Pelicans 259
New Orleans Pelicans 290
New York Giants 15, 20, 68–69, 112–113, 135, 152, 215, 224
New York Journal-American 8, 17, 21, 28, 297
New York Mets 22, 77, 96, 120, 127, 150, 205, 277, 282–283, 297
New York Mirror 17, 21
New York Post 13, 15, 184, 228, 241, 263, 272, 289
New York Times 8, 19–20, 27–28, 30, 33, 37, 40, 49, 54, 58, 75, 105, 149, 166, 187, 194, 207, 217, 228, 258, 272
New York Tribune 10
New York World-Telegram 17, 53, 184, 216
Newcombe, Don 142

Newhouser, Hal 113, 212
Nicaragua 242
Nichols, Chet 83, 285
Nixon, Russ 74–75, 82, 88
Norman, Bill 146, 232
Northern League 42, 248
Nuxhall, Joe 104–105, 123–127

Oakland Athletics 71–72, 210, 252–253
Oakland Oaks 170
O'Dell, Billy 170
O'Doul, Lefty 170
Ogle, Jim 14
Oklahoma City 89ers 97
Oklahoma City Indians 174
Omaha Cardinals 237–238
O'Neill, Steve 212
Orr, Jack 13
Osborne, Bobo 149
Ostby, Burt 42
Osteen, Claude 138, 251
O'Toole, Jim 288–289
Owen, Mickey 136

Pacific Coast League 74, 96, 99, 117, 139, 170, 181, 199, 202–203, 226, 231, 242, 248, 259, 283
Paducah Chiefs 203
Pagliaroni, Jim 89, 159
Paige, Satchel 27, 248
Palmquist, Ed 99–100
Pampa Oilers 180
Paparella, Art 229
Pappas, Milt 2, 76, 120, 224, 233, 263–270, 276
Parker, Dan 17, 21
Patterson, Floyd 255
Paul, Gabe 125, 141, 190, 203, 225, 250
Pearson, Albie 121, 213
Peary, Danny 1, 169
Peete, Charlie 237
Pepe, Phil 184, 207
Perranoski, Ron 252
Perry, Gaylord 71–72, 94–95
Perry, Jim 71–73, 77, 109–110, 218, 250
Pesky, Johnny 131, 157
Philadelphia Athletics 36, 87, 101
Philadelphia Phillies 81, 84–85, 104, 144, 182, 245, 261
Phillips, Bubba 61, 109
Pierce, Billy 46, 94, 96–97, 209, 211–216
Piersall, Jimmy 8, 129, 197, 255
Pinson, Vada 288
Pioneer League 199
Pittsburgh Pirates 3, 20, 48, 50, 54, 57, 84, 199–200, 210, 236, 238, 245, 253, 290–292

Pizarro, Juan 27, 166, 180, 183, 207–211
Player of the Year Award 165, 295
Pocatello A's 128
Poholsky, Tom 177
Popular Mechanics 29
Portland Beavers 130, 203–204, 226
Posada, Leo 129
Povich, Shirley 16–17, 69, 138
Powell, Boog 239
Power, Vic 73, 243
Powers, Jimmy 17
press 1, 7–8, 4–14, 17, 21, 38–39, 108, 169, 132, 150–151, 154, 162, 184–185, 193, 206–207, 216–217, 227, 235–236, 257–258, 263–264, 271–273, 279, 295–298
Princeton University 135
Puerto Rican League 208

Quinn, John 80

Ramos, Pedro 58, 62–63, 100–101, 243
Rand, Dick 200
Raytown, Missouri 49, 54, 223, 295
Reading Indians 45, 248
Reichler, Joe 19, 216
Reitz, Bob 273
Reniff, Hal 98, 192
Reston, James 20
Reynolds, Debbie 216
Richards, Paul 53, 76, 120, 170, 212–213, 224, 265–267, 275–276
Richardson, Bobby 2, 24, 40, 63, 88–89, 95, 100, 106, 110, 117, 119, 122, 126, 130, 134–135, 139, 152, 165, 167, 172, 175, 182, 192–193, 197, 205, 214–215, 218, 230, 240, 247, 254, 261, 270, 273, 284, 293–294
Richmond Virginians 64, 98, 106–107, 226
Rigney, Bill 119, 221
Rizzuto, Phil 190, 285
Roarke, Mike 261
Robinson, Aaron 212
Robinson, Brooks 54, 77, 224
Robinson, Earl 78, 270, 278
Robinson, Floyd 180
Robinson, Frank 266–267, 288, 293
Robinson, Jackie 163, 249
Robinson, Murray 27, 229
Rochester, New York 295
Rochester Red Wings 45
Rogan, Bullet 27
Romano, John 2, 72, 75–76, 109, 111, 154

Index

Rookie of the Year 42, 46, 48, 71, 80, 136, 248
Root, Charlie 141
Rose, Pete 185
Roseboro, John 18, 252
Rudolph, Wilma 295
Runge, Ed 127, 158, 271
Runnels, Pete 190
Ruth, Babe 1–5, 8–28, 30–34, 36, 38–39, 46, 50, 52, 56, 58, 101, 108, 131–133, 150–151, 154, 159, 162, 165, 167–169, 171, 184, 186–188, 193, 206–207, 215–218, 221, 227, 234, 236, 241, 247, 254–257, 262, 265, 270–274, 278–279, 284, 287, 294–295, 297–298
Ruth, Claire 216, 278–279

Sacramento Solons 259
Sadecki, Ray 283
Sadowski, Ted 63–64
Sain, Johnny 38, 72, 102, 144, 251
St. Louis Browns 33, 140, 176
St. Louis Cardinals 33, 57, 90–91, 123, 140, 177, 200, 203, 224, 236–238, 252, 283, 292, 298
St. Louis Post-Dispatch 17
St. Petersburg, Florida 56–57, 297
Salinas Packers 76
Salt Lake City Bees 175, 242
San Diego Padres 268
San Diego Padres (PCL) 74, 127, 139, 220, 231, 242, 245, 248, 261
San Francisco, California 138, 156, 162, 214
San Francisco Chronicle 18
San Francisco Giants 40, 69, 90, 94, 96, 135, 161, 172, 178–179, 213–214, 277, 298
San Francisco Seals 96, 117, 136
San Jose Bees 221
Schaffer, Jimmie 175
Scheffing, Bob 43, 145, 147, 149, 230, 232, 235, 260
Schilling, Chuck 286
Schoendienst, Red 283
Schwall, Don 159, 274, 280–281
Schwarz, Alan 11–12
Score, Herb 48
Seattle Rainers 170, 181, 203, 282
Seaver, Tom 277
Severini, Thomas 36
Shaw, Bob 93–96, 103, 189, 196
Shecter, Leonard 1, 13, 44, 49, 241, 246, 287
Sheehen, Joseph 30, 217
Sheehy, Pete 20
Sheldon, Rollie 76, 87, 89, 91, 98, 115, 135, 149, 151–152, 156, 159
Sherry, Larry 260, 281

Shibe Park (Philadelphia) 33
Shreveport Sports 89, 129, 180
Siebern, Norm 50, 122
Sievers, Roy 18, 95
Simmons, Curt 283
Simpson, Dick 266
Sisler, Dave 135–139, 143
Sisler, Dick 135, 139
Sisler, George 135
*61** (movie) 1, 263, 296
Skowron, Bill "Moose" 56–57, 65, 70, 73, 83, 87, 115–117, 122, 126, 130, 140, 143, 149, 157, 176, 179–180, 223, 229–230, 238, 241, 253–254, 257, 259, 261–262, 270, 289
Slocum, Frank 168
Smith, Al 93
Smith, Lyall 235
Snyder, Russ 120, 204
Soar, Hank 256
Song, Alex 36
South Atlantic League 207, 223
Southern Association 74, 195, 242, 290
Spahn, Warren 18, 80, 124, 149, 196, 208
The Sporting News 2, 16–17, 19, 21, 55–56, 61, 88, 102, 106, 121, 125, 133, 136, 153, 157, 165–166, 168, 170, 180, 187, 197–198, 203, 215, 242, 244, 251, 259–260, 263, 266–267, 295
Sports Illustrated 1, 18, 25, 28–29, 32, 217
Sportsman's Park (St. Louis) 33
Spring, Jack 220
Stafford, Bill 68, 76, 87, 98, 108, 126, 134–135, 149, 165, 168, 182, 195, 214, 219, 221, 228, 259, 281, 284, 289–290, 293
Stage Deli 109, 284
Stallard, Tracy 83, 281–287
Stanky, Eddie 277
Stann, Francis 18, 25
Stengel, Casey 51–52, 106, 114, 162, 176–178, 224
Stephens, Gene 104
Stevens, Bob 18
Stewart, Bob 298
Stigman, Dick 2, 241–246, 251, 254
Stobbs, Chuck 87
Stock, Wes 271
Stone, Dean 97
Stoneman, Horace 214
Stottlemyre, Mel 220
Sturdivant, Tom 239
Sultan of Swat Award 56, 273, 295
Sun (Baltimore) 272
Swift, Bob 97

Tagliabue, Emil 216
Tebbetts, Birdie 141–142, 182, 250
Temple, Johnny 84
Terry, Ralph 2, 23, 75–76, 83, 87, 95, 98, 100, 105, 111, 167–168, 218, 223, 229–230, 242, 258, 270–271, 289, 294
Texarkana Bears 180
Texas League 69, 89, 111, 180
Texas-New Mexico League 180
That Touch of Mink (movie) 219
Thomas, Lee 67, 107
Thomson, Bobby 15
Three-I League 44
Throneberry, Marv 50
Tiger Stadium 32, 59, 111, 255, 258
Tighe, Jack 59, 147
Toledo Mud Hens 101, 195, 226
Topping, Dan 50, 66, 78, 280
Toronto Maple Leafs 152–153, 155
Tresh, Tom 40
Triandos, Gus 224, 263, 270
Trimble, Joe 17
Tsitouris, John 125
Tucson, Arizona 45–46, 48
Tulsa Oilers 44, 91, 111, 124, 283
Turley, Bob "Bullet Bob" 63, 76, 83–84, 87, 92–93, 98, 110, 145, 148, 176, 178
Turner, Jim 177

Umont, Frank 180
United Press International 296
Universal Studios 219
University of Oklahoma 41

Vancouver Mounties 76, 99
Vargo, Eddie 125
Vecsey, George 40
Veeck, Bill 46, 50, 209
Venezuela 118
Vernon, Mickey 137, 139, 143, 164, 197–198, 201, 204–205
Versalles, Zoilo "Zorro" 154, 252
Vidalia Indians 242
Vincent, Al 124
Vincent, Fay 17
Virgil, Ozzie 119

Wade, Ben 200
Wagner, Charlie 117
Wagner, Leon 65, 225
Walker, Dixie 85
Walker, Harry 90
Walker, Jerry 76, 166, 223–226, 276
Walker, Stanley 10
Walters, Bucky 69
Washington Post 16–17
Washington Senators 2, 12, 26,

37, 56, 67–70, 80, 82, 87, 95, 97, 112, 118, 125, 129, 134–135, 137–139, 143, 153, 159, 163–164, 171, 173–174, 189–191, 194–199, 201–206, 213, 223–224, 235–236, 239–240, 249, 251, 265
Washington Star 17–18, 25, 202
Webb, Del 50, 206
Weiss, George 45, 50
Wertz, Vic 86
White, Jo-Jo 42, 44–45, 47, 142
Wichita Braves 208
Wilhelm, Hoyt 114, 161, 170, 237, 264, 266, 271, 275, 291
Wilks, Ted 33, 249
Williams, Dick 78, 239, 269
Williams, Smokey Joe 27
Williams, Ted 113–114, 142, 147, 191, 231, 276, 296
Wills, Maury 232
Wilson, Hack 21, 38
Wilson, Red 72
Wingard, Ernie 27
Wolf, Bob 208
Wood, Jake 229, 259
World Series 2–4, 23, 39–40, 45, 51, 54–55, 94, 111, 117, 123, 142, 144, 164, 176–179, 191, 196, 211, 213–214, 232, 238, 241, 245, 251, 266, 277, 283, 284, 287–289, 292–294, 298
Wrigley Field (Los Angeles) 32, 64, 132–133, 219–221, 290
Wyatt, Whit 195–196
Wynn, Early 27, 74–75, 84, 94, 112, 114, 157, 163–166, 196, 209, 225
Wynn, Joe 163

Yankee Stadium 27, 32, 50, 61–62, 71, 93, 134, 145, 159, 172, 186, 191, 215, 219, 241, 275, 284–285
Yastrzemski, Carl 284
York, Rudy 131
Yost, Eddie 105
Young, Dick 14–15, 17, 19, 168

Zachary, Tom 27
Zimmer, Don 197
Zipfel, Bud 194, 239
Zumbrun, Forrest 223
Zumbrun, Lori Beth 223

www.ingramcontent.com/pod-product-compliance
Lightning Source LLC
Chambersburg PA
CBHW060335010526
44117CB00017B/2838